THE CAMBRIDGE HISTORY OF
CHINESE LITERATURE

*

VOLUME I
To 1375

The Cambridge History of Chinese Literature gives an account of three thousand years of Chinese literature accessible to non-specialist readers as well as scholars and students of Chinese. From the beginnings of the Chinese written language to the lively world of Internet literature, these two volumes tell the story of Chinese writing, both as an instrument of the state and as a medium for culture outside the state. The volumes treat not only poetry, drama, and fiction, but early works of history and the informal prose of later eras.

The first volume begins with the question of the Chinese written language and the earliest inscriptions, dating from the late second millennium BC. In doing so it traces the beginnings of one of the longest continuous literary traditions in the world. By the end of the period there was a fully evolved commercial print culture, encompassing both writing in the older classical language and an emerging urban vernacular. The chapters in this volume chart the rise and fall of major dynasties and the role of the court in literary production, the cultural influences of other Asian countries, including the introduction of Buddhism, and the social and material contexts of the most important authors. The contributors keep in mind the traditions that preserved classical texts as much as the conditions that originally produced them.

THE CAMBRIDGE
HISTORY OF
CHINESE LITERATURE

*

Edited by

KANG-I SUN CHANG AND STEPHEN OWEN

*

VOLUME 1

To 1375

*

Edited by

STEPHEN OWEN

CAMBRIDGE
UNIVERSITY PRESS

CAMBRIDGE UNIVERSITY PRESS
Cambridge, New York, Melbourne, Madrid, Cape Town,
Singapore, São Paulo, Delhi, Dubai, Tokyo

Cambridge University Press
The Edinburgh Building, Cambridge CB2 8RU, UK

Published in the United States of America by Cambridge University Press, New York

www.cambridge.org
Information on this title: www.cambridge.org/9780521855587

© Cambridge University Press 2010

First published 2010

Printed in the United Kingdom at the University Press, Cambridge

A catalogue record for this publication is available from the British Library

ISBN 978-0-521-85558-7 Hardback

only available or a two-volume set:

ISBN 978-0-521-11677-0   2-volume set

Contents

Contents

Contents

Contents of Volume 2

Contributors

Kang-i Sun Chang is the inaugural Malcolm G. Chace '56 Professor of East Asian Languages and Literatures at Yale University. Her primary areas of research are classical Chinese literature, lyric poetry, gender studies, and cultural theory/aesthetics. She is the author of *The Evolution of Chinese Tz'u Poetry* (Princeton, 1980), *Six Dynasties Poetry* (Princeton, 1986), and *The Late Ming Poet Ch'en Tzu-lung: Crises of Love and Loyalism* (New Haven, 1991). She is also co-editor (with Ellen Widmer) of *Writing Women in Late Imperial China* (Stanford, 1997), and compiler and co-editor (with Haun Saussy) of *Women Writers of Traditional China* (Stanford, 1999). Her most recent book is *Journey through the White Terror: A Daughter's Memoir* (Taipei: National Taiwan University Press, 2006). She has also published several books in Chinese about American culture, feminism, literature, and film.

Ronald Egan is Professor of Chinese at the University of California, Santa Barbara. His works include book-length studies of Ouyang Xiu and Su Shi, as well as a translation of the selected essays of Qian Zhongshu, *Limited Views: Essays on Ideas and Letters* (Cambridge, MA, 1998). His most recent work is *The Problem of Beauty: Aesthetic Thought and Pursuits in Northern Song Dynasty China* (Cambridge, MA, 2006).

Michael A. Fuller is Associate Professor of Chinese Literature at the University of California, Irvine. He is the author of *An Introduction to Literary Chinese* (Cambridge, MA, 1999), *The Road to Eastslope: The Development of Su Shi's Poetic Voice* (Stanford, 1990), and the chapter "Sung Dynasty *shih* poetry" in *The Columbia History of Chinese Literature* (2001).

Michel Hockx is Professor of Chinese at SOAS, University of London. His research centers on modern and contemporary Chinese literary media and institutions, as well as modern Chinese poetry and poetics. His major publication is *Questions of Style: Literary Societies and Literary Journals in Modern China, 1911–1937* (Leiden, 2003).

Wilt L. Idema studied Chinese language and culture at Leiden University. Following study in Japan and Hong Kong, he taught at Leiden University from 1970 to 1999. He has taught Chinese literature at Harvard since 2000. He has published widely in both English and Dutch on Chinese vernacular literature of the last four dynasties. His most recent English-language publications include *The Red Brush: Writing Women of Imperial China* (co-authored with Beata Grant; Cambridge, MA, 2004); *Personal Salvation and Filial Piety:*

Two Precious Scroll Narratives on Guanyin and Her Acolytes (Honolulu, 2008); and *Meng Jiangnü Brings Down the Great Wall: Ten Versions of a Chinese Legend* (Seattle, 2008).

MARTIN KERN is Professor of East Asian Studies at Princeton University. He has published widely on ancient Chinese literature, history, and religion. His current work addresses the intersection of poetic expression, ritual performance, and the formation of Zhou cultural memory and identity. His most recent books are *The Stele Inscriptions of Ch'in Shih-huang: Text and Ritual in Early Chinese Imperial Representation* (New Haven, 2000) and the edited volume *Text and Ritual in Early China* (Seattle, 2005).

DAVID R. KNECHTGES is Professor of Chinese Literature at the University of Washington. His publications include *Two Studies on the Han Fu* (Seattle, 1968), *The Han Rhapsody: A Study of the Fu of Yang Hsiung* (Cambridge, 1976), *The Han shu Biography of Yang Xiong* (Tempe, AZ, 1982), and *Wen xuan: Selections of Refined Literature* (Princeton, 1982, 1987, 1996). He is the editor of Gong Kechang's *Studies on the Han Fu* (New Haven, 1997), and co-editor (with Eugene Vance) of *Rhetoric and the Discourses of Power in Court Culture* (Seattle, 2005).

WAI-YEE LI is Professor of Chinese literature at Harvard University. She is the author of *Enchantment and Disenchantment: Love and Illusion in Chinese Literature* (Princeton, 1993) and *The Readability of the Past in Early Chinese Historiography* (Cambridge, MA, 2007), and co-editor of *Trauma and Transcendence in Early Qing Literature* (Cambridge, MA, 2006). In collaboration with Stephen Durrant and David Schaberg, she also translated *Zuozhuan* (Seattle, forthcoming).

SHUEN-FU LIN is Professor of Chinese Literature at the University of Michigan. Author of *The Transformation of the Chinese Lyrical Tradition: Chiang K'uei and Southern Sung Tz'u Poetry* (Princeton, 1978) and *The Pursuit of Utopias* (in Chinese, 2003), he is also co-editor of *The Vitality of the Lyric Voice: Shih Poetry from the Late Han to the T'ang* (Princeton, 1986), and co-translator of Tung Yueh's (Dong Yue) *The Tower of Myriad Mirrors: A Supplement to Journey to the West* (Berkeley, 1978; revised edn, Michigan, 2000).

TINA LU is Professor of Chinese Literature at Yale University. She is the author of *Persons, Roles, and Minds: Identity in* Peony Pavilion *and* Peach Blossom Fan (Stanford, 2001) and *Accidental Incest, Filial Cannibalism, and Other Peculiar Encounters in Late Imperial Chinese Literature* (Cambridge, MA, 2008).

STEPHEN OWEN is James Bryant Conant University Professor at Harvard University, with joint appointments in the Department of Comparative Literature, and in East Asian Languages and Civilizations. His primary areas of research interest are premodern Chinese literature, lyric poetry, and comparative poetics. Much of his previous work has focused on the middle period of Chinese Literature (200–1200), and he is currently engaged in a complete translation of the Tang poet Du Fu. His most recent books are: *The Late Tang: Chinese Poetry of the Mid-ninth Century* (Cambridge, MA, 2006), *The Making of Early Chinese Classical Poetry* (Cambridge, MA, 2006), *An Anthology of Chinese Literature: Beginnings to 1911* (New York, 1996), *The End of the Chinese "Middle Ages"* (Stanford, 1996), *Readings in*

Chinese Literary Thought (Cambridge, MA, 1992), *Mi-lou: Poetry and the Labyrinth of Desire* (Cambridge, MA, 1989), *Remembrances: The Experience of the Past in Classical Chinese Literature* (Cambridge, MA, 1986), and *Traditional Chinese Poetry and Poetics* (Madison, WI, 1985).

SHANG WEI is Wm. Theodore and Fanny Brett de Bary and Class of 1941 Collegiate Professor of Asian Humanities, and Professor of Chinese Literature at Columbia University. His research interests include print culture, book history, intellectual history, and fiction and drama of the late imperial period. His book *"Rulin waishi" and Cultural Transformation in Late Imperial China* (Cambridge, MA, 2003) addresses the role of ritual and fiction in shaping the intellectual and cultural changes of the eighteenth century. His other publications are mainly concerned with *Jin Ping Mei cihua* (*The Plum in the Golden Vase*), late Ming culture, and fiction commentary in the Ming and Qing periods. He is the co-editor of several books, including *Dynastic Crisis and Cultural Innovation from the Late Ming to the Late Qing and Beyond* (Cambridge, MA, 2005).

XIAOFEI TIAN is Professor of Chinese Literature at Harvard University. Her research interests include Chinese literature and culture, manuscript culture, book history, the history of ideas, and world literature. She is the author of *Tao Yuanming and Manuscript Culture: The Record of a Dusty Table* (Seattle, 2005) and *Beacon Fire and Shooting Star: The Literary Culture of the Liang (502–557)* (Cambridge, MA, 2007). Her Chinese-language publications include a book on the sixteenth-century novel *The Plum in the Golden Vase* (2003; revised edn, 2005); a book on Sappho (2004); a book on the history, culture, and literature of Moorish Spain (2006); and several works of translations, as well as a number of collections of poetry and essays. She is currently working on a book about visionary journeys in early medieval and late imperial China.

JING TSU is Assistant Professor of Chinese Literature in the Department of East Asian Languages and Literatures at Yale University. She specializes in modern and contemporary Chinese literature, as well as Chinese intellectual and cultural history. Her research areas include science and popular culture, race, nationalism, dialects, and diaspora from the nineteenth century to the present. She is the author of *Failure, Nationalism, and Literature: The Making of Modern Chinese Identity, 1895–1937* (Stanford, 2005) and *Literary Governance: Sound and Script in Chinese Diaspora* (Cambridge, MA, forthcoming).

DAVID DER-WEI WANG is Edward C. Henderson Professor of Chinese Literature at Harvard University. He specializes in modern and contemporary Chinese literature, late Qing fiction and drama, and comparative literary theory. His works include *Fictional Realism in Twentieth-Century China: Mao Dun, Lao She, Shen Congwen* (New York, 1992), *Fin-de-siècle Splendor: Repressed Modernities of Late Qing Fiction, 1849–1911* (Stanford, 1997), and *The Monster that Is History: Violence, History, and Fictional Writing in Twentieth-Century China* (Berkeley, 2004).

STEPHEN H. WEST received his Ph.D. from the University of Michigan in 1972. He began his teaching career at the University of Arizona in 1972 and subsequently taught at the University of California, Berkeley from 1986 to 2004, where he was the Louis Agassiz

Professor of Chinese. He currently serves as Director of the Center for Asian Research, and is Foundation Professor of Chinese Language in the School of International Letters and Cultures at Arizona State University. He teaches courses in the prose and poetry of late medieval China (the Song and Yuan dynasties), urban literature of the twelfth and thirteenth centuries, and early Chinese drama. His research specialties are early Chinese theater, and the urban culture and cultural history of the late medieval period.

MICHELLE YEH is Professor of East Asian Languages and Cultures at the University of California, Davis. Her work focuses on modern Chinese poetry, comparative poetics, and translation. She is the author of *Modern Chinese Poetry: Theory and Practice Since 1917* (New Haven, 1991), and is the editor and translator of the *Anthology of Modern Chinese Poetry* (New Haven, 1992). She co-edited and co-translated *No Trace of the Gardener: Poems of Yang Mu* (New Haven, 1998) and *Frontier Taiwan: An Anthology of Modern Chinese Poetry* (New York, 2001). She has also published several books in Chinese, including *Essays on Modern Chinese Poetry* (1998), *From the Margin: An Alternative Tradition of Modern Chinese Poetry* (2000), and *A Poetics of Aromatics* (2005).

Preface

The two-volume *Cambridge History of Chinese Literature* traces the development of Chinese literary culture over three millennia, from the earliest inscriptions to contemporary works, including the literature of the Chinese diaspora. Our purpose is to provide a coherent narrative that can be read from cover to cover. In order to achieve consistency and readability, our contributors have consulted with one another throughout the writing process, particularly when subject areas and time periods overlap from one chapter to the next. We have carefully considered the structure and goals of each individual chapter, as well as the best point at which to break the history into two volumes so as to add to, rather than detract from, the understanding of the reader.

Literary history as practiced in China has been shaped both by premodern Chinese categories and by nineteenth-century European literary history; historical accounts of Chinese literature in the West have in turn been shaped by Chinese practices, whose categories have become habitual even though the result often seems strange to Western readers. In these volumes, we have the opportunity to question these categories. In particular, we have attempted as much as possible to avoid the division of the field into genres and to move toward a more integrated historical approach, creating a cultural history or a history of literary culture. This is the most natural approach to the earliest time periods, and still relatively easy in the middle period, but becomes increasingly difficult in the Ming, the Qing, and the modern period. It is possible, however, to achieve our goal by providing a clear framing of the general cultural (and sometimes political) history. For example, the Tang chapter in Volume 1 has not been divided into the standard categories of "Tang poetry," "Tang prose," "Tang stories," and "Tang ci." Rather, we will explore the period in terms of "The age of Empress Wu," "The reign of Emperor Xuanzong," and so on, treating poetry, prose, anecdote books, and stories as part of a cohesive historical whole. Similarly, the chapter discussing early and mid-Ming literature in Volume 2 is divided into "Early Ming to 1450," "The period from 1450 to 1520," and "The period from 1520 to 1572," with each section focusing on topics of literary culture such as "Political persecution and censorship," "New perspectives on place," "Exile literature," and so on. Issues of genre do need to be addressed, but the historical context of a given genre's appearance and its transformations clarifies the role of genre in ways that are made difficult by a genre-based organizational scheme.

A problem one encounters when using this historical approach is that there are a number of works that evolved over a long course of history and as such do not belong to a single historical moment. This primarily involves popular material of the vernacular culture, which appears relatively late in the textual record, but often has older roots. This issue has been handled by Wilt Idema (Chapter 5 of Volume 2), who has worked to dovetail his treatment with the authors of the historical chapters.

Due to the size and complexity of our undertaking, we have decided not to encourage extended plot summaries, and instead have favored short synopses of novels and longer plays. In addition, much of Chinese literature is in the form of relatively short works. The standard Chinese approach (as well as the approach of other Cambridge histories of literature) has been to focus on individual authors. Inevitably, our approach also involves the discussion of some of the great writers throughout the ages. Apart from those authors whose lives (real or invented) have become part of the reading of their works, however, we have in many cases focused on types of situations or writing rather than on individuals.

Maintaining a coherent narrative becomes more difficult in the Ming, Qing, and modern periods, as literature becomes more diverse and the options for its dissemination increase. In order to restrict this history to a reasonable size and scope, we have chosen not to discuss the literatures of linguistic minorities in the present-day PRC. Our historical approach also compels us to exclude literature written in Chinese in Korea, Vietnam, and Japan, although the circulation of literary texts between China and other East Asian countries is touched upon when the exchange is integral to the history of Chinese literary culture itself.

Histories of literature are inevitably shaped by the academic conventions and standard categories of a given national literature, as much as by the material itself. In the case of Chinese literature, the periods, names, generic terms, and conventional translations of Chinese words can occasionally pose a substantial barrier to even the most enthusiastic reader. We therefore have tried as much as possible to find ways to present our material in ways that will not pose unnecessary difficulties to readers familiar only with Anglo-European traditions.

We have tried to be consistent with the translations of terms and titles, although contributors have been urged to use their own best translations for the titles of works confined to their own period. Each initial occurrence of a book title in the text will be given in translation first and then succeeded by a transliteration of the original Chinese title in parentheses. Unless otherwise specified, all translations in these chapters are the work of the contributors. The Chinese characters in book titles, terms, and names are not given in the text; in most cases they can be found in the Glossary at the end of book.

Given length and space constraints, sources are not referenced in footnotes but are often mentioned in the text itself. The bibliographies are very selective; in particular, due to the magnitude of publications in Chinese, we have omitted from the bibliographies works of Chinese scholarship to which the editors and authors of these chapters are deeply indebted.

Acknowledgments

An undertaking of this magnitude can be carried to completion only with the support of many individuals and institutions. The Acknowledgments here is to ensure that the "unsung" heroes and heroines are celebrated. We are grateful to Linda Bree of Cambridge University Press for suggesting the idea to Kang-i Sun Chang (I came in later), and to the Council on East Asian Studies at Yale University for supporting the initial workshop and the index. Another individual who deserves special words of gratitude is Eleanor Goodman for preparing the Index.

It is, perhaps, unusual to thank one's contributors. Most were prompt with their submissions; all were responsive to editing and a pleasure to work with.

I must thank my co-editor Kang-I Sun Chang for her general oversight of the whole enterprise, ever reminding me of what needs to be done and taking care of endless details.

I thank Tian Xiaofei, not only for putting up with long hours and an editor's anxieties, but also for stepping in to help me when there was simply too much to do.

I want to give very special thanks to my graduate student Wangling Jinghua, who served as a second copy-editor. She was always ready to help out in checking over things for proper form and adherence to the guidelines. The errors that remain are my oversight, but she has caught a great many.

SO

Introduction

Chinese shares with Sanskrit and Hebrew the privilege of being one of the longest continuous literary traditions. The antiquity of each of these traditions has murky origins that are to some degree shaped by later construction, additions, and editing. Each culture, however, never lost sight of its early texts, which served as reference points as the traditions transformed over millennia. In the course of millennia and spreading over large geographical regions, Chinese and Sanskrit in particular amassed a vast corpus of literary texts, which are still read and studied.

Apart from inscriptions, which survive because of their durable media, the received tradition of Chinese literature begins in the first quarter of the first millennium BC and has continued with a steadily increasing volume of production. Students in primary schools all over China still read selections of texts from antiquity and the medieval period, though heavily annotated. Paper, which proved to be the most successful medium for the written word, gradually came into general use probably in the first and second centuries AD. Paper could not compare to parchment or vellum for durability, but neither did the production of a book require whole herds or flocks; like its equally inexpensive competitors, papyrus and palm leaves, paper enabled levels of circulation that made literary texts more than isolated treasures. China, moreover, had state-sponsored printing by the tenth century and a flourishing commercial printing industry by the late eleventh century. As Europe later discovered, paper and printing were a winning combination for the dissemination of knowledge.

When books and writings are produced, they are gathered, stored, then scattered with losses, after which they are only partially recovered. Before texts are stabilized by some form of cultural authority – religious, political, or scholarly – they tend to grow or shrink or generally transform. Readers often seek a lineage of distinct moments in literary history, represented by texts that belong to some single moment in the past. More often, particularly before the age of print, we find sediments of textual change by which later generations shaped the textual legacy according to their later interests – through recopying, editing, and emendation.

In China there was a long tradition of scholarship that sought to assess and conserve the textual legacy. Our first extant catalogue of the imperial library dates from the end of the first century BC. A continuous tradition of bibliography followed thereafter, mostly state-sponsored before the twelfth century, but with significant contributions by private bibliographers thereafter. Emperors felt a particular responsibility to conserve the textual legacy; edicts were issued seeking rare books, which were then copied and disseminated; imperial libraries went up in flames, and new edicts were issued. Attrition happens; much was, thankfully, lost; but much also was preserved and lovingly conserved by a very bookish culture. We are more aware of the transformations of the pre-print textual legacy in China than in some other cultures precisely because we know so much about that legacy. The history of a textual culture is not something simply given by that culture's greatness; it is a history of motives and material that is continuously re-creating that culture's past for the needs of some present moment.

A "history of Chinese literature" might mean several different things. It could include all literature written in the Chinese language, whose classical form was commonly used as a written medium for literature in Korea, Vietnam, and Japan. A "history of Chinese literature" might include all literature from within the political borders of modern China, a territory that encompasses many languages and some old and extensive literary traditions that are quite independent of Han Chinese literature. In these volumes we adopt a more restricted definition of the field: literature produced and circulated in Han Chinese communities, both those communities within the borders of modern China and diaspora communities. Even though not all the authors discussed were ethnically Han Chinese, all participated in a Han Chinese culture.

This apparently simple definition begs many questions. It can only be based on ethnic self-identification of communities spread across millennia and the assumption of a common identity among what linguists would recognize as different but closely related languages. Like all such "imagined communities," it is essentially tied to a polity that is now a "nation state." The Chinese state's relation to Han Chinese communities outside the polity and their own relation to that polity remain a contested issue.

No matter how we try to contain literary history, the enterprise has become far more complicated than it seemed when this genre of scholarship reached its first mature form in the early nineteenth century. Two centuries ago it was self-evident to literary historians that there was a unity between language, ethnicity, and the nation state, either as a historical fact or as an aspiration. Even then there were often communities inside nation states speaking – and often writing – in other languages. We recognize further complications now. There were classical languages, sometimes radically distinct from the spoken language, that could constitute the bulk of literary production, but were entirely or in large measure excluded from histories of "national literatures." There were and still are macaronic languages, languages changing under the pressure of translation, national languages spreading and mutating in colonies and former colonies, diasporas and multiethnic immigration.

All these phenomena present problems for literary history, and they clearly show the degree to which literary history as a modern enterprise has been tied to the nation state and its interests, supplying it with a continuous cultural history. If no nation state formed, literary history of a particular ethnic group often became the affirmation of a cultural history of a "people," tied to a language that justified the possibility of such a state.

Although Chinese literature served the purpose of constituting a shared cultural identity of a class long before the modern period, the modern writing of Chinese literary history, which first reached full maturity in the 1920s, has clung to that nineteenth-century belief in the unity of language, ethnicity, and the polity. For almost a century it has continuously retold a Han Chinese epic, recounting the history and continuity of Chinese literary culture from antiquity to the present, spread across a huge territory.

This brings us to the Chinese language and what became, in the twentieth century, the language politics that has resulted in a two-volume *Cambridge History of Chinese Literature*, rather than a volume called *The Cambridge History of Classical Chinese Literature* and a volume called *The Cambridge History of Vernacular Chinese Literature*. In Western Europe one would not have used the same word for both volumes: the first would be called "Latin," and the second, one of the European vernaculars – let us say "Italian" to invoke a parallel case, in which Italian was until relatively recently not a national language but the "vernacular," *volgare*. The fact that in China the same word is used for both volumes and in Europe different words are used is "political," both in the usual sense and in the cultural sense.

As is well known, Chinese is a character-based language. The consequences are generally less well understood. The pronunciation of the same character has varied greatly through the history of the language and across the large linguistic area of distinct, but related, languages and dialects. In addition,

Chinese has only the unrecognized traces of an archaic morphology; it seems uninflected. If the original function of a written grammar was a way to control regional variation and historical change in language, Chinese did not need a written grammar because of the variable pronunciation of characters and the apparent lack of morphology. As in all languages, the words and the patterns changed over time in different places, but the variation of pronunciation made it seem that a simple "classical Chinese," based on the language of antiquity, was no more than the proper formal written form of the existing spoken language. Until the language reforms of the 1920s the situation in China was closely analogous to a teacher considering a student's writing exercise in American English: "gotta" (representing the spoken language), "got to" (spoken language translated into the written language), "have to" (informal, but acceptable in some written venues), and "must" (formal, "proper" written usage). Chinese was, indeed, very much like English in recognizing such differences as a question of register, while accepting all these variations as the same language ("Chinese," "English").

There was nothing in Chinese like artificially normalized Sanskrit and the multiple regional and historical Indic vernaculars, each distinct and recognizable, which constituted the exceedingly complex linguistic literary map of India (where variations in register of the kind described above would each be proper to a language type with a different name). There was not even any clear binary opposition between "classical" and "vernacular" Chinese until the nineteenth century and the beginnings of the language politics that culminated in the 1920s, when it was explicitly described on the model of the opposition between Latin and the European vernaculars. As in many literary cultures, in Chinese certain styles and linguistic features became associated with different kinds of writing. Again, English offers very instructive parallels: if one read the lyrics of "gangsta rap" from a CD and saw "must" in the transcription of a recited "gotta," there would be a comic dissonance of generic linguistic codes that corresponds very well to the proprieties of registers in Chinese. Once initiated, remarkably few of these genre styles ever disappeared; the Chinese literary language grew by generically segregated accretions until the new vernacular literature of the twentieth century. The older Chinese literary language is perhaps best understood as a range of registers, varying between "refined" (*ya*) and "common" (*su*), or between "ancient" and "modern" ("modern" understood as a style normalized between the sixth and eighth centuries). What is now called "vernacular" is the "common" (*su*) side of the first axis; but there was no norm even here. The lively vernaculars of drama (with different vernaculars for plays in the northern and southern traditions) were different from the lively vernacular of short stories and novels, which was in turn different from the vernacular of dialectical song lyrics. Everything was bound to genres and the register appropriate to a given genre.

It was in the interest of the European nation states to stress the distinction between their own normative vernaculars (keeping in mind that national vernaculars transformed all linguistic difference within their borders into "dialect") and a European Latin that crossed national boundaries without a passport. By long history determined to remain a single polity, China had different interests: there could be only one national vernacular, and a story was needed by which a single classical became a single vernacular, affirming both the integrity of the territory and the continuity of the culture.

China's cultural critics and literary historians of the 1920s transformed a placid map of linguistic registers and associated genres into an agonistic narrative of the struggle between a dead "classical" language and a living "vernacular" language. Hu Shi, one of the most prominent intellectuals of the 1920s generation, dated the beginning of the struggle to the first century BC. This was a literary history with an agenda, and the many literary histories written in Chinese since the 1920s and 1930s still carry the traces of that agenda. If that was a period in which a new China was struggling to emerge out of a very old China, literary history was an agonistic epic of the struggle of the written vernacular against the deadening dominance of classical Chinese. The end of the story, the final victory of the modern national literary vernacular in the 1920s, was assumed beforehand.

The northern Mandarin that became the national literary vernacular is no more the vernacular of large parts of China than classical Chinese was. The power of mass media, however, allows it to influence and change those languages far more effectively than classical Chinese ever could.

Recent literary historiography has struggled with many of the inherited assumptions of the genre; these are deeply engrained and still very much a part of literary history in many places. One such assumption, closely tied to some putative organic integrity of the people, is the integrity of the literary tradition. The entrances of other cultural traditions are often seen as "alien" to the national genius and accepted only when assimilated and domesticated, stamped with the "native genius."

Chinese culture is often considered in splendid isolation, both within China itself and from the outside. Such a presumption invites us to consider an alternative narrative by which the resilience of Chinese culture has been a function of its ability to adapt to and assimilate foreign cultures. There were, indeed, two periods when China was profoundly transformed by outside influences. The first of these was with the introduction of Buddhism in the early medieval period; the second of these is more commonly recognized, when China assimilated European culture from the late nineteenth through the twentieth centuries.

For six centuries, between the Eastern Han and the early Tang, China was engaged in the most monumental translation project that the world had ever seen or would again see until the explosion of translations in European languages in the nineteenth century. A vast corpus of utterly unfamiliar and often very sophisticated cultural material was imported from South Asia and translated, accompanied by careful reflection on the problems of translation. The pressures exerted by Sanskrit on the target language produced a language that we now refer to as "Buddhist Chinese," and it was in this language that Buddhism was further exported to Korea and Japan. Chinese secular culture spread along with it.

Like the Latin of the Vulgate Bible, Buddhist Chinese was a remarkable combination of the straightforward vernacular and a very foreign conceptual discourse. Chinese Buddhist discourse was segregated, culturally and bibliographically, from secular discourse, and there was significant native resistance to Buddhism on the grounds of Buddhism's "foreignness" and the way in which its values came into conflict with Han Chinese values. Segregation, however, never succeeds. Translated texts and a new conceptual discourse that grew out of translation were a major presence in the Chinese discursive world, in the form of readings, lectures, debates, and stories. Buddhism profoundly transformed the Chinese language, the conceptual universe, and narrative.

A profound transformation from outside influence is often troubling to those who wish to believe in some primordial autonomy of a tradition. Scholars of Chinese culture, indeed, often feel comfortable only with the late-bloomer in Buddhist sects, Chan (Zen), which is seen as Buddhism acceptably domesticated. By and large Chinese scholarly discourse focuses on how China changed Buddhism, rather than on how Buddhism changed China (as modern political scholars often like to talk about how China changed and domesticated Marxism).

The contrary argument also has much to recommend it. A culture may be enriched and strengthened by the coexistence of values that can never be perfectly reconciled. The argument has been made regarding the confrontation of the Greco-Roman tradition with the values of the Jewish tradition through Christianity. So it can be argued that, after its first flowering in antiquity, the

Chinese tradition became great because of the fruitful opposition of irreconcilable values, from Buddhism and from the indigenous tradition.

Indian and Central Asian monks were welcome in China, and Chinese monks undertook the long journey to study in India; this was a cultural encounter that very many Chinese desired. The later encounter with European culture came in a very different mode, with foreign concessions, European warships supporting *its* missionaries, and social upheavals that followed from major technological changes. China still felt the fascination of this encounter, but the level of threat and hostility far surpassed the general response to the introduction of Buddhism. Europeans and Americans came to China, and some Chinese went to study in Europe and America, as in the seventh century Xuanzang had gone to study in a Buddhist academy in South Asia. One great difference from the medieval situation was that in the late nineteenth and early twentieth centuries there was a mediator through which European culture could be encountered in a form already translated into an East Asian context (and using Chinese characters). This was Japan, in whose universities countless Chinese students gathered, and where they learned Western novels, medicine, and revolution.

The impact of European literary culture on Chinese literature has been questioned in interesting ways. Did China produce its own modernity (perhaps jolted by its contact with the European powers), or was modernity a European import? The alternative answers to the question may both be true. One story tells us that long before European culture imposed itself on the Chinese world, the Chinese language was developing on its own the capacity to give a complex representation of human experience in vernacular narrative. The other story is that the impact of European forms of expression and ideas (in translation) exerted such a pressure on the language that it had to change. These very different stories agree on one point: certain kinds of written classical Chinese were incapable of directly representing these changes.

The supporter of European culture will have to significantly modify the definition of the "novel" in order to exclude *The Plum in the Golden Vase* of the late sixteenth century (at the latest). Chinese fiction was already everywhere in East Asia when European fiction made its appearance in East Asia in the nineteenth century. The introduction of European fiction profoundly changed the market of literary exchange, but it did not introduce the "novel."

The two "true stories" still exist: the indigenous transformation of the possibilities of representation and new forces from outside through translation. The contemporary achievements of Chinese literature bear witness, a second time, to how the Chinese tradition is strengthened by internalizing the foreign. Perfect "domestication" is impossible; irreconcilable values must live together. China has always learned and made fruitful use of what it needed.

A new literary history is the opportunity to reexamine categories, both those from premodern China and those introduced in the new literary histories of the 1920s. Reexamination does not mean wholesale rejection; it simply means testing old categories against the evidence. Old habits will still sometimes linger on.

We have asked our contributors to avoid too sharp a division between "classical" and "vernacular" literatures, until that begins to be a concern in the late nineteenth century. From the Chinese tradition itself there are sharp divisions, but they are genre divisions rather than "classical" and "vernacular" divisions. The historical integrity of genre is itself a problem that all literary historians must face. A Renaissance vernacular eclogue will be closer to Vergil than to a sonnet by the same Renaissance writer, though his or her sonnets may be closer to Petrarch. A similar situation was true in China. The danger for the literary historian, however, is a set of increasingly atomized genre histories giving no sense of the variety of interests in a period or in a particular writer. We have asked our authors in these volumes to try to think of periods as integrals in order to counteract the tendency to think only in terms of genre.

One area in which we have sometimes departed from the received tradition is in periodization. Sometimes our periods correspond to traditional period divisions, but at other times they may differ by more than a century. One consequence of the identification of literature and the polity was periodization of literature by dynasties and reigns. This remained true even for the radically innovative literary historians of the twentieth century.

Virtually every scholar of Chinese literature knows on some level that in many cases dynastic periodization does not accurately represent major changes in cultural and literary history, but the habit is so deeply engrained that it still defines the chapter structure in virtually every literary history. The usual way of addressing the obvious inadequacies of dynastic periodization is by saying that the beginning of a dynasty "continued" the style of the preceding era. The disadvantage of such a tactic is that the formal division discourages scholars from thinking across dynastic boundaries to reflect on such continuities as a single phenomenon. Every literary history, for example, starts anew with the Tang, or the short Sui dynasty that preceded it, representing the newly unified empire. A more persuasive account begins in the north before unification, with the influx of southern literary men and southern culture, and continues through the first reigns of the Tang; this account involves the politically victorious north coming to terms with the cultural power of the south.

We will generally keep the dynastic terms in the earlier periods, but sometimes we will redefine them. Our "cultural Tang" begins in 650, rather than 617, when the dynasty was actually founded; on the other hand our "cultural Tang" extends through the Five Dynasties and sixty years into the Song, when a distinctly new Song cultural turn became clear. The advantages to such an approach outweigh its awkwardness.

We have endeavored to take into account the material culture that was the basis of the production and circulation of texts. The period covered in the first volume witnessed the two most significant events: the invention and spread of paper as the medium of writing and the spread of printing in the eleventh century. If the corpus of texts that can be reliably dated to the roughly two centuries of the Eastern Han vastly outnumbers literary texts from the two centuries of the Western Han, part of the reason may be the introduction of paper and consequently the wider circulation of written texts.

We have tried to take some account of the ways in which earlier works were preserved and shaped by the judgment of later ages. If two centuries of Northern Dynasties writing (from the fifth and sixth centuries) are almost invisible, it is not because the northerners were illiterate or culturally incompetent. We see, in dramatic ways, the prejudice against them in the seventh-century sources on which we largely depend. A good literary historian always learns that there are very few cases of permanent consensus; the most famous figures often need time to appear, and the canon of one age is the target of another. Almost any American who reads Chinese poetry in translation knows of "Cold Mountain" (Hanshan). "Hanshan" was a minor poet in China until very recently. In Japan this collection of poems (let us disbelieve single authorship) was attached to Chan Buddhism, and by this association a selection of the works was included in an influential series of anthologies in the 1950s. The poems then attracted the attention of the sinologist Burton Watson and the poet Gary Snyder, and their renditions invited yet other renditions. Their popularity in America drew attention first in Taiwan and later in mainland China. There are now a number of excellent Chinese commentaries and studies of Hanshan. The Hanshan poems clearly deserve the attention that is now given them; so long as a text is preserved, history has strange, sometimes roundabout ways of rectifying unfair neglect.

Literary history shares one characteristic in common with histories of the other arts: a version of literary history is itself already part of the literature about which one writes. This simply means that writers write and readers read within a virtual literary-historical narrative that is essential to both writing and reading. If a scholar demonstrates that an "Elizabethan" sonnet was actually written in 1930, that changes the meaning of the text to such a degree that we are forcibly reminded that we can read only inside a conventional literary-historical narrative that tells us how to take certain things. Borges's "Pierre Menard, Author of *Don Quixote*" is always with us.

China was and still is very much such a historicist culture, with the account of literature serving as a mainstay in a larger cultural history. The contemporary literary historian can neither simply reproduce the standard account nor disregard it. The challenge we have tried to face here is to write a literary history that does not simply repeat the standard narrative. Ultimately this can be achieved only by making the formation of standard literary-historical narrative itself part of our own account.

The first volume of *The Cambridge History of Chinese Literature* begins with the question of the Chinese written language and the earliest inscriptions, dating from the late second millennium BC; it continues to the end of the fourteenth century. We move from inscribed bones and tortoise plastrons to a fully evolved commercial print culture, encompassing both writing in the older classical language and an emerging urban vernacular. During this long span, writing and its interpretation passed from the special competence of a very small scribal class attached to royalty to the defining characteristic of the elite of a large empire, with varying degrees of literacy extending throughout the population.

Almost half this period is covered in Martin Kern's chapter, which brings the story from the earliest writing down to the end of the first century BC, from the traces of archaic ritual to a sophisticated ancient empire, the Han. Archaeological discoveries and a critical reading of the evidence from received texts have radically transformed our understanding of this period. Throughout most of imperial China and the modern period, Chinese antiquity seemed like merely an earlier version of the textual world that succeeded it. The disruption of transmission of early texts was often blamed on the legend of the Qin burning of the books in the last part of the third century BC. We now pose questions about the oral transmission of some texts and the venues of writing, with due consideration of the material media – often bulky rolls of bamboo slips. Archaeologically recovered manuscripts have given us a very different view of early writing and suggest the degree to which the received textual tradition was reconstructed for the needs of archivists working in the imperial library at the very end of antiquity.

David Knechtges's chapter, covering the first through third centuries AD, saw the introduction of paper, which seems to have come into general use in the second century. It should be no surprise that this same period saw a dramatic increase in the number of preserved texts. Writing seems to have often been a family tradition, organized around fathers, mothers, sons, and daughters. "Literature" in this context was not the specialized field it later became, but rather part of a larger arena that included history, learning in the Classics, and the production of texts for social needs, such as commemorative inscription. The collapse of the Eastern Han at the end of the second century was a traumatic event, and we see a striking increase in private texts, including personal poetry.

War, with brief periods of stability, took up much of the third century; In the second decade of the fourth century the ruling Jin dynasty collapsed under pressure from invading peoples of the north. Xiaofei Tian picks up the story in 317, with the flight of the dynasty and many elite families south of the Yangzi river. Over the course of more than two and a half centuries a distinctly southern culture developed, in which literature, particularly poetry, played an important role. This period also saw the rapid spread of Buddhism, culminating in what was a true Buddhist dynasty, the Liang, in the first half of the sixth century. The Liang, with its literary criticism, literary history, anthology-making, and bibliographical work, became the mediator through which the earlier literary tradition was transmitted to later ages.

The sudden and unexpected collapse of the Liang in the middle of the sixth century sent many southerners, with their immense cultural confidence, seeking a place in the courts of north China. This was a period of political and cultural consolidation, during which China was reunified, first under the brief Sui dynasty, and then under the Tang. During the first half of the seventh century the textual remains of the devastation of the second half of the sixth century were gathered and inventoried. Literary scholarship was institutionalized in the court, which remained the center of literary production.

Beginning in the 650s the empress of the weak Emperor Gaozong gradually took over the business of ruling; after Gaozong's death and the very brief installation of two of her young sons on the throne, she declared herself the sole ruler and eventually proclaimed her own new dynasty, the Zhou. This was Empress Wu, who reigned until her death in 705. In Stephen Owen's chapter we see how she gathered her own literary courtiers, no longer from the old families with cultural prestige, and added the composition of poetry to the literary examination. After her death the Tang was reestablished, but she had begun a process by which literary composition extended to ever wider circles of the elite as a means to participate in a unified culture and advance in the central government. The center of literary production – poetry, prose, anecdote, and literary scholarship – gradually moved away from the court and became the defining competence of a class. The striking achievements of Tang literature are in part due to its production and circulation in expanded communities of changing values and fashions that no longer were centered on the court.

The styles and range of Tang literature continued through the regional states that formed in the dissolution of the Tang around the turn of the tenth century and into the Song dynasty, founded in 960 and consolidating its power in the decades that followed. Where Ronald Egan picks up the story in the 1020s profound changes in the culture were becoming apparent in literature. Printing, first undertaken by Buddhist establishments and the state, made books available on an unprecedented scale. Commercial printing became more widespread toward the end of the eleventh century. A reformed examination system made recruitment of the elite more truly meritocratic than the old Tang patronage system. Daoxue – Confucianism revived in a new key – questioned received authority in understanding the Confucian Classics. New genres, such as song lyrics, miscellanies, and connoisseur literature, became popular. The old Tang genres took on a new aspect – sometimes genial and reflective, sometime erudite in ways made possible by the availability of books.

The swift fall of the Song's northern territories in 1127 left China again divided, with the Song reestablished in the south. The north was ruled by a Jurchen dynasty called the Jin. Michael Fuller and Shuen-fu Lin present this period, particularly the Southern Song, with its large, rich cities and thriving economy. The loss of the north to a non-Han people provoked an outpouring of poetry that we might call "patriotic," a sense of identification with an ethnic polity and its territory, rather than simply loyalty to a particular dynasty. The position of Daoxue continued to grow, and the distrust of literature that had always been part of Daoxue left literature with a diminished role in the state and in society. If literature had lost something of its old cultural moorings, it was more widely practiced than ever, with societies devoted to writing both poems and song lyrics, and a growing output of criticism.

In the north the Jin felt acutely the cultural power of the Southern Song, and it tried to define itself in opposition, as carrying on earlier Song literary traditions, traditions of what had become the "Northern Song." The Jin, however, was the first to suffer the impact of the Mongols, who overran the Jin in 1234 and the Southern Song in 1276. Stephen West's chapter gives us a new view of the literature of the Mongol dynasty, called the Yuan, of how Jin and Song intellectuals came to terms with a new kind of government that did not follow the Chinese model, a model that had come to seem both universal and eternal. The Yuan was a multiethnic empire, and many who wrote in Chinese were not ethnically Han. A vernacular urban culture, with entertainments from theater to storytelling to lively vernacular songs, had made its first appearance in the Song; by the Yuan it emerged even more into print culture.

The Yuan was collapsing by the mid-fourteenth century and officially fell in 1368. The beginning of the Ming was populated by writers who had risen to prominence in the Yuan. The Ming founder, the Hongwu Emperor, laid waste to that world; and when the literary world gradually recovered at the beginning of the fifteenth century, the continuity had been broken and was to be recovered in a new mode.

Early Chinese literature, beginnings through Western Han

MARTIN KERN

I. The Chinese language and writing system

The earliest evidence for the Chinese language, and for the Chinese script as its writing system, is found in oracle bone and bronze inscriptions from the site of the Late Shang (ca 1250–ca 1046 BC) royal capital near modern Anyang, located in the northernmost part of modern Henan Province. From there to the present day, a continuous line of development can be drawn for both language and script that has served the expression of Chinese literature over the last three millennia. The Chinese script is one of only a handful of instances in human history where writing was invented independently, and it is the only originally invented writing system still in use today. Over time, it was adopted to write not just Chinese but also other East and Southeast Asian languages such as Korean, Japanese, and Vietnamese, thereby extending the reach of the Chinese literary tradition significantly beyond the boundaries of its spoken language.

The Late Shang oracle inscriptions (*jiaguwen*) scratched into bovine shoulder bones and turtle plastrons were records of communications with the royal ancestral spirits. Since their initial discovery in 1899, more than 150,000 fragments of such inscriptions have been found. They range in length from just a few to several dozen characters and preserve accounts of royal divinations on a wide range of topics – the well-being of the king, military success, the timeliness of sacrifices, the weather, and so on – that affected both the person of the ruler and the prosperity of his state. Incised into the very material used for divination, these inscriptions recorded the king's successful communication with his ancestors and were hence of both religious and political significance. The second group of Late Shang texts, far smaller in number, were inscriptions cast into elaborate bronze vessels (most prominently food and wine containers) that were used in ancestral sacrifices. The Shang had produced ritual bronzes since at least the fifteenth century BC, but inscriptions appeared only around 1250 BC. In their vast majority, these earliest bronze inscriptions (*jinwen*) contained only one to five characters to denote the donor and the sacrificial purpose of the bronze vessel. However, both bone and bronze inscriptions from the late second millennium BC show the Chinese writing system as sophisticated and well developed, indicating that its origin and development might reach further back in time. Moreover, the inscriptions, while not created for mere archival purposes or the recording of history, seem based on writings that were first composed on perishable materials like wood and bamboo. Nothing suggests that writing at the Shang capital was limited to oracle records and bronze inscriptions; instead, all other writing on less durable surfaces has simply disappeared.

What is not an accident of preservation, though, is the fact that the early Chinese limited the use of their most precious and prestigious materials to those writings that had the closest connection to their religious practices of divination and the ancestral cult. The same observation still holds for the Western Zhou (ca 1046–771 BC). While oracle bone inscriptions soon disappeared under the new dynasty, the production of bronze ritual artifacts, both inscribed and uninscribed, proliferated enormously; bronze vessels, bells, ritual weapons, and so on must have numbered in the tens, if not hundreds, of thousands. Moreover, Western Zhou bronze texts on occasion extended to hundreds of characters and became more regular in both their visual appearance and the use of rhyme, meter, and onomatopoeia. At the same time, these aesthetic devices also appeared in the earliest transmitted writings of Chinese literature: the core layers – most likely dating from the ninth and eighth centuries BC – of the *Classic of Documents* (*Shangshu* or *Shujing*), the *Classic of Poetry* (*Shijing*), and the *Classic of Changes* (*Yijing*). Unlike the inscriptions, these texts are preserved in the standardized orthography in which all received writings from the early period have come to us.

The initial move to standardize the forms of Chinese characters dates from the Qin (221–207 BC) dynasty and was part of the overall administrative standardization enacted by the newly founded imperial rule. During the four centuries of the subsequent Western (202 BC–AD 9) and Eastern (AD 25–220) Han dynasties, including Wang Mang's brief Xin dynasty (r. 9–23) in the middle, the texts of antiquity were transcribed into the then standard script. This script was further refined over the course of the Six Dynasties (220–589). In the course of this development, the number of characters proliferated greatly by the systematic application of semantic classifiers – graphic elements to indicate different categories of meaning – to graphically distinguish homophonous but semantically different words, finally matching the sound, meaning, and written form of a word with far greater precision than before. The crowning achievement of these scholarly efforts was the character dictionary *Cut Rhymes* (*Qieyun*), arranged by tone and rhyme, that Lu Fayan (fl. 581–601) and his collaborators completed in 601.

Today, the Chinese script – not counting the simplified forms created in the People's Republic of China – encompasses perhaps 80,000 characters, with the actual number contingent on how variant writings are counted. By comparison, Shang oracle bone inscriptions include fewer than five thousand different characters; the Thirteen Classics (*shisan jing*) of the Confucian canon, containing diachronic textual layers from the Western Zhou through the Han dynasties, total 6,544 different characters; *Cang Jie*, a dictionary attributed to the Qin chancellor Li Si (d. 208 BC) and further elaborated upon by Yang Xiong (53 BC–AD 18), included 5,340 characters; and Xu Shen's (ca 55–ca 149) *Explanation of Simple Graphs and Analysis of Composite Characters* (*Shuowen jiezi*) was originally composed of 9,353 different characters and in addition included 1,163 variant forms (the received version of the dictionary includes 10,700 characters). These numbers illustrate the gradual development of the writing system. A first peak, reflecting Eastern Han scholastic attempts to create a standardized inventory of writing and, hence, normative readings of the Classics, emerged with the *Shuowen jiezi* around AD 120; yet it was the later differentiation of characters through the systematic addition of semantic classifiers that multiplied the repertoire of the written language.

A certain number of Chinese characters show obvious pictographic origins. This fact has given rise to the misperception that Chinese characters in general are pictographs (images of things) or ideographs (images of ideas). They are, instead, logographs, writing the words of the Chinese language. As such, they primarily represent not ideas but sounds and hence function by and large like the letters and graphs of other writing systems, if considerably more cumbersome. Yet Chinese characters also possess specific features that have influenced the development of Chinese writing, literature, and even culture in general. Because the characters represent syllables, and because the vast majority of early Chinese words were monosyllabic, individual characters wrote individual words in classical literature. At the same time, the syllables of any Chinese dialect number merely in the hundreds; even while further differentiated by different tones, this tightly limited repertoire of sound resulted in very large numbers of homophonous words. Prior to the large-scale post-Han differentiation and standardization of writing, the pervasive homophony of words combined with a limited repertoire of characters led to the promiscuous use of "loan characters" (*jiajiezi*); that is, characters being "borrowed" to write a whole range of homophonous words. This widespread phonetic use of the writing system infused a considerable potential of ambiguity into all but the most pedestrian administrative pieces of writing and shows that writing – especially the writing of the texts of high antiquity – functioned properly only within a framework of interpretation, commentary, transcription, and personal instruction. All received Chinese texts from classical antiquity have reached us through the filter of these hermeneutic practices that continuously served textual continuity. At least through the late Six Dynasties, the writing system was not able to arrest the textual tradition; in order to continue, the tradition – and with it the writing system – had to evolve dynamically.

A second characteristic of Chinese characters, very much matching the isolating nature of the Chinese language, is their immutable form. Without profuse use of grammatical particles (*xuci*, also known as "function words") – something normally avoided in classical literary writing – the written language was both extremely economical and seriously underdetermined in terms of tense, number, gender, and syntactical relations. Moreover, the proliferation of dialects over the vast geographic expanse of the realm of spoken Chinese, and diachronic changes within these dialects, are rendered moot and invisible by the stability of the characters. Yet, perhaps even more importantly, the stability of the characters has created an illusion of linguistic and cultural stability that generated a formidable reality in its own right: a continuous literary tradition of three millennia where any newly written text could be enriched by expressions from various earlier written texts without necessarily giving the appearance of stylistic antiquarianism or phonetic incompatibility. Since pre-imperial times, this phenomenon has led to the perpetuation of a literary koine that, while changing incrementally over time, was firmly guarded in its fundamental identity and continuity as it encompassed an ever-expanding universe of texts.

The third feature of Chinese characters that has contributed to the power and coherence of the written tradition is their use to write foreign words that were either phonetically transcribed or genuinely translated into Chinese. During the Six Dynasties, when Buddhism made its powerful entry into Chinese civilization, thousands of new terms and names found their way into the Chinese language. Written with existing Chinese characters that at the same time maintained their conventional use to write indigenous Chinese words, the foreign additions to the Chinese dictionary were easily naturalized and became part of the Chinese intellectual and literary tradition.

Finally, the basic monosyllabic structure of most Chinese words, cast into individual and immutable characters, provided the rhythms for both poetry and prose. Classical Chinese seems to fall naturally into simple rhythms of beats that are also words: the xx | xx structure of the *Classic of Poetry*, the xx | xxx meter of the classical poem in the five-syllable line, the alternating sequences of four and six characters in parallel prose, the four-syllable-line structure of proverbs and slogans, and other metric forms give the classical language a profoundly rhythmical appearance. The resulting regularity of poetic meter lends itself most naturally to the aesthetics of end-rhyme and parallelism, two defining formal features of Chinese literature that can be traced throughout the tradition.

These characteristics of the classical written language contributed forcefully to a tradition of Chinese literature that by now has continued well into its fourth millennium. Part of the attraction and cultural force of the writing system was based in its early mythology, which described the system of Chinese characters as not artificially devised but found in nature, imagining writing as an element of cosmic order. In the absence of a creator god, the order of writing was seen as emerging from the natural world and revealed to the sages of high antiquity. Xu Shen's postface to his *Shuowen jiezi* provides the mature statement of this mythology of writing, and indeed of civilization as a whole:

> When in the time of antiquity Bao Xi [Fu Xi] ruled the world as king, he looked up and perceived the images in the skies, looked down and perceived the model order on the earth. He observed how the patterns of the birds and beasts were adapted to the earth. Nearby he took [his insights] from himself; further away he took them from the things of the world. Thereupon he first created the eight trigrams of the *Classic of Changes* in order to transmit the models and images ... When Cang Jie, the scribe of the Yellow Emperor, saw the claw and hoof traces of birds and beasts, he recognized that these could be distinguished in their forms and differentiated from one another. [Thus] he first created incised writing ... When Cang Jie first created writing, he probably made images of forms according to their categories; thus, [his simple characters] are called "patterns" [*wen*]. Later, these were increased in number through the mutual combination of elements of mimetic form and sound; [these complex characters] were called "graphs" [*zi*].

Here, the invention of the Chinese script is both a civilizational feat of the ancient sages and an act of "finding" writing in nature, tracing the origins of writing to both history and the natural cosmos and envisioning the script as a representation of order that encompasses and comprehends both. This view of the origin of the Chinese script became enormously influential over the following centuries, extending into the cosmologies of literature, calligraphy, and painting. The idea that literature was an order of nature remained at the core of literary theory as expressed in Lu Ji's (261–303) "Poetic Exposition on Literature" (Wen fu), in Liu Xie's (ca 467–ca 522) *The Literary Mind and the Carving of the Dragon* (*Wenxin diaolong*), and even in Tang and Song ideas about "ancient-style literature" (*guwen*).

Xu Shen's account is rooted not only in ancient mythology, but also in one of the philosophical core texts of early China, the "Appended Phrases" (Xici, or Xici zhuan). This text, also known as the "Great Tradition" (Dazhuan) and likely dating from the third century BC, is a cosmological treatise that became appended to the *Classic of Changes* as one of the so-called "ten wings" (*shiyi*) of philosophical elaboration that by Han times were attributed to Confucius (551–479 BC?). Yet in the "Appended Phrases," writing – in its initial stages of "knotted cords" (*jiesheng*) and "scratched notations" (*shuqi*) – appears merely as one of many civilizational achievements, including agriculture, traffic, commerce, and so on; it is not yet connected to the culture heroes of high antiquity, nor is it related to the cosmological eight trigrams. This difference between the earlier and the later accounts points to the development of a textual culture during the early centuries of the Chinese empire when writing and literature became gradually established as the supreme expression of culture. The early Chinese term for writing-as-culture is *wen*, which originally denotes any kind of natural or human "pattern." Before the empire, the term was not restricted to "writing" but used broadly for "cultural accomplishment," especially in ritual demeanor and performance, including the "patterns" of music and material ornament. It was only in late Western Han times, around the middle of the first century BC, that *wen* began to denote primarily "writing." This shift was more than a change in meaning of a single word: it signaled an overall move of the cultural core from ritual to textual expression. It generated a cultural history of the written text together with the institutions to sustain it – first and foremost the imperial bureaucracy and its civil examination system – that remained intact and in place throughout the rise and fall of succeeding imperial dynasties. In this continuity, the written tradition constituted its own sovereign realm, parallel and always superior to the reality of imperial rule, and explicitly imbued with the capacity not only to express human emotion and thought, but to reflect the nature and condition of social and cosmological order. Yet despite the powerful interpretation that the later tradition has exerted over its origins, it is imperative not to project this later understanding of *wen* into the twelve centuries of Chinese writing before the late Western Han cultural shift.

II. Inscriptions on oracle bones and bronze artifacts

Shang dynasty oracle records are brief, seemingly bureaucratic documents of religious practice that lack any literary aesthetics. Following an act of royal divination during which the bone or plastron cracked under the local application of intense heat, an inscription was added right next to the crack – the pattern of which presumably represented the response from the ancestral spirits – to record the original divination charge in an alternating pair ("It may rain / It may not rain") as well the diviner or king's prediction according to the cracks. On occasion, a verification of the royal prediction was added at a later point. In addition, the inscriptions routinely provide the notation of the date of the divination as well as the name of the diviner. Especially during the early reign of King Wu Ding (r. ca 1200–1181 BC), oracle questions covered the entire range of royal activities (sacrificial rituals, military expeditions, agriculture, meteorology, astrology, natural calamities, hunting) along with matters concerning the personal well-being of the king (toothaches, dreams, illnesses, births). After King Wu Ding, however, divinations became not only far more numerous but also increasingly limited to matters of the royal ancestral sacrifices, suggesting that divination became a more formalized routine. The oracle questions of Anyang did not allow the unexpected: phrased in formulaic yes/no alternatives and thus strictly limiting the range of possible answers, they expressed the confidence of the living in a predictable world where the spirits were not considered capricious – or, perhaps, the desire to impose limits on spirits the King and his diviners did consider capricious.

While the Late Shang kings placed great emphasis on the continuity with their venerated ancestors to whom they also sacrificed, it is less clear why they produced so many oracle records. These records were sometimes carved weeks after the divination; moreover, there is a considerable number of used but uninscribed bones and plastrons. It is unlikely that the inscriptions were meant as historical records. Their dating system of the sixty-day cycle gave neither a year notation nor the name of the king; the unwieldy shape of bones and plastrons, especially in light of their sheer numbers, made them cumbersome to stack and keep track of. Moreover, some very large characters were apparently meant for display while others were not only incised but also filled with red color. The yes/no alternatives were written in beautiful symmetry, and in a number of cases, the same inscriptions were repeated over a series of bones or plastrons. None of these efforts added informational value to an archival use. Thus the records' main purpose may have been to show the king in his prerogative to communicate with the Shang royal ancestors and to secure their blessings. The aesthetic features of the inscriptions, their semantic ossification over time (which evidently did not render them less valuable), their confidence in a universe that could be divined and explained, and the way in which they frequently show the king as religious agent ("The king, testing the charge, said: . . . ") all contributed to the ritual and political representation of the Shang kings. In this the oracle records are related to the only other group of texts extant from high antiquity in durable material, the Shang and Western Zhou inscriptions on bronze paraphernalia used in the ancestral sacrifices. These texts belonged to the same political and religious contexts as the oracle inscriptions, and both bodies of early writing must therefore be considered in light of one another.

While ritual bronze vessels pre-date the period of the divination records by more than two centuries, the casting of inscribed objects arose only around the time of the oracle inscriptions. It then developed rapidly under the Zhou dynasty, who had overthrown the Shang in roughly 1046 BC and maintained the royal capital in the Wei river valley of modern Shaanxi Province until driven eastward by non-Zhou invaders in 771 BC. It is this period of nearly three centuries – retrospectively called the Western Zhou – and especially its early reigns, that to later historical imagination became the golden age of political order and civilization, providing the cultural framework and moral orientation for the subsequent literature of Eastern Zhou (771–256 BC) and early imperial times. While the Western Zhou rulers soon abandoned the bone and plastron oracles of the Shang for new forms of divination, they developed the art of bronze casting to a level of technological and aesthetic sophistication unseen in any other early civilization. They did so on a very large scale, producing thousands, perhaps tens of thousands of bronze objects that show a dazzling array of forms and designs. These precious objects belonged entirely to the royal and aristocratic elite, who used them primarily in ancestral sacrifices and further at secular occasions such as banquets. The earliest Zhou bronzes seem eccentric and inferior compared to the Late Shang artifacts, but gradually the Western Zhou developed its own formal language for what were the most precious artifacts of the time. The casting of ritual bronzes was not entirely limited to the royal court, but it appears that throughout Western Zhou times it mostly remained to some extent under court authority, as did the inscriptions. Bronzes from the early part of the dynasty have been discovered in tombs spread along a northern Chinese corridor that extends from the Wei river area eastward along the Yellow river. Yet after the mid-tenth century BC, bronzes were largely concentrated in the Wei river core region of the Western Zhou, where they have been found both in tombs and, tightly and carefully packed, in storage pits. These pits from the latter half of the Western Zhou, when the dynasty began its political and military decline, were apparently dug to hide the bronzes from invaders until their owners could retrieve them at a later, more secure time. This time never came after the Western Zhou was displaced eastward to the area of modern Luoyang in 771 BC.

The bronze inscriptions before the mid-Western Zhou reign of King Mu (r. 956–918 BC) are rather irregular in their visual layout. In their vast majority, they contain only single characters or brief phrases of five characters or fewer, simply naming the donor of the bronze artifact, yet a small number of individual vessels could enter into long accounts. The most extensive inscription known so far, that of the famous Mao Gong tripod, contains 498 characters and surpasses even the longest hymns from the *Classic of Poetry*. With very few exceptions, all vessel inscriptions were cast on the inside of either the vessel, its lid, or both, while the outside was aesthetically defined through the vessel shape and often elaborate ornament that included rich geometrical designs as well as abstract yet imposing representations of animal shapes and monstrous faces (*taotie*). Most of the early vessels were of limited size – rarely surpassing fifty centimeters in diameter – that revealed their delicate features only upon close and careful inspection. During the ancestral sacrifices, their inscriptions were covered with the offerings and could not be read (except, perhaps, by the descending spirits invited to partake of the food and wine). The viewing public of these artifacts was firmly circumscribed, comprising only the lineage members and their guests in the sacrifices and banquets, or in the case of the royal house including high-ranking officials as well as diplomats from subordinate or neighboring polities. The lineage members would have been able to associate the individual bronzes, which were kept for generations, with specific ancestors. While inscribed vessels were particularly prized, numerous bronzes were cast without inscriptions. However, due to the sheer demand of economic, technological, cultural, and social resources that were on display in such an exquisitely crafted artifact, even uninscribed vessels were still fully capable of signifying the donor's merits and recognition. For these merits, recognized by the royal court and recorded on bamboo, the casting and possession of a bronze vessel was granted.

Over the course of the Western Zhou, the average bronze inscription grew in length to comprise several dozens of characters. Not by accident, most of the longest and historically informative inscriptions date from the mid-tenth century BC onward, a period of profound social, political, and ritual reforms. These inscriptions show a number of new developments following King Zhao's (r. 977/975–957 BC) disastrous military campaign southward, which resulted in complete defeat and the death of the king. During the following reign of King Mu, power was no longer as concentrated in the royal family as it had been before; instead, large numbers of official appointments were given to members of an institutional elite not related by blood. Meanwhile, the eastern part of the Zhou realm appears to have slipped from royal control, as the archaeological record shows inscribed vessels from the mid- and late Western Zhou period being largely limited to the Wei river capital region. In this time of crisis, administrative reforms led to a more complex bureaucracy and inspired more elaborate forms of court ritual, most prominent among them the ceremony of royal appointment. The larger size and bolder ornament of the vessels suggests that rituals were now conducted in front of larger, less intimate audiences. Vessels were now produced in much greater numbers and appeared increasingly in sets that reflect the sumptuary rules of social hierarchy. Unified in both material design and linguistic expression, they testify not only to new forms of mass production but also to the increased degree of sociopolitical institutionalization and control that the royal court exerted over its shrinking sphere of influence. This is further expressed through the proliferation of official titles and the detailed accounts of bureaucratic and ritual procedure in the inscriptions from this period.

The appointment inscriptions provide a standardized account of a court procedure that was as ceremonial as it was bureaucratic. In a solemn ritual, the king (or sometimes a high-level aristocrat) issued a charge (*ming*) to the appointee and bestowed (*ci*) on him the lavish insignia and paraphernalia appropriate to his status and task. The charge, written on a bundle of bamboo slips, was first read out loud and then handed over to the appointee. After the ceremony, it served as the basis for the bronze inscription to be cast in the appointee's name. Within the appointee's ancestral sacrifices, the inscribed words were then perhaps transformed back into speech and integrated with the presentations of food and wine, dance, music, and song.

These longer inscriptions are composed according to a fixed tripartite structure. The first part, usually the most extensive, provides the record of speeches from the appointment ceremony. In its fullest form, this record first details the appointee's self-presentation of his ancestors' and his own merits, followed by the royal response of approval and charge of appointment. These statements are sometimes introduced by the formulae "I, X, said" and/or "the king approvingly said" – on occasion abbreviated to the simple verb "said," with the subject eliminated – that reflect the oral performance of the appointment ceremony. More often, however, only one of the two highly ritualized speeches is cast in the vessel, with the other one being only implied. While the appointee's speech is more individualized in its account of past merits, the royal speech is almost entirely codified according to a standard format.

In the second and much shorter part of the inscription, the donor dedicates his vessel ("I have made this precious . . . "), identifying the artifact and sometimes also the specific ancestors to whom he will sacrifice with it. This self-referential part marks the making and sacrificial use of the inscribed artifact as an act of virtue and defines the donor's place vis-à-vis his illustrious forebears. While the record of the appointment ceremony presents the donor's past achievements as the prerequisite for the casting of the vessel, the statement of dedication, moving from past to present, focuses on the casting and use of the artifact itself. Finally, the third part consists of a formulaic and often rhymed prayer through which the donor asks his ancestors for their future blessings as the response to his sacrifices.

In their announcements of merit, Western Zhou bronze inscriptions of a certain size concern a range of topics, including records of royal appointments, land contracts and other legal agreements, marriages, diplomatic visits, military achievements, and others. Yet while such details are prized by modern scholars for their historical information, they were also the easiest to dispose of: the vast majority of inscriptions are shorter and tend to comprise merely the dedication and prayer. Further condensed, an inscription contained only the dedication identifying the donor through the formulaic "I, X, have made this vessel" or, in the extreme case, simply giving his name. While these inscriptions – not to mention the thousands of uninscribed artifacts – evidently defy any purpose of recording historical detail, they still point to their donor's accomplishments, without which no right to cast such a vessel would have been granted.

The rigorous ritual regime that governed the appointment inscriptions can be gathered from five late Western Zhou inscriptions that provide a fairly comprehensive picture of the ceremony. These inscriptions date from around 825 to 785 BC and recognize different individuals in different positions, but they are largely reproduced verbatim down to the list of awarded insignia. The Feng tripod inscription (809 BC) of ninety-seven characters reads as follows:

{Part 1} It was the nineteenth year, the fourth month, after the full moon, the day *xinmao*. The king was in the Zhao [Temple] of the Kang Palace. He arrived at the Great Chamber and assumed his position. Assisted to his right by Intendant Xun, [I,] Feng entered the gate. [I] assumed [my] position in the center of the court, facing north [toward the king]. Scribe Liu presented the king with the written order. The king called out to the Scribe of the Interior, X, to announce the written bestowal to [me,] Feng: "[I bestow on you] a black jacket with embroidered hem, red kneepads, a scarlet demi-circlet, a chime pennant, and a bridle with bit and cheek pieces; use [these] to perform your service!" [I] bowed with my head touching the ground. {Part 2} "[May I, Feng,] dare in response to extol the Son of Heaven's greatly illustrious and abundant blessings and on account of this make for my August Deceased Father, the Elder Zheng(?), and his wife Zheng [this] precious tripod!" {Part 3} "May [I enjoy] extended longevity for ten thousand years! May sons of sons, grandsons of grandsons, forever treasure [this tripod]!"

The uniformity of such inscriptions points to the ritual institutions of the Zhou royal court of King Xuan (827–782 BC), to the existence of a royal archive that maintained the continuous identity of royal announcements over decades, and to the legal stature of the document. Just at the time when the appointment ceremony became a major part of Western Zhou administration and ritual, inscriptions on legal contracts also appeared in larger numbers, typically listing the names and titles of the officials who served as witnesses at the time of the legal agreement. Similarly, the appointment inscriptions included the names and titles of the officials who recited the charge and hence were witnesses to the appointee's claim to his inscribed vessel. As a result, each inscription became part of a larger ritual continuum that was further expressed through the formulaic standardization of the shape and ornamentation of bronze vessels. This overarching stability in both language and bronze design suggests that by the second half of the tenth century, the casting of bronze inscriptions, especially those recording royal appointments, was largely under centralized control. By contrast, even when some of the highest officials such as the "scribes" (*shi*) noted above commissioned vessels on their own authority, they were comparatively crude in their bronze work and sometimes semiliterate in their writing.

Western Zhou bronze inscriptions are in many respects the fountainhead of Chinese literature. Their texts emerged from meticulously scripted court rituals and were presented in the religious context of elaborate sacrifices to the ancestors, fusing political legitimacy and religious communication into a single form of expression. Their underlying set of religious beliefs was oriented toward the humans of previous generations whose spirits were considered still present and powerful. Cast into precious and durable artifacts of display, bronze inscriptions were more than just silent writings: their gradually emerging aesthetics of rhyme, meter, onomatopeia, and other euphonic elements indicate that they were meant to be recited and heard.

As such, bronze inscriptions were both more and less than historical records. Their formulaic rhetoric left little room for historical detail but idealized the past in a standardized idiom. This linguistic structure embodied the ideology of the ancestral sacrifice itself, namely the continuity with the models of the past; furthermore, they recorded not what had happened but what was to be remembered. Thus, while dozens of Western Zhou bronze inscriptions offer accounts of war, none records a defeat; even King Zhao's disastrous campaign is retold as having successfully "tamed" the southern regions. Yet, at the same time, bronze inscriptions were also much more than the archival records that presumably contained a fuller (and more accurate?) version of the past: their mode of commemoration produced the moral and political paradigms of history and identity; their poetic idiom spoke at once to the spirits of the dead and the community of the living; their repetition in sets of bronze vessels marked the status of the donor entitled to these sets; their aesthetic form, shimmering from the depths of the most exquisite of artifacts, showed them as insignia of great attainment; and the very fact of their existence displayed writing itself as a conspicuous expression of religious and political power.

The mid- and late Western Zhou elite were aware of these qualities of inscribed artifacts. Moreover, in offering an increasingly elaborate account of court ritual and royal administration, the bronze texts came to exhibit the self-consciousness of a hereditary class of "scribes" or "makers of records" (*zuoce*) as the highest-ranking officials at court. No inscription portrays them involved in the actual process of writing; instead, they oversaw the production of writing and performed its ritual presentation. Their most famous exemplar is Scribe Qiang, who around 900 BC, or perhaps one generation later, had a simple yet elegant bronze water basin of 47.3 centimeters in diameter inscribed. When excavated from a pit near Zhuangbai (Fufeng, Shaanxi) in December 1975, it was accompanied by 102 other bronze vessels – seventy-three of them bearing inscriptions – that mostly came from four generations of his family of royal secretaries. Its 16.2-centimeter-high exterior base and wall bear a bird ornament in the flat, continuous ribbons familiar from other bronze vessels of the middle Western Zhou period. The inscription is cast on the vessel's otherwise unadorned interior.

In it – likely as a statement of merit – Scribe Qiang presented himself as a member of the Western Zhou court, boasting a distinguished ancestral line of royal secretaries. A master of the dynasty's political and cultural memory, he traced and praised the genealogy of the Western Zhou kings and then paired them in no less eulogistic fashion with the line of his ancestors who had, one after the other, served the succeeding Zhou rulers. This text is the most powerful self-representation of an early Chinese functionary of writing known so far, testifying to the mature ritual institutions of the Western Zhou court as well as to the donor's self-awareness as the heir to a lineage of royal secretaries. The 276 characters (including nine ligatures) are cast into two beautifully symmetric columns of nine vertical lines each. Each line comprises fifteen characters evenly spaced apart; only in the final line, the carver of the mold accommodated twenty characters. This slight mark of imperfection illustrates two conflicting goals: first, it suggests a preexisting text that could not be shortened by even a mere five characters. Second, while the carver could have begun another vertical line, he chose, or was instructed, not to do so – clearly to preserve the balance of columns. Striking a remarkable compromise, he respected both the integrity of the text and the symmetry of its display. Compared to most other vessel types that in their appearance are defined by shape and ornament while more or less hiding their inscriptions on the inside, the open surface of the water basin was ideal for displaying two columns of elegant characters, promoting, above anything else, an image of calligraphic beauty and order that eloquently bespeaks the awareness of the visual power of Chinese writing even in this very early period. Scribe Qiang's water basin inscription was meant to be seen.

In the first column, Scribe Qiang eulogizes the lineage and achievements of the Zhou royal house, presumably concluding with his own ruler. In the second half, starting almost precisely at the column break, he lists and praises his own ancestors and their accomplishments, finally ending with his own person. The symmetrical order of the text is further enhanced by its literary aesthetics of mostly four-syllable-line verse and the regular use of end rhyme; in their coherence, both features are unusual for their time. Most remarkably, Scribe Qiang applied rhyme and meter to the two long genealogies but not to the final prayer section, reversing the usual aesthetic choice of most other inscriptions. He thus granted the weight of aesthetic emphasis not to the prayer but to the narrative that defined both himself and his ancestors in their intimate relation to the Zhou kings.

In its synthesis of visual appearance, literary aesthetics, and narrative structure, Scribe Qiang's inscription is the epitome of order and regularity. It represents the ideal political order of the Zhou royal lineage, the ideal order of the Qiang family line, and, finally, the ideal order of the written artifact. The combination of Zhou dynastic memory, perfected literary form, and superb visual display reveals an extreme degree of authorial self-consciousness; likewise, the scribe's vocabulary significantly exceeds the repertoire of other inscriptions. While this inscription has no match in the archaeological record of its period, it shows the possibilities of writing in the royal institutions of political and religious ritual around 900 BC. The only comparable example so far, this one coming from the early eighth century BC, is found in the Qiu *pan*-water basin, excavated in 2003 together with twenty-six other inscribed vessels from a pit in Yang jiacun (Meixian, Shaanxi). Here again, in a text of 372 characters that includes a royal appointment charge, the genealogy of Zhou kings is provided in the service of the praise of one's ancestors, who are eulogized for having served the individual kings. The royal genealogies presented in these inscriptions prove the continuity of political memory preserved in the archival records that could be selectively applied to the vessel inscriptions. With the latter, any specific instance of memory could be extended to whole series of bronze paraphernalia or divided and distributed over a series of artifacts, especially, though not exclusively, in bell inscriptions. At the same time, the literary aesthetics of a text – rhyme, meter, onomatopoeia, and so on – depended on oral recitation to come to life in the multimedia performance of the ancestral sacrifice.

Following the fall of the Western Zhou in 771 BC and the eastward relocation of their capital to the area around modern Luoyang (Henan), the royal prerogative to commission inscribed bronze vessels was increasingly assumed by the lords of the states of the Spring and Autumn Period (771–481 BC). The decline of royal authority and rapid disintegration of the Zhou realm into numerous polities, culminating in the centuries of warfare during the Warring States Period (476–221 BC), is directly reflected in the rhetoric of the inscriptions. Bronze donors no longer referred to the Son of Heaven as the sole origin of power but instead – as on a set of bells cast by the lord of Qin around 700 BC – usurped the royal claim of responding directly to Heaven and being in charge of the realm. While the individual states developed distinct regional styles in their bronze décor, the language of their inscriptions remained the Western Zhou ritual idiom which, as a result, became increasingly ossified and atavistic. The linguistic differences across far-flung regions and several centuries were silenced in the stereotyped diction of the inscriptions. The number of long inscriptions presenting the donor's accomplishments to his ancestors declined in favor of shorter, preconceived formulae that spoke more to the living than to the spirits. More extensive texts such as the inscriptions cast by King Cuo of Zhongshan (r. 323–313 BC) expressed a claim for secular political authority largely divorced from the earlier forms of religious communication. Not accidentally, King Cuo's long texts extolling the feats of their donor in beautiful gold-inlaid calligraphy appeared on the outside of the vessels, signifying a new mode of representation for an audience comprising, first and foremost, members of the political community.

Especially from the mid-tenth century BC onward, the bronze inscriptions of Western and Eastern Zhou times – texts unmarred by later editing – are closely related to the early hymns and royal speeches preserved in the received *Classic of Poetry* and the *Classic of Documents*. They were used in the same ceremonial contexts, are written in the same idiom of archaic ritual language, display the same (and over time shifting) concerns with religious communication and political authority, and are primary expressions of an early Chinese cultural memory and identity that was to be secured through elaborately orchestrated ritual performance. While the great historical narratives of the *Poetry* and the *Documents* are not replicated in the inscriptions, they share with the latter the formal and functional paradigms of early literary expression. Like the material of bronze, the poetic speech of these received texts was both exquisite and durable, expressing what must not be forgotten and providing the format in which memory, distilled from history, could be secured. The physical site common to both the inscriptions and the earliest layers of the transmitted Classics was the ancestral temple – an arena for ritual performance and itself the spatial embodiment of memory and identity.

Linguistic evidence, including reference to official titles, ideological concepts, ritual procedures, and administrative structures, suggests that the bulk of the early layers of the *Poetry* and the *Documents* comes from this time of political reorganization and ritual reform. These classical texts, valorized as the hallmark of Zhou civilization, apparently emerged when the Zhou began to experience themselves in a time of crisis and loss, forever separated from their glorious early days. To the late Western Zhou, these days were now to be remembered as irretrievably past. Thus the memory of the dynastic founders, kings Wen and Wu, celebrated in the *Poetry* and the *Documents*, is very rarely invoked in early Western Zhou inscriptions but becomes decidedly more emphatic in late ones; likewise, the expression "Son of Heaven" (*tianzi*) as the designation of the king becomes common only during the middle of the Western Zhou and truly prominent only toward its end. The "Mandate of Heaven" (*tianming*), in traditional historiography a centerpiece of early Western Zhou rule and rhetoric and found in a number of early *Poetry* hymns and *Documents* royal speeches, is all but invisible in Western Zhou inscriptions. Considering this evidence, it appears that the speeches and hymns traditionally associated with the early reigns of the Western Zhou were, in fact, already expressions of remembrance of a golden age lost. Like the bronze inscriptions, the hymns and speeches are devoted not to history but to memory. Late Western Zhou bronzes are not interested in recent events or rulers but in the idealized moment of Zhou origin, as are the hymns and speeches.

III. The *Classic of Poetry*

Chinese poetry emerged from the ancestral sacrifices and political rituals of the Western Zhou, where it was produced by court officials. In its early stage, this poetry is best understood formally as a mode of intensified, rhythmic speech or song that included the use of end rhyme, meter, and onomatopoeic expressions that often took the form of rhyming, alliterative, and reduplicative binomes – two-character compounds that were usually euphonic in nature. In somewhat irregular fashion, these elements appear already in the earliest Western Zhou bronze inscriptions. Following the mid-Western Zhou, and especially over the course of the Eastern Zhou period, their systematic use in inscriptions increased steadily, though never reaching the level of pervasive coherence exhibited in the received version of the *Classic of Poetry*. One should not, however, apply the most rigid formal definition to Western Zhou poetry, especially as our current version of the *Classic of Poetry* is the product of later editing and systematization. A somewhat looser understanding of poetry as intensified, rhythmic speech, directed at both the spirits and the political elite, also allows us to better appreciate the continuity of such speech across the different "genres" of ritual hymns, bronze inscriptions, and the royal pronouncements of the *Classic of Documents*. These expressions form the backbone of early historical consciousness, mythological remembrance, and political representation.

In addition to the *Documents* and the *Poetry*, the third transmitted text probably dating from late Western Zhou times is the *Classic of Changes*, originally a divination manual that over the course of Warring States and early imperial times was transformed into a cosmological text complete with a series of philosophical commentaries known as the "ten wings." Since Han times, when the core text became attributed to the duke of Zhou (r. 1042–1036 BC) and its commentaries to Confucius, the *Changes* was considered the most fundamental of the Five Classics (*wu jing*), generating an enormous amount of speculative philosophical scholarship that culminated in the Song dynasty "Learning of the Way" (*daoxue*, often translated as "neo-Confucianism"). Modern scholarship has identified poetic passages and nature imagery in the earliest layers of the *Changes* that seem parallel to those of the *Poetry* and reflect another use of archaic song. The "line statements" (*yaoci*) to the six lines of each of the sixty-four hexagrams show a preference for the four-syllable-line meter and an irregular use of end rhyme. While the traditional reception of the *Changes* has not paid much attention to this aesthetic dimension of the textual core, it has been rediscovered in recent efforts to understand the *Changes* as a work of religious practice. At a minimum the poetic form of the original divination manual testifies to the overall coherence of intensified speech across the range of Western Zhou religious expression; to speak in poetry was to speak with truth and authority.

The same applies to the declamations in rhythmic speech that are attributed to the early Zhou kings and preserved in the *Documents* – majestic harangues that in part have been interpreted as dramatic libretti and stage directions for the steps of ritual dances. Yet the most comprehensive and lasting representation of archaic Chinese poetry is the corpus preserved in the *Poetry*, an anthology of songs that encompasses the voices of rulers as well as those of the common people, verses of mythological remembrance and celebration, as well as lyrics of love and hope, solitude and despair. It is this all-embracing view of human existence, expressed in the solemn and straightforward diction of pre-classical Chinese, that has established the *Poetry* as the foundational text of Chinese literature. This is not to say that its songs should be subsumed under the category of the "lyrical" as opposed to dramatic and epic forms of expression. While the individual text of ancient Chinese literature is incomparably shorter than, say, those of the Greek epics or plays, the *Poetry* contains magnificent examples of polyvocal performance texts alongside extensive narratives that over the course of a series of short poems establish, albeit in compressed form, the foundational story of Zhou civilization.

The received *Poetry* contains 305 songs that are traditionally dated, if without specific evidence, to between 1000 and 600 BC. None of the songs is attributed to a particular author, although four of its ritual hymns contain self-referential statements that seem reminiscent of a bronze vessel donor's statement of dedication, as in the example of "Lofty the Southern Mountain" (Jienanshan, *Mao* 191): "Jiafu has made this recitation / in order to lay bare the king's disorder. / Use it to change your heart / in order to nourish the ten thousand states."

A few ritual hymns show tenuous links to texts in the *Documents*, while other songs seem to reflect on historical events from Eastern Zhou times; yet in no case can authorship be established. Moreover, the attempts of

Han and later scholars to assign individual songs, or groups of songs, to specific historical circumstances are retrospective assertions of dubious origin. The same uncertainty applies to many of the received interpretations of the ancient verses, as has become clear from recently excavated Warring States and early Han manuscripts, which for now provide the earliest discussions of the songs – and differ decidedly from all received readings. For more than two millennia, the *Poetry* has remained hermeneutically inexhaustible, continuously transcending the historicity of all its interpretations.

While several pre-imperial texts – including the *Analects* (*Lunyu*) and the recently excavated manuscript "Confucius' Discussion of the *Poetry*" (Kongzi shilun) of ca 300 BC – show Confucius involved with the anthology, it was Sima Qian (ca 145–ca 86 BC) in his *Records of the Historian* (*Shiji*) who first attributed the compilation to him, noting that Confucius had chosen the "three hundred" songs from an existing corpus of three thousand. This statement may primarily reflect an early imperial tendency to relate all of the Five Classics in one way or another to Confucius, by then the model sage and primary classicist who was believed to have opened the connection to the civilization of the early Zhou through his writing, editing, and interpretation of the Classics. The *Analects*, a compilation of short sayings and dialogues believed to come from subsequent generations of disciples, cites "the master" as having characterized the *Poetry* on various occasions. With the ancient songs, "one can inspire, observe, unite, and express resentment" as well as learn "in great numbers the names of fish, birds, beasts, plants, and trees" (*Analects* 17/9); those who fail to study them "have nothing to express themselves with" (16/13) and are like a man who "stands with his face straight to the wall" (17/10); moreover, the goal was not mere memorization but the ability to properly apply the songs in social intercourse (13/5). Early criticisms, as in *Master Mo* (*Mozi*), subsequently ridiculed the classicists (*ru*, a term that only in specific contexts denotes the followers of Confucius) for being consumed with singing, dancing, and putting to music the "three hundred songs" (*Mozi* Chapter 48). The two sides confirm what is apparent from both the received tradition and an increasing number of newly excavated manuscripts on wood, bamboo, and silk: the *Poetry* was by far the most prominent and most quoted text in Warring States and early Han times. It was not merely a particular text used by the classicist tradition; it was the text around which this tradition arranged itself.

The received anthology is divided into four sections, comprising 160 "Airs of the States" (*guofeng*), seventy-four "Minor Court Hymns" (*xiaoya*), thirty-one "Major Court Hymns" (*daya*), and forty (mostly sacrificial) "Eulogies" (*song*), an early division that is now confirmed by excavated manuscripts. In the received text, the "Airs of the States" are further divided into fifteen sections named after a range of Eastern Zhou geographical regions and states. These extend roughly along the course of the Yellow River from modern Shandong in the east to modern Shaanxi – the Western Zhou capital area – in the west, associating the ancient songs with the northern heartland of Western and early Eastern Zhou China, and hence also with the language of the bronze inscriptions. Whereas the four-syllable meter was fully developed by the time of the Scribe Qiang inscription but rarely applied consistently in inscriptions, it is observed in roughly 95 percent of all lines in the received *Poetry*. Quotations in Warring States and early Han manuscripts show a slightly more varied meter – suggesting later standardization and/or the existence of early parallel versions – but by and large attest to the regularity of form by the fourth century BC. The dominant four-syllable meter, with a slight caesura between the second and the third characters, most likely emerged with the earliest layers of the anthology, the ancestral and banquet hymns performed to the slow and heavy rhythms of bells, drums, and chime stones.

In terms of content, a line can be drawn between the "Airs of the States" and the hymns and eulogies. The latter comprise mostly sacrificial eulogies, extensive court panegyrics, and the great dynastic hymns recalling the foundation and rise of the Zhou. The former, by contrast, are mostly shorter lyrics composed in simple formulaic language that frequently seem to assume the voice of the common folk: songs of love, courtship, and longing; of soldiers on campaign and hardworking farmers; of political satire and bitter protest. While Warring States and early imperial texts frequently invoked the "Major" and to some lesser extent also the "Minor Court Hymns" and "Eulogies," the later (post-Han) tradition clearly favored the "Airs of the States" for the presumed authenticity of their personal and political sentiments.

In recent years, fragments from the *Poetry* have appeared in six excavated manuscripts: the "Confucius' Discussion of the *Poetry*" from ca 300 BC, a fragmentary manuscript of slightly more than a thousand characters on twenty-nine partially broken bamboo slips that, written in the calligraphy of the southern state of Chu and probably looted from a tomb in modern Hubei, was acquired in Hong Kong by the Shanghai Museum; two versions of the "Black Robes" (Ziyi) text – one from Guodian (Jingmen, Hubei; ca 300 BC), the other again in the Shanghai Museum – that the tradition has preserved in the Han dynasty compilation *Records of Ritual* (*Liji*); the "Five Forms of Conduct" (Wuxing) from Guodian, with another version, now including an elaborating commentary, from Mawangdui tomb no. 3 near Changsha (Hunan; tomb closed 168 BC); and a fragmentary version of the anthology, containing sixty-five songs known from the "Airs of the States" and four from the "Minor Court Hymns," that was found in Shuanggudui (Fuyang, Anhui; tomb closed 165 BC). These manuscripts on silk (Mawangdui) and bamboo (all others) have confirmed the received text of the *Poetry* in two ways: with a single exception, all quoted poems can be found in the extant anthology, and the individual characters, while written with numerous graphic variants, represent the sounds, and hence likely the words, of the text as we know it. By 300 BC at the latest, a canonical anthology similar to the present one was already in place, if still far from the later standardization in orthography and interpretation.

The received version of the anthology is known as the *Mao Tradition of the Poetry* (*Mao shi zhuan*) and attributed to the otherwise obscure scholar Mao Heng of the third to second century BC. In Han times, it was known as one of four hermeneutic traditions of the *Poetry* and was patronized by Liu De, Prince Xian of Hejian (r. 155–129 BC), the older brother of Emperor Wu (r. 141–87 BC) and a man famously fond of ancient writings. The other three traditions – the *Lu Poetry* (*Lu shi*), *Qi Poetry* (*Qi shi*), and *Poetry of [Mr.] Han [Ying]* (*Han shi*) – had been endowed with chairs at the Imperial Academy under Emperor Wu, while the *Mao Tradition* received this status only under Emperor Ping (r. 1 BC–AD 6). Over the course of the Eastern Han, however, the *Mao Tradition* began to eclipse the other "three lineages" (*sanjia*) partly as the result of a debate that favored versions of the Classics in "ancient script" (*guwen*) over those in "modern script" (*jinwen*) – versions first written down or transcribed in Han times. While in fact none of the four traditions was written in "ancient" (pre-Qin) script, advocates of the *Mao Tradition* argued that its text had descended from the first generation of Confucius' disciples and was therefore of supreme authenticity and authority. Strong support for the *Mao Poetry* came from the *guwen* partisan Xu Shen, who in his *Shuowen* dictionary quoted the *Poetry* overwhelmingly from the Mao version. In the next step, Zheng Xuan (127–200), the greatest and most influential Eastern Han commentator on the Five Classics, complemented the *Mao Tradition* with his own interpretation. The resulting *Commentary to the Mao Tradition of the Poetry* (*Mao shi zhuan jian*) became the base text for the *Poetry* in the imperially commissioned *Correct Meaning of the Five Classics* (*Wujing zhengyi*) of AD 642; in 653 it was made the authorized commentary, confirming the *Mao Tradition* as the imperial version of the *Poetry*.

In Zheng Xuan's own time, the *Mao Tradition* was still secondary to the *Lu Poetry*, the exegetical tradition founded by Shen Pei. Shen was the student of a student of the late Warring States thinker Xun Kuang (or Xun Qing, ca 335–238 BC), the principal author of the late third-century BC *ru* (classicist) text *Xunzi*, and became appointed as imperial "erudite" (*boshi*) for the *Poetry* under Emperor Wen (r. 180–157 BC). The influence of the Lu exegesis can be traced across a range of Western Han sources and as late as AD 175 was chosen for the inscriptions of the Five Classics on stone stelae erected outside the Imperial Academy. The catalogue of the Western Han imperial library, compiled after 26 BC and preserved in abbreviated form in the "Monograph on Arts and Writings" (Yiwen zhi) of Ban Gu's (32–92) *History of the Han* (*Han shu*), lists fourteen works from all four Han traditions; yet according to the catalogue in the *History of the Sui* (*Sui shu*; completed AD 657), the Qi and Lu traditions had died out during the third and fourth centuries and even the only work still known from *Mr. Han's Poetry* – *Mr. Han's Exoteric Tradition of the Poetry* (*Hanshi waizhuan*), a text later reconstituted – was no longer being taught. Meanwhile, subcommentaries to the *Mao Tradition* had greatly proliferated.

These developments, spanning the third through the seventh centuries, postdate the original compilation of the *Poetry* by at least five hundred years and have erased most traces of early poetic hermeneutics. No independent evidence supports the claims for the early authenticity and hence superiority of the *Mao Tradition* – claims deeply tied to the Eastern Han quest for cultural tradition and political legitimacy. According to Han political discourse, the *Poetry*, together with the other Classics, fell victim to the large-scale book proscription that the chancellor Li Si engineered under the Qin First Emperor (Qin Shihuang, r. as emperor 221–207 BC). Yet because the *Poetry*, unlike some other (and most later) texts, was preserved also in oral memory, it could be reconstituted under the Han dynasty. The Han account of the "burning of the books" is dubious, however, and may primarily reflect the ideological needs of both the Han court classicists and the ruling house; traces of official patronage of the *Poetry* are abundantly present in early imperial sources such as the Qin First Emperor's stele inscriptions and early Han state ritual hymns (see below). Furthermore, the manuscript fragments from both before and after the Qin show the same type and degree of textual variation.

The received sequence of the four sections of the *Poetry* runs opposite to their presumed chronological appearance, with the "Eulogies" and "Major Court Hymns" considered the earliest parts of the collection. The "Eulogies" consist of thirty-one "Eulogies of Zhou" (Zhou song), four "Eulogies of Lu" (Lu song), and five "Eulogies of Shang" (Shang song). Of these, the "Eulogies of Zhou," with their lack of stanza divisions, relatively irregular meter, near absence of rhyme, and general lack of aesthetic polish, appear as the most archaic group of songs and are widely believed to reflect the original language of early through mid-Western Zhou times. These mostly very short pieces – twenty of them comprising fewer than fifty characters – are sacrificial hymns addressed to the early ancestors of the Western Zhou royal house, ending with Kings Cheng (r. 1042/35–1006 BC) and Kang (r. 1005/3–978 BC). (By contrast, the "Eulogies of Lu" and "Eulogies of Shang" are much later pieces that in length and elaborate poetic form concur largely with the "Major Court Hymns.") The first "Eulogy of Zhou" in the received anthology, "Clear Temple" (Qing miao; *Mao* 266), is the song with which the Duke of Zhou purportedly sacrificed to King Wen (r. 1099/56–1050 BC), father of the dynastic founder King Wu (r. 1049/45–1043 BC). Since Eastern Zhou times, this text has been celebrated as the model of a sacrificial hymn:

> Ah! Solemn is the clear temple,
> reverent and concordant the illustrious assistants.
> Dignified, dignified are the many officers,
> holding fast to the virtue of King Wen.
> Responding in praise to the one in Heaven,
> they hurry swiftly within the temple.
> Greatly illustrious, greatly honored,
> may [King Wen] never be weary of [us] men.

Six other "Eulogies of Zhou" (*Mao* 271, 285, 293, 294, 295, 296), all of them similarly brief, have been reconstructed as a continuous narrative that was enacted in dance, mimetically representing the conquest of the Shang by King Wu. All the "Eulogies of Zhou" are difficult to date, although their pronounced commemorative gesture may place them at a greater distance to the early kings than is traditionally recognized. Notably, several hymns refer to Kings Wen and Wu – twice even to King Wen's "statutes" or "models" (*dian*) – and some also refer to the "Mandate of Heaven" and to the king as the "Son of Heaven." In bronze inscriptions, these concepts become prominent only in the latter half of the Western Zhou.

Whatever their specific date, the Zhou temple hymns were part of a repertoire of music and dance, with their words self-referentially describing the sacrifices at which they were performed. Extolling the sacrificial service as an act of filial piety, they praised the ancestors and prayed for their blessings in response. This self-referential gesture, common to both hymns and bronze inscriptions, was at the core of a ritual system founded on the principle of reciprocity between the dead and the living. By describing the very ritual in which they were performed, some of the longer – and most likely later – sacrificial hymns celebrated the spirits as much as the act of celebration itself, creating a verbal display of ritual and social order. Furthermore, the seventy-two lines of the great sacrificial hymn "Thorny Caltrop" (Chuci, *Mao* 209), organized in six stanzas of equal length, follow the steps of the sacrifice by describing the ritual participants in their different roles and marking their separate speeches through rhyme change and other formal devices. The result was the polyvocal script for a ritual drama to be performed in the ancestral temple. As such, the text both accompanied the sacrifice and perpetuated it in hymnic speech. It was a text for both the present and the future, beginning with the invocation of memory by a religious specialist: "Thorny, thorny is the caltrop, / so we remove its prickles. / Since times of old, how is it done? / We plant the panicled millet, the glutinous millet: / . . . " Then, after describing in detail the complete success of the sacrificial action and the proper behavior of all its actors, the hymn addressed both the living and their future descendants with the prayer ubiquitous in Zhou bronze inscriptions: "Sons of sons, grandsons of grandsons, / never fail to continue these [rites]!"

This hymn from the "Minor Court Hymns" is a far more consciously constructed account of the ancestral sacrifice, compared to the archaic "Eulogies of Zhou." In its systematic retelling and extreme linguistic regularity (likely a feature of Eastern Zhou composition and editing), it did not describe any particular performance but the blueprint and essence of all such performances; it embodied the performances of the past as long as the hymn was sung in the commemorative rituals of subsequent generations. As such hymns were thought to have emerged directly from the archaic sacrifices, they came to stand for the ritual order of old itself. According to the late fourth-century BC *Mencius* (*Mengzi*), "When the traces of the [ancient] kings were extinguished, the *Poetry* vanished."

Even more than the sacrificial "Eulogies," the "Major Court Hymns" served as the primary texts of early Chinese religious and cultural memory. They are marked by extensive length (in a number of pieces several hundred characters), a striking regularity in ceremonial diction, and a grand vision of the foundation of the Zhou and its way of rulership. From the perspective of the "small prefaces" (*xiaoxu*) that accompany each song in the *Mao Tradition*, the "Major Court Hymns" proceed largely chronologically, beginning with a series of hymns in praise of Kings Wen and Wu and ending with two songs that criticize King You (r. 781–771 BC) under whom the Western Zhou finally collapsed. Judging from their contents, the "Major Court Hymns" appear to include pieces for both sacrificial rites and court banquets as well as songs clearly related to the appointment ceremony, especially "The Jiang and the Han" (Jiang Han, *Mao* 262). Within this poetic history of the Western Zhou, a group of five texts (*Mao* 236, 237, 241, 245, 250) have been identified as the master narrative of the life of King Wen; in addition, the first of the "Major Court Hymns" titled "King Wen" (Wen wang; *Mao* 235) and another one titled "King Wen Has Fame" (Wen wang you sheng, *Mao* 244) are entirely devoted to his praise. King Wen is further mentioned in two more hymns (*Mao* 240, 255, the latter being the king's harangue directed toward the last Shang king, a text reminiscent of the *Documents* speeches). The "Mandate of Heaven" is mentioned, in one form or another, in no fewer than five of the hymns of praise (*Mao* 235, 236, 241, 249, 255). Considering the formal coherence and sustained narrative of commemoration together with their emphasis on King Wen and the "Mandate of Heaven," and comparing these aesthetic and ideological features to Western Zhou bronze inscriptions, a late Western Zhou date, at the earliest, seems most plausible.

As a repertoire of mythical commemoration and an inventory of ritual expression, the "Major Court Hymns" compare to the great epics of early Greece even without matching them in scope. Their greatest difference from the latter might be overall absence of glorification of battle; unlike the Homeric epics, the Chinese hymns minimize the account of martial detail. Instead, like the royal speeches enshrined in the *Documents*, the court hymns emphasize the moral "mandate" as the source of Zhou civilization and superiority that was represented in the appropriate ritual demeanor of the king and his appearance of "majestic terror" (*weiyi*). Accordingly, the foundational myth of the Zhou origin is one not of warfare but of the invention of agriculture, related in the great hymn "She Bore the Folk" (Sheng min) that tells the story of Lord Millet (Hou Ji). With him, history begins: his miraculous birth, his survival as an infant among wild animals, his invention of agriculture and the planting of millet, his sacrifices to the spirits. Like "Thorny Caltrop," the hymn finally leads to the present, recalling Lord Millet's sacrifices as the blueprint for those now given to him:

> Truly – our sacrifices, what are they like?
> Some hull (the grain), some scoop it;
> Some sift it, some tread it.
> Washing it, we hear it swish, swish;
> Distilling it, we see it steam, steam.
> Now we consult, now we consider;
> We take southernwood to sacrifice the fat,
> We take a ram to flay it.
> Now we roast, now we broil;
> To rouse up the following year.

> We load the wooden vessels,
> The wooden vessels, the earthen vessels.
> As the fragrance begins to rise,
> The god on high is calmed and delighted.
> How good the fragrance is indeed!
> Lord Millet founded the sacrifice,
> Luckily, without fault or offense,
> It has reached the present day.

In the historical and philosophical writings of Warring States and early imperial China, the "Major Court Hymns" – hermeneutically unproblematic and unambiguous in their moral intent – were the primary texts invoked to "prove" an argument with the authority of antiquity. Quotations from the hymns served to condense a historical situation or discursive point into a single expression that would sum up, and define, the issue at hand. While quotations from the *Poetry* appear across a wide range of texts, they were used with particular intensity by that diverse group of thinkers who referred to themselves as classicists, *ru*, and were engaged with a defined body of textual learning. The "Six Virtues" (Liude) manuscript from Guodian shows that by 300 BC at the latest, the core of this set of learning had coalesced as the "Six Arts" (*liuyi*); in Han times, these were narrowed into the Five Classics: the *Poetry, Documents, Changes, Spring and Autumn Annals,* and *Rites*, no longer including the "art" and textual body of "Music." In Warring States times, a basic text (*jing*) existed for each of these, giving rise to a growing body of further elaborations both oral and written; yet likely because of their formal coherence, their direct historical relation to high antiquity, their eminent usability for citation, and their poetic diction that invited easy memorization and oral transmission, no text was more prominent than the songs from the *Poetry*. Thus the *Zuo Tradition* (*Zuo zhuan*) and the *Discourses of the States* (*Guoyu*), the two largest historical narratives of the fourth century BC, show songs from all sections of the anthology being recited at interstate diplomatic meetings, indicating a universal circulation uninhibited by cultural differences across the Eastern Zhou states. The mutual understanding of speakers of different dialects in the medium of the *Poetry* suggests that the songs were performed in a literary koine that transcended any local idiom. This elite koine was likely the "elegant classical speech" (*yayan*) that Confucius is said to have used for the *Poetry*, the *Documents*, and matters of ritual (*Analects* 7/18). To speak in this idiom was to perform the memory of classical culture – a memory "transmitted, not created" (*Analects* 7/1).

Quoting and reciting the *Poetry* was primarily a matter of oral practice. Regardless of the writings recently excavated from a small number of elite tombs, the manuscript culture of Warring States China must have been of limited depth and breadth. The available stationery was either too bulky (wood and bamboo) or too expensive (silk) for the extensive copying of texts and their circulation over vast distances. References to writing and reading, as well as to the economic, material, or educational conditions of textual production and circulation, are extremely scarce in the early literature, which instead consistently depicts learning in personal master–disciple settings (likely supported by writing as aide-mémoire and educational practice). While local writing of technical, administrative, legal, economic, military, and other matters existed in the different regions of the Warring States, the extensive circulation of the Classics probably did not depend on writing. No pre-imperial source speaks of the circulation of the Classics as writings, or of the profound difficulties involved in transcribing them among distinctly different calligraphic and orthographic regional traditions. Not one of the numerous invocations of the *Poetry* in the *Zuo Tradition* and the *Discourses of the States* mentions the use of a written text; invariably, they show the ability of memorization and free recitation – in the literary koine mentioned above – as the hallmark of education.

In Warring States times, no particular written version of the *Poetry* (or the *Documents*) was considered primary or authoritative. Only the institutionalization of official learning (*guanxue*) at the Qin and Han imperial courts led to written versions of the Classics taught at court, especially at the Imperial Academy founded in 124 BC, and called for textual stabilization and standardization. Yet excavated manuscripts even from Western Han times still display the characteristics of classical texts primarily memorized and only on occasion written down locally. The more than 1,400 characters of *Poetry* fragments in manuscripts from the late fourth through the mid-second centuries BC show a ratio of textual variants consistently in the range of 30 to 40 percent of all characters. This ratio does not include different conventions in writing the same character, and it easily doubles once one removes the most common and simple characters from the equation. Yet these variants are overwhelmingly merely graphic, showing a text unstable in orthography but stable in sound. While the calligraphy of the early manuscripts was bound to regional conventions and scribal idiosyncracies, the text that was written, and that could be sounded out, transcended such differences. Meanwhile, the sheer amount of graphic variation combined with the archaic poetic idiom of the

Poetry would have made private reading impossible. To identify and understand the text, one would have had to already know it. The manuscripts thus support the scenario of direct, primarily oral, teacher–disciple transmission that is described in traditional sources and over time gave rise to a variety of hermeneutic approaches and teaching lineages.

IV. The "Airs" and the early hermeneutic traditions

Chinese poetic hermeneutics, and literary thought in general, likely emerged from the use of poetry in specific historical situations such as illustrated in the *Zuo Tradition* and the *Discourses of the States*. In these contexts of educated diplomacy, quotations from the *Poetry* were invoked to encode meaning in polite speech of shared cultural experience. While the "Major Court Hymns" and "Eulogies," and to a lesser extent also the "Minor Court Hymns," offered relatively unproblematic narratives of morality and virtuous rulership, the hermeneutical challenge arose with lines from the "Airs of the States." These songs, often deceptively simple and formulaic, allowed for a wide range of applications according to specific circumstances. A song, stanza, or couplet from the "Airs" could not be reduced to a presumed single original meaning of its words; it came to mean different things on different occasions. In fact, authorship and original composition were not at stake; the only two of the 160 "Airs" that refer to their own composition do so anonymously: "It is because of his narrow heart, / that I have made this satire" ("Dolichos Shoes" (Ge ju), *Mao* 107); "The man is not good, / so I sing to accuse him" ("The Gate to the Tomb" (Mu men), *Mao* 141).

In the widespread use of the *Poetry* in the *Zuo Tradition* and the *Discourses of the States*, single stanzas were presented to make a point; none of the transmitted "Airs" or "Court Hymns" is ever cited in full, and only one – very short – of the "Eulogies." While this practice was later criticized as "breaking a stanza off [from its context] to generate meaning" (*duanzhang quyi*), it made sense to an audience that did not presume any such fixed or original context but accepted the "Airs" as a repertoire of texts freely available for sophisticated, indirect communication. In this hermeneutic approach, it was the situational presentation and reception that endowed the "Airs" with ever-renewed meaning and significance. Furthermore, in occasional ensemble performances of the songs, their meaning rested not in the words alone but also in their musical presentation. In *Analects* 9/15, Confucius says that he had rectified the ritual music so that the "Court Hymns" and "Eulogies" were all arranged in their proper order; elsewhere (8/15), he notes how the coda of

"Fishhawks" (Guanju, *Mao* 1) "fills the ear." According to the *Zuo Tradition*, Ji Zha, a prince from the southeastern (allegedly semi-barbarian) state of Wu, in 544 BC visited the northeastern state of Lu, the home state of Confucius where the old rituals of Zhou were still maintained. When the prince was treated to a musical performance of the entire *Poetry*, he perspicaciously commented on the condition of the individual states as their music was presented to him. Here, the performance of the songs, both textual and musical, was the visible and audible emblem of good order – or its opposite.

It is not always clear what a particular song conveyed in a specific situation, as in the case of "Zhongzi, Please!" (Qiang Zhongzi, *Mao* 76), which in the *Zuo Tradition* (Duke Xiang, 26th year (547 BC)) is recited in order to achieve the release of the marquis of Wei from imprisonment in Qin:

> Zhongzi, please!
> Do not leap into our hamlet,
> do not break the willow trees we have planted.
> How would I dare to care for them,
> yet I am fearful of my father and mother.
> Zhongzi is truly to be loved,
> yet the words of father and mother
> are also truly to be feared.
>
> Zhongzi, please!
> Do not leap across our wall,
> do not break the mulberry trees we have planted.
> How would I dare to care for them,
> yet I am fearful of my older brothers.
> Zhongzi is truly to be loved,
> yet the words of my older brothers
> are also truly to be feared.
>
> Zhongzi, please!
> Do not leap into our garden,
> do not break the sandalwood trees we have planted.
> How would I dare to care for them,
> yet I am fearful of the many words by the people.
> Zhongzi is truly to be loved,
> yet the many words by the people
> are also truly to be feared.

Nothing in this song relates to an imprisoned ruler, nor did subsequent readers dwell on this interpretation. Instead, the *Mao Tradition* took the song into a new direction by connecting it to another, unrelated anecdote from the *Zuo Tradition*. In this historical application, the song criticized a ruler of the state of Zheng who in 722 BC failed to avert disaster by allowing his younger brother to usurp ever greater power until he finally could be subdued only by military force. This reading, too, cannot be substantiated from the lyrics proper and, beginning in Song times, has been rejected by later commentators. Zheng Qiao (1104–1162) understood the song as "the words of a licentious eloper" that had nothing to do with the historical story advanced by the *Mao Tradition*. Zheng's interpretation was accepted by Zhu Xi (1130–1200) in his *Collected Traditions of the Poetry* (*Shi jizhuan*) that after the Mao and Zheng Xuan exegesis became the single most influential commentary on the anthology. Modern readers, disposed toward taking the "Airs" as originally folk songs, have understood "Zhongzi, Please!" as the words of a young woman who fears that her lover's impetuosity will compromise her social reputation.

The case is typical of how the *Mao Tradition* interpreted the "Airs" as composed in response to specific circumstances and hence – once these circumstances could be identified – as historical documents. More than any other early interpretation, the *Mao Tradition* was focused not on the application or reception of the "Airs" but on their purported specific moment and historical significance of textual composition. In this, it appropriated a formula that appears in several early texts, most succinctly in the third- or second-century BC "Canon of Yao" (Yaodian) of the *Documents*: "poetry expresses intent" (*shi yan zhi*). In the "Canon of Yao," this was followed directly by the phrase "song makes words last long" (*ge yong yan*), emphasizing performance and its mnemonic force to give poetry its duration. By contrast, the "Great Preface" (Daxu), presumably composed by Wei Hong in the first century AD and included with the *Mao Tradition* some time before Zheng Xuan, dropped the second half of the statement to focus entirely on the act of original composition. The seminal statement on the nature and purpose of both the *Classic of Poetry* and Chinese poetry in general, the "Great Preface" reflected a strong notion of authorship indicative of early imperial thought. In some of its most important parts, this statement was developed out of contemporaneous ideas about music that are preserved in the "Records of Music" (Yueji). Combining Warring States and Qin–Han material, this chapter from the *Records of Ritual* elaborates on ideas from earlier texts such as *Xunzi* and some of the Guodian manuscripts that discuss music as an expression and instrument of cosmic and social order. With only the slightest modifications in language – mainly replacing the terms "tones" and "music" with "words" and "poetry" – the "Great Preface" restates the central passage from the "Records of Ritual" on the nature of composition:

The poem is where the intention goes. In the heart it is intention; sent forth in speech, it is the poem. The affections are moved within and take on form in speech. When speaking them is insufficient, one sighs them. When sighing them is insufficient, one draws them out by singing. When drawing them out by singing is not sufficient, unconsciously the hands dance them, and the feet tap them. The tones of a well-governed era are at ease and lead to joy; its rulership is harmonious. The tones of an era in turmoil are bitter and lead to anger; its rulership is perverse. The tones of a perishing state are lamenting and lead to longing; its people are in difficulty.

In this vision, music and poetry sprang involuntarily from the perceptive human mind after it was affected by an external impulse. The resulting artifact was an immediate individual response to a specific historical experience that was generated by the fundamental participation of the human mind in the workings of the cosmos. The human author was not a creator in the Aristotelian sense but produced an expression that was at once specific and universal. It served as a concomitant, immediate response to historical circumstances and could thus be interpreted as authentic judgment. In the *Zuo Tradition* and *Discourses of the States*, this judgmental function was assigned to the recitation of existing anonymous poems; in the "Great Preface" as well as in the individual "small prefaces" to individual songs, it was transposed to the moment of original poetic composition. The *Mao Tradition* thus epitomized the reading of the *Poetry* as historical documents, constituting the historical interpretation of individual songs such as "Zhongzi, Please!" as well as the overall arrangement of the "Airs" in groups of poems under the names of different states. Thus the apparently geographic division of the "Airs" according to regions is in truth a moral one. In the Mao arrangement and interpretation, the first two sections – the eleven "South of Zhou" (Zhou nan) and fourteen "South of Shao" (Shao nan) songs – collectively represent the moral virtue of the early Zhou royal house, with the "South of Zhou" poems specifically focused on the royal wives. By contrast, entire sections like the ten "Airs of Chen" and all but the first of the twenty-one "Airs of Zheng" purportedly criticized the lack of morality in the leaders of these states. Zheng Xuan, in his preface to the *Mao Tradition*, further systematized this approach by grouping both the "Court Hymns" and the "Airs" into those of "moral orthodoxy" (zheng) and others of "deviation" (bian), where the "orthodox" poems are panegyrics and the "deviant" ones songs of political satire and admonition. With the emphasis on poetry as a direct reflection of its time, the panegyrics (most of the "Eulogies" and "Major Court Hymns") were believed to come from the glorious days of the early Western Zhou, while the political satires (most of the "Minor Court Hymns" and, with the exception of the two opening sections, the "Airs") were located in later times of disorder.

The framework of historical interpretation had far-reaching consequences for the use of literature for the entire Chinese tradition. It established the songs of the *Poetry* as an account of political and cultural rise and decline and its presumed anonymous authors and reciters as moral judges of their own ages. Already in the *Zuo Tradition* and the *Discourses of the States*, poetry recitation is frequently portrayed as a means by which ministers and advisers admonished their rulers. The *Mencius*, next to the *Analects* the most influential early philosophical work of the *ru* tradition, quotes a (lost) "Great Oath" (Taishi) chapter from the *Documents* as saying that Heaven judges the king through the eyes and ears of the common people. To the *Mao Tradition*, this is the origin of poetry: voices from among the common folk or morally upright ministers who speak truth to power. Not a few of the "Airs" and "Minor Court Hymns" indeed complain about acts of injustice such as the hardships of soldiers on campaign or the injustice done to peasants on their fields. Thus "Big Rat" (Shi shu, *Mao* 113) in three formulaic stanzas of minimal variation gives voice to the farmers who toil in vain:

> Big rat, big rat,
> Do not eat our millet.
> Three years we have served you,
> Yet you have not been willing to care.
> At last we are going to leave you
> And move to that happy land.
> Happy land, happy land,
> Where we shall find our place. (Stanza I)

Similarly, "Minister of War" (Qi fu, *Mao* 185), also in three brief and repetitious stanzas, complains about the misery of the troops:

> Minister of war!
> We are the king's claws and teeth.
> Why have you rolled us into misery,
> With no place to settle or rest?
>
> Minister of war!
> We are the king's claws and teeth.
> Why have you rolled us into misery,
> With no place to arrive and rest? (Stanzas I, II)

In the three stanzas of "Northern Gate" (Bei men, *Mao* 40), a man resents the duties imposed by his government and at the same time accuses Heaven of showing no mercy:

> I go out the northern gate,
> My worried heart distressed, distressed.
> Destitute indeed and poor,
> With no one knowing my hardship.
> It is over now, alas!
> Heaven, truly, has done it –
> Alas, what can it be called?
>
> The king's affairs come to me,
> The government's affairs are ever heavier on me.
> When I come in from the outside,
> The folk in the house all take turns to scold me.
> Heaven, truly, has done it –
> Alas, what can it be called! (Stanzas I, II)

Similarly, Heaven is held responsible in the three stanzas of "Yellow Birds" (Huang niao, *Mao* 131), which describes three different men, each one close to death:

> *Jiao-jiao* cry the yellow birds
> Settling on the jujube tree.
> Who followed Lord Mu?
> Ziju Yanxi!
> Truly, this Yanxi,
> Of a hundred men the finest!
> He draws close to the pit,
> Trembling, trembling in terror.
> Heaven, the azure one,
> Slays our good man!
> If one could ransom him, ah –
> A hundred men for this life! (Stanza I)

In Han times, this song was related to an event of 621 BC, narrated in the *Zuo Tradition*, when three brothers and 174 others were sacrificed to follow Lord Mu of Qin into the grave; accordingly, the song was attributed to "the people of Qin" (Zheng Xuan) who deplored the fate of their "three good men." While such songs are easy to appreciate in their outspoken satirical message, many others are not nearly as straightforward and have been subjected to elaborate decoding. A specific feature of many "Airs" is an opening nature image followed by a juxtaposed human situation. Here, nature imagery serves as an implicit analogy to human affairs, a rhetorical technique identified as "evocation" or "stimulus" (*xing*) in the poetic tradition. Due to its indirect nature, "evocation" has proven a rather difficult concept to define, but according to the Mao reading, it governs a song like "The Peach Tree Lush" (Tao yao, *Mao* 6):

> The peach tree lush, lush,
> Blazing, blazing its flowers.
> This girl goes out to marry,
> Suiting well her [new] house and family. (Stanza I)

The following two stanzas are close repetitions of the first but develop the "blazing flowers" first into "ripening fruits" and then into "luxurious leaves." In the Mao interpretation, these images evoke the vitality of youth together with the appropriate timeliness of growth and development: as the fruits ripen to their fullness, so does the girl reach the proper time of marriage. This analogy is then further developed into a praise of morality and social order, as it radiates from the royal court downward to the common folk: in the ideal world of the early Zhou, the young women will not miss the right time of marriage.

While the specific historical interpretations of the *Mao Tradition* were often doubted by later readers, the "Airs" themselves – songs of love and courtship, pleasure and joy, frustration and anguish – have survived over two millennia of imperial and modern China. Their simple and often charming diction has conveyed a sense of dignity and sincerity, endowing the poetic voice with a superior capacity for truth, immediacy, and compassion that has inspired the Chinese literary tradition to the present day. Yet the reception of the *Poetry* had no room for aesthetic concerns; not one of the early commentators appreciated them as examples of beautiful or well-crafted language. The task of the Mao interpretation was to create, or to reconstruct from sources no longer known, a historical context for each of the "Airs," and it did so through two separate but complementary forms. The first of these are the "Minor Prefaces" attached to each of the 305 songs that consist of a succinct, usually single-phrase, statement and a longer elaboration of it, as in the case of "Yellow Birds":

> "Yellow Birds" laments the three good men. The people of the state, in criticizing Lord Mu for having people follow him into death, made this poem.

The distinction between the two parts of the preface might suggest that the initial statement preceded its subsequent elaboration chronologically and may have been attached to the song quite early, even in pre-imperial times. By contrast, the historically explicit second part of the preface seems to reflect the particular reception of the "Airs" within the overall institutionalization of textual learning at the late Western Han imperial court. It was at this time when a distinctly historical perspective on the Five Classics became preeminent and was taught to thousands of students at the Imperial Academy. Such teaching further required the fixation of a standardized, unambiguous text that no longer depended on individual instruction in a personal teacher–disciple setting. In addition to the historicization provided by the prefaces, it was again only the *Mao Tradition* that furnished such a standard text by adding numerous glosses of individual words (*xungu*). No such glossing is known from the pre-imperial period, and no text was in greater need of it than the archaic verse of the *Poetry* that especially in many of the "Airs" offered neither a sustained narrative nor a specific argument, but instead relied on principles such as "evocation" to create meaning out of highly underdetermined poetic expression. The most dramatic illustration of what the *Mao Tradition* accomplished, and how it differed from earlier readings of the "Airs," are the three stanzas of "Fishhawks," the first song in the received anthology:

> *Guan-guan* cry the fishhawks
> On the islands in the river.
> Pure and fair, the virtuous lady,
> A good companion to the prince.
>
> Long and short grows the watercress,
> Left and right one plucks it.
> Pure and fair, the virtuous lady,
> Waking and asleep he seeks her.
> Seeking her, he does not get her,
> Waking and asleep he thinks of her.
> Longing, oh, and longing,
> He tosses and turns from side to side.
>
> Long and short grows the watercress,
> Left and right one pulls it.
> Pure and fair, the virtuous lady,
> With zithers small and large one befriends her.
> Long and short grows the watercress,
> Left and right one picks it.
> Pure and fair, the virtuous lady,
> With bells and drums one delights her.

In this song in four-syllable lines, the Mao commentary glosses the first word, a reduplicative binome, as "harmonious sound," and the second word, an assonant binome, as a kind of bird that lives in separation. This nature image, filling the entire first line, is then interpreted as evocative of the virtue of the queen (by the later tradition identified as the wife of the Zhou founder, King Wen): she is in harmonious company with her lord but keeps the appropriate distance in order not to debauch him. With line three, this reading is further solidified in the description of the lady. The first word, the near-rhyming binome *yaotiao*, is glossed as "secluded and noble," while the epithet for the lady is read as "good." Together, these word glosses generate the meaning that the "Minor Preface" then elaborates upon, establishing a specific hermeneutic procedure in which evocative nature images are decoded as illustrations of human relations and behavior.

The interpretation of "Fishhawks" also sets the tone for the first section of the anthology, the eleven "South of Zhou" poems that have been hailed as the paradigm of the "orthodox airs" since Zheng Xuan. Furthermore, the *Mao Tradition*, transmitted through Zheng Xuan's commentary, came to serve as a model of reading not only for the ancient songs but also for poetry in general, including new compositions from late Eastern Han times onward. Yet up to then, the Mao reading had been the exception, not the rule. The Lu tradition – the dominant reading of the "Airs" in Han times – took the song as specific criticism of King Kang's sexual indulgence and neglect of duties; similarly, the Qi and Han interpretations read the song as a satire on excessive behavior. Some Eastern Han and later texts such as Zhang Chao's (fl. ca 190) "*Fu* Ridiculing '*Fu* on a Maidservant'" (Qiao qingyi fu) maintained that "Fishhawks" functioned as a satire because it confronted King Kang with an illustration of true virtue – a reading that could thus accommodate Mao glosses such as "goodness," "harmonious separation," or "secluded and pure." It is dubious, however, that this interpretation represented the original Lu (or Qi or Han) tradition of the *Poetry*. Other early texts like the *Xunzi*, Liu An's (175–122 BC) "Tradition of 'Encountering Sorrow'" (Lisao zhuan), or Sima Qian's *Records of the Historian* seem to have understood "Fishhawks" and the "Airs" in general as expressions of sexual desire. Such a reading cannot accept the specific Mao glosses for "Fishhawks," which suggests that the four Western Han hermeneutic traditions differed not merely in their graphical choices but also in their understanding of the words represented by these graphs. Meanwhile, those who took the "Airs" as expressions of desire did not consider them immoral; they "satisfy the desires but do not lead to transgressing of the right stopping point" (*Xunzi*), they "express a fondness or sexual allure but do not lead into licentiousness" (Liu An), and their expression of "erotic desire does not surpass appropriate demeanor" (Qi reading). In this interpretation, the "Airs" and "Fishhawks" are not political satires of a specific historical background and purpose but general vehicles of moral edification, dovetailing with Confucius' statement (*Analects* 3/20) that "'Fishhawks' expresses pleasure but does not lead into licentiousness, expresses sorrow but does not cause harm." The same interpretation has now been found in two early manuscripts: both the "Five Forms of Conduct" from Mawangdui and "Confucius' Discussion of the *Poetry*" in the Shanghai Museum collection state that "'Fishhawks' uses the expression of sexual allure to illustrate the case for ritual propriety." In other words, the expression of sexual desire was not considered problematic but a strategic form of guidance, beyond such desire, to proper social conduct. From at least the late fourth century BC onward, this seems to have been the standard interpretation of "Fishhawks" and the "Airs" – and in the Shanghai Museum manuscript it is explicitly associated with Confucius, the purported compiler of the *Poetry*.

Compared to these readings as well as to the satirical interpretation, the *Mao Tradition* introduced a decidedly new understanding of the "Airs" in general and "Fishhawks" in particular. Moreover, through its prescriptive word glosses, the *Mao Tradition* effectively created a new text that was phonologically consistent with the long-established *Poetry* anthology but established a new interpretation and definition of its words. Fixed in both orthography and meaning, it served the needs of early imperial "official learning" (*guanxue*). Methodologically, the Mao reading reversed the earlier practice of flexibly applying the hermeneutically underdetermined songs to historical situations; now, a definite historical context was established to determine their purported single original purpose and meaning. Through its glosses and "Minor Prefaces," the *Mao Tradition* prepared the ground for the argument of the "Great Preface" that poetry was the response to specific historical circumstances.

The extent of this rewriting of the text of the *Poetry* is apparent from a comparison between "Fishhawks" and several other "Airs." The key word in the second line of "Fishhawks," *yaotiao* (Mao: "secluded and noble"), appears in entirely different characters not only in the Mawangdui "Five Forms of Conduct" but also, written with the characters *yaojiao*, in "The Moon Appears" (Yue chu, Mao 143) – a song from the "Airs of Chen" that according to its Mao preface "criticizes fondness of sexual allure" and those in office who "are not fond of virtue but delighted in glorifying sexual allure." Here, *yaojiao* is understood as the sensual attraction of a young woman, that is, in precisely the sense the satirical reading of "Fishhawks" seems to understand *yaotiao* there. Furthermore, the Mawangdui "Five Forms of Conduct" manuscript elaborates on "Fishhawks" as follows:

> If [the man's desire] is as deep as this, would he copulate next to his father and mother? Even if threatened with death, he would not do it. Would he copulate next to his older and younger brothers? He would not do it either. Would he copulate next to the countrymen? He would not do it either. [Being fearful] of father and older brother, and only then being fearful of others, is ritual propriety. Using the expression of sexual allure / desire as an analogy to ritual propriety is to advance [moral conduct].

This discussion of parents, brothers, and countrymen does not directly bear on the text of "Fishhawks" but is parallel to the concerns about sexual desire raised in "Zhongzi, Please!" It was thus only in the *Mao Tradition* that "Fishhawks" was placed in a paradigmatic opposition to both "The Moon Appears" and "Zhongzi, Please!" – in earlier readings, these texts were discussed from the common perspective of sexual temptation and its resolution in moral propriety.

The later tradition reacted in mixed ways to the *Mao Tradition*, which had become orthodox by Tang times. Song dynasty scholars such as Ouyang Xiu (1007–1072), Su Zhe (1039–1112), Zheng Qiao, Lü Zuqian (1137–1181), and Zhu Xi were critical of many of the Mao historical readings of the "Airs" (though, curiously, not in the case of "Fishhawks"). They proposed to free the *Poetry* from the Mao readings that they judged as obscuring straightforward expressions of folk sentiment. In the minds of these scholars, the meaning of the "Airs" was still open to direct access. In this spirit, Zhu Xi's *Collected Traditions of the Poetry* – the version of the anthology that ruled supreme in the imperial examinations from 1315 through 1905 – consisted of the merely necessary word glosses and some succinct evaluations of meaning. Yet even while arguing new readings of the songs, it still could not escape the power of the Mao glosses. In particular, Zhu Xi and other Song readers struggled to explain why the anthology included texts such as "Zhongzi, Please!" when Confucius had famously stated that the *Poetry* could be "covered in one phrase: no wayward thoughts!" (*Analects* 2/2). On this dilemma, only the newly excavated manuscripts – texts long eliminated from the received tradition and not available to Song or later imperial readers – offer a fundamentally new perspective. These manuscripts not only question the validity of the *Mao Tradition* but also vigorously refute the later – especially modern – reading of the "Airs" as original folk songs that express their meaning on the plain surface of their words. Both the Mawangdui "Five Forms of Conduct" and the

Shanghai Museum "Confucius' Discussion of the *Poetry*" lay out a hermeneutic process that takes the textual surface of the text as an analogy or "illustration" (*yu*) for moral edification. While these sources do not reach back to the original composition of the songs, and perhaps not even to the initial compilation of the anthology, they document an early mode of reception popular among the Warring States classicists who claimed Confucius as their intellectual ancestor. Whether or not Confucius was indeed the compiler of the *Poetry*, the hermeneutic approach attributed to him in the Shanghai Museum manuscript of ca 300 BC was the dominant one that carried the anthology into the early empire. Without it, the "three hundred songs" might have disappeared just like almost all other poetry from pre-imperial times. While texts like the *Zuo Tradition* show traces of songs outside the received anthology, sometimes including brief quotations, not a single complete stanza comparable to those from the "Airs" has survived. Only once has a body of texts been retrieved that, in its theme of a hunting excursion, its tetrasyllabic form, and its poetic imagery, shows similarity to the "Court Hymns": a cycle of verse engraved into a Warring States set of ten round stone blocks – so-called stone drums – that were first mentioned in literary sources of the seventh century AD. They include more than 460 still legible characters and are kept in the Beijing Palace Museum. Their existence shows both the original production of poetry outside the received anthology and its later near-complete disappearance. The songs of the *Poetry* became canonical through their early appropriation by the *ru* classicist intellectual lineage, and they have survived ever since because of their continuously evolving hermeneutic possibilities.

V. The royal speeches in the *Classic of Documents*

The only other text of the Five Classics that in Warring States and early imperial times was frequently mentioned alongside the *Poetry* is the *Classic of Documents*, an anthology of speeches, historical narratives, and cosmological treatises. Its core – hailed as the fountainhead of both political philosophy and historical writing – comprises a series of royal speeches some of which may date from the late Western Zhou. Composed in a formulaic, rhythmic, and partly rhymed diction, these ceremonial speeches are attributed to rulers from high antiquity to the Xia, Shang, and Zhou dynasties. They are centrally concerned with political legitimacy obtained through the "Mandate of Heaven" (*tianming*) – a concept, however, that bronze inscriptions mention with some frequency only from late Western Zhou times onward.

References to specific *Documents* chapters can be found across Warring States texts, including newly excavated manuscripts. By the late fourth century BC, and possibly much earlier, a certain body of texts was gaining canonical stature that at least partially corresponds to our received version of the text. However, while more than 90 percent of all early *Poetry* quotations have counterparts in the transmitted anthology, only about a third of *Documents*-style quotations are found in the received classic. Excavated manuscripts further show that compared to the *Poetry*, the wording of *Documents*-style texts was far more unstable, perhaps because their diction was not as strictly guarded by rhyme and meter as the ancient songs. Furthermore, the *Documents* are virtually never quoted as "documents" (*shu*) in the way the *Poetry* is routinely cited as "poetry" (*shi*). Instead, they are mentioned by titles that may or may not concur with the chapter titles of the received text.

Of all Warring States texts, only the third-century BC *Xunzi*, edited at the late Western Han imperial court, concurs in all its *Documents* quotations with the received text. In Warring States and even Western Han times, an evidently much larger body of *Documents*-style texts – or separate compilations of such texts – circulated in the political discourses of different intellectual lineages. As a result, the textual history of the received anthology is exceedingly complex.

First, the text contains various layers whose composition seems to reach from late Western Zhou to Qin and Western Han times. Second, the history of the text during Qin and Han times remains unclear. Third, the received version of the text in the *Correct Meaning of the Five Classics* is attributed to the *Documents* expert and descendant of Confucius Kong Anguo (d. ca 100 BC). According to an account that includes various embellishments and contradictions, Kong's version of the text had been retrieved from the walls of Confucius' former residence where it had survived the Qin book burning until it was finally discovered some time between 154 and 128 BC. This version in pre-Qin "ancient script" (*guwen*) purportedly correspond to twenty-nine known chapters in the Western Han "modern script" plus material of sixteen additional ones. The text was lost with the fall of the Western Jin dynasty and the destruction of the palace library in 311. The canonical version included in the *Correct Meaning of the Five Classics*, the ancient-script *Hallowed Documents* (*Shangshu*), is based on a *Hallowed Documents of Kong Anguo* (*Kong Anguo Shangshu*) presented by a certain Mei Ze in 317 after the constitution of the Eastern Jin. It now included fifty-eight chapters, of which thirty-four, according to their titles, corresponded to the twenty-nine chapters of the Western Han text. The authenticity of the remaining chapters was doubted already in Song times, but only Yan Ruoqu (1636–1704) proved them to be forgeries, containing both newly fabricated texts and fragments from other early sources. Hui Dong (1697–1758) and others further corroborated Yan's work, effectively dividing the received text into two halves: the forged ancient-script chapters on the one hand, and the twenty-nine Western Han modern-script chapters on the other.

This, however, still does not clarify the provenance of the Western Han *Documents*. Han and later sources report that the Qin official erudite (*boshi*) Fu Sheng (b. 260 BC) had hidden his copy in a wall to save it from the Qin proscription of 213 BC, yet the wall fell victim to the turmoil of the Qin–Han transition. Emperor Wen (r. 180–157 BC) then ordered the court official Chao Cuo (d. 154 BC) to visit Fu Sheng and orally retrieve his "explanation" (*shuo*) of the text. Wei Hong (mid-first century AD), in a lost preface to (Kong Anguo's?) ancient-script *Documents*, noted that the old and frail Fu Sheng "could not speak properly." His unintelligible utterances were translated by his daughter, yet Chao Cuo understood her dialect only in parts. While much of this saga is dubious – for example, as a Qin court erudite, Fu Sheng was exempted from the proscription and did not have to hide his *Documents* copy – consistent emphasis is placed on the disrupted and imperfect oral transmission of Fu Sheng's text as opposed to Kong Anguo's ancient-script version found in the wall of Confucius' own house. This theme resonates with Eastern Han ancient-script ideology. As with the *Poetry*, nothing suggests that the *Documents* were lost under the Qin; more likely, the text existed in different versions, oral and written, that followed different lines of transmission.

Whatever its early history, the *Documents* anthology is highly eclectic and reflects not just a single intellectual source or lineage. Its chapters range from eighty-six to 1285 characters in length and are organized into the "Documents of the Yu and Xia Dynasties" (Yu Xia shu), "Documents of the Shang Dynasty" (Shang shu), and "Documents of the Zhou Dynasty" (Zhou shu). Among the twenty-nine Western Han chapters, four "Documents of the Yu and Xia" concern the mythological heroes Yao, Shun, Gao Yao, and Yu, or claim to be their direct speeches. Five "Documents of the Shang Dynasty" chapters chronicle the rise and fall of the Shang. The following nineteen chapters of the "Documents of the Zhou Dynasty" begin with the "Oath at Mu" (Mu shi), in which King Wu addresses his troops before his decisive attack on the Shang, and ends with the "Oath of Qin" (Qin shi), a speech set in 632 BC that culminates in the assertion that the well-being of the state was based in the person of an autocratic ruler. Many of these speeches are titled either "oath" (*shi*) or "announcement" (*gao*) and combine elements of proclamation, admonition, and terrifying threats. The dating of all of these texts is uncertain. Linguistic evidence suggests that especially the purportedly earliest speeches, those attributed to the rulers of the Shang and earlier, are in fact Warring States or Qin–Han fabrications. By contrast, the earliest parts of the *Documents* are a group of twelve speeches attributed to the early Western Zhou rulers, most notably the five long "announcements" traditionally believed to have been made by the Duke of Zhou, acting as regent for King Cheng (r. 1042/35–1006 BC): the "Great Announcement" (Da gao), "Announcement to Kang" (Kang gao), "Announcement on Alcohol" (Jiu gao), "Announcement to Shao" (Shao gao), and "Announcement at Luo" (Luo gao). In each of these, the Duke of Zhou – traditionally also credited with the composition of the *Classic of Changes* and the first of the "Eulogies of Zhou" – presents in a highly ceremonial idiom the principles of rulership and ritual order, grounding the claim for political legitimacy in religious practice: the texts refer to the ancestors, the order of sacrifice, the consultation of oracles, cosmic portents, and the Mandate of Heaven that the Zhou kings are anxious to maintain.

The overall diction of the early speeches is one of ceremonial gravity and solemnity. It is intensified through rhythmic phrasing (often falling into a four-syllable meter), repetitions of various kinds, frequent exclamations like "Alas!" at the beginning of a paragraph, catalogues (as in the lists of dignitaries and functionaries), and the regular use of fixed formulae like "I, the small child" (*yu xiao zi*) that are also familiar from bronze inscriptions. A passage from the "Many Officers" (Duo shi) speech may illustrate this style; here, the Duke of Zhou addresses the officers remaining from the overthrown Yin (Shang) dynasty:

> It was in the third month when the Duke of Zhou commenced [his government] in the new city of Luo. He made an announcement to the officers of the [former] Shang king: "The king speaks to this effect: 'You, remaining officers of Yin! Merciless and severe Heaven has sent down great disaster on Yin. We, the Zhou, assisted in its Mandate, and with Heaven's bright majestic terror we executed the royal punishment, rectified the Mandate to Yin and made it end according to God . . . [The last Shang king] was greatly licentious in his dissolution; he neglected the brightness of Heaven and the respect due to the folk. It is because of this that God on High did not protect him and sent down disaster as great as this . . . Ah! I declare to you, the many officers: I, only because of this, have transferred and settled you in the west; it is not because I, the One Man, take it as my virtue to disturb your calm. This is indeed the Mandate from Heaven – do not go against it! I do not dare to be dilatory – do not resent me! . . . ' The king says: 'I declare to you, the many officers of Yin: Today, since indeed I have not killed you, it is that I give you this order again: Today, I have made a great city here in this place of Luo. I, indeed, in the four quarters have none whom I reject. Moreover, you, the many officers:

with zeal and fervor, hasten to be our subjects! Be much obedient! . . . If you are greatly reverential, Heaven itself will favor and pity you. If you are not greatly reverential, you not only will not have your land, I will also apply the punishments of Heaven on your persons. Today, yours it is to dwell in your city and perpetuate your residence . . . '

No specific evidence suggests that the speeches like "Many Officers" were given by their purported speakers. Their linguistic features, repeated claims for the Mandate of Heaven, and references to specific administrative procedures and functionaries show clear parallels to mid- and late Western Zhou bronze inscriptions and seem to mark them as products of retrospective imagination, composed not by founding heroes but by their later descendants, who commemorated and celebrated the feats of their forebears. As such, the speeches contained the memory of the early Western Zhou model rulers as speaking in their own voices. While the tradition is entirely silent on the institutional framework in which the early speeches played their role and were preserved, their ceremonial rhetoric and presumed commemorative nature may plausibly situate them in the ancestral sacrifice and other court rituals that asserted both memory and identity. In this hypothesis, the speeches were part of the multimedia experience of dance, music, and recitation. Their commemorative gesture places them, together with the "Major Court Hymns," in the later part of the Western Zhou dynasty: a time of crisis that was forever removed from the dynastic founders – and all the more in need of their memory.

VI. Warring States narrative literature and rhetoric

With the single exception of the "Announcement to Kang," citations of the early *Documents* speeches are exceedingly rare in Warring States texts. This stands in sharp contrast to the presumably youngest chapters of the *Documents* that claim to contain the voices from mythological antiquity but, in fact, present elaborate schemes of cosmological, numerological, and bureaucratic order popular among late Warring States thinkers. Examples of these chapters are the "Great Plan" (Hong fan), the "Merits of Yu" (Yu gong), the "Canon of Yao" (Yao dian), or the "Plans of Gao Yao" (Gao Yao mo). Their ideal images of a cosmo-political order emerged in direct response to the instability of the Warring States period, a time of incessant warfare during which all political thinkers shared the quest for political unity that had no reality beyond the memory of high antiquity. A prominent example of such imagination is the "Canon of Yao," which shows the mythical ruler Shun on a cosmic journey through his realm. In a repetitive, monotonous account intimating total order and standardization, the ruler embarks in the middle month of each season toward the cardinal direction correlated to it in "Five Phases" (*wuxing*) cosmology, ascends the primary mountain there, and exerts his sovereignty through a fixed order of ritual activities:

> In the second month of the year, [Shun] went east to visit those under his protection and arrived at [Mount] Venerable Dai. He made a burnt offering and in the correct sequence performed "gazing from the distance" sacrifices to the mountains and streams. Then he gave audience to the lords of the east, regulated the [calendar of the] seasons and months, rectified the [designations of the] days, and unified the pitch-pipes and the measures of length, capacity, and weight.

Similarly, the "Merits of Yu" shows Yu as the ordering force in a mechanical and predictable universe: he measures the known realm, regulates its waters, cultivates its mountains, develops its plains, organizes agriculture, divides the world into nine spheres, and distributes both land and surnames. Likewise, "The Great Plan" presents the cosmic ruler in the center of a numerology scheme that encompasses both the natural and the political worlds.

The amalgamation of cosmology and political mythology is a typical phenomenon of late Warring States times, rhetorically anticipating the unification of the Chinese realm. No early Chinese text advocates an alternative to a unified rule; instead, a number of works composed around the Qin unification are joined by their trust in a centralized, well-ordered cosmos and state. Their ideal natural and social universe is open to human comprehension and prediction because its dynamics are not erratic but governed by principles of regularity. This regularity is expressed in numerological systems – most comprehensively in the correlative philosophy of the Five Phases – that were mapped onto time (seasons), space (directions), social structures (administration and so on), and a host of other matters.

Thus the late Warring States(?) *Rituals of Zhou* (*Zhou li*) – first promoted by Liu Xin (d. AD 23) at the end of the Western Han and later one of the Thirteen Classics – arranges the administrative institutions according to the "offices" of Heaven, Earth, and the four seasons. For each office, the exact (if highly schematic) number of bureaucrats at the different ranks is noted, on the whole reproducing the numerological order of the universe as the order of political administration and its ideal textual description. While the *Rituals of Zhou* has been associated with either the Qin imperial court or Wang Mang's Xin dynasty (AD 9–23) – both regarded as illegitimate by the later tradition –

its scholasticism matches that of other late Warring States and early imperial texts. For example, *Mr. Lü's Spring and Autumn Annals* (*Lüshi chunqiu*), compiled under the patronage of the Qin chancellor Lü Buwei (d. 235 BC), discusses the ideal administrative order in twelve core chapters (completed 239 BC) that are dedicated to the twelve months of the year. Similarly, the "Merits of Yu" and the "Great Plan" impose numerology on geography and thus turn the actual landscape of early China into mythological space. The same is true for two other late Warring States works: the *Tradition of King Mu* (*Mu tianzi zhuan*) and the *Classic of Mountains and Seas* (*Shanhai jing*). The former text was excavated from a tomb in AD 281, with its four core chapters likely dating from the mid-fourth century BC. It recounts in highly formulaic and systematic fashion the Western Zhou king Mu's legendary celestial journey to the west, culminating in his sojourn with the Queen-Mother of the West (Xiwangmu), who grants him a romantic encounter at Jasper Pool in the Elysium of the Kunlun mountains. Here, King Mu is no longer a mere historical figure; he is a cosmic sovereign who converses with a host of spirits on whom he graciously bestows entire catalogues of splendid gifts.

It is unclear how widely this mythological narrative, built around the trope of the celestial journey, circulated in late Warring States times. It did not, however, enter the tradition of historical narrative. The abundance of anecdotal and fictional elements in works like the *Zuo Tradition* notwithstanding, some lines – however tentative and inconsistent – were drawn between the downright fantastic (and therefore didactically irrelevant) and the historically and morally plausible. This may also explain the isolated position of the *Classic of Mountains and Seas*, an ethno-cosmography of the strange lands and their bizarre inhabitants beyond the Chinese realm. While a text titled *Classic of Mountains and Seas* is first mentioned in the *Records of the Historian*, the received version is a work of many chronological layers; only Chapters 1–5 may reach back into Warring States times. The text abounds with specific geographic detail such as the distances between places, but these are largely schematic and as a whole create more a mandala-like cosmic diagram than any realistic geography. Like the "Heavenly Questions" of the *Verses of Chu* (*Chuci*; see below), the *Classic of Mountains and Seas* was reportedly written to existing illustrations (not to be confused with later illustrated versions of the text). Such a connection to visual representation is quite possible, although the exact relation between text and image remains unclear.

If texts like the *Tradition of King Mu*, the *Classic of Mountains and Seas*, and perhaps many other writings devoted to the strange and the transcendent – the kinds of things Confucius "did not talk about" (*zi bu yu*; *Analects* 7/21) – were on the margins of the early prose tradition, the mainstream of Warring States narrative was profoundly historical. It developed from the *Spring and Autumn Annals* (*Chunqiu*) that already in the *Mencius* is attributed to Confucius and in Han times became part of the Five Classics. Covering the years from 722 to 481 BC, the *Annals* provides brief annalistic entries from the perspective of twelve generations of rulers from the small northeastern state of Lu, the home state of Confucius. The *Annals* was not the only text of its kind; in Warring States times, the very term "Spring and Autumn" (*chunqiu*; perhaps more correctly "Springs and Autumns"), which refers to the continuous rise and fall of ruling houses, was generally used for annalistic accounts that various Eastern Zhou states kept in their archives. The *Annals* records events about other states of the realm but only in their relation to the state of Lu and from a Lu perspective. Far more inhibiting to the reading of the *Annals*, however, is the extreme brevity of the individual entries, the limitation to a small number of events per year, and the formulaic diction of the text. To function as an archival text that could be consulted about the past, it must have been substantiated by a host of additional records. In its received version, the text is in urgent need of further explanation.

According to the *Mencius* (III.B.9), Confucius had compiled the *Annals* in response to a world in turmoil and decline. From the beginning, the text was understood as moral judgment. According to the *Mencius*, Confucius expected to be both understood and condemned on the basis of the *Annals*; and after he had completed the text, "rebellious subjects and deceitful sons were frightened." Despite the terse and factual nature of the *Annals*, its author is portrayed as a moral authority. His writing both rectifies the past and offers moral guidance. As with the exegesis of the Five Classics altogether, the interpretation of the *Annals* takes its decisive turn in Western Han times. Like the *Poetry*, the *Annals* was seen as encoded language; in fact, due to its extremely terse and formulaic wording, the text was virtually incomprehensible without further elaboration. The central commentary to the *Annals*, dominant from the early Han through the mid-first century BC, was the *Gongyang Tradition* (*Gongyang zhuan*), which elevated Confucius to the status of a "plain" – that is, uncrowned – "king" (*suwang*). He did not equal an actual ruler but was above all rulers by submitting them to his own moral judgment.

The *Gongyang Tradition* is said to have begun with Confucius' disciple Zi Xia, from whom it continued orally for some four hundred years to an otherwise unknown erudite, Mr. Gongyang, who during the reign of Emperor Jing (r. 157–141 BC) first wrote the text on bamboo and silk. The account is impossible to verify, but by the time of Sima Qian, the *Annals* had become the master text of Spring and Autumn history with the *Gongyang Tradition* as its principal exegesis. Its most illustrious proponent was Dong Zhongshu (ca 179–ca 104 BC), who attracted thousands of students, among them Sima Qian. In Western Han times, none of the Five Classics was more directly applied to questions of imperial rule than the *Annals*. In 51 BC, Emperor Xuan (r. 74–49 BC) personally presided over a court debate – led by Xiao Wangzhi (ca 110–47 BC), the Grand Tutor to the heir apparent – on the Five Classics at the Stone Canal Pavilion (*shiqu ge*) within the imperial palace. The meeting of twenty-three court scholars had been triggered by the ascendance of a new *Annals* exegesis, the *Guliang Tradition* (*Guliang zhuan*), as a challenge to the *Gongyang* interpretation. The debate was immensely political and over several months led to written discussions on various topics, many of them related to matters of ritual propriety and social order. On each of the more than thirty questions under debate, the final pronouncement was left to the emperor, who thus assumed his own authority over the Classics. In the end the *Guliang Tradition* was given preference over the *Gongyang* and received its own chair at the Imperial Academy.

The high-profile debate over the *Annals* testifies to their importance at the Western Han court. It implied a series of assumptions on a notoriously underdetermined text, that, in order to mean anything at all, had to be imbued with profound yet hidden authorial intent. Thus, in addition to the *Poetry* and the *Changes*, the *Annals* was the third of the Five Classics that called for complex hermeneutic procedures and generated a large field of learning engaging thousands of scholars. The study of the *Annals* assumed particular urgency because its lessons could be directly applied both to Han rule and to Han historical writing. Thus Confucius, now the preeminent historian of old, became a powerful model for Sima Qian, to whom, in turn, we owe the only substantial biographical account of Confucius. This account created the very model the Han historian then set out to follow.

The Western Han understanding of the *Annals* was rooted in three notions: "praise and blame" (*baobian*), "subtle phrasing" (*weiyan*), and "rectification of names" (*zhengming*). Together, they defined the purpose and supreme stature of the historian: his work served as a tool of historical criticism, as a warning for the present and future, as a standard of language, and, by its nature as a textual artifact, as a retrospective rectification and replacement of history itself. Thus the famous last entry in the *Annals*, dating to the fourteenth year of Duke Ai (481 BC), reads, "The fourteenth year, spring. In the west, hunters caught a unicorn." The *Gongyang* comments,

The unicorn is a beast of benevolence. It arrives under the rule of a [true] king. Without a [true] king, it does not arrive . . . Confucius said: "How could it come! How could it come!" He grasped his inner sleeve and wiped his face; tears soaked his seams . . . When the hunters caught the unicorn in the west, Confucius said: "My way has ended."

Gongyang and *Guliang* both subject the *Annals* to a question-and-answer catechism that probes deeply into the text. They operate on the assumption that Confucius had used "subtle phrasing" to encode moral judgment, and that commentary could decode the text back into plain language. To this end, *Gongyang* and *Guliang* explore the meaning of each word in the *Annals* through a tripartite procedure. First, they insist that historical writing is conveyed in strict and precise language. Second, they propose that deviations from that normative phrasing are purposeful and can be identified. Third, these deviations also follow precise rules and, if properly decoded, will demonstrate how a deviation in phrasing reflects the deviation in moral behavior that the historian was trying to expose. In this spirit, each entry in the *Annals* could be decoded as moral judgment and offered examples from the past as lessons for the present. This was particularly true for anomalous natural phenomena of which numerous instances were reported in the *Annals*. These accounts were readily available to scholars like Dong Zhongshu or the *Guliang* expert Liu Xiang (79–8 BC), who used them to explain any irregular cosmic events of their own times, such as eclipses, droughts, floods, unusual atmospheric phenomena, the appearance of strange plants and animals, or aberrant movements of the stars and planets.

While the *Gongyang* and *Guliang* traditions offer paradigms of historical judgment and the encoding of praise and blame, their catechistic format stays close to the *Annals* and is limited to the events reported there. The third "tradition" (*zhuan*) that in Han times became related to the *Annals* was that by a Mr. Zuo, whose *Zuo Tradition* is only loosely connected to the *Annals* but at the same time offers by far the most extensive narrative account of Spring and Autumn history. The *Zuo Tradition* is the most important and most fascinating work of pre-imperial historical writing and in many ways served as both source and model for Sima Qian's *Records of the Historian*. It is traditionally attributed to Zuo Qiuming, an obscure figure of the fifth century who is briefly hailed for his moral judgment by Confucius in *Analects* 5/25. While the *Zuo Tradition* was one of the central sources for Sima Qian, it was only Liu Xiang's son Liu Xin who recommended the work for imperial canonization with the argument that its text was in ancient script and thus more trustworthy than the *Gongyang* and *Guliang* traditions that had relied merely on oral transmission. To many a scholar in late imperial China, Liu Xin was the bête noire of the Han: a man who not only had betrayed the Western Han imperial house of Liu (to which he was directly related) by serving the "usurper" Wang Mang, but was also a forger of several classics – especially the *Zuo Tradition* and the *Rituals of Zhou* – in order to provide ideological support for Wang's "New" (*Xin*) dynasty. This claim by Kang Youwei (1858–1927) and others, that Liu Xin had forged the *Zuo Tradition*, has been discredited; in general, the composition of the work is now dated into the late fourth century. Following the historical framework of the *Annals*, it includes a wealth of documents and speeches woven into the narrative proper. It remains unclear to what extent these are based on authentic, and thus indeed very early, written records. While certain stylistic features seem to distinguish the chronologically earlier narratives from the later ones, numerous instances of proleptic speech – predictions of future events that almost all turn out to be true – indicate a strong retrospective authorial or editorial hand.

Despite these uncertainties, the *Zuo Tradition* is rightfully celebrated as a masterpiece of grand historical narrative. It constitutes the single most important historical narrative from the years 722 to 468 BC; that is, thirteen years beyond the last entry in the *Annals*. The text is replete with narrative detail and dramatic encounters, with a highly complex architecture in which extensive strings of anecdotal narrative develop in parallel, overlapping, and recurrent patterns. It also is hailed for its didactic orientation. Instead of offering authorial judgments or catechistic hermeneutics, the *Zuo Tradition* lets its moral lessons unfold within the narrative itself, teaching at once history and historical judgment. This combination of historical account, narrative aesthetics, and didactic persuasion is fundamentally self-contradictory: both rhetorical brilliance and didactic purpose tend to undermine the modern reader's trust in the historical account – yet to the literary tradition, it was precisely this powerful combination that has elevated the *Zuo Tradition* to its preeminent stature of a classic in the Confucian canon.

In narrative tension and dramatic episodes, the *Zuo Tradition* leaves little to ask for: battles and fights, royal assassinations and the murder of concubines, courage and cowardice, deception and intrigues, excesses of all colors, oppression and insurgence, appearances of cosmic portents and ghosts. Infused with an emphasis on sincere personal intent and emotion, the narrative offers a panorama of human existence that – not unlike the "Airs of the States" – locates the roots of truth and morality less in the rulers than in their subjects. As a whole, the text continuously illustrates the importance of social order and ritual hierarchy precisely because it recounts so vividly the catastrophic consequences of their failure. Meanwhile, despite its overarching didacticism, it also leaves moments of ambivalence and moral inconsistency that testify to disparate anecdotal traditions.

The dominant narrative strategy is related to the absence of an authorial voice. Instead, through predictions, flashbacks, and extensive dialogues, the narrative threads, which often span years and decades, are both held together and reflected upon in the thoughts and speeches of the historical protagonists themselves. History appears driven not by the events proper but by the choices and deliberations of its individual agents, who routinely provide the justifications for, and explanations of, their own actions. In this rhetorical framework, the bare outcome of a conflict is far less important than the moral choices it makes explicit. These choices tend to be presented at an early stage of the specific narrative, inviting the reader to predict the result of the conflict together with the historical actors' own predictions. In the *Zuo Tradition*, history becomes a moral and predictable universe of social and ritual order. Violations of this order are recognizable, and their consequences are foreseeable. Success and failure are not a matter of brute force but result from the degree to which the moral order and its externalization in ritual form are observed. Those who violate the rules, who act ruthlessly toward the common folk, or who ignore sagely advice, are doomed. Such judgment unfolds without authorial interference and is often left implicit, yet by entering the *Zuo Tradition* universe, the audience – the Chinese elite versed in the Classics and their moral imperatives – was well prepared to follow its logic.

Individual anecdotes are on occasion also capped by brief moral verdicts attributed either to Confucius or to an anonymous "superior man" (*junzi*). In these remarks, the *Zuo Tradition* becomes related to the ethical and political program of Warring States *ru* classicists. Most likely, these verdicts were attached at the time when the vast array of anecdotal narratives were cast into the grand narrative of the received text; one may speculate that they – much like the prefaces to the songs of the *Poetry* – served the purposes of a particular teaching lineage to distill both historical knowledge and moral teaching into compact formulae. Most importantly, they make the *Zuo Tradition* speak directly to those in power, reminding them of the historical precedents and inevitable consequences of their own actions. As a whole the text thus assumes a single voice that embodies the totality of voices of ministers, advisers, "old men," and other named or anonymous figures who consistently present their rulers with political advice and remonstrations to remind them of their moral duties and of the predictable regularities of history. These voices, together the voice of the *Zuo Tradition*, speak with elegance and authority; they represent the historical actors as well as "Confucius" and the "superior man" – yet ultimately they represent the very classicists who compiled the *Zuo Tradition*. Rulers who heed them succeed; those who do not heed them fail. As such the *Zuo Tradition* is not a disinterested account of the past but a text directly tied to the specific political and philosophical persuasions of Warring States classicists. It is, in every sense of the word, their text.

The constructed, patchwork-like nature of the narrative becomes apparent in the many instances of inserted didactic episodes, brief vignettes of exemplary situations that must have existed independent of the context into which they were finally embedded. These brief passages may represent an earlier anecdotal style that is much more prominent in the other great historical narrative dating from the Warring States period, the *Discourses of the States*. Sima Qian attributes this text likewise to Zuo Qiuming, but the *Discourses* follows a different organization and is more philosophical and rhetorical treatise than continuous narrative. A number of parallel passages shared by the *Zuo Tradition* and *Discourses* may reveal a widely available repertoire of traditional knowledge circulating in various written and oral versions. Additional parallels are found between the *Zuo Tradition* and *Master Yan's Spring and Autumn Annals* (*Yanzi chunqiu*), another collection of anecdotal writing. Containing mainly the remonstrations that Yan Ying (d. 500 BC) purportedly delivered to Lord Jing of Qi (r. 547–489 BC), this text oscillates between history, rhetoric, and didactic purpose. Its 215 episodes, compiled into eight chapters in late Western Han times, likely date from the late Warring States period and display the trope of the morally superior adviser even more pointedly than the *Discourses* and the *Zuo Tradition*.

The twenty-one chapters of the *Discourses* are a rich collection of speeches and dialogues, interspersed with narrative and discursive passages, which are assigned to eight Western and Eastern Zhou states: Zhou, Lu, Qi, Jin, Zheng, Chu, Wu, and Yue. The chapters are named after their states ("Discourses of Zhou," "Discourses of Lu," and so forth) and in themselves are chrono-logically ordered, ranging from the tenth century BC to 453 BC. However, the interest of the *Discourses* in the eight states is decidedly uneven, as the distribution of its 245 episodes reveals: while the mighty Eastern Zhou state of Jin is represented with 127 entries (in the current text arranged in nine chapters), the small state of Lu – Confucius' home state, where purportedly the Western Zhou ritual traditions were still maintained – receives no fewer than thirty-seven, exceeding both the royal state of Zhou (thirty-three pas-sages) and Lu's powerful northeastern neighbor Qi (eight). This distribution may be another reflection of *ru* classicism and its preoccupation with Lu – a state both noble and powerless, exemplifying as a polity what Confucius, the "uncrowned king," embodied as a person.

Han sources may thus be correct in locating the compilation of the *Discourses* not entirely separately from that of the *Zuo Tradition*; both are devoted to the same moral purpose and historical paradigms under which they organize a wide variety of materials. Both abound in references to recitations of songs from the *Poetry*, performed as elements of diplomatic discourse and political remonstration. Given these similarities with the *Zuo Tradition*, the Jin dynasty commentator of the *Discourses*, Wei Zhao (d. 273), called the *Discourses* the "exoteric tradition" (*waizhuan*) to the *Annals*. While the text itself shows no such specific relation, the connection of the *Discourses* with the historical and political consciousness of Warring States *ru* classicists, to whom the *Annals* was the primary account of history, is unmistakable.

Altogether, the large corpus of Warring States anecdotal and philosophical writing (on the latter, see below) was framed in historical terms and over time became organized in a series of compilations, many dating from as late as Western Han times. Instead of authors, we must think of compilers, and probably groups of compilers; individual authorship, if existing at all before the third century BC, was an extreme exception. Not only do the texts themselves withhold any information to identify their authors – no excavated manuscript so far contains a reference to its author – but the substantial pieces of traditional lore that appear repeatedly, and then in strikingly different versions, across a range of compilations from the fourth through the first centuries BC, amply testify to the fluidity of such material beyond geographical and political boundaries. Even the – in this context often overstated – divide between the multistate world of the Warring States and the early empire is questionable. We know next to nothing about the specific ways in which this lore developed, was circulated, and became transmitted to the late Western Han court classicists who organized the textual world of early China in the way we know it. An outstanding example of a narrative that found its way into a whole series of texts is the story of Wu Zixu, a refugee from Chu who became a key political adviser and military leader in the southeastern state of Wu. The *Zuo Tradition* gives most of its account on Wu Zixu in eight entries dating from 522 through 484 BC; the *Discourses* concentrates the story into a period of only twenty-two years while dramatically embellishing its details; *Mr. Lü's Spring and Autumn Annals* provides further, increasingly bizarre additions; and in Chapter 66 of the *Records of the Historian*, the story becomes refocused on Wu Zixu's moral choices. Finally, two probably Eastern Han anecdote compilations complete the retellings: the *Book on the Incomparability of Yue*

(*Yue jue shu*) and, most extensively, the *Spring and Autumn Annals of Wu and Yue* (*Wu Yue chunqiu*), recounting the struggle between the states of Wu and Yue at the southeastern Chinese periphery. On this increasingly rich basis, later versions continued to elaborate on Wu Zixu (who gradually became the epitome of filial piety), including a "transformation text" (*bianwen*) manuscript found at Dunhuang.

The fantastic proliferation of detail in the Wu Zixu story provides abundant evidence not for specific authors but for the motives, interests, and literary techniques common to them all. The building blocks of early Chinese prose are historical anecdotes focused on exemplary individuals and their thoughts, words, and actions. They are driven not by chronology but by direct speech and dramatic dialogue that reveal the protagonists' inner worlds. Where the cosmic or ancestral spirits interfere, they do so in predictable responses to human action and intent. The emphasis on speech and dialogue exposes the constructed nature of prose rhetoric: the great speeches of early Chinese narrative, beautifully phrased and yet ever-changing across parallel accounts, are the words of ritual propriety (or failure thereof) as imagined by later generations. They are at once the most fictional and the most powerful elements of historical narrative – true not because they had ever been spoken but as ideal and prototypical speech.

The emphasis on the spoken word in early China – references to the importance of writing are next to absent – extends far beyond history. Speeches and dialogues structure much of philosophical writing (the early layers of the *Analects*, the *Mencius*, but also the core sections of the *Mozi* and the *Zhuangzi*) that, in turn, takes on the framework of the historical anecdote. Yet the primacy of oral persuasion culminates in another body of texts centered on the figure of the "itinerant rhetorician" (*youshui*) or "political strategist" (*zhongheng jia*). Their accounts are the pseudohistorical *Intrigues of the Warring States* (*Zhanguo ce*), compiled by Liu Xiang between 26 and 8 BC from at least six different collections of remonstrations (*jian*) and persuasions (*shui*). The *Intrigues* contains 497 entries relating to the seven big domains of Warring States times (Qin, Qi, Chu, Zhao, Wei, Han, and Yan), as well as to the Zhou royal house and the minor states of Song, Wei, and Zhongshan. The origins of the anecdotes are unknown, and the textual history of the *Intrigues* is problematic. The earliest commentary is attributed to Gao You (ca 168–212), but the current text is based on a reconstruction of Liu Xiang's compilation by Zeng Gong (1019–1083) which gave rise to two editions of different arrangement: while Yao Hong's (ca 1100–1146) version presumably follows Liu Xiang's initial order of the text according to states, Bao Biao's (1106–1149) edition – revised and annotated by Wu Shidao (1283–1344) – abandons the geographical for a purely chronological sequence of the entries.

A short text of twenty-seven entries that has been found separately among the silk manuscripts from the Western Han Mawangdui tomb no. 3 contains a number of direct parallels to the *Intrigues*. Further parallels appear in the *Records of the Historian* and in the "Forest of Persuasions" (*Shui lin*) chapters of the *Han Feizi*. Altogether, a large body of rhetorical writings beyond the *Intrigues* must have circulated widely in the early empire. As they appear in several sources, these materials show an early rhetorical tradition – alive for several centuries before reaching Liu Xiang – quite distinct from the moral universe of *ru* classicist learning. Paying no attention to the hallowed *Poetry* and *Documents*, these "persuasions" show expertise in the craft of rhetoric that was forged among strategists who traveled between the various states to offer their political and military advice. While early China did not produce systematic treatises on rhetoric and did not develop anything like the lexicon and the professional and institutionalized training of rhetoric of ancient Greece and Rome, discussions of rhetorical techniques are preserved in sources like the "Smooth Persuasions" (*Shun shui*) of *Mr. Lü's Spring and Autumn Annals*, the "Difficulties of Persuasion" (*Shui nan*) of *Han Feizi*, or the "Arrayed Traditions of Fortune-Tellers" in the *Records of the Historian*. These texts do not discuss specific rhetorical figures but emphasize strategies of persuasion such as the need to explore one's counterpart's thoughts or the use of historical analogy and precedent. Yet it is mostly the individual *Intrigues* episode that reveals the basic techniques of early Chinese oratory. A common rhetorical strategy is to explore a situation from two possible outcomes that both lead to the same conclusion, as in the brief anecdote "A Person Who Presented the Drug of Immortality to the King of Jing" (*Intrigues*, Chu, 4):

Someone presented the drug of immortality to the king of Jing. The receptionist ushered him in when an attendant asked: "Can it be consumed?" – "It can." Thereupon the attendant snatched the drug and consumed it. The king was angry and sent a man to execute him, but the attendant sent someone to persuade the king: "Your subject has asked the receptionist, and the receptionist said it could be consumed; thus, your subject consumed it. In this, your subject is without fault; the fault rests with the receptionist. Moreover, the visitor had presented the medicine as the drug of immortality. If your subject consumed it and were then executed by the king, it would be the drug of mortality. If the king executes your innocent servant, it will be clear to everyone that the king has been deceived." Thereupon the king did not execute him.

In the vast majority of persuasions, the principal scenario is the same: a strategist speaks to the ruler who follows advice or fails to listen. As such, the *Intrigues* reflect the political circumstances of the Warring States era, when competing states were in constant need of political and military advice. The traditional image of the Warring States themselves is largely shaped by the persuasions that display the cynical pursuit of strategic advantage. What the rulers in the *Intrigues* request, and what the "itinerant persuaders" deliver, is clever advice beyond the moral concerns set forth in the speeches of the *Zuo Tradition* and the *Discourses of the States*. Unlike *ru* classicist discourse, the speeches of the *Intrigues* pull out all the stops of deceit and manipulation, demonstrating not the elegance of virtuous speech but the efficiency of amoral, if not downright immoral, verbal craft. The *Intrigues* thus occupy an ambivalent position where admiration for eloquence and disapproval of the unscrupulous ploy converge. Both Confucius in *Analects* 15/11 and 17/18 and Mencius (V.A.4) denounce crafty speakers who, according to the *Analects*, are able to "overturn family and state." Yet the most brilliant, if certainly fictional, condemnation of crafty political rhetoric is found in the *Intrigues* itself. This condemnation is attributed to the master rhetorician Su Qin, who tries to move King Hui of Qin to take military action against the anti-Qin alliance of the time. Su Qin traces the decay of political power to a lack of military prowess and to the emergence of excessive rhetoric. To make this point, Su Qin, in a marvelous self-referential turn, overwhelms the king with the full force of oratory, delivering a rushing, hendiadys-laden tri- and tetrasyllabic harangue with rhyme changes after every couplet:

> As soon as rules and statutes were complete,
> the people mostly assumed crafty manners.
> When writings and documents became dense and murky,
> the common people lived in hardship.
> Those above and below resented each other,
> the folk had nothing to put them at ease.
> The more shining the words and brilliant the reasoning,
> the more weapons and shields arose.
> Despite eloquent words and sumptuous adornment
> battles and attacks did not cease.
> Profusely they recited refined phrases,
> yet all under heaven remained in disorder.
> Tongues withered, ears became deaf,
> yet one did not see achievement or merit.

. . .
Today, the succeeding rulers
are ignorant about the supreme way.
They all are:
muddled in their teachings,
chaotic in their rule,
confused by words,
mystified by speech,
deluged by disputation,
drowned by phrases.

In this verbal cascade, language is more than the vehicle of meaning; Su Qin creates the very reality he sets out to denounce. In Western Han times this particular use of oral rhetoric became one of the defining features of the dominant court genre of literature, the poetic exposition (*fu*; see below). It carried with it both the splendor and the moral ambiguity of persuasive speech – and for this came to be rejected by the later Confucian tradition.

VII. The question of literacy

While the *Zuo Tradition* and the *Discourses* are genuine Warring States works, the oratory of the *Intrigues* and discussions of rhetoric found in texts from the late third and early second centuries BC are somewhat later constructions of Warring States political discourse. Much of the *Intrigues* is historically unreliable – if perhaps no more so than some aspects of the Wu Zixu legend – but the text reflects genuine practices of diplomacy and debate during the era of political disintegration and interstate conflict from, roughly, 500 through 200 BC. After the foundation of the Qin empire in 221 BC, the new politics of intellectual and material unification and standardization put an end to the "discourses of the hundred lineages" (*baijiayu*) of Warring States times, the classical era of Chinese philosophical debate. The expository prose of the Warring States is written in "classical Chinese," which – compared to the archaic language of the *Poetry* and the core layers of the *Documents* and *Changes* – is characterized by a lucid and smooth style. As a whole, this body of texts created the intellectual foundations of the Chinese empire. The *ru* classicists in particular composed a new body of expository texts around the *Poetry* and the *Documents* that secured these canonical works as the primary source of cultural authority. This new corpus of philosophical prose established the *ru* scholars as the principal interpreters and guardians of the Classics – men who, like Confucius in *Analects* 7/1, "trustfully delight in antiquity." Meanwhile, other intellectual lineages developed their own responses to the changing needs of an increasingly complex society and its diverse fields of traditional and emerging knowledge.

The specific origins of Warring States intellectual discourse are difficult to grasp. Traditional ideas that relate purportedly very early texts to specific authors – like the *Laozi* coming from the sixth century BC – are a Han dynasty phenomenon and fraught with dubious assumptions about the original integrity of individual "books" and the identity of their putative authors and audiences. No archaeological or traditional evidence inspires confidence in high rates of literacy in, say, 500 BC. Pragmatic writing for economic, administrative, legal, military, and other technical purposes had been in existence since Western Zhou and probably even late Shang times, although no wide-ranging evidence such as we find in ancient Mesopotamia or Egypt exists to support more specific conclusions. Some form of schooling, including its economic and cultural resources from buildings to textbooks, must have been available to the aristocratic elite as well as – for functional literacy in daily transactions – to lower strata of administrators, judges, and practitioners of medical and other specialist knowledge. Traditional historiography relates the composition of expository prose to the lowest rank of the hereditary aristocracy, the "servicemen" (*shi*) who lived in the capitals of the various states or moved from state to state. For example, Xun Kuang, the principal author of the *Xunzi*, is said to have traveled from the eastern states all the way to Qin in the west.

It would be adventurous to project the practices of writing known from the late fourth century BC onward, and then especially from the Han imperial state, to earlier centuries, or to relate low-level functional literacy to the composition of philosophical prose. Administrative tasks relied on the technology of writing in ways philosophical discourse did not. Beginning with the late Shang oracle records and extending to the texts of Western Zhou bronze inscriptions, one can identify anonymous specialists in writing at the royal court. The *Rituals of Zhou*, a text that purports to outline the institutions of the Western Zhou but reflects Warring States ideals of political and cosmological order, lists a total number of 366 government offices and mentions acts of reading and writing for 42 of these. However, the vast majority of governmental offices – real or imagined – produced and kept written texts. This fact is reflected in the general "outlines of offices" (*xu guan*) that introduce the six major sections of the *Rituals of Zhou*, as in the outline for the highest office of the state, that of the prime minister (*dazai*) in the Ministry of State (*tianguan*):

Prime minister, one man in the rank of one of the six ministers (*qing*); Vice prime ministers (*xiaozai*), two men in the rank of Ordinary grand master (*zhong dafu*); Assistant ministers of state (*zaifu*), four men in the rank of Junior grand master (*xia dafu*); Senior servicemen (*shangshi*), eight men; Ordinary servicemen (*zhongshi*), sixteen men; Numerous junior servicemen (*lü xiashi*), thirty-six men; Storehouse keepers (*fu*), six men; Scribes (*shi*), twelve men; Aides (*xu*), twelve men; Runners (*tu*), one hundred and twenty men.

The sequence of positions is typical and reflects the ranks of government officials: the three levels of servicemen (*shi*) were still part of the nobility, but the four ranks of storehouse keepers, scribes, aides, and runners were not; their members were recruited from commoners. The storehouse keepers were in charge of storing official documents and contracts; the scribes, usually double the number of storehouse keepers, were their subordinates who created these writings. According to Zheng Xuan's commentary, both groups were appointed not by the ruler but by the respective ministers, which reflects their relatively low status.

Altogether, the *Rituals of Zhou* lists for the regular offices of the central government 442 storehouse keepers and 994 scribes, plus those for administrative units beyond the central government (including 101 scribes). Whatever its factual substance, this account clearly points to large numbers of minor officials charged with the production and storage of documents, and thus to an extensive amount of pragmatic writing. This is consistent with evidence from recently excavated manuscripts. Direct archaeological evidence for the status of government scribes comes from the late third-century BC Qin statutes, written on bamboo, that were excavated in 1975 from Shuihudi (Yunmeng, Hubei) tomb no. 11 (sealed 217 BC). The tomb occupant, a man named Xi who lived from 262 to 217 BC, began his career as a local scribe (*shi*) at the age of eighteen or nineteen (244 BC) and was promoted to the position of a prefectural scribe (*lingshi*) three years later. In that capacity his responsibilities included the investigation of criminal cases; in 235 BC, he was promoted to a higher legal position. This biography suggests that the position of scribe, although hereditary in the state of Qin, was an entry position to be taken at a young age, immediately after being trained in an office that the Qin statutes identify as "study room" (*xueshi*); the main prerequisite was the ability to recite and write a text of a certain length.

The *History of the Han* and the postface of the *Shuowen jiezi* note that a scribe had to master a text of nine thousand characters in length; by contrast, a number of five thousand characters is noted in a recently excavated legal manuscript from Zhangjiashan (Jingzhou, Hubei) tomb no. 247, "Statutes and Ordinances of the Second Year" (Ernian lüling, probably referring to the year 186 BC), that includes a "Statute on Scribes" (Shilü). Both the Shuowen and the "Statute" give the students' age as seventeen sui (sixteen years according to Western counting) before they were examined for the position of scribe, which corresponds to the entry-level position mentioned for the Shuihudi tomb occupant. The difference in the number of characters may itself be nothing more than a scribal error based on the similarity of the graphs for "five" and "nine" in Warring States script.

It is difficult to gauge how many different characters a text of five thousand or nine thousand graphs contained, but considering the nature and rank of the scribal position, it was certainly far below what was needed to read the Classics. The Western Han administrative wooden slips from Juyan (Edsengol, Inner Mongolia/Gansu) show evidence that they were written by scribes of only limited education. Depending on the nature of the text an aspiring scribe had to master for low-level administrative tasks, the number of different graphs may have been in the low four digits, if not much fewer. His scribal competence for producing pedestrian documents was fundamentally different from composing expository prose with its frequent references to the archaic classics.

At the same time, the technology of writing was far more instrumental to administrative, economic, and legal procedures than to the philosophical debate. Warring States expository prose is replete with references to the dialogical teacher–disciple relationship and to the primacy of committing knowledge to memory (while remaining virtually silent on acts of writing). If these sources – texts that finally ended up as the edited written artifacts we now have – are at all to be trusted, the technology of choice in philosophical argument, political oratory, and the perpetuation of the canon was memorization, not writing. For Warring States times, it remains to be shown that the ability to write was the hallmark of superior education and self-cultivation, or of the cultural elite in general. It may well have been the domain of menial clerks on the one hand, and of the servicemen (shi) on the other. While the former operated on the basic level of functional literacy, the latter – as coming from the lowest rank of the traditional aristocracy – had good reason to master a technology that on occasion supported their primarily oral discourses and may have granted them the attention of the ruling elite and, possibly, a perspective of upward mobility. Be this as it may, none of the early philosophical masters – Confucius, Mencius, Mozi, Zhuangzi, and so on – is said to have been the writer of the entire text later circulated under his name. (The exception is Laozi, who only according to later pious legend wrote his work of "five thousand characters.") Texts like the *Analects* or the *Mozi* are about the early masters, not by them. For all works of expository prose prior to the late third century BC (when real authors like Xun Kuang and his student Han Feizi entered the picture), we must assume a mode of gradual composition and compilation along the literacy / orality continuum. The more widespread textual circulation in pre-imperial times is assumed, the larger the space for oral transmission and recomposition becomes – never precluding the writing down of a text on whatever specific occasion. Either way, all received Warring States texts were reshaped through the editorial work by scholars at the Han imperial court.

For two millennia, the perception of Warring States intellectual discourse has been shaped by these scholars and their views of textual composition. While the recent manuscript finds have invited challenges to these views, they do not establish a new vision of early Chinese textuality that could compete in scope and depth with the received accounts produced in Han times. It remains next to impossible to approach the newly excavated texts without constant reference to the overall framework designed by Han thinkers – a framework that not only aligned an existing textual tradition with a grid of powerful categories but, in fact, was responsible for shaping and editing the tradition. We cannot approach Warring States expository prose without considering the nature and scope of Han dynasty editorship and textual classification.

VIII. The Han construction of Warring States textual lineages

Sima Tan (d. ca 110 BC), father of Sima Qian and the first author of the *Records of the Historian*, is credited with the first outline of Warring States thought which he organized in "six intellectual lineages" (*liu jia*): yinyang cosmologists, *ru* classicists, Mohists, terminologists (*mingjia*), legalists (*fajia*), and Daoists (*daojia*). Sima Tan did not, however, identify specific texts under these headings. In 26 BC, Emperor Cheng (r. 32 BC–7 BC) ordered Liu Xiang to assemble and collate the writings from across the empire and to compile the imperial library catalogue "Categorized Listings" (*Bielu*). In around 6 BC, Liu's son Liu Xin shortened the catalogue into the "Seven Summaries" (*Qilüe*), which Ban Gu in the late first century AD then further abbreviated into the "Monograph on Arts and Writings" in his *History of the Han*. The result was a broad survey of the enormous textual heritage that had accumulated by the fall of the Western Han, and it is here where we first see individual works assigned to specific intellectual lineages, reflecting the views of the

Han literary and political elite and giving pride of place to the Classics and the texts of the "hundred lineages." The vast fields of technical writing such as those on religion or the occult arts, which have become visible from excavated manuscripts, were undoubtedly known but are significantly underrepresented in Ban Gu's account. Thus the imperial catalogue was not a disinterested collection and description of all available materials, but rather reflects a selective and prescriptive vision of the textual heritage superimposed on a far more eclectic, less neatly divided universe of Warring States writing. Liu Xiang and his collaborators, as well as Liu Xin and Ban Gu, were court classicists to whom the canon of the Five Classics was both the source and the summit of all thinking and writing, as elaborated upon in the *ru* classicist exegetical traditions that had developed around these hallowed works of antiquity. The Five Classics were the "arts" (*yi*) proper, perfected and all-encompassing, to which all other "writings" (*wen*) were both subordinate and oriented.

The "Monograph on Arts and Writings" begins with a brief historical introduction from a late Western/early Eastern Han conception of early Chinese literary culture. According to Ban Gu, the "subtle phrasing" (*weiyan*) and "great principle" (*dayi*) of antiquity had been lost after Confucius and his immediate disciples, and the resulting uncertainty led to diverse hermeneutical and teaching traditions for each of the Classics. Following the (purported) large-scale destruction of classical learning under the Qin, the old texts had been collected only in fragments at the Han imperial court until Emperor Cheng's edict of 26 BC.

After this sketch, Ban Gu presents the resulting textual order in six divisions. The first three of these were devoted to the philosophical and literary heritage:

- The texts and hermeneutic traditions of the "six arts" (*liuyi*), including the "art," or classical learning, of music that by Han times had been lost. In addition to the *Changes, Documents, Poetry, Rites, Music,* and *Spring and Autumn Annals,* this supreme category also included the *Analects* and the *Classic of Filial Piety* (*Xiaojing*) – both primers in Han elite education – as well as the glossaries of "elementary learning" (*xiaoxue*) that facilitated the access to the Classics.
- The writings of Warring States and early Han philosophical "masters" (*zhuzi*), arranged under the rubrics of the *ru* classicists, Daoists, *yinyang* cosmologists, legalists, terminologists (or "sophists"), Mohists, strategists (*zonghengjia*), writers of miscellaneous learning (*zajia*), agriculturists (*nong jia*), and folklorists (*xiaoshuojia*).
- Songs and poetic expositions (*shifu*) mostly of Han times.

The following three categories of Ban Gu's catalogue contained a broad range of technical writings:

- military writings (*bingshu*);
- cosmological, calendrical, and prognostic writings (*shushu*);
- pharmaceutical and medical writings (*fangji*).

Liu Xiang personally collated the texts of the former three divisions and supervised those of the latter three. Working from vastly disparate materials, he and his collaborators had to select, decipher, collate, and arrange their texts; in addition, they transcribed them in current script onto new sets of bamboo slips, producing a new body of standardized texts. For each text Liu submitted to Emperor Cheng the work itself, a table of contents, a description of the various sources, information on the author, details regarding the collation, and a general discussion. All received early writings have come to us through this filter of textual evaluation, ordering, and rewriting. All excavated manuscripts so far available that pre-date Liu Xiang's efforts and have counterparts in the tradition differ in their internal arrangements from the received versions. Where it is possible to judge these differences, the received text seems less compelling than the manuscript version. The example of the "Black Robes" chapter from the *Records of Ritual* is particularly illustrative: while the manuscript versions in the Guodian and Shanghai Museum collections develop a consistent political argument on the ruler–subject relation, the differently arranged paragraphs of the received text appear as a series of individual statements, or clusters of statements, that lack cohesion or logical progression. Where the manuscript versions are tightly structured around a sequence of quotations from the *Poetry* (and, to a much lesser extent, the *Documents*), the same quotations in the received text are partly applied to different paragraphs and structured in a looser and somewhat redundant fashion. As a result, the received texts seem doubly deficient: first, the loss of the coherent political argument shows a deterioration in meaning, with a line of clear reasoning transformed into a series of disjointed statements; second, the loss of the earlier version's tight textual organization points to the erosion of mnemonic structure. In all likelihood the Guodian and Shanghai Museum manuscripts contain a coherent text that lent itself easily to memorization. The *Records of Ritual* version, by contrast, reflects an institutionalized imperial culture of writing and reading where texts were not primarily memorized and internalized but studied and stored on stationery. In the imperial collection of writings, the circulation and preservation of texts and ideas no longer depended on their intrinsic mnemonic structure. Liu Xiang's editorial choices were meaningful and appropriate to the imperial environment of official learning but not necessarily the best reconstructions of ancient texts that originally functioned in a very different cultural context.

Another striking case is that of the three Guodian manuscripts of ca 300 BC that, taken together, constitute a text containing parts of the received *Laozi* but in a different order of paragraphs. At the same time, the "*Laozi* C" manuscript from Guodian is physically indistinguishable from a previously unknown cosmogony that the modern editors have labeled "Grand Unity Gives Birth to Water" (Taiyi sheng shui) and that may well have been an integral part of the proto-*Laozi* materials. To further complicate the matter, the "Grand Unity" manuscript itself can be divided into two distinct parts, written on two distinct groups of bamboo slips, that may have been separately interspersed with the "*Laozi* C" materials. Altogether, the Guodian manuscripts seem to show an ongoing textual formation of the *Laozi* text in the late fourth century BC (whereas two complete copies of the received text, dating from early Western Han times, have been found at Mawangdui). Even if the Guodian collection were merely an idiosyncratic selection from a larger body of material similar to the received *Laozi*, it would suggest that the text was open to manipulation rather than firmly established.

Yet another example of remarkable textual change can be found with the bamboo text that the Shanghai Museum editors have titled "The Father and Mother of the Folk" (Min zhi fumu), also of around 300 BC. This manuscript text is parallel both to most of the "Discourse on Ritual" (Lun li) chapter in the Han dynasty compilation *Family Sayings of Confucius (Kongzi jiayu)* and to roughly the first half of the *Records of Ritual* chapter "Confucius Dwells at Leisure" (Kongzi xian ju). Unlike either of these received texts, however, "The Father and Mother of the Folk" sets out with a question regarding a couplet from the *Poetry* hymn "Drawing Water from Afar" (Jiong zhuo, Mao 251), posed by Confucius' disciple Zi Xia: how does a ruler become rightly called "the father and mother of the people?" From here, the tightly structured, partially rhymed text develops, in five steps, Confucius' discussion of song, ritual, and music. While the text has survived in two separate versions, neither is identical to the manuscript; although the received texts adhere to the basic formal structure, they show different arrangements of the material, together with a host of lexical changes. Furthermore, the manuscript's emphasis on "Drawing Water from Afar" as the starting point of the entire discussion (to which it then also returns later) has disappeared. Thus either the textual material existed in several parallel versions, with the manuscript and the received texts being just three instances among others, or the received versions reflect two instances of strong editorship that did not shy away from cannibalizing an earlier text to create something new and quite different in both form and meaning.

Not all excavated manuscripts with received counterparts reveal such dramatic changes, though none of them – especially in the internal arrangement of its sections – fully concurs with its counterpart. The complex history of texts in early China is too poorly understood to determine the actual relations between two or more different versions of a single text. What is clear, however, is the degree to which early imperial scholarship has interfered with the textual heritage far beyond merely exegetical debates. The salaried Western Han court classicists had to create new, normalized texts out of numerous bundles of bamboo slips that more often than not were in considerable disarray or in competing and divergent orthography. Han scholars like Liu Xiang literally wrote their own imperial versions of the earlier texts by making orthographic and lexical choices, but also, even more fundamentally, by deciding which writings were to be included under a specific title – that is, as a "book." While the learned men of pre-imperial times must have had ways to refer to texts by titles, the vast majority of excavated manuscripts do not show them; only in a few cases were titles written on the back end of a bundle of bamboo slips, visible once the bundle was rolled up. Collections like the *Records of Ritual* were compiled as "books" with "chapters" only in early imperial times. What was eventually to become a "book chapter" was earlier an individual treatise in its own right, which circulated independently from the other "chapters" with which it finally came to be grouped.

This is not to say that pre-Han manuscripts did not display a sense of textual integrity. The tight, rhythmic structure of both the "Black Robes" and the "Father and Mother of the Folk" manuscripts show more, not less, awareness of textual structure than their received counterparts. Furthermore, the Guodian and Shanghai Museum manuscripts use punctuation marks in the form of black dots or hooks to indicate the end of individual sections, and the "Black Robes" text from Guodian has a note "twenty-three" appended to indicate the number of its paragraphs. Together with the punctuation marks at the end of each paragraph, this note confirms a notion of textual order. If the received "Black Robes" chapter of the *Records of Ritual* indeed evolved from something like the manuscript version, a later editor not only changed the order of paragraphs but also expanded the text: the received version of twenty-four paragraphs contains two additional ones while combining two of the manuscript paragraphs into one. As with the "Father and Mother of the

Folk," the received version, most likely a Han product, has replaced an earlier textual order with a new one.

The Han imperial catalogue, and indeed our entire perspective on the pre-imperial tradition, is thus an intellectual artifact of the early empire. Its view of mutually exclusive Warring States "schools of thought" has overplayed their differences and understated unmistakably common ideas that connect, for example, *ru* classicist ritualism to "legalist" realism (as manifest in the *Xunzi*). Heterogeneous compendia like *Mr. Lü's Spring and Autumn Annals*, the second-century BC *Huainanzi*, the *Records of Ritual*, or even the *Documents* are not accidents of ideological confusion. As compilations of a variety of earlier texts (*Documents, Records of Ritual*) or the product of a larger group of scholars (*Mr. Lü's Spring and Autumn Annals, Huainanzi*) they were more the rule than the exception. No manuscript-yielding tomb from late Warring States or early Han times can be identified with a specific philosophical lineage. The tomb occupants, presumably sponsors (of some social stature) of the writings they were buried with, show widely eclectic interests. In short, the manuscript situation makes us question some of the hard distinctions Liu Xiang and his collaborators produced in response to the challenge to organize an enormous amount of disparate bamboo writing into "books" complete with authors and titles.

Furthermore, only some 10 percent of all excavated manuscripts have counterparts in the received tradition, and only a few others can be related to entries in the "Monograph on Arts and Writings." Tombs have yielded an impressive amount of technical writing: texts on divination, astrology, calendrical calculations, exorcism, pharmacology, and medical questions stand side by side, and often overlap, with works that detail legal, bureaucratic, and military procedures. Of the 278 titles of technical writing listed in the Han catalogue, two have survived through the later imperial tradition. While the "Monograph on Arts and Writings" was already selective, the later tradition, with its focus on the classics, historical texts, philosophy, and poetry, had even less room for the far more diverse riches of early Chinese textuality. For the history of literature, these newly discovered works are important because they hold the potential to illuminate a host of references (especially in the field of religion) that were self-explanatory to the contemporaneous readers of early and medieval literature but became obscure to later ages.

The manuscript finds also do not support traditional ideas about Warring States and Han intellectual and cultural geography. Contrary to the ideological view of the northeast as the center of the classical tradition and of the south as semi-barbarian, most canonical texts of *ru* classicist learning excavated so far come from southern tombs. Indeed, all pre-imperial and early imperial manuscript evidence for the *Poetry* comes from the south – the area of the ancient state of Chu – with the tombs of Guodian, Mawangdui, and Shuanggudui also yielding a substantial number of other *ru* classicist texts, as does the Shanghai Museum corpus that is likewise written in Chu script. While the identity of the Guodian tomb occupant remains unknown, the Mawangdui tombs belong to the family of Li Cang (d. 185 BC), who was ennobled as marquis of Dai and appointed chancellor of the princedom of Changsha in the early years of the Han dynasty. The Shuanggudui tomb in Fuyang (Anhui) belongs to Xiahou Zao (d. 164 BC), the marquis of Ruyin, who was, like Li Cang, a high-ranking member of the early Han political and cultural elite.

In the north, only three other excavated sites, all dating to Han times, contain similar writings: tomb no. 40 from Bajiaolang (Dingxian, Hebei Province) with a version of the *Analects*, fragments from the *Xunzi*, and a number of other Han writings on bamboo slips; tomb no. 6 from Mozuizi (Wuwei, Gansu) with parts of several *Ceremonial Ritual* (*Yili*) chapters on wooden and bamboo slips; and ruins of houses and watchtowers at Lop Nor (Ruoqiang, Xinjiang) with an *Analects* fragment of only ten characters on one wooden slip. Altogether, the geographical distribution of excavated texts of classical *ru* learning may be partly explained as accidents of preservation and excavation. While future excavations may yield new evidence for *ru* writings in northeastern burials, it has at least become clear that classical learning was actively pursued, and perhaps with particular enthusiasm, also in other regions, especially in the south.

IX. The texts of Warring States philosophical and political discourse

While the limited manuscript finds expand and challenge the traditional view of Warring States intellectual discourse, the imperial catalogue remains a powerful guide to the received corpus of early expository prose. Its compilation was not external or posterior to the texts it lists but concomitant with the editorial process that produced these texts from earlier materials. As a result, the Warring States period came to be seen through the prism of competing "schools of thought" in dialogue with one another. Yet while some texts refer in general (usually pejorative) terms to other intellectual lineages and their fundamental tenets, they do not present themselves as the result of an actual intellectual "debate" among their authors or proponents, nor do they engage in direct confrontation based on mutual citation. The works of Warring States expository prose are best seen as collections of ideas and anecdotes associated with certain eminent masters.

The most important of these masters was Confucius, who is prominently recognized in many texts both received and excavated. "His" principal text, the *Analects*, a collection of hundreds of sayings and anecdotes, is invisible in the Warring States context, although unattributed textual parallels can be identified in other early texts. The text contains different chronological layers possibly ranging from the fifth century through the early empire. As a discrete collection of Confucius' sayings, dialogues with his disciples, and succinct characterizations of his conduct and ideas, the *Analects* came into focus only in the curriculum of the Western Han Imperial Academy when three different versions are said to have existed. Toward the end of the Western Han, Zhang Yu (d. 5 BC) – tutor to Emperor Cheng as crown prince – produced an authoritative synthesis of the text that has not survived. Following its Western Han canonization, the *Analects* inspired a new edition and commentary by Zheng Xuan that likewise is lost; the received text is based on He Yan's (190–249) edition that drew on both the Zhang and the Zheng versions. Thereafter the text attracted numerous commentaries throughout premodern China; most importantly, it became one of the "four books" in Zhu Xi's curriculum.

Like other Warring States works, the *Analects* shows its principal "master" (*zi*) as a man of speech, not of writing. The anecdotes, arranged in twenty chapters in the received version, are mutually independent and do not amount to a systematic and sustained argument as we find in late third-century texts such as *Xunzi* or *Han Feizi*. Stylistically, the *Analects* are terse, sometimes even cryptic, yet the book as a whole is centered on matters of ritual (*li*) and social order together with the ideals of humaneness (*ren*) and rightness (*yi*) and the process of constant learning (*xue*). Apparently, none of these concepts was important before Confucius, who seems to have developed them against the decline of social and moral order, promoting self-cultivation and adherence to the spirit of antiquity as expressed in the *Poetry* and the *Documents*. The Confucian "superior man" was a student and practitioner of cultural memory, a man of profound self-inspection, and a model of both personal humility and moral authority. This "superior man" cultivated himself and taught others, but he did not compromise his moral principles for political influence. A particularly long and famous anecdote that illustrates this ideal is *Analects* 11/26, where Confucius asks four of his disciples about their ambitions:

Zilu answered immediately, "Given charge of a state of a thousand chariots that is hemmed in between great states, suffering from military invasion and moreover visited with famines, I would within three years give the people courage and a sense of the right direction." The Master smiled at him. "Qiu, what about you?" "Given charge of an area of sixty or seventy leagues square, or just fifty or sixty, I would within three years fill the needs of the people. [Yet educating them] in ritual and music I would leave to a superior man." "Chi, what about you?" "I am not saying I am able, but I wish to learn. At the services in the ancestral temple or at diplomatic gatherings, I would like to act as a minor assistant, clad in the proper cap and robes." "Dian, how about you?" After he stopped plucking the zither, letting the last notes fade off, [Dian] put the zither aside and stood up. "My wishes are different from those of the other three." The Master said: "What harm is there in that! Let's just each express our intentions." "In late spring, after the spring clothes are completed, I would with five or six young men and six or seven boys go bathing in the River Yi. We would enjoy the breeze above the Rain Dance altar and then return home, chanting." The Master sighed deeply: "I am with Dian."

The anecdote concludes with Confucius expressing to Dian his discontent with the other three and their focus on statecraft, even in the superficial modesty of Chi. By contrast, the text implies, Dian had rightly focused on self-cultivation, from his initial zither playing to his desire for chanting poetry in spring.

Defined by learning, comportment, and morality, the ideal of the "superior man" was not confined to the aristocracy but accessible to men like Confucius himself who dwelled on the fringes of power and prestige. To the tradition responsible for the compilation of the *Analects*, Confucius thus represented a new possibility of being a sage. Himself oriented toward the Western Zhou, the Confucius of the *Analects* and various other Warring States and Han texts was a model that could be followed, a figure of recent memory who had established the very way of remembering. More than any other master of Warring States philosophy, the persona of Confucius was created and perpetuated by those who cast themselves as his successors. Citations attributed to him appeared across a wide range of texts, many of them transmitted and some – like "Confucius' Discussion of the *Poetry*" – finally known from excavated manuscripts. His undistinguished career did not impede such worship but lent him authenticity: in an era of turmoil and decline, it established the master as the true moral authority vis-à-vis those corrupted by power.

Far beyond the philosophical reception of the *Analects*, the persona of Confucius proved meaningful to many aspects of the later literary tradition.

The balance between demeanor (*wen*) and substance (*zhi*) that the master had attributed to the "superior man" (*Analects* 6/18) became an important trope of literary discourse, beginning already with the late Western Han critique of the poetic exposition (*fu*). Confucius' steady emphasis on the *Poetry* as the noblest expression of Chinese civilization and his purported role as editor of the anthology secured the preeminent stature of poetry in the literature of premodern China. His turn to the golden past of the early Western Zhou established a culture of remembrance and nostalgia for "antiquity" (*gu*, *Analects* 7/1) that in medieval times developed into a major theme of Chinese poetry. His "subtle phrasing" and historical criticism made him the prototype for both historians and literary authors, who cast themselves in his image of moral judges and political advisers. His celebration of a community of learning, singing, and mutual understanding (*Analects* 11/25) provided the model for groups like the mid-third-century "Seven Worthies of the Bamboo Grove" (*Zhulin qixian*), where like-minded friends cultivated their interests in philosophy, music, poetry, and the Classics. And finally, his attention to self-cultivation even under adverse conditions, and the choice of the "superior man" to retreat from public service at times of political corruption and danger (*Analects* 8/13, 11/24), converged with Zhuangzi's critique of civilization (see below) to stimulate the powerful literary trope – most famously in the work of Tao Qian – of the writer in reclusion. In sum, Confucius became the ideal person and the ideal author, with the Five Classics held up as the fountainhead of all genres of literary writing. His model was available to scholar–officials of the imperial state as well as to those who declined to serve their rulers.

By the late fourth century BC, the *ru* classicist scholars who in one way or another were inspired by Confucius had generated a wealth of other texts. The Guodian corpus alone contains ten shorter essays that show conceptual and terminological affinities with the ideals of the *Analects*, the *Mencius*, and the *Xunzi*; texts like the "Black Robes," furthermore, have invited much speculation about the lost textual corpus that in Han times was associated with the figure of Confucius' grandson Zi Si. By the late third century BC several distinct teaching lineages of *ru* classicist provenance were in existence, most visibly those represented in the *Mencius* and the *Xunzi*.

The late fourth-century BC *Mencius* frequently refers to Confucius and shares many of the central positions of the *Analects*. Its protagonist, Meng Ke, was born in the small northeastern state of Zou next to Confucius' home state of Lu, and – according to Sima Qian – was taught by one of Zi Si's disciples. Compared to the *Analects*, the *Mencius*, a work compiled by later generations of followers of "Master Meng" (Mengzi; Latin "Mencius"), shows a distinctly more mature and systematic architecture of expository prose. Later authors cherished the elegant text, which alternates short sayings with extensive dialogues elaborating specific philosophical arguments, as a model of Warring States prose. Each of its seven chapters is divided into two halves and devoted to Master Meng's dialogues with one or more historical figures: rulers, other philosophers, or disciples. The anecdotes and conversations are longer, more complex, and more historically minded than those of the *Analects*; only the final chapter of the *Mencius* is reminiscent of the short aphorisms so typical of the *Analects*.

Until recently, the *Mencius* could have been called the first work to systematically employ quotations from the *Poetry* to support specific arguments, routinely introducing them with the words "A [song from the] *Poetry* says" (*shi yue*) and concluding with the statement "this [the preceding argument] is what [the song] is about" (*ci zhi wei ye*). However, some Guodian and Shanghai Museum manuscripts such as the "Five Forms of Conduct" or the "Black Robes," while lacking the elegant Mencian style of anecdotal narrative, now show a similar use of the *Poetry* and may well pre-date the *Mencius*. Unlike the manuscripts, including "Confucius' Discussion of the *Poetry*," the *Mencius* at one point (V.A.4) offers an early discussion on how to interpret the *Poetry*. Challenged by the casuist thinker Xianqiu Meng over the song "Northern Mountain" (Beishan, *Mao* 205), which seemingly puts the virtues of political loyalty and filial piety into conflict, Mencius gives his own interpretation of the text and then states a hermeneutical principle that invokes the late Warring States paradigm of "poetry expresses intent": "In explaining a poem, one may not use the rhetorical pattern to violate the phrases, and one may not use the phrases to violate the [author's] intent. [Instead,] one uses [one's comprehension of] the meaning to return to the [author's] intent – this is how one grasps it!"

Here and elsewhere the *Mencius* gives a sense of philosophical competition and, especially compared to the *Analects*, active engagement with the moral and political issues of its age. Fundamental positions such as the claim that human nature is inherently good (VI.A) are developed in conversations with contemporaneous thinkers or disciples, while moral and political counsel to various rulers tends to focus on specific issues. In its most daring passages, the *Mencius* sides with the people against their ruler: the Mandate of Heaven is only given to the just and benevolent sovereign; those who tyrannize their folk are no longer rulers in the proper sense but common criminals, and their elimination shall be regarded as just punishment, not regicide (I.B.8). With positions like this, the *Mencius* contributed to the Warring States ideal of the political philosopher as an incorruptible agent of truth and justice. In the wake of Han Yu's (768–824) program of "ancient-style prose" (guwen), the Mencius was canonized as a model of moral, intellectual, and stylistic clarity; in Song times, the text became one of Zhu Xi's "four books" and, furthermore, was added to the ru canon of the henceforth Thirteen Classics.

Meanwhile, the late third-century BC work Xunzi underwent a different development. The Xunzi may be the first voluminous work of expository prose written largely by a single author, Xun Kuang, who happened to be the teacher of both Han Fei (ca 280–ca 233 BC) and the Qin imperial chancellor Li Si. A text of sharp and consistent rationality, which developed the hitherto most systematic discussions on the core ru themes of ritual, music, and social order, the Xunzi exerted strong influence on Han dynasty thought and writing. When after 26 BC Liu Xiang compiled the thirty-two chapters of the received text, he had to choose from a body of bamboo writing ten times this size (including repetitions of the same material) that in one way or another was associated with the Xunzi. With its blend of traditional ru classicist ideas and pragmatic analyses (including, for example, of military matters), the Xunzi offered what the new empire needed: the legitimacy derived from classicism joined with a realist's approach to strong government. In this Xunzi transcended both Han Feizi's radical realism and the utopian idealism of the Mencius. Its claim that human nature was bad and needed to be formed by discipline and morality placed it in direct opposition to the Mencius. After the Han the Xunzi lost out. Its earliest known commentary by Yang Liang dates only from Tang times, and with the Song canonization of the Mencius, the text was excluded from the orthodox transmission line (daotong) of ru classicist ideology.

Most other Warring States works had a less distinguished reception and little impact on later literature. The Master Zi Si (Zi Sizi), a body of texts attributed to Confucius' grandson Zi Si that the Han shu "Monograph on Arts and Writings" lists with twenty-three bamboo bundles, is lost except for, perhaps, four chapters of the Records of Ritual: "Black Robes," "Records of the Dikes" (Fangji), "Records of Exemplary Demeanor" (Biaoji), and "Doctrine of the Mean" (Zhongyong). Together with the "Great Learning" (Daxue), these chapters contain the vast majority of classical quotations in all of the Records of Ritual: eighty-two from the Poetry, thirty from the Documents, and six from the Changes; eight other quotations are no longer identifiable. By comparison, there are just twenty-one Poetry quotations in the forty-four remaining chapters (all clustered in nine of them) and a roughly equal number of other quotations. In the four presumed Zi Sizi chapters, quotation is part of a recurrent formulaic structure: a brief passage begins with the formula "the master said" (*zi yue*), is then followed by a philosophical statement, and capped with a quotation. "Records of the Dikes" (thirty-eight paragraphs), "Records of Exemplary Demeanor" (fifty-four paragraphs), and "Black Robes" (twenty-four paragraphs in the received text) are entirely composed in such fashion; in "Doctrine of the Mean" the sections are much longer and less uniform in structure. Outside these four chapters, no part of the *Records of Rituals* contains a series of paragraphs all beginning with "the master said." If these chapters are indeed part of a larger *Zi Sizi*, that text – likely compiled by Zi Si's disciples – may have used a unique rhetorical structure to build its arguments tightly around the ancient classics.

The Mohists, next to the *ru* classicists the only identifiable intellectual lineage of Warring States times, were best known for their doctrine of "universal caring" (*jian'ai*) and their opposition to aggressive warfare, waste of resources, and ritualism, but never exerted any political influence; their different intellectual currents, at least three of which were compiled into parallel chapters of the received *Mozi*, had dried up already in Western Han times. Likewise, the so-called "terminologists" (*mingjia*) or casuists Hui Shi and Gongsun Long, while (like the late Mohists) contributing to the development of rhetoric and logic, never gained political influence and were inconsequential for the development of literature. By contrast, the rhetorically brilliant *Han Feizi* (late third century BC), attributed to Han Fei but also containing early Han material, provided the most cogent summary of pragmatic realism and rebuttal of the *ru* classicist orientation toward the ancient past. From Liu Xiang's late Western Han perspective, however, the text was tainted by its association with the "legalist" (*fa*) harshness of Qin imperial rule. As such, it was grouped with the *Book of Lord Shang* (*Shangjun shu*) attributed to Shang Yang (d. 338 BC), mastermind of the political and military reorganization that led to Qin's powerful rise after approximately 350 BC.

The actual impact of these major (and many other minor) texts in their Warring States contexts is difficult to assess. Aside from the major texts of the *ru* classicist tradition, however, only two Warring States works remained influential far beyond their own times: the *Laozi* (also the *Classic of the Way and the Power – Daode jing*), since Han times attributed to an obscure figure called Lao Dan or Li Er from the sixth century BC, and the *Zhuangzi*, the single work of Warring States prose that comes close to later concepts of "literature" as a form of art. The two texts were to become the seminal works of philosophical Daoism from Eastern Han times onward. From early Western Han times, two complete silk manuscripts of the *Laozi* were found in Mawangdui tomb no. 3. The text contains eighty-one short, rhythmic, and often rhymed paragraphs of exceptionally abstract style that are divided into two sections: the "Classic of the Way" (paragraphs 1–37) and the "Classic of the Power" (38–81) – an order that is reversed in both Mawangdui versions. The Guodian bamboo texts include three manuscripts containing material known from the first sixty-six paragraphs of the received *Laozi*, albeit in different sequential order. The traditional recension of the Heshang Gong *Laozi* was likely formed some time after the third century, parallel to other commentaries that were often philosophical treatises in their own right. These treatises – Wang Bi's being the most important one – paved the way for numerous interpretations and philosophical elaborations that have continued ever since. Both the *Laozi* and the *Zhuangzi* focus on the spontaneous and natural "Way" (*dao*), yet only the *Laozi* appears as a political treatise on rulership, advocating quietism and non-interference (*wuwei*) in the natural course of the universe. At the same time, the *Laozi* shows connections to the mystic "Inner Cultivation" (Neiye) chapter of the *Guanzi*, a wide-ranging, convoluted compendium mainly of political and economic thought, as well as to the medical, cosmological, and legalist treatises of the third and second centuries BC that have been found in both transmitted (*Han Feizi*) and excavated (Mawangdui manuscripts) texts. In early Han times, the *Laozi* became further related to a body of texts developed around the mythical Yellow Emperor (Huangdi). The designation Huang-Lao, used in the *Records of the Historians*, may have denoted an amalgam of authoritarian rule, mystic cosmology, and self-cultivation. Yet while Huang-Lao thought did not develop beyond the second century BC, the meditative and mystic streaks of the *Laozi* maintained their appeal. In the religious "Heavenly Masters" Daoism (*tianshidao*) of Zhang Daoling (fl. 142 AD), the figure of Laozi was elevated to the top of the spiritual pantheon; meanwhile, the text *Laozi* was cherished by philosophers and poets who sought for themselves a spiritual way of "spontaneity" (*ziran*), self-cultivation, and distance from social conventions. Especially in the context of the third and fourth centuries, aspects of the *Laozi* (and the *Zhuangzi*) converged with some fundamental ideas of the *Analects*. Learned writers like Guo Pu (276–324), Sun Chuo (314–371), or Tao Qian (365?–427, also known as Tao Yuanming) – to name just the most famous – were equally versed in both traditions and referenced them side by side in their own compositions.

While the *Laozi* owed its popularity primarily to its poetic mysticism, the *Zhuangzi* is the most appealing Warring States work of prose. No trace of the *Zhuangzi* has yet been found in any archaeological context, but the limited number of manuscript findings so far precludes us from relating this absence to the idiosyncratic and extremely unconventional nature of the

Zhuangzi. The received text is the version prepared by Guo Xiang (d. 312), whose commentary is a dense, often highly abstract philosophical treatise. An earlier commentary by Xiang Xiu (third century AD), one of the "Seven Worthies of the Bamboo Grove," is only preserved in fragments. All thirty-three chapters of the present *Zhuangzi* are accepted as compositions from the fourth through second centuries BC, with the seven "inner chapters" (*neipian*) as their core and most original writings. These are traditionally attributed to Zhuang Zhou, who according to the *Records of the Historian* lived in the fourth century BC. By contrast, the fifteen "outer chapters" (*waipian*) and eleven "miscellaneous chapters" (*zapian*) contain heterogeneous material from various sources, including writings that reflect a particular focus on the well-being of the self, a doctrine associated with the Warring States philosopher Yang Zhu. An imperial edict of 742 elevated the *Zhuangzi* to Daoist canonical status under the title of *True Classic of the Southern Flowerland* (*Nanhua zhenjing*). Like the *Laozi*, the *Zhuangzi* is believed to come from the old southern state of Chu.

The "inner chapters" develop the core ideas of philosophical Daoism: a life of natural spontaneity; unity of the human inner self with the cosmic "way"; distance from social obligations and political engagement; acceptance of death as natural transformation; praise of the useless and the aimless; contempt for social values, hierarchies, and conventional reasoning. These themes are further elaborated upon in the anecdotes of the "outer" and "miscellaneous" chapters that accumulated over time as colorful lore around the figure of Zhuang Zhou. In this spirit, the "miscellaneous" Chapter 32 contains a vignette on the master's own death:

> When Master Zhuang was about to die, his disciples wanted to give him a lavish funeral. Master Zhuang said: "I take heaven and earth as my inner and outer coffins, the sun and the moon as my pair of jade disks, the stars and constellations as my pearls and beads, the ten thousand things as my funerary gifts. With my burial complete, how is there anything left unprepared? What shall be added to it?" The disciples said: "We are afraid that the crows and kites will eat you, Master!" Master Zhuang said: "Above ground I'd be eaten by crows and kites, below ground I'd be eaten by mole crickets and ants. You rob the one and give to the other – how skewed would that be? If you take the uneven to create evenness, then the even is yet uneven. If you take the unproven for proof, then the proven is yet unproven. The clear-sighted man is merely used by others, but the man of spiritual insight produces proof. The clear-sighted man has been inferior to the man of spiritual insight for long already! And yet the fool holds on to what he sees and projects it onto others. His achievement is just exterior, and isn't it pitiable?"

While other Warring States philosophical texts advance ideals of sociopolitical order, the *Zhuangzi* is fundamentally opposed to any such order imposed on the individual. Apart from their philosophical radicalism, the "inner chapters" also come closest to a notion of fictional writing. Their anecdotal format and mention of historical figures accords with Warring States historical narrative and expository prose, yet the text subverts its historical references through dazzling imagination, hyperbole, and explicit fictionalization. Its imaginary tales and parables are poetic (with ample use of rhyme and other euphonic structures) and humorous, with frequent flashes of sarcasm, shocking images, and an outspoken disdain for the deepest notions of moral thought and ritual propriety.

Many *Zhuangzi* anecdotes display a fictional, even fantastical, nature. A recurrent technique is the shift of events into the sphere of dreams where, for example, a skull, speaking from the perspective of the dead, may serve as conversation partner. In the most famous anecdote, the ambivalence of dream and reality itself becomes the topic: Zhuang Zhou wakes up from a dream of being a butterfly – yet now, "he did not know whether he was Zhou, who had dreamt being a butterfly, or a butterfly who dreams being Zhou." Throughout the text, the conventional order of things is reversed: those who maintain their uselessness – like human cripples or crooked trees – will not be exploited but live out their allotted time, the social obligations of mourning for the dead run against the natural course of existence, life and death are different phases in the larger scheme of cosmic transformation, and the hallowed texts of old are the dregs of people long dead. Strenuous instruction violates true comprehension and mastery of any art (like wheel-making or butchering), which arises only from one's complete adaptation to the task. In numerous parables, the social order is rejected as opposed to the natural one.

The text furthermore uses sharp-witted sophistry to resolutely drive conventional logic into absurd conclusions, challenging rationality itself. It shows the manipulative power of eloquent speech together with its limits and possible transcendence. In this, the *Zhuangzi* influenced the "profound learning" (*xuanxue*) of early medieval times as much as the paradoxical riddles of Chan (Japanese "Zen") Buddhism; at the same time, its philosophy of natural spontaneity and rejection of public service, as well as its mythological fantasies and exuberant imagery, inspired poets, philosophers, and writers of fiction – such as Six Dynasties "Accounts of the Strange" (*zhiguai*) – from Han times onward. The modern term for fiction, *xiaoshuo*, incidentally, appeared first in the *Zhuangzi*, where it means "trivial talk," perhaps of folklore.

X. The *Verses of Chu*

The anthology *Verses of Chu* contains a series of late Warring States and Han dynasty poems, some of them long, others brief, associated with the southern literature and cultural geography of ancient Chu. Unlike the *Poetry*, the *Verses of Chu* never received imperial recognition, but their influence on all later Chinese literature is no less tangible and significant. By late Warring States times, the state of Chu had developed its own distinct forms of cultural expression (religion, mythology, painting, music, literature) while also remaining fully exposed to the northern traditions, as the evidence of Chu tomb manuscripts amply proves. People in Chu spoke their own dialect, or dialects, and had developed their own calligraphic forms, yet both were clearly Chinese and concurred with their counterparts in the north. The southern poets were entirely familiar with the northern literary tradition while developing their own, highly sophisticated art of literary expression. The earliest texts of the southern anthology are dated to the fourth or third centuries BC, but their poetic brilliance suggests a much larger, and earlier, literary tradition. Outside the anthology proper, the influence of the southern lyrics is clearly manifest in the poetic expositions (*fu*) and shorter songs (*ge*) of Western Han times.

The Western Han taste for Chu poetry, music, and material culture may partly stem from the southern origins of the imperial family. When Liu Bang, the Han founding emperor (Han Gaozu, r. 202–195 BC), had his state sacrifices arranged, his ritual hymns were performed to "Chu melodies" (*Chu sheng*). The Western Han poetry attributed to members of the imperial family shows common traits with the language and rhythms of the *Verses of Chu*, and the *History of the Han* notes the performance of Chu songs at the imperial court. Wang Yi's *Chapter and Verse Commentary to the Verses of Chu* (*Chuci zhangju*), the basis of the received version of the anthology, attributes roughly half of the songs to Qu Yuan (ca 340–278 BC) and several others to his shadowy third-century "successors" Song Yu and Jing Cuo; however, a number of the Qu Yuan songs are evidently Han imitations. The first anthology of Chu lyrics may go back to Liu An, king of Huainan and uncle of Emperor Wu, whom the tradition credits with the "Summoning the Recluse" (Zhao yinshi) poem in the *Verses of Chu*. Liu An – or the scholars assembled at his court – also authored a commentary on "Encountering Sorrow" (Lisao), the longest and most prominent poem of the anthology. Wang Yi mentions that Liu Xiang, on the basis of Liu An's earlier compilation, had assembled the next version of the *Verses of Chu*, and he attributes to Liu the penultimate series of poems in the anthology, "Nine Laments" (Jiutan), which are then followed by Wang's own "Nine Yearnings" (Jiusi). The received text under the title *Supplementary Commentary to the Verses of Chu* (*Chuci buzhu*) represents Hong Xingzu's (1070–1135) reorganization of the Wang Yi text. It includes Wang Yi's original exegesis, the Tang dynasty commentaries on the pieces included in the sixth-century *Selections of Refined Literature* (*Wenxuan*), and Hong Xingzu's own annotation that partly departs from Wang's. Influential later commentaries that often reject Wang's readings include Zhu Xi's *Collected Commentaries to the Verses of Chu* (*Chuci jizhu*) and Wang Fuzhi's (1619–1692) *Thorough Explanations to the Verses of Chu* (*Chuci tongshi*).

The *Verses of Chu* differs from the older *Poetry* in its topics, imagery, language, and meter – and, most significantly, must have differed in its (no longer retrievable) musical style. The *Verses of Chu* includes references to the geography and flora as well as to the mythological world of the south. Its rich imagination, especially in the early poems, seems to connect it to the paintings on luxurious lacquerware and silk found at richly furnished Chu aristocratic tombs, including the 433 BC tomb of the Marquis Yi of Zeng (Zeng Hou Yi) in Suixian (Hubei) and the tombs at Mawangdui. The paintings show large numbers of mythological beings riding the clouds or dwelling – as in the famous silk banner from Mawangdui – in the spirit worlds.

The vivid meter and rapid changes of rhyme in the *Verses of Chu* likely reflect southern musical styles that in their tempi and versatility differed starkly from the solemn and slow melodies associated with the hymns from the *Poetry*. Archaeological finds of both string and wind instruments point to the performance of elegant and lithe melodies in contrast to the classical music dominated by bells, drums, and chime stones. Likewise, the somewhat static repetition of syllables in the *Poetry* has made room for a wealth of rhyming and alliterative binomes, and the largely uniform four-syllable meter is replaced by a diversity of verse structures, including alternations between poetry and prose, and variations of the four-syllable form through addition of recurrent particles. The typical couplet of the "Nine Songs" (Jiuge) – perhaps the earliest series of poems in the anthology – has two equal lines of four, five, or six syllables plus the rhythmic particle *xi* after the second or third syllable. In "Encountering Sorrow," the pattern is further developed by moving the *xi* to the end of the first line while adding another (constantly varying) particle in the middle of each line; the result is a continuous flow of ten words (plus three particles) able to carry a narrative style. This lively rhythm is further accelerated by a slight pause after the first beat: dum dum-dum *particle* dum-dum *xi* / dum dum-dum *particle* dum-dum. Since Han times, this so-called *sao* meter was particularly popular in laments over personal misfortune.

Framed as a celestial journey, the 187 couplets of "Encountering Sorrow" – the longest poem of pre-imperial China – unfold a melancholic narrative of political ambition and frustration that from its earliest reception was interpreted through the tragic biography of its presumed author Qu Yuan. Since Jia Yi's (200–168 BC) "Lament for Qu Yuan" (Diao Qu Yuan), the text was read as the elegy of a neglected and banished worthy. In Han times alone, Liu An, Sima Qian, Liu Xiang, Yang Xiong, Liang Song (d. 83 AD), Ban Gu, and Wang Yi have all contributed to this interpretation. The *Records of the Historian* provides the principal information on Qu Yuan, but Jia Yi's "Lament for Qu Yuan" and the patchwork nature of Sima Qian's account show the existence of earlier and possibly diverging sources. The biography in the *Records* seems to combine at least two partly contradictory sources, one of which refers to the protagonist as Qu Ping. The emerging figure of Qu Yuan / Qu Ping is a minister of Chu, related to the ruling house but slandered by rivals at court, who had warned his ruler against a disastrous military engagement; his advice was not heeded, and he was instead banished to the south, where he wandered around aimlessly and finally drowned himself in the Miluo river. Different sources place "Encountering Sorrow" either before or after the moment of banishment. Either way, in Qu Yuan we meet the first literary author of China identified by name and furnished with a biographical rationale for his writing – a rationale conspicuously reminiscent of the numerous neglected advisers in the *Zuo Tradition* and *Discourses of the States*. Moreover, the reading of "Encountering Sorrow" as self-expression and lament corresponds to the purposes of writing that the "Great Preface" attributes to the unknown authors of the *Poetry*.

The protagonist of "Encountering Sorrow" expresses his inner virtue by donning a wealth of beautiful and aromatic plants – yet only to finally realize that they, and moral integrity, are no longer prized:

> In profusion I already had this inner beauty,
> And added to it superb comportment.
> I dressed in fragrant river rush and secluded angelica,
> Twined autumn thoroughwort to make for my girdle.
> . . .
> The three kings of old were pure and perfect,
> And thus the flocks of sweet fragrance were in their proper place.
> Diversely combined were the layered pepper and cinnamon,
> How would sweet clover and angelica alone be strung together?

. . .

I fashioned waterlilies into a robe,
Gathered lotus to make a skirt,
No one understands me, it is over now,
Only my inner self is true and fragrant.

. . .

The times are in tumult, rapidly changing,
How can I linger for long?
Thoroughwort and angelica are changing and no longer fragrant,
Iris and sweet clover are transforming and turn into straw.
How can these fragrant plants of old
Today have now turned into worthless mugwort?

Throughout the protagonist's mystic journey, his erotic desire, fantasies of immortality, and sovereign command of the cosmic spirits – all metaphors for political ambition – alternate with passages of lament and complaints about a world upside down. To Han readers, the political allegory was unmistakable, and Wang Yi interpreted "Encountering Sorrow" within the same moral–historical framework that the Mao exegesis had already brought to the *Poetry*. This political reading of "Encountering Sorrow," clearly suggested by the poem itself, was then extended to other songs of the anthology. Like the Mao reading of the *Poetry*, Wang Yi's approach to the *Verses of Chu* was explicitly challenged only in Song times.

Modern scholars have doubted the historical persona of Qu Yuan, his authorship of "Encountering Sorrow," and the biographical reading of the text. To Han and later traditional scholars, these issues were off-limits. Qu Yuan was the prototypical poet driven by unbearable despair. To Sima Qian, Qu Yuan – almost as much as Confucius – was a primary ancestor in spirit, and numerous later authors saw his fate as a precursor of their own. Jia Yi's "Lament for Qu Yuan" and Yang Xiong's "Refuting 'Encountering Sorrow'" (Fan Lisao) criticized Qu Yuan's escapism into suicide, but Sima Qian's sympathetic view of a tragic hero prevailed: having tried in vain to avert catastrophe from his ruler and state, Qu Yuan ultimately paid the highest price for his morally superior stance. In modern times, Wen Yiduo (1899–1946) and Guo Moruo (1892–1978), writing during the Japanese invasion of 1937–1945, recast Qu Yuan in their own terms: the exemplary patriot, the politically engaged intellectual, and China's "first poet of the people."

The *Records* biography includes two more songs related to Qu Yuan's life that are also found in the *Verses of Chu*: "The Fisherman" (Yufu), a dialogue with a rustic commoner where Qu Yuan explains himself as the single "clear" person in a "muddy" world, and "Embracing Sand" (Huai sha), a lament that Qu Yuan "made" (*zuo*) immediately before drowning himself. In the *Verses of Chu*, "Embracing Sand" is one of the "Nine Declarations" (Jiuzhang), a cycle of poems attributed to Qu Yuan that, however, seem like later imitations of "Encountering Sorrow." Composed in the *sao* style, they aim to capture Qu Yuan's poetic spirit and sentiment of desolation. The same is true for "The Fisherman," "Divining the Abode" (Bu ju), and the cycle "Nine Changes" (Jiubian) that is attributed to Song Yu. All these songs, likely dating from the third and early second centuries BC, contribute to the Qu Yuan legend. Most of them are monologues that use the topoi established in "Encountering Sorrow" – the plant imagery, the unsuccessful journey – to complain about the unjust world. They also develop a new depiction of nature far beyond the brief and simple images known from the "Airs of the States": long, intense descriptions of bleak environments that correspond to the disconsolate state of human existence.

Beginning with "Encountering Sorrow" and then further developed in the subsequent Qu Yuan tradition, a new poetic lexicon unfolds that becomes the hallmark of the Western Han poetic exposition (*fu*): entire catalogues of natural phenomena, cast in the literary form of rhyming and alliterative binomes. The cosmic journey, which takes the protagonists across vast distances and through a rapid succession of landscapes, provides the narrative framework for such descriptions, opening new vistas and their poetic catalogues at every turn. All but one of these journeys are unsuccessful. The exception is "Roaming Afar" (Yuan you), a long piece of 178 lines depicting the ecstatic and mystical flight to the four directions and, finally, the utopian center of the "great beginning" (*taichu*). Likely dating from the second century BC, the poem combines the sensualistic language of the spirit voyage with fantasies of natural elixirs and the attainment of transcendence. Oscillating between religious dreams of immortality and the exploration of the natural cosmos, "Roaming Afar" prefigures the medieval poetry and prose of alchemical experiments and Daoist thought. The precious plants of "Encountering Sorrow" are no longer allegories of inner purity but the source of dietary and spiritual perfection.

Apart from "Encountering Sorrow," which provided the stylistic and thematic template for much of the *Verses of Chu*, the "Nine Songs" (Jiuge), which possibly pre-date "Encountering Sorrow," exerted profound and lasting influence on later Chinese literature. According to Wang Yi, Qu Yuan composed these poems during his banishment in the south where he encountered the "excessive" religious practices of the common people; on this occasion, he adapted and refined their songs to give expression to his personal frustration and political criticism. This Eastern Han reading (maintained also by Hong Xingzu) combined two political tropes of its time: the pejorative view of the south as semi-barbarian and "excessive" (*yin*), and the purpose of poetry as an expression of personal intent. However, unlike "Encountering Sorrow," the "Nine Songs" offer little to support such an interpretation unless one decoded each of their images in a narrow and tendentious fashion. In fact, the earliest poetic reception accepted the songs fully as religious chants to the cosmic deities of Chu: during the two decades after 114 BC, Emperor Wu's court poets adapted the diction and vocabulary of the "Nine Songs" for a new set of state sacrificial hymns, the "Songs for the Sacrifices at the Suburban Altars" (*Jiaosi ge*). As so much of the musical, literary, religious, and material culture of third- and early second-century Chu was present in Western Han – and especially Emperor Wu's – imperial representation and court entertainment, this reception was likely based on some direct knowledge of southern religious rites and their chants. Writing more than two centuries later, Wang Yi, on the other hand, transposed the meaning of the "Nine Songs" onto the plane of political rhetoric.

The "Nine Songs" unfold a pantheon of cosmic spirits that were partly indigenous to the south and partly – like the two "Masters of Fate" (*siming*) or the "Lord of the (Yellow) River" (*hebo*) – shared with the religious culture of northern China. Possibly a repertoire of hymns performed at seasonal rituals, their received sequence might contain a certain performative order, with the first song, "Great Unity, August Emperor of the East" (Donghuang taiyi), invoking the spirits and the last one, "Offering Rites to the Souls" (Li hun), sending them off. "Great Unity" shows parallels with the first of Emperor Wu's hymns: it begins with divining an auspicious day for the sacrifice, notes the offerings and ritual music, and finally concludes with a self-referential statement on the success of the performance, stating that the cosmic spirit has assumed his place among the sacrificial community. The formulaic structure resonates with both the subsequent Western Han sacrificial hymns and the venerated models of old, the hymns of the *Poetry* and their contemporaneous bronze inscriptions. The "Nine Songs" may have served to establish the contact with the cosmic spirits and, simultaneously, to celebrate and reaffirm this communication. Thus the final song briefly states the conclusion of the ritual and its eternal perpetuation.

The altogether eleven hymns are devoted to nine spirits and in addition recall the "Fallen of the State" (Guoshang) before ending with "Offering Rites to the Souls." The title "Nine Songs" for a series of eleven poems has found various explanations, three of which seem relatively persuasive without being mutually exclusive: that "nine" as the highest number of classical numerology signifies "completeness" more than any specific number, and was for this reason used for the various cycles of the *Verses of Chu*; that "nine" refers to the nine spirits worshipped in the cycle; or that the "Nine Songs" includes two pairs of songs so that at each performance, perhaps seasonally adjusted, only one song of each pair was actually performed.

Beyond both the religious reception and political interpretation, and ultimately far more influential than either one, is the inspiration the "Nine Songs" gave to later poetry. The two most beautiful and influential pieces are to the goddesses of the Xiang river, "Lady of the Xiang" (Xiang jun) and "Consort of the Xiang" (Xiang furen). Speaking in the voice of a male shaman, these songs depict the unsuccessful quest for an erotic encounter with the goddess. In both songs, the shaman embarks on a spirit journey through the watery and lush landscape of southern Chu, mapping a hallucinatory world onto the real geography. The magical landscape is filled with precious exotic plants that the shaman now uses for his own purposes. The principal literary structure is, as in "Encountering Sorrow," the richly varied catalogue of intense description. And yet his quest ends in frustration, as in "Lady of the Xiang":

> With cinnamon oars and thoroughwort sweeps
> I cut through the ice, piled up the snow.
> Figs I was plucking in the water,
> For lotus I reached in the treetops.
> With hearts divided, the go-between toils,
> Her love was not deep and lightly broken.
> The stream rushed swiftly between stones, shallow and shallow,
> My flying dragons went soaring and soaring.
> As her joining was faithless, resentment lasts long,
> Untrue to her vow, she told me she had no time.

The unfulfilled quest for a tryst with the elusive goddess established a new language of erotic desire that was subsequently refined and expanded in ever-new variations: Cao Zhi's (191–232) "Poetic Exposition on the Goddess of the Luo River" (Luoshen fu), the "Poetic Exposition on Gaotang" (Gaotang fu) attributed to Song Yu (but most likely of a Six Dynasties date), the *yuefu* series "Mount Wu so High" (Wushan gao), the palace-style poetry of Qi and Liang times, Li He's (791–817) sensual and morbid fantasies of Elysian goddesses, and even Bai Juyi's (772–846) "Song of Everlasting Regret" (Changhen ge) all draw extensively on the diction of the "Nine Songs." Meanwhile, the vocabulary of cosmic sovereignty and grandiose representation of songs like

"Great Unity, August Emperor of the East" appealed to later depictions of imperial authority and its ritual manifestations. And finally, the "Fallen of the State" became a political topos for lamenting the martyrs of great causes. When Kang Youwei (1858–1927) remembered in emotional verses Tan Sitong (1865–1898), the executed activist of the "Hundred Days Reforms" from Hunan (the core area of ancient Chu), the language of the "Nine Songs" was his best possible choice.

Within the *Verses of Chu*, one more work and one sequence of three texts stand out for their uniqueness and highly developed diction changing between religious sentiment and literary rhetoric. The first are the 172 mostly tetrasyllabic verses of the "Heavenly Questions" (Tianwen), a catalogue of questions that begins with the origin of the universe and continues to mythical and cosmic phenomena. The main part, comprising more than 80 percent of the text, is devoted to the mythology and history of Chu, told in mostly chronological order, up to 506 BC. Parts of the text seem cryptic and perhaps incomplete; moreover, much of its underlying mythology was lost early on. Originally, the text must have been embedded in a larger context of legends and ritual practice. Wang Yi, who again resorts to a biographical and political reading, suggests that when Qu Yuan wandered aimlessly through the south, he rested in the ancestral temples of former kings and worthies, where he found murals of mythological and historical narratives. He thus wrote his questions directly to these paintings from where they were later copied and put into the form of the "Heavenly Questions." Wang Yi's account was perhaps inspired by stone carvings as well as wall paintings in Eastern Han temples and tombs, yet archaeology has produced a wealth of much earlier paintings on silk and lacquerwork that already for late Warring States and early Western Han times prove the technical and imaginative maturity of pictorial representation in ancient Chu aristocratic culture: the star map on the lacquered suitcase from the tomb of the Marquis Yi of Zeng, the Chu silk manuscript from Zidanku (Changsha, Hunan) of around 300 BC, the funerary banner and representations of comets from Mawangdui, and others. In addition, the *History of the Han* mentions pictorial representations at the suburban altars, a depiction of astral bodies on an imperial military banner, and images of imperial ancestors inside the Western Han imperial palace – all perhaps inspired by the southern origins of the imperial house. In short, Wang Yi's conjecture of a pictorial background to the "Heavenly Questions" may not be entirely implausible; at the very least, both the sophisticated cosmological and mythological images from Chu tombs and the equally developed literary art of the *Verses of Chu* must have emerged from the same southern aristocratic culture. Incidentally, the protagonist of "Encountering Sorrow" – presumably Qu Yuan – declares himself the scion of the Chu royal clan.

To appreciate the aristocratic origins of the *Verses of Chu*, one may leave aside Wang Yi's narrow biographical–political readings and their Western Han precursors in the writings of Jia Yi, Sima Qian, and Yang Xiong. As soon as one removes this interpretation, or at least its extension from "Encountering Sorrow" to the "Nine Songs" and "Heavenly Questions," the early layers of the *Verses of Chu* become more clearly visible as the product of Chu and Han court writing. The "Nine Songs" and "Heavenly Questions" may indeed have been the literary rearrangement of archaic religious knowledge whose original form, function, and context we no longer know. They may have emerged from rituals of sacrifice and religious commemoration where ancient knowledge and identity were ascertained and perpetuated. In the state of Chu, which had long been part of the Zhou realm but in Warring States times increasingly developed its own forms of artistic expression, cultural identity meant the fusion of archaic Zhou traditions with indigenous traits of Chu historical memory and imagination. References to a wide and eclectic pantheon of spirits show the learned authors of "Encountering Sorrow," the "Nine Songs," and "Heavenly Questions" being familiar with sources both northern and southern.

The same is true for the last major genre of the early part of the *Verses of Chu*. The two long pieces "Summoning the Soul" (Zhao hun) and "Great Summons" (Da zhao) are literary reworkings of shamanistic incantations to call back the soul of the dying or the deceased, a religious ritual detailed in the *Ceremonial Ritual*. The two texts are largely parallel and follow a simple sequence: speaking in the voice of the ritual specialist, they call back the soul by describing in long catalogues the horrors waiting in each of the four directions (and, in "Summoning the Soul," also above and below); this terrifying description is then contrasted with even more elaborate accounts of the sensual pleasures and luxury of court life ready for the returning soul to enjoy:

> O Soul, come back!
> Do not descend into that dark realm
> Where the Lord of the Earth lies in nine coils.
> With his horns cutting sharp,
> His back humped, his bloody flanks,
> He is hounding men, pacing fast.
>
> . . .
>
> O Soul, come back!
> Return to your old abode!

. . .

The chambers faced with minerals, and kingfisher wings
Suspended from carnelian hooks;
Quilts covered with kingfisher pearls,
Glowing with even light.
Thin gauze covers the walls,
Brocade canopies are spreading out.
Ribbons and plaits patterned and plain,
Knotted to half-disks of agate.

Following the (altogether much longer) description of the palace chambers, "Summoning the Soul" then continues with extensive descriptions of the court beauties populating them; next, the text lists the rare delicacies of a banquet before ending with the celebration of a veritable orgy. Finally, shifting into a more measured diction, a coda (*luan*) recalls a former hunting expedition with the king – possibly King Xiang of Chu (r. 298–263 BC) – who is also the addressee of the text.

In their boundless imagination and hyperbolic language, the two "Summons" are related to the rhetoric of the "persuasions" as well as to the grand form of the Western Han poetic exposition (*fu*, see below). Yet the "Summons" also inspired a far more sober variation on their theme of "calling back" a departed soul. This is the poem "Summoning the Recluse" (Zhao yinshi), presumably composed at Liu An's southern court. "Summoning the Recluse" – which later readers saw as an expression of Liu An's personal and political troubles – is no longer devoted to the departed soul but to a royal prince (*wangzi*) of high character who has withdrawn from public life into seclusion in nature. The ideal of the recluse was long established by Liu An's time, and credible Western Han sources mention eremites living in the mountains. Entirely new and of far-reaching influence, however, was the poetic expression given to it in "Summoning the Recluse." Beyond other early visions of nature, this poem imagines the natural environment of the mountain as a utopian alternative to the social realm – not, however, as an ideal landscape but as a hostile and utterly dangerous space where the prince "cannot linger long." The wilderness is the sphere of both salvation and deadly threat, a complex balance created from the correspondences between landscape description and the recluse's inner world of inconsolable melancholy. The princely recluse does not flee into comfort; his moral principles cause him terrifying hardship. In this poem, nature is at once the actual space of reclusion and the metaphor for the trouble and affliction visited upon the man of high character who refuses to compromise his rectitude. "Summoning the

Recluse" is the poetic voice not of escapism but of incorruptible steadfastness, with uncounted echoes resounding throughout the literary tradition of imperial China. A member of the moral aristocracy, now in opposition to raw political power, the "prince," like the Confucian "superior man" or the Qu Yuan of "Encountering Sorrow," was a model to emulate.

XI. The poetry of the early empire

The poetry of imperial China begins with the Qin First Emperor. After completing his final conquest and establishing the unified empire in 221 BC, the emperor, accompanied by his court classicists (*ru*), toured the newly conquered eastern regions and between 219 and 210 BC erected seven stele inscriptions on mountaintops or otherwise historically significant locations. At each location, the imperial entourage performed sacrifices to the cosmic powers, recited the emperor's historical merits and carved the eulogy into stone. Six of the seven inscriptions are included in the *Records of the Historian*; the remaining one from Mount Yi (Shandong province) was well-known in Tang times and has been transmitted in collections of stone rubbings. A recarving of the stele, dating from AD 993, is preserved in the "Forest of Stelae" (*beilin*) in Xi'an.

Little is left of the inscriptions. A stone fragment of ten characters, purportedly from the Mount Tai inscription, is of dubious authenticity; in addition, a fragment from the inscription on Mount Langye (Shandong) includes only lines of a secondary inscription that the First Emperor's son, the "Second Generation (Emperor)" (Ershi, r. 210–207 BC), is said to have added, in 209 BC, to his father's monuments. Several traditional sources have attributed the inscriptions, both text and calligraphy, to the Qin chancellor Li Si, while some modern scholars have speculated that the primary inscriptions on Mount Tai and Mount Yi were actually retrospective creations of the son.

All seven inscriptions commemorate not only the unification but also the act of their inscription and recitation, historicizing both the emperor's accomplishments and their immediate recognition. These texts comprise either seventy-two or thirty-six lines, regular in both line length and the use of rhyme. Their diction, vocabulary, and political rhetoric recall and continue the hymns of the *Classic of Poetry* and pre-imperial bronze inscriptions, celebrating the unification not as an act accomplished by military success but as the establishment of good moral order. While invoking the earlier religious language of political representation, they are no longer limited to the audience of the ancestral temple but address the spirits of the entire cosmos within the framework of a new political ritual: the imperial tour of inspection. Their relative uniformity across both geographical distances and a ten-year period suggests that the texts followed a blueprint designed by textual and ritual classicists at the Qin imperial court, many of whom had been recruited from the newly conquered eastern states. Written in the unified script of the Qin empire, they inscribe the new political order into chosen, usually religiously significant, sites of nature, integrating the former states and their religious geography into the new universal polity of Qin. In their teleological account, they transform the eastern states from subjects of their own history and memory into objects of Qin imperial historiography and religious representation, as in the inscription on the eastern vista of Mount Zhifu (Shandong) in 218 BC:

> Since the sage's laws initially arose,
> He cleansed and ordered the land within the borders
> And abroad punished the cruel and violent.
> His martial terror radiating in all directions,
> He shook and moved the four poles,
> Seized and extinguished the six kings.
> Far and wide he unified all under Heaven,
> Disaster and harm were finally put to rest,
> And forever halted were clashes of arms.
> The August Divine Emperor's shining virtue
> Regulates and orders the realm,
> Inspecting and listening, he is not idle.
> He creates and establishes the great principle,
> Brilliantly arranges the assembled implements,
> Making all have their insignia and banners.
> The officials in service honor their divisions,
> Each understanding his task,
> And affairs have no doubts or uncertainties.
> The black-haired people are changed and transformed,
> The distant and near share unified measures,
> In approaching the old, they eliminate fault.
> The constant duties are now fixed,
> Later successors will continue the deed,
> Forever upholding the sage's rule.

The second cycle of imperial poetry, immediately following the Qin inscriptions, is of a similar nature: seventeen hymns that the Han founding emperor Gaozu used in his ancestral sacrifices. These "Songs of a Pacified Age for the Inner Halls" (Anshi fangzhong ge), composed between 202 and 195 BC, were likely created by another group of court classicists partially inherited from the Qin. In their classical diction, once again oriented toward the Zhou hymns and bronze inscriptions, the hymns display an attempt toward ritual continuity and textual tradition that transcended the social and political turmoil surrounding the fall of the Qin. Performed to "Chu melodies" (*Chu sheng*, reportedly composed by the emperor's otherwise unknown consort Lady Tangshan), the hymns show only occasional traces of the southern poetic idiom familiar from the *Verses of Chu*, yet fused with the solemn diction of political liturgy:

> Thoroughwort and fig issue their scent,
> Moving back and forth the cinnamon flowers.
> Piously we present Heaven's rites,
> Complying with the radiance of sun and moon.
> [The spirits] mount the four dragons of profound mystery,
> Dashing in circles and moving around.
> Feathers and banners in rich abundance,
> Lush indeed, spreading far and farther.
> The Way of filial piety continuous with our age,
> We display the brilliant order of ritual!

While the Qin inscriptions and Han hymns were important for the political and religious representation of their newly established polities, the dominant genre of Han poetry was the "poetic exposition" (*fu*) that for Western Han times is best understood as a genre of rhapsodic performance. In early China, the literary term *fu* appears in three partially overlapping meanings: as the verb "to recite" or "to present" (as in poetry recitations in the *Zuo Tradition*); as one of the three poetic modes *fu* (exposition), *bi* (comparison), and *xing* (evocation) named in the *Rituals of Zhou* and the "Great Preface" and subsequently applied to the songs of the *Classic of Poetry*; and as the term denoting the Han dynasty genre of "poetic exposition." In Han times, the word *fu* is interchangeable with a series of homophones or near-homophones that all mean "to display" or "to spread out," linking the genre to the poetic mode of "exposition." A recently excavated manuscript from Yinwan (Lianyungang, Jiangsu), the "Poetic Exposition on the Spirit Crow" (Shenwu fu) of approximately 10 BC, where the word *fu* is written with a variant character, has confirmed this interpretation. *Fu* thus refers to both the comprehensive exposition of a certain subject and its rhapsodic presentation, the latter being captured in the formula "to recite without singing is called *fu*" (*History of the Han*, "Monograph on Arts and Writings"). Without providing a complete tally, the "Monograph" lists the titles of 1,004 *fu* mostly of Western Han times. Today, only a few dozen *fu* are extant from before the end of the Western Han, most of them in mere fragments.

The genre was largely undefined in both form and content. Virtually any poetic text of a certain length could be called *fu*, occasionally also in alternation with terms like "eulogy" (*song*) or "(elegant) phrases" (*ci*). Later sources distinguish specific subsets of the *fu*, such as the "sorrows" (*sao*), in the tradition of "Encountering Sorrow"; the "lament" (*diaowen*); compositions in seven parts, or "sevens" (*qi*); and the dialogical "staged discussions" (*shelun*, also called "responses to questions," *duiwen*). These terms began to be used as genre designations soon after the Western Han; thus no fewer than thirteen "sevens" are known by title from Eastern Han times alone. Likewise, the staged discussions or responses to questions – compositions where the protagonist successfully defends himself against unjust accusations – generated their own tradition, the origins of which were retrospectively traced to Dongfang Shuo's (154–93 BC) "Responding to a Guest's Objections" (Da ke nan) and Yang Xiong's "Justification against Ridicule" (Jie chao). The genre died out in the fourth century, leaving merely nineteen titles on record.

For Western Han times, such distinctions are anachronistic; strictly speaking, the concept of genre seems to have emerged only over the second and third centuries. "To recite without singing" points more to a performative mode than to literary form, and this mode applied, for example, also to inscriptions. Thus, apart from the short song (*ge*) largely associated with the southern literary tradition, the Western Han term *fu* covered the entire gamut of poetic forms and topics, ranging from Jia Yi's four-syllable-line philosophical meditation "The Owl" (Funiao fu) to Dong Zhongshu's lament of personal frustration, "The Gentleman Is Not Accepted in His Times" (Shi buyu fu); from Sima Xiangru's (179–117 BC) grandiose celebration of the imperial park, "Excursion Hunt of the Son of Heaven" (Tianzi youlie fu) to Mei Gao's (fl. ca 130–110 BC) impromptu pieces with which he constantly entertained the emperor; from elaborate expositions on individual items such as Wang Bao's (d. 61 BC) "The Panpipes" (Dongxiao fu) to Yang Xiong's compositions of moral admonition. Musical instruments, trees, screens, ballgames, or dog races were topics just as valid as accounts of the imperial rituals, processions, and architecture. The personal reflection in the mode of Jia Yi, Dong Zhongshu, or Sima Qian – the latter being credited, perhaps spuriously, with a "Lamenting the Gentleman Who Is Not Accepted in His Times" (Bei shi buyu fu) – was the exception; the rule was compositions for delectation, rhetorical display, and moral edification. The audience for these pieces was the ruler – regional or imperial – and his courtiers, who enjoyed them not through individual reading but at oral performances. While no few of the highest officials – indeed Emperor Wu himself – composed *fu*, literary talent did not lead to an official career but at best some minor appointment. Ban Gu characterized the most prolific of all *fu* authors at Emperor Wu's court, Mei Gao, as a man who "was not well versed in classical learning but played the buffoon in the manner of the comedians and delighted in frivolous jokes when composing *fu* and eulogies." Like Dongfang Shuo, a man known for his occasionally bizarre jokes, Mei Gao complained about being treated as a jester.

The Western Han *fu* was related to the southern literary tradition known from the *Verses of Chu*, but its true origin lay in late Warring States rhetorical display and political persuasion. During the early Han reigns, the *fu* was not promoted at the imperial court but emerged at the southern princely courts of Wu (under Prince Liu Pi, r. 195–154 BC), Huainan (Liu An), and Liang (Liu Wu, r. 168–144 BC), which attracted numerous political thinkers, philosophers, rhetoricians, and literary talents. Accordingly, the language and imagination of Mei Sheng (father of Mei Gao, d. 140 BC) and Sima Xiangru, the two greatest stylists of their time, show decidedly southern characteristics in the mold of the *Verses of Chu*. Jia Yi, a native of Luoyang whose "The Owl" is the earliest known Han text called *fu*, wrote in the southern exile of Changsha (Hunan). Mei Sheng hailed from southeastern Huaiyin (Jiangsu), while the three most prominent authors from the reign of Emperor Wu to the end of the Western Han – Sima Xiangru, Wang Bao, and Yang Xiong – all came from Shu (Sichuan); in addition, the *History of the Han* mentions that Wang Bao was skilled in the recitation of Chu poetry, apparently a special and noteworthy art. Indeed, works attributed to Jia Yi and Wang Bao are included in the *Verses of Chu*. The "Monograph on Arts and Writings" credits Liu An with eighty-two *fu* and his courtiers with another forty-four.

The great age of the *fu* began after Emperor Wu, at the age of seventeen, ascended the imperial throne in 141 BC. He soon began to call the southern literary talents to the imperial court at Chang'an – an eclectic group that included rhetoricians like Zhuang Zhu (d. 122 BC), Zhufu Yan (d. 126 BC), and Zhuang Ji (ca 188–105 BC, also called Yan Ji); fortune hunters like Sima Xiangru; and entertainers like Mei Gao. While the old and frail Mei Sheng died en route to the capital, Sima Xiangru, whom the *History of the Han* credits with twenty-nine *fu*, arrived around 136 BC. (The account that Sima was called to Chang'an after the emperor had personally "read" one of his works, however, is clearly a product of later imagination.) Mei Sheng's "Seven Stimuli" (Qi fa) is the earliest extant example of the southern "grand *fu*" (*dafu*), the early climax of the Han *fu*. The grand *fu* is marked by length (running up to five hundred lines or more), a dialogical structure reminiscent of Warring States face-to-face persuasions, a brief historicizing prose introduction, an irregular meter, the alternation of rhymed and prose passages, constant and extreme hyperbole, the use of rare words (especially onomatopoeia and rhyming), alliterative and reduplicative binomes, a loose use of parallelism within couplets, and extensive descriptive or enumerative catalogues of various phenomena. On the whole, the grand *fu* is designed as a spectacle of language, celebrating at once the subject it expounds upon and its own poetic brilliance. It expresses an extreme sensitivity to language as rhetorical embellishment and aural display, overwhelming its audience in cascades of intricate sound patterns. In its greatest examples, the language of the *fu* mimetically reproduces the very phenomenon it describes, such as in Mei Sheng's account of a tidal bore as the sixth of seven enticements by which a "guest from Wu" tries to cure a Chu prince from an illness caused by overindulgence in luxury and pleasure. Pushing the prince's sensual imagination and perception to its limits, the text for some eighty lines races along with the wave it describes:

> Revolving and rushing, a glistening halo,
> front and rear conjoined and connected.
> Lofty and lofty, lifted and lifted,
> roiling and roiling, raging and raging,
> pressing and pressing, climbing and climbing,
> a layered fortress of multiplied strength,
> doubled and diverse like the lines of troops.
> Rumbling and roaring, booming and crashing,
> pushing and turning, surging and rolling –
> truly, it cannot be withstood!

Except for impromptu compositions *à la* Mei Gao, it is not clear who performed the *fu* at court and in which context. Did Sima Xiangru and Yang Xiong, purportedly both stutterers, perform their own *fu*? In Sima Xiangru's largely spurious biography in the *Records of the Historian*, which seems to extol the moral and aesthetic attitudes of Yang Xiong's time about a century later, the poet is said to have "presented" (*zou*) his "Great Man" (Daren fu), stirring Emperor Wu into a flash of megalomaniac delusion where he felt as elated as if "traversing the clouds" and "roaming Heaven and Earth." The dialogical format of many *fu* that created an arena of rhetorical competition may even suggest polyvocal performances, or at least theatrical techniques to represent the different voices. Furthermore, these competing voices were often explicitly fictionalized, such as those of "Sir Vacuous" (Zixu), "Master Improbable," and "Lord No-Such" in Sima Xiangru's "Excursion Hunt of the Son of Heaven."

Such texts reproduced late Warring States modes of persuasion and verbal embellishment and presented the art of verbal discourse itself as a source of endless pleasure and entertainment. Thus Sima Xiangru's "Excursion Hunt" – in the *Selections of Refined Literature* divided into two distinct texts, "Sir Vacuous" (Zixu fu) and "The Imperial Park" (Shanglin fu) – is far more than an account of the imperial hunt. In a grandiose spectacle of language, it turns the actual park into a mythical landscape inhabited by the creatures of the universe and traversed by the cosmic sovereign. Every wonder of the world becomes part of the larger wonder of verbal artistry, enjoyed by the very emperor who is celebrated in the poetic exposition. Like Mei Sheng's "Seven Stimuli," the text concludes with a shift from the delight in sensual pleasure (including the pleasure of language) to a lesson in moral edification. After indulging in a slaughter of cosmic proportion followed by a veritable orgy with strong sexual overtones, the subject of the text – the emperor – turns suddenly inward and questions his excesses:

> Thereupon, in the midst of drinking and the rapture of music, the Son of Heaven becomes dazed and contemplative, as if having lost something. He says, "Alas! This is too extravagant! I spend my leisure time with [the sensual pleasures of] watching and listening, waste the days with nothing to do! . . . I am afraid that later generations will become dissolute and dissipated; if they proceed on this path, they will not turn back."

The emperor then ends the feast with a solemn speech in which he extols modesty and morality, immersion in the Classics, and selfless care for the folk. The dramatic semantic shift from excess to contemplation is mirrored in Sima Xiangru's language: the extravagant rhythms and sound patterns used to describe the royal hunt are now replaced by the simple dignity of classical four-syllable verse. The text itself thus embodies the transformation of an unrestrained and violent ruler into an archetypal sage-king of old. Having initially mirrored the splendor of imperial pleasure, it now creates a textual model for a sage ruler. This rhetorical performance is found in the works of Sima Qian and Mei Sheng as well as in the "Great Summons" poem from the *Verses of Chu*. In "Seven Stimuli," after all sensual enticements have failed, it is enough to merely mention the "important words and marvelous doctrines" (*yaoyan miaodao*) to finally cure the prince of his illness:

> The guest said, "Now I shall present to your Excellency the masters of methods and arts, possessed of talent and sagacity, thinkers like Zhuang Zhou, Wei Mou, Yang Zhu, Mo Di, Bian Juan, and Zhan He. Let us have them discourse on the essential and the subtle of all under Heaven, giving order to the right

and the false. With Confucius and Laozi surveying what is presented, and with Mencius holding the bamboo tally and counting, not one of ten thousand cases will go amiss. These indeed are the important words and marvelous doctrines of all under Heaven. I wonder whether your Excellency might like to hear them." Thereupon, the prince leaned upon his table, rose, and said, "My mind has become clear as if I had already completely heard the words of the sages and disputers." Profusely, his perspiration issued forth, and all of a sudden, his illness was gone.

Through playful fictionalization, relentless hyperbole, and bold pursuit of a modernist literary taste, the grand *fu* of early and mid-Western Han times revealed itself as an illusion for everyone to see through, celebrating the double pleasures of splendid poetic delight and its simultaneous transcendence in classical learning and moral ideals. Later generations were, however, deeply suspicious of this fusion of the monitory and entertaining functions of literature, especially as the unrestrained display of verbal eloquence was rooted in the morally dubious tradition of late Warring States "wandering persuaders." Beginning in the mid-first century BC, a conservative critique of Emperor Wu's modernist court culture emerged, which, within decades, culminated in a radical reevaluation of the *fu*. The most forceful criticism, which still carries weight to this day, was delivered by Yang Xiong, the most influential literary author of the late Western Han. Originally an admirer and imitator of Sima Xiangru's style, albeit always with a more pronounced moral perspective, Yang rejected the *fu* later in life. In his autobiography (included in the *History of the Han*) and in the second chapter of his *Exemplary Sayings (Fayan)* – a work written in imitation of the *Analects* – Yang provided the first explicit definition and critique of the *fu* and the first sustained argument of literary criticism in early China. According to Yang, the purpose of the *fu* is "indirect admonition" (*feng*); yet by "adducing analogies," using "extremely gorgeous and lavish phrases," and grandly exaggerating its topic, the *fu* achieves just the opposite: its addressee, the emperor, merely indulges in its aesthetic marvels while missing its moral message. Thus, with ornate language overpowering didactic purpose, "it is clear that the *fu* only encourages and does not restrain." Withdrawing from further *fu* writing, Yang juxtaposed the recent compositions with the poetic mode of "exposition" (*fu*) in the ancient *Classic of Poetry*: "The *fu* of the men of the *Poetry* are gorgeous and provide standards; the *fu* of the epideictic poets are gorgeous and lead to excess."

This didactic stand on the nature and purpose of literature was embraced and canonized by Liu Xin – whom Yang seems to have held in some light distaste – and then Ban Gu: the entire discussion of the *fu* in the "Monograph on

Arts and Writings" directly descends, via Liu Xin, from Yang's critique. Going beyond Yang, Liu Xin's voice in the "Monograph" turns this critique into a tripartite historical narrative of cultural decline: originally, the dignitaries of antiquity had presented (*fu*) works from the *Classic of Poetry* on diplomatic missions, to exert moral influence, and to express their personal thoughts; next, with the political and moral collapse of the Zhou social order, such recitation gave way to expressions of personal suffering and frustration that served, at the same time, as political admonitions. For these, Liu Xin names two authors: Qu Yuan, whose works were regarded as *fu* in the Han, and Xun Qing, the author of the *Xunzi*, Chapter 26 ("Fu") of which contains five poetic riddles that share some of the formal characteristics of the Han *fu* (rhyme, meter, rudimentary dialogue) together with a complaint about the morally corrupt world. Liu Xin not only places the beginning of the true moral *fu* with Qu Yuan and Xun Qing; in a third step, he also sees its end right there: all subsequent authors, beginning with Qu Yuan's "successors" Song Yu and Jing Cuo, "vied to compose phrases greatly gorgeous and grossly aggrandizing" and thus "drowned the meaning of indirect suasion and moral illustration" of the genre. Two generations later, however, Ban Gu, author of the *History of the Han* and the leading poet of court eulogies and *fu* of his time, used the preface to his "The Two Capitals" (Liangdu fu) to praise the Han *fu* as "a class of the ancient *Poems*." Concerned with the historical stature of the Han dynasty, he marvels at the more than one thousand *fu* listings in the imperial library catalogue and equates the cultural splendor of the Han with that of high antiquity. Departing from the rigor of Liu Xin's critique, Ban Gu lists the illustrious poets from the Emperor Wu reign onwards and an impressive group of high-ranking officials – men whose *fu* "were second only to the Court Hymns and Eulogies [of the *Classic of Poetry*]."

While Liu Xin emphasizes the remonstrative purpose of the *fu*, and Ban Gu the eulogizing one, both agree with Yang Xiong's vision of an autonomous literary author and consider Qu Yuan to be its first incarnation. Nevertheless, Liu Xin's argument that the *fu* originated in the expression of personal sentiment largely upsets the Western Han history of the genre. Instead of recognizing the combination of entertainment, panegyric, and moral persuasion that seems to have defined the *fu* at Emperor Wu's court, Liu Xin focuses on a type of *fu* that for most of Western Han times was marginal at best. As Jia Yi and Yang Xiong had expressed their discontent with Qu Yuan's mere lament and suicide, Liu Xin establishes him as the primary model to follow. Only a few examples of these "frustration *fu*" are known: those purportedly written by Dong Zhongshu and Sima Qian, "Lamenting Time's Fate" (Ai shiming) attributed to Zhuang Ji and included in the *Verses of Chu*, Dongfang Shuo's "Responding to a Guest's Objection," Yang Xiong's "Dissolving Ridicule," and Ban Jieyu's (Favorite Beauty Ban, d. ca 6 BC) "Self-Commiseration" (Zidao fu), in which she laments her fate as an imperial concubine. The literature monograph in the *History of the Han* notes collectively the existence of a mere dozen pieces of "Miscellaneous *Fu* on the Loyal and Worthy Failing in Their Aims" (Za zhongxian shiyi fu).

As the development of the *fu* was part of the new court culture established by Emperor Wu, Yang Xiong's and Liu Xin's later critique of it belonged to a much larger conservative cultural reorientation, which, toward the end of the Western Han, culminated in the overall rejection of Emperor Wu's court literature, music, and ritual representation. In military, political, and fiscal terms, Emperor Wu had stretched the resources of the young empire in three decades (ca 130–100 BC) of rigorous expansion into Central Asia and northern Vietnam, and toward the Korean peninsula. Following this expansion, foreign goods and customs came to Chang'an and received an enthusiastic reception at court. Furthermore, the southern aesthetics and religious practices from the old region of Chu were introduced to the official state sacrifices. Sometime between 114 and 111 BC, Emperor Wu greatly revitalized and expanded an institution that had existed since Qin times, the imperial Bureau of Music (Yuefu). Under the leadership of the poet and musician Li Yannian – brother of Emperor Wu's favorite consort, Lady Li (Li furen) – this office was part of the imperial privy and thus outside the ritual bureaucracy. Producing the music for both court entertainment and state rituals, the office welcomed contemporary tunes from the various Chinese and even foreign (including Central Asian) regions. At different times between 113 and 94 BC (earlier dates given in the *History of the Han* are doubtful), a set of nineteen "Songs for the Sacrifices at the Suburban Altars" was created. Several of their tunes celebrated cosmic omens – the appearance of strange animals and plants, the discovery of an ancient tripod, unusual atmospheric phenomena – interpreted to signal cosmic approval of Emperor Wu's rule. The hymns were presented in the imperial ancestral temple and at the newly established, lavishly adorned altar to the supreme cosmic deity Grand Unity (Taiyi) located in Ganquan, about 110 kilometers northwest of Chang'an. Their diction is close to the sensual expression of both the "Nine Songs" and some of Sima Xiangru's *fu*, although their traditional association with Sima, who died in 117 BC, seems spurious.

It is for these qualities that Emperor Wu's entire court culture – vivacious music, modernist poetry, rich adornment of the imperial altars – was finally rejected in late Western Han times. In 32–31 BC, Chancellor Kuang Heng and Chief Censor Zhang Tan petitioned to change the wording of the hymns and to restore the dignified music of old (as opposed to the "licentious tunes" of the present). Their critique of the imperial altar to Grand Unity exemplifies the entire program:

> The purple altar is decorated with patterned ornament, multicolored carvings, and white–black and black–azure counterchange patterns. Moreover, it has jade equipment and [representations of?] female musicians. Its stone altars and shrines for the immortals, buried carriages with simurgh-bells, red horses and strong foals, and [wooden] figures of dragon steeds cannot find their models in antiquity. According to the principle of the burnt offerings to the [cosmic] emperors at the suburban altar that Your Subjects have learned, one [simply] sweeps the ground and sacrifices – this is venerating substantial simplicity . . . Everything relating to the artificial adornment of the purple altar, female musicians, carriages with simurgh-bells, red horses and strong foals, dragon steeds, and stone altars, should appropriately not be maintained.

In 7 BC, the Bureau of Music was dismantled and 441 of its 829 musicians dismissed. The remaining 388 were transferred to the Ministry of Rites, and the hymns on cosmic omens were deleted from the ritual repertoire. At precisely the same time, scholars like Liu Xin and others moved to establish new traditions of learning in the Five Classics – exegetical works like those of the *Mao Tradition* and the *Zuo Tradition* – that purportedly were of higher antiquity, and thus of superior moral authority, compared with the more recent interpretations (see below).

Beyond the *fu* and the ritual hymns, the range of poetry that can be dated with certainty to Western Han times is more limited than is traditionally assumed. The *History of the Han* includes only two early Western Han songs that are partially in the five-syllable line. Both of them are brief: a lament by Lady Qi, consort of the founding emperor Gaozu, and the following poem in which Li Yannian praises his sister's beauty:

> In the north, there is a beauty;
> Unique in her own era, she stands alone.
> With one glance, she topples a city;
> with a second glance, she topples a state.
> How could we not know her toppling the city and toppling the state?
> Yet such a beauty will be hard to find again.

All other songs in the five-syllable line attributed to early Western Han times appear only in sixth-century or later sources. Four other partly five-syllable-line songs included in the *History of the Han* are dated into the second half of the first century BC. To the literary tradition, this did not matter: by late Six Dynasties times, the anonymous "Nineteen Old Poems" (Gushi shijiu shou), the also anonymous eighteen "Songs for the Short Pan-pipe and the Nao Bell" (Duanxiao naoge, apparently military songs), poems attributed to Li Ling (d. 74 BC) and Su Wu (140–60 BC), and a whole series of other anonymous songs and ballads were assigned a Western Han date. At this time, many of them were labeled *yuefu* – "Music Bureau (songs)" – after the designation of the Western Han institution presumably in charge of their composition and performance. While the literature monograph in the *History of the Han* notes the existence of 314 short songs (ge), most of them were clearly ritualistic in nature, and none can be matched with the anonymous songs anthologized in Six Dynasties times.

The later assumptions about Western Han poetry are related to the idea that the Bureau of Music was devoted to collecting the folk poetry from the "lanes and alleys." According to Eastern Han and later sources, the Zhou kings had already sent out messengers to gather such songs in order to gauge popular sentiment. This idea became widespread and influential in Eastern Han times but cannot be ascertained for pre-imperial or even Western Han times. If the practice of collecting folk songs at court indeed existed, it was not yet the profound political trope envisioned by Eastern Han scholars.

This is not to say that there was no Western Han poetry beyond the *fu* and the state ritual hymns. The *Records of the Historian* and especially the *History of the Han* contain many songs attributed to members of the imperial family and several other important historical figures. Some poems are metrically close to the "Nine Songs" and thus suggestive of southern tunes, yet the *History of the Han* extends the term "Chu melodies" (*Chu sheng*) also to pieces in classical verse in the four-syllable line. As no traces of Han music have been preserved, it remains speculative to fill the term with specific contents; in literary terms, it may have referred to meter and rhythm, to Chu dialect words and pronunciations, or to the use of rhyme that gradually shifted away from the classical conventions of the *Classic of Poetry*. After being still observed in the Qin stele inscriptions and Emperor Gaozu's ancestral hymns, these conventions weakened significantly already with the rhymed parts of the *Huainanzi* and the early Han dynasty layers of the *Verses of Chu*. "Chu melodies" may hence have referred to a combination of musical and linguistic features; however, the Han songs associated with "Chu melodies" are far removed from the intricate imagery and ornate vocabulary of the "Nine Songs."

All the songs included in Han dynasty historiography that are attributed to prominent figures share several features: they are intensely personal, relatively short, and simple and straightforward in their expression; moreover, they all are attributed to moments of personal despair, often with the protagonist extemporizing the song on the verge of his or her imminent demise. Thus Xiang Yu (232–202 BC) sang in desperation when surrounded by Liu Bang's troops in 202 BC; Liu Bang sang – and danced – "The Great Wind" (Dafeng ge) at the end of his life, worrying about his succession; after Liu Bang's death, Lady Qi sang while being incarcerated by the Empress Dowager (and suffered horrible physical mutilation and the killing of her son in response to her lament); Liu You (prince of Zhao, d. 181 BC), slandered and imprisoned by the Empress Dowager's clan, broke into song while being starved to death; Liu Dan (prince of Yan, d. 80 BC) and his consort exchanged songs at a banquet before Liu committed suicide because of his failed *coup d'état*; Liu Xu (prince of Guangling, d. 54 BC) sang (and then killed himself) at a banquet, incriminated in a witchcraft case against the emperor; Emperor Wu fell into a poetic lament over the death of his favorite consort, Lady Li; and Liu Xijun, a Han princess, agonized in song over her fate in Central Asia:

> My family married me off to the other end of Heaven;
> far away they gave me to a foreign land, to the King of Wusun.
> A domed hut is my chamber, felt are the walls.
> I take flesh as my food, sour milk as my drink.
> Dwelling here, I always long for my soil – my heart is wounded.
> I wish I were a yellow swan, returning to my old homestead.

These extemporized performances of song and dance, drenched in the tears of the protagonists and their audiences, mark the climactic moments of the historical narratives they are embedded in. In most cases, the song is quoted as the protagonist's last utterance.

The *Records of the Historian* includes such songs not just in the biographies of Western Han figures but also for earlier heroes such as Qu Yuan (with "Embracing Sand"); Jing Ke (d. 217 BC), who sang before trying to assassinate the Qin First Emperor; or the brothers Boyi and Shuqi, who chose starvation over "eating the grain of Zhou" after the violent conquest of the Shang dynasty. Such quotation of song was a rhetorical device of early historiography, adding drama and authenticity to the historical narrative. It is highly dubious how any such song – performed just once – could have been transmitted to the historian, especially in cases like those of Qu Yuan (who sang in utter isolation), Liu Xijun (who was in a faraway land), Boyi and Shuqi (who starved as hermits in the mountains), or those dying in prison. Yet all these songs were plausible to the early historians and their audience as truthful utterances in moments of suffering and death. Most likely the songs were integral to the biographical lore, written and oral, that had formed over decades before reaching Sima Qian and Ban Gu, and were thus part of a larger culture of poetry performance and historical imagination. In this they reflected the dictum that "poetry expresses intent" and emerged as the natural and immediate response to an actual experience, especially one of suffering. As poetry served to dramatize and authenticate the historical narrative and to condense the essence of this narrative into the stable and durable medium of song, it also reaffirmed the Han view of poetry as something intensely personal and autobiographic. This view – noticeable also in Liu Xin's emphasis on the "frustration *fu*" – corresponded to the Mao interpretation of the *Classic of Poetry*: where historiography showed song as emerging from history and individual experience, the Mao reading attempted to retrieve such history and authorship from the songs. For the next two millennia, this expressive theory of literature, enshrined in the "Great Preface," remained the single most influential statement on the nature and purpose of Chinese poetry.

In addition to the songs by prominent historical figures, the early historical texts include dozens of anonymous ditties and proverbs that are attributed to "the people of Chang'an," "all under Heaven," "the villagers," "the folk," or even children. In the *History of the Han*'s coverage of the final decades of the Western Han dynasty, appearances of such songs were regarded as quasi-natural omens foretelling political and social disaster. Where songs and proverbs are quoted in this way, they are invariably validated by the subsequent historical events, betraying the ordering hand of the historian. As with the poetry attributed to named individuals, anonymous songs were seen not as artificial creations but as inevitable phenomena in a cosmos that was at once natural and political.

XII. Western Han historical and anecdotal narrative

The relation between poetry and historiography did not originate in Western Han times. Nevertheless, while in the *Zuo Tradition* and the *Discourses of the States* quotations from the *Classic of Poetry* far outweighed the occasional anonymous ditty, Han historiography showed a decisive shift from recitation to composition-in-performance, and thus a strong emphasis on genuine authorship. This emphasis now also marked historical writing itself. The single monument of Western Han historiography, and by far the largest Western Han narrative text altogether, is the *Records of the Historian*, a privately composed work that began with Sima Tan and was completed by his son, Sima Qian. Especially since Song times, the work has become tightly connected to Sima Qian's autobiography and read both as historical account and as the expression of its author's resentment and political criticism. This was not the dominant reading of the text before late Six Dynasties times, at the earliest. One must therefore contextualize not only the *Records* but also its later interpretations, instead of anachronistically collapsing the former into the latter. The three principal extant commentaries to the *Records* are Pei Yin's (fifth century) *Collected Explanations* (*Jijie*), Sima Zhen's (eighth century) *Retrieving the Hidden [Meaning]* (*Suoyin*), and Zhang Shoujie's (eighth century) *Correct Meaning* (*Zhengyi*).

The 130 chapters – the final chapter being Sima Qian's account of his work and life, and Sima Tan's outline of the "six lineages" – cover the time from the mythical Yellow Emperor to roughly 100 BC. In a radical departure from earlier annalistic narrative, the text is organized in five sections: twelve "Basic Annals" (*benji*) cover in terse annalistic format the dynasties and reigns from the Yellow Emperor to Sima Qian's own Emperor Wu (the received chapter on the latter being a later substitution); ten "Tables" (*biao*) note in geographic and chronological order the main events and historical protagonists since 841 BC; eight "Monographs" (*zhi*) discuss the technical subjects of ritual, music, calendrics, astrology, sacrifices, waterways, and agronomy; thirty chapters of "Hereditary Families" (*shijia*) trace the hereditary nobility of the major Zhou states, including the family of Confucius, down to the dignitaries enfeoffed by the early Han emperors; and sixty-nine "Arrayed Traditions" (*liezhuan*) provide individual and group biographies – including such subjects as *ru* classicist scholars, mild or cruel officials, roaming knights, sycophants at court, jesters, fortune-tellers, assassins, and merchants – as well as accounts of several non-Chinese neighbors and regions from Korea to Vietnam and Central Asia.

The circulation and early reception of the *Records* is not sufficiently clear. The received text contains a significant number of later additions, interpolations, and substitutions of original chapters. An early layer of explicitly marked additions, spreading across a number of chapters, came from Chu Shaosun (ca 105–ca 30 BC), an imperially appointed erudite (*boshi*). Sima Qian's biography in the *History of the Han* speaks of ten lost chapters, of which by the first century AD only the titles had survived. The third-century commentator Zhang Yan identifies these chapters as the two "Basic Annals" of emperors Jing and Wu, the three "Monographs" on ritual, music, and warfare, the "Table" of early Western Han generals and high officials, the "Hereditary House" of the princes of Qi, Yan, and Guangling, and the three "Arrayed Traditions" of diviners, fortune-tellers, and Fu Kuan and Jin Shi. Except for the "Monograph" on warfare, all these chapters are included in the received *Records of the Historian* and hence are regarded as later replacements (the "Basic Annals" of Emperor Wu largely duplicates the "Monograph" on the *feng* and *shan* sacrifices). The authenticity of other chapters, especially several that have counterparts in the *History of the Han* and may have been reconstructed from that work, remains under discussion. Beyond these direct interventions, the *Records of the Historian* – like all early texts – underwent substantive later editing that probably went beyond mere orthographic standardization. The assumption of Sima Qian as the single author of the *Records*, and of the text as his personal response to the suffering inflicted upon him, is thus complicated by three facts: the principal authors include both Sima Tan and Sima Qian, and it seems dubious to attribute specific sections to one or the other; both authors accepted hundreds of earlier sources into their work; and the *Records* contains significant portions of later additions and rewritings. As a result, the vast text has frustrated attempts to find a coherent interpretation both of the historical account and of Sima Qian's authorial self-expression.

The complex narrative structure of the *Records* contributes to its appearance as a text of multiple perspectives. Most historical protagonists appear not only in a number of chapters across the five divisions, but also within the "Arrayed Traditions," where their actions intersect with those of their contemporaries. Events are related in different versions and may often reflect sources of different types, and individual biographies – for example, the Qu Yuan account – are clearly a patchwork of diverse materials. Modern scholarship has identified about seventy different sources of the *Records* by title, with many more remaining in obscurity. The term "arrayed traditions" may refer not to the overall lineup of chapters but to the compilation of different oral and written narrative traditions within each chapter. This has not prevented later imperial scholars – not to mention virtually all modern Chinese and Western readers – from taking the *Records* as a monument of Sima Qian's self-expression. This reading is based especially on two partially overlapping texts attributed to him: his autobiography in Chapter 130 and the "Letter in Response to Ren Shaoqing" (Bao Ren Shaoqing shu) preserved in his biography in the *History of the Han*. These two writings, taken together, provide a dramatic account of how and why Sima Qian began and ended his work as a historian, an account that places the *Records* squarely into the emerging Western Han ideas of strong authorship, the compulsive production of literature out of suffering and frustration, and the powerful truth claims related to such literary creation. It shows the *Records* not only as a work of historical writing, but – very much like the poetic performances it relates – as a text that itself is driven by historical necessity.

According to Sima Qian's account, his father Sima Tan, Emperor Wu's court astrologer involved in calendar calculation, divination, and the correct performance of the imperial sacrifices, died in 110 BC out of grief and despair over having been excluded from the most solemn cosmic ritual, the imperial *feng* and *shan* sacrifices. On his deathbed, he bequeathed to his son the charge to complete his private work of history. The second, no less dramatic, moment came a decade later, when in 99 BC Sima Qian defended the general Li Ling, who during a campaign beyond China's borders had surrendered to an overwhelming enemy. Sima Qian fell into disgrace and was ordered to choose between suicide and castration. He opted for the unbearable shame of the latter in order to complete the *Records*. Explaining his choice as driven by his sense of duty, he offers a noble genealogy of earlier writers – among them King Wen of Zhou, Qu Yuan, Confucius, Zuo Qiuming, and the anonymous authors of the *Classic of Poetry* – who all had composed their works when in dire straits. Thus Sima Qian presented himself as the filial son of his father and the successor of earlier moral paragons, eager to rescue the worthy men of the past from oblivion while simultaneously securing the lasting memory of himself and his father for the "sages and nobles of future generations." In terms heavily charged with religious overtones, Sima Qian stated his intent to "explore the junction of Heaven and Man, comprehend the transformation of past and present, and establish the exposition of one lineage" – that is, to explore human history in a cosmic framework, and to transcend the biological end of his family through its textual future of a newly established intellectual tradition. If authentic, this account is the earliest extant self-interpretation of a literary author and a fundamental statement on the nature and purpose of writing. Here Sima Qian presented himself as a most self-conscious author and one obsessed with the posterity of his name. At the same time the *Records* is the earliest text to establish a series of sages – King Wen, Confucius, Qu Yuan, and so on – as strong authors in Sima's own image.

The autobiographical reading aligned the *Records* closely with the *Spring and Autumn Annals* that in Western Han times – prominently by Sima Qian's teacher Dong Zhongshu – was interpreted as Confucius' historical judgment expressed through "subtle words" (*weiyan*) of "praise and blame" (*baobian*). In the *Records* this criticism was seen as directed at Sima's own ruler, Emperor Wu. Large parts of the text are indeed devoted to the four decades from 141 (the date of Emperor Wu's ascent) to roughly 100 BC when Sima stopped writing. Moreover, Sima's sometimes (though not consistently) sharp criticism of the Qin First Emperor as a tyrant and megalomaniac, deluded by fantasies of immortality, has been read as being ultimately directed at Emperor Wu, who in later Western Han times was cast in similar terms.

Sima Qian's explicit authorial presence in the *Records* itself is limited to certain chapters (e.g. the introductions to some of the "Tables") and to brief comments appended at the end of each chapter. The narrative proper unfolds as a seemingly objective record, driven by events and the moral forces of history. This pattern of writing follows the model of the *Zuo Tradition* – one of Sima Qian's key sources – with its appended judgments under the name of the "Gentleman" or Confucius. In the *Records* the historian's comments are often intensely personal. He tries, on occasion, to rationalize a course of events that contradicts both reason and morality; elsewhere, he expresses frustration over the impossibility of doing so. He points to a protagonist's moral deficiencies or praises his character; he explains improbable outcomes or defers to an unfathomable Heaven as the ultimate force behind them. He sighs over what he finds in his sources or concludes with series of real or rhetorical questions. Altogether, the comments reveal his moral and rational stand and show him as both narrator and judge of history, retrospectively setting right what history had allowed to go wrong.

By far the most lively parts of the *Records* are the biographies presented in the "Arrayed Traditions." Rich in minute detail, vivid in narrative and description, and dramatic in the frequent use of dialogues and flashbacks, they focus on concrete situations that display the protagonists' personalities. Attention to supernatural phenomena and uncounted instances of well-crafted speech may raise questions about the narrative as a truthful and authentic account, stacking the literary qualities of the *Records* against its factual reliability. Eastern Han writers like Ban Gu and Wang Chong (27–ca 100) complained about Sima's interest in the fanciful, but later readers – especially Song and later advocates of "ancient-style literature" (*guwen*) – have cherished his stylistic eloquence and forceful expression as the reflection of Sima's personality.

Among the biographical chapters, the first – the "Arrayed Traditions of Boyi and Shuqi" (Chapter 61) – deserves particular attention as it frames the narrative with extensive considerations about the historian's purpose and moral predicament. The brief narrative relates how the noble brothers Boyi and Shuqi preferred starvation to a life under the Zhou dynasty that had just violently overthrown the Shang. The historian faces a dilemma of judgment: here were the loyal subjects whose ruler had been killed, there was King Wu of Zhou who had ended the oppressive Shang rule (and in the process had neglected piety toward his just-deceased father). Sima Qian sides with Boyi and Shuqi, but only through a series of rhetorical questions that lead him to query the justice of Heaven: "I am deeply confused by this – is this what is called the Way of Heaven? Is it true? Is it false?" He quotes both the ancient Classics and Confucius, whom he praises for having preserved the memory of Boyi and Shuqi. Like so many other good men of the "cliffs and caves," Sima Qian self-consciously concludes, these virtuous hermits would have fallen into oblivion were it not for the effort of the historian to preserve their names.

This reflection on the duties of the historian shows him interested in more than the bare facts. His charge is to create the memory of the past as a model for the present and the future. Thus, according to an "adage from among the rustics" – quoted in Jia Yi's lengthy essay "Finding Fault with Qin" (Guo Qin lun) that is in turn included in Sima's appended judgment to the "Basic Annals of the Qin First Emperor" – "those who do not forget past affairs will be the master of the future." Toward this end Sima Qian presents himself as a tireless researcher who travels the empire to gather local memories, searches the archives of old and laments that the Qin had destroyed all records except their own, or weighs the available evidence and on occasion considers it insufficient.

While the *Records* is the largest and most prominent work of Western Han narrative literature, it is not isolated. It draws on a number of earlier works such as Lu Jia's (ca 228–ca 140 BC) *Spring and Autumn Annals of Chu and Han* (*Chu Han Chunqiu*, a work surviving only in fragmentary quotations and borrowings) that details the founding of the Han dynasty. Parts of its vast repertoire of anecdotes are further shared with other Han compilations. In the "Arrayed Traditions," anecdotes from oral and written sources are organized to create specific biographies; in other texts, such anecdotes are retold in smaller, mutually independent units that may more accurately reflect their original form of transmission. The earliest of these compilations is *Mr. Han's Exoteric Tradition of the Poetry* (mid-second century BC), with 306 historical anecdotes illustrating philosophical or moral thought. Each passage closes with a quotation from the *Classic of Poetry*, and the text is considered part of Han Ying's exegetical tradition of the *Poetry*. About a third of Han Ying's anecdotal material can be found in Warring States texts, and other parts appear elsewhere in Han writing, testifying to the general popularity of such anecdotes both before and after the establishment of the empire. While Sima Qian became viewed as the author of the *Records*, Han Ying, lacking a personal agenda, has been perceived as a compiler of anonymous material. The same is true for the other four transmitted Western Han collections of historical narrative that are all attributed to Liu Xiang, the imperial collator and bibliographer. In comparison, Sima Qian's perceived authorship of the vast and variegated *Records* is completely unique in all of Western Han times, as is his writing, on either wood or bamboo, of a personal letter of such remarkable length.

Liu Xiang's anecdote collections are the *Intrigues of the Warring States* (with some parallels in a silk manuscript from Mawangdui), the *Matters Newly Arranged* (*Xinxu*), the *Garden of Persuasions* (*Shuiyuan* or *Shuoyuan*), and the *Biographies of Exemplary Women* (*Lienü zhuan*). After the voluminous *Intrigues* (see above), the next-largest collection is the *Garden of Persuasions*, containing 639 (of a presumed original 784) sections in the received text. The *Persuasions* is also closely related to the *Matters Newly Arranged* that contains 166 sections; in addition, fifty-nine more fragments are known. In the "Monograph on Arts and Writings," the two titles appear as a single, ambiguous listing that combines the received titles as *Xinxu shuiyuan*, which may in fact refer to only a single work, a *Newly Arranged Garden of Persuasions*. Both collections are organized by topic and serve as repertoires of moral illustration, especially between rulers and ministers. *Biographies of Exemplary Women* is likewise arranged topically, in this case according to six cardinal virtues represented by the individual women. Each set of virtues ("motherly deportment," "worthiness and sagacity," "humaneness and wisdom," "purity and obedience," "chastity and rightness," "judgment and comprehension") is given its own chapter and illustrated by fifteen examples; in addition, the concluding seventh chapter furnishes fifteen instances of "waywardness and depravity." (Chapter 8 of the received text, complementing the seven categories, is a later addition.) Like Liu Xiang's other collections, the *Biographies* is historical and didactic in outlook. It introduces women from high antiquity through the Western Han, and from royal wives to peasant ladies, in each case illustrating their exemplary behavior through a brief anecdote. At the end of each anecdote, the compiler enters the text. First, he quotes briefly from the *Classic of Poetry* and adds the formula known from *Mencius* and other texts, "this is what [the text] is about" (*ci zhi wei ye*). Then he concludes with a separate rhymed appraisal of eight four-syllable lines, which is introduced by the words "the appraisal says" (*song yue*). Thus imitating the appended authorial statements of the *Zuo Tradition* and the *Records of the Historian*, Liu submits his text as a supplement to historical narrative. Didactic in intent, it presents the *Classic of Poetry* as the single canonical text that encompasses all human behavior.

Despite their historical gestures and didactic purpose, Liu Xiang's compilations depart from the grand narratives of the *Zuo Tradition* and the *Records* in the arrangement of their material. The latter combine a wide range of sources into elaborate, integrated stories; Liu Xiang groups individual anecdotes under topical categories. This choice shows a methodic compiler from the end of the Western Han determined and explicit in his didactic purpose. Through their systematic arrangement, his texts give clear guidance to the reader; they are unambiguous in their moral positions and straightforward in language, lending them to a wide circulation that no longer depended on personal instruction or learned hermeneutic efforts. In particular the *Biographies of Exemplary Women* came to enjoy broad popularity and inspired numerous later works in praise of female virtue. Since Eastern Han times images of Liu Xiang's female paragons were placed on the walls of houses, temples, and tombs, and illustrated versions of the book had circulated since the early Six Dynasties. By contrast, the fifteen titles of "trivial talk" (*xiaoshuo*) that are listed in the "Monograph on Arts and Literature," some of them comprising hundreds of chapters, fell by the wayside and are no longer extant. Presumably less didactic in outlook, their anecdotes may have lacked the support of the post-Han tradition to be continuously circulated and preserved.

In addition to poetry and historical narrative, a large number of texts in other formats were composed over the two centuries of the Western Han. Some – for example, philosophical works, technical treatises, or interpretations of the Classics – are listed in the "Monograph on Arts and Letters"; others, such as edicts and petitions, personal letters and inscriptions, or all kinds of administrative, legal, and economic records, are generally not. While only a fraction of the titles listed in the "Monograph" are transmitted, recently excavated manuscripts from numerous sites point to a large amount of writing that never entered the imperial catalogue. Cao Pi's (187–226) "Discussion of Literature" (Lun wen) lists "petitions and discussions," "letters and discourses," "inscriptions and dirges," and "songs and poetic expositions" as the primary genres of writing, pointing to a notion of literature that was defined by its pragmatic purpose and application. Inscriptions, dirges, and personal letters appear to have become common only in Eastern Han times. The famous letter exchange between Li Ling and Su Wu, for example, is of dubious authenticity; the earliest credible exchange still extant is the one between Liu Xin and Yang Xiong over Yang's dialect dictionary, *Regional Expressions* (*Fangyan*). Given that paper became only gradually available after approximately AD 100, the writing of long personal letters – either on the bulky materials of wood or bamboo, or on expensive silk – was certainly not the norm. Letters by soldiers, local administrators, and envoys, or – on behalf of the dead and buried with them – to the authorities of the netherworld (for example, at Mawangdui) are now archaeologically documented, but they are a far cry from the elaborate and intensely personal composition attributed to Sima Qian. Archaeology has produced very large numbers of legal, administrative, military, and economic documents written on wood and bamboo. From the imperial court to the local administration in even remote border areas (as in evidence, for example, from manuscripts finds in Juyan, Inner Mongolia/Gansu), Western Han government agencies produced a continuous stream of bureaucratic writing. Neither the *Records of the Historian*, the *History of the Han*, nor Liu Xiang in his compilation of the imperial library catalogue paid much attention to this type of bureaucratic and technical writing.

XIII. Qin and Western Han political and philosophical discourses

Liu Xiang appears to have most valued those kinds of Western Han texts that corresponded to the prestigious writings from earlier times, including historical narrative, the exegesis of the Classics, and philosophical discourse. Of these the later tradition has preserved but a handful of major Western Han works, erasing the vast majority of early texts and with them much of the intellectual context of the surviving ones. While a small but coherent body of writings has thus come to define Western Han intellectual and literary history, several of even these texts are later imperial reconstructions. As a result, the authenticity of some key texts of early Western Han political discourse – among them Jia Yi's *New Writings* (*Xinshu*), Lu Jia's *New Discourses* (*Xinyu*), and Dong Zhongshu's *Luxuriant Dew of the Spring and Autumn Annals* (*Chunqiu fanlu*) – are shrouded in doubt.

Lu Jia's *New Discourses* in twelve sections set out the traditional principles of good rulership and was purportedly composed at Emperor Gaozu's request. Jia Yi's *New Writings* includes "Finding Fault with Qin," Jia's petitions to Emperor Wen (r. 180–157 BC), historical anecdotes, and discussions of ritual. Both texts have come to represent traditional political thought from the early years of the Western Han and are closely related to the imperial court, where both Lu and Jia served as officials. Both authors point to the purported moral corruption and political failures of Qin in order to legitimize Han imperial rule. Addressing the pragmatic needs of successful rulership, their arguments are rooted in Warring States classicist political thought and supported by quotations from the Classics. Their ideal ruler is frugal, oriented toward the examples of the early Zhou kings, and intent on self-cultivation and ritual propriety. He rewards the worthy and the virtuous, listens to his advisers, and adapts his decisions to the new circumstances of a changing world. This notion of "changing with the times," advocated already by Qin officials like Li Si and later often despised as an expression of Qin "legalism," was a key argument in Western Han classicist political thought and appears in a diverse range of texts including the *Records of Ritual*, the *Huainanzi*, and a series of imperial edicts, petitions to the throne, and court debates throughout Western Han times.

The emphasis on change and "newness" (*xin*, a word that recurs in titles of Western Han political writing) was in an uneasy relationship with a concomitant claim for reviving pre-Qin "antiquity" (*gu*). The master metaphor of the divide that separated past and present was the purported destruction of classical culture under the Qin and its subsequent resurrection by the Han. This ideological construct developed gradually over the course of the Han and has served as the foundational myth of imperial, and now post-imperial, Confucianism ever since. Meanwhile, the idea of "timeliness" or "changing with the times" connected Western Han political and administrative needs to contemporaneous cosmology. The three largest compendia of late pre-imperial and early imperial political and cosmological thought – all three profoundly eclectic – are *Mr. Lü's Spring and Autumn Annals* of 239 BC, the *Huainanzi* of 139 BC, and the *Records of Ritual* that comprise a range of texts from late Warring States through Western Han times. They all contain versions of the "Monthly Ordinances" (*Yueling*) that define the ideal ruler as acting – both ritually and administratively – in accordance with cosmic time and cyclical change. This notion is further expressed in the "Canon of Yao" of the *Classic of Documents* (placing the chapter squarely into late Warring States or even Qin times) and several additional chapters of the *Huainanzi*. Over the course of the Western Han, it became fully integrated with the correlative cosmology of the Five Phases. In this cosmology, the emperor became a cosmic sovereign at the center of the universe, who through his actions secured the well-being of his domain as well as of the natural cosmos altogether.

With *Mr. Lü's Spring and Autumn Annals* composed on the eve of Qin imperial unification and the *Records of Ritual* compiled into a single work not before late Western and possibly Eastern Han times, the largest and most influential Western Han philosophical text is the *Huainanzi*, compiled by a large group of scholars at Liu An's southern princely court of Huainan. It was likely a challenge to Emperor Wu's political and cultural authority, and Liu An, the emperor's cousin and rival, in 122 BC was finally forced into suicide. The text shares the language, mythology, and imagery of other southern writings (the *Verses of Chu*, the *Zhuangzi*, the early *fu*) and makes frequent use of rhyme. Drawing on diverse strands of political and philosophical thought, it outlines a cosmological order that integrates ancient mythology, the notion of the self-perfected "true man" (*zhenren*) as the ideal of a cosmic ruler, and Five Phases correlative thought. Like *Mr. Lü's Spring and Autumn Annals*, the work is listed among the "miscellaneous" or "mixed" traditions (*zajia*) in the "Monograph of Arts and Writings." Already in Eastern Han times it attracted commentaries by Xu Shen and Gao You (ca 168–212, also the earliest commentator of *Mr. Lü's Spring and Autumn Annals*) with which it is still transmitted.

The Han integration of cosmology and political thought replaced the ancient notion of political legitimacy, rooted in genealogy and expressed in the ancestral sacrifice, with one in which the ruler answered directly to the cosmic powers. This notion enabled Emperor Wu's grandiose claims of universal sovereignty that were celebrated in a new set of cosmic sacrifices, ritual court hymns, and poetic expositions; yet over the course of the Western Han, it served the court scholars and learned officials better than it did their monarchs. Their arena consisted of edicts, petitions to the throne, and court debates – new forms of writing that developed together with the imperial state and were considered eminent forms of refined literary expression.

Numerous Western Han examples of edicts and petitions are preserved in the *Records of the Historian* and the *History of the Han*. Often shaped by the rhythmic speech of traditional rhetoric (sometimes even employing rhyme and four-syllable meter), they draw on analogies and historical precedent and evoke the Classics. While prepared for specific occasions, these texts are not ad hoc utterances but stylistically sophisticated political arguments that were, presumably, preserved in the imperial archives. Cases of substantially different versions of the same text, however, suggest that even documents of central importance could be subject to later rewriting, or reimagining. In their political philosophy, many petitions share a view of the world as an organic and well-ordered universe open to cosmological as well as moral explanation. Extensive political arguments could be developed within the framework of correlative cosmology and supported by quotations from the Classics in their new Western Han interpretations. Thus in his famous three statements to the emperor that Dong Zhongshu presented in 136 BC, he portrayed the ruler as a universal sovereign in communication with the universe. Heaven was seen as directly responsive to good or bad rulership; omens and natural disasters were warnings to the ruler. When a fire broke out in the founding emperor Gaozu's funerary park in 135 BC, Dong accordingly drew on events recorded in the *Spring and Autumn Annals* to argue against Emperor Wu's practices of ancestral worship and continued from there to offer further policy recommendations. These almost led to his execution and seem to have cautioned Dong against further interpretations of contemporary portents. Nevertheless his use of historical precedent to read cosmic events in political terms remained intact.

Following Dong Zhongshu, all major Western Han interpreters of cosmic portents were, first of all, scholars steeped in the Five Classics – especially in the *Spring and Autumn Annals*, the *Classic of Changes*, and the *Classic of Documents* – who could demonstrate how the Classics were eminently applicable to contemporary matters. This becomes clear with the extensive "Monograph on the Five Phases" (Wu xing zhi) that uses the framework of Five Phases cosmology to list and discuss the numerous auspicious and inauspicious omens from the Spring and Autumn period down to the Western Han. Its most prominent voices after the *Gongyang* scholar Dong Zhongshu are Jing Fang (77–37 BC), Sui Meng (originally Sui Hong, fl. ca 78 BC), Xiahou Sheng (fl. ca 70 BC), Liu Xiang and his son Liu Xin, Gu Yong (d. 8 BC), and Li Xun (fl. ca 5 BC). Each of these men, credited with impressive accounts of omen interpretation, was a specialist in one of the Classics. Consequently, during the first century BC, a large new corpus of texts submitted the Classics to an exegesis driven by cosmological and prognostic speculation. These esoteric writings, later labeled "prognostic apocrypha" (chenwei), were, however, subsequently excluded from the commentarial tradition and have survived only in fragments of quotation.

Over the first century BC, omen interpretation became a powerful way by which the court classicists asserted their authority toward the emperor. The imperial promotion of traditional learning had produced a new class of thousands of scholars, educated both privately and at the Imperial Academy, who came to occupy offices high and low in the central government. Within less than two centuries, the scholarly elite of early imperial China had thus positioned itself as a formidable, self-sustaining, and continuously reproducing power at the heart of the Chinese empire, organized around a body of supremely authoritative texts from antiquity. These texts were not under the emperor's control; on the contrary, they served to limit his actions and ambitions. The court-appointed *ru* classicist erudites had maneuvered themselves into a win–win situation: virtuoso insiders of imperial politics, their familiarity with the Classics provided them with the moral high ground and critical stance toward the emperor.

XIV. The status of the Classics

The texts around which their learning was arranged were the Five Classics. The term *wu jing*, a Western Han coinage, initially overlapped with the older one of the "six arts" (*liu yi*) that was still used in Liu Xiang's imperial catalogue and the subsequent "Monograph on Arts and Writings." At the time of the Stone Canal Pavilion discussions (51 BC), the canon of music – from the beginning likely a loose assembly of writings – had receded into the background, leaving the classics of *Changes, Documents, Poetry, Spring and Autumn Annals,* and *Ritual* as the foundation of court-sponsored *ru* classicist learning. The Five Classics were in many respects problematic and unwieldy: much of them was composed in terse archaic language that required commentary to become fully intelligible to a Han audience; they were transcribed into the new standard script and as such open to questions about authenticity and accuracy; each Classic gave rise to a number of competing exegetical traditions, some sponsored by the court, others not; and as presumably perfect texts, written and edited by the sages (especially Confucius, who in one way or another now became related to all of them), they embodied the unquestionable ideal of political and moral order. The imperial court, eager to draw political legitimacy and moral authority from the ancient writings, responded to these issues repeatedly.

   The first move was the proscription of private book ownership by the Qin dynasty in 213 BC, following Chancellor Li Si's argument that the *Classic of Poetry* and the *Classic of Documents* were used to denigrate present rulership. While the people outside the court were allowed to keep manuals on agriculture, divination and other technical subjects, only the erudites at court could study the Classics. The proscription, aimed at suppressing the "talk of the hundred intellectual lineages" (*baijia yu*), remained in place until 191 BC. Since Eastern Han times, the Confucian tradition has interpreted the decision of 213 BC as a wholesale destruction of classical learning and has further connected it to reports that, in 212 BC, the Qin had executed more than 460 scholars in the capital. This traditional account has served Confucian identity remarkably well, but there are several problems with it. First, no text before Sima Qian's *Records of the Historian* mentions the execution, and no text before Wei Hong's first-century AD preface to a (since lost) version of the *Classic of Documents* identifies the *ru* classicists as the victims of the execution. The earliest known source for the famous formula "burning the books and executing the *ru* classicists" (*fenshu kengru*) to condemn Qin cruelty and anti-classicism is the preface to the forged Kong Anguo version of the *Classic of Documents* that emerged in AD 317. Second, the early sources report in unison that the Qin court employed erudites (*boshi*) for the study of the Classics, among them the *Documents* scholar Fu Sheng and the ritual expert Shusun Tong (fl. ca 209–195 BC). In 213 BC, the erudites were granted a monopoly to study, teach, and probably also edit the Classics; they also designed the imperial rituals and inscriptions. Those said to have triggered the First Emperor's ire that then purportedly led to the mass execution were two well-known "masters of methods" (*fangshi*) – that is, representatives of non-canonical learning – and no *ru* classicist scholar known by name is reported to have suffered under the Qin. Third, extensive references to the Classics, especially to the *Documents* and the *Poetry*, can be found in Qin and early Han official writing, suggesting the continued availability of these texts at court. Furthermore, quotations from the Classics in excavated manuscripts before and after the presumed bibliocaust show no difference in the degree of classical learning.

It therefore appears that the Qin court classicists were not the victims but, if anything, the beneficiaries of the proscription of private learning. Their stance was further strengthened in 136 BC when – in a move remarkably parallel to that of the Qin – Emperor Wu of the Han proclaimed the *ru* Classics as the sole objective of official learning. While erudites were appointed to each of the Five Classics, the learning of the "talk of the hundred intellectual lineages" was censored. As a group the *ru* erudites had meanwhile successfully maintained their presence at court, securing a ritual and textual continuity from the Qin through the Western Han. Recently excavated manuscripts, especially the bamboo slips from Zhangjiashan, have confirmed the same Qin–Han continuity also in the legal and administrative realm. Altogether, the traditional account of collapse and revival of classical learning seems at least greatly exaggerated if not largely a self-serving assertion by later generations of Confucians.

From the Qin through the Han, the officially appointed erudites were in charge of the Classics, controlling not only the interpretation but also the very text of the received canon in its different versions. The establishment of the Imperial Academy (Taixue) in 124 BC further solidified the status of the Classics. While most appointments in the central administration of the empire were still based on recommendation and inherited status, proficiency in at least one of the Five Classics was now officially promoted as a career path. The double quest for eloquent literary expression and political engagement, honed through the study of the classical texts and practiced in exegetical writing as well as in the production of petitions, discursive essays, and other court documents, conjoined the interests of the imperial state and its classical scholars.

This is not to say that classical scholarship was always the exclusive domain of the imperial court. Well into Emperor Wu's reign, princely courts like those of Liu An in Huainan and Liu De in Hejian rivaled and sometimes surpassed the Chang'an court in the sponsorship of classical learning and literary production. Liu De, the patron of the *Mao Tradition*, was famous for his love (and physical possession) of old writings in pre-Qin script, and he nourished a culture, complete with its own group of erudites, that promoted classical ritualism and the study and performance of elegant orthodox music. Emperor Wu's energetic appropriation of the Classics at the imperial court may thus be understood as an attempt to gain control over the textual resources of traditional authority. It parallels his efforts to summon the literary talents and masters of political debate – two groups of eloquent speakers and writers that largely overlapped – from the southern princely courts to Chang'an. Both the study of the Classics and the performance of poetic rhetoric were directly tied to the emperor's quest for political legitimacy and cultural prestige. As noted above, poetic expositions like those attributed to Mei Sheng and Sima Xiangru turned explicitly to the Classics to underscore their message of moral edification.

Considering the imperial ambition to concentrate classical learning in the hands of the official erudites, it is remarkable that at no time during the Western Han was adherence to any particular exegesis enforced. When classical learning became the "official learning" (*guanxue*), and when its proponents turned from Warring States independent thinkers to Qin and Han court appointees, the study of each of the Five Classics was not reduced to a single tradition but continuously allowed for competing interpretations. These diverging teachings could each receive a chair at the Imperial Academy, which by the time of Emperor Ping was home to thirty erudites for the Five Classics, reportedly teaching more than three thousand students. We do not know how studying at the academy was organized, or how closely the official teachers interacted with their students. Yet it is clear that the promotion of official learning led to a flurry of discussions and writings on the Five Classics as well as to their application to political issues and matters of ritual representation. One result of these constant debates was the compilation of learned petitions, such as in the case of the Stone Canal Pavilion conference of 51 BC. Another outcome was an increasing number of written commentaries of various kinds, including works of word glosses, exegetical and narrative traditions, illustrative anecdotes, and so-called "chapter-and-verse" (*zhangju*) commentaries on individual Classics that are said to have been excessively long and detailed, sometimes running to over a million words. Little is left of the many chapter-and-verse commentaries from late Western and then Eastern Han times, but the ones we still have – such as Wang Yi's commentary on the *Verses of Chu* – do not seem to fit that pejorative characterization.

In addition to commentaries and the use of the Classics in literary composition and political argument, another aspect of late Western Han textual culture built around the Classics was the compilation of glossaries and dictionaries. The only extant glossary that presumably dates from pre-imperial times is *Approximating Elegance* (*Erya*), a text of probably late Warring States origins that is first mentioned in the *History of the Han* and quoted repeatedly in Eastern Han sources; its earliest known commentary was written by Guo Pu. *Approximating Elegance* was likely created as a collection of word glosses on the Classics; thus, in the *History of the Han*, the text was listed next to the *Classic of Filial Piety* (*Xiaojing*) and the *Analects* that in Western Han times both served as primers. It was treated as a canonical text from late Six Dynasties times and in the Song finally became one of the Thirteen Classics. Under the section "elementary learning" (*xiaoxue*), the "Monograph of Arts and Writings" contains entries of four other early lexicographic works that are lost: the *Scribe Zhou* (*Shi Zhou*), a text attributed to a Western Zhou official but almost certainly a late Warring States text; the *Eight Character Forms and Six Techniques* (*Bati liuji*) of unknown origins; the *Cang Jie* glossary, named after the legendary inventor of the script and attributed to the Qin chancellor Li Si; and the *Fan Jiang* by Sima Xiangru. In addition, it notes the existence of several other Qin and early glossaries that partially overlapped with the *Scribe Zhou* or were compiled into a larger *Cang Jie* of more than three thousand characters.

In late Western Han times, a new series of other lexicographic works appeared: the *Jijiu* by Shi You, director of the palace gates under Emperor Yuan; the *Yuanshang* attributed to Li Chang, court architect under Emperor Cheng; and several works by Yang Xiong. Yang compiled the dialect glossary *Regional Expressions* (*Fangyan*), also known under the title *Separate Graphs* (*Biezi*), the *Compendium of Glosses* (*Xunxuan*), the *Cang Jie Tradition* (*Cang Jie zhuan*), and the *Cang Jie Compendium of Glosses* (*Cang Jie xunzuan*). Except for the much longer *Regional Expressions* – a work still extant – all these glossaries are listed in the "Monograph" as rather short texts of a single bamboo bundle (*pian*) each. Following Yang, the palace attendant Du Lin compiled two more glossaries in the *Cang Jie* tradition.

With the exception of *Regional Expressions*, all these works were fundamentally concerned with two aspects of the Chinese script: first, the correct reading of pre-Qin classical texts and their "ancient," that is, non-standardized character forms; and second, the mastery of the newly established official (clerical) script established under the Qin. In other words, the glossaries served both classical learning and the use of the script in the administration of the early empire – the two central uses of writing in the Qin and Western Han. Their accumulation toward the end of the Western Han, the concomitant imperial collection of books from around the empire, and Liu Xiang's systematic account of the textual heritage all signal the beginning of a new era in the importance of the written text. It is precisely at this time that Liu Xin promoted the superiority of the *Zuo Tradition* over those of the *Gongyang* and *Guliang* on the grounds of an argument whose time had finally arrived: that the former text was written in "ancient script" while the latter two had only recently been transcribed from oral tradition.

2

From the Eastern Han through the
Western Jin (AD 25–317)

DAVID R. KNECHTGES

I. Eastern Han literature

Overview

The Eastern Han dynasty (25–220), also known as the Later Han, formally began on August 5, AD 25 with the accession of Liu Xiu (5 BC–AD 57) as emperor. His posthumous imperial title was Guangwu (r. 25–57). The Eastern Han lasted until November 24, 220, when the last Han emperor abdicated to Cao Pi (187–226), the founder of the Wei dynasty (220–265). Historians conventionally treat the Eastern Han as a restoration, for it was not technically a new dynasty but the return of imperial authority to a member of the Liu clan, which had lost its claim to the throne during the Xin dynasty (9–23) of Wang Mang (45 BC–AD 23). It took Liu Xiu about a decade to gain control over the entire realm. One of his main rivals was Gongsun Shu (d. 36), who set up a powerful regime in Shu (modern Sichuan). After much difficulty, Liu Xiu's army defeated Gongsun Shu in December of AD 36.

The Eastern Han established its capital at Luoyang. Although the Eastern Han ruling family had the same surname as the ruling family of the Western Han, their background was quite different. They represented the powerful landowning class, and much of their power was based on the support of prominent families, several of which had a strong interest in literature and scholarship. The first three reigns of the Eastern Han, from about 25 to 88, were a time of domestic stability and foreign expansion. The power of the clans of imperial consorts and the eunuchs was curtailed, and the Han was able to take advantage of a power vacuum in the north to regain control over parts of Central Asia.

After 88, the political climate began to deteriorate at the Han court. Members of the consort clans and eunuchs assumed positions of power to the point where by the middle of the second century AD the court was virtually dominated either by the consort clans or eunuchs, or in some reigns by both. This led to disaffection on the part of the scholar–official class. In 167, a group of scholar–officials, supported by large landowners, tried to oust the eunuchs from their privileged position. The result was a disastrous defeat for the scholar–officials. They were all dismissed from their positions, some were executed, and many were sent into exile. The large landowners continued the struggle against the eunuchs. In 184 the military strongman Yuan Shao (d. 202) led an attack on the eunuch stronghold in Luoyang that resulted in the massacre of over two thousand eunuchs.

The last twenty years of the second century saw an increasing number of popular uprisings. One important rebellion was led by a man who claimed inspiration from the Daoist thinker Laozi. The activities of this group, known as the Yellow Turbans, led to the formation of the Daoist church. The task of suppressing the uprisings fell to various generals who had taken advantage of the breakdown in imperial authority to establish local power bases. One of these men was a warlord from the northwest named Dong Zhuo (d. 192). In 189 Dong Zhuo seized Luoyang and put his own emperor on the throne. He then moved this emperor to Chang'an, which became the new capital. In 192, however, Dong Zhuo was assassinated by his own men.

Cao Cao (155–220), the son of a man who had been adopted by a eunuch, became the most famous and powerful of the current warlords. Beginning from a power base in the northeast, by 197 Cao Cao had established an independent kingdom. When Cao Cao died in 220, his son Cao Pi forced the Han emperor to cede the imperial throne to him, officially ending the Han dynasty.

During the Eastern Han writings began to circulate more widely. One reason for this new development was the increasing use of paper as writing material. Early in the Han and before, writing had been done on wood, bamboo, and silk. Wood and bamboo were bulky and cumbersome, and silk was expensive. As papermaking technology improved, it proved to be the most economical and easiest medium on which to write. By the second century AD, the eunuch Cai Lun (d. 121) had significantly improved the methods for making paper. In 105, while serving in the directorate for imperial manufactures, he devised a process of making paper from hemp, mulberry bark, and fishing nets. In the second century, we begin to see increased circulation of texts written on paper. Cui Yuan (d. 143) wrote in a letter to Ge Gong (ca 70–ca 130) that he was sending him a text in ten fascicles; however, because silk was too expensive, he copied it out on paper. There is also evidence of the circulation of paper letters. Zhang Huan (104–181) expressed delight at receiving a friend's letter written on paper. He says that he has read it so often, the paper has become tattered and the ink faded. Yan Du (ca 100–167), in a letter to Zhang Huan, thanks him for his letter written on four sheets of paper.

The increased use of paper does not mean that older media of textual transmission disappeared. In 87, a new edition of the *Observances of the Han* (*Han yi*) in 150 bamboo tablets was prepared. Numerous bamboo tablet texts, including administrative documents, medical prescriptions, calendars, personal letters, and portions of the Classics, have been found in Eastern Han tombs. Silk also continued to be used as a medium for writing in this period. The most famous examples are the two Eastern Han silk letters discovered by Aurel Stein at Dunhuang in 1908. Stone still was considered the most important medium for preserving authoritative versions of the Confucian Classics. In 175, Emperor Ling (r. 168–189) ordered the carving of the Classics on stone tablets that were erected east of the Lecture Hall of the imperial university. The project was completed in 183.

As in the Western Han, the imperial court was a major center of literary production. Much of the writing produced at the imperial court consisted of "bureaucratic" forms such as edicts and petitions. At the beginning of the Eastern Han, the petitions largely concerned the accession of Liu Xiu and issues relating to the establishment of the new regime in Luoyang. At the end of the dynasty, from November 21 to December 10, there was a flurry of documents including edicts, commands, letters, and petitions urging Cao Pi to accept the abdication of the last Han emperor. In the writings submitted at the beginning and end of the Eastern Han, the arguments were often based on the ideology of the prognostication texts (*chen wei*), which were extremely popular among the literati during the Eastern Han. The prognostication texts often claimed to be commentaries on the Classics. Thus they were called "weft texts" (*wei shu*) to distinguish them from "woof texts" (*jing*), which are the Confucian canonical works. Such works were produced throughout the Eastern Han.

The imperial court also produced some poetic writing. As in the Western Han, poets wrote *fu* to commemorate court occasions and imperial activities such as sacrifices, hunts, and imperial progresses. Poets at the court also composed "*fu* on things" (*yongwu fu*) to celebrate the presentation of tribute items from foreign states or gifts from prominent individuals. Other rhymed forms of writing that emanated from the court were the eulogy (*song*), inscription (*ming*), admonition (*zhen*), and dirge (*lei*).

Not all writing in the Eastern Han was the product of the court. Not only were there many writers who did not reside at the court, even men who spent most of their careers at the court composed major works that were not part of their court duties. Most of the *fu* composed by the leading *fu* writers of the Eastern Han were not composed at the imperial court. For example, Zhang Heng composed his famous "*Fu* on the Two Metropolises" as a private individual, and there is no evidence that he presented it to the court. The poetry (*shi*) and *yuefu* of the Eastern Han were also largely by private persons, and, except for a few ritual pieces, were not composed at the imperial court.

The Eastern Han saw the writing of much expository literature. Although some of the expository writings concerned official scholarly issues and were written for the court, most of the more original works were written by private individuals, many of whom lived in retirement. For example, Wang Chong (27–after AD 100) wrote his eighty-five-chapter *Discourses Weighed* (*Lun heng*) in the remote southeastern area of Shangyu (modern Zhejiang). His work was not well known until Cai Yong (133–192) and Wang Lang (d. 228) discovered it during their residence in the southeast during the late Eastern Han.

Throughout the Eastern Han, certain families distinguished themselves as scholars and writers. Although few of these families achieved high position or exercised great power at the imperial court, some of their writings were influential in their own time, or at least achieved some modicum of "immortality" in Chinese literary history.

The Ban family and its contemporaries

The most distinguished scholarly and literary family of the early Eastern Han was the Ban family. The Ban family had originally lived in the southern state of Chu, but at the end of the Qin period (ca 210 BC) a man named Ban Yi fled to the northern area of Loufan (modern Yanmen, Shanxi), where he made a large fortune raising horses, cattle, and goats. Ban Yi's descendant Ban Kuang (fl. 30 BC) served at the imperial court during the reign of Emperor Cheng (r. 32–7 BC). His daughter was Emperor Cheng's concubine, Favored Beauty Ban, who was an accomplished poet. Ban Kuang moved the Ban family residence to the capital area. Ban Kuang's sons were all scholars.

The most distinguished of Ban Kuang's sons was his second son, Ban You. He served in several court positions and then assisted Liu Xiang in editing the texts in the imperial library. Emperor Cheng even summoned him to lecture and recite texts for him, and as a reward the emperor gave him duplicate copies of works in the imperial library. Thus the Ban family owned one of the largest private libraries of the Han.

At the beginning of the Eastern Han, the most prominent member of the Ban family was Ban Biao (3–54), nephew of Ban You. Because Ban Biao moved the family home to Anling (northeast of modern Xianyang, Shaanxi), the

Eastern Han Bans are identified as natives of Anling. When Chang'an was under siege by the rebellion of the so-called Red Eyebrows in 25, Ban Biao fled to join the staff of Wei Ao (d. 33), who had established an independent regime in southeastern Gansu. Ban Biao remained in Wei Ao's service about four years, leaving in 29 after failing to dissuade Wei Ao from challenging Liu Xiu for the imperial throne. It was at this time that Ban Biao wrote his famous "Discourse on the Mandate of Kings" (Wang ming lun), in which he argues that accession to the imperial throne is governed by a succession cycle determined by Heaven. Although Ban Biao's essay is usually read as a defense of the Liu clan's legitimacy and is the first of a number of Eastern Han works praising the merits of the imperial house, it was also a political tract addressed to Wei Ao to dissuade him from his imperial ambitions. We clearly see that Wei Ao was the intended recipient in Ban Biao's repeated point that it would be folly for any man not blessed by Heaven to seek the imperial throne.

Although in his essay Ban Biao implicitly recognized Liu Xiu as the legitimate heir to the Han throne, he did not join the imperial court in Luoyang immediately, but went instead to serve on the staff of Dou Rong (16 BC–AD 62), a regional leader who held sway in western Gansu. From this time on, the Ban family had a close relationship with the Dou family. Around AD 36 Ban Biao accompanied Dou Rong to the imperial capital of Luoyang, and Emperor Guangwu, who was impressed with the petitions Ban had composed on behalf of Dou, appointed him prefect of Xu (modern Xuzhou, Jiangsu). He did not stay in this position long, however, and soon resigned on grounds of illness. Ban Biao then turned his attention to scholarship, especially history. He wrote "several tens of fascicles" of a history that served as a basis for his son Ban Gu's *History of the [Former] Han* (*Han shu*). After serving briefly in minor posts, Ban Biao died in 54.

Ban Biao is best known for his "*Fu* on a Northward Journey" (Bei zheng fu). He wrote it in 25, while he was traveling to Tianshui from Chang'an. The piece is clearly inspired by Liu Xin's *fu* on the travel theme, "*Fu* on Obtaining My First Emolument" (Sui chu fu). There are several lines in Ban Biao's piece that are clearly derived from Liu Xin's *fu*. This is a good example of the increased circulation of writings that is evident in this period.

"*Fu* on a Northward Journey" is the first of a number of poetic travelogues written in the Eastern Han. In this piece Ban Biao gives an account of his visit to actual sites that he viewed on his journey to Tianshui. Most of the sites are historical places that invoke memories of the past, not only famous historical figures and places, but also the history of the Ban family. At one point Ban Biao tells of making a detour to a place named Niyang. This would have taken him near the area of Loufan, where his ancestor Ban Yi had settled. Upon arriving here, Ban Biao laments that his family's ancestral temple is in disrepair, for members of the Ban family no longer reside here.

Ban Biao's oldest son was Ban Gu (32–92), the principal compiler of the *History of the Han*. Ban Gu's twin brother Ban Chao (32–102) was a famous military man and Central Asian explorer, and his younger sister Ban Zhao (ca 49–ca 120) was one of the most distinguished female scholars in Chinese history. Aged twenty-two when his father died in AD 54, Ban Gu returned to the family home in Anling and spent a period pondering what path in life he should follow. As a means of resolving his dilemma, he wrote a long poem titled "*Fu* on Communicating with the Hidden" (You tong fu). This long and complex piece is written throughout in *sao*-style prosody and borrows extensively from the Qu Yuan poems in the *Verses of Chu*. Like his father, Ban Gu was concerned about his family legacy. At the beginning of the *fu*, he gives a brief history of the family, recounting their origins in the south and their move to the north at the end of the Qin period. He then tells of his father's flight from the capital at the time of the fall of the usurper Wang Mang. He even refers to Ban Biao's account of these events in his "*Fu* on the Northward Journey."

After lamenting his lack of accomplishment (he had yet to undertake an official career), Ban Gu then relates his encounter with what he calls "the hidden men." The hidden men are the spirits who offer him advice and guidance. Ban Gu's contact with them does not involve the conventional imaginary journey through the heavens, but a dream journey to a mountain where he gazes upon their spectral forms. The role of the spirits, however, is the same as in Qu Yuan's "Encountering Sorrow": they dispense counsel to the troubled poet. Ban Gu eventually receives advice from an oracle divined by none other than the Yellow Emperor. In the epilogue he quotes Confucius and Mencius to support his belief that the moral man "must keep himself intact," "adopt what is right," and, above all, not die an early death from grief and excessive self-pity.

The "*Fu* on Communicating with the Hidden" is a notable example of the *fu* used for a new purpose, in which the poet in effect writes a philosophical essay in rhyme. Rather than simply venting frustration, Ban Gu uses his *fu* to explore the question of how the moral man should view fate and fortune. In typical *fu* fashion, he strings together a series of exempla and allusions, all of which make the point that fortune, whether good or bad, is constantly changing, and that whatever fate decrees is inevitable. Given this situation, the moral man must all the more adhere to his principles, and by virtue of the example of his adherence to them, he can make his influence felt, perhaps not in his own time, but in later ages.

Ban Gu did not immediately embark on an official career, but remained at home in Anling engaging in scholarly pursuits, primarily the task of completing his father's sequel to Sima Qian's *Records of the Historian*. As he began his work, someone reported to Emperor Ming (r. 58–75) that Ban Gu was "privately revising the national history." The main concern of the court was probably what kind of an account Ban Gu would write about the fall of the Western Han and the rise of the Eastern Han. The emperor had Ban Gu arrested and the family library confiscated. His brother Ban Chao interceded on his behalf, and the emperor ordered Ban Gu released. In the same year Ban Gu was assigned to the Magnolia Terrace to compile the annals of the first Eastern Han emperor, Guangwu, along with biographies of important figures of that era. In 64, Ban was promoted to the rank of gentleman and put in charge of collating books in the imperial collection. The emperor was so impressed with the quality of Ban Gu's scholarship that in 66 he granted him permission to resume compilation of his Western Han history, on which he worked for over twenty-five years until his death in AD 92.

During Emperor Ming's reign, in addition to compiling his history, Ban Gu continued to write *fu*. It was probably during this period that he wrote his longest and most famous *fu*, "*Fu* on the Two Capitals" (Liang du fu). The two capitals of the title are the Han metropolises of Chang'an and Luoyang. Chang'an, the western capital, was the capital of the Western Han. Luoyang, the eastern capital, was the capital established by Emperor Guangwu, who reconstructed the old Southern Palace that remained from the Western Han. Guangwu's successor, Emperor Ming, continued to expand the palace complex, and between 60 and 65 the Northern Palace was reconstructed. It was probably during this period that Ban Gu composed "*Fu* on the Two Capitals."

Ban Gu considered his *fu* important enough to write a preface in which he presents his views on the history of the *fu* and its proper function. In the first line of the preface, Ban asserts that the *fu* was a genre or "outflow" of the *Classic of Poetry*. Ban Gu probably derives his definition of *fu* from the exegetical tradition that placed *fu* among the six principles of the *Classic of Poetry*. *Fu* of the six principles is, however, not the name of a literary genre, but designates a technique of recitation or composition that involves direct exposition unencumbered by tropes or rhetorical flourishes. Ban Gu extends this sense of *fu* to signify a putative genre of the *Classic of Poetry*. By Ban Gu's time there was no clear distinction between *fu* as a poetic principle and *fu* as a literary form, and in fact the features of the *fu* form itself very likely led Han exegetes to define *fu* of the poetic principles as direct exposition.

Ban Gu does not stress *fu* in the sense of exposition, but rather links it with one of the true genres of the *Classic of Poetry*, the "Hymns" (*song*). In one section of the preface, Ban gives a brief history of the genre, and in his account he stresses that during the Western Han, when the *fu* began to flourish, it was primarily a court-centered activity, particularly during the reign of Emperor Wu, who appointed officials to office for their writing skills. Ban Gu mentions two functions that the *fu* had at the imperial court: "Sometimes it was for the purpose of expressing feelings of the emperor's subjects and conveying subtle criticism and advice, and other times it was for the purpose of proclaiming the ruler's virtue and demonstrating the utmost loyalty and filial obedience." Although Ban Gu acknowledges that the *fu* had two functions – one eulogistic, and the other suasive – he strongly emphasizes that the primary function of the form was to praise the grand accomplishments of the ruler.

Ban Gu considered the *fu* primarily a praise genre whose primary function was to celebrate the glory and power of the Han empire. It must be remembered that the Eastern Han restoration was only slightly over a generation old when Ban Gu wrote the "*Fu* on the Two Capitals," and undoubtedly he felt an obligation to write a panegyric to commemorate this grand achievement. Ban Gu may have had another, more immediate purpose of writing a rebuttal to an earlier *fu* composed at the beginning of the Eastern Han by Du Du (d. after 78), "*Fu* Discoursing on the Capital" (Lun du fu). Du Du, who was a native of the Chang'an area, presented this piece to Emperor Guangwu in 42 to persuade him to move the capital from Luoyang back to Chang'an. Du Du's *fu* consists almost exclusively of argumentative rhetoric and is structured around a debate between Du and a guest. Although Du Du declares in his preface, which is directly addressed to the emperor, that the proper place for the capital is Chang'an, not Luoyang, he pretends to champion the choice of Luoyang. The language he uses, however, clearly betrays his bias in favor of Chang'an. In the preface he refers to Luoyang as an area of "poor and barren soil." In the body of the poem, he calls Luoyang "stagnant water in a well" and "that mud puddle Luo City." Even in the portion of the *fu* where he pretends to present the case in favor of Luoyang, he stresses the superiority of Yongzhou, the area in which Chang'an is located.

Ban Gu must have been aware of Du Du's *fu*, for in the preface he refers to "aged men from the western territory," who, "hoping for a kind glance from the emperor, lavishly praise the old institutions of Chang'an and hold that Luoyang is a shabby place." He then declares that he has written the "*Fu* on the Two Capitals" in order "to present an exhaustive account of the things that dazzle and daze the Chang'an multitudes and rebut them by means of the patterns and institutions of the present."

Like Du Du, Ban Gu structures his *fu* around a debate between a guest, who is the protagonist speaking on behalf of the Western Capital, and a host, who argues the case for Luoyang. The Chang'an section, which is titled "*Fu on the Western Capital*," contains a lavish account of Chang'an: its strategic position near the Hangu Pass; its past prosperity; the imperial palace complex, including the women's apartments, office buildings, libraries, courtyards, and gardens with all of their supernatural appurtenances; and the grand spectacle of the imperial hunt.

The second section of the *fu*, titled "*Fu on the Eastern Capital*," describes Luoyang in the Eastern Han period. The spokesman for Luoyang, the Eastern Capital host, begins by telling of the founding of the Eastern Han by the Sage Emperor, Guangwu. The account effusively praises the founder's great deeds, which rival the accomplishments of the greatest rulers of the past, including the founders of the Shang and Zhou. Ban Gu follows this panegyric to Guangwu with a tribute to Guangwu's successor, Emperor Ming. Ban especially praises him for his revival of classical ritual principles, which he applied to the reconstruction of the capital. At the appropriate seasons, the emperor holds a ritual hunt for the purpose of "practicing maneuvers," and everything is done according to the classical ritual norms. Unlike his Western Han counterpart, the Eastern Han emperor exalts frugality and moderation.

The Western Capital guest is completely overwhelmed by this eloquent presentation of the ethical and ritual superiority of Luoyang over Chang'an. As the guest is about to leave, the host tells him he will instruct him with five poems. The guest then reads the poems and declares: "Excellent, indeed, these poems! Their principles are more correct than those of Yang Xiong. Their content is more real than that of Sima Xiangru."

Three of the five poems are in four-syllable lines and praise the ritual buildings Bright Hall, Circular Moat, and Divine Tower. Emperor Guangwu had the Bright Hall constructed in 56, approximately a kilometer from the main southern gate of the capital. In 59 Emperor Ming performed a sacrifice to the Five Lords here. The Circular Moat, also constructed in 56, was a ritual hall located about a half kilometer east of the Bright Hall. In 59, Emperor Ming performed the Great Archery and Entertaining the Aged ceremonies here. The Divine Tower, located slightly south of the Bright Hall, served as the imperial observatory from which the stars, moon, sun, clouds, and "ethers" were watched. The construction of these ritual buildings was strongly supported by most scholar–officials at this time.

The two sections of the *"Fu* on the Two Capitals" represent two distinct styles and cultural values. The *"Fu* on the Western Capital," with all of its effusive ornamental rhetoric, is typical of the writing associated with the Western Han *fu* epideictic tradition beginning with Sima Xiangru and Mei Sheng. *"Fu* on the Eastern Capital," which is written in much plainer language that in many cases borrows from the Classics of *Documents*, *Poetry*, and the *Rites*, represents a moderate style consistent with canonical norms. Ban Gu must have been familiar with Yang Xiong's severe criticism of the *fu* as an effective didactic instrument, and he clearly shared Yang's view that the primary function of literature was moral suasion. Ban Gu's use of the grand, ornamental style in the Chang'an section is appropriate for the portion of the *fu* that celebrates the age in which the epideictic rhapsody flourished, while the classical diction and straightforward style in the Luoyang portion is better suited to the age of the restoration that Ban Gu portrays as the embodiment of propriety and moderation. Unlike the court rhapsodies of Sima Xiangru and Yang Xiong, there is no doubt at the end of the poem what Ban Gu's message is. He clearly believes that the Eastern Han is morally and culturally superior to the Western Han, and one cannot detect in his account of Luoyang any subtle moral reprimands to the emperor; on the contrary, there are only words of praise. He utterly jubilates over the devotion to ritual of the Eastern Han emperors – particularly Emperor Ming, to whom he presented the piece.

During the reign of Emperor Ming's successor, Emperor Zhang (r. 75–88), Ban Gu received more honor and acclaim at the imperial court. In approximately 78, Emperor Zhang promoted Ban Gu to marshal of the Black Warrior Gate, a position with more prestige and a higher salary (a thousand bushels of grain). In 79 the emperor assigned Ban Gu the task of editing the proceedings of an important scholarly conference on the Classics held in the White Tiger Hall. Although some scholars question the attribution, Ban Gu has often been credited with a summary of the discussions entitled *Comprehensive Discussions in the White Tiger Hall* (*Bohu tong yi*).

Serving with Ban Gu at the court at this time was Fu Yi (ca 47–92), who also came from the capital district. Emperor Zhang was an ardent devotee of literature, and Ban Gu and Fu Yi often composed pieces upon imperial command. Excerpts from two eulogies Ban Gu wrote for imperial inspection tours to the south and east have been preserved. One court poem Fu Yi composed during this period was a ten-part "Eulogy to Xianzong" (*Xianzong song*) that praises the achievements of Emperor Ming, who had died in 75.

Although only a few lines of the piece survive, judging from its title it must have been similar to the eulogistic odes that conclude Ban Gu's "*Fu* on the Two Capitals."

Ban Gu spent his final years on the staff of Dou Xian (d. 92), who was an elder brother of Emperor Zhang's empress. Dou Xian was the great-grandson of Dou Rong, whom Ban Gu's father Ban Biao had served before he went to the imperial court at the beginning of the Eastern Han. During the time of the Dou family's ascendancy, there was a literary salon sponsored by Dou Xian. In AD 88 Dou Xian led a successful expedition against the Northern Xiongnu, and as a result his influence increased considerably; his power to recommend men for official appointments in particular contributed to a growing fear of him among court officials. Distinguished writers such as Ban Gu, Fu Yi, and Cui Yin (30?–92) served on his staff. Dou placed them in charge of "literature" and the literary pieces by members of Dou Xian's entourage reputedly were "the best of the age." The compositions that members of Dou Xian's salon composed included some *fu*. What survives mainly consists of praise poems for Dou Xian's military achievements.

Although Dou Xian received much honor and acclaim for another successful Xiongnu expedition, in 92 Emperor He (r. 89–106), suspecting him of plotting a revolt against the throne, had him arrested and sent to his estate, where he was forced to commit suicide. As Dou Xian's supporter, Ban Gu was dismissed from office. The prefect of Luoyang, who had harbored a grudge against Ban Gu, ordered his arrest. Ban Gu died in his sixty-first year in the capital's prison.

The work for which Ban Gu is best known is *History of the Han*. The work actually begins before the formal founding of the Han. The earliest events it records concern the fall of the Qin and the struggle between Liu Bang and Xiang Yu (ca 209 BC). It ends with the fall of Wang Mang (AD 23). One of the reasons Ban Biao decided to write his sequel to the *Records of the Historian* is because he had reservations about Sima Qian's history. For example, he faulted Sima Qian for quoting selectively from the Classics, commentaries, and the philosophers. Although Ban Biao gave credit to Sima Qian for his vast knowledge, he criticized his judgments as superficial, and accused him of favoring Huang-Lao thought, while denigrating the Five Classics. Ban Biao also faulted Sima Qian for glorifying profiteers in the chapter on "money-makers" and men who took the law into their own hands in the section on "knights-errant."

Ban Biao took issue as well with some of the formal features of the *Records of the Historian*. He considered it wrong of Sima Qian to have elevated Xiang

Yu and Chen She to the status of rulers by putting their accounts in a "basic annal," while including members of the Han imperial family such as the kings of Huainan and Hengshan in the biographies section. In his sequel Ban Biao decided to eliminate the section on hereditary houses and include only annals and biographies.

The *History of the Han* consists of one hundred chapters. It is divided into twelve annals (one for each of the Western Han emperors); eight tables, including one on the Han bureaucracy and genealogical tables of various noble houses; ten monographs on such subjects as rites, music, the calendar, geography, economy, and bibliography; and seventy biographies and accounts. How much of Ban Biao's history Ban Gu incorporated in the *History of the Han* is difficult to determine. Certain chapters, such as the "Annals of Emperor Yuan" and "Annals of Emperor Cheng," have been credited to Ban Biao. The appraisals at the end of some of the biographies also are attributed to Ban Biao. At the time of Ban Gu's death in 92, he had not completed the tables and the "Monograph on Astronomy." His younger sister Ban Zhao finished compiling them with the aid of Ma Xu, who was an expert in mathematics.

The *History of the Han* is a rich source for the study of Han history and literature. The literal meaning of the book is "writings of the Han," and in this sense the title reflects the archival quality of the work, for much of it consists of quotations, some running to many thousands of characters, from various types of writing, including imperial edicts, petitions to the court, essays, *fu*, eulogies, and even poems. One scholar has counted 1,170 Western Han works that are contained in the *History of the Han*. In this respect, the *History of the Han* provides more examples of Western Han writing than does the *Records of the Historian*. In certain biographies, the *History of the Han* includes texts of writings that were excluded from the parallel biography in the *Records of the Historian*. For example, in the biographies of Jia Yi and Dong Zhongshu, the *History of the Han* inserts texts of petitions that these two important thinkers presented to the court on political and philosophical matters. These writings are excluded from the *Records of the Historian*.

For the period before Emperor Wu, the conventional view is that the *History of the Han* faithfully copies the *Records of the Historian* account. However, one can find a number of significant additions that Ban Gu and his co-compilers made to the *Records of the Historian*. For example, both the *Records of the Historian* and *History of the Han* have chapters devoted to Emperor Gaozu's minister Xiao He (Sima Qian gave him an account in the Hereditary Houses section, while Ban Gu put it in the Biographies). The *History of the Han* version is the same as that of the *Records of the Historian*, except at the point at which Liu

Bang captures the Qin capital of Xianyang. Although there was an agreement that whoever entered the Hangu Pass first would be named king of Qin, Xiang Yu reneged on the agreement and assigned Liu Bang to the remote area of Ba and Shu, naming him king of Han. The *Records of the Historian* does not record Liu Bang's reaction to this insult. However, the biography of Xiao He in the *History of the Han* contains a long passage that recounts Liu Bang's bursting into anger, only to be calmed down by Xiao He, who advised him not to take on the superior force of Xiang Yu at this time, but rather use the resources of the Ba and Shu area to strengthen his position to launch a campaign against Xiang Yu at a later time.

For the reign of Emperor Wu, Ban Gu provides much more detailed accounts than Sima Qian. Although Ban Gu is generally regarded as the more sober historian, some of his accounts of Emperor Wu's reign read more like romance than history. For example, Ban Gu includes long biographies of Li Ling (d. 74 BC) and Su Wu (d. 60 BC), who were held prisoner by the Xiongnu. Li Ling receives little mention in the *Records of the Historian*, and Su Wu is not mentioned at all. Ban Gu turns their story into a fully fledged romance. Ban Gu does the same with the account of Emperor Wu's favorite concubine, Lady Li. He includes a dramatic episode after her death in which a magician conjures up her spirit. Even the account of the poet Sima Xiangru, details of which are virtually the same in both *Records of the Historian* and *History of the Han*, may represent a Sima Xiangru romance that had gradually developed before Ban Gu's time. Several scholars have argued in fact that the *History of the Han* version of Sima Xiangru's biography is earlier than the *Records of the Historian* version.

Ban Gu's younger sister, Ban Zhao, was one of the leading writers and scholars of the reigns of Emperor He and Emperor An (r. 107–125). Although Ban Gu had been executed as a member of the Dou Xian faction, in 92 Emperor He summoned Ban Zhao to the Eastern Institute, where she was put in charge of completing her elder brother's history of the Former Han. He also summoned her to the palace to serve as tutor to the empress and the imperial concubines. At the court she was called Cao Dagu or "Auntie Cao." Ban Zhao was on intimate terms with Empress Dowager Deng (81–121), who dominated the court during much of the Emperor He and Emperor An reigns.

Another of Ban Zhao's functions was to write *fu* on unusual objects that were presented to the emperor. Poems that describe objects are known in Chinese as *yongwu* (poems or *fu* "on things"). They include pieces on birds, animals, plants, stones, household articles, buildings, musical instruments, even insects. Around the year 101 Ban Zhao composed a *fu* on a large bird, probably a Parthian ostrich, that her brother Ban Chao had brought to the court from Central Asia. Titled *"Fu on the Great Bird"* (Da que fu), this piece is a good example of a "poem on things" written under imperial auspices. Unlike the elaborate epideictic court pieces of the Former Han, Ban Zhao's text is written in simple, straightforward language, and is pure eulogy that praises both this marvelous bird from the west and the Han emperor, whose rule is so virtuous and proper that he is rewarded with marvelous tribute from afar.

Ban Zhao has two other *fu* on objects, both of which survive in fragments: *"Fu on the Cicada"* (Chan fu) and *"Fu on the Needle and Thread"* (Zhen lü fu). The extant excerpts from the *"Fu on the Cicada"* show this to be a typical poem "on things" that presents the various attributes of the cicada: its shrill chirping, sipping of dew, and swift metamorphosis. In her *"Fu on the Needle and Thread"* Ban Zhao virtually personifies the needle and thread, attributing to them moral virtues: the needle is "true and straight" and "pierces and penetrates." Together with the thread, its traces are "broad and wide" as it "mends flaws."

In 95 Ban Zhao's son Cao Cheng received his first official position, that of chief of Changyuan prefecture (modern Changyuan, Henan) in Chenliu commandery. Ban Zhao accompanied her son to his post, and to record her 530-*li* journey from Luoyang to Changyuan she wrote a poetic travelogue, *"Fu on an Eastward Journey"* (Dong zheng fu). *"Fu on an Eastward Journey"* contains a vivid account of the places through which Ban Zhao and her son passed. Ban Zhao's visit to historic places evokes memories of the past. For example, not far from Changyuan, she saw the ruins of Pucheng and recalled that this was where Confucius' disciple Zi Lu had served as an official. Ban Zhao's visit to the tomb of Qu Boyu, a famous Wei official whom Confucius admired, led her to reflect on the importance of maintaining a reputation for virtue. Ban Zhao's *fu* is more than a travelogue. It also is full of advice for her son on his official career. Ban Zhao even seems to equate the journey with her son's career. In one place she refers to the road in a double sense: first, as the road actually traveled, and second, as a metaphor for the proper path her son should follow through life. She advises him that he should keep to the "great way" and not take byways and shortcuts. The final lines of the *fu*, which stress the virtues of caution, diligence, humility, quietude, and elimination of desire, appear to be Ban Zhao's maternal advice for her son as he is about to enter official service: he should be circumspect, hardworking, modest, tranquil, and moderate in his desires.

The Cui family

Another distinguished literary family of the Eastern Han was the Cui. Their ancestral home was Anping in Zhuo commandery (modern Anping, Hebei), and they were the ancestors of the famous Cui clan of Boling that became prominent in the Six Dynasties and the Tang. The first known literary man among the Cui clan is Cui Zhuan (fl. ca AD 20), a famous scholar who reluctantly served under Wang Mang. When Liu Xiu first took the throne, Cui Zhuan was recommended for a position but declined on the grounds that he was ashamed of his former service with Wang Mang. He then became a recluse scholar, and compiled a large work on the *Classic of Changes*. Cui Zhuan composed a short *fu* titled "Consoling My Feelings" (Wei zhi fu) in which he expresses regret that he had served Wang Mang against his will.

Cui Zhuan's grandson Cui Yin (30?–92) was a prominent writer and scholar during the reigns of Emperor Ming and Emperor Zhang. He studied at the Imperial Academy at the same time (ca 52) as Ban Gu and Fu Yi. Rather than taking an official position, however, Cui Yin devoted himself to the study of ancient texts. When one of his contemporaries ridiculed him for his failure to pursue an official career in about AD 59, he composed "Expressing My Purpose" (Da zhi) in imitation of Yang Xiong's "Justification against Ridicule." Like Yang Xiong's piece, "Expressing My Purpose" is constructed as a dialogue between the anonymous critic and himself. To persuade Cui Yin that official service is the proper course, the critic enumerates the glorious accomplishments of Emperor Ming, notably his visit to the Circular Moat where he promotes classical learning and honors worthy officials. Cui Yin follows with a long reply in which he argues that the present age is so peaceful, even men with the abilities of the great statesmen and strategists of the past are not useful to the state. He declares that he is not opposed to accepting official appointment. It is simply that the time and conditions are not right for him to serve.

If Cui Yin did not wish to accept a formal post at the court, this did not prevent him from composing literary works for the court. Thus, when Dou Rong died in 62, Cui Yin composed a poem lamenting his death. Ban Gu composed a eulogy for the same occasion. In the year 75 Cui wrote a eulogy upon the death of Emperor Ming. Cui Yin continued to write praise pieces under imperial auspices. Between 84 and 86, Emperor Zhang undertook four imperial progresses to each of the four directions, and Cui Yin composed long eulogies celebrating each of these affairs, also praising the accomplishments of the early Eastern Han rulers.

Admiring Cui Yin's literary skill, Emperor Zhang recommended him to Dou Xian, who soon accepted him as a member of his large entourage. Cui Yin wrote several letters to Dou Xian. In one of them he admonishes him for his arrogance and misuse of his status as elder brother of the Empress Dowager Dou. He even bluntly warns him about the consequences of his arrogant behavior: "After the founding of the Han down to the reigns of Emperor Ai and Emperor Ping, there have been twenty consort families, but only four were able to preserve their clans and keep themselves intact." After receiving numerous reprimands of this sort, Dou Xian could no longer tolerate Cui Yin and had him appointed as a magistrate in the remote outpost of Changcen, which is located in modern Korea. Rather than take up a position in such an isolated place, Cui Yin returned home and died there in 92.

Cui Yin wrote a *fu* on the imperial capital titled "Returning to the Capital" (Fan du fu). In his preface Cui Yin says that he wrote the piece to rebut the proponents of Chang'an who opposed the choice of Luoyang as capital. Like Ban Gu, Cui Yin considered the Eastern Han capital superior to Chang'an not because of its geographic location, but because of the moral qualities fostered by its rulers. Thus he praises Emperor Guangwu for following the customs of the ancient sage rulers and for his devotion to ritual, including the establishment of the three ritual sites, the Bright Hall, Circular Moat, and Numinous Tower.

Du Du and Feng Yan

Not all members of prominent families had successful careers at the early Eastern Han imperial court. There are two examples of men who were descendants of prominent families from the capital district of Chang'an who were distinguished writers but never were able to gain court acceptance: Du Du (ca 20–78) and Feng Yan (ca 20 BC–ca AD 60).

Du Du was from the Du clan of Duling (northeast of modern Chang'an county, Shaanxi). His great-great-grandfather was the Former Han minister Du Yanian (d. 53 BC). Du Yanian was the first to establish the home of the Du clan in Duling. Du Du showed vast learning already in his youth, but because he did not observe the proper niceties of etiquette, the people of his home area did not treat him with respect. Du Du then was imprisoned for offending a local official. The general Wu Han had just died (in 44), and Emperor Guangwu issued an edict inviting scholars to compose elegies for him. Composed from prison, Du Du's elegy so impressed the emperor that he issued Du Du a pardon. Shortly after his release Du Du composed the "*Fu* Discussing the Capital." A few years later Du Du served as a commandery instructor in the capital area. Because he suffered from an eye ailment, however, he did not enter the capital for over twenty years.

Frustrated because he had failed to obtain distinction as an official, Du Du then decided to pursue a military career. Du Du's younger sister was married to a member of the powerful Ma family, and through her influence Du Du was able to obtain a position with Ma Fang (d. 101), who was undertaking an expedition against the Qiang. Du Du died in battle at Yegushan (northwest of modern Qingyang, Gansu) in 78.

According to Du Du's biography in the *History of the Later Han*, he had written eighteen literary pieces in various genres, including *fu*, dirges, laments, letters, an "admonition for daughters," and miscellaneous prose. The only complete extant *fu* is "*Fu* Discussing the Capital." There are fragments of four other *fu*. The most interesting of these is "*Fu* on Shouyang Mountain" (Shouyang shan fu). This is a dialogue between Du Du and the ancient recluses Bo Yi and Shu Qi. When King Wu of Zhou conquered the Yin, they refused to serve the Zhou and went into reclusion on Mount Shouyang. Du Du tells of his encounter with the two recluses, who explain that they had followed King Wu's father King Wen, but could not accept King Wu because he used force of arms to conquer the Yin. One wonders whether this is a subtle statement of Du Du's disaffection with the Eastern Han dynastic founder, Emperor Guangwu, who did not reward Du Du with the honors and positions that someone from his distinguished family deserved.

Feng Yan also was a native of Duling. His remote ancestors had once lived in Shangdang (near modern Changzhi in southeastern Shanxi). Feng Yan's great-grandfather was Feng Fengshi (d. ca 39), a high court official during the later Western Han. It was he who moved the family home to Duling. In his youth, Feng Yan was much admired for his erudition. When Emperor Guangwu took the throne in 25, Feng waited two years before seeking to join his court, as a result of which Guangwu and some of his advisers considered Feng untrustworthy. Except for a one-year term as prefect in the northeast in 28, Feng Yan did not hold office until AD 43, when through the influence of two brothers of Guangwu's Empress Yin, he obtained the position of retainer to the metropolitan commandant.

In 52 Emperor Guangwu decided to arrest and even put to death the retainers of powerful clans who resided in the Chang'an area. Feng Yan barely escaped punishment but was forced to return home to Duling, where he shunned contact with friends and relatives for several years. Feng Yan spent the remainder of his years living in retirement in the area of Xinfeng (northeast of modern Lintong, Shaanxi). Feng Yan did not fare any better when Emperor

Ming took the throne in 58, for many people criticized Feng's writing as being more form than substance. He continued to remain at home in retirement, finally dying in poverty in around AD 60. The compiler of the *History of the Later Han* knew of some fifty works by Feng Yan in various genres, including *fu*, dirges, inscriptions, discourses, notes, and even an autobiography. He also mentions three essays, none of which survives.

Feng Yan's most famous piece is a long *fu* titled "*Fu* on Making Clear My Aim" (Xian zhi fu), one of the earliest autobiographical *fu*. Feng Yan wrote this piece late in life after he had retired to Xinfeng. He precedes the *fu* with what is called a "disquisition on self" that is the equivalent of a preface, though partially in rhyme. In the preface, Feng Yan complains that he had early in his career formulated various stratagems and plans, but no one had ever heeded them. As a consequence he was never able to realize his ambitions and now must live in extreme poverty. He tells of taking up residence in Xinfeng, from which he had a clear view of the old Western Han capital of Chang'an. Feng Yan then reflects on his family history and laments that the ancestral tombs, presumably meaning those in the old family home of Shangdang, are no longer tended. Regretting that in his old age he has no achievement or merit, he declares his intention to make a living raising crops and livestock. At the end of the preface, Feng states that he has written a *fu* in which he recounts his travels. The travel is of two kinds, first to actual places that he visits near his new home and to the west near his ancestral home of Shangdang, and then an imaginary journey where he encounters historical sites and figures from the past. Thus Feng Yan combines the older form of the imaginary journey with the newer poetic travelogue that we have seen in the *fu* of Liu Xin, Ban Biao, and Ban Zhao.

The *fu* portion is a long piece written in *sao*-style meter with heavy borrowing from the poems in the *Verses of Chu*. In addition to the travel theme, one of the striking features of the piece is Feng Yan's complaint about the decline of his once distinguished family. In the opening section he laments that he has experienced nothing but sorrow and misery his entire life, and he fears he will die without achieving fame. As Feng journeys further to the west, he treks through the Taihang Mountains of Shanxi. When he comes to Hukou, which was a pass located near his ancestral home of Shangdang, he laments that the family graves there have long gone untended. There are similar lines in Ban Biao's "Northward Journey."

Feng Yan then begins a long account of his new form of livelihood, farming. He compares himself with such legendary "farmers" as the Divine Husbandman, the reputed inventor of the plowshare and plow handle, and Lord Millet, who is credited with determining suitable places to plant millet and soy beans. When he gazes out from the Long Mountains that stretch from Shaanxi to Gansu, he can see the entire expanse of the ancient states of Qin and Jin. He is then reminded of two of his ancestors who lived in this area during the Warring States and Qin periods.

Up to this point, Feng Yan gives an account of his actual journey. However, in the next section his roaming is purely in the realm of the imagination. In four lines he makes a complete circuit of the world, followed by an account of his visit to sites associated with famous figures of the past. Although he heaps praise on such exemplary men, Feng expresses contempt for the schemers and persuaders of the Warring States period. Then, as the day turns to dusk, he consults two recluses, one of whom is none other than Shu Qi, the recluse with whom Du Du had an imaginary dialogue in his *"Fu on Shouyang Mountain."* After consulting a few more recluses, Feng Yan decides to return home. In the final section of the *fu* is one of the earliest descriptions of the delights of living in reclusion in the countryside, a theme that becomes more common after the Han.

Huan Tan and Wang Chong

In the early Eastern Han we begin to see the emergence of a number of independent, highly critical thinkers, who began to question traditional assumptions, including those of the dominant Confucian school. The first of these was Huan Tan (23 BC–AD 56, alternatively ca 43 BC–AD 28, or 40 BC–AD 31). Huan Tan's native place was Xiang County in Pei commandery (modern Huaibei City, Anhui), but he may have been born near the Western Han capital of Chang'an, where his father served at the imperial court during the reign of Emperor Cheng (r. 32–7 BC). Huan Tan's father was a specialist in music and served during the reign of Emperor Cheng as director of imperial music. Huan Tan inherited his father's expertise in music and served in the music office through the end of the Western Han and in the reign of Wang Mang. Huan Tan probably helped compose the ceremonial court music commissioned by Wang Mang. During this time he became a good friend of Yang Xiong. Already at this time Huan Tan was known for his outspokenness and his habit of criticizing other scholars.

When Emperor Guangwu established the Eastern Han, his grand minister of works Song Hong recommended Huan Tan for a position at the court. He actually praised Huan as the equal of Yang Xiong, Liu Xiang, and Liu Xin. However, given his age and former high status, his positions were rather low: gentleman consultant and servitor in the palace.

Huan Tan did not shrink from giving Emperor Guangwu advice. Emperor Guangwu justified his legitimacy partially based on what were called *chen*, or prognostication texts, that contained oracular statements predicting the rise of a ruler who had exactly the same name and family background as Emperor Guangwu. Huan Tan was very much opposed to the prognostication texts, and he presented Emperor Guangwu with a petition, urging him to ban them on the grounds that they were "strange and fabulous" reports concocted by experts in the occult arts to deceive the emperor. According to Huan Tan, this was contrary to principles of the Five Classics. Huan Tan made the same argument sometime later, perhaps in the year 28, when Emperor Guangwu summoned Huan Tan to the court to question him about his views on the prognostication texts. This reply was tantamount to questioning the basis for Guangwu's legitimacy as emperor. Furious at this point, Emperor Guangwu accused Huan Tan of "criticizing the sages" and ordered him to be executed. Only after Huan Tan had kowtowed until the blood flowed from his forehead was he pardoned. After this, Huan Tan never returned to the court. He died at more than seventy years of age, en route to his position as assistant administrator of Lu'an (modern Lu'an City, Anhui).

Huan Tan compiled a collection of essays titled *New Discourses* (*Xin lun*). The original text, which Huan Tan presented to Emperor Guangwu, consisted of twenty-nine sections. One chapter, however, titled "Way of the Zither," was not complete, and Emperor Zhang (r. 76–88) ordered Ban Gu to complete it. The original *New Discourses* had been lost by the time of the Song period. The extant versions are reconstructions.

If Huan Tan presented the *New Discourses* to Emperor Guangwu, he must have done so before he fell out of favor for objecting to the prognostication texts. From the fragments of his treatise, we can see that Huan Tan maintained the same critical view of conventional ideas and beliefs that he exhibited in his criticism of the prognostication texts. The titles of some of the chapters indicate his critical and skeptical attitude: "Observing Evidence," "Reprimanding Wrong," "Awakening Insight," "Correcting the Classics," and "Discerning Error." Although the work is highly fragmentary, one can find numerous statements by Huan Tan questioning the existence of immortals, supernatural occurrences, magic, and alchemy.

Huan Tan also was strongly interested in literature, and there is one chapter devoted to the *fu*: "Discussing the *Fu*." Regrettably, there are only four short fragments from this section extant. The *New Discourses* fragments have somewhat more to say about music, a field in which Huan Tan was an acknowledged expert. Unlike his friend Yang Xiong, Huan Tan showed a preference for the "music of Zheng"; that is, the new popular music as opposed to the older classical form. Among the fragments is a short passage in which Yang Xiong reprimands Huan Tan for his interest in the new music. Huan Tan clearly held Yang Xiong in high regard, even ranking Yang's *Great Mystery* as the equal of the Five Classics.

Because the *New Discourses* exists only in fragments, there are few long essays in the reconstructed text. There is, however, one interesting extended treatise in which Huan Tan uses the analogy of a candle and flame to illustrate the process of life and death and explain the relationship between body and spirit. This piece happens to survive because it is quoted in the Buddhist anthology *Collection of Writings on the Propagation of the Light* (*Hongming ji*) compiled by the Buddhist monk Seng You (435–518), who included it in a set of essays concerning the relationship of body and spirit. Although Huan Tan's authorship has been questioned, most authorities accept it as genuine.

One of Huan Tan's most ardent admirers was his younger contemporary Wang Chong (27–after AD 100). Wang Chong was a native of the southeastern area of Shangyu in Guiji (modern Shangyu City, Zhejiang). His ancestors had originally lived in the north, but the family moved south when one of his ancestors was rewarded with a small fief in Guiji. However, within a year he lost the fief, and he then took up farming to make a living. Wang Chong's great-grandfather, grandfather, uncles, and father were all irascible ruffians who became involved in feuds with other families. Wang Chong's father and brothers were thus forced to move to Shangyu, where Wang Chong was born in AD 27. At the age of seventeen or eighteen (AD 43–44) he went to Luoyang to study at the Imperial Academy. One of his teachers may have been Ban Gu's father Ban Biao. Wang Chong did not have money to buy books, and he could only browse them on the bookstalls in Luoyang; however, he reputedly had such a good memory that he could remember virtually anything that he had read, and thus he acquired a vast knowledge of texts.

Around AD 54 Wang Chong left the capital and took up a career in the local administration. Wang Chong eventually gave up his official career and returned home to Shangyu, where he devoted himself full-time to study and writing. His major work is *Discourses Weighed* (*Lun heng*). Wang Chong reputedly kept brush and book knife (used to erase bamboo strips and writing boards) by the windows, doors, and walls of his house so that he could always have access to writing implements. If accurate, this anecdote shows that paper was still not widely available, at least in some areas of China in the early Eastern Han.

The received version of *Discourses Weighed* consists of eighty-five chapters in thirty fascicles. One chapter, number forty-four, has no text. Scholars have debated whether the *Discourses Weighed* originally contained a hundred or more chapters (Wang Chong mentions in his autobiography that his work "is just a hundred chapters"). Wang Chong probably composed the *Discourses Weighed* over a long period of time. The earliest chapters date from the time he was in Luoyang. He composed the latest chapters near the end of his life.

Wang Chong says that his main purpose in composing the *Discourses Weighed* is "to show contempt for falsity and nonsense." He devotes much of the treatise to debunking what he considered to be the ridiculous and far-fetched notions of his day. Three of the chapters concern what Wang Chong called "exaggeration": "Verbal Exaggerations," "Exaggerations of Scholars," and "Exaggerations in the Classics." There are nine chapters devoted to exposing "falsehoods." For example, in "Falsehoods in Written Accounts," Wang Chong argues that the accounts of Yao and Shun having died in the south are wrong. He also disputes the myth that the tidal bores in Zhejiang were caused by the vengeful spirit of Wu Zixu.

Wang Chong was highly critical of many hallowed traditions, including those of the Confucian school. In two chapters of *Discourses Weighed*, "Questioning Confucius" and "Criticizing Mencius," he presents a subtle critique of passages in the *Analects* and *Mencius*. Wang Chong also questions the conventional theory that natural disasters and anomalous events are evidence of Heaven's displeasure with the emperor's conduct of government. He devotes two chapters, "Falsity of Prodigies" and "Falsity of Anomalies," to this issue. Wang Chong also was skeptical of belief in immortals and ghosts. Chapters that concern these issues are "Falsehoods of the Daoists, "On Death," "Fabrications about Death," "Accounts about Demons," and "Evaluating Ghosts."

The style of *Discourses Weighed* is very lively, and Wang Chong deliberately tried to write clearly and simply. Wang Chong's language perhaps even shows evidence of being a more faithful representation of the spoken language of his time than that of any other Han writer. Wang Chong also has extended remarks about the issue of "creation" of writings and how he views his role with respect to the tradition of the sages who "created" rather than simply transmitted. Wang claims that his role was neither that of a creator nor that of a transmitter, but rather that of a critic who composed *lun* or "critical discourses."

In several chapters Wang Chong challenges the view common among most Han thinkers that antiquity was a golden age of perfect order and peace and that the past is superior to the present. For example, at the beginning of "Questioning Confucius" he faults the scholars of his time for thinking that the views of the ancients are more profound than those of thinkers of the present. In the chapter titled "Treating All Ages as Equal" Wang Chong rejects the notion that people of antiquity were better-looking, stronger, and lived longer than people of the present. He argues that the era of the Han in which he lives is as good as that of the ideal ages of antiquity. He then follows with four chapters in which he provides evidence for the greatness of the Han, especially the reigns of the first three Eastern Han emperors, whom he praises as the equal of the sage rulers of remote antiquity. Thus even the most skeptical writer of his age sings the praises of the Han imperium.

Two newly emerging prose genres: the inscription and admonition

During the early Eastern Han writers began to compose in two closely related prose forms, the *ming* (inscription) and *zhen* (admonition). The inscription is a writing that was carved on almost any object. In ancient times, however, metal was the most common material used. Bronze vessels were inscribed as early as the Shang period, but many of the early inscriptions include only the name of the vessel's owner and maker. Later, especially during the Zhou, much more elaborate inscriptions were inscribed. Some of these inscriptions contain admonitions, while others are eulogistic, and contain effusive praise, usually for a ruler.

During the Eastern Han, inscription composition became a highly developed art. Several famous writers are authors of the texts of inscriptions. One of the best-known of the Han inscriptions is the "Inscription on the Ceremonial Mounding of Mount Yanran" by Ban Gu. Ban Gu was commissioned to write this piece to celebrate the military victory of the Han general Dou Xian (d. 92) over the Northern Xiongnu. The inscription was inscribed on a stone monu-ment erected on Mount Yanran (located in modern Mongolia). The piece is preceded by an introduction that explains the circumstances for which the inscription was composed. It is followed by the text of the inscription, which is rhymed and in the prosodic pattern of the "Nine Songs" of the *Verses of Chu*.

Some of the early Eastern Han inscriptions are less solemn compositions. There are, for example, inscriptions on chess, writing brushes, zithers, arrows, saddles, bridles, mats, even beds. One prolific writer of this type of inscription is Li You (44–126). Li You was a native of Luo in Guanghan (north of modern Guanghan, Sichuan). Nothing is known about him until approximately AD 96, when Emperor He summoned him to the Eastern Institute to compose *fu* upon imperial command. The palace attendant Jia Kui had recommended his writing as similar to the famous Shu (Sichuan) writers Sima Xiangru and Yang Xiong. Li You was then appointed foreman clerk of the Magnolia Terrace. From this time on, for nearly forty years, Li You had a distinguished official career. He died at the age of eighty-three while serving as a minister in the kingdom of Le'an (modern Shandong).

Li You is best known for the inscriptions that he composed for Emperor He. There were originally 120 pieces in the set. Eighty-six inscriptions, many of them in fragments, survive. There is a wide variety of topics. There are inscriptions on places and buildings such as the Yellow River, the Luo river, the Hangu Pass, the Bright Hall, the Grand Academy, the Circular Moat, the Eastern Institute, the Yong'an Palace, the Cloud Terrace, the Deyang Hall, the soccer field, the capital city walls, various lodges, the Shanglin Park, the capital city gates, the well and stove. There are also inscriptions for various objects: zither, flute, water clock, screen, pillow, writing brush, knife, sword, bow, arrow, crossbow, shield, saddle, bridle, bed, armrest, mat, walking stick, sambar-tail chowry, mirror, incense burner, ink, cap, slippers, boat and oars, chariot, cauldron, plate, cup, goblet, winnowing sieve, chess, lamp, and scale. Most of these pieces are written in four-syllable-line form, and are virtually indistinguishable from poems.

The companion genre to the inscription is the *zhen*. The word *zhen* literally means "needle" or "acupuncture." As the name of a literary form, the term became extended to designate a composition that "exhorted" or "admonished" persons to good conduct. The *zhen* usually is a short piece written in four-syllable lines. In the Han dynasty, most *zhen* were monitory pieces that prescribed the duties and moral qualities required of a particular government office. The first writer to compose sets of admonitions was Yang Xiong. Yang Xiong composed twelve admonitions on the provinces and twenty-five admonitions on official offices. By Eastern Han times, however, nine of his admonitions were missing or in fragments. In the early Eastern Han, scholars such as Cui Yin, his son Cui Yuan (78–143), and Liu Taotu (ca 70–ca 130), a member of the imperial family with scholarly inclinations, added sixteen additional pieces. In the mid-Eastern Han, Hu Guang (91–172) added four more. Hu Guang arranged the pieces in order, provided a commentary, and gave it the title "Admonitions on the Official Offices" (Bai guan zhen).

The textual history of this work is complicated, and different sources, even different editions of the same source, disagree on the authorship of individual admonitions. The admonitions are rhymed and are usually written throughout in four-syllable lines. They often extend for thirty lines or more. The piece begins by giving a history of the office, including examples of both proper and improper use of the position in ancient history. The admonition always concludes with a moral message cautioning office-holders to be wary of abusing their position. For example, the admonition on the privy treasurer (attributed to Yang Xiong) says: "Failure has never resulted from restraint, / But it always results from extravagance."

Although most admonitions seem to be general statements of moral principles, some were written as reprimands addressed to specific persons. One such admonition was written by Cui Qi (ca 90–ca 150), who was a kinsman of Cui Yuan. In his youth Cui Qi went to the capital to study, and he obtained a reputation for his vast learning and skill at writing. In around 126, he was recommended as "filial and incorrupt," and appointed gentleman at the imperial court. Some years later, he entered the service of a powerful member of the consort clan, Liang Ji (d. 159), who then was serving as governor of Henan. Cui Qi was offended by Liang Ji's abuse of his position and frequently admonished him, though to no avail. He then composed a long four-part "Admonition on the Consort Clan" (Wai qi zhen). In the three stanzas, Cui Qi recounts the calamities that resulted from rulers who gave their consorts free rein at the court. He cites the examples of the wives of the last rulers of the Xia and Shang, who lost their states because of their infatuation with their consorts. The final stanza is a frank reprimand to Liang Ji.

The middle period of Eastern Han

The middle Eastern Han conventionally refers to the reigns of four rulers, Emperor He (r. 89–105), Emperor Shang (106), Emperor An (r. 107–125), and Emperor Shun (r. 125–144). All of these emperors came to the throne as young boys, and for much of their reigns they were under the control of the consort clans. As we have seen, during the first three years of Emperor He's reign, the court was under the control of the Empress Dowager Dou and her elder brother, Dou Xian, who served as regent. Although Emperor He eliminated Dou Xian in 92, the family of Empress Deng, Emperor He's consort, had great power and influence throughout Emperor He's reign and into Emperor An's reign. When Empress Deng died in 121, the Deng family was replaced by the family of Emperor An's consort, Empress Yan. The Yan clan fell from imperial favor with the accession of Emperor Shun in 125. Emperor Shun, who was ten years old at the time of his accession, selected as empress Liang Na, who was nine years his senior. Serving as regent during Emperor Shun's reign were Liang Na's father, Liang Shang (d. 141), followed by his son Liang Ji (d. 159). The Liang family, especially Liang Ji, was ruthless in suppressing any opposition to its policies.

Another group that had great power and influence at the imperial court in the middle period of the Eastern Han was the eunuchs. The eunuchs first began to play an important role during the reign of Emperor He, who eliminated Dou Xian with the aid of the eunuch Zheng Zhong (d. 114). One faction of eunuchs also was instrumental in the installation of Emperor Shun, who rewarded them by bestowing on them noble titles and fiefs that could be inherited by their adopted sons.

The scholar–officials of this period became increasingly critical both of the consort clan and of the eunuchs. We have already mentioned above Cui Qi's unsuccessful attempts to reprimand Liang Ji. Other prominent writers were to continue this practice until the end of the Eastern Han. Another new cultural development in this period was the emergence of the polymath scholar. Before this time, the most prestigious field of learning was the Classics. Classical scholarship tended to be rather specialized, and most scholars would establish expertise in a single Classic. By the middle Eastern Han, scholars began to broaden their intellectual interests. We have seen already in the early Eastern Han the examples of "comprehensive scholars" (tong ru) such as Huan Tan and Wang Chong, who did not confine their interests only to the Confucian canon. Huan Tan was a leading expert in music, and Wang Chong shows in his *Discourses Weighed* a catholic interest in nearly all fields of study. The next generation of scholars included several important polymaths, Zhang Heng, Ma Rong, and Cui Yuan.

Zhang Heng

The most famous writer of the middle period of the Eastern Han is Zhang Heng (78–139), who was a distinguished scholar, poet, and scientist. He came from a prominent local family of Xi'e in Nanyang commandery (north of modern Nanyang City, Henan), which was the home area of the Eastern Han founder Emperor Guangwu. In his youth, Zhang Heng distinguished himself in his home area with his learning and literary skill. At about the age of fifteen (ca AD 93), he traveled to the Chang'an and Luoyang areas and began drafting a *fu* on the two Han capitals.

Zhang returned to Nanyang around AD 100, where he assumed the post of master of documents under Bao De (d. 111 / 113), governor of Nanyang from 100 to 111. Zhang was only twenty-three at the time, but because of his superior literary skills he was commissioned to compose inscriptions, dirges, and other works on Bao De's behalf.

Around 107 Zhang Heng completed his masterpiece, the "*Fu* on the Two Metropolises." He also wrote a set of appraisals on the scholars of the local academy in Nanyang, which Bao De had restored. This is one of several works by Zhang Heng that show his strong identification with his home area, most notably his "*Fu* on the Southern Capital" about Nanyang. Because Nanyang was the native place of the Eastern Han founder Emperor Guangwu, it was called the Southern Capital. Throughout the *fu* Zhang celebrates Nanyang as if it were the equivalent of the imperial capital.

In 108, after Bao De was transferred to the capital, Zhang returned to Xi'e to resume his scholarly studies. He did research in mathematics and astronomy and wrote a commentary to Yang Xiong's *Great Mystery*, a work that he regarded as comparable to the Five Classics. This is a good example of the polymath scholar's attempt to expand the canon. In about the year 112 Zhang Heng received an invitation to the capital on the basis of his expertise in astronomy and mathematics. However, he was assigned to the low position of palace gentleman, which was basically an entry-level rank. It was during this time that Zhang invented a number of mechanical devices, including a self-propelled three-wheeled south-pointing chariot and a wooden eagle that reputedly could fly on its own. Such works did not earn Zhang much acclaim, for in the view of the traditional scholar, the skill to build a machine or even expertise in astronomy and mathematics were considered low-level "arts" that a proper gentleman should not pursue.

Two years later (114) Zhang was promoted to attendant gentleman to the masters of writing. This, however, was also a very low position with a stipend of only four hundred bushels of grain. During this time Zhang continued his scientific studies. In 115 Zhang Heng took up the post of imperial astrologer, which was still relatively low (only six hundred bushels). In that same year he made a topographical map that survived at least to the Tang. Zhang Heng's contributions in the field of astronomy come from this period. In 117 he constructed an armillary sphere that was used to locate astral positions in the heavens.

Emperor An died on April 30, 125. He was succeeded by Emperor Shun (r. 125–144), who was only ten years old at the time of his accession. During his reign, the eunuchs came to dominate the court. In the same year that Emperor Shun took the throne, Zhang Heng was summoned to his former position of imperial astrologer. The prospect of returning to a post that he had occupied already for seven years did not sit well with Zhang Heng. He also may have been criticized by some members of the court who faulted him for devoting too much of his energy to scholarly and scientific endeavors. Zhang Heng wrote a dialogue in the manner of Yang Xiong's "Justification against Ridicule" to defend himself. This work is "Responding to Criticism."

Although dissatisfied with his status at the court, Zhang Heng continued to do scientific investigations. In 132, he constructed a seismograph, which is regarded as the earliest machine of its type in world history.

During the early 130s, Zhang Heng became increasingly concerned about corruption at court and the usurpation of imperial authority by members of the consort clan and the eunuchs. In 130 he presented to Emperor Shun a long petition blaming the eunuchs' usurpation of imperial prerogatives for the recent drought and earthquake. In 134 Zhang Heng was finally promoted to a high position, palace attendant, a rank with a salary of two thousand bushels of grain. In this capacity he had the duty to offer advice to the emperor. On one occasion Emperor Shun called Zhang Heng into his private quarters and asked him who were the most despised men in the realm. The eunuchs, fearing that he would name them, made threatening glances at him, and Zhang gave an evasive answer. Eventually, however, they began to slander Zhang to the emperor. Zhang then composed a long *fu*, "Pondering the Mystery," to express his frustration.

In 136 Zhang Heng left his central government post to take up the position of chancellor of Hejian (its administrative center, southeast of modern Xian County, Hebei). Zhang Heng was a strict administrator, and after learning the names of those who had violated the law he had them arrested. For this deed he earned the respect and admiration of the Hejian people. In 138 Zhang Heng decided to retire from office, and he returned to his home in Xi'e. In 139 Zhang Heng was summoned out of retirement but died after serving briefly as master of writing.

Zhang Heng was a prolific writer. His *fu* compositions are especially notable. He wrote long epideictic pieces such as "*Fu* on the Two Metropolises" (Er jing fu) and "*Fu* on the Southern Capital" (Nan du fu). Zhang also is the first *fu* writer to write a large number of shorter pieces. His earliest known *fu*, "*Fu* on the Hot Springs" (Wen quan fu), recounts a visit to the hot springs baths at Mount Li, located east of Chang'an and later the site of the famous Tang Huaqing Palace. Zhang Heng portrays the area as open to the public, and he has a delightful description of crowds of people "clustering like schools of fish" and "thronging thick as mist" to enjoy the healing waters of the hot springs. In another piece, "*Fu* on the Grave Mound" (Zhong fu), Zhang describes the construction of a tomb. In "*Fu* on the Dance" (Wu fu), which is a fragment, Zhang recounts a performance of the seven-plate dance that he had once seen. Another piece on an original theme is "*Fu* on Settling the Passions" (Ding qing fu), in which the poet describes a beautiful woman whose erotic charms he finally resists at the end of the poem. Only ten lines of Zhang Heng's poem survive, but the extant fragments contain most of the conventional features of the theme, including the catalogue of the lady's features and the conceit of erotic desire ("I wish to be the powder on your face"). Poets of the late Eastern Han, Wei, and Jin periods wrote *fu* on this same theme, all of which have titles that are variations of the phrase "settling the passions." The most famous work is *"Fu on Quieting the Passions"* by Tao Qian (365?–427).

Zhang Heng's masterwork is the *"Fu on the Two Metropolises."* Having spent over ten years gathering material to compose the piece, Zhang Heng must have considered the writing of this *fu* a form of scholarship. This is a new concept of the function of the *fu* genre. According to Zhang Heng's biography in the *History of the Later Han*, Zhang wrote this *fu* as an imitation of Ban Gu's *"Fu on the Two Capitals"*; however, a fragment of a preface to Zhang's *fu* contained in a Tang dynasty commonplace book indicates that Zhang wished to present an alternative to the account of Chang'an and Luoyang by Ban Gu. Zhang Heng's treatment of the two Han capitals differs radically from that of Ban Gu. Unlike Ban Gu, who found nothing wrong with his age, Zhang Heng verges on satire in his portrayal of the Han court.

The "Two Metropolises" is in two parts, *"Fu on the Western Metropolis,"* and *"Fu on the Eastern Metropolis."* At the beginning of the "Western Metropolis" two protagonists are introduced, and they begin to debate the merits of Chang'an and Luoyang. The Chang'an representative is Lord Relying-on-Nothing, and the spokesman for Luoyang is a Master Where-Live. The Western Metropolis protagonist portrays the city of Chang'an as a center of luxury and prodigality, in which succeeding generations outdid each other in extravagant indulgence.

One obvious difference between the two pairs of capital *fu* by Ban Gu and Zhang Heng is that Zhang Heng wrote his two poems at a time when the choice of where to locate the capital was no longer an issue. Zhang Heng, in fact, wrote his *fu* not in Luoyang, but while he was still residing in his home area of Nanyang. Perhaps for these reasons Zhang did not feel compelled to praise Luoyang as effusively as did Ban Gu. Thus Zhang Heng's treatment of the two capitals contains much satire and sardonic comment. While Ban Gu's account of the Western Capital is rather bland and straightforward, Zhang Heng, through the persona of Lord Relying-on-Nothing, presents a series of satirical portraits of the most egregiously uncivilized pursuits of the Western Han. The irony that pervades these accounts is more sustained than the relatively short satirical asides found in Sima Xiangru or even Yang Xiong. For example, Zhang Heng cleverly ridicules the Western Han Emperor Wu for his failure to see through the deceptions of the humbugs who offered him recipes for attaining immortality. Zhang describes the shady dealings of the hawkers and peddlers of the marketplace and sarcastically comments on the undeserved respect accorded to wealthy merchants. Zhang Heng even makes fun of scholars, perhaps those of the New Text School, whose main occupation was the writing of long, detailed, and often irrelevantly far-fetched explanations of passages in the Classics.

Another way in which Zhang Heng's *fu* differs from Ban Gu's is in the amount of detail and concrete description it provides. Ban Gu's account of Chang'an and even Luoyang is rather sparing of details and devoid of concrete description. Zhang Heng, by contrast, includes long descriptive passages on various aspects of life in the two Han metropolises. One long section describes the games, sports, and entertainment that took place at the Lodge of Peaceful Joy located in the Shanglin Park. Zhang describes acrobats, weightlifters, pole-climbers, jugglers, fire-eaters, and various processions of "floats" and marchers in animal and bird costumes.

The "*Fu* on the Eastern Metropolis" is Master Where-Live's rebuttal to the Western Metropolis protagonist's speech. His main point is that the most praiseworthy quality of Luoyang was its moderation and simplicity, and, unlike Chang'an, it "did not rely on strategic strongholds," but adhered to classical ritual principles. In this respect Zhang Heng's *fu* is similar to Ban Gu's "Two Capitals," which as we have seen essentially is a celebration of the ritual revival of the early Eastern Han. Zhang Heng devotes even more attention to ritual performance than does Ban Gu. He praises the Peaceful Joy Lodge, which Emperor Ming had ordered constructed outside the Upper West Gate of Luoyang (probably in imitation of the Peaceful Joy Lodge of the Western Han imperial park that Zhang Heng had described in great detail in the "*Fu* on the Western Metropolis"). In contrast to his portrayal of the Western Han Peaceful Joy Lodge as a center of lavish spectacles, Zhang Heng depicts the Eastern Han counterpart as a model of moderation and restraint. The main distinction between treatments of ritual in Ban Gu and those in Zhang Heng is that Zhang Heng provides more concrete and detailed description. A good example is the long section Zhang Heng devotes to a ritual known as Grand Exorcism. This ceremony was performed at the end of the year to expel all evil spirits and other malevolent forces that accumulated during the year. Knowing Zhang Heng's skepticism about spirits and matters pertaining to the supernatural, it is possible that his account of this ritual actually is a satire, or perhaps a parody of an actual demon-exorcism spell.

Another of Zhang Heng's great *fu* poems is "Pondering the Mystery." This long poem of 436 lines is written almost exclusively in the regular

"*Sao*-style" form. It also borrows extensively from *Verses of Chu* pieces, particularly "Encountering Sorrow" and "Far Roaming." Zhang Heng uses the standard fragrant plant allegories, the metaphors of the mistreated steed and the solitary nesting phoenix, the lament about the impending approach of old age, and other *sao* conventions to create a persona similar to that of Qu Yuan.

"Pondering the Mystery" is primarily important as a refutation of the melancholy pessimism of the Han frustration *fu* tradition. In his *fu* Zhang expresses remarkable confidence in a moral order, and his appeal to that order not only provides him comfort and solace from his grief, but also offers the source of confidence he needs in order to dispel his doubts and confusion. In contrast to earlier *sao* poets, Zhang Heng's persona is not burdened with vacillation, but emerges at the end decisive and certain that his solution is correct.

The question that Zhang Heng poses for himself in the *fu* is the following: in the face of a corrupt world of slander and malice, should he escape to a realm far from his home, or should he remain in the world and, in spite of adversity, persist in the cultivation of his own virtue? To resolve the question, Zhang undertakes a long imaginary journey. His travels follow the standard ritual sequence: east, south, west, and north. In none of these places does he find anything to offer him comfort or relief from his despair. Eventually Zhang visits the palace of Heaven, where unlike Qu Yuan, who was refused admission to the celestial palace, the gatekeeper allows him to enter. As he next makes a brief tour of the constellations, one feels that it is Zhang Heng the astronomer speaking as he tells of his hunts in the Blue Grove, the hunting park of Heaven. Zhang soon begins to doubt the efficacy of his distant wandering; he declares that escape from the world is not necessary and resolves to return to his home, where he continues to study the ancient Classics, write poetry, and lead the life of a country scholar. Although his journey to Heaven seems full of triumph and ecstasy, Zhang Heng does not, as does the protagonist of "Far Roaming," end his journey in Daoist transcendence. On the contrary, Zhang rejects this possibility and resolves instead to return to the human world.

Zhang Heng's refusal to leave the human world not only has to do with his skepticism about the possibilities of celestial flight and contact with immortals (he cites Confucius himself when he says "Heaven cannot be scaled"), but is related as well to his view that the unseen forces of Heaven, which determine fate and fortune, lie beyond the ken of man. If man tries to know these things, he can make tragic mistakes in interpreting them.

Because Zhang Heng believed that the unseen world could be neither known nor trusted, he had to reject the idea of the imaginary journey. The only thing trustworthy or knowable that emanated from Heaven was its moral order, which was the source of human ethical principles. Thus, even though one could not understand the workings of fate and fortune, it was possible, through ethical conduct, to receive Heaven's blessing. Ethical principles, which are the laws of human activity, could be found only by remaining in the human world. Zhang Heng believed that ethical principles must operate in the human world, and even though he believed that the times in which he lived were corrupt and immoral, because of his confidence in a moral order he found the notion of mystical escape repugnant.

In the final portion of "Pondering the Mystery," Zhang describes the bucolic scene of the countryside where he lives (or hopes to live) and his great delight in leading the life of a country gentleman. He elaborates on this theme in the short but much celebrated "Fu on Returning to the Fields," which he most likely wrote when he decided to retire in 138. In the opening lines of this piece, Zhang characterizes his life up to this point as a "long roaming in city and town," referring to his service at the imperial court in the capital. Zhang expresses dissatisfaction with his career as an official. He was unable to provide advice to the throne, and the reason for this is not entirely his fault, for he did not live in a time of good rule. Zhang then declares his resolve to bid a final farewell to worldly affairs.

In the remaining lines of the piece Zhang describes his new abode, an estate in the countryside. Although in the title Zhang says he is returning to the fields, he does not actually do any farming. He shoots birds with corded arrows and catches sand dabs in a brook. He obtains great pleasure from roaming his estate by day, and returning to his "thatched hut" at night to play the zither, read "the writings of the Duke of Zhou and Confucius," and write literary works. This *fu* is the first Chinese poem that self-consciously poses the delights of the bucolic lifestyle as an alternative to living in the city and court. The countryside that Zhang describes is an idealized hermitage that serves as a model for subsequent depictions of rural life, including the great master of bucolic "fields and gardens" verse, Tao Qian.

Zhang wrote a number of prose works, several of which are quite famous. Some of these works are products of his polymath interests. He wrote treatises on mathematics and astronomy, the most important of which is "The Sublime Model" (Ling xian), which he may have written in 118. In this essay, he depicts the heavens as shaped like an egg that encased the earth inside like a yolk. In approximately 132 Zhang presented one of his most famous petitions concerning the prognostication texts. After pointing out that these texts appeared only relatively recently, in the reign of the last two Western Han emperors Ai and Ping, Zhang cites examples of historical inaccuracies and anachronisms in various prognostication texts. He attributed such writings to "fabricators who sought approval and wealth." Zhang concludes by urging Emperor Shun to confiscate the "prognostication charts and texts and completely ban them." Zhang thus is clearly following in the skeptical tradition of Huan Tan and Wang Chong.

Ma Rong and Cui Yuan

Two of Zhang Heng's acquaintances were Ma Rong (79–166) and Cui Yuan (78–143), both of whom, like Zhang Heng, had broad intellectual interests. Ma Rong was a skilled writer, a scholar and teacher of the Classics, and a musician who excelled at playing the zither and flute. He is another example of the polymath culture that becomes more common by the end of the Eastern Han.

Ma Rong was the grandnephew of the famous general Ma Yuan (14 BC– AD 40), and besides his scholarly interests, Ma continued the family tradition of expertise in military matters. Ma Rong's most famous *fu* is the "Eulogy on the Guangcheng Park" (Guangcheng song), which he wrote in 118 to protest against the "pacifist" policies espoused by members of the Deng clan, policies that were very influential at court during this period. Guangcheng was the hunting and military review area of the Eastern Han. Although Ma Rong titled his piece *song* ("eulogy"), it does not differ from the grand epideictic *fu* of Sima Xiangru and Yang Xiong. It contains long catalogues of plants, animals, birds, and aquatic creatures, and uses a number of rare and difficult words. Unlike earlier pieces on hunting parks, however, Ma Rong's eulogy does not contain any criticism of hunting, but, on the contrary, uses his elaborate description of the park and the activities that take place there as an argument to persuade the court to reverse its policy of de-emphasizing military affairs.

Ma Rong continued the practice of writing *fu* on objects. His best-known piece of this type is "*Fu* on the Long Flute" (Chang di fu). This is one of a number of early *fu* written about musical instruments. Ma's piece is a long descriptive poem full of difficult language. It has the usual features of a *fu* on a musical instrument: (1) a description of the place from which the bamboo used to make the flute comes: the shady slopes of the Zhongnan Mountains south of Chang'an; (2) an account of the perils of cutting down the bamboo to use in making the flute; (3) a description of the making of the flute; (4) words of praise about the beauty of the flute music; and (5) an exposition on the effects the flute music has on humans and the natural world.

Ma also composed *fu* on games. His *"Fu* on Chaupar" (Chupu fu) is on a board game that originated in India. The Chinese believed that Laozi "invented" the game during his travels in Central Asia. Ma Rong's piece is the earliest account of chaupar and provides valuable information about terminology and method of play. Ma also wrote a *"Fu* on Encirclement Chess" (Wei qi fu), which is one of the earliest extant pieces on the game of Go. Ma portrays the chess match as a game of military strategy.

Ma Rong is an example of the newly emerging "universal scholar" (*tong ru*). Not only was he well versed in music and writing, he also had catholic interests in texts. In addition to writing commentaries and explications of the canonical works such as the *Classic of Filial Piety*, the *Analects*, the *Classic of Poetry*, the *Classic of Changes*, and the *Classic of Documents*, he also wrote commentaries to non-canonical texts such as "Encountering Sorrow," *Huainanzi*, and *Laozi*.

Cui Yuan was the second son of Cui Yin. In 95 he went to Luoyang, where he studied with Jia Kui (30–101). Cui Yuan attained knowledge of astronomy, calendrical and mathematical sciences, and the *Classic of Changes*. It was at this time that he became good friends with Zhang Heng, who had just gone to Luoyang to study at the Imperial Academy. Cui Yuan shared Zhang Heng's interest in Yang Xiong's *Great Mystery* and wrote a commentary to this text. Also a renowned calligrapher, Cui Yuan was one of the earliest masters of cursive script and composed an essay on cursive script titled "The Configuration of Cursive Script."

Cui Yuan was a prolific writer. His biography in the *History of the Later Han* says that he wrote seventy-five pieces in various genres. He especially excelled in the writing of letters, notes, inscriptions, and admonitions. Most of his extant work consists of inscriptions and admonitions. His best-known work is "Inscription Placed to the Right of My Seat" (Zuo you ming), which is included in the *Selections of Refined Literature*. It is written throughout in five-syllable lines, and it actually can be read as a poem in the five-syllable meter.

Two southerners: Wang Yi and Wang Yanshou

Contemporaneous with Ma Rong and Zhang Heng are two natives from Yicheng (modern Hubei) in the old southern area of Chu, Wang Yi (fl. 130–140) and his son Wang Yanshou (ca 118–ca 138). Wang Yi is best known for his commentary to the *Verses of Chu*. In about 114 he went to Luoyang to present the accounts from his home commandery. He then obtained a position as collator of texts in the imperial archives. Wang Yi may have earned his appointment by virtue of presenting his commentary to the *Verses of Chu* to the court at this time. Wang Yi's commentary does not survive in its original form and is only available in a Song dynasty version, the *Supplementary Commentary to the Verses of Chu (Chu ci buzhu)* by Hong Xingzu (1070–1135). The form of Wang Yi's commentary is distinctive, for in many places he uses rhyme to paraphrase the original text. Some of his paraphrases form seven-syllable-line poems.

Wang Yi included a long piece of his own in the *Verses of Chu* titled "Nine Longings" (Jiu si). It is in nine sections plus a coda, all written in the "Nine Songs" meter. This is a typical imitation of the Qu Yuan poems and has all the topoi of the *Verses of Chu*, including the imaginary journey, the portrayal of the world as upside down, and the lament of the worthy man who fails to meet a propitious time.

Little is known about Wang Yanshou. During his youth, he accompanied his father to Lu where they studied Classics and computation with a scholar who lived in the Mount Tai area. On his return to Yicheng from Lu, Wang drowned crossing the Xiang River. He was just over twenty years old at the time.

Like Ma Rong, Wang Yi and Wang Yanshou expanded the range of *fu* topics. Wang Yi's extant works include "Fu on the Loom" (Ji fu), which is a poetic description of the weaver's loom, and "Fu on the Lychee" (Lizhi fu), which celebrates the most famous fruit of the south. Wang Yi's *fu* is the earliest known poetic description of it. Regrettably, both of these pieces are fragments. Wang Yanshou has one complete piece, "Fu on the Hall of Numinous Brilliance in Lu" (Lu Lingguan dian fu), which is preserved in the *Selections of Refined Literature*. In this piece written in the grand epideictic style, Wang Yanshou describes a famous palace located southeast of the Confucian temple in Qufu, Shandong. It is a masterpiece of description and provides the most detailed literary record of a Han palace's construction and architectural features.

There are two other shorter *fu* attributed to Wang Yanshou, "Fu on a Dream" (Meng fu) and "Fu on the Macaque" (Wangsun fu). If these works are genuine, they show Wang Yanshou's precocious originality as a *fu* writer. In "Fu on a Dream," the poet poetically exorcizes a horde of demons that had appeared to him in a dream at night. The "Fu on the Macaque" is a poem about the primate known in English as the rhesus macaque or rhesus monkey (*Macaca mulatta*). The poet uses colorful and unusual rhyming and alliterative binomes to describe the eyes, nose, mouth, ears, teeth, and other bodily features of this remarkable animal that lives in a dense forest deep in the mountains. There it romps and plays with other macaques, who seem impossible to catch. Their only weakness is wine. A hunter sets out a bowl of wine, and the macaques race each other to drink it up. They then fall asleep in a drunken stupor and are taken away to a stable where onlookers gape at them. Some scholars have claimed the beast of this poem is Wang Yanshou's "self-representation," or that it represents a man who gets into trouble because of his inability to restrain his carnal desire. However, it could simply be a poetic account of an actual event that he observed.

End of the Eastern Han

The final years of the Eastern Han include the reigns of three emperors, Huan (r. 146–168), Ling (r. 168–189), and Xian (r. 189–220). Emperor Huan came to the throne at the age fourteen, and for the first thirteen years of his reign he was under the control of the regent Liang Ji and Liang Ji's sister, Empress Liang. In 159 Empress Liang died, and Emperor Huan, with the support of eunuchs, purged the Liang clan from office. Relying on their favored position at the imperial court, the eunuchs began to establish their power base, largely at the expense of the scholar–officials, some of whom presented strongly worded petitions to the emperor protesting eunuch abuses.

Emperor Huan died on January 25, 168 without naming an heir. A group of officials and eunuchs installed a twelve-year-old boy as emperor on February 17, 168. This was Emperor Ling (r. 168–189). Initially, Emperor Ling was supervised by a three-man regency consisting of Dou Wu (d. 168), Chen Fan (ca 90–168), and Hu Guang (91–172). In late summer and fall of that year, Dou Wu and Chen Fan conspired to have eunuchs who had dominated the court under Emperor Huan purged. Their plot, however, failed when the eunuchs overpowered the small band of soldiers who supported Chen and Dou. Chen Fan was killed in prison, and Dou Wu, facing the prospect of capture, committed suicide. The eunuchs dominated the imperial court through the entire reign of Emperor Ling.

The eunuchs first moved against those who had conspired against them. They executed eight officials whom they charged with "factionalism," along with their supporters, parents, and sons. They then initiated the "great proscription" that resulted in banning anyone even remotely connected with the anti-eunuch partisans from serving in office. The proscription continued until 184, when a eunuch official at the court advised Emperor Ling that its severity was one of the causes of the Yellow Turban uprising that began in that year. One of the results of the proscription was increased dissent on the part of scholar–officials, who began even to question the moral authority of the imperial court.

In 189, Emperor Ling passed away. His successor was a thirteen-year-old ruler named Liu Bian, who is known by his posthumous title of Emperor Shao (r. May–September 189). The real power at the court was in the hands of Liu Bian's mother, Empress Dowager He, and her half-brother, the general-in-chief He Jin (d. 189). Up to this time, the court had been dominated by eunuchs. He Jin devised a plan to eliminate them. He summoned the warlord Dong Zhuo (d. 192) to lead his army toward the capital of Luoyang, hoping to force the Empress Dowager He to dismiss the eunuchs. In retaliation, the eunuchs assassinated He Jin on September 22, 189. Dong Zhuo deposed Liu Bian and installed his brother Liu Xie as emperor. This was Emperor Xian (r. 189–220), who became a puppet of Dong Zhuo. In 190 a coalition of eastern commanders including Yuan Shao (d. 202) and Cao Cao (155–220) led an attack against Dong Zhuo. In April 190 Dong Zhuo burned Luoyang and removed the young emperor to Chang'an, along with the remaining members of the Han imperial court. On May 22, 192, Dong Zhuo was assassinated by his own followers.

By 193 Cao Cao was the supreme military power in north China. In 196 he took Emperor Xian under his protection and installed him in Xuchang. In 210 Cao Cao made the city of Ye (modern Linzhang, Hebei) his primary residence, and thus he established a second court in addition to the one in Xu. By 208 Cao Cao had achieved supremacy over most of his rivals. His position was that of chancellor. In August of 208 he led his army south on a campaign against Liu Biao (d. 208) in Jingzhou (modern Hubei). After Liu Biao died of natural causes, Cao was easily able to obtain the surrender of Liu Biao's son, Liu Cong. Cao Cao's only setback was in December of 208, when his army was routed in the famous Battle of the Red Cliff.

In his later years, Cao Cao solidified his power in the north and continued to wage campaigns against his two main rivals, Sun Quan (182–252) in the southeast and Liu Bei (162–223) in the southwest. He also established a policy of recruiting officials based on their talent rather than on social status or wealth. To solidify his power, however, he granted important positions to his own sons. In 211 he named Cao Pi (187–226) vice-chancellor. His other sons received marquisates. In 216 Cao Cao assumed the title of king of Wei and established Cao Pi as his heir designate. By the time of his death in 220, Cao Cao had prepared the way for the establishment of the Wei dynasty (220–264).

Late Eastern Han discourses

During the late Eastern Han, the favored form of expository writing was the "discourse" (lun). Some disaffected men wrote many discourses that were then compiled into collections. One of the earliest of such works is the *Discourses of a Hidden Man* (*Qianfu lun*) by Wang Fu (ca 90–ca 167). He lived in reclusion to the end of his life and devoted himself to writing critical essays from about 111 to 129. Most of the thirty-six chapters of the *Discourses of a Hidden Man* concern contemporary issues. For example, in the chapter "Examining Merit," Wang criticizes the recruitment system that resulted in the recommendation of unqualified men for positions. In "Boundaries of Friendship" he complains that the recommendation system, which relied on favoritism and family connections, inhibited the formation of true friendship. In another chapter, "Extravagance," Wang denounces the lavish lifestyle of his wealthy contemporaries. In "Devotion to the Fundamental" he faults artisans and merchants for creating useless ornamental goods that only serve to deceive the people. He also accuses writers of poetry and *fu* of composing "carved and lovely" writings simply to become admired by their contemporaries.

A somewhat later discourse writer is Cui Shi (ca 120–170), who was the son of Cui Yuan. Cui Yuan was on good terms with Wang Fu. Cui Shi wrote a series of critical essays that were collected in a work that usually goes under the title of *Discourses on Government* (*Zheng lun*). This work survived through the Tang period, but apparently was lost in the Song period. Cui Shi probably began writing the *Discourses on Government* around 151, for he mentions in one of his essays that the Han had flourished for over 350 years, which would coincide with 151. He continued to add to it throughout the remainder of his life. Cui Shi's thought is highly colored by legalism, which is reflected in Cui's acceptance of the idea that there are no constant norms for human society and that remedies for the ills of the time must be determined by the circumstances. Cui Shi then sets forth a program to implement the reward and penalty system of the ancient legalists. He especially criticizes the Western Han emperor Wen for eliminating capital punishment.

One of the most original thinkers at the end of the Eastern Han was Zhongchang Tong (180–220). After refusing appointments from regional governors, he eventually (ca 207) received a position on the staff of Cao Cao. It was also at this time that he began writing a series of essays that he titled *Forthright Words* (*Chang yan*). After Zhongchang Tong died in 220, Miao Xi (186–245) presented a copy of the book to Cao Pi, who had just taken the throne of the Wei dynasty.

Only portions of *Forthright Words* are extant. They show that Zhongchang Tong was a highly original thinker. He admired Cui Shi's *Discourse on Government* and is reported to have said: "every ruler should have a copy written out and placed by his seat." Like Wang Chong, Zhongchang Tong did not accept the idea that Heaven controlled human fate. In commenting on the founding of the Western Han and Eastern Han, he criticized "those who only understand the way of Heaven, but lacked plans formulated by men," as belonging to "the cohort of shamans, quacks, diviners, and priests, and stupid people who were not worth considering seriously." Zhongchang Tong's most original essay is "On Order and Disorder," in which he portrays human history as an irreversible process leading to deterioration and chaos.

Zhao Yi

We have seen that at the end of the Han traditional values no longer held their appeal to some members of the scholar–official class. We also begin to see some men overtly engaging in an eccentric mode of conduct. One of these eccentrics was Zhao Yi (ca 130 –ca 185), who was a highly original writer, especially in the *fu* form. Zhao Yi's biography in the *History of the Later Han* described him as a man of great gifts who often offended people with his arrogant manner. In 167 his fellow townsmen expelled him from his native place. As a response he wrote a piece titled "Justification against Expulsion" (Jie bin). Although the piece does not survive, judging from its title it must have been an imitation of Yang Xiong's "Justification against Ridicule."

Zhao Yi was frequently in trouble with the authorities, and around 173 he was charged with a crime and sentenced to death. A friend interceded on his behalf, and Zhao Yi received a pardon. After making a brief visit to the capital in 178, Zhao Yi returned to his home commandery. He received ten invitations to take office, all of which he declined. He died at home around the year 185.

Zhao Yi's most famous work is "*Fu* on Satirizing the World and Denouncing Evil" (Ci shi ji xie fu), which is an excellent example of late Han satire. It is a bitter complaint directed against the great clans and possibly the eunuchs who held sway during this period. Zhao Yi refers to these people in blunt language, calling them flatterers and pile-lickers who cower and cringe before the political magnates. Zhao openly specifies the source of the ills of his age: the ruler's close advisers, who prevent good advice from reaching his ears. In such a situation, there is little a man of integrity can do. Zhao Yi forthrightly declares that he prefers not to live in this corrupt age:

> I would rather starve and freeze during a fruitless year of Yao and Shun,
> Than be full and warm in a rich year of the present.
> To die by following the truth is not death;
> To live by going against what is right is not living.

Zhao Yi's *fu* differs from other frustration *fu* of the Han in its frankness and bold expression. Although it is in rhyme, it is as much a polemic as it is a poetic composition. The style is almost the antithesis of the epideictic *fu* style, and the language is plain and unadorned. By the end of the Eastern Han this style of *fu* becomes more pervasive.

Cai Yong

Cai Yong is another example of the late Han polymath. He was an expert on astronomy, mathematics, music, classical scholarship, painting, and calligraphy, and was the most accomplished writer of grave inscriptions in his time. He was from a prominent family in the commandery of Chenliu (modern Henan). His parents died when he was young, and he was raised by his uncle Cai Zhi, who was one of his first teachers. He also studied with the renowned scholar and official Hu Guang (91–172). Until he was nearly forty, Cai Yong avoided official service. However, he gained a reputation for his composition of grave inscriptions. In the early 170s Cai Yong took up his first positions at the imperial court, the most important of which was as textual editor in the Eastern Institute library. Together with other scholars he worked on the compilation of the *Han Records of the Eastern Institute* (*Dongguan Han ji*). Around this time Cai also wrote the *Solitary Judgments* (*Du duan*), a collection of notes dealing mainly with ritual, ceremonies, and official titles. He also reputedly wrote the text for the stone-inscribed version of the Classics that Emperor Ling had ordered in 175.

In 177 and 178, Cai Yong presented a series of petitions commenting on important issues of governance. At this time Cai Yong became involved in the controversy over a new academy, the Hongdu Gate School. Formally instituted in March 178, it had been in actual existence for several years before this time. In the late 170s, Emperor Ling began to appoint men to his court not on the basis of their knowledge of the Classics, but on their ability to compose *fu* and write in "bird script," an ornamental style of calligraphy used for pennants and tallies. Members of the scholarly establishment began to criticize the officials who were appointed to the Hongdu Gate School on the grounds that such minor skills were not proper tests of ability to undertake official duties. In one of his petitions, Cai Yong derides the literary works produced by these vulgar upstarts as mere entertainment: "With students competing for profit, writers [of *fu*] teem like bubbles in a frothing cauldron. The most eminent among them draw somewhat upon the moral teachings of the Classics, but the lowest of them string together vulgar sayings in the manner of entertainers and jesters." Although none of the writings of the Hongdu Gate School students and scholars survives, based on Cai Yong's description of them they must have been similar to the humorous and witty pieces written by Mei Gao and Dongfang Shuo in the Western Han. Emperor Ling must have revived this practice. From a conventional Confucian perspective, this kind of poetry lacked moral seriousness and would have been considered improper.

In one of these petitions Cai Yong denounced the corruption and abuse of power of the eunuchs, who retaliated by charging him with a crime. Cai was sentenced to be executed, but a sympathetic eunuch official made a special plea to the emperor, and Cai was sent to Shuofang (modern Inner Mongolia) to work as a convict laborer. Although the emperor pardoned Cai Yong the following year, the eunuchs continued to harass him, and he fled to the southeast where he lived incognito until 189, when the warlord Dong Zhuo summoned Cai Yong to serve in his administration. Dong treated Cai with great respect and appointed him to high office: attending secretary, then secretary in charge of documents, and finally master of documents. In 190 Cai Yong was appointed general of the gentlemen of the household of the left. When Dong Zhuo sacked Luoyang and moved the emperor to Chang'an, Cai Yong went with him as his close adviser. In 192, after Dong Zhuo was assassinated, Cai Yong was arrested and died in prison.

Cai Yong was a prolific writer. According to his biography in the *History of the Later Han*, his corpus consisted of 104 works, including poetry, *fu*, epitaphs, dirges, inscriptions, encomia, admonitions, laments, discourses, prayers, petitions, and notes; works on the script, ritual, and music; and an "instruction for daughters." He has a total of sixteen *fu* attributed to him, but only three are complete. The most famous of his *fu* is "*Fu* on Recounting a Journey" (Shu xing fu) that Cai Yong wrote in the autumn of 159 when he was traveling from his home in Chenliu to the capital in response to a summons from the eunuch Xu Huang to perform on the zither. Cai traveled as far as Yanshi (just east of the capital), became ill, and was able to return home. He then composed this *fu* to provide a poetic record of his journey. Like the earlier travel *fu* by Liu Xin, Ban Biao, and Ban Zhao, Cai Yong's piece is an account of the historical sites he passed on his journey. Most of the historical events to which Cai alludes are examples of men who improperly arrogate authority to themselves, or who engage in treachery and deceit. In addition to his reflections on history, Cai also has vivid descriptions of the landscape. For example, he portrays the rugged mountains of the Hulao area (modern Sishui, Henan) as a place of twisting peaks, dark valleys, jagged cliffs, and plunging ravines that are difficult to cross in the wind and rain. Strong gusts blow from the mountains, the air is "biting cold," and clouds block the view in all directions. The darkness that envelops him is more than just bad weather. It rather represents the unpropitious political climate of the times. Thus at Yanshi he halts to ponder the prospect of a change in the weather, and as he gazes at the gloomy sky, his sadness only increases. Finally, after two days, he looks west toward Luoyang, and as he sees the sun begin to break through, he feels a momentary happiness.

His joy, however, quickly ends. As he is about to continue on to the capital, the poet recalls the corruption and arrogance of those in power. Although he does not mention them by name, it is clear that those whom he satirizes in the following lines are the eunuchs, whose lust for power is insatiable and who quickly suppress all dissent:

> The august house is resplendent, as if dwelling in Heaven;
> From a myriad directions they come, gathering like stars.
> The honored and favored fan their fires of lust even hotter;
> All guard profit without cease.
> When a front coach overturns not far ahead,
> The rear teams dash forward, racing to catch up.
> They exhaust their multifarious craft on terraces and towers,
> While the people dwell in the open, sleep in the wet.
> They waste fine grain on birds and beasts,
> While those below eat chaff and husks without the kernels.
> They grandly bestow liberal generosity on fawning flatterers,
> But in impeaching loyal protest, they are swift and sure.

At this point, Cai utterly despairs at the thought of continuing his journey to the capital, resolving to turn around and head for home. Cai Yong concludes his *fu* with an epilogue, written in the four-syllable line modeled on the *Classic of Poetry*, in which he declares that his purpose in writing the piece was to make a poetic account of the sites he had visited in order to examine the deeds and legends of the past.

Cai Yong's "*Fu* on Recounting a Journey" is a good example of the travel *fu* used for both personal expression and political comment. In his opening lines, Cai specifically says that he wrote the piece "to proclaim his deep-felt feelings" and thus he clearly conceived of the fundamental purpose of the piece as a means of personal expression. Cai Yong's *fu*, however, combines personal expression with political and social comment to a much greater degree than those of his predecessors. Although Liu Xin, Ban Biao, and to some extent Ban Zhao also engaged in social and political criticism, they directed that criticism against historical figures and did not comment directly on the contemporary situation. Their criticism had contemporary relevance only by analogy. Thus

Cai Yong's *fu*, with its long description of the rain-soaked terrain through which he journeyed and the extended satire of the men in power, is a much more immediate and politically focused piece than its precursors.

Although Cai Yong did not write any long epideictic *fu*, the range of his topics is quite broad. One *fu* that comes close to replicating the grand display style of the Western Han is "*Fu* on the Han River Ford" (Han jin fu). It is the first extant *fu* on a river. The thirty-seven-line fragment presents an account of the Han river, from its origins in the mountains of Gansu, its passage south to Xiangyang, to its entry into Dongting lake. Several pieces such as "*Fu* on the Writing Brush" (Bi fu) and "*Fu* on Strumming the Zither" (Tan qin fu) reflect Cai's personal interests, for he was an accomplished calligrapher and zither player.

Another unusual work is "*Fu* on Dwarfs" (Duanren fu). The piece, which may be complete, consists of a preface followed by a "song." The entire piece, including the preface, is written in rhyming four-syllable lines. This is a very unusual form for the *fu*. In the song section, Cai Yong introduces a series of avian images to portray the appearance of dwarfs: small roosters, little grebes, green pigeons, quail hens, hoopoes, and woodpeckers. He then compares them to two types of horse and various insects: locusts, crickets, chrysalids, and silkworms. The final section consists of a variety of analogies: door post, roof support, damaged chisel head, broken ax handle, hand drum, and shoe mallet. This *fu* displays the kind of wit and humor that clearly was part of the court *fu* tradition. Mei Gao's compositions at Emperor's Wu's court probably were similar to this. Thus, even though Cai Yong criticized the Hongdu Gate School *fu* compositions, it is possible that he too composed in this more "vulgar" style to conform to the aesthetic taste of Emperor Ling's court.

Perhaps the most innovative of Cai Yong's *fu* are those on erotic desire. One piece, "*Fu* on Curbing Excess" (Jian yi fu), was inspired by Zhang Heng's "*Fu* on Settling the Passions." Only fourteen lines of this piece survive. The extant portion has a description of a beautiful lady followed by a statement of the persona's desire for her. Cai Yong uses the "I would like to" trope that Zhang Heng used in "Settling the Passions." Instead of powder on the lady's face, Cai Yong desires to be the reed tongue of a mouth organ (*sheng*) in the lady's mouth.

Such erotic writing is found in two of Cai Yong's other *fu*: "*Fu* on the Maidservant" (Qingyi fu) and "*Fu* on Harmonious Marriage" (Xiehe hun fu). In the former piece Cai Yong celebrates the beauty of a lowly maidservant and even indicates his erotic desire for her. This piece aroused the wrath of Cai's contemporary, Zhang Chao (ca 150–200), who wrote a *fu* titled "*Fu*

Ridiculing "*Fu* on the Maidservant'" (Qiao Qingyi fu) to reproach Cai Yong for his violation of decorum. "*Fu* on Harmonious Marriage" describes a wedding ceremony replete with a description of the alluring beauty of the bride and even a few lines re-creating the scene in the bridal bed.

Although like most Chinese literary genres the stele inscription (*beiwen*) has an ancient pedigree, it was in the late Eastern Han that this form, especially the grave inscription, began to flourish. Liu Xie makes this point in the chapter of "Dirges and Stele Inscriptions" in the *Literary Mind and the Carving of the Dragon*: "Beginning in the Eastern Han, stelae and stone tablets rose up like clouds." Over three hundred stele inscriptions dating to the Eastern Han period have been preserved, and about half of these are grave inscriptions. The inscription was carved on a stone tablet that was placed before the shrine or tomb of the deceased. The inscription was usually in two parts: a prose preface followed by a rhymed verse conclusion.

The most prolific writer of stele inscriptions was Cai Yong. His extant works contain the titles of forty-one stele inscriptions, most of which seem to be complete. Only a few of these attributions have been questioned. Cai Yong began writing grave inscriptions in his early twenties. His first extant work is the inscription he wrote for Cai Lang (d. 153), who perhaps was one of Cai Yong's relatives. Before he took up his first post in 171, he wrote grave inscriptions for prominent persons, including Yang Bing (92–165), a high court official, who was one of the most outspoken opponents of the eunuchs in the 160s, and Du Shang (117–166), a regional governor who had distinguished himself quelling bandit uprisings in Jingzhou (modern Hubei).

Cai Yong composed a stele inscription and a tripod vessel inscription for one of the most uncompromising opponents of the eunuchs, Zhu Mu (100–163). Cai Yong also composed stele inscriptions for the contemporary recluse scholars Guo Tai (128–169) and Juan Dian (95–169). Guo Tai was one of the most celebrated student leaders of the Imperial Academy during the 160s. When he retired to his home in Jiexiu, Taiyuan (southeast of modern Jiexiu County, Shanxi), he reputedly attracted a following of over a thousand students. He died at the young age of forty-two, and over a thousand people attended his funeral. Cai Yong's grave inscription for Guo Tai was greatly admired and was included in the *Selections of Refined Literature*. Juan Dian may have been from Cai Yong's home commandery of Chenliu. Cai Yong may also be the author of the famous "Stele Inscription for Wangzi Qiao." Wangzi Qiao was a Daoist immortal who had a tomb north of Meng (northeast of modern Shangqiu City, Henan).

After Cai Yong took up office in the capital in 171, he continued to write stele inscriptions. In 172, he composed two grave inscriptions for his teacher Hu Guang, who passed away in that year. Because Hu Guang was somewhat unprincipled in his later years, some scholars have faulted Cai Yong for "toadying to the grave." However, given Cai's close connections with Hu Guang, it is not surprising that he wrote so effusively about his teacher.

Even after he left the court in 178 and went into exile, Cai was active writing grave inscriptions. Among Cai Yong's most famous stele inscriptions are the three epitaphs he wrote for Chen Shi (104–186), who died in 186 at the age of eighty-four. Chen Shi, a native of Xu in Yingchuan (southeast of modern Zhengzhou), was a man of humble background who served in local administrative posts, never rising to high office. In his later years, he received numerous requests to take office at the court, but he declined each invitation. Known for his tolerance and forbearance, at the time of his death it is said that 30,000 people went to mourn him. Cai Yong actually received a commission to write the first of the grave inscriptions from the governor of Henan. This piece, under the title "Grave Inscription for Chen Taiqiu," was included in the *Selections of Refined Literature*. Perhaps because Chen Shi did not have a distinguished family pedigree, Cai Yong dispenses with the usual account of family history and enumerates instead his moral qualities. The preface is also notable for including a rhymed eight-line dirge in four-syllable-line pattern. Cai Yong also provides an explanation of Chen Shi's posthumous name, Master Exemplar of Refinement. The rhymed inscription is relatively short (twelve lines) compared with the long preface. However, in the inscription Cai Yong grieves that with Chen Shi's death "profound words" (of the sages) have been "cut off" and "this culture of ours" has perished. Cai thus combines the group grieving for Chen Shi with a lament on the decline of the dynasty.

Eastern Han poetry

Poetry in the Eastern Han consists of verse in a variety of forms. The oldest form is the four-syllable-line pattern that was used in most of the poems in the *Classic of Poetry*. Another form is the "Chu Song" pattern that was derived from the "Nine Songs" in the *Verses of Chu*. Two forms are new in the Han, the five-syllable line and the seven-syllable line.

The best documented of these four forms is the four-syllable-line poem, which generally was reserved for serious purposes and occasions. It was also used for expressions of political criticism and personal sentiments. For example, in the Western Han, Wei Meng (ca 228–ca 156 BC) is credited with composing "Poem of Admonition" (Feng jian shi) in five four-syllable-line stanzas to criticize the dissolute behavior of Prince Liu Wu of Chu (d. 154 BC). Writing such poems may have been a family tradition in the Wei family. Wei Meng's sixth-generation descendant Wei Xuancheng (fl. 42 BC) composed two sets of four-syllable-line poems, one of which he directed as a warning to his descendants.

In the Eastern Han, some poets used the four-syllable-line form to compose praise songs in the manner of the eulogies of the *Classic of Poetry*. For example, Liu Cang (ca 30–83), prince of Dongping, who was one of the most learned members of the Eastern Han imperial family, composed the lyrics for a ritual ceremony in the temple that was built in honor of Emperor Guangwu after his death on March 29, AD 57. In AD 60, Liu Cang led the court discussions concerning the proper songs and dances that should be used in the temple ceremony in honor of Emperor Guangwu. The song composed by Liu Cang was the "Dance Song of the Martial Virtue." The extant text is a song in fourteen four-syllable lines. At the end of his "*Fu* on the Two Capitals," Ban Gu inserted three four-syllable-line verses praising the three ritual structures – the Bright Hall, Circular Moat, and Divine Terrace.

Other writers continued the practice of using the four-syllable-line form to write about their personal and family history. The best example of this kind of piece is "Fulfilling My Aims" by Fu Yi. In the second stanza, he refers to his descent from none other than Fu Yue, who according to legend had been a laborer at the earthen walls at the cliffs of Fu. Upon meeting him, King Wu Ding of Shang appointed him minister. Without mentioning their names, Fu Yi also refers to his ancestors who obtained noble titles during the Western Han.

Zhu Mu (100–163) used a four-syllable-line poem to conclude a letter "breaking off friendship" with Liu Bozong. When Zhu Mu had formerly served as prefect and attending secretary, he had taken Liu in and treated him well. After Liu rose to a high position, he acted in a most imperious manner toward Zhu. Zhu then sent him a letter severing relationships with him. Attached to the letter was a poem of sixteen lines of four syllables each in which he compares Liu to a greedy and rapacious owl who "feasts on stinking rotten flesh."

Perhaps the most artful of the Eastern Han four-syllable-line poems was a two-stanza poem by Zhongchang Tong (180–220) titled "Recounting My Aims" (Xian zhi shi). In the first stanza he compares himself to four creatures: a bird that leaves no imprint behind, a cicada that has sloughed off its skin, a snake that has shed its scales, and a dragon that has lost its horns. He then rides the clouds without the aid of reins, and gallops upon the wind without any feet. Dew forms his curtain, and he makes a meal of midnight vapors. He finally reaches the state in which he does as his heart desires and is oblivious to all human affairs.

In the second stanza, he declares that he will "convey his grief to heaven, / and bury his cares in the earth." He even vows to abandon the Classics and the philosophical texts:

> I shall cast aside the Five Classics,
> Destroy the "Airs" and "Odes."
> The hundred thinkers are trivial and confused,
> Let me submit them to the fire.

He ends the poem by stating his intention to leave the world altogether.

The poetic form whose origins are most commonly attributed to the Han period is the five-syllable-line poem. The study of five-syllable-line poetry in the Han is complicated by the paucity of authentic texts preserved from Han times. The *History of the Han* records one five-syllable-line poem, the famous "Song of a Beauty" attributed to the court musician Li Yannian (d. ca 87 BC). According to the *History of the Han*, Li Yannian performed this "song" before Emperor Wu. In the song he described an enchanting lady, whose beauty could "overthrow cities and states." The lady that Li Yannian was describing just happened to be his younger sister, whom Emperor Wu immediately recruited for the imperial harem. She died at a young age, and Emperor Wu grieved for her for many years. There are multiple versions of the "Song of a Beauty." The version in the *History of the Han* is not a perfect five-syllable-line poem, for the penultimate line is in eight syllables. The account of Lady Li in the *History of the Han* also reads more like romance than a history, and perhaps some skepticism about the date of "Song of a Beauty" may be warranted. It conceivably is an early Eastern Han rather than a Western Han piece.

The earliest source of five-syllable-line poems that are attributed to the Han period is the "Monograph on Music" contained in the *History of the Song* compiled by Shen Yue (441–513) in the first decade of the sixth century. Shen Yue includes texts of anonymous pieces he designates "ancient songs" that are conventionally considered Han *yuefu*. A good number of them are in five-syllable-line form. However, we do not know what Shen Yue's sources were, and it is questionable whether the received texts of these ancient songs are of Han date even if they are based on musical pieces that were once performed in the Han period (there is some evidence that some of the *yuefu* titles such as "Accompanied Songs" did exist in the Eastern Han). Two sixth-century anthologies, the *Selections of Refined Literature* and *New Songs of the Jade Terrace*, contain a few five-syllable-line poems that the compilers attribute to the Han period. The largest collection of putative Han five-syllable-line poems is the *Collection of Yuefu Poetry (Yuefu shiji)* compiled by Guo Maoqian in the late twelfth century. Guo based himself on the sources mentioned above as well as several now lost collections of *yuefu* that date from the sixth and seventh centuries.

The problem with these sources is not only their relatively late dates, but also the contradictory information that they provide about authorship and dates. For example, different sources designate the *yuefu* poem "On the Dike" as either an anonymous Han poem, or a piece by Cao Cao, Cao Pi, or Cao Pi's consort Lady Zhen. In addition, there are variant versions of what purports to be the same poem. Guo Maoqian tried to resolve this problem by claiming that the simpler or shorter version was a Han original, and the more elaborate version a revision prepared by musicians in the third or fourth century. However, recently Jean-Pierre Diény has argued that the musical versions are earlier than the so-called Han originals.

Perhaps the most famous example of contradictory claims about authorship is the "Nineteen Old Poems." "Nineteen Old Poems" is the title that the *Selections of Refined Literature* gives to a group of anonymous five-syllable-line poems. Other Six Dynasties sources attribute all or some of these pieces to known poets. The *New Songs of the Jade Terrace* credits eight of them to Mei Sheng. Liu Xie in *Literary Mind and Carving of the Dragon* mentions that "some attribute them to Mei Sheng," except for "Solitary Bamboo" (Poem VIII in *Selections of Refined Literature*), which is ascribed to Fu Yi (d. ca 90). Liu Xie says that "by comparing their style [with other poems], one can deduce that they are works of both the Western and Eastern Han." There undoubtedly were more than the nineteen "old poems" preserved in the *Selections of Refined Literature*. Zhong Rong (d. 518) mentions that there were forty-five pieces in addition to fourteen imitated by Lu Ji. The *Selections of Refined Literature* preserves twelve of Lu Ji's imitations. Zhong Rong then adds that the forty-five pieces "of old were thought to have been composed by Cao Zhi [192–232] and Wang Can." Zhong Rong does not comment on the credibility of this attribution. He only remarks that the "'Old Poems' are now so remote and obscure it is difficult to determine their authors or period." However, Zhong deduces from their style that they are "compositions of the Han [which ruled by virtue of] the Fire Phase."

Most scholars now believe that it is impossible to determine the authorship of these poems. We cannot even be certain whether the poems are of Han date. The "Old Poems" show traces of "folk" elements, notably formulaic phrases that can be found in the anonymous *yuefu* songs (e.g. "We are daily parted farther from each other – Poem I," "A traveler came from a distant place – Poem XV," "I wish we could be a pair of crunkling cranes" – Poem V). These are, however, features shared with known literati pieces written in the last several decades of the Eastern Han, and thus the occurrence of putative folk song devices does not constitute evidence that the "Old Poems" are popular pieces.

The prosodic form of all nineteen poems is the five-syllable line. In almost every line there is a caesura after the second syllable. Rhyme occurs in even-numbered lines. This is a very mature form of the five-syllable-line verse. A dominant theme that is found in nearly half of the poems is the sadness of separation (see Poems I, II, VI, VIII, IX, X, XVI, XVII, and XIX). Most of these poems concern separated lovers, or express the grief of an abandoned woman. This is a theme that is shared by both anonymous "Han" *yuefu* and literati poems of the late Eastern Han.

Poems in the five-syllable-line form are also attributed to famous Han scholars. Ban Gu's five-syllable-line poem, titled "Poem on History," is important, for, if genuine, it would be the first extant five-syllable-line poem on a historical theme. It praises a young girl named Tiying, who, after her father had been put into prison, volunteered to be a government slave if the authorities would release her father. However, the first mention of the piece is a letter from Lu Jue to Shen Yue dated 494, and the earliest texts are from the seventh and eighth centuries. Although most scholars accept the attribution to Ban Gu, recently some scholars have raised questions about its authenticity.

To Zhang Heng is attributed a five-syllable-line poem titled "Song of Concordant Sounds." The earliest source for this piece is *New Songs of the Jade Terrace*. The poem is written in the voice of a new bride, who declares her desire to offer devoted service to her husband. The piece traditionally has been interpreted as a poem expressing the official's desire to give loyal service to his ruler. However, the song is remarkable for its frank expression of erotic desire and, if genuine, may be related to such pieces as Zhang Heng's "*Fu* on Settling the Passions."

The *New Songs of the Jade Terrace* attributes to Cai Yong a *yuefu* titled "Song of Watering Horses at a Great Wall Grotto." The *Selections of Refined Literature*, however, records it as an anonymous piece. Thus most scholars do not accept the attribution to Cai Yong. Cai Yong's collected works contain a second five-syllable-line piece, the "Poem on the Kingfishers." The poem is a good example of an allegory in which the kingfishers represent grateful protégés of a kindly lord. The authenticity of this poem has not been challenged.

The received corpus of five-syllable-line poems attributed to the Eastern Han includes several well-known pieces whose authenticity is problematic. For example, the *New Songs of the Jade Terrace* contains three poems attributed to one Qin Jia, a native of the northwest who during the reign of Emperor Huan (r. 147–168) was sent to present the accounts of his locality in Luoyang. While he was gone, his wife became ill and had to return home to her parents. Being unable personally to send her off, Qin Jia reputedly sent three poems to her. His wife, Xu Shu, replied with one poem. Although few scholars have questioned the authenticity of these poems, it should be noted that there is no biographical account or record of these poems by this husband and wife before the *New Songs of the Jade Terrace*.

"Southeast Fly the Peacocks" (Kongque dongnan fei), also known as "Wife of Jiao Zhongqing" (Jiao Zhongqing qi), is another poem for which the earliest textual record is the *New Songs of the Jade Terrace*. This ballad is the longest narrative poem of pre-Tang literature. It relates the story of the wife of one Jiao Zhongqing, a minor official of Lujiang, who was expelled from her husband's household by her mother-in-law. She vowed not to remarry. When her family tried to force her to remarry, she committed suicide by drowning. Upon hearing this news, Jiao Zhongqing hanged himself on a tree in his courtyard. Although the story is based on events of the late Han era, the received version of the poem contains linguistic and other features that show that parts of the piece must have been written after the Han. It very likely is a composite poem that was revised repeatedly until the sixth century.

Another writer of the Eastern Han to whom long narrative poems have been attributed is Cai Yan (ca 178–after 206; alternatively ca 170–ca 215), the daughter of Cai Yong. She was married at sixteen to a man from the illustrious Wei family of Hedong. After he died, she returned to her parents' home in Chenliu (modern eastern Henan). Sometime in the early 190s, during the Dong Zhuo insurrection, she was abducted by a band of non-Chinese raiders. She eventually ended up in the hands of the Southern Xiongnu, who resided in the Fen river valley of southern Shanxi, near Pingyang. She lived with the Southern Xiongnu for about twelve years and became the wife of a Xiongnu chieftain and bore him two children. Finally, around 208, Cao Cao arranged for her to be ransomed. She returned to her home and married Dong Si of Chenliu, who was one of Cao Cao's provincial functionaries.

Cai Yan is credited with three poems that recount the story of her abduction, a five-syllable-line poem titled "Song of Grief and Anger" (Bei fen shi), a poem in the "Chu song" style by the same title, and "Song of the Tartar Whistle in Eighteen Stanzas" (Hu jia shiba pai) in a modified "Chu song" style. The authenticity of all of these poems has been questioned. Few scholars now accept the attribution to Cai Yan of the two songs in the "Chu song" meter.

One important argument against authenticity is that the landscape described in all three poems is Central Asian steppe, which does not fit the landscape of southern Shanxi where, according to the historical sources, she lived. Some scholars who defend the authenticity, at least of the five-syllable-line poem, have argued that Cai Yan lived during her captivity not in southern Shanxi but in Inner Mongolia, which had a steppe landscape that would match that of the poem. There is a chronological problem, however, in that the first line of this poem refers to the end of the Han dynasty. According to Cai Yan's biography in the *History of the Later Han*, Cao Cao ransomed Cai Yan around 208. The Han dynasty ended in 220. Thus, if Cai Yan wrote this poem, she would have waited twelve or more years to do so; moreover, she probably did not live as late as 220 and thus could not have known about the fall of the Han.

II. The Jian'an period

Overview

The Jian'an period (196–219) is the last reign period of the Eastern Han. Although it is a Han reign title, Jian'an also is the name of a literary period that approximately coincides with the actual political period. The Jian'an literary period begins in about 190 and extends to the death of Cao Zhi (192–232) in 232. In this period the five-syllable-line verse form reached maturity. Already by the mid-190s, poets such as Wang Can (177–217) were writing poems in this form. The older four-syllable-line form, however, did not go out of style and in fact may have been more commonly used than the five-syllable-line form. The most important poetic genre of this period continued to be the *fu*. Some 240 *fu* are known for the Jian'an period. Although many of these pieces are fragments, the extant corpus reveals a wide variety of *fu* pieces, including many group compositions on set topics.

Prose writing also flourished during the Jian'an period. The letter and petition were written in great numbers. One new form of the petition is the "expression" (*biao*), a form that many writers used to express their personal feelings. There are thirty-four "expressions" credited to Cao Zhi alone. Extant letters include correspondence between several writers. Many of these letters are also on personal matters.

The Jian'an period was a time of much debate and argument, and the discourse was a common literary form. Discourses include discrete essays as well as large collections. For example, in 217, Cao Pi (187–226) compiled *Normative Discourses* (*Dian lun*), a collection of twenty essays on matters pertaining to the quest for immortality (Cao Pi denounces it), history (notably assessments of Han emperors), literature, stories about famous swords, and even an autobiography. In 230 his son Emperor Ming had it carved on six stone stelae, thus showing the importance of this text in the Jian'an era. Cao Pi even sent a copy written on silk to his rival Sun Quan in Wu.

The only complete essay in this collection is "Discussing Literature." This work is often hailed as the first declaration of independence for literature. For example, Cao Pi is the first to divide literature into four classes and identify the style that is best suited for each group. He also attributes to writing the quality of "breath" or "vitality (*qi*) that a writer imparts to his composition. However, at the end of the essay Cao Pi defines "writing" (*wenzhang*) as the "great undertaking that pertains to managing the state." Although Cao Pi modifies this claim by going on to specify that it is through literature that a man can be known in later ages, the type of writing to which Cao Pi attaches highest value is moral and political philosophy. He singles out one contemporary work as the most exemplary form of writing, the *Discourses on the Mean* (*Zhong lun*) by Xu Gan (170–217 or 218). Xu Gan had earlier served the Cao court where he wrote both poetry and *fu*. In 216, he retired to a country village where he gave up writing poetry, *fu*, stele inscriptions, and other genres of belles-lettres. He then wrote the *Discourses on the Mean*, a work that was intended "to propagate the greater meaning of the Way." Cao Pi's endorsement of Xu Gan's work shows that he did not conceive of literature as fully autonomous.

It is commonly thought that Jian'an literature flourished primarily because of the literary interests of Cao Cao and his sons. It is certainly true that Cao Cao and his two sons, Cao Pi and Cao Zhi, were among the foremost patrons of literature. In Xuchang, where in 196 Cao Cao had taken the last Han emperor (Xian, r. 190–220) into his "protection," a number of prominent writers gathered in the early years of the Jian'an era. These writers included Kong Rong, Mi Heng, and Yang Xiu.

Kong Rong (153–208) was a twentieth-generation descendant of Confucius. Known for his biting wit and outspoken manner, he rose to prominence in his native Lu (modern Qufu, Shandong) around 190, when he established a new city to care for refugees of the Yellow Turban uprising. Kong Rong fled to Xu in 196 and held several high positions on Cao Cao's staff, even daring to object to the proposal to reinstate corporal punishment. Annoyed with Kong's insolence and criticism of his usurpation of imperial prerogatives, Cao Cao eventually had him executed in 208.

Kong Rong was a patron of young scholars, among whom was Mi Heng (173–198), a precocious but eccentric young talent who often offended his patrons with his sharp rebukes and arrogant manner. When Mi Heng arrived at Xu in 196, Kong Rong composed a petition recommending him to the court. This piece is a much-admired work of parallel prose. After suffering repeated insults from Mi Heng, Cao Cao had the impudent young man sent to Liu Biao. In 198 Mi Heng was executed by the local satrap, Huang Zu, who could not tolerate Mi Heng's insolence. Mi Heng is best known for his "Fu on the Parrot" (Yingwu fu). The parrot of this piece represents Mi Heng himself, who like the parrot is confined in the "gilded cage" of the stultifying court society of his time, where he is constantly offending his patron because of his inability to control his tongue.

Yang Xiu (175–219) was a native of Huayin in Hongnong (modern Shaanxi). He came from a distinguished family of men who served in the highest positions of the central administration. Upon his arrival in Xu in 196, Yang Xiu became friends with Kong Rong and Mi Heng. Although Cao Cao admired Yang Xiu for his intelligence and quick wit, he eventually became suspicious of his loyalty and had him executed. Most of his writings have been lost. One of his pieces from the time he lived in Xu is a *fu* celebrating the construction of the new palace in Xuchang.

Although the Cao family played an important role in promoting literature, especially after they established their "capital" in Ye, it is misleading to claim that Jian'an literature was exclusively the product of the Cao family literary salon. In fact, the earliest works of Jian'an literature were not written under the patronage of the Caos, but at the court of Liu Biao (d. 208) in Jingzhou (in modern Hubei). Liu Biao, who was a native of Gaoping (south of modern Jining, Shandong), became inspector of Jingzhou in 190. He established his headquarters at Xiangyang (modern Xiangfan City, Hubei). In the early 190s, as a result of the turmoil in north China, a number of prominent writers and scholars came to Jingzhou and formed an important literary and scholarly coterie at the Jingzhou court.

One of the first writers to come to Jingzhou was Handan Chun (ca 130–ca 225), a leading authority on various types of script, and perhaps second only to Cai Yong as a writer of grave inscriptions. He arrived in Jingzhou in 191 and remained there until 208, when after Liu Biao's son surrendered to Cao Cao he received a cordial reception from the Cao family. In 193 both Wang Can and Po Qin joined Liu Biao's staff. Po Qin (ca 170–218) was a native of Yingchuan (near Xuchang) and was well known as a writer of lyric poems and *fu*. When he arrived in Jingzhou, Liu Biao treated him with special deference.

Wang Can (177–217) came from a distinguished family of Gaoping. As a young boy he had impressed Cai Yong, who turned over his library to him. Although Wang Can's family had a special connection with Liu Biao, who was also from Gaoping, Wang Can did not receive the deferential treatment accorded Po Qin. Liu Biao, in fact, was rather contemptuous of Wang Can, whom he considered "unattractive" and much too rude and casual. Wang Can spent fifteen years in Jingzhou, and during this time he wrote some of his most famous poems. Wang Can's most admired poems come from this period, notably the "Sevenfold Laments." Wang Can wrote the first of these poems in 193, just as he departed from Chang'an for Jingzhou. He recounts during his journey south an encounter with a woman who had to abandon her child. Although this is a common theme of the anonymous *yuefu*, Wang Can artfully uses the mother's abandonment of her child as a counterpart to his own abandonment of relatives and friends in the north, from whom he is separated.

During the fifteen years he spent in Jingzhou, Wang composed many poems, including the second of his "Sevenfold Laments" (Qi ai), in which Wang expresses a longing to return to his home in the north. He wrote three poems in the four-syllable-line form which he presented to other members of Liu Biao's entourage. Also while in Jingzhou, Wang Can composed his most famous piece, "*Fu* on Climbing a Tower" (Deng lou fu). Wang Can wrote this piece after climbing a wall tower at the southeast corner of the city of Maicheng, which was located at the confluence of the Zhang and Ju rivers, about fifty kilometers northwest of modern Jiangling. He begins the *fu* by describing what he sees from the tower. He sees the Zhang river, with its small tributary that connects with the twisting Ju river and its long sandbars. To his rear he sees hills and a long plain, and in front he gazes upon wet marshlands. The area also is the site of grave mounds, and the land is rich with flowers, fruit, and millets. However, as beautiful as the scene is, the poet is not happy in this place:

> Though truly beautiful, it is not my home!
> How can I remain here even briefly?

The literary salon in Ye

After the surrender of Liu Biao's son to Cao Cao in 208, the center of literary activity shifted to the Cao family salon in Ye. Most of the leading writers of the period took up residence in Ye and participated in the literary gatherings hosted by members of the Cao family. Among the Jian'an writers, there are seven who traditionally have been granted an honored place in Chinese literary history. They are the "Seven Masters of the Jian'an" (*Jian'an qizi*). The names of the members of this *Pléiade* already appear in a work of the Jian'an period, the "Discussing Literature" chapter of Cao Pi's *Normative Discourses* written around 217. They include Kong Rong, Chen Lin (d. 217), Wang Can, Xu Gan, Ruan Yu (ca 167–212), Ying Yang (170?–217), and Liu Zhen (170?–217). Kong Rong had been executed in 208, and thus does not properly belong with these Ye literary luminaries. Many of the works written for the gatherings at Ye are group compositions of *fu*. Some of them are short pieces written about precious objects that were presented to the Cao family. For example, there is a series of *fu* titled "The Agate Bridle" (Ma'nao le fu) composed by Cao Pi, Chen Lin, and Wang Can. According to the preface to Chen Lin's *fu*, Cao Pi obtained an agate, which he had made into a jeweled bridle. He then had other members of his entourage write *fu* about it. Another similar group of *fu* is on the *juqu* or *musāragalva*, a precious stone, possibly coral, that was one of the seven precious things of the Western Regions. Wang Can, Ying Yang, Xu Gan, Cao Pi, and Cao Zhi all wrote *fu* titled "The *Musāragalva* Bowl" (Juqu wan fu).

The salon environment at Ye also facilitated the circulation of literature. For example, Chen Lin mentions in a letter that Cao Zhi had shown him a copy of a *fu* on a tortoise that he had composed. In a letter to Yang Xiu, Cao Zhi mentions that his good friend Ding Yih (175?–220) once asked him to polish up a "small piece" that he had written. Writings even circulated over long distances. Chen Lin, who was in the north, was able to see a copy of a *fu* written in the south by Zhang Hong (169–229) on a pillow made of a burl of Phoebe nanmu, a hardwood of the laurel family.

The Cao family also hosted numerous feasts at which the host and the guests composed poems. There is an entire group of such pieces titled "Lord's Feast" (Gong yan). Authors include Cao Zhi, Wang Can, Ying Yang, Liu Zhen, and Ruan Yu. Some of them may have been written for a banquet hosted by Cao Pi.

In addition to literature, Cao Cao mastered other arts such as calligraphy, board games, and music. His interest in music extended both to the classical (*ya*) type and to popular forms. When Liu Biao's son surrendered to him in 208, Cao Cao acquired the services of the music expert Du Kui (d. ca 225), who had fled to Jingzhou in the 190s. Cao Cao had him compose the formal music for his court. It was, however, the popular or "new music" that most interested Cao Cao. Cao Cao is said to have set many of his poems to music. Indeed, all of the extant poems attributed to Cao Cao are *yuefu*, and the texts preserved in such works as Shen Yue's "Monograph on Music" show traces of musical versions, including indication of stanzas and notation of which lines are to be repeated. Cao Cao, Cao Pi, and Cao Zhi also wrote *yuefu* in mixed patterns of three-, four-, five-, and six-syllable lines. Cao Pi even wrote a *yuefu* that employs the seven-syllable line throughout the piece.

Cao Cao favored the four-syllable-line pattern. He also is one of the first poets to use the *yuefu* to write about his personal experience and contemporary events. For example, "Ballad of Dew on the Shallots" and "Ballad of Wormwood Village" recount the destruction and disorder that resulted from Dong Zhuo's seizing the last Han emperor and razing of the capital, Luoyang.

Cao Cao wrote seven poems on the theme of "wandering as an immortal" (*youxian*). Poems on this theme usually portray the persona traveling far off into the heavens, where he visits the haunts of the immortals. He drinks magic potions and ingests immortality-conferring drugs. Scholars usually trace the origins of poetry on "wandering as an immortal" to the imaginary journey pieces of the *Verses of Chu*, especially "Far Roaming." The more immediate stimulus for representing the quest for immortality was the Daoist religion, which had emerged in the second half of the Eastern Han and was firmly established by the Jian'an period. There are numerous Eastern Han mirrors, bowls, tomb mural paintings, and stone reliefs that depict immortals. The anonymous *yuefu* attributed to the Han period also include poems on this theme. The Cao family itself, including Cao Cao, had some knowledge of religious Daoism. Cao Zhi wrote extensively on the subject. He wrote ten *yuefu* on the immortals. Cao Zhi in his "Discourse on Analyzing the Way" (Bian dao lun) says that his father recruited experts on breath control, the "arts of the bedchamber," and macrobiotics. Cao Zhi goes on to explain that the powers of these men were exaggerated, and the main reason that Cao Cao recruited them was to restrain them from deluding the people. Cao Zhi is credited with a second essay, "Discourse on Resolving Doubts" (Shi yi lun), in which he recants his earlier views. However, some scholars have doubted the authenticity of this work.

The bulk of Cao Cao's surviving writings consist of prose. He has a total of 150 prose works, including letters, commands (*ling*), prefaces, petitions, and instructions (*jiao*). Cao Cao may be the most prolific writer of commands in the Chinese literary tradition. His most famous piece in this form is "Command Relinquishing the Prefectures and Clarifying My Basic Aims." Although the ostensible purpose of the piece is to proclaim Cao Cao's wish to relinquish possession of three of his four fiefdoms, it is also a work that combines autobiography with self-advertisement.

The Jian'an period writers exchanged letters with each other, and members of the Cao family and the members of their entourage were prolific letter writers. Many of the letters contain important information about the literary activities of the Cao court, as well as occasional remarks about individual writers and compositions. Although not a member of the Cao family "salon," one of the most prolific letter writers was Ying Qu (190–252), a younger brother of Ying Yang. He has a total of thirty-four extant letters, many of which express the delights of living the life of a gentleman farmer in the countryside.

The Jian'an period also saw the compilation of literary collections and treatises on literature. In 218, Cao Pi compiled a collection of the writings of Xu Gan, Chen Lin, Ying Yang, and Liu Zhen, who had died during the epidemic of 217–218. Cao Zhi made a collection of seventy of his *fu* pieces, and after his death the emperor ordered that a collection of one hundred of Cao Zhi's writings be prepared. Two copies of this collection were made, one for the palace library and one for circulation outside the imperial court. Ying Qu even compiled a collection of letters, the *Grove of Letters* (*Shu lin*) in eight scrolls, which regrettably has not survived. It was probably a collection of Ying's own letters.

Cao Zhi and Cao Pi

Cao Pi and Cao Zhi are conventionally portrayed as rivals who competed to be named their father's successor. The competition between Cao Pi and Cao Zhi for designation as heir was fierce and involved intrigue and scheming on both sides. Cao Zhi's reckless behavior eventually resulted in the loss of his father's favor. One particularly serious offense was the riding of his chariot down the speedway of the palace and going out through the major's gate, possibly in 217. Thus, in November or December of 217, Cao Cao finally named Cao Pi heir designate. Upon Cao Cao's death on March 20, 220, Cao Pi sent all of his younger brothers to their fiefs. Cao Pi's main rival, Cao Zhi, was charged with showing disrespect for the throne by getting drunk and insulting the royal envoy. Cao Pi degraded him to the rank of marquis, and ordered Cao Zhi's partisans, Ding Yi and his younger brother Ding Yih, put to death. Throughout Cao Pi's reign and that of his nephew, Cao Rui (206–239, r. 226–239), Cao Zhi clearly was unhappy with the treatment he received from his emperor brother and nephew, who not only did not assign him any important court position, but transferred him from one fief to another so that he could not establish any permanent power base. One of the perennial subjects of the study of Cao Zhi's writings is the extent to which they express complaint about his frustrated official career. Hans Frankel's seminal article published in 1964 was an important contribution to pointing out the circularity of the attempts to read autobiography into Cao Zhi's writings, especially his poetry.

Cao Zhi is not alone among the Jian'an period writers whose poems have been read autobiographically, even in pieces that do not specify place or time. For example, Cao Cao's "Ballad of Suffering in the Cold" (Ku han xing), which is a poem written in the voice of a common soldier longing for home, is conventionally read as an account of Cao Cao's military campaign against Gao Guan in the Huguan area of Shanxi in 206. Cao Pi's "Unclassified Poem" (Za shi) is a poem on the common theme of a traveler longing for home, employing most of the conventions of the anonymous *yuefu* tradition. As early as the Tang, however, scholars have interpreted the homesickness as a metaphor for Cao Pi's feeling of frustration at being unable to be of service to the state.

Some of the poems of this period do have a clear connection with contemporary events. One good example is Cao Zhi's long seven-part poem "Presented to Cao Biao, Prince of Baima" (Zeng Baima wang Biao shi). During the early Wei period, Cao Pi had sent all of his brothers to their fiefs, and they could only visit the capital with special permission. In the summer of 223, Cao Zhi and two other brothers, Cao Biao and Cao Zhang, were allowed to come to the capital to participate in the seasonal festival. Shortly after he arrived in the capital, Cao Zhang died. Some sources claim that Cao Pi had him poisoned. After the festival was over, the brothers had to return to their homes. Cao Zhi wanted to travel part way with Cao Biao, but Cao Pi would not allow this. Outraged at this treatment, Cao Zhi wrote this seven-part poem recounting his travels but also expressing grief at the death of Cao Zhang and his resentment that he must separate from the prince of Baima. The poem combines several themes, including the hardships of travel, a lament for his deceased brother, and affection for Cao Biao. At the end of the piece, Cao Zhi even expresses skepticism about the quest for immortality.

Another issue concerns the relative literary achievement of the two Cao brothers. Although the vast majority of critics and scholars consider Cao Zhi the superior writer, there are some dissonant voices, including that of Liu Xie, who in Chapter 47 of his *Literary Mind and the Carving of the Dragon* argues that critics had wrongly depreciated Cao Pi's talent because he occupied the imperial throne and placed too high a value on Cao Zhi's writing because he had lived in straitened circumstances. Wang Fuzhi (1619–1692) also championed Cao Pi over Cao Zhi. He even claimed that only two of Cao Zhi's forty-three *yuefu* were worth reading. He condemned the others as "feeble and wasted like worm-infested peaches or bitter pears."

Most modern critics, however, do not concur in the assessment of Liu Xie and Wang Fuzhi, and Cao Zhi is generally regarded as the most important Chinese writer after Qu Yuan and before Tao Qian. Although the extant versions of Cao Zhi's collected works are Ming and Qing dynasty reconstructions, many of his important poems and prose pieces have survived intact. Cao Zhi was a prolific *fu* writer. According to Liao Guodong, Cao Zhi has sixty-three *fu* pieces credited to him. Although most of these are not complete, this still represents an impressive corpus of composition that began in his youth and continued until his death.

One of Cao Zhi's earliest compositions was a *fu* on the Bronze Bird Terrace, constructed by Cao Cao in 210. At a gathering held at the terrace probably in 212, Cao Zhi composed the *"Fu* on Ascending the Terrace" (Deng tai fu), in which he describes the view from the terrace and pays tribute to the achievements of his father. Another of Cao Zhi's early pieces was the *"Fu* Relating Sorrow" (Xu chou fu), which he wrote in 213 on the occasion of the betrothal of his two young sisters to the Han emperor. According to the preface, Cao Zhi's mother was saddened at the prospect of her young daughters becoming imperial concubines, and she had Cao Zhi compose a *fu* to lament their fate. In the *fu* Cao Zhi assumes the persona of a young girl, who has no choice but to accept her lot of being selected for the imperial harem. Another personal piece is *"Fu* on Homeward Thoughts" (Gui si fu) written in 213 to record a visit to the Cao family native place in Qiao. This short fragment contains a vivid description of the wasted condition of the town.

Many of Cao Zhi's *fu* were written for social occasions and include pieces that were part of a group composition. Such pieces include "Grieving over the Downpour" (Chou lin fu), "Rejoicing at the Clearing Rain" (Xi ji fu), "White Crane" (Bai he fu), "Pagoda Tree" (Huai fu), and "The Willow" (Liu fu). One of Cao Zhi's more inventive pieces is the "The Hawk and the Sparrow" (Yao que fu), a dialogue between a hawk and sparrow, in which the sparrow uses his clever wit to convince the hawk not to kill him. This piece, written in a colloquial style, is an example of the "vernacular *fu*" (su fu). Another similar work is the "Discourse on the Skull" (Dulou shuo), which is inspired by the famous story of Zhuangzi's dialogue with a skull that he finds by the side of the road. Zhang Heng in the Eastern Han is credited with a similar piece.

Cao Zhi's best-known *fu* is *"Fu* on the Luo River Goddess" (Luoshen fu). According to tradition, the Luo River Goddess is Fu Fei, who was the daughter of the ancient culture hero Fu Xi. She drowned in the Luo river and was subsequently worshiped as the Luo River Goddess. Cao Zhi composed "Luo River Goddess" in imitation of the "*Fu* on the Goddess" attributed to Song Yu. His motivation in writing the piece has long been the subject of speculation. There is the tradition that the Luo River Goddess actually stands for Empress Zhen, the wife of his elder brother Cao Pi, with whom Cao Zhi reputedly was in love; however, this account clearly does not accord with historical circumstances and should not be given serious consideration. The *fu* is also read as a frustration poem in which Cao Zhi uses the beautiful goddess to represent Cao Pi, who, after becoming emperor, refused to grant Cao Zhi an important position in the Wei regime. As in Qu Yuan's quest for Fu Fei in "Encountering Sorrow," Cao Zhi's brief encounter with the Luo River Goddess is understood to represent his abortive quest to receive a government post in which to demonstrate his loyalty and talent. This interpretation is more credible than the previous one, but there is no solid evidence that the poem is a political allegory.

Cao Zhi has an even greater number of poems. However, different editions contain varying numbers of pieces, ranging from seventy-three in the Ming movable-type edition to 101 in the collection prepared by Zhu Xuzeng (fl. 1837). Cao Zhi also began to write poetry during his early years. In addition to the many occasional poems he composed for the gatherings in Ye, he wrote several personal poems. One of these is "Sending off Master Ying" or "Sending off the Messrs. Ying" (Song Ying shi). Cao Zhi possibly wrote this poem for Ying Yang as Ying was about to leave for a post in the north. Some sources claim that Ying in the title refers to both Ying Yang and his younger brother Ying Qu (190–252). In the poem Cao Zhi describes his visit to Luoyang, which was in ruins after being sacked by Dong Zhuo in 190.

Cao Zhi's poetry also reflects the activities of the elite of his period. One such piece is "Ballad of the White Horse" (Bai ma pian), which tells of the deeds of young knights-errant. The poem may also express Cao Zhi's longing to achieve fame on the battlefield. Another piece of this type is "The Fighting Cock" (Dou ji shi), which describes a cockfight held at a palace feast. This probably is another group composition, for both Liu Zhen and Ying Yang wrote poems on the same subject.

One of the major themes of Jian'an verse is that of the abandoned woman. Poems on this theme are usually written in the persona of a woman who has been abandoned by her husband or lover and left alone to grieve. Both Cao Pi and Cao Zhi wrote poems and *fu* on this topic. They wrote *fu* to the title of "The Divorced Wife" (Chu fu fu), as did Wang Can and Xu Gan. These are likely group compositions. Whether these pieces refer to a contemporary divorce is a matter of debate among scholars. Cao Pi did compose several *fu* about contemporary women. His "The Daughter of Cai Bojie" (Cai Bojie nü fu), of which only the preface survives, tells of the ransoming of Cai Yan from the Xiongnu by Cao Cao. In Cao Pi's "The Widow" (Gua fu fu) the author assumes the voice of the wife of Ruan Yu, who grieves at the passing of her husband, who died in 212. Cao Pi also wrote a poem by the same title. Wang Can wrote a matching *fu* piece.

III. The Zhengshi period

Overview

When Cao Pi's successor Emperor Ming died in 239, he left no son as his heir. He thus named as his successor a young boy who was only distantly related to the Cao clan (if at all). Assisting him were co-regents, Cao Shuang, a grandnephew of Cao Cao, and Sima Yi (179–251), a prominent general. In 249 Sima Yi overthrew Cao Shuang and seized power for himself. The reign period between 240 and 248 is known as the Zhengshi period. During this time, the power of the ruling Cao clan began to erode, and the Sima clan gained increasing power.

The Zhengshi period was important in intellectual history for the emergence of the ontological philosophy known as "abstruse learning," or "arcane learning." The two leading proponents of this system of thought were He Yan (ca 190–249) and Wang Bi (226–249). The basic idea of these two thinkers was that non-being or non-actuality (*wu*) was the source from which all "actual" events or being (*you*) emanate. Basing themselves primarily on concepts taken from the *Laozi*, He Yan and Wang Bi developed the idea that since non-being was the basis of all existence, everything that happened was spontaneous and natural (*ziran*). All action should thus be natural and spontaneous, not dictated by moral precepts or predetermined patterns of behavior. The individual has the right to decide what is proper for each situation. Wang Bi, in his commentary to *Laozi*, Chapter 42, made this view clear:

> I am not one to force someone to follow my ideas, but I use naturalness to show the ultimate principles. Comply with them and one will obtain good fortune. Oppose them and one will obtain bad fortune. Thus, when a person teaches someone, if he opposes the teaching, he brings misfortune upon himself.

Another important arcane-learning thinker is Guo Xiang (d. 312), who was an expert on the *Laozi* and *Zhuangzi*. Men of his age rated him "second to

Wang Bi." Guo Xiang is attributed with an extensive commentary to the *Zhuangzi*, which is the source of Guo's thought.

The Zhengshi period also was the golden age of "pure conversation" (*qingtan*). This was a special type of discourse that developed out of the late Han dynasty practice of "characterology"; that is, formulating terse and cryptic characterizations of a person's abilities and moral qualities. In the Zhengshi period, "pure conversation" involved discussions on politics, philosophy, scholarship, and aesthetics.

The Seven Worthies of the Bamboo Grove

Some of the leading practitioners of "pure conversation" were famous writers and thinkers of the late Wei dynasty. One famous group is the so-called Seven Worthies of the Bamboo Grove (Zhu lin qi xian) that reputedly gathered on the country estate of Xi Kang (223–262) for drinking, composing literary works, and engaging in "pure conversation." Xi Kang's estate was located in the area of Shanyang (north of modern Jiaozuo City, Henan) at Bailu Mountain in the foothills of the Taihang Mountains. The seven included: Xi Kang, Ruan Ji (210–263), Xiang Xiu (ca 221–ca 300), Liu Ling (ca 221–ca 300), Wang Rong (ca 224–305), Shan Tao (205–283), and Ruan Xian (234–305). Scholars generally consider this group a fiction created several generations later when the ideas of the two most prominent "members" of the group, Ruan Ji and Xi Kang, were in vogue in the capital, Luoyang.

Ruan Ji

Two of the Seven Worthies are important writers. The first is Ruan Ji. Ruan Ji was the second son of Ruan Yu (d. 212), one of the Seven Masters of the Jian'an. Ruan Yu died when Ruan Ji was only two. Ruan Ji grew to adulthood at the beginning of the Wei dynasty. Traditional accounts say that he had few inhibitions, yet never expressed strong emotion. Although he was rather studious and a skilled writer, he enjoyed climbing mountains and exploring rivers, often going out for days at a time. Two of his favorite texts were *Laozi* and *Zhuangzi*. He also was a heavy drinker and skilled at playing the zither.

However well qualified for a government career, Ruan Ji spent much of his life trying to avoid serving in office. Although he was politically connected and even admired by some powerful members of the Sima clan, he was largely successful in declining appointments. Ruan Ji did serve briefly as a governor of the commandery of Dongping (north of modern Ji'ning, Shandong). The last position Ruan Ji held was that of colonel of infantry. In the late Wei period, this was a relatively low rank (fourth grade) and may even have been a sinecure. Ruan Ji reputedly sought this position after hearing that in the kitchen of the infantry command there was a large supply of ale made by an excellent brewer.

Ruan Ji had a profound interest in Daoism. He wrote several essays that espouse Daoist ideas. One of his best-known prose pieces is "Discourse on Understanding Zhuangzi" (Da Zhuang lun). The essay, written in a quasi-*fu* style, is a dialogue between a "Daoist," simply designated "Master," and a group of Confucian officials, who, hearing of the Daoist's outrageous ideas, express their doubts about his theories. The Daoist master then follows with a long exposition on Zhuangzi's theory of "non-distinction among things" (*qi wu*). His main argument is that all the varied things of the cosmos and nature are the product of "a single undifferentiated vital breath." Thus all things are part of a single organism or "body." Humankind obtains its bodily form through a process that occurs spontaneously, "by itself" (*ziran*). The human body is a microcosm of this spontaneous process. It is accumulated "breath" of *yin* and *yang*, and human nature is the "proper disposition of the Five Phases." Given that everything is from the same body, there is no distinction between big and small, life and death.

The essay is not a complete rejection of Confucian ideas. At the end of the essay, the Master even declares that Zhuangzi's book is not worthy of mention, for he does not discuss the primordial period of remote antiquity when society was simple and uncomplicated by artificial contrivances. According to the Master, Zhuangzi's greatest contribution was to teach people how to avoid harmful things and to nurture one's body so that the spirit will become purified. This has the beneficial effect of inculcating "loyalty and sincerity," and creating social order. This kind of blending of Daoist and Confucian thought is common among the arcane-learning thinkers.

Ruan Ji did show an inclination for the religious variety of Daoism, especially the tradition associated with prolonging life and seeking immortality. He claimed to have engaged in the search for immortals and for a mythical superman known as the Great Man. Ruan wrote a long *fu*-like essay, the "Biography of Master Great Man" (Daren xiansheng zhuan), on this hoary personage. Ruan Ji identifies the Great Man as a Daoist adept who resides on Mount Sumen (in modern Hui County, Henan). Some sources identify Master Great Man with the famous Sun Deng, a hermit who lived in a cave on Mount Sumen. He was an expert on Daoist breathing exercises.

Ruan Ji was a highly accomplished master of the five-syllable-line poem. His extant verse consists almost entirely of a single group of eighty-two five-syllable-line poems titled "Singing My Feelings" (Yonghuai shi). This group of poems does not form a cycle, but is a collection of poems that Ruan Ji wrote over a long period of time. Some of these poems show a direct influence from the Jian'an poets, especially Cao Zhi. Ruan Ji differs from the Jian'an poets in his more bookish and learned style. Many of his "Singing My Feelings" poems are full of historical allusions and quotations from a wide variety of sources. In addition, most of Ruan's poems do not make use of the *yuefu* conventions to the same degree that those of Jian'an writers do. Ruan's poems are rather "pure lyrics" that concentrate on the subjective expression of intense emotion. Thus melancholy and personal frustration are his most common themes.

Traditionally, scholars have attempted to read into Ruan Ji's poems all manner of political and social comment imaginable. Many of the poems are interpreted as veiled satires of the despotic Sima court. Already in the Six Dynasties period, some poets and literary critics recognized that whatever political and social comment Ruan might have intended in his poems was virtually impossible to uncover. Yan Yanzhi (384–456), who was one of the earliest commentators on Ruan's verse, remarked that "even though the purpose of his poetry rests with satire, his writing is full of concealment and evasion, and many ages later, it is difficult to fathom his real feelings."

There is, however, no question that some of Ruan's poems are satirical. We simply cannot identify in many cases the specific target of his barbs. "Singing My Feelings" LXVII is an excellent example of Ruan Ji's penchant for poking fun at the more ritual-minded men of the day. He portrays them as men who only are concerned with the outer form of ritual. They walk bent like musical chimes holding their jade insignia. When no longer bound by ritual restraints, they expose themselves as hypocrites. In other poems Ruan Ji denounces the excesses of the rich and powerful (as in LXXII). He also wrote some poems that seem overtly political. In XVI Ruan Ji recounts a visit to the ancient site of Daliang (modern Kaifeng), which was the capital of Wei during the Warring States period. As he looks toward Daliang he describes a gloomy and ominous scene. Birds and beasts are fleeing, the cold north wind is blowing, and the "yin breath" forms frost. Ruan Ji even mentions the ominous movements of the Quail Fire constellation, which according to an account in the *Zuo Tradition* augured the ancient domain of Jin's conquest of the state of Guo. Some commentators think that Ruan Ji is referring to the plot of the Sima clan (the lords of the latter-day Jin) to overthrow the Wei. The poem ends with the poet feeling sad and lonely. He finally declares that even though he wastes away because of frustration with the decay and gloom he sees about him, he will not be concerned about it.

Ruan Ji's "Singing My Feelings" contains many poems on the quest for immortality. A number of these pieces seem to be expressions of a desire to escape from the travails of the world (see XXIV, LVII, XXXV). In other poems in the set (e.g. LXXVIII, LXXX) Ruan Ji even indicates doubts that it is possible to achieve immortality. Thus he says in the second couplet of LXXX: "On the Three Immortal Peaks I would seek Red Pine and Wangzi Qiao, / But through time immemorial, who has ever met them?" However, there are several poems in which Ruan seems to attain an almost mystical state, as in LXXXI: "Would it not be better to cast aside the things of the world, / And ascending the Mountain of Brightness, attain the state of drifting at ease?"

Xi Kang

The second great writer of the Seven Worthies is Xi Kang (223–262), also pronounced as Ji Kang. Xi Kang came from a wealthy family of Confucian scholars. His father held several high positions. He died when Xi Kang was an infant, and Xi was raised by his elder brother, Xi Xi, and his mother, née Sun. Xi Kang had a strong interest in Daoism, the study of which he began at an early age. Like Ruan Ji, he cultivated the image for himself of a person who acted spontaneously and did not follow conventional rules.

Xi Kang was one of the leading spokesmen of his age for Daoist quietism, as well as for the more esoteric aspects of Daoism that involved the techniques called "nurturing life" (yang sheng). Around the year 243 Xi Kang wrote an essay titled "Discourse on Nurturing Life" (Yang sheng lun), in which he argued that it was possible for some men to live as long as a thousand years. In order to achieve the maximum life span, one had to follow certain practices, some mental and some physical. The mental practices primarily involve divesting oneself of emotions and avoiding such worldly concerns as wealth and honor. Emotions are harmful because they agitate the mind and thus sap physical vitality. The pursuit of wealth and honor is bad because when one has position and status, one is faced with more problems and more dangers, and thus has more to worry about. The physical practices for prolonging life include various breathing exercises and calisthenics, and the ingestion of certain herbs and drugs, as well as a dietary regimen that specifies the avoidance of meat, alcohol, and the grains. In order to achieve long life, the best method is to remain calm and avoid passion.

Sometime in the 240s Xi Kang married a princess of the Cao clan. As a result of his marriage, Xi received a low-ranking post at the court. Around 245 he received the honorific title of grandee without specified appointment, which was a sinecure. He then moved to Shanyang, located about sixty kilometers northeast of Luoyang. Xi Kang remained here for most of the rest of his life.

Although Xi Kang expressed his distaste for official service, he did not completely avoid politics. In 255 he considered raising an army in support of the anti-Sima revolt but backed out after Shan Tao advised him not to get involved. It may have been as a result of his contemplated involvement in this revolt that Xi Kang went into hiding for several years. Xi Kang perhaps joined the recluse Sun Deng, who lived in the mountains of Ji prefecture, about forty kilometers east of Shanyang.

Xi Kang's contempt for conventional society and government service is best reflected in a letter he wrote to his friend Shan Tao in 261. In that year Shan Tao was about to leave the bureau of selection, and he recommended Xi Kang as his replacement. Xi Kang then wrote the "Letter to Shan Tao Breaking off Friendship," in which he expressed his indignation at being asked to abandon his principles.

Xi Kang's contempt for conventions and authority eventually led to his death. In 261 Xi Kang became embroiled in a family dispute between his friend Lü An and the friend's elder brother, Lü Xun. Both Lü An and Xi Kang ended up being arrested. An old enemy, Zhong Hui (225–264), held the post of metropolitan commandant, in which capacity he was in charge of preserving the moral customs in the area around the capital. On Zhong Hui's recommendation that Xi Kang and Lü An be put to death for sedition and treason, Xi Kang was then taken to the Eastern Market of Luoyang and executed, probably in 262 (one source says 263).

Among Xi Kang's extant writings there are sixty poems, over half of which are in four-syllable lines. Many of them are on themes that we find in Ruan Ji's verse – the quest for immortality and the escape from the dangers of the world. He has one particularly well-known eighteen-part piece titled "Presented to the Flourishing Talent upon Entering the Army (Zeng xiucai ru jun); there also is one pentasyllabic poem by the same title. The commonly accepted interpretation is that Xi Kang addressed the poems to his elder brother Xi Xi. After the establishment of the Jin dynasty in 266, Xi Xi went on to hold the post of governor of Yangzhou, under the very men who were responsible for executing his younger brother in 262 or 263. There is evidence that the two brothers held divergent views on politics and on the entire question of the value of official service. The title of the piece indicates that Xi Kang must have written this set of poems when his brother first began his political career, presumably in a military position. The basic themes of the set of poems are two: first, to recount how someone dear, presumably his brother, has abandoned his ideals and compromised his principles by entering government service; and second, to relate Xi Kang's own progress in withdrawing from the profane world into Daoist escapism. Throughout the series Xi Kang uses the image of birds to symbolize himself and his brother.

Xi Kang was an accomplished zither player and an expert on music. He wrote a long essay titled "On the Non-emotional Nature of Music" (Sheng wu ai le lun), in which he argues that music has no intrinsic emotion. The emotion is only felt by those who are affected by the music. Another of Xi Kang's famous pieces on music is the "Fu on the Zither" (Qin fu). Xi Kang attaches to the *fu* a preface in which he tells of his lifelong passion for music, which he claims "can guide and nourish spirit and breath, relax and harmonize the emotions and feelings." He then mentions the practice of writing *fu* on the subject of musical instruments. He first mentions some of the conventions of these pieces: a description of the material from which the instrument is made, and the rugged and perilous qualities of the location where this material is produced. Xi Kang then faults earlier writers of *fu* on musical instruments for their lack of knowledge of music. He then praises the zither as the noblest of all instruments.

In the *fu* proper, Xi Kang follows convention first by describing the geographic region in which the paulownia, the tree from which the best zithers are made, grows. In a long rhapsodic passage on the mountains and rivers, Xi Kang portrays the area as one inhabited by hermits and immortals, who go there not only to escape the entanglements of the profane world, but to cut wood from which to make a zither. He then follows with an account of the construction of the zither, its tuning, and the zither music itself, with special mention of various tunes. He ends the *fu* with a description of the effects the zither music has on those who hear it. In the finale, Xi Kang praises the zither as the musical instrument for the perfected man.

IV. Western Jin literature

Overview

The Western Jin, the official dates of which are 265 to 317, is the only period between the end of the Han dynasty and the Sui when the Chinese empire was unified. Even under the Western Jin the hard-won unity and stability were short-lived and fragile. The first Western Jin emperor, Sima Yan (236–290, r. 265–290), did not conquer the southeastern kingdom of Wu until 280. The second Western Jin emperor, Sima Zhong (259–306, r. 290–300), was mentally retarded, and real power rested for much of his reign in the hands of his consort, the Empress Jia (Jia Nanfeng, d. 300). The period from 300 to 306, characterized in Chinese accounts as the era of the "Insurrection of the Eight Princes," is a time of increasing internal conflict, frequent palace coups, and civil war among members of the Sima clan. The Western Jin control of north China began to erode in the early fourth century as sinicized Tibetan, Altaic, and Turkic kingdoms began to encroach upon the northern border areas. In 311 the Xiongnu army captured and destroyed Luoyang – they reputedly put to death some 30,000 Jin officials. The Jin emperor was captured and taken to the Xiongnu capital, where he was murdered in 313. By 316 the entire area north of the Yangi river was in the hands of various non-Han peoples. In April 317, Sima Rui (276–322) established the capital at Jiankang and assumed the title of emperor of the Eastern Jin, thus beginning the period of division known as the Northern and Southern Dynasties.

Although its days of peace and stability were short, the Western Jin, at least before 300, was a period of remarkable intellectual, scholarly, and literary activity. The first Jin emperor undertook to establish ties with the kingdoms of Central Asia, and once again merchants began traveling the old trade routes to the commerce centers of Central Asia: Khotan, Kucha, Qarashar, and Ferghana. In addition to commerce, these Central Asian kingdoms were also centers of Buddhism, and it was from the cities on the Central Asian trade route that Buddhism spread into the Middle Kingdom. Thus it is no accident that it was during the Western Jin that Buddhism began to establish itself as a significant presence, at least in north China.

The Western Jin also is important for remarkable works of scholarship, some of which have endured to the present day. One of the great scholars of the Wei and early Jin was Huangfu Mi (215–282), a profligate in his youth who in his twentieth year decided to devote himself to serious study. He was never without a book, even when planting his fields. Huangfu Mi is the compiler of an important biographical collection, the *Lives of High-Minded Gentlemen* (*Gaoshi zhuan*).

Western Jin scholars did especially important work in textual scholarship and the writing of commentaries. The most distinguished textual scholar of the time was Shu Xi (263–302). In 279 a large cache of bamboo documents was discovered in a Zhou dynasty tomb located in Ji commandery near modern Ji County, Henan. These texts, known as the "Ji Tumulus Texts," included the *Bamboo Annals*, *Account of the Travels of Emperor Mu of Zhou*, versions of the *Classic of Changes*, and several collections of fabulous tales.

Although the Western Jin is not generally known as a time of great Confucian learning, the study of the Classics flourished during this period. It was during the Western Jin that Du Yu (222–284) made his monumental study of the *Zuo Tradition*. His commentary on this work became the standard and is still invaluable in helping us interpret this text.

Perhaps the most learned scholar of all during this period was Guo Pu (276–324), who lived into the early Eastern Jin. In addition to his commentary to the great *Erya* lexicon, he also wrote commentaries to such works as the *Regional Expressions (Fangyan)*, a Han dynasty dialect dictionary, the *Classic of Mountains and Seas* (a collection of fabulous lore concerning various places, some real, some imaginary), and the *Travels of Emperor Mu*. Thanks to Guo Pu, we now have some idea how to read the abstruse language of these works, much of which would be unintelligible today without his explications.

Another important contribution to Chinese scholarship of the Western Jin was the general anthology. The general anthology is a collection of various writings arranged by genre. The best-known of these collections is the *Collection of Literature Arranged by Genre (Wenzhang liubie ji)* compiled by Zhi Yu (d. 312). Zhi Yu is usually regarded as the inventor of the general anthology. The *Collection of Literature Arranged by Genre* was a large work of sixty scrolls. Although it is now lost, it included most of the major forms of poetry and prose, and was an important precursor to the monumental *Selections of Refined Literature* compiled in the sixth century. There were also other large collections from this same period. The *Zuo Tradition* scholar Du Yu compiled a fifty-scroll anthology titled *Excellent Writings (Shan wen)*; however, this work also does not survive.

When one examines Western Jin literature as a whole, one is immediately struck by its variety, not only the variety of genres and styles, but of subject matter and themes. The diversity of genres is something clearly recognized in this period by critics, and also by the anthologists, who for the first time arranged literary works by genre. Whereas around 220 Cao Pi in his "Discoursing on Literature" identified only "four classes" of writing, Lu Ji in his "*Fu* on Literature" (Wen fu), written around 300, extends the number of literary types to ten. What is particularly significant about Lu Ji's discussion of genre is that not only is he conscious of the diversity of literary forms, he also confidently identifies the qualities that each form should have. Although none of the genre anthologies of the Western Jin survives, even the few fragments of Zhi Yu's discourse on literature tell us that he had a catholic view of literature and that his anthology included a wide variety of literary types. The major genres of Western Jin literature are the poem, the *fu*, and various types of prose: the letter, expository essay, memorial, dirge, grave inscription, and lament, just to mention the more common ones.

A large amount of poetry survives from the Western Jin. Over half of the poems are in the four-syllable line, which was still highly favored. Some literary men such as Shu Xi, Fu Xian (249–294), and Lu Yun (262–303) wrote almost exclusively in the four-syllable-line form. Shu Xi even composed a six-poem set to supply lyrics for pieces in the *Classic of Poetry* for which only the titles had survived. Pan Yue (247–300) and his friend Xiahou Zhan (243–291) also prepared "reconstructions" of the same poems. One of the most common occasions for composing four-syllable-line poems was when writing to friends. Lu Yun wrote 110 stanzas of four-syllable-line poems, and most of them were sent to friends or relatives. He has a total of seventeen stanzas to Zheng Feng (fl. after 280) and ten to Sun Zheng (d. 303) all in the four-syllable line. Zheng has twenty stanzas written to Lu Ji, and Sun has ten. Zheng's and Sun's poems survive because they have been preserved in Lu Yun's collected works (Lu's collection is one of the few collections from this period that has survived in relatively good condition). Even writers who favored the five-syllable line wrote long four-syllable-line pieces. Pan Yue and Lu Ji sent many poems written in this form to friends, relatives, and colleagues.

The *yuefu* was still a favored form throughout the Western Jin. The scholar Fu Xuan (217–278), who bridges the Wei and Western Jin, wrote a large number of *yuefu*. Ninety-one of the 129 pieces in his collection are *yuefu*. Although fifty-three of these are formal ceremonial pieces, the remainder were composed to putative "popular" *yuefu* tunes. Although Fu Xuan's *yuefu* are in a variety of prosodic patterns, his best-known pieces are in the five-syllable line. Several of them are either written in a female persona or express sympathy toward a female figure. This perhaps reflects the continuation of the influence of Cao Zhi, who was one of the most admired writers during this period.

One can also find similar pieces in the smaller corpus of Zhang Hua (232–300), the statesman and author of the famous "compendium of medieval knowledge," the *Treatise on Manifold Subjects* (*Bowu zhi*). He has a set of five "Love Poems" (Qing shi) all written in the persona of an abandoned wife pining away for her absent husband. Zhang Hua even wrote one poem in which he speaks out against the ills of his time. Titled "Frivolity" (Qingbo pian), this long *yuefu* is a complaint against the extravagance and self-indulgence of the rich young dandies, who dress in fancy finery and spend all their time feasting, drinking, and cavorting with pretty women.

The Western Jin was a period of great prosperity for some, and it is possible to find examples of the kind of wastrels and spendthrifts that Zhang Hua portrays in his poem. There were several men who accumulated astounding riches, which they did not hesitate to flaunt before the eyes of their contemporaries. Perhaps the richest plutocrat of the time was Shi Chong (249–300), owner of the renowned Golden Valley (Jingu) villa located northwest of Luoyang. Famous for its scenic spots, the villa was the site of gatherings and banquets attended by distinguished statesmen and literary men.

In 296, Shi Chong hosted a large party at his estate attended by high officials and prominent men of the area who gathered there to pay tribute to Shi Chong and another official who was about to depart for Chang'an. The guests roamed about the estate, climbing hills to look at the view or sitting together on the edge of a stream. They listened to music played by zithers and mouth organs. Each person was obliged to compose a poem. Whoever could not write a poem had to drink three dipperfuls of wine. Thirty of the participants composed poems, and Shi Chong wrote a preface to the poems in which he describes the estate. Although only one poem, a piece by Pan Yue, survives, the Shi Chong gathering shows that group composition still flourished in this period.

Pan Yue

The most versatile writer of the Western Jin is Pan Yue, whose collection contains a remarkable number of pieces that reflect on his own personal situation and show a poignancy that is rare in earlier verse. Pan Yue came from a prominent family of officials. He married the daughter of Yang Zhao (d. 275), one of the leading military figures of the time. Pan Yue's career alternated between periods of service in the court and assignments to the provinces. Throughout his life he was confronted with the question that occupied many of his contemporaries: whether to fulfill the obligation to serve or to give it all up and retire to the countryside. Pan Yue actually did retire for two years. Between 295 and 297 he lived in his country villa located on the banks of the Luo river in Gong prefecture in the foothills of the Mang Mountains. Already in his "Autumn Inspirations" (Qiu xing fu), written in 278 at the age of thirty-two, Pan Yue declared his desire to leave official service and take up residence on his country estate.

Around 295 Pan Yue was a member of the entourage of Empress Jia's nephew, Jia Mi (d. 300). Jia Mi gathered around him a coterie of men who were known as the "Twenty-Four Friends." This group included some of the most distinguished literary men of the day, including Shi Chong, Zhi Yu, Du Yu, Zuo Si (ca 250–ca 305), and Lu Ji and his younger brother Lu Yun.

During his retirement, Pan Yue wrote his famous "*Fu* on Living in Idleness" (Xianju fu), in which he contrasts the frenetic pace and danger of his life as an official with the carefree and lazy existence he found in his country retreat in the company of his mother, wife, and children. Pan Yue would have fared better if he had remained in retirement, for in September of 301 he was falsely charged with collaborating with a group plotting insurrection. Pan Yue was arrested and executed, along with his aged mother, his elder brother, and his two younger brothers, as well as all of their children.

Pan Yue was ranked as one of the best poets of the Six Dynasties period. The sixth-century critic Zhong Rong includes him among eleven poets he places in the top rank of *Gradations of Poets*. In addition to his accomplishment as a writer of poems, Pan Yue was a master of other genres, including the *fu* and various prose forms, especially the lament, dirge, and grave inscription. Later critics were not always as kind as Zhong Rong, but one quality of Pan Yue's verse that almost all critics acknowledged was the expression of emotion. Pan Yue stands out in the Western Jin period as a poet who expresses deeply felt sentiments in his verse. This characterization especially pertains to Pan Yue's three "Poems Lamenting the Deceased" (Daowang shi), written to mourn the death of his wife, who died in 298. In the first poem he mentions the conflict he faces between following his "personal desires" to remain home and grieve for his beloved mate and the summons to official service.

Pan Yue wrote two other pieces mourning his wife: "*Fu* Lamenting the Deceased" (Daowang fu) and "Mourning the Eternally Departed" (Ai yongshi wen). In these pieces Pan describes the funeral observances for his wife and in the process provides a great deal of useful material relating to medieval Chinese death rituals. "Mourning the Eternally Departed" contains an especially affecting passage in which Pan Yue pours out his heart as he observes his wife's coffin being sealed in the tomb. In these pieces, Pan Yue actually violates ritual strictures in the piece. For example, the term he uses for the cart that carries his wife's coffin is "dragon hearse," which normally should be reserved for the burial coach of a ruler.

Pan Yue is the foremost writer of threnodic literature in the Western Jin. His dirges (*lei*) are not perfunctory pieces, but heartfelt expressions of grief for friends and relatives. Among his best-known works in this genre are "Dirge for Regular Attendant Xiahou" (Xiahou changshi lei), written for his friend Xiahou Zhan, who died suddenly in 291, and "Dirge for Ma, Overseer of Qian" (Ma Qian du lei), written for Ma Dun, who died in prison in 297. Pan Yue also wrote moving laments for his in-laws. The best known of these are "Dirge for Yang Jingzhou" (Yang Jingzhou lei), written in 275 upon the death of his father-in-law Yang Zhao, whom he held in high regard. His "*Fu* on the Widow" (Guafu fu), written around 278, was written on behalf of his wife's younger sister, who was married to Ren Hu, a boyhood friend of Pan Yue. In "*Fu* on Recalling Old Friends and Kin" (Huai jiu fu) Pan Yue recounts his visit to the grave sites of his father-in-law and his two sons, Yang Tan (d. 278) and Yang Shao.

Lu Ji and Lu Yun

Lu Ji and Lu Yun came from an illustrious family of the Wu state (223–280). Their grandfather Lu Xun (183–245) was chancellor of Wu, and their father Lu Kang (226–274) was grand minister of war. In 280, when the Jin conquered Wu, Lu Ji and Lu Yun retired to the family estate in Huating (near modern Shanghai). In 289 Lu Ji and Lu Yun, probably in response to a special summons from the Jin emperor, went to Luoyang, where they began a career with the Western Jin. In 301 Lu Ji became chief aide to one of the Jin princes who was involved in the Insurrection of the Eight Princes. In August 303, the prince put Lu Ji in command of an army to put down an insurrection led by a rival prince. On November 3, 303, Lu Ji's army suffered a devastating defeat. Shortly thereafter, Lu Ji was charged with disloyalty and arrested. Lu Ji was put to death by one of the prince's underlings. His entire family, including Lu Yun, was executed.

Lu Ji probably is best known for his "*Fu* on Literature," which was mentioned above. He was a great poet as well, and although his verse lacks the fervent emotion and poignancy of Pan Yue, he is a superb craftsman. He is the acknowledged master of the parallel couplet, which became an important feature of classical Chinese verse from the Western Jin on.

Lu Ji was proud of his Wu heritage, and when he first arrived in Luoyang he encountered hostility from some members of the northern elite. Lu Ji was also offended by what he considered violations of the traditional norms of etiquette and ritual that he observed in the capital. In 294 Lu Ji accepted a position on the staff of Sima Yan, who was stationed in the southeast. In 296 Lu Ji was summoned back to the capital, where he was appointed gentleman of palace writers. To celebrate Lu Ji's return, Jia Mi commissioned Pan Yue to compose in Jia Mi's name a long poem in four-syllable lines titled "Presented to Lu Ji, Written on behalf of Jia Mi" (Wei Jia Mi zuo zeng Lu Ji). Lu Ji replied with a poem in the same meter and of the same length titled "Replying to Jia Mi" (Da Jia Changyuan).

Although Pan Yue's poem is ostensibly intended to welcome Lu Ji back to the capital, he manages to hurl a few insults Lu Ji's way, first by referring to his home state of Wu as a usurper regime, and then by calling him a southern sweet-peel orange that when transplanted to the north becomes the inferior coolie orange. What he implies is that Lu Ji the southern aristocrat is now a vassal of a new master, the ruler of the Western Jin.

Lu Ji's response closely follows the content and form of Pan Yue's poem. Unlike Pan Yue, he speaks of his native Wu state in more favorable terms, comparing it to a soaring dragon. In the opening lines of the final stanza, Lu Ji refutes Pan's characterization of him as an orange. Lu tells him that he should have compared him not to a tree but to something more durable and valuable, "southern gold."

Lu Ji wrote extensively in the *yuefu* form. About half of his extant poems are *yuefu*. Many of the titles are those that had been used by the Jian'an period poets. Both Fu Xuan and Zhang Hua also wrote poems to these titles. In some of Lu Ji's *yuefu* he is clearly reworking the earlier model. For example, "Ballad of 'To My Gate Came a Traveler with Carriage and Horse'" (Men you ju ma ke xing) is a rewriting of a *yuefu* by Cao Zhi. Zhang Hua wrote a similar *yuefu* piece. It is possible that the Lu Ji and Zhang Hua poems were group compositions.

Lu Ji is also well known for his imitations of the so-called anonymous "old poems" of the Han. The *Selections of Refined Literature* contains twelve of these poems, of which eleven are rewritings of the poems in the "Nineteen Old Poems" group. The art of imitation has a long history in the Chinese literary tradition. Already in the Han, poets were writing imitations of the *Verses of Chu*. By the late Han, poets wrote variations of the *fu* attributed to Song Yu. By the Western Jin, poets became quite skilled in rewriting, often in more elegant language, lines and even entire poems from the earlier literary tradition. These include poems but also *fu*. For example, Pan Yue says that he wrote "Fu on the Widow" as an imitation of the Jian'an period *fu* written for the widow of Ruan Yu. A number of the lines closely emulate lines in the Jian'an writers' compositions. Fu Xuan wrote imitations of the *Verses of Chu* poems "Summoning the Soul" and "Heavenly Questions" that survive only in fragments. His "Fu on the Plum" is probably inspired by the "Ode on the Orange." Lu Yun's collection contains a nearly complete work, "Nine Commiserations" (Jiu min), which is an attempt to rewrite the "Nine Declarations" attributed to Qu Yuan.

Zhang Xie, Zuo Si, and Zuo Fen

The Western Jin is also the period in which landscape verse begins to emerge. The recluse poet Zhang Xie (d. 307), most of whose collection unfortunately has been lost, has left a few poems that show rich and vivid descriptions. His verse is full of twisting mountain trails, raging rivers, towering trees, roaring tigers, shrieking cranes, drenching rain, and howling wind. Zhang Xie has a set of ten "Unclassified Poems" (Za shi), which are remarkable pieces, particularly in their creative use of imagery. Most of these poems are landscape pieces that describe the horrors as well as the delights of nature. One of his favorite images is rain, the destructive power of which he vividly portrays in "Unclassified Poem" X in which he portrays the rain as a demonic force that creates a destructive flood.

A contemporary of Zhang Xie is Zuo Si, a scholarly man who spent much of his career writing a long *fu* on the three states of Shu, Wu, and Wei. When his sister Zuo Fen (ca 255–300) was selected for the imperial harem in 272, the Zuo family moved to Luoyang, and Zuo Si became acquainted with some of the leading scholars of the capital. Zuo Si only briefly served as an official, twice as an aide to one of the Sima princes and once as assistant in the palace library. He retired in 300. Zuo and his family left the capital in 302 for Jizhou (modern Ji County, Hebei), where he died a few years later of an unspecified illness.

Zuo Si's masterwork is the "*Fu* on the Three Capitals" (Sandu fu). Zuo Si devoted ten years to this long work, which occupies nearly three chapters of the *Selections of Refined Literature*. Zuo considered his *fu* as much scholarship as poetry, and he thoroughly researched his subject before putting brush to paper. Zuo Si was reputedly so absorbed in his project that he kept brushes and paper everywhere, even in the privy, so that if a line came to him, he could immediately write it down. After Zuo completed his *fu*, the piece did not meet with the acclaim he had expected. Realizing that he needed endorsement from a notable personage, he showed it to Huangfu Mi, who honored him by writing a preface. Another notable scholar–poet of the time, Zhang Zai (d. ca 304), wrote a commentary to the section on the Wei, and the scholar Liu Kui (fl. ca 295) wrote both a preface and a commentary to the Wu and Shu portions of the piece. It is said that Lu Ji, who once had planned to write a similar *fu*, abandoned the idea after seeing Zuo Si's poem. Soon the "*Fu* on the Three Capitals" became very much in demand, and reputedly the price of paper in Luoyang rose because so many important families wanted to obtain copies of it.

Zuo Si wrote a long preface to the piece in which he criticized the *fu* of the leading Han *fu* writers such as Sima Xiangru, Yang Xiong, Ban Gu, and Zhang Heng for their use of excessive hyperbole and lack of verisimilitude. Zuo Si then declares that in writing the "*Fu* on the Three Capitals" he has researched and verified every detail:

When I first thought of writing "Three Capitals" in imitation of "Two Metropolises," for the mountains and streams, cities and towns, I consulted maps. Birds and animals, plants and trees, I have verified in gazetteers. Each of the popular ballads, songs, and dances is consistent with local custom, and all of the prominent personages are based on old traditions.

In spite of his claims to maintaining verisimilitude, Zuo Si's *fu* contains almost as much exaggeration and fabulous lore as the Han *fu* writers he condemns. The section on the Wei reads almost like a panegyric to the Jin, which claimed succession from the Wei.

Zuo Si has eight "Poems on History" (Yong shi) in the *Selections of Refined Literature*. Although the title indicates they are on historical themes, most of the poems concern two or more historical figures. The first of these is not on a historical theme at all, but is a brief "autobiography." He writes about his youth, when he "plied the writing brush" and "read all manner of books." At this time there were military engagements on the frontier, and even though he was not a warrior clad in "armor and helmet," he read the military strategy works of Sima Rangju. His goal was to defeat the state of Wu as well as the western Qiang. "Looking left, I cleanse the Yangzi and Xiang, / Gazing right, I pacify the Qiang tribes." For his merit he did not expect any noble rank. After his work was done, he would simply make a "long bow and return to the cottage in the fields."

In other pieces Zuo Si does write about historical figures. In the third poem of the set he praises Duangan Mu and Lu Zhonglian, two Warring States figures who saved the state in which they lived from being invaded by the army of the powerful state of Qin. Zuo Si praises these two men for not accepting rewards for their achievements. Zuo Si devotes the entire sixth poem to a single person, Jing Ke, who attempted to assassinate the Qin First Emperor. Zuo Si does not praise Jing Ke's martial skills, but his integrity and unwillingness to toady to the rich and powerful. "Gazing from on high, he looks down upon the four seas, / How were powerful magnates worth his consideration?" Zuo Si ends the poem by declaring his preference for men of low status to the noble class:

> Although the noble consider themselves noble,
> I view them as dirt and grime.
> Although the mean demean themselves,
> I consider them as valuable as thirty thousand catties.

One of Zuo Si's heroes was Yang Xiong, the solitary scholar who was content to live in a humble house writing his *Exemplary Sayings* in imitation of the *Analects* of Confucius and his *fu* in imitation of the works of Sima Xiangru. Although he was not recognized in his own time, "After many centuries, / His fine name has won unique acclaim throughout the world."

Zuo Si also wrote two poems on the theme of "summoning the recluse." In the first of these pieces, he portrays the abode of the recluse as a pristine preserve free from human artifice.

> One has no need for strings and reeds,
> For the hills and streams have their own clear sound.
> Why have whistling and singing,
> For the dense trees sigh sadly on their own.

Zuo Si ends the poem by throwing away the pins that fasten his cap of office to his hair. Lu Ji also wrote poems on this same theme.

Zuo Si's younger sister, Zuo Fen, was also a skilled poet. In 272 she was selected as a member of the imperial harem, not for her beauty (she apparently was rather homely), but for her literary talent. In 274 Zuo Si presented her with a set of poems in four-syllable lines titled "Sorrow of Separation, Sent to My Younger Sister." Zuo Fen replied with the short poem "Heartfelt Feelings on Separation." She also wrote upon imperial command a long *fu*, "Thoughts on Separation," in which she complains of being sequestered in the harem without being able even to see members of her own family. Zuo Fen was in demand at the court to write formal compositions. In 276 she composed a dirge upon the death of Empress Yang. She also wrote a dirge for Emperor Wu's daughter, Princess Wannian, who died in 298. Zuo Fen's collected works in four scrolls, which existed in the sixth century, was lost by the early Tang. Most of the surviving works are fragments. However, she wrote *fu* and odes (*song*) on some of the same objects as the male poets of her day. These include *fu* on the anemometer, peacock, parrot, white dove, pine and cypress, and water bubble, and odes on the chrysanthemum and turmeric. Zuo Fen also wrote a large number of encomia in praise of virtuous women of the past.

Western Jin fu

In the Western Jin there were not many grand epideictic pieces like Zuo Si's "*Fu* on the Three Capitals." The more favored form was the "*fu* on objects." The two most prolific writers of *fu* on objects are Fu Xuan and his son Fu Xian. The elder Fu has fifty-seven extant *fu*, while his son has thirty-seven, and most of these are poems on objects. Between them, their corpus is a veritable encyclopedia of poems on every imaginable subject. Fu Xuan has pieces on the wind, clearing after rain, spring, summer, and winter; the writing brush and inkstone; the round fan and the anemometer; such musical instruments as the zither, lute, and reed pipe; ale; the games of pitch-pot and pellet chess; flowers and plants, including turmeric, honey bush, hollyhock, yellow day lily, chrysanthemum, and milfoil used for divination; such fruits as the melon, the pomegranate (which was a favorite subject of the Western Jin poets), the plum, peach, orange, jujube, and even the grape; and several types of tree, including the ubiquitous willow, and the mulberry, whose fruit he celebrates. Fu Xuan was especially fond of birds, and he has *fu* on the pheasant, hawk, parrot, and fighting cock. One of his pieces appears to be a dialogue between a hawk and hare and is similar to Cao Zhi's "*Fu on the Hawk and Sparrow.*" Other pieces on the animal world include several *fu* on horses, and one delightful poem on a fleet-footed racing dog.

Fu Xian has almost the same diversity of subjects as his father. He has two *fu* on rain (one in which he rejoices in the rain, the other in which he complains about it), and a piece expressing his feelings about the approach of the cold season. Like his father, Fu Xian also wrote a *fu* on the *xiangfeng* anemometer. Although he has no *fu* on the writing brush, he does devote one to the topic of paper, which had only been in existence since the Eastern Han. He wrote three pieces on fans, including a rather unusual fan made of feathers. Among household articles, there are *fu* on the comb, mirror, and candle. Plants do not figure as prominently in his *fu* corpus as they did in Fu Xuan's. There are only two such pieces, one on coltsfoot, and the other on the honey bush, a piece inspired by his father's *fu* on the same subject. Of trees, he devotes poems to the mulberry, the paulownia, and the shrubby althaea. Of the avian species, Fu Xian selected the parrot, the swallow, and a speckled dove for poetic description. One bird poem on the fabled *feng* or phoenix is a response to the famous *fu* on the wren by Fu Xian's contemporary, Zhang Hua, who used the tiny wren to illustrate the moral that it is the small insignificant creature that is best able to avoid harm. In Fu Xian's view, the only creature truly able to avoid all harm is the phoenix.

One part of the animal world to which Fu Xian devoted special attention is the insect realm. He has two separate pieces on the cicada, and one each on the greenfly (the proverbial symbol of the slanderer), the mayfly, the firefly, and the click beetle, known in Chinese as the *koutou chong* or "kowtowing bug" because it had the habit of nodding its head whenever someone touched it.

Jao Tsung-i has observed that the Western Jin *fu* poets and critics placed increased emphasis on "investigating reality" (*he shi*). The vast diversity of *fu* treating the variety of life in the natural world may be a reflection of this tendency. It is striking to note that, with the exception of Guo Pu, who actually lived into the Eastern Jin, the major writers of the Western Jin did not compose much escapist verse. Indeed, one finds among the *fu* of this period a strong interest not only in the natural world, but in the human world as well. Some of the subjects treated by Western Jin poets are quite mundane. One remarkable piece is the "Discourse on the Divinity of Money" (Qian shen lun) by Lu Bao (fl. 300). Concerned about the avarice and greed of his time, Lu wrote under an assumed name an essay in *fu* style satirizing what he characterized as the deification of money.

During the Western Jin period, *fu* writers begin to break away from the epideictic Han *fu* tradition and write in a simpler, more direct style on mundane and humble subjects. Rather than celebrating the glory and grandeur of the empire, poets who lived in grand mansions laud the virtues of humble living. Pan Yue, for example, wrote *"Fu on My Tiny House"* (Xia shi fu), in which he relates how he remains unperturbed and content, even in the face of searing summer heat and drenching rain that enter his humble cottage.

The poet who wrote on the most the mundane and humble subjects is Shu Xi. Shu Xi has five *fu* extant. Several of them show a playful, jesting quality that his contemporaries condemned as vulgar. One such piece is his *"Fu on Pasta"* (Bing fu). In the typical manner of the *fu*, the *"Fu on Pasta"* gives an encyclopedic account of various doughy foods such as noodles, steamed buns, dumplings, and pancakes, which in this period had the generic name of *bing*. The remarkable quality of the *"Fu on Pasta"* is the amount of specifying detail that Shu Xi provides. Shu Xi's description of *bing* not only includes the kind of encyclopedic display of learning that is typical of the epideictic rhapsody, it also contains a good deal of humor.

Shu Xi shows his penchant for humor in another of his *fu*, the *"Fu on Nearby Roaming"* (Jin you fu). This piece is a parody of the well-known *Verses of Chu* poem "Far Roaming." "Far Roaming" is a poem celebrating the celestial wanderings of a Daoist mystic who finds the profane world much too small for his grand vision. The wanderer of Shu Xi's rhapsody is a recluse who is content to live in a country dwelling, and who, unlike the Daoist traveler of the *Verses of Chu*, is not weary of the ordinary world. Rather than riding around the heavens in a dragon-drawn coach, the "nearby wanderer" mounts a rickety firewood cart drawn by a weary buffalo. He shares a well with two households, and his garden is only a hundred paces from his house. Instead of climbing up to the stars, he scrambles over his wicker gate, and "lingers about in nearby roaming."

Shu Xi's other *fu* also are of interest: "Encourager of Agriculture" (Quan nong fu), a satire directed against the corrupt tax officials who reduced the levies on farmers who bribed them with meat and ale; "*Fu* on the Poor Family" (Pin jia fu), a remarkably graphic portrayal of the hardships endured by a family who live in a leaky thatched hut, with nothing to eat but grass and leaves; and "*Fu* on Reading" (Du shu fu), an amusing piece that celebrates the delights of reading aloud in a humble cottage.

The best of the Western Jin writers of *fu* perhaps is Pan Yue. Pan Yue wrote on a variety of subjects, many of them personal. He wrote a long 767-line *fu* recounting his journey from Luoyang to Chang'an in 292. Titled "*Fu* on the Westward Journey" (Xi zheng fu), this piece is mainly a poetic record of the historical sites through which Pan passed. Just west of Luoyang, Pan Yue's infant son died at a post station called Thousand Autumns. In a passage the like of which is rarely found in the *fu* of this or any period, Pan Yue tells of this event, and notes the irony of contrast between the name of the post station and his son's short life span (seven weeks).

Pan Yue has many other remarkable *fu*, including a detailed account of the sport of shooting pheasants with a crossbow, his celebration of living in retirement in the country that has already been mentioned, and a marvelous piece on that noble Chinese musical instrument the reed organ (*sheng*).

Lu Ji and Lu Yun both wrote *fu*. Twenty-five *fu* pieces survive under Lu Ji's name; however, only two of these are complete: "*Fu* on Literature" and "*Fu* on Lamenting the Departed" (Tan shi fu), which he wrote in the year 300 to lament the death of friends and relatives who had recently passed away. Although Lu Yun has only eight *fu* extant, all of them are complete. This is a valuable corpus, for it gives a rare insight into complete texts rather than excerpts. Lu Yun even admitted in a letter to Lu Ji that his literary ability did not lie in composing either four-syllable or five-syllable verse. Rather, his skill was in writing *fu*.

Liu Kun, Lu Chen, and the transition to the Eastern Jin

Most of the leading writers of the Western Jin died early in the first decade of the fourth century. Zhang Hua, Pan Yue, and Shi Chong were executed in 300; Lu Ji and Lu Yun were put to death in 303; Zuo Si and Shu Xi probably died around 305; Zhi Yu and Zhang Xie did not live beyond 311. There are only two Western Jin figures who wrote during the period from about 306 to the fall of the Western Jin in 317 – Liu Kun (271–318) and Lu Chen (285–351). Liu Kun came from a distinguished family. His mother was from the Guo family of Taiyuan, and he married a woman from the Qinghe Cui family. He spent the first thirty-six years of his life in Luoyang. In the 290s he was a member of the court group called the Companions of Jia Mi. In 306 he went north to take up a position as regional inspector of Bingzhou (modern Shanxi), where he served for ten years until he was driven out of the area by the Jie chieftain Shi Le (274–333) in 316. He fled to the neighboring province of Youzhou (modern Hebei), where he was put to death by the Xianbei leader Duan Pidi (d. 322) in 318.

Lu Chen was from the famous Lu clan of Fanyang (modern Zhuozhou, Hebei) and was related to Liu Kun by marriage. He was the nephew of Liu Kun's wife, née Cui. Lu Chen joined Liu Kun's staff in 315, the year before Liu Kun fled to Youzhou. Lu Chen accompanied Liu Kun to Youzhou, but soon took a post with Duan Pidi. After Liu Kun was executed in 318, Lu Chen served various Xianbei and Jie warlords. He was killed in battle in early 352.

The bulk of Liu Kun's extant writing consists of prose. He is best known for his petitions. His earliest petition is one he wrote at Huguan (southeast of modern Changzhi, Shanxi) while he was on the way to take up his post at Bingzhou in 306. Liu Kun was moved by the plight of the people in this area, which had recently been raided by a Xiongnu army. He describes long lines of refugees on the road, many of whom are reduced to selling their wives and children. Two lines are similar to lines found in late Eastern Han and Jian'an period poetry that describe the devastation wrought by the invaders: "Bleached bones cover the fields, and the voices of wailing are filled with sorrow and pain."

From the time of Emperor Min's surrender to the Xiongnu to the end of March of 317, Liu Kun presented a series of four petitions urging Sima Rui (276–322) to assume the Jin throne. The fourth and most famous of these petitions titled "Urging the Succession" (Quan jin biao), which is contained in the *Selections of Refined Literature*, is considered a model example of Six Dynasties parallel prose.

Although Liu Kun only has three poems extant, he is mainly remembered as a poet. His best-known piece is "Song of Fufeng" (Fufeng ge) that Liu Kun wrote in 306 when he was on his way from Luoyang to take up his post in Bingzhou. Liu Kun portrays himself as a warrior who has reluctantly left Luoyang. He sadly moves through a bleak landscape where the chilly wind blows. He regrets that he is separated from his family, and is distressed that he has consumed all of his travel provisions. In the concluding stanzas he compares himself first to Confucius, who also ran out of provisions while traveling, and then to the Western Han general Li Ling, who despite his loyal service was charged with treason. Liu Kun perhaps worries that if he is defeated at Bingzhou, he may suffer the same fate as Li Ling. The most striking feature of the piece is the poet's use of the language and conventions of Jian'an and Wei period poetry. It is as if Liu Kun simply cut and pasted phrases from here and there to put his poem together. This kind of verse was relatively rare in 306, and one would like to know if Liu Kun wrote any more pieces of this kind.

At the time that he took up his post with Duan Pidi, Lu Chen wrote a letter to Liu Kun along with a long four-syllable-line poem in twenty eight-line stanzas to express regret that he must leave Liu Kun. In both the letter and the poem, Lu Chen recasts phrases that were popular among the arcane-learning thinkers. Instead of using them to make abstract philosophical points, however, he employs the rhetoric of arcane learning to convey the depth of his regard for Liu Kun.

Liu Kun wrote a letter and a set of eight twelve-line poems in reply to Lu Chen. The letter is interesting for Liu Kun's confession of his youthful attraction to the eccentric mode of conduct that prevailed among the elite in Luoyang in the 290s. He then tells of his youthful interest in Zhuangzi's theory of placing all values at the same level and not making distinctions, and of his admiration for the "unrestrained abandon" of Ruan Ji. Liu Kun says that these intellectual pursuits led him to disdain the conventional concern with good and bad fortune, life and death, good and evil. He also believed that one should be dispassionate and avoid feeling either sorrow or joy.

In the next section of his letter, Liu Kun tells Lu Chen that he had changed his earlier view. He now considers that "Lao Dan and Zhuang Zhou put forth errant nonsense, and Ruan Ji engaged in reckless behavior." Why did he come to this conclusion? Liu Kun basically changed his mind because of his personal experience. He had seen the Jin state fall, and many friends and family members, including his parents, had been killed. As much as he tried to dispel his sorrow, he could not do so.

In the poems, Liu Kun portrays the Western Jin as a state that has effectively fallen. To answer Lu Chen, he portrays him as a solitary bamboo stalk that, though growing alone, is a flourishing plant with lush leaves, supple branches, rich fruit, and lovely stems. This presumably is intended to represent Lu Chen's talent and moral virtues. Since Lu Chen, the bamboo stalk, has turned out so well, Liu Kun has no concerns about his leaving his service.

Liu Kun and Lu Chen continued to exchange poems, this time using the five-syllable line. These poems show gradually increasing tension between the two men that may have led to an open rift. One source of the tension is the perception by Lu Chen and some of his contemporaries that Liu Kun had imperial ambitions. There indeed may be some truth to the charge that Liu Kun was not a fully loyal servant of the Jin. What the writings of Liu Kun and Lu Chen show is that the transition to the Eastern Jin was a complicated matter for some members of the elite. Liu Kun, who began his career as a favored insider at the Luoyang court, suddenly in 306 took up a regional post in the strategic province of Bingzhou. For over a decade he contended with a succession of rival overlords in the north. Liu Kun was thus not so much a loyal defender of the Jin house, which by then was defunct, but a regional governor who tried unsuccessfully to establish his own regime in the north.

From the Eastern Jin through the early Tang (317–649)

XIAOFEI TIAN

I. Literature of the fourth century

The Eastern Jin (317–420): an overview

In 317, Sima Rui (276–322), a member of the Jin royal family, assumed the title of the king of Jin in the old Wu capital, Jiankang, and acted as the new regent of the Jin regime. In the following year Sima Rui formally took the throne as the Jin emperor and would be known to posterity as Emperor Yuan. Jiankang was to the southeast of the former Jin capital, Luoyang; hence, in the tradition of the Zhou and Han dynasties, the regime founded by Sima Rui was designated the Eastern Jin.

The territory of the Eastern Jin was much diminished, with the North fallen under the rule of rival states, and the southwest (modern Sichuan) dominated by the Cheng-Han kingdom until 347; but territorial reduction is not necessarily proportionate to intellectual vigor and cultural splendor. The Eastern Jin and the ensuing four dynasties in the South – Song, Qi, Liang, and Chen – represent a richness of cultural accomplishment on a scale unparalleled in pre-Tang China. Jiankang was to grow into a thriving metropolis, the world's most populated city in the early sixth century, with a population twice that of Constantinople, and, above all, a dazzling cultural and intellectual center that lasted until a northern dynasty, the Sui, united China in 589 and ordered the city razed to the ground. During this period of division commonly referred to as the Northern and Southern Dynasties, the south, for the first time in Chinese history, ceased being a periphery to the Chinese heartland in the Yellow River valley.

During these centuries the south remained mostly free from large-scale war and destruction, offering an opportunity for literary and scholarly undertakings. In the Eastern Jin the fate of the empire was controlled by a number of great families that had immigrated from the north. These families nevertheless needed the weakened imperial government to maintain a balance of power. With the maneuvers of a few brilliant statesmen and able generals, the Eastern Jin enjoyed relative peace and prosperity for about a century, despite several rebellions, the threat of its northern foes, and the émigré families' clashes with the local southern elite. The great families not only controlled the court politics but also asserted their cultural authority in literature and the arts. Most Eastern Jin writers and artists were members of aristocratic clans, or at least of the gentry, who had the social and economic advantages to devote themselves to literary production.

At the beginning of the fourth century, the cultural atmosphere of the south was remarkably different from that of the former Jin capital, Luoyang. The "arcane discourse" (xuanyan) on the Laozi and Zhuangzi embraced by the Luoyang elite had never penetrated the south, and noted southern literary figures of the early Eastern Jin, such as Gan Bao (d. 336), Ge Hong (283–343), and Yu Yu (ca 270s–330s), publicly condemned the open scorn of conventional social norms that was associated with those who practiced arcane discourse. Yet their very disapproval of contemporary emulation of such northern cultural fashions indicated just how much the south had fallen under the influence of the northern émigré elite. "Pure conversation" continued to be fashionable; and as Buddhism gained influence in court, Buddhist scriptures, particularly the Vimalarkīrti-nirdeśa Sūtra, became part of arcane discourse. The Eastern Jin elite, however, never allowed themselves to be carried away by spiritual pursuits. The powerful minister Yu Liang (289–340), a skillful interlocutor on the Zhuangzi and Laozi, was known for his strict observance of propriety; another famous statesman, Xie An (320–385), staged a show of nonchalance on the eve of a historic battle that was to determine the fate of the Jin empire; but after throwing a grand party, he went home and duly dealt with the military matters awaiting his decision. The fourth century, on the whole, was a period of convergence of diverse influences, a period of delicate balance between the northern and southern ways of life and scholarship, cultural sophistication and panache and a down-to-earth practicality brought about by the precarious political situation.

By the fourth century, paper was becoming the most important writing medium. Lightweight and easy to use, it contributed to the proliferation of writing. The bibliographical section of History of the Sui (Sui shu), compiled in the early seventh century, recorded the literary collections of about 140 Eastern Jin men and women, a number almost twice that of the Han writers. Papermaking in the Eastern Jin was facilitated by the utilization of local raw materials, such as rattan, grown primarily in southeastern China. When Wang Xizhi (303–361), the renowned calligrapher and writer, was serving as magistrate at Guiji (modern Shaoxing, Zhejiang), Xie An asked him for paper and reportedly received the entire stock of the county storehouse, which amounted to 90,000 sheets. In 402 Huan Xuan (369–404), the rebel general who proclaimed himself emperor, issued an edict: "In the ancient times there was no paper, and so bamboo slips were used; the use of bamboo slips had nothing to do with showing respect. From now on, all bamboo slips should be replaced with yellow paper." This edict shows that although bamboo and wooden slips had not entirely disappeared from use, the practice was fast fading. Yellow paper, treated with an insecticidal dye, lasted longer than plain paper, and was commonly used for important official documents.

Paper was cheap, but only relatively and not by any absolute standard. Ge Hong, a learned scholar and devoted Daoist, reminisced that in his youthful days, because of strained family circumstances, he had to make economical use of paper by writing on both sides of a sheet; as a result, few people could read what he wrote. Another telling example is that of the historian Wang Yin, a learned man from a humble family background. Slandered by his ambitious colleague Yu Yu, a member of the southern elite who was also engaged in the writing of the Jin history, Wang Yin was dismissed from office. He managed to finish writing the history of the Jin only with the help of Yu Liang, who "provided him with paper and brush." The cases of Ge Hong and Wang Yin demonstrate that with the Eastern Jin elite's monopoly of the resources of writing, it was quite unthinkable for socially underprivileged people to produce literary compositions, let alone large tomes.

Literary composition was primarily an aristocratic affair in the Eastern Jin. It served diverse functions in social life. Poetry was written at court banquets or private parties, on excursions to scenic sites, or as letters exchanged between friends. Despite the increasing popularity of five-syllable-line poetry, the four-syllable line still seemed to be the dominant verse form, particularly in public circumstances. The Western Jin scholar Zhi Yu had insisted that four-syllable-line poetry was normative, a view that prevailed until the fifth century, when poetry in the five-syllable line became firmly established as the predominant form.

Even more than poetry, prose played a prominent role in the social world. Apart from public prose forms such as petitions to the throne, proclamations, or epitaphs for famous personages, the traditional genre of *fu* continued to be important and proved instrumental in the dynasty-building project of the Eastern Jin. The writing of histories flourished in the fourth century, as both official and private enterprises. In conjunction with an intensified awareness of regional and familial identities, the compilation of dynastic histories was paralleled by that of the histories of clans and regions as well as geographic treatises. Dynastic histories emphasized the macrocosmic interests of the state, while accounts of places, clans, and particular groups of people such as recluses, filial sons, and noted women tended toward the local and the individual.

Closely related to the writing of history were collections of "strange tales" or "anomaly accounts" (zhiguai) that gave account of supernatural phenomena, exotic locales, and fantastic flora and fauna. As a genre of writing it parallels what Western classical scholars call "paradoxography," writings about marvels. This new genre came into maturity in the Eastern Jin, with Gan Bao's In Search of the Supernatural (Soushen ji) as its representative work. Although regarded in modern times as marking the "birth of Chinese fiction," in this period the recording of such tales was undertaken not as a literary endeavor, but rather in the spirit of chronicling true occurrences or at least preserving ancient documents for future generations. The language of such tales, which are never very long, is usually plain and straightforward, and their narrative pattern betrays a strong influence of the historian's style.

The Eastern Jin saw a remarkable growth of landscape representation in prose, poetry, and painting. Landscape was an essential element in the so-called "poetry of arcane discourse" (xuanyan shi) of the fourth century, a poetry drawing heavily upon the terminology and concerns of the philosophy expounded in the Laozi and Zhuangzi as well as in Buddhist doctrine, which was enthusiastically accepted by more and more members of the Eastern Jin elite. For the early medieval Chinese, however, nature was not just the object of aesthetic appreciation, but was also populated with gods, goddesses, spirits, and goblins, and dotted with magical plants. Recluses sought peace and quiet in the mountains, and Daoist adepts sought immortality and transcendence. These two roles were undistinguishable, as many recluses in the third and fourth centuries went into the mountains with the explicit purpose of finding herbs and minerals for making elixirs. Acquiring the ultimate truth embodied in nature and acquiring the ingredients for immortality drugs turned out to be two sides of the same coin, as they both pointed to transcendence. "Wandering as an immortal" (youxian) was a popular poetic topic in the Eastern Jin. Becoming a recluse, another important theme, shared the element of shunning the madding crowd with poems on "wandering as an immortal." In the hands of the late Eastern Jin poet Tao Yuanming (365?–427, also known as Tao Qian), the conventional vocabulary and images of poems on reclusion were transformed into a much more personalized poetry not only about the poet's decision to withdraw from public service, but, more importantly, about how he lived and struggled with his decision from day to day. Tao Yuanming's writings were a testimony to discovering and justifying the values of private life as opposed to the demands of the public world; this aspect of his work was deeply embedded in the cultural and intellectual contexts of his age.

Social uses of literature

Many early Eastern Jin writers straddled the two halves of the Jin dynasty, and the northern elite suffered the most from the chaos of the last Western Jin years. Kong Yan (268–320), a descendant of Confucius and a well-known scholar and historian, crossed the Yangzi river and sought refuge in the south between 307 and 311. A few fragments from a work of his entitled *An Account of Being in Adversity* (*Zaiqiong ji*) deserve mention because they are the only surviving record of the devastation of the north, offering a glimpse into the experience of one individual and his family during the civil wars. One section reads,

> The bandits broke into our home. At the time, we had over three thousand bolts of silk and cloth, as well as garments and utensils, in the house. I told the maids and servants to bring them all out and display them in the courtyard, so that the bandits could take whatever they wanted. Thereby the bandits vied with one another to seize our belongings and could not spare a moment to kill us.

Another section reads,

> I sent a messenger to inform Sun Zhongkai, the magistrate of Yiyang, of our deprivation and obtained from him two bolts of silk and one broken carriage. I sold the carriage for three bolts of silk, which I then exchanged for one bushel of rice and twenty decalitres of acorns to feed the thirty-five people in our household. For about three months, this was all we had to live on. Everyone was as bony as the joints of a crane's legs and wore a pallid complexion.

The first decades of the fourth century were transition years in many senses, and writings, even private writings such as the sections cited above, took on a public dimension as testimony to trauma and dislocation. The regime, newly established in the south, was faced with the task of not so much "restoring" Jin rule as starting all over again, in a strange land that spoke a different tongue (the Wu "dialect"), followed different customs, was notorious for its humid climate, and had always been considered "barbarian" by those from the Chinese heartland. As Emperor Yuan of the Jin "felt ashamed of lodging in another people's state," the northern émigrés sought to win the acceptance of the old ruling class of the Kingdom of Wu and aspired to transform themselves from refugees into colonial masters. To justify and consolidate its rule, the new dynasty appealed, among other things, to the power of words. Eastern Jin literary history therefore must begin with Guo Pu (276–324), the émigré *littérateur* whose writings both recounted the pains of displacement at the fall of the Western Jin and celebrated imperial power reestablished in the south, figuring significantly in the construction of a new cultural space.

Guo Pu was born into a family of minor officials and grew up in Wenxi (modern Wenxi, Shanxi). His biography in *History of the Jin* (*Jin shu*) describes him as a taciturn man learned in Confucian Classics, passionate about ancient scripts, and skillful in the occult arts. Around 310 he left his hometown and fled southeast from the Xiongnu general Liu Yuan's forces. The journey through the war-torn and deserted towns in the Yellow River region was narrated in his *"Fu* on Exile" (Liuyu fu), and it was perhaps when he was stopping at Luoyang that he wrote *"Fu* on the Hundred-foot Tower" (Baichilou fu), in which he lamented the fate of the Jin ruling house and expressed nostalgia for his native soil. After crossing the Yangzi river, Guo Pu joined the staff of Yin You, the magistrate of Xuancheng (modern Xuancheng, Anhui). In 311 he accompanied Yin You to Jiankang, and won the admiration of the grand minister Wang Dao (276–339), who often consulted Guo Pu on divination matters concerning the fate of the new regime.

What established Guo Pu's reputation as a writer was a poetic exposition he composed around 317, *"Fu* on the Yangzi river" (Jiang fu). According to He Fasheng, the fifth-century compiler of *The History of the Jin Restoration* (*Jin zhongxing shu*), Guo Pu had written this *fu* as a tribute to the restoration of the Jin. The first *fu* to date praising the Yangzi river, it demonstrated Guo Pu's erudite learning, his familiarity with esoteric lore and obscure words. In its highly rhetorical style, the epideictic *fu* was an attempt to imitate the rich and powerful Yangzi river itself, giving a detailed, hyperbolic account of the river's origin in the mountains of Sichuan, its eastward flow to the sea, its exotic water creatures and wondrous products, the trees and plants growing on its banks, as well as mythical beings and historical personages associated with it. Describing the river as not only fertilizing the southern provinces, but also setting a boundary "between China and outland," Guo Pu confirmed imperial rule in the south as representing orthodox Chinese culture; indeed, he elevated the Yangzi river to a status equal to that of the Yellow River, the river of the "Central Plain" which had always been considered the most venerable river in China.

Although Guo Pu declared that the wonders of the Yangzi river could not be fully conveyed in writing, he did try to re-create the river by means of words. Language sometimes preceded reality, as was the case of Guo Pu's "*Fu* on Making Sacrifices to Heaven in the Southern Suburbs" (Nanjiao fu). Making sacrifices to Heaven in the southern suburbs of the capital city was an important imperial ritual, which validated the legitimacy of the dynastic rule. When Guo Pu composed his *fu* in 318 and presented it to the throne, the Eastern Jin regime was so new that no altar had yet been established in the southern suburbs. Emperor Yuan nevertheless appreciated Guo Pu's lavish description of the imaginary ceremony and appointed him assistant editorial director in charge of the compilation of the dynastic history. A year later, after having the matter debated among the courtiers, Emperor Yuan decided to reinstate the southern suburbs sacrificial rite. It would not be far-fetched to assume that Guo Pu's *fu* had played a part in Emperor Yuan's resolution.

Guo Pu was only one of the writers of the "restoration generation" who devoted themselves to the glorification of Jin rule in the south. When Emperor Yuan first assumed the title of king of Jin in 317, a white rabbit was presented to the throne as a propitious omen. Wang Yi (276–322), a cousin of the prime minister, Wang Dao, and a celebrated calligrapher and painter, penned a "*Fu* on the White Rabbit" (Baitu fu) in commemoration of the event; another courtier, Zhang Jun, wrote "An Ode to the White Rabbit" (Baitu song). In 318, Wang Yi composed "*Fu* on the Restoration" (Zhongxing fu) and proffered it to Emperor Yuan. The *fu* itself is lost, but Wang Yi's letter to the throne accompanying it is still extant.

Su Jun's rebellion of 327 devastated Jiankang and left the imperial palaces in ruins, but Wang Dao held his ground against the proposal to move the capital. The rebuilding of the palace complex began in 330, and was completed just in time for holding a New Year's Day celebration ceremony attended by all courtiers and foreign emissaries in early 333. This event was recorded in the much-acclaimed "*Fu* on the Southern Capital" (Yangdu fu) by Yu Chan (ca 294–347), an important émigré writer of the early Eastern Jin.

Yu Chan was a kinsman of the minister Yu Liang, and served in a series of minor official posts from around 322. "*Fu* on the Southern Capital" was written in the "capital *fu*" tradition. After it was finished, Yu Chan showed it to Yu Liang, who praised it as being on a par with Zhang Heng's *fu* on the western and eastern metropolises and with Zuo Si's "*Fu* on the Three Capitals." Yu Liang's admiration greatly enhanced the value of Yu Chan's *fu*, which enjoyed enormous popularity in its day. Xie An, however, thought differently: "[Yu Liang's remark] was improper. [Yu Chan's *fu*] is merely 'building a house under a house.' It emulates its predecessors in everything, but cannot avoid being narrow and cramped." Xie An's criticism of Yu Chan's *fu*, which employed an architectural metaphor, echoed the Eastern Jin émigrés' attitude toward the city of Jiankang, the imperial palace, and even of the entire south: Wang Biaozhi (295–367) used the same words, "narrow and cramped," to describe the imperial palace; Wang Dao's grandson Wang Xun (350–401) said that the south itself was "cramped" compared to the Chinese heartland. Just as Xie An, who believed in the symbolic significance of architecture, had the entire imperial palace rebuilt in 368, Cao Pi (ca 326–386), a well-known writer, composed another "*Fu* on the Southern Capital." Yu Chan's and Cao Pi's poetic expositions played a role no less crucial than Xie An's project in the dynastic building program of the Eastern Jin: Jiankang was as much a city of brick and stone as a city of words.

Eastern Jin public prose boasted a number of outstanding writers. Many eminent political figures had large literary collections, which must have contained various forms of writings intended for practical purposes. Yu Liang's was a graceful, fluent style. His letter to the throne in 323 declining the appointment of secretariat director, which managed to inject a sense of sincerity and earnestness into a formulaic form, was a fine example of its genre. Huan Wen (312–373), the powerful general who conquered the Cheng-Han kingdom in 347 and recovered Luoyang briefly during one of his northern campaigns, was a prolific writer with a collection of forty-seven scrolls. His letters to the throne recommending the Shu recluse Qiao Xiu for office in 347 or proposing to reestablish Luoyang as capital in 362 combined lucidity with a dignified elegance.

As the Eastern Jin regime was constantly engaged in battles with its northern foes or internal rebels, military proclamations (*xi*) became a much-practiced genre. A fragment of Huan Wen's proclamation against the northern "barbarians" was cited by the critic Liu Xie (ca 460s–520s) as having "a virile style." Yu Chan's extant writings include several proclamations composed on behalf of military commanders. Yuan Bao (373–413), a learned scholar, was one of the last acclaimed Eastern Jin writers of public prose. He had penned a vigorous proclamation against the rebel forces of Shu (modern Sichuan) in early 413.

Death, the most intensely private event in human life, was a social occasion on which many funerary genres converged. By eulogizing the accomplishments of the deceased in highly stylized prose, or expressing the grief of the living, or both, these genres provided a vital link between the worlds of the living and the dead, serving both a social, ceremonial purpose and a personal one. In 318, Emperor Yuan gave special permission to have a stone stele erected for the tomb of Gu Rong, an influential member of the southern elite. This led to the gradual revival of stele inscriptions (*bei wen*), which had been prohibited in 205 and then again in 278; they were once again banned at the suggestion of the historian Pei Songzhi (372–451) during the Yixi reign (405–418). Sun Chuo (314–371), one of the most versatile Eastern Jin writers, had been asked to compose stele inscriptions for renowned public figures such as Wang Dao and Yu Liang. His dirge (*lei*) for Yu Liang won the admiration of his contemporaries, even though Yu Liang's son was repelled by Sun Chuo's exaggeration of his friendship with the late grandee, which was taken to be Sun Chuo's way of glorifying himself. His dirge for Wang Meng (309–347) was likewise reputedly dismissed by Weng Meng's grandson.

Unlike stele inscriptions, there could be many dirges for one deceased person. After Chi Chao (336–377), a sociable man, passed away, more than forty people, including his peers and inferiors, wrote dirges for him. While a dirge was usually composed soon after a person's death, a sacrificial address (*ji wen*) might be written long afterwards, and its most distinguishing characteristic is directly speaking to the dead. A number of sacrificial addresses from this period survive. Yu Chan's "Condolence for Scholar Jia" (Diao Jiasheng wen), written in 339, is essentially a sacrificial address. Jia Yi, the Western Han writer banished to the humid land of Changsha, had written a condolence for the ancient poet Qu Yuan, in which he expressed sorrow for his own situation; Yu Chan's condolence was composed upon seeing a portrait of Jia Yi at Changsha. In contrast with the sacrificial prayers addressed to ancient personages or famous contemporaries, Tao Yuanming's sacrificial addresses to his sister, Madame Cheng, in 407, and to his cousin, Tao Jingyuan, in 411, are touchingly personal.

The most singular sacrificial address of the Eastern Jin, however, was the one Tao Yuanming wrote for himself (Zi ji wen), in which he compared death to a journey home, and the ritual offering to a farewell banquet. Looking back at his life of "drinking and composing poetry," he stressed that it was different from that of most people, who strove for accomplishments and immortality. The address ended with musing: "Life was truly difficult, / I wonder how death will be?" While scholars have used ingenious emendations to date this unique piece to Tao Yuanming's last year of life, its earliest extant source, *Classified Extracts from Literature* (Yiwen leiju), which was compiled in 624, gave its date as 407, twenty years before Tao Yuanming's death. This would not have been impossible, given the popularity of another funerary genre, the "pallbearers' song" (*wan ge*), which was not only sung at funerals but also treated as an entertainment form. An Eastern Jin prince, Sima Xi (316–381), was fond of pallbearers' songs, as was the historian Yuan Shansong (d. 401), who would have his attendants sing pallbearers' songs while going on outings.

Tao Yuanming wrote three pallbearers' songs in the tradition of his literary predecessors, Miao Xi, Fu Xuan, and Lu Ji.

Eastern Jin epistolary literature consists of both prose and poetry. While most prose letters are either political or personal in nature, sometimes they are discourses on contemporary issues or contributions to an epistolary debate. Thanks to the Buddhist anthologies compiled in the sixth and seventh centuries, many letters exchanged on religious topics are preserved. The only extant works by Luo Han (295–371?), who was included in "Biographies of Literary Men" in the *History of the Jin*, are his correspondence with the historian Sun Sheng (300–371), on the subject of reincarnation. Huan Xuan's letters addressed to several recipients in 402, as well as their replies, are important documents regarding whether Buddhist clergy should pay homage to the ruler, a major point of controversy in the clashes of church and state. One of Huan Xuan's correspondents was the renowned monk Huiyuan (334–417), who was moved to compose a lengthy treatise on the subject afterwards.

Although some might be later forgeries, a batch of several hundred letters by Wang Xizhi (303–361) and Wang Xianzhi (344–386) deserve special mention. The letters were preserved because the father and son were considered two of the greatest calligraphers of all times, and their handwritten notes were highly valued. These letters are usually short, casual, apparently dashed off without the usual care attending the writing of more serious epistles, but exuding a whimsical charm. One note by Wang Xizhi reads, "I am sending you three hundred oranges. It is not the time of frost yet, so I could not obtain more." Another note by Wang Xianzhi reads, "Qing and others have already arrived. Did the goose get better? I am very concerned." Although not initially prized for their literary merit, these letters were a source of inspiration for late Ming informal prose.

Two woman writers, Sun Qiong (fl. 320s) and Chen Chen, left some interesting letters. Sun Qiong's letter to her cousin, in defense of her fondness of pet swans, argued that an obsession was not necessarily a morally dangerous thing – a dispute that was to become a prominent theme in the connoisseur culture of late imperial China. Chen Chen's letter to her sister, Madame Liu, expressed doubt about their brother Chen Hong's use of *Laozi* and *Zhuangzi* terminology in his dirge for their late father, stressing the superiority of Confucian values. Chen Chen was one of four sisters who were all well known for their literary talent; one of the sisters, Chen Fen, was the mother of Xu Miao (344–398), a learned scholar and writer, and of Xu Guang (352–425), a ritual specialist and historian. Chen Fen had a collection in five scrolls, from which a fragmentary *fu* on pomegranate is extant. Eastern Jin elite women were generally well educated, and a number of them left literary collections, which, however, sadly met with the fate of Eastern Jin literature in general, with only a fraction surviving.

Poetry continued to play an important social role. Half of the extant poetic *oeuvre* of Guo Pu consists of "exchange poems" (*zengda shi*) in the four-syllable line. Poems such as these, with their archaic meter and pompous phrasing, were out of favor in the later times and were largely preserved in *The Grove of Texts from the Literature Office* (*Wenguan cilin*), a seventh-century anthology. Thanks to this anthology, we are able to see a rather different picture of Jin poetry, and realize that, despite the increasing popularity of poems in the five-syllable line, poetry in the four-syllable line remained dominant, especially under formal social circumstances. Guo Pu and Sun Chuo, primarily known for their poems in the five-syllable line today, composed many poems in the four-syllable line, presenting or replying to their associates. In 323 Yu Liang, Guo Pu, Wen Qiao (288–329), Yang Man (274–328), and Huan Wen's father, Huan Yi (276–328), gathered by the Blue Stream in the Jiankang suburbs; Huan Yi composed a poem to "show the four worthy gentlemen and express his feelings." The "four worthy gentlemen" presumably responded with verse.

Guiji, famous for its beautiful scenery, was where many literati members chose to set up residence. Xie An, Wang Xizhi, Sun Chuo, Li Chong (d. 350s), Xu Xun (d. 361), and the monk Zhidun (314–366) all lived there at one point, and formed a close literary circle. Several of them participated in the famous gathering that took place on the third day of the third month (April 22), 353. Forty-one people (or forty-two according to another source) got together at Lanting, commonly rendered as the "Orchid Pavilion," in observance of the Lustration Festival celebrating the arrival of spring. Twenty-six guests composed poems, and it seems that each of them was asked to write one poem in the four-syllable line and one in the five-syllable line. Those who failed to produce a poem had to drink three goblets of ale as a penalty. Although its authenticity remains a topic of heated debate, Wang Xizhi's preface to the collection of the poems remains one of the best-known landscape essays in Chinese literary history, as well as one of the most celebrated calligraphy pieces. Largely due to this preface, the gathering at Lanting has acquired a legendary status in Chinese literary culture, itself the subject of poems, plays, paintings, and decorative arts.

As the writer Yuan Hong (328–376) put it in the preface to his encomia on the famous courtiers of the Three Kingdoms period, the composition of poetry and eulogies "sometimes sings forth feelings and nature, and sometimes recounts virtue and glorifies accomplishments." One of the essential "uses" of literature, or of all writing, is commemoration. Two genres, eulogy (*song*) and encomium (*zan*), serve the function well. The distinction between the two genres is not always clear, and they lie somewhere between poetry and prose. Cao Pi's eulogy on Huan Wen's military campaign to the Shu region in 347, for instance, reads like a poem in the four-syllable line. A rarer example is the poet monk Zhidun's eleven encomia on buddhas and bodhisattvas written in the five-syllable line, which, although included in the *Complete Jin Prose* compiled by Yan Kejun (1762–1843), are of exactly the same form as poetry.

Accounts

During the Eastern Jin, the compilation of dynastic histories flourished, both as a public project and as a private passion. In 317 Wang Dao asked Emperor Yuan to establish a History Bureau, which he described as "the foundation of the imperial enterprise." Emperor Yuan consented, and appointed Gan Bao assistant editorial director, who compiled an acclaimed history of the Western Jin (*Jin ji*). In the following year Wang Yin and Guo Pu were also assigned to the office. Using his father's work as a basis, Wang Yin produced a *History of the Jin* (*Jin shu*) in ninety-three scrolls, while his rival, Yu Yu, completed one in forty-four scrolls. Xie Shen (ca 292–344), Sun Sheng, and Xu Guang all compiled their own versions of Jin history. Embracing an anti-mainstream notion of imperial legitimacy and the succession of power, Xi Zuochi (d. 384), a learned scholar, compiled *Annals of the Han and Jin* (*Han Jin chunqiu*) on the premise that the Jin had received its mandate to rule from the Han, not from the Wei. Fragments of these works can be found in sources such as the historian Pei Songzhi's annotations of *History of the Three Kingdoms*, completed in 429.

In conjunction with the writing of dynastic histories was a burgeoning interest in giving accounts of people, families, and places. Cao Pi, a descendant of the Wei royal family, produced *An Account of the Cao Clan* (*Caoshi jiazhuan*); Yu Yu, a native of Guiji, compiled *A Standard Record of Guiji* (*Guiji dianlu*), as well as *Biographies of the Yus* (*Zhu Yu zhuan*). Xi Zuochi, a native of Xiangyang (modern Hubei), composed *Account of the Elders of Xiangyang* (*Xiangyang qijiu ji*). *Record of the Kingdom of Huayang* (*Huayangguo zhi*) by Chang Qu (291?–361), a famous scholar of the Cheng-Han kingdom in Sichuan, is the earliest extant regional history, and certainly one of the best regional histories produced in this period.

There were biographies of specific social groups, such as Ge Hong's *Biographies of Recluses* (*Yinyi zhuan*) and *Biographies of Virtuous Officials* (*Liangli zhuan*), or Yuan Hong's account of the lives of the Seven Worthies of the

Bamboo Grove (*Zhulin mingshi zhuan*); there were also biographies of single persons, such as Kang Hong's biography of Shan Daokai, a Dunhuang monk with supernatural powers who came to the south in 359, or Tao Yuanming's biography of his maternal grandfather Meng Jia. In the tradition of Ruan Ji's "Biography of Master Great Man" (Daren xiansheng zhuan), Tao Yuanming also composed the famous fictional autobiography, "Biography of Master Five Willows" (Wuliu xiansheng zhuan), which clearly inspired Yuan Can's (421–478) "Biography of the Master of Wonderful Virtue" (Miaode xiansheng zhuan).

The prolific Daoist writer Ge Hong – mainly known for *Outer Chapters of the Master Who Embraces Simplicity* (Baopuzi waipian, fifty essays dealing with social, political, and cultural issues) and *Inner Chapters of the Master Who Embraces Simplicity* (Baopuzi neipian, twenty essays on esoteric matters) – was also the author of a hagiography entitled *Biographies of Divine Transcendents* (Shenxian zhuan). All three works are extant, though not in their complete form. *Biographies of Divine Transcendents*, like most pre-Tang collections, has been reconstructed from a variety of later texts such as encyclopedias, commentaries, and hagiographic compilations. Its two major recensions are both from late Ming; that is, the sixteenth and seventeenth centuries. According to Ge Hong's own statement, it had been finished by 317. It records the lives of more than a hundred figures from antiquity down to Ge Hong's own age who had obtained "transcendence" and become immortal beings with extraordinary powers. Despite its fantastic nature, it is important to bear in mind, in the context of Ge Hong's age and his personal belief system, that *Biographies of Divine Transcendents* was not intended as fiction, but as a record of actual facts, on a par with his two other accounts of recluses and virtuous officials.

The same can be said of the historian Gan Bao's *In Search of the Supernatural* (Soushen ji). This work was lost after the Northern Song and reconstructed in the sixteenth century. The recompilation contains more than four hundred items, ranging from one sentence to more full-blown narratives, about anything considered out of the ordinary, such as prophetic dreams, animal spirits, ghosts, and demons. It is the defining work of the loosely defined genre named *zhiguai*, "strange tales" or "accounts of anomalies." Though not the first in this genre, it is exceptional in its scope and variety. In the preface, Gan Bao claimed that he had compiled this work from various written and oral sources to show that "the spirit world is no fabrication." In fact, much of the material in *In Search of the Supernatural* on omens and portents also appears in dynastic histories.

Many Southern Dynasties works in the genre of "anomaly accounts" are anonymous or of uncertain authorship and date, surviving only in bits and pieces. *A Sequel to In Search of the Supernatural (Xu Soushen ji* or *Soushen houji)* was attributed to Tao Yuanming in as early as the sixth century. Its present version is a late Ming recompilation, which has apparently mixed in a number of items from other works. Many scholars contest the attribution of authorship, primarily on the ground that Tao Yuanming's worldview as perceived in his other writings made it highly unlikely that he would be interested in "affairs of ghosts and spirits." Tao Yuanming, however, did write a series of poems on reading the *Classic of Mountains and Seas* and *Travels of Emperor Mu*, showing his familiarity with writings on fantastic subjects. The famous poet Yan Yanzhi (384–456) also said in his dirge for Tao Yuanming that Tao had always been fond of "strange writings."

Zu Taizhi (fl. ca 389–402), the great-grandfather of the famous scientist Zu Chongzhi (429–500), was himself a *zhiguai* compiler and produced *Accounts of Anomalies (Zhiguai).* A few items survive, including a humorous story about an aristocrat's romantic encounter with a pretty girl who turned out to be a sow spirit.

Another work that deserves mention is *Responsive Manifestations of Avalokiteśvara (Guangshiyin yingyan ji),* produced by Xie Fu, a Buddhist layman. The original collection, which contained a dozen accounts of Bodhisattva Avalokiteśvara's manifestations to devout believers in distress, was given to Fu Yuan, the father of the famous minister Fu Liang (374–426). After the work was lost during the Sun En Rebellion in 399, Fu Liang rewrote seven items from memory. These items were first supplemented by the fifth-century scholar–official Zhang Yan, and then again by Zhang Yan's kinsman, Lu Gao (459–532), so that the entire work consists of eighty-six tales, a twelfth-century manuscript copy of which is preserved in Japan. It is the earliest extant collection of Buddhist miracle tales in the Chinese tradition.

Parallel with the development of accounts of anomalies were collections of anecdotes about past and present celebrities. These anecdotes, light and often whimsical, were immensely popular with contemporary readers. Pei Qi's *Forest of Tales (Yu lin),* written in 362, was so admired that every elite family was said to have had a copy of it, until Xie An voiced his disapproval and said that the two items concerning himself were made up and had no basis. Nevertheless, the best-known work in this genre, *A New Account of Tales of the World (Shishuo xinyu)* from the early fifth century, incorporated many items from *Forest of Tales.* The image of the Eastern Jin projected in these two works, characterized by sophistication, panache, and more than a dash of socially sanctioned eccentricity, has come to define the age. In both cases historical veracity was secondary to the attraction of a good story.

Other works of the same nature include Sun Sheng's *Miscellaneous Tales* (*Za yu*), Guo Chengzhi's (fl. ca 373–418) *Master Guo* (*Guozi*), and *Stories Current in the Wei and Jin* (*Wei Jin shiyu*) by an obscure writer, Guo Ban. The last work, though criticized by the historian Pei Songzhi as "vulgar and inferior," was popular with contemporary readers for having recorded many "unusual occurrences." All these works are only extant as fragments.

One must also mention *A Miscellaneous Record of the Western Capital* (*Xijing zaji*), a collection of anecdotes about the Western Han, some fantastic and some mundane, produced between the third and sixth centuries, some say by Ge Hong, some say by Wu Jun (469–520) or Xiao Ben (d. 552). Many of these accounts became favorite topics in later literary writings. The collection has a colophon by Ge Hong, who claimed that it was from an unfinished chronicle of the Han penned by the first-century scholar Liu Xin. According to the colophon, Ban Gu's *History of the Han* was entirely based on Liu Xin's work, but there were about 20,000 words which Ban Gu did not use, and of these abandoned words Ge Hong made an epitome in two scrolls, which he named *A Miscellaneous Record of the Western Capital*. While the attribution to Liu Xin is almost certainly spurious, the authenticity of the colophon is also questionable, which would, interestingly, make the work the forgery of a forgery. The colophon nevertheless provides a fascinating picture of the perceived relation between orthodox dynastic history and the "miscellaneous records" – be they accounts of anomalies or of human affairs.

Introspective landscape: poetry and prose

Landscape first became a conspicuous element in literature and the arts during the Southern Dynasties. The Eastern Jin elite were deeply influenced by Buddhism, which was dubbed the "doctrine of images" because of its emphasis on teaching through visual means. For the Eastern Jin elite, landscape was a grand image (*xiang*), and the perception, interpretation, and very construction of this image were contingent upon the workings of the individual mind. Imagination was therefore a full verb indicating image-making. While geographic treatises began to appear in large quantity in this period and continued in the fifth and sixth centuries, the rise of landscape representation in the fourth century was, in many ways, as much a movement inward as outward; that is, the heightened interest in physical nature was but an extension of the primary engagement with the inner world of a particular person. It is for this reason that imaginary landscape is such a prominent motif in Eastern Jin literature. Sun Chuo's famous "Fu on Roaming the Heavenly Terrace Mountain" (You Tiantai shan fu), much appreciated by his contemporaries, relates an imaginary journey that may have been inspired by looking at illustrations. The famous painter and writer Gu Kaizhi's (ca 345–406) "Account of Painting the Cloud Terrace Mountain" (Hua Yuntai shan ji) describes a projected painting of an envisioned mountain. Painter, Buddhist layman, and recluse Zong Bing's (374–443) "Preface to Painted Landscape" (Hua shanshui xu) suggests that the painted landscape is no less real than a real landscape. Xie An's niece Xie Daoyun wrote "A Song of Mount Tai" (Taishan yin), alternatively known as "Ascending the Mountain" (Deng shan), and yet, throughout most of the Eastern Jin, Mount Tai was in the much-contested northern territory. Xie Daoyun's poem might very well have been inspired by real historical event, when the Jin army, led by none other than her brother Xie Xuan (343–388), briefly recovered the Mount Tai region in 384. It is highly unlikely, however, that she had ever traveled there in person.

In the "Stele Inscription for the Grand Marshall Yu Liang," Sun Chuo praises the deceased minister for being able to "face mountains and waters with *xuan*." *Xuan*, an important concept in the *Laozi* that has been variously rendered as "dark," "profound," "abstruse," "mysterious," "esoteric," or "arcane," was widely used in general religious, philosophical, and cultural discourse in the fourth century, indicating the attribute of the ultimate truth, or, as in Sun Chuo's inscription, the mental state of residing in the ultimate truth. For the Eastern Jin elite, facing the landscape alone was not enough; one must possess the right attitude to appreciate it. It was no coincidence that one of the most popular sūtras in this period was the Vimalarkīrti-nirdeśa Sūtra, whose very first chapter, "Buddha's Kingdom," teaches that what one is determines what one sees. As the famous monk Sengzhao (384–414) wrote in his commentary on the Vimalarkīrti-nirdeśa Sūtra: "The pure land is but the shadow and echo of one's mind."

In the well-known preface for poems on an excursion to Stonegate Mountain, written in the year 400 by an anonymous member of the Buddhist circle around the monk Huiyuan, the lesson is that without the right state of mind, the beauty of the landscape would not have been revealed. One message repeatedly encountered in the poetry and prose of the Eastern Jin is that it is not landscape itself that appeals to the viewer, but a "profound observation" (*xuanlan*) that illuminates the myriad images of "what is naturally so" (*ziran*). The mind is so powerful that it overrides even the physical environment. Hence Tao Yuanming's famous lines:

> I built a cottage in the human realm,
> yet there is no noise of horse and carriage.
> I ask you, how can that be so?
> When mind is far, the locale becomes remote.

The same notion is conveyed in Wang Xizhi's poem about the celebrated Lanting gathering: "Although sounds of nature are various and uneven, / they are all endearing upon reaching *me*."

Both Sun Chuo and his friend Xu Xun were illustrious poets of arcane discourse, but no complete poem by Xu Xun survives. Another important poet was the monk Zhidun. "On a Buddhist Monk in Meditation" (Yong chansi daoren), based on a painting by Sun Chuo, is a prototype of "poetry on paintings" (*yonghua shi*), an important subgenre in later times. In contrast with "encomium on painting" (*huazan*), which usually focuses on the moral character of the person being painted, Zhidun's poem describes the landscape in Sun Chuo's painting and enables us to catch a glimpse of what the painting was like. Zhidun's "Singing My Feelings" III (Yonghuai), like Sun Chuo's *fu*, relates an imaginary ascent of the Heavenly Terrace Mountain. "Singing My Feelings" II, a poem on reading and contemplative visualization, anticipates Tao Yuanming's thirteen poems on "Reading the Classic of Mountains and Seas" (Du Shanhai jing). Tao's series begins with the poet's reading in an early summer garden, in a familiar, everyday setting, and goes on to a fantastic cosmic journey undertaken in the imagination and inspired by his reading material. These poems, along with Sun Chuo's "*Fu* on Roaming the Heavenly Terrace Mountain," descend from the tradition of the ethereal wanderings of the *Verses of Chu*, but in the Eastern Jin texts the roaming is generally carried out in the mind.

The monk Huiyuan, who set up residence on Mount Lu (in modern Jiangxi) around 380, was not only an extremely influential personage in Chinese Buddhism, but also a prominent literary figure. His extant work includes letters, treatises, prefaces, an inscription on Buddha's shadow, and a poem on Mount Lu. His "Account of Mount Lu" (Lushan ji), composed in the early 400s, is a beautiful landscape essay.

Long before becoming a Buddhist shrine, Mount Lu had been associated with Daoist immortals and recluses, whom Huiyuan mentioned in "Account of Mount Lu." He also related that once "a man of the wilds" saw a person wearing the garb of a Buddhist monk ascending to the mountaintop and vanishing into the clouds. "At that time those with literary abilities were all amazed [and wrote about the happening]." This seemed to be the occasion on which Zhan Fangsheng, a late fourth-century poet known primarily for his landscape poetry, composed a poem in the four-syllable line, "On the Immortal of Mount Lu" (Lushan shenxian shi). The preface to the poem dates the incident to 386. Zhan Fangsheng's poem, though about a Buddhist, not Daoist, immortal, clearly belongs to the tradition of poems on "roaming as an immortal."

Yu Chan wrote a number of poems on "roaming as an immortal," but Guo Pu is considered the representative poet of this genre. The sixth-century anthology *Selections of Refined Literature* includes seven of Guo Pu's poems on roaming as an immortal; three others and a number of fragments, all in the five-syllable line, are preserved in later sources. The critic Zhong Rong (d. 518) observes in his *Gradations of Poets* (*Shipin*) that Guo Pu's poems on roaming as an immortal "sing forth his frustration [with society] and have nothing to do with the mood of immortals." This observation does not, however, apply to all of Guo Pu's extant poems on roaming as an immortal, some of which explicitly employ the terminology of alchemy to portray gathering ingredients for an elixir in the mountains and breathing exercises, focusing exclusively on the pursuit and attainment of transcendence. Zhong Rong also notes that Guo Pu's poems "go against the mystical tradition," yet this statement has a textual variant that reverses its meaning. The more typical poems on roaming as an immortal in Guo Pu's extant *oeuvre* form an interesting contrast with the pieces chosen by *Selections of Refined Literature*, which are more diverse in their content. This reminds us that in dealing with pre-Tang literature, we are very much at the mercy of our sources. The sixth- and seventh-century anthologies and encyclopedias largely determine what we see today, and may offer a rather skewed picture of the literary reality.

A remarkable group of Daoist poems from the fourth century, rarely mentioned in Chinese literary history, has a direct bearing on the poetry of arcane discourse as well as on poetry of roaming as an immortal. Yang Xi (330–386), a Daoist priest, claimed that he received visitations from Daoist deities, who dictated the poems and asked him to transcribe them. Using esoteric terms and fantastic images, these poems describe the pleasures of the heavenly realm and exhort the mortals to perfect themselves and achieve transcendence. They show the influence of Buddhist scriptures, in which *gāthās* in the four- or five-syllable line are a popular form of expounding the Buddhist doctrine. Two poems about the body and spirit, for instance, contain lines taken almost verbatim from the Seven Maidens Sūtra, which was translated into Chinese in the third century. Earnest and solicitous, the deities in Yang Xi's poems occasionally manifest a sense of humor by playfully adopting Wu dialect.

Other topics of poetry and fu

Of the large poetic output of the Eastern Jin, only a fraction is extant, but even such a small number of poems show a variety of topics going far beyond the usual perception of Eastern Jin poetry as being all about arcane discourse. Yang Fang (fl. 323), a learned scholar, left five love poems, "Joining in Pleasure" (Hehuan shi). Cao Pi's "On Listening to Fulling Clothes at Night" (Ye ting daoyi) was the earliest extant poem on what was to become a popular subject in later poetry. Yuan Hong, the author of a history of the Eastern Han and of biographies of celebrity figures from the Wei and Western Jin, was also known for his poems on history (yongshi shi). Poems on impoverished gentlemen by Jiang You (ca 307–364) and Zhang Wang (fl. 340s) depict poverty in vivid terms, and Zhan Fangsheng extols the pleasures of reclusion: they were the precursors of the great poet Tao Yuanming, who will be discussed in a separate section below.

Eastern Jin writers continued to write fu on natural phenomena, places, and things, and further expanded the traditional repertoire of topics, such as Xie Shang's (308–357) "Fu on Discourse" (Tan fu), or Yuan Hong's "Fu on Singing" (Ge fu). Zu Taizhi, the author of Account of Anomalies, even composed a fu on the ears of the ancient philosopher Xunzi. A number of fu are about specifically southern topics, such as Wang Biaozhi's "Fu on Mount Lu" (Lushan fu), Cao Pi's "Fu on the Xiang Region" (Xiangzhong fu), or Jiang You's "Fu on Bamboo" (Zhu fu). Sometimes, a writer would simply take an old topic and give it an interesting twist: while Shu Xi had written "Fu on Pasta" in the Western Jin, Yu Chan composed "Fu on Unsavory Pasta" and related the occasion for composition in the preface.

The yuefu songs

One cannot talk about Eastern Jin literature without mentioning a corpus of poems known as the southern yuefu songs, which, in their current form, probably largely originated from the urban entertainment quarters or palace performers. There are two major groups: "Sounds of Wu" (Wusheng ge) and "Western Tunes" (Xiqu ge). The 330-odd Sounds of Wu songs are believed to represent the Wu region of the lower Yangzi river with Jiankang as its center; the Western Tunes songs, 142 in total, are from the central Yangzi region, particularly the Jiangling and Xiangyang areas (in modern Hubei). Most of these songs are quatrains in the five-syllable line and sing of romantic love, in a female or male voice. Different lyrics may share one tune title, which probably indicates a melody type. Puns were a favorite device: "lotus" and "love" (*lian*) or "filaments [in the lotus root]" and "longing" (*si*) are among the most common. Many songs are composed in the form of "paired songs" (*dui ge*), representing a man and a woman in a dialogue. Simple in diction but witty, sometimes bold and saucy, sometimes tender and sentimental, these songs are remarkably different from the old *yuefu* poetry and exerted a palpable impact on the development of the literary quatrain.

The fascination of the elite with the Sounds of Wu began in the fourth century, not surprisingly, among the northern immigrants, but in most cases it is impossible to tell exactly when the extant lyrics were produced, since they continued to be composed and sung throughout the Southern Dynasties. Even if a tune title might have been created in the Eastern Jin or Liu-Song, the lyrics to the same title could have been written in a much later era. The songs we have now are preserved in the twelfth-century *Collection of Yuefu Poetry* (*Yuefu shiji*), which had used, among other things, a now lost *Record of Music from Past and Present* (*Gujin yuelu*) compiled by the monk Zhijiang in 568 as its source. A large number of the southern *yuefu* were probably first gathered in the sixth century. Although often referred to by modern scholars as "folk songs," the southern *yuefu* were performed in court and transmitted by court musicians; many were composed by court singers, literati members, and sometimes even the emperors themselves. This is not to deny that the songs had their roots in contemporary popular culture, but their transmission was mediated by the interests of the southern elite, and, as such, represent not so much the creation of the "common folk" as that of the aristocratic imagination.

A few *yuefu* songs are attributed to known Eastern Jin figures, all elite northerners: Sun Chuo, Wang Xianzhi, and Xie Shang. Xie Shang was said to have once sat on a folding chair, played the balloon guitar, and sung "The Song of the Great Road" (*Dadao qu*) on the gate tower of a Buddhist monastery in the marketplace; "none of the people in the marketplace knew he was one of the highest-ranking ministers." As the song itself played with the notion of being incognito, what Xie Shang pulled off was "class cross-dressing." It was not because the Southern Dynasties went through a cultural "vulgarization," but because by imagining themselves as the southern commoner, their social and cultural Other, the aristocratic immigrants were able to sustain and confirm their own identity in a land which they inhabited as refugees, settlers, and colonial masters.

Literary criticism

Judging from the extant material, the Eastern Jin was not an age in which literary criticism flourished. Ge Hong voiced his views of literature in the

Outer Chapters of the Master Who Embraced Simplicity, but much of his discussion concentrates on philosophical work, consisting of a series of treatises and known as the writings of the Masters (*zishu*), which he explicitly distinguished from "poetry, *fu*, and miscellaneous prose pieces." For Ge Hong, the "writings of the Masters" were not only a part of literature (*wen*), but also the best part: while poetry and *fu* seemed to him "shallow" and "scrappy," the "writings of the Masters" could rectify the wrongs of the world and establish the writer's eternal fame. Typical of his age, Ge Hong acutely felt his own belatedness in the tradition and hence the need to defend the modern "writings of the Masters" against the canon of sagely writings from antiquity. As a by-product of his argument, he claimed that contemporary poetry and *fu* were much more sophisticated than classical literature, citing Guo Pu's "*Fu* on Making Sacrifices to Heaven in the Southern Suburbs" as more ornate than the odes from the *Classic of Poetry*, and thus superior. Ge Hong's statements about poetry are, however, largely driven by immediate rhetorical purposes and thus lack consistency. At another point, he remarked that ancient poetry gave admonition, and so was better than modern poetry, which was pure flattery.

Li Chong was a prolific writer and bibliographer, and the only Eastern Jin literary figure known to have written a work of literary criticism, *Literary Grove Treatise* (*Hanlin lun*), which may have been compiled when Li Chong was organizing the imperial book collection. The bibliography section of the *History of the Sui* records the *Treatise* in three scrolls, but mentions that the work was listed in fifty-four scrolls in the sixth century. The fifty-four scrolls may have constituted the *Literary Grove* (*Hanlin*), an anthology of writings in a variety of genres mainly by Wei writers, and were perhaps separate from the three-scroll *Treatise* discussing the characteristics of different genres and making critical comments on these writings. Only a few fragments from the *Treatise* survive.

Tao Yuanming

Tao Yuanming (also known as Tao Qian, 365?–427) is considered one of the greatest classical Chinese poets. His great-grandfather, Tao Kan (259–334), was a native of the south, some say of non-Han ethnicity, and rose from a humble family background to become one of the most influential political and military figures in early Eastern Jin. By the time Tao Yuanming was born, the fortunes of the Tao clan had declined, though it was still considered a prominent southern noble family. Tao Yuanming served in several official posts, but never held any high position. His last appointment was that of a county magistrate at Pengze, a place not far away from his hometown of Xunyang (in modern Jiangxi). In 405, upon the death of his sister, he resigned and went home. He spent the rest of his life in reclusion, although he kept up his friendships with local and court officials, drinking and exchanging poetry with them. Like many other gentry members, he owned farming land and had tenants.

The life of reclusion is the major topic of Tao Yuanming's writings. Many of his poems describe the process of arriving at the decision to withdraw from public life, or, after the decision was made, explaining and justifying his choice. In the last years of Tao Yuanming's life, Liu Yu (363–422), a powerful general who had earlier suppressed a major rebellion, deposed the last Jin emperor and founded the Liu-Song dynasty in 420. Shen Yue (441–513), who wrote the first biography of Tao Yuanming in the *History of the Song (Song shu)*, completed in 488, claimed that Tao Yuanming had refused to serve because he was a Jin loyalist. No such sentiment, however, can be found in Tao Yuanming's extant writings; instead, Tao Yuanming makes it clear that his decision is driven by his personal inclination toward a private life of leisure and spontaneity, as opposed to the demands and pressures of the public world.

Tao Yuanming is certainly not the first Chinese poet to write poems on reclusion, but his uniqueness lies in the fact that he transforms the conventional vocabulary and stock images of poetry on reclusion into a highly personalized poetry, and combines traditional themes and forms with a complex individual voice. More than anyone before him, his poetry alludes to the particular circumstances of the poet in the historical here and now rather than to a generic gentleman-recluse. Such gestures of individuation can be seen as part of a larger discursive tendency from the third century on, as witnessed by the short prefaces attached to poems and *fu* relating the real-life occasions of composition. Tao Yuanming, however, integrates the narrative element into his poetry itself, making it effectively a poetry of autobiography, even if this autobiography is a highly constructed self-image rather than an "objective" documentary.

In contrast with the formal social verse written by his contemporaries, Tao Yuanming used a simple, unpretentious language to record the events of daily life as well as his thoughts and feelings. The simplicity of his style should not, however, obscure the poet's self-consciousness and sophistication, which are rarely found in his contemporaries' rhetorically more elaborate, but emotionally less complicated, writings. Tao Yuanming introduced new topics into his poetry, such as begging, moving house, encountering a fire, and harvesting dry rice. He was the first known poet to extensively use calendar dates in his often lengthy and descriptive poem titles, which became a common practice in later times.

Tao Yuanming was well-read and made constant references to his readings in his work; the *Analects* and *Zhuangzi* were among his favorite texts. Instead of drawing upon their terminology in a merely decorative way, he took his readings seriously. "Drinking Alone during Incessant Rain" (Lianyu duyin), for instance, gives an interesting twist to the theme of roaming as an immortal by describing a different sort of "roaming in transcendence" achieved through drinking; the entire poem is built around *Zhuangzi* passages in which wise men maintain inner peace despite material hardship and changes on the outside brought about by ravages of time.

Tao Yuanming is sometimes described as writing a poetry of "fields and gardens." If so, this is no innocent poetry extolling pastoral pleasures or the harmony between nature and man: in his poems, weeds are forever threatening to overwhelm the fragile human order imposed on farmland, and a farmer must remain vigilant to keep the forces of nature at bay. He must also conserve his resources and take stock. Tao Yuanming is intensely concerned with *cheng*, a word meaning "harvest," "ripeness," "completion," and "achievements" in general. His poems are in many ways a defense of private values against public values, the personal fulfillment and happiness of an individual against the claims of public life.

Among Tao Yuanming's prose pieces, "The Record of Peach Blossom Spring" (Taohuayuan ji) is one of the most beloved texts in classical Chinese literature. It describes a utopian community where there are no usual social constraints such as taxation and hierarchy, and everyone lives in contentment. Hidden away in the mountains, the community is accidentally discovered by a fisherman. Later, the fisherman tries to retrace his steps, but he can never find the community again. The story of the Peach Blossom Spring has inspired numerous writings in later times and become a minor literary tradition in itself.

About 120 poems by Tao Yuanming are extant, most of which are poems in the five-syllable line. The first known editor of Tao Yuanming's collection was Xiao Tong (501–531), Crown Prince Zhaoming of the Liang. Both Xiao Tong and his younger brother Xiao Gang (503–551), better known as Emperor Jianwen of the Liang, deeply admired Tao Yuanming's writings. In the following centuries of the Tang dynasty, Tao Yuanming was appreciated largely as a drinker and as a recluse. Although a small number of Tang poets were clearly influenced by his style, he remained one of many famous Six Dynasties poets until he was singled out as *the* Six Dynasties poet by the Northern Song luminary Su Shi (1037–1101) and his followers, about five hundred years after Tao Yuanming's death. Their choices in textual editing of the many variants in Tao Yuanming's works confirmed their image of Tao Yuanming as a tranquil, spontaneous recluse with little interest in the poetic craft. The most revealing example is the case of "gaze" (*wang*) and "see" (*jian*), the two textual variants in one of Tao Yuanming's most famous poems, "Drinking" (*Yinjiu*) V, whose opening lines are cited in a preceding section. The couplet in question reads:

> Picking chrysanthemums by the eastern hedge,
> I see/gaze at South Mountain in the distance.

Su Shi insisted that "see" was the original word used by Tao Yuanming, because, for Su Shi, "see" indicated a more spontaneous attitude than "gaze," and thus was more true to what Su Shi perceived to be the poet's personality. Since that moment of ideological editing, "see," not "gaze," has become part of the standard version.

In part because of the increasingly prominent role of printing, editors and scholars of the Northern Song first began to notice and become passionately concerned with disagreements among various manuscript copies. Commonplace opinions about Tao Yuanming had a profound impact on the choice of textual variants, when Northern Song literary scholars were often faced with "dozens of textual variants" for just one word in Tao Yuanming's writings. Editorial decisions became invested with ideological significance, and throughout Tao Yuanming's collection we see numerous cases in which the choice of one textual variant over another makes a great difference in understanding a poem. While we cannot know which variant is "right," we can see to some degree the historical motivation for choosing one variant over another and the version or versions of Tao Yuanming that have been suppressed by such choices. The case of Tao Yuanming is particularly illuminating for understanding the problems of manuscript culture and how the desire for a particular image of a poet could transform a potentially more complex figure into a cultural icon. We also realize the extent to which pre-Song literature has come down to us through the mediation of Northern Song literary values, when printing changed the entire landscape of literary scholarship.

Literature of the Sixteen Kingdoms

As the Eastern Jin consolidated its power in the south, the north was divided under the rule of a series of non-Chinese regimes known as the Sixteen Kingdoms. The literature of the Sixteen Kingdoms is poorly preserved in early Tang encyclopedias, our best sources for pre-Tang northern literature, perhaps largely due to early Tang literary taste as well as prejudice against what was considered the illegitimate rule of "barbarian usurpers." The extant writings, except for Buddhist writings conserved in sixth- and seventh-century Buddhist compilations, are largely gleaned from the *History of the Jin* (*Jin shu*). The nature of our source, *History of the Jin*, and the scanty material conserved in encyclopedias and Buddhist compilations, make a more objective assessment of northern literary output in the fourth century virtually impossible, but, judging from the titles mentioned in the histories and the writings that remain, the Sixteen Kingdoms were by no means a cultural desert as painted in some literary-historical accounts, and northern literature in this period may have been just as sophisticated as that of the south. The account given below, though not exhaustive, allows us to glimpse the state of literature in the Sixteen Kingdoms. We may be limited by our sources in dealing with early medieval literature, but in acknowledging the limitation, we already begin to change the established literary-historical account.

The Xiongnu ruler of the kingdom of Han, Liu Cong (d. 318), composed over a hundred poems on "Stating My Feelings" (Shu huai) and around fifty *fu* and eulogies. The Latter Zhao ruler Shi Hu (295–349), a tyrant who nevertheless admired the Confucian Classics, sent someone to copy the "stone Classics" in Luoyang and had them collated. In 337, a black jade seal was discovered and offered to Shi Hu, and the Secretariat Director Wang Bo composed "A Eulogy to the Dark Seal" (Xuanxi song). In 342, in response to another precipitous omen, 107 courtiers presented "A Eulogy to the Imperial Virtue" (Huangde song). Among the Latter Zhao courtiers, Xu Guang (299?–333), Xu Xian (ca 240s–330s), Fu Chang (d. 330), and Wei Sou (d. 350) were all known for their literary skills.

The Särbi (Ch. Xianbei) rulers of the kingdom of Yan were highly sinicized. Murong Huang (297–348) was an erudite scholar of Confucian Classics and authored *Canon of Admonishments* (*Dian jie*) in fifteen chapters. Murong Huang's son Murong Jun (319–360) loved discoursing with his courtiers on Classics, history, and literature, and produced over forty pieces of literary writings. Other known Yan men of letters include Huangfu Zhen, who wrote more than forty poems and *fu*, Feng Yi (d. 365), Miao Kai, Han Heng, and Song Gai.

The Yan was conquered in 370 by the Former Qin ruler Fu Jian (338–385), who came from the Di tribe. Fu Jian did much to revive the study of the Classics, and on many occasions asked his courtiers to compose poetry at court banquets. In 378 some Central Asian kingdoms sent Fu Jian well-bred steeds as a gift, which Fu Jian declined in order to demonstrate his lack of avarice. About four hundred courtiers composed poems to commemorate the event. Fu Jian's younger brother Fu Rong was a skilled interlocutor in the arcane discourse and a gifted writer, who had "never failed to write a *fu* when ascending high, or to produce a dirge when attending a funeral." His *"Fu* on the Buddha"* (Futu fu) was "magnificent and sumptuous," a widely acclaimed piece. He died during Fu Jian's ill-fated southern campaign in 383. Fu Lang, the son of Fu Jian's cousin, capitulated to the Eastern Jin in 384. He was the author of *Master Fu* (*Fuzi*), a work in the tradition of the *Zhuangzi*. Some fragments are still extant. Arrogant and sharp-tongued, Fu Lang offended the powerful minister Wang Guobao and was executed in 389. He composed a poem in the five-syllable line before his death, which is extant.

Many Former Qin courtiers were known for their literary accomplishments. Wang Meng (325–375), Fu Jian's most trusted minister, had a collection in nine scrolls, although only a few letters survive. Zhao Zheng (fl. 374–399), another noted figure, participated in the compilation of the dynastic history; composed songs in the four-, five-, and seven-syllable line to admonish Fu Jian; and contributed to the translation of Buddhist scriptures between 381 and 385. Wang Jia (d. 386), a Daoist recluse, authored *An Account of Things Overlooked* (*Shiyi ji*). This is a collection of accounts of anomalies, recording strange occurrences from antiquity down to the Jin. By the sixth century the original form of the collection was lost, and it was recompiled by the otherwise unknown writer Xiao Qi, who appended a preface as well as commentaries to the original text. The work is extant.

A woman writer, Su Hui, composed the famous palindrome poem (*huiwen shi*), 840 words in all, expressing longing for her husband Dou Tao, an exiled governor. She reportedly wove the poem into a piece of brocade and sent it to him. A fragment is preserved in the Tang *Encyclopedia for Beginners* (*Chuxue ji*). The extant full version has a preface attributed to Empress Wu of the Tang (624–705), but both might be spurious.

In the fourth century, Liangzhou (modern Gansu and Qinghai) was a cultural center in the northwest. Zhang Jun (307–346), the governor of Liangzhou, had a collection in eight scrolls. Of his two extant *yuefu* poems in the five-syllable line, the one entitled "Dew on the Onion Grass" (Xielu xing) is clearly an imitation of Cao Cao's poem of the same title in terms of structure and phrasing; it relates the fall of the Western Jin, and ends with a vow to exterminate all the "barbarians." Xie Ai (d. 353) was an important Liangzhou writer, although nothing has survived from his collection. He and a fellow writer, Wang Ji, were highly praised by the fifth-century critic Liu Xie. Song Xian (ca 271–352), a Liangzhou recluse, wrote a commentary on the *Analects*, and composed poetry and eulogies "in many tens of thousands of words."

Liangzhou was conquered by the Former Qin. After the Qin fell, a general, Lü Guang (337–399), took control of Liangzhou in 385, and established the Latter Liang. The Latter Liang soon disintegrated into the Northern Liang, the Southern Liang, and the Western Liang. The founder of the Western Liang, Li Gao (351–417), was an accomplished writer and an enthusiastic patron of literary and scholarly activities. A work produced by Li Gao and his courtiers, *Eulogies to the Hall of Reverence* (*Jinggong tang song*), was still extant in the seventh century. Li Gao's "*Fu* on Expressing My Aims" (Shuzhi fu) is one of the few northern literary writings surviving from this period. It is a grand piece, although one cannot help suspecting that it was preserved in a Tang source because Li Gao was considered the ancestor of the Tang royal family. Among Li Gao's courtiers, Liu Bing (d. 440) was the most learned and prolific. He compiled *History of the Liang* (*Liang shu*) and *Record of Dunhuang* (*Dunhuang shilu*), among other things.

The Northern Liang ruler, Duan Ye (d. 400), had composed poetry and *fu* while in the service of Lü Guang. He was replaced by Juqu Mengxun (d. 433), probably of Xiongnu origin, who appointed Kan Yin, the author of the *Record of Thirteen States* (*Shisan zhou zhi*), to lead a team of thirty scholars to collate the Classics and the works of the Masters, which amounted to over three thousand scrolls. In 426 Juqu Mengxun dispatched his son, Juqu Maoqian, to the south on a mission to acquire books; among the books requested were the *Classic of Changes*, collections of individual authors, and a copy of *In Search of the Supernatural*. The gifts were repaid: in 437, Juqu Mengqian sent a batch of books in 154 scrolls to the south, including the above-mentioned collection of Xie Ai.

In the far north, Helian Bobo (d. 425), a Latter Qin general of Xiongnu descent, founded the kingdom of Xia in 407. In 413, he built the fortress of Tongwan. A lavish inscription in the four-syllable line composed by Hu Yizhou (or his son Hu Fanghui) is still extant, along with a lengthy, finely wrought preface.

During the Former and Latter Qin (386–417), Chang'an flourished as a center of religious activity. The translation of Buddhist scriptures, supported by the Qin rulers, was carried out on a large scale under the supervision of the eminent monk Dao'an (314–385), who compiled the first systematic catalogue of translated sūtras, and reached a new level with the arrival of the famous Kuchean monk Kumārajīva (344–413) in 401. Dao'an and Kumārajīva left fascinating discussions on translation theory and the nature of Sanskrit and Chinese languages. Kumārajīva's disciple Sengzhao was an influential Buddhist thinker and a prolific, refined writer. His letter to Liu Yimin, a noted lay member of the Mount Lu Buddhist community in the south, and his dirge for Kumārajīva, are both elegant compositions. Another disciple, Daoheng, penned a long, eloquent treatise in defense of the Buddhist faith, written in the traditional form of a hypothetical dialogue between the author and an imaginary challenger.

It was from Chang'an that a monk named Faxian (ca 340–421) set out in 399 on an arduous pilgrimage to India. Fourteen years and some thirty kingdoms later, he boarded a merchant ship from Ceylon and returned to China. He reached Jiankang in the following year and recorded his travels in *Account of the Buddhist Kingdoms* (*Foguo ji*). A precursor to the monk Xuanzang's (600–664) famous *An Account of the Western Regions in the Great Tang* (*Da Tang xiyu ji*), Faxian's work, completed in 414, is the first extensive travelogue written by a Chinese about his experiences in foreign lands.

II. Literature in the south: the fifth century

An overview: 420–479

The Song dynasty, founded by Liu Yu, lasted from 420 to 479. It is commonly referred to as the Liu-Song to distinguish it from the later Song dynasty (960–1279). Liu Yu died soon afterwards; his son Liu Yilong (407–453), Emperor Wen, began a thirty-year rule known as the peaceful reign of Yuanjia (424–453). Liu Yilong was assassinated by his son, who was then overthrown by his brother Liu Jun (Emperor Xiaowu, r. 454–464). The turbulent last decades of the Song were filled with palace coups, uprisings, and killings within the imperial family. In 479 the last Song emperor was forced to abdicate in favor of a distant relative, Xiao Daocheng (427–482), who founded the Qi.

Fifth-century literary-historical accounts credited Yin Zhongwen (d. 407) and Xie Hun (d. 412) as initiating a move away from the "arcane" poetic style popular in the Eastern Jin. Each of these two poets has only one poem extant, in addition to a few fragments; and it is difficult to ascertain the extent of their innovation. There was indeed real, profound change in the literary realm, but it took place on a much more extensive scale than the achievements of two poets.

The fifth century was an age of reaching out to faraway time and space. It is characterized by a sense of vast possibilities and geographical expansion brought about by military campaigns to north China and religious adventures into the foreign land and back. Buddhist monks like Faxian traveled to Central and Southeast Asia and brought back scriptures and stories of the exotic lands and people. More geographical accounts appeared than ever before. Poets gave poetic accounts of their journeys through earthly nature, represented by the works of Xie Lingyun (385–433), the first major landscape poet in Chinese literary history. The impulse to explore hitherto uncharted territory even stretched to the territory of the other world, as we have the first prose accounts of journeys to hell in this period, not gleaned from Buddhist sutras, but related by people who claimed to have come back from death.

There was also expansion in temporal terms, as this period in literary history was one of retrospection. We find many poems written under old *yuefu* titles of the Wei and Western Jin, and poems with such titles as "Imitating the Old [Poem]" (Ni gu), "Emulating the Old [Poem]" (Xiao gu), "Following the Old [Poem]" (Yi gu), "To the Old [Title]" (Dai gu), or "The Old Mode" (Guyi). Yan Yanzhi (384–456) wrote a ninety-line "Ballad of Qiuhu" (Qiuhu xing) in the five-syllable line, the longest narrative ballad of the time and twice the size of the Western Jin poet Fu Xuan's "Ballad of Qiuhu" in the five-syllable line on the same subject. One-fifth of Xie Lingyun's extant poetic *oeuvre* is *yuefu* poems. Of the younger generation, Bao Zhao (414?–466), the third major Liu-Song poet after Yan Yanzhi and Xie Lingyun, was a champion of *yuefu* poetry.

Many Liu-Song poets composed "imitations" of specific old poems, in much the same way as the earlier poets Fu Xuan and Lu Ji had done. He Yan's (413–458) "Swaying Solitary Bamboo" (Ranran gusheng zhu) furnishes a typical example: it is a line-by-line imitation of the model text, elevating the linguistic register of the model text. Sometimes a poem title indicates which poem is being imitated by citing the first line of the model text; sometimes, however, the title could have been supplied by later editors. Xie Lingyun's cousin, Xie Huilian (407–433), wrote a poem, "To the Old [Title]" (Daigu shi), which has a variant title, "Imitating 'A Visitor Comes from Afar'" (Ni Ke cong yuanfang lai), "A Visitor Comes from Afar" being the first line of an "old poem."

The model texts, however, are not always extant, such as in the case of the Song prince Liu Shuo's (431–453) "To 'Holding back Tears and Hitting the Long Road'" (Dai Shoulei jiu changlu shi). Sometimes, if a poem is simply entitled "Xiao gu shi," like the one by Yuan Shu (408–453), we do not know whether the poet is imitating a specific model text that is no longer extant, or whether "Xiao gu shi" is being used as a general term, so that it reads "Poem Emulating the Old" rather than "Emulating the Old Poem." Sometimes, the poet imitated the "style" (*ti*) of an earlier writer rather than a specific poem, such as Wang Su's (418–471) "Emulating Infantry Commandant Ruan [Ji]'s Style" (Xue Ruan Bubing ti). Poems like these show an intensified awareness of the individual styles of different poets, a sense of the continuation of literary tradition.

In the 440s, Liu Shuo composed more than thirty imitation poems and was praised by his contemporaries as a modern Lu Ji. Occasionally, instead of imitating an entire poem, he would take a passage and make it into a separate poem. The last six lines of a famous old poem, "Chang'an Has Narrow Alleys" (Chang'an you xiaxie), or its alternative version, "Meeting" (Xiangfeng xing), describe the wives of three brothers: two of the wives are weaving, while the wife of the youngest brother is playing music. Liu Shuo was the first to turn this passage into a six-line poem, "The Sensual Charms of the Three Wives" (Sanfu yan). Many fifth- and sixth-century poets composed to this and another spin-off title, "The Middle Wife Weaves the Yellow Floss" (Zhongfu zhi liuhuang); somehow, the three sisters-in-law metamorphosed into the three wives of one man. Liu Shuo's brother, Emperor Xiaowu, likewise turned a passage from the Wei poet Xu Gan's poem into a separate quatrain, "Ever Since You Left" (Zi jun zhi chu yi), which then became a standard *yuefu* title.

What could have triggered this revival of interest in "old poems" and old *yuefu* titles? This is a question not easy to answer. It might have been a fad started by one or two famous writers; it might have had to do with the "discovery" of a repertoire of *yuefu* lyrics hitherto unknown in the South. In 417, Liu Yu carried out a successful northern expedition, conquered the Latter Qin, and recaptured Chang'an. Among his loot were four thousand scrolls of books, and, even more important, 120 court musicians. These musicians had belonged to the Former Qin and were taken by the Western Yan army in 385; later, when the Latter Yan defeated the Western Yan in 394, the musicians fell into the hands of Murong Chui. Murong Chui's successor, Murong Chao, offered them to the Latter Qin ruler Yao Xing in an exchange for Murong Chao's mother and wife, both detained in Chang'an. The musicians finally returned to Chang'an in 407, only to be taken south by Liu Yu. These musicians clearly maintained a living tradition by oral transmission of music and lyrics; their presence made an important difference to the cultural landscape. Eastern Jin court music greatly benefited from the migration of the northern musicians, once in 355, and once again in 383; but the acquisition of the 120 court musicians in 417 was the largest gain of all.

Eastern Jin poets who had earlier used "Imitation" in their titles – Yuan Hong, Xie Daoyun, Tao Yuanming – all had relations with people who had access to the northern musicians. Yuan Hong, the author of a fragmentary

"Imitating the Old [Poem]," was appreciated and employed by Xie Shang, a musician himself and the major figure in reviving court music by working with the new northern musicians who arrived in 355. Xie Daoyun's brother Xie Xuan was the very general who defeated Fu Jian in the battle of the Fei river in 383, after which the Eastern Jin obtained a number of Fu Jian's musicians. Xie Daoyun's "Imitating Courtier Xi's Poem on the Pine Tree" (Ni Xi zhongsan Yong song) is a close imitation of the third-century poet Xi Kang's poem entitled "Roaming as an Immortal" (Youxian). Tao Yuanming, who has a series of eight poems entitled "Imitating the Old [Poems]," was on close terms with Wang Hong and Yan Yanzhi, both closely involved in Liu Yu's northern expedition in 416 and 417; Tao also addressed a poem to a Clerk Yang when the latter was sent to see Liu Yu at Chang'an. The most telling coincidence was the composition of fifteen songs, all to old *yuefu* titles, by He Chengtian (370–447), a learned scholar, historian, and scientist, "at the end of the Yixi reign [405–418]." "At the end of" has a textual variant that reads "in the middle of," but since one of the songs praises Liu Yu's suppression of an uprising in 415, "at the end of" is more likely. Seven of the songs are in the five-syllable line, five are in a mixture of three- and seven-syllable lines, one is in the three-syllable line, one is of lines of various lengths; only one is in the four-syllable line. This forms a remarkable contrast with the thirteen ancestral temple songs, all in the four-syllable line, composed by Cao Pi and Wang Xun, produced after obtaining the northern musicians in 383. While poems in the four-syllable line continued to be composed on formal occasions, the popularity of the five-syllable line was on the rise.

As the Eastern Jin reaped cultural benefit through military victories, literary scholarship also experienced a boom. The great Xie clan, whose status had risen dramatically in the second half of the fourth century as a result of Xie An and Xie Xuan's achievements, contributed greatly to this literary prosperity, probably in no small measure due to their privileged access to the northern manuscript tradition. At the beginning of the fifth century, Xie Hun and his cousins, including Xie Lingyun, often gathered at his residence in the Black Robe Lane and discussed literature, forming an exclusive group known as the famous Black Robe Xies. A *Basics of Literature Divided by Genre* (*Wenzhang liubie ben*) is attributed to Xie Hun in the bibliography section of the *History of the Sui*; it does not survive, but could have been an epitome of the *Collection of Literature Divided by Genre* by the Western Jin writer Zhi Yu. Another work listed under Xie Hun's name in the bibliography section of the *History of the Tang* is the *Garden of Collections* (*Ji yuan*) in sixty scrolls, which was clearly an anthology of individual literary collections. Xie Hun's familiarity with the literary tradition is shown in a poem fragment, which borrows a line verbatim from an old *yuefu* title, "Joining the Army" (Cong jun xing), even if the poem itself is not a *yuefu*.

Xie Lingyun compiled a *Collection of Poetry* (*Shi ji*) in fifty scrolls, an anthology that was faulted by Zhong Rong for indiscriminately "including every poem he saw." Xie Lingyun is credited with another poetry anthology, "The Fine Blossoms of Poetry" (*Shiying*) in nine scrolls; he also made an epitome of the *Collection of Poetry* (*Shi ji chao*). Other single-genre anthologies produced by Xie Lingyun include a *fu* collection (*Fu ji*), a collection of palindrome poetry (*Huiwen ji*), and a collection of the "Sevens" (*Qi ji*). All these were probably compiled when he served as director of the imperial library from 426 to 428 and was commissioned to organize the imperial book collection. Of the younger generation, Xie Zhuang (421–466), another famous literary member of the Xie clan, compiled collections of encomia, dirges, and inscriptions.

Xie Hun, Xie Lingyun, and Xie Zhuang were not the only writers devoted to making anthologies. Literary scholarship in the early fifth century flourished, perhaps because of the availability of new material, but also because of the encouragement of emperors and princes. Emperor Wen established an Academy of Literature in 439, along with Academies of Classics, Arcane Learning, and Historical Studies. Emperor Xiaowu and Emperor Ming (466–472) were both avid literature lovers. Emperor Ming compiled the *Record of Literature of the Eastern Jin* (*Jin jiangzuo wenzhang zhi*), as well as collections of poetry and *fu*.

Many other literary compilations were produced during this period, including a thirty-scroll *Collection of Woman Writers* (*Furen ji*) compiled by Yin Chun (379–438), the first of its kind. Though none of these compilations survives, their listings in the *History of the Sui* bibliography testify to the richness of literary activity in the early fifth century. This forms a sharp contrast with the relative quietness of the fourth century, for which only a handful of identifiable collections are recorded, such as Li Chong's *Literary Grove*, and a nine-scroll collection of poems on expressing one's aims (*Baizhi shi*) attributed to Gan Bao.

In conjunction with the revival of *yuefu* and their interest in "old poems," fifth-century writers developed an acute sense of the literary past, and true historical accounts of poetry appeared. Tan Daoluan's *Sequel to [Sun Sheng's] Annals of the Jin* (*Xu Jin Yangqiu*), a work of the early fifth century, relates the history of poetry from the Jian'an period, the Western Jin, all the way to the Yixi era (405–418). The basic narrative revolves around the rise and fall of "the poetry of arcane discourse," which Tan Daoluan described as beginning with Guo Pu's poetry in the five-syllable line and becoming predominant with Sun Chuo and Xu Xun. "It was not until the Yixi era that Xie Hun changed it." Tan Daoluan's remarks represent a widely accepted view of the poetry of the third and fourth centuries, repeated by later critics such as Shen Yue, Liu Xie (ca 460s–520s), and Zhong Rong, and remains the standard account today. The low esteem in which the Eastern Jin poetry was held had a lasting influence, and has serious consequences for its preservation.

The fifth and sixth centuries were a crucial period for the formation of a canon of early Chinese poetry. Although the *Classic of Poetry* and the *Verses of Chu* were always cited as the distant origins, the Jian'an period was seen as the true beginning of poetry, primarily poetry in the five-syllable line. In the early fifth century, Xie Lingyun wrote a poetic series in the five-syllable line entitled "Imitating the Poems of the Wei Crown Prince's Gathering at Ye" (Ni Wei taizi Yezhong ji), which consists of eight poems in the voices of Cao Pi, Cao Zhi, and six of the Seven Masters of the Jian'an period. In the brief preface to each poem, Xie Lingyun attempts to capture each poet's essential characteristic in terms of content or style, but the poems themselves do not show distinctive stylistic differences. In contrast, Jiang Yan's (444–505) thirty poems in the five-syllable line, "Various Forms" (Za ti), probably composed toward the end of fifth century, imitate twenty-nine specific poets from the Han to the fifth century arranged in chronological order (the first being an imitation of an unspecific "old poem"), and clearly attempt to convey the individual style of each poet.

In the preface, Jiang Yan calls the reader's attention not only to period differences ("The Chu ballads and Han airs are not of one frame; Wei creations and Jin products have two forms"), but also to regional differences ("On the other side of the Yellow River and in the south of the Yangzi river, the methods of composition are quite different"); he asks for sympathetic acceptance without comparative judgment. Jiang Yan's attempt at a historical understanding of poetry marks an important moment in the making of literary history; his awareness of regional differences in styles and tastes also mirrors the increasingly self-conscious comparison between north and south in the late fifth century, which would continue into the sixth century and contribute to the formation of the cultural identities of the north and south, culminating in the Sui and Tang, the conquest dynasties that unified China and brought north and south together.

Fifth-century literary criticism made a distinction between *wen* (rhymed writings, including poetry and *fu*) and *bi* (unrhymed writings serving more practical purposes), first explicitly made in the mid-fifth century by

Fan Ye (398–445), the author of the *History of the Later Han* (*Hou Han shu*), and in remarks by Yan Yanzhi that were later elaborated in greater detail by Liu Xie; the distinction marks the initial attempt to separate belles-lettres from public prose forms.

While major prose forms of the fifth century did not vary greatly from earlier eras, parallelism became increasingly intricate, and shorter, lyrical *fu* were in vogue. Xie Huilian's *"Fu on Snow"* (Xue fu) is a tour de force. Set in a pseudo-historical narrative framework, with the Western Han prince of Liang and his courtiers as central characters, the *fu* gives a layered discourse on snow by assuming multiple voices of the different courtiers, each in a distinctive style. In many ways, it evokes Xie Lingyun's poems imitating the gathering of Ye, inspired by a historical imagination typical of its age. Xie Huilian's influence can be detected in Xie Zhuang's *"Fu on the Moon"* (Yue fu) and Jiang Yan's *"Fu on the Lamp"* (Deng fu), the latter also a rather close imitation of *"Fu on the Wind"* (Feng fu) of the Han.

Two rather long *fu* that survive more or less intact from the Liu-Song are Xie Lingyun's *"Fu on Dwelling in the Mountains"* (Shanju fu) written around 425, complete with his own annotations, and *"Fu on the Sea"* (Hai fu) written in 463 by Zhang Rong (444–497), a writer known for his love of idiosyncrasy. The grandeur and comprehensiveness of the *"Fu on Dwelling in the Mountains"* evoke the Han writer Sima Xiangru's magnificent *fu* on the imperial park, but Xie was only describing his private estate. While the real-life magnitude of Xie's estate was certainly impressive enough to be a match for the Han imperial park, it was Xie's extravagant discourse that constituted more of a challenge to imperial authority. In this aspect, Xie Lingyun seemed to be clinging to the aura of the Eastern Jin, when the great families were more powerful than the imperial house; but the Liu-Song was a different age, and Xie was eventually executed as a consequence of his aristocratic brashness.

Writings and social life

Poetry and prose serving public functions nevertheless continued to occupy an important place in social life. In 454 a woman writer, Han Lanying (fl. ca 454–494), presented a *"Fu on Dynastic Restoration"* (Zhongxing fu) to Emperor Xiaowu and was subsequently appointed tutor to palace ladies. Two capital *fu* were composed in this period, a *"Fu on the Eastern Capital"* (Dongdu fu) by Kong Huan (d. 470s), which is no longer extant, and a *"Fu on the Wu Capital"* (Wudu fu) by an otherwise unknown Xiahou Bi, which survives in fragments. The most famous *fu* on a metropolis produced in the fifth century, however, is *"Fu on the Weed-covered City"* (Wucheng fu) by Bao Zhao. It gives a moving account of the glorious past and desolate present of a ruined city, identified as Guangling (modern Yangzhou) in an old note. The retrospective impulse, so common in the Liu-Song literature, is here manifested in the lament over an unnamed city whose splendor lay in the past.

The most famous public writings from this period were commissioned by emperors. Yan Yanzhi's "Fu on the Russet and White Horse (Zhebaima fu), a polished piece rich with horse lore, was written in 441 in commemoration of a piebald horse that had been a favorite steed of the Liu-Song emperors. Two prefaces to collections of poems composed on the Lustration Festival in spring, one by Yan Yanzhi in 434 and one by Wang Rong (467–493) in 491, were widely acclaimed. In 462, Lady Yin, Emperor Xiaowu's favorite consort, passed away. Xie Zhuang's dirge mixes the four-syllable line, a more common form for a dirge, with the *Verses of Chu* meter, which recalls Cao Zhi's dirge for his brother Cao Pi and achieves a poignant effect.

In the fifth century there also appeared parodies of public prose which use animal or plant characters, such as those written by Yuan Shu, who compiled a ten-scroll collection of humorous prose, or "The Bamboo's Accusation of Plantain" (Xiuzhu tan ganjiao wen) by Shen Yue. The monk Baolin authored a proclamation against demons and spirits. The writer Kong Zhigui's (447–501) "Proclamation on Behalf of North Mountain" (Beishan yiwen) is a famous mock-proclamation written in well-crafted parallel prose, speaking from the perspective of the mountain god to tease the author's friend Zhou Yong (fl. ca 460–489) for renouncing reclusion in the mountain.

The preservation of grave memoirs (*muzhi ming*) as literary texts by known writers was a new phenomenon in the fifth century. Unlike stele inscriptions, grave memoirs were buried inside the tomb. Earlier grave memoirs were generally rather simple, but beginning in the third century, perhaps in response to the prohibition of stele inscriptions, the grave memoir became more elaborate, assuming characteristics of the stele inscription. It typically consists of a prose account of the deceased and a rhymed inscription in the four-syllable line. In the fifth century, Yan Yanzhi composed a grave memoir, no longer extant, for a courtier, Wang Qiu (393–441). Emperor Xiaowu's grave memoir for his brother Liu Hong (434–458) and Xie Zhuang's grave memoirs for He Shangzhi in 460 are two of the earliest extant grave memoirs by known writers. It was perhaps around this time that writers began to keep copies of grave memoirs and included them in literary collections. Among other funerary writings, Xie Huilian's "Sacrificial Address to an Ancient Tomb" (Ji guzhong wen), speaking to nameless dead unearthed during a construction project in the early autumn of 430, is a rather original specimen of its genre.

Many histories were compiled in the fifth century. Fan Ye's *History of the Later Han* (*Hou Han shu*) and Shen Yue's *History of the Song* (*Song shu*), which was based on the work of several predecessors and presented to the throne in 488, survive in good shape. Numerous literary writings are preserved in these two histories. In the *History of the Song*, the monograph on music is one of our best sources for court songs performed from Han to Song. Shen Yue's commentary on Xie Lingyun's biography is an important piece of literary criticism: in the context of discussing poetic euphony, it gives an elaborate account of literary history from the pre-Qin period to Shen's own day, and upholds Yan Yanzhi and Xie Lingyun as two great literary models for later ages.

A new prose genre, the "communication" (*qi*), appeared in the Liu-Song. It was originally a memo to the throne or a member of the royal family, frequently, though not exclusively, used in expression of gratitude to the emperor or a prince for a gift. As such, it may be described as a "thank-you note" written in increasingly elaborate language. In late fifth century, these "thank-you notes" evolved into short pieces of elegant parallel prose, describing the gift with rich allusions and in exquisite terms, suggesting a miniature *fu* on an object. The presentation of a gift thus became mutual, with the thing bestowed requited with the representation of the thing given back to the giver.

Xie Lingyun

Xie Lingyun, a haughty, hot-tempered aristocrat given to a luxurious style, was a scion of the great Xie clan of the Eastern Jin. In 405, the year when Tao Yuanming resigned from the post of magistrate of Pengze, Xie Lingyun entered public service at the age of twenty. His career was a bumpy one. After Liu Yu died in 422, his young son succeeded him; unable to get along with the regents, Xie Lingyun was banished from the capital to serve as the magistrate of Yongjia (modern Zhejiang). In the following year, Xie Lingyun resigned and returned to his home estate at Guiji. He was called back to the capital in 426 as the director of the imperial library, but two years later he resigned again. Back at his home estate, Xie Lingyun's hauteur caused a strained relationship with the local magistrate, who in 430 sent a letter to the throne accusing Xie Lingyun of plotting a rebellion. Xie Lingyun went to the capital to exonerate himself. He was detained in the capital, and during this period he participated in the project of rendering an elegant translation of the Mahāparinirvāṇa Sūtra. Emperor Wen, unwilling to let him go home again, appointed him to a post in Linchuan (modern Jiangxi) in the early 432, where Xie Lingyun again neglected his official duties, as he had done at Yongjia, to explore the landscape. He came into conflict with the emperor's brother, and resisted arrest with armed force. The emperor exiled him to Guangzhou in the far south, where he was accused of being involved with an uprising and was executed in 433.

Xie Lingyun is many things: writer, scholar, Buddhist theorist; his "Discourse on Distinguishing the Essentials" (Bianzong lun) is a brilliant exegesis of the "Sudden Enlightenment" theory championed by the monk Zhu Daosheng (d. 434). He is, however, first of all a great poet. A few extant poems are datable to Xie Lingyun's early career; these are mostly in the four-syllable line and belong to the social verse in the "presentation/reply" mode. His poetic career took off at the same time that his political career suffered setbacks; his most memorable poetry began in 422, during his first exile to Yongjia. From then on, he turned out a steady stream of remarkable poems. They were so popular with his contemporaries that as soon as a new poem arrived at the capital, people vied with one another to make a copy of it.

Xie Lingyun was a younger contemporary of Tao Yuanming. They shared a number of friends, including Yan Yanzhi. Xie had most likely read and was influenced by the older poet's works. For instance, he continued Tao's practice of giving elaborate titles to his poems to mark their specificity in terms of time and place. Xie's style, however, remains distinctive: while Tao uses simple vocabulary and is easy to read in that sense, Xie's poetry is highly wrought, known for its difficult diction, dense allusions, and crafted parallelism. Despite the superficial divergence, the two poets nevertheless share much more than is commonly realized. Both poets took their readings seriously, and use their readings to mirror, question, justify, and make sense of their experiences. Both struggle with the world of nature: Tao Yuanming by reclaiming farmland from wilderness and worrying about his crops and himself – his life's work as a poet – being overgrown and overtaken by weeds and mortality; Xie Lingyun by wresting meaning from mountains and waters, and by structuring the manifold of Nature and the manifold of his experiences, thoughts, and feelings into a significant whole that is imprinted with his personal perception and understanding, culminating in a moment of enlightenment.

Xie Lingyun is traditionally credited for having transformed the poetry of "arcane discourse," decorated with landscape couplets, into a fully fledged landscape poetry. Like all clichés there is some truth to such a claim. But Xie's biggest innovation lies in his crafting of a landscape poetry that is personal, intense, and poignant in its emotional complexity, and in his representation of a body moving through landscape. Depictions of landscape in earlier poetry are often generic and scattered in perspective; in contrast, Xie presents a landscape observed by an assiduous traveler in motion, a physical journey literalized in minutely observed details of nature. Moreover, the long narrative titles of his poems allow no ambiguity as to the time and place of his sightseeing. We may well imagine that when his contemporaries read his poetry, they felt that they were there with him. The fascination with "witness reports from afar" in the fifth century both motivated and contributed to the popularity of Xie's poetry. The emphasis on the very process of one's physical journey also proffers a secular version of contemporary Buddhist advocacy of a long process of hard work before achieving enlightenment.

Xie Lingyun was an active explorer of nature, known for taking arduous trips to appreciate the beauty of the landscape. He was well equipped to do so, as he had a sizable labor force at his disposal. He once employed several hundred retainers to cut a path through a forest all the way from his home estate to a town many miles away; the commotion alarmed the local authorities, who mistook them for mountain bandits. Yet, despite his large entourage, a sense of loneliness permeates Xie's poems. This certainly reflects the stringent class hierarchy in early medieval China: surrounded by servants who were unable to share with him an appreciation of beauty, the great nobleman lamented his solitude. Xie Lingyun's class-blindness is redeemed from irony by his capacity to transform his sense of solitude into powerful poetry. "On Visiting Nanting" (You Nanting), focusing on a brief period of clearing up at dusk after hours, perhaps days, of rain, is a moving contemplation of lingering illness, old age, and mortality, which culminates in an illuminating moment of resolution before imminent darkness, followed with the question: "For whom can I clarify my dreams and hopes?"

The poet finds his loneliness reflected in the solitude of nature. In "Ascending the Lonely Isle in the Middle of the River" (Deng jiangzhong guyu), he writes, "Its numinous quality is appreciated by none; / it conceals immortals, yet who will spread the word?" He sometimes sees himself as an understanding friend to nature, as in "The Stone Chamber Mountain" (Shishi shan), which ends with the following couplets:

> The numinous realm has lain hidden for long;
> now it is as if communing with an appreciative companion.
> Conjoined pleasure allows no words:
> plucking a fragrant blossom, I play with the cold branches.

This brings to mind the ending of Tao Yuanming's famous "Drinking" poem, in which he picks chrysanthemum at the eastern hedge, gazes at South

Mountain, and muses, "Therein is some true significance; / I want to explain it, but have lost the words." If Xie Lingyun had indeed had Tao Yuanming's poem in mind, he ingeniously turned the original text around so as to end his poem with an evocative image. Such an ending is quite striking when compared with conventional poetic conclusions with a statement of thought or emotion, and it plays into an increasingly important aesthetic principle about poetry being able to convey what is beyond words.

In his last years the landscape in Xie Lingyun's poetry, though still majestic, exotic, and beautiful, becomes increasingly desolate. The poet not only has no companions to converse with, but also faces a nature that is devoid of gods, immortals, strange beings, even recluses, whom he has learned about in his readings, but fails to find in reality. When he gazes at landscape, it no longer offers the poet any philosophical principle that brings order and comfort; instead, he is staring at a world that has lost its luminosity, and the poet feels an acute sense of belatedness. In "Entering the Mouth of Pengli Lake" (Ru Pengli hu kou) he writes,

> The numinous creatures no longer manifest their marvels,
> and extraordinary beings conceal their spiritual essence.
> The Golden Unguent obscures its brilliant light,
> water sapphires have ceased their flowing warmth.

"Entering the Third Valley of Mayuan Where Huazi Hill Stands" (Ru Huazi gang shi Mayuan disan gu), a poem composed in the year before his death, compares the hill, empty of "feathered beings" (i.e. immortals) and written records, to an "empty fishtrap."

Xie Lingyun writes an erudite poetry, drawing widely on earlier literature. His landscape is the darkly exotic textual landscape of the *Verses of Chu*; the way he seeks to convey the totality of experience by incorporating many details evokes the exhaustive description of *fu*. His parallel couplets often consist of one line representing a mountain scene and the next line representing a water scene, or vice versa; thus the couplet instantiates the Chinese conceptual category of landscape, "mountains-and-waters" (*shanshui*). The fifth century was prone to a strict formal structure in poetry and extreme density in diction, exemplified by Yan Yanzhi's work; but because of his extraordinary talent, Xie Lingyun manages to animate the period style. Although disparaged for being a "heavy-handed craftsman" during the Northern Song, an opinion still shared by many today, Xie Lingyun was praised in his day for being "as natural as a fresh lotus blossom" in contrast with Yan Yanzhi's "mixed colors and carved gold," a judgment that reminds us that critical categories must be historicized.

Even more than Tao Yuanming, Xie Lingyun exerted a palpable influence on the subsequent development of Chinese poetry, inspiring many followers in the fifth and sixth centuries, not the least his younger contemporary Bao Zhao, who learned from Xie Lingyun, among other literary predecessors, and went in another direction.

Yan Yanzhi

Yan Yanzhi was the public writer par excellence. Many of his prose pieces were composed for public purposes, and almost half of his extant poems, about twenty in all, were written to imperial command. His style is elegant and formal, no doubt appropriate to the occasion; but when the occasion is over, the poem itself is forgotten, fitting only as a model text for an aspiring courtier. His two *yuefu* ballads and a series of poems on five of the Seven Worthies of the Bamboo Grove are among his more interesting compositions. *Instructions from the Courtyard* (*Ting gao*), a didactic work for his sons, contains some comments on literature and anticipates the more famous work of his clansman, the sixth-century writer Yan Zhitui's *Family Instructions of the Yan Clan* (*Yanshi jiaxun*).

Yan Yanzhi was considered a great writer in his time. Even Zhong Rong, who complained that Yan had misled an entire generation with his heavy use of allusions, accorded him a grudging respect. Yan's influence was strongly felt in the mid-fifth century, despite the increasing popularity of the two younger writers, Bao Zhao and Tang Huixiu. Zhong Rong cited a number of Yan Yanzhi's faithful followers from this period, including Qiu Lingju (fl. ca 430s–480s) and Xie Lingyun's grandson, Xie Chaozong (d. 483). The public poetry of Xie Zhuang also adopted the Yan Yanzhi style, which Zhong Rong described as "elaborate and dense." In his private poetry, however, Xie Zhuang was much more relaxed and lucid. His poems in lines of varied lengths are remarkable experiments in poetic forms.

Bao Zhao and Jiang Yan

The early fifth century was a time of looking back and rediscovering former masters; no one did this with more originality and panache than Bao Zhao. Born into a humble family, Bao Zhao spent his official career mostly on the staffs of various princes. In 466 he was killed by imperial soldiers during a failed insurrection attempt by the young prince he served.

Despite an intense renewal of interest in earlier poetry, it would be a mistake to regard the Liu-Song poets as slavish imitators, for they were anything but that. Bao Zhao is a good example. In many ways, he was typical of his age.

On the one hand, of about two hundred poems he left, eighty-six were *yuefu*, and twenty-five were imitations of anonymous old poems or known poets, including Liu Zhen, Ruan Ji, and Tao Yuanming; on the other hand, he wrote a great number of landscape poems in which one detects Xie Lingyun's influence. Both in his *yuefu*, for which he is best known, and in his landscape poetry, Bao Zhao shows something distinctly his own.

Bao Zhao was the first poet we know of to write poems in the seven-syllable line without rhyming in every line; instead, he adopted the abcb rhyme pattern. This seemingly small difference from Han, Wei, and Jin poems in the seven-syllable line, which always rhyme aaaa, was nevertheless significant, because the old seven-syllable line could be seen as a combination of four- and thee-syllable lines, and could be treated as two lines, not as one. Bao Zhao's was therefore a very different meter, and it proved crucial in the subsequent development of seven-syllable poetry. He also composed a quatrain in the seven-syllable line, "Listening to a Singing Girl at Night" (Ye ting ji), with an aaba rhyme scheme. Bao's contemporary, Tang Huixiu, whose poems were contemptuously referred to by Yan Yanzhi as "street songs," composed another seven-syllable-line quatrain with the same rhyme pattern. These are the earliest extant seven-syllable-line quatrains proper, an extremely important poetic form that first began to develop in the Southern Dynasties.

Bao Zhao's *yuefu* are lucid and direct, remarkably free from the mannered density and formality of many Liu-Song poems. He is at his best in songs on romantic and military themes, perhaps because both themes benefit from theatricality and bravado, qualities Bao Zhao possessed in abundance. Though he had never been to the north, Bao Zhao was the true ancestor of a poetic subgenre dubbed "frontier poetry" (*biansai shi*), which often involves an exaggerated description of the cold, harsh weather of the northern frontier, displaced into the legendary past of the Han dynasty. Bao Zhao's most famous *yuefu* series is "Hard Traveling" (Xinglu nan): its eighteen poems read like dramatic monologues, delivered by an impassioned, anguished speaker.

Bao Zhao loves to shock his readers by employing unusual imagery; he is also more attentive to the effect of individual words than anyone before him. This tendency is particularly pronounced in his landscape writings, which are mannered and tortuous, completely unlike his *yuefu*. In the "Inscriptional Essay of Guabu Hill" (Guabu shan jiewen), he wrote that the hill occupies such a lofty position that "rivers and tributaries [seem like] tears and mucus, mountains and peaks, warts and protuberances." The poem entitled "Going to Jingkou and Passing through Zhuli" (Xing Jingkou zhi Zhuli) opens with a couplet on a close-up scene of towering branches and jagged rocks, an abrupt beginning atypical of the poetic structure of this period; it then portrays a menacing nature, with the "sound of pines" "concealed" in layered ravines, the ice "closing," the cold growing "stalwart," and the twilight shadows "forcing themselves upon" the lonely traveler.

While Bao Zhao's *yuefu*, with their dramatic personae and situations, manifest a powerful individuality, his landscape poems, written in his own voice, largely lack the kind of intensely personal quality that Xie Lingyun's landscape poems possess. A nineteenth-century critic complained, quite justly, that Bao Zhao's poem on ascending Mount Lu could have been about any mountain and by any poet (in the sense of being "impersonal"). Stylistically, however, these poems do manage to achieve a distinctive manner by avoiding conventional word combinations and using startling images. Bao Zhao's conscious pursuit of a striking effect earned him the reputation of being "perilous" (*xian*), a quality frowned upon by court poets of the late fifth century and the sixth, who aimed for a lucid grace, known as "clarity" (*qing*), in poetic expression, but Bao Zhao's style was influential in his lifetime and after his death. In the words of a contemporary poet, Bao Zhao and his friend Tang Huixiu "quite affected the crowd" in the 450s and 460s. The work of Jiang Yan, a younger poet, provides good evidence.

Jiang Yan came from a declining elite family. In 474 he offended a prince he served and was demoted to a provincial administrative position. Two years later, the prince was killed in a failed insurrection, and Jiang Yan was called back to the capital by Xiao Daocheng, who founded the Qi dynasty in 479 and put Jiang Yan in charge of drafting edicts. Jiang Yan enjoyed a smooth official career from this point on, but in his later years a rumor went around that he had "exhausted his literary talent." We do not know if the rumor started because he wrote less, or because his style went out of fashion, or both. Jiang Yan was enfeoffed as the earl of Liling after the Liang dynasty was founded in 502, and died shortly after.

Jiang Yan was notably one of the first writers to edit his own literary writings, which were divided into a *Former Collection* (*Qianji*) compiled around 480 and a *Latter Collection* (*Houji*). Each collection spanned ten scrolls. An "Autobiographical Account" (*Zixu*) was appended to Jiang Yan's *Former Collection*, a practice that was common with dynastic histories and philosophical works. This forms a striking contrast with the attitude of the Eastern Jin writer Ge Hong, who referred to the writing of poetry and *fu* as a waste of time and stressed the importance of philosophical treatises in the autobiographical account included in his *Outer Chapters of the Master Who Embraced Simplicity*. While lengthy treatises in the style of "Masters Literature" such as the *Zhuangzi* or *Huainanzi* continued to be produced in large numbers in the third and fourth centuries, in the fifth century they largely disappeared, and the importance attached to those treatises seems to have been transferred to literary collections, as evidenced by the kind of care invested in preparing it by the author himself. Jiang Yan's contemporary Zhang Rong was the first known writer to give titles to collections of his literary writings.

Even though his active life spanned three dynasties, Jiang Yan was a late Liu-Song poet in spirit. He left behind few *yuefu*, but he was good at imitating literary predecessors: his "Various Forms" so vividly convey different styles of individual poets that in later times some of them were mistaken for originals; he also wrote poems emulating Cao Pi and Ruan Ji. The ability to imitate, however, seems to be Jiang Yan's most distinctive characteristic, for his poetry is filled with echoes of earlier poetry, most notably the *Verses of Chu*, Xie Lingyun, and Bao Zhao in particular. Jiang Yan's landscape poems, not as painfully mannered as Bao Zhao's and yet falling short of the graceful ease of the Yongming (483–493) poets, uneasily sit somewhere in the middle. From time to time, Jiang Yan turned out a surprisingly good poem, but overall his poetry is more inspired than inspiring.

Jiang Yan is better known for his *"Fu on Sorrowful Frustration"* (Hen fu) and *"Fu on Separation"* (Bie fu), which describe different types of frustration or different occasions of separation. Although they are commonly dated to Jiang Yan's exile years, there is no internal textual evidence to support such a claim.

Liu Yiqing and his literary entourage

Liu Yiqing (403–444), the prince of Linchuan, was an important figure on the fifth-century literary scene on account of several famous compilations produced either by himself or under his auspices. Liu Yiqing was a nephew of the founding emperor of the Song. In his youth, he had been a skillful rider, but as he grew older, he turned his attention to literature, "gathering literary men from near or far." Yuan Shu, Lu Zhan (d. 454), He Changyu (d. 443), and Bao Zhao all served under him.

The most famous work attributed to Liu Yiqing is a collection of over a thousand anecdotes taken from various sources. Originally entitled *Tales of the World* (Shishuo), it is better known by its later appellation, *A New Account of Tales of the World* (Shishuo xinyu). It was intended for the reading pleasure of an elite circle and portrays such circles, often referred to by the insiders as "people of our kind" (*wobei*). The issue of social class, a key concern in the stringent hierarchical society of early medieval China, plays an overwhelming role. The historical period covered in the *Tales* begins with the Western Han and ends with the early fifth century, but its focus falls on the Eastern Jin. In many ways, the *Tales* was a nostalgic construction, which presents a romanticized image of a bygone era characterized by wit, panache, and elegance. The compilers often seem to have been willing to sacrifice historical accuracy for the sake of a good story, although in this case truthfulness was not as important as what was taken to be true.

The current version of the *Tales* is divided into thirty-six categories, such as "Graceful Tolerance," and "Stinginess and Meanness." These categories represent a set of interpretive frameworks for the anecdotes, for the category under which an anecdote is listed implies the compiler's value judgment. Rather than arguing for "mis-categorization" of certain items as later commentators sometimes did, it is more important to understand the rationale behind the grouping of the anecdotes.

The *Tales* inspired many later imitations and must have been popular in its day. Not long after it was produced, there appeared two sets of annotations, one by Shi Jingyin (fl. ca 480s), and the other by Liu Jun, also known as Liu Xiaobiao (462–521). The latter is famous for its erudition and pertinence, and survives in its entirety.

Other important compilations attributed to Liu Yiqing include a collection of anomaly accounts, *Records of the Invisible and Visible Worlds* (*Youming lu*), and a collection of Buddhist miracle tales, *Proclamations of Manifestations* (*Xuanyan ji*), which was probably compiled in Liu Yiqing's late years when he became a devout Buddhist.

Paradoxographic collections continued to be produced in the fifth century, such as *Garden of Marvels* (*Yiyuan*) by Liu Jingshu (fl. ca 410s–460s), *Qi Xie's Records* (*Qi Xie ji*) by Dongyang Wuyi, and *Accounts of Strange Things* (*Shuyi ji*) by Zu Chongzhi (429–500). Buddhist influence is clearly present, as in the large number of accounts of retribution and reincarnation, and vivid portrayals of journeys to Hell. More collections of Buddhist miracle tales appeared. Wang Yan's (fl. ca 450s–500s) *Signs of the Invisible World* (*Mingxiang ji*), inspired by the author's relationship with a miraculous statue of a bodhisattva, is a well-known collection, of which 131 tales survive.

The rise of the literary quatrain

The quatrain, a major poetic form since the Tang, is in Chinese literally "cut-off lines" (*jueju*), a term which probably owes its name to the social practice of writing "linked verse" (*lianju*): two or more poets would take turns composing a quatrain, each responding to and expanding the previous poet's passage; when a quatrain receives no response, it became "broken lines" (duanju) or "cut-off lines" (jueju).

The earliest extant linked verse was attributed to Jia Chong (217–282) and his wife, Lady Li, included in the sixth-century anthology *New Songs of the Jade Terrace* (Yutai xinyong). Its authenticity, however, is dubious, nor is its form, with each party composing one couplet, typical. If we discount this example, then the earliest linked verse is found in Tao Yuanming's collection. Xie Hui (390–426) produced linked verse with his nephew before their execution in 426. Bao Zhao's collection also contains several sets of linked verse. Hence we may be certain that linked verse was a well-established practice in the early fifth century. By the early sixth century, the writing of linked verse became more elaborate, as participants were assigned rhyme words by an arbiter.

The term *jueju* itself must have appeared by the fifth century, as Emperor Ming of the Song (r. 465–472) once commented on the poet Wu Maiyuan's (d. 474) work: "This man has nothing else besides linked [verse] and cut-off [lines]." A Song prince, Liu Chang (435–498), composed "broken lines" (duanju) when escaping to the north in 465. *Jueju* is sometimes referred to as a "short poem" (duanju), as in Zhong Rong's *Gradations of Poets*, or the *History of the Southern Qi* (Nan Qi shu) written by Xiao Zixian (489–537) in the early sixth century.

Stimulated by the popularity of the southern *yuefu* songs, the composition of quatrain, independent of the writing of linked verse, became increasingly common in the late fifth century. Some of the best quatrains were written by the Qi poet Xie Tiao (464–499), who used simple language to create complex nuances in a compact form.

Almost no linked verse was written in the seven-syllable line except for the famous "Boliang-style linked verse," which reportedly originated in the second century BC, when Emperor Wu of the Han commanded each of his courtiers to produce one rhyming seven-syllable line at a banquet held on the Boliang Terrace. This set of linked verse, long considered inauthentic, was preserved in the *Unofficial Biography of Dongfang Shuo* (Dongfang Shuo biezhuan), an anonymous prose narrative probably produced in the third or fourth century or even much later. The date is corroborated by the imitation of the "Boliang style" composed by Emperor Xiaowu and his courtiers in 455, the first in a stream of imitations of the "original" text. If, however, Emperor Xiaowu had seen the "Han" Boliang linked verse in some other source lost to us, the set recorded in the Dongfang Shuo story might have been an imitation of Emperor Xiaowu's set, rather than vice versa.

The Yongming generation

The Qi dynasty, founded by Xiao Daocheng in 479, enjoyed a brief period of peace under the rule of Xiao Daocheng's son Xiao Ze (Emperor Wu, r. 483–493). The year 493 was disastrous for the Qi royal family: first the Crown Prince Wenhui (458–493) died; half a year later, the emperor himself passed away. The crown prince's eldest son succeeded to the throne, only to be killed by a distant cousin, Xiao Luan (452–498), a year later. After installing and then quickly deposing another young emperor, Xiao Luan himself seized the throne in 494. The last years of the Qi saw a series of intrigues, murders of royal family members, and insurrections. In 498 Xiao Luan died of illness. His heir, Xiao Baojuan, better known as Marquis of the Eastern Darkness (his posthumous title), was only a teenage boy, and a notorious tyrant. His bloody rule was ended by a clansman, Xiao Yan (464–549), who established the Liang dynasty in 502.

Qi literature is characterized by two important new phenomena: princely sponsorship of literary activities and a group of writers who not only shared close friendship and wrote poetry together, but also consciously embraced the same literary values. The central figure was Xiao Ziliang (460–494), the prince of Jingling. In 487, he moved into the Western Residence at Rooster Cage Mountain in the suburbs of Jiankang, and turned it into a flourishing cultural and religious center, described in the *History of the Qi* as unprecedented south of the Yangzi river. The possibility that Liu Yiqing had relied on his literary attendants in the compilation of *Tales of the World* and other collections remains no more than scholarly speculation; in Xiao Ziliang's case we know for certain that he commissioned the compilation of *An Epitome of Books of the Four Categories* (*Sibu yaolüe*) in a thousand scrolls. The "four categories" referred to Confucian Classics, histories, the writings of the Masters, and literary collections.

Xiao Ziliang may not have been the first imperial prince to bring together men of letters to compile large works, but his salon was distinguished by the fact that its regular members were all known writers in their own right, unlike, for example, the obscure or anonymous contributors to the philosophical work *Huainanzi* compiled under the Western Han prince Liu An. The relationship between the prince and his salon members is also different from before, as the prince treated them as friends rather than as attendants. Indeed, the most illustrious members of the salon were referred to by their contemporaries as the "Eight *Friends* of the Prince of Jingling." They were Shen Yue, Fan Yun (451–503), Ren Fang (460–508), Xie Tiao, Xiao Yan, Wang

Rong (467–493), Lu Chui (470–526), and Xiao Chen (?–529), the leading writers of the Yongming generation. Yongming, "Eternal Brilliance," was the name of the reign spanning 483 to 493, and the poetic style of this group, with its emphasis on tonal euphony, became known as the Yongming style. These eight friends later met with very different fates – Wang Rong and Xie Tiao were executed in their prime, Shen Yue and Ren Fang lived on to be admired as grand literary masters in the early sixth century, and Xiao Yan became emperor and ruled for nearly fifty years. As they gathered in the prince of Jing-ling's salon in the 480s, none of them, however, could foresee what awaited them in the not too distant future.

A genteel man and devoted lover of literature, Xiao Ziliang was famous for treating men of letters with hospitality. Writers composed to Xiao Ziliang's command or wrote companion pieces to his poems. Speed was much valued in group compositions. During a night gathering at the prince's residence, those present were asked to complete a poem of eight lines by the time a candle burned down one inch; one of the regulars at the prince's protested that this was not difficult enough, so he and several others set a shorter limit for themselves by striking a bronze gong and finishing their poems before the echo faded away. At these gatherings poets often wrote short but witty "poems on things" (yongwu shi), which describe either an object in the room, such as a musical instrument, a mat, or a mirror stand; or a thing of nature, such as a plant, a bird, snowflakes, or the moon. "Poetry on things," which became an important subgenre in later times, owed its origin to the migration of fu topics and represented a significant expansion of material for poetry.

Xiao Ziliang was also a pious Buddhist. He frequently invited famous monks to give lectures on Buddhist scriptures at his residence. Some of the monks were well versed in Sanskrit metrics; with Xiao Ziliang's personal participation, they experimented with "new sounds" of sutra-chanting. It has been pointed out by many scholars that Xiao Ziliang's keen interest in Buddhist psalmody was a key factor in the invention of a new tonal prosody by three of the "Eight Friends," Wang Rong, Shen Yue, and Xie Tiao. The new tonal prosody involved the "discovery" of the "four tones" (sisheng), the bifurcation of the four tones into "light" and "heavy" sounds, the demand for alternating uses of light and heavy sounds within a line and a couplet, and the prohibition of the "eight defects" (babing) in euphony. This prosody was perfected by the Tang poets and became the basis of "regulated poetry" (lüshi). According to Zhong Rong, Wang Rong was primarily responsible for these prosodic innovations, yet Shen Yue's name came to be most frequently associated with the new prosody, probably because he was the one who defined, theorized, and defended the tonal rules, both in his commentary on Xie Lingyun's biography in the *History of the Song*, and in his reply to a challenger, Lu Jue (472–499). Lu Jue had written Shen Yue a letter, not criticizing the tonal rules per se, but protesting Shen Yue's assertion that no one before had had any conscious knowledge of them. Lu Jue was eloquent, but he clearly misunderstood the tonal rules and confused a number of different issues.

The new prosody was very significant in the development of classical Chinese poetry, but in literary-historical terms, even more important was the princely agency in carrying out cultural projects: it anticipated the state-sponsored cultural work in later times as a way of asserting imperial cultural authority. Apart from *An Epitome of Books of the Four Categories*, Xiao Ziliang also commissioned extracts of thirty-six Buddhist scriptures and asked Shen Yue to compile *Biographies of Noble Recluses* (*Gaoshi zhuan*).

The immediate product of the prince's salon was a close-knit literary community. What differentiated this community from previous groups of writers such as the Seven Masters of the Jian'an or the Twenty-Four Friends of Jia Mi was the fact that its major members shared certain conceptions about poetry and strove to put them into practice. The attention paid to tonal euphony was one of their common traits, yet it must be understood in the literary ambience of the era, as part of a larger transformation of literature, particularly poetry in the five-syllable line, which had clearly become the most privileged genre by this time. Shen Yue's famous statement defined the larger goal: "Literary writings should follow the three rules of 'easiness': an allusion should be easy to understand; words should be easy to recognize; the whole piece should be easy to read out loud." In other words, the Yongming poets were against obscure allusions, difficult diction, and rugged style; "fluency and smoothness" (*liubian*) became the new poetic ideal. As Xie Tiao said, a good poem should be "round and beautiful, rolling and turning like a pellet."

Shen Yue and Xie Tiao were articulating values; the real-life literary scene in the late fifth century was more diverse. Although it had come to seem stiff and archaic, poetry in the four-syllable line continued to be written on solemn public occasions, or when the young Wang Rong wanted to impress his cousin, the powerful minister Wang Jian (452–489), who was indeed duly impressed. Yan Yanzhi was still widely emulated, and Jiang Yan had a circle of admirers who did not care much for Shen Yue and Xie Tiao's more modern style. When Emperor Wu of the Qi asked Wang Jian which contemporary poets were good at writing poetry in the five-syllable line, he answered, "Xie Fei has acquired his father's richness, and Jiang Yan shows sensitivity." Xie Fei (441–506) was famous for his precocity, but not a single poem by him survives;

he was the son of Xie Zhuang, whose public poetry was characterized by his heavy use of allusions. Wang Jian himself was more a learned scholar than a talented poet. He was known to offer small prizes in the Imperial Secretariat for those who could come up with the largest number of textual citations concerning a given object. The use of dense allusions in poetry was apparently still a popular practice: both Ren Fang and Wang Rong were accused of it by Zhong Rong. Ren and Wang, however, were better known for their public prose; the true master of poetry among the "Eight Friends," as commonly acknowledged by contemporaries and posterity, was Xie Tiao.

Xie Tiao, like Xie Lingyun, was a descendant of the illustrious Xie clan; his mother was a Liu-Song princess. Xie Tiao began his official career at eighteen, and the Yongming era was the happiest period of his life. In 491 he was assigned to the staff of a young prince and left for the provinces. The prince was a lover of poetry and admired Xie Tiao too much for the comfort of other staff members; slandered by a jealous colleague, Xie Tiao was soon called back to the capital. In the last years of his life Xie Tiao witnessed many bloody court intrigues and violent deaths of friends. Lacking Shen Yue's ability to navigate in troubled waters, Xie Tiao lived in constant apprehension. In 498 his father-in-law, a general, plotted an insurrection; Xie Tiao informed on him, leading to the execution of his wife's family. This, as one can imagine, took a toll on Xie Tiao's marital life: he had to constantly hide from his wife, who reportedly carried a knife under her clothes to kill him. In the next year, he was again unwillingly involved in a conspiracy. This time, he lost his own life.

In some of Xie Tiao's landscape poems one may still detect Xie Lingyun's influence, but on the whole Xie Tiao's poetry is devoid of the dense and rugged quality of his Liu-Song predecessors. Compared with Xie Lingyun, whose parallelism is relatively simple and straightforward, Xie Tiao achieves a greater intricacy in his parallel couplets, and his poems are marked by an easy, graceful flow of measured and refined expression. "Clarity" or "purity" (*qing*) is the quality commonly attributed to Xie Tiao's poetry: this word had immense resonance in the political and social culture of early medieval China, for it was also the term used to describe prestigious offices commonly occupied by scions of great clans, as well as a person's character, abilities, and moral caliber in "characterology." In literary criticism *qing* usually refers to a lucid style; it accords with Xie Tiao's own poetic ideal of graceful smoothness and decorous sophistication, the ideal of an aristocrat courtier in the context of court poetry. This ideal was to achieve even more impressive results in the southern court of the following century.

Two minor poets of this period, Wang Sengru (463–521) and Liu Yun (465–517), lived well into the sixth century and served the Liang dynasty, but in their youth they were both members of Xiao Ziliang's salon. Liu Yun, a scion of an old northern émigré noble family, befriended and patronized Wu Jun (469–520), a native southerner from a humble background. Wu Jun was exposed to the elegant capital style of the elite Yongming group through Liu Yun, but his poetry manages to combine well-crafted parallelism with the directness of old *yuefu* ballads, and achieves a rather distinctive style. The mannered bravado in Wu Jun's poems, especially those on frontier themes, is clearly the legacy of Bao Zhao. Unlike Bao Zhao, however, Wu Jun lets the extravagant *yuefu* voice slip into his social poetry. He loves to adopt the persona of a chivalrous cavalier from the north in poems presented to friends, referring to himself as "a messenger from Longxi," even "a lad of You and Bing." Longxi, You, and Bing were all northern regions where Wu Jun, a native southerner, had never set foot.

Wu Jun was also an accomplished prose writer. His three extant letters are celebrated pieces of landscape writing. "A Discourse on Pasta" (Bing shuo) is set in a pseudo-historical narrative frame like Xie Huilian's "*Fu* on Snow"; however, Wu Jun makes use of a much more recent past event: Liu Yu's expedition to the city of Chang'an in 417.

Wu Jun's dramatic talent is best displayed in an anomaly account entitled *Sequel to Qi Xie's Records* (*Xu Qi Xie ji*), which is much more elaborate and sophisticated than most of the earlier anomaly accounts. Wu Jun chose to write a sequel to this particular work, *Qi Xie's Records*, probably because of regional affinity, as *Qi Xie's Records* was compiled by a native of Dongyang (modern Jinhua, Zhejiang), not far from Wu Jun's hometown. One story is modeled on a tale in *Records of Powerful Ghosts* (*Linggui zhi*) by a Mr. Xun (fl. ca 405), which in turn originates from the *Sūtra of Miscellaneous Parables* translated by Kang Senghui (d. 280). Although earlier compilers of anomaly accounts had also drawn on previous sources, Wu Jun seemed to have gone further by consciously and deliberately rewriting them.

Qiu Chi (464–508), the poet Qiu Lingju's son, was also in the capital during the Yongming era. Although Qiu Lingju was known for emulating Yan Yanzhi, Qiu Chi's poetic style was very much influenced by the Yongming poets, particularly Xie Tiao. A poem composed at a parting banquet in the year 500 contains the couplet, "Nest is empty – the early bird has flown away; / water poppies all in a mess, as young fish play." This clearly derives from Xie Tiao's couplet in "An Outing to the Eastern Field" (You Dongtian): "Fish play, new lotuses are stirred; / birds scattering, remaining blossoms fall." Qiu Chi's most famous composition is an eloquent letter written in 506 on behalf of a Liang prince to persuade an insurgent general to capitulate.

Another well-known poet who carried on the Yongming legacy was He Xun (d. 518?), the great-grandson of the scholar and writer He Chengtian. He Xun was well received in the capital; he was admired by the senior poets Fan Yun and Shen Yue, and befriended by Wang Sengru, Liu Yun, and Qiu Chi. In a poem presented to Qiu Chi, He Xun reminisced how they had once discussed literature together. After He Xun died, Wang Sengru edited his writings in eight scrolls. In the early sixth century, He Xun and the famous court poet Liu Xiaochuo (481–539) were often spoken of as equals, although critics in the capital reportedly commented that He Xun's poetry "suffers from a sense of bitterness, and has a poor, needy air, not as gracious as Liu Xiaochuo's." This comment confirms that grace, which was tantamount to, among other things, a decorous expression of sentiments, was the ideal of court literature. Nevertheless, He Xun's literary reputation continued to grow after his death. His collection was brought to Luoyang and was appreciated by the northern court. A younger generation of poets in the Liang, led by the Liang princes, held He Xun up as a model along with Xie Tiao and Shen Yue.

Shen Yue, the eldest of the "Eight Friends," was an extremely important figure. He was a skillful prose stylist and a fine poet, yet his significance in literary history was not based on his writings alone, but on his role as a patron and arbiter. This was especially true in the early sixth century, when he was advanced in age and in official status. With the rule of Xiao Yan, another of the "Eight Friends," a new era began.

III. Literature in the south: the sixth century

The rule of Emperor Wu and the rise of a cultural elite

The Liang dynasty, spanning the first half of the sixth century, represented the apex of the cultural achievement of the Southern Dynasties. It was characterized by an unusually robust cultural spirit, a keen awareness of the literary past, and a conscious desire to sort out and make sense of the received textual tradition and to be innovative. This period witnessed the redistribution of cultural capital in society and the rise of a new cultural elite. Both bear directly on the literary production of the Liang and had a lasting impact on the sociopolitical structure of premodern Chinese society. For this reason, before we delve into Liang literature, it is necessary to briefly review social stratification in the south in early medieval China.

Medieval Chinese society was characterized by a rigidly defined social hierarchy. The basic distinction was between gentry (*shi*) and commoners (*shu*). Gentry status was recorded in the register of a household, customarily referred to as the "Yellow Register" because, according to a conventional explanation, it was written on yellow-dyed paper. The gentry enjoyed exemption from taxes and corvée labor, and had privileged access to offices. After the northern immigrants came to the south in the early fourth century, they gave a further twist to social inequality by discriminating against native southerners in official appointments. Emperor Wu had to strike a delicate balance between the conflicting interests of different social classes and groups. Aware that he could not root out the entrenched political and economic system without causing major upheavals, he sought to make the inherited system work to the better advantage of the state, and he succeeded to a remarkable degree. The key reforms he carried out regarded the systems of education and recruitment, closely related institutions with great cultural significance.

An imperial edict of 505 decreed that those who did not have a thorough understanding of one Confucian Classic were not allowed to serve, unless he proved to be a person of extraordinary talent. At the same time Emperor Wu restored the Imperial Academy and demanded that schools be set up in prefectures and commanderies. Erudites of the Five Classics, first set up by Emperor Wu of the Han in 136 BC, were reestablished in the Imperial Academy, with one person responsible for each Classic and in charge of one branch or academy. According to the *History of the Sui*, "In the past admission to the Imperial Academy was limited to noble scions. The Emperor [Wu of the Liang] desired to acquire young talents, and so the five academies all let in gifted students of humble origin, and there was no enrollment limit." This was to have a considerable impact on upward social mobility.

Emperor Wu also had the examination system reinstated. Those who answered the examination questions well and showed a good understanding of the Classics would be appointed. This opened up the road to social advancement and overcame some of the conventional prejudices in official appointments against members of the lower gentry, native southerners, and late-coming northern immigrants. Great literary value was attached to examination questions, as testified by the fact that the genre was represented in *Selections of Refined Literature*, but the most important consequence of the reinstatement of the examination system was the close, tangible connection established between cultural and political values. A certain semblance of social mobility (because people who could afford an education did not, after all, come from the lowest rung of the social ladder) acted as a powerful stimulus for the acquisition of knowledge. If scions of great houses had to take the examinations like sons of the "lesser families," then even if they had to hire someone else to write answers or bribe the examiners, as sometimes happened, the message was nonetheless clear: lineage, though still of vital importance, was no longer the only standard in judging a person. It was, in fact, during the Liang that we begin to see a new criterion being formed for evaluating people: the possession of cultural capital in the form of scholarly and literary accomplishments.

Emperor Wu was the central figure in the rich and diverse cultural landscape of the first half of the sixth century. It was his grand vision for the empire that made the Liang dynasty in many ways a cultural and intellectual pinnacle in pre-Tang China. His tireless devotion to literary and scholarly undertakings went far beyond any of his imperial predecessors, both in terms of his personal involvement and in terms of the imperial sponsorship of various large-scale cultural projects.

At banquets and on outings, Emperor Wu invariably asked his courtiers to compose poetry and bestowed gifts of gold and silk on those whose writings stood out. To anyone who presented a *fu* or an ode to the throne, he always tried to give audience. He addressed poems to his courtiers, sometimes praising their literary talent, sometimes teasing their slowness in poetic composition. Emperor Wu was himself a prolific writer. The collection of his literary works, now lost, consisted of 120 scrolls; even though it had doubtless included a large amount of political writings, the size was nevertheless remarkable. Many of his prose pieces and poems, including a number of lovely *yuefu* songs, survive. His "*Fu* on Filial Pining" (Xiaosi fu) and "*Fu* on Cultivating Pure Karma" (Jingye fu) both have lengthy prose prefaces that offer a fascinating account of his life circumstances and spiritual pursuits. He also edited *A Collection of Fu of Various Dynasties (Lidai fu)*, which he commanded his courtiers Zhou Xingsi (d. 521) and Zhou She (469–524) to annotate. A fervent Buddhist known as the "emperor bodhisattva," he authored several hundred scrolls of commentary on Buddhist scriptures, but he also wrote a commentary on the *Laozi* and commentaries on a number of the Confucian Classics. His exegesis of "The Doctrine of the Mean" (Zhongyong) was one of the few early independent commentaries on that work before it became part of the canonical "Four Books" in the twelfth century. In the winter of 541, the emperor, aging but vigorous as ever, completed a twenty-scroll work, *The Corrective Word of Confucius*, and composed a poem to commemorate the occasion. This work was subsequently used as a textbook in the Imperial Academy.

Many of the writers appreciated and promoted to prominent positions by Emperor Wu were, significantly, members of the lower gentry and native southerners, who traditionally had been politically and culturally marginalized. Conscious of their less privileged social status, they strove for recognition through cultural achievements, and formed a close literary community that was characterized by making literature "family business" as well as by intermarriages. Thus the old family politics of the Southern Dynasties, sustained by strategies such as intermarrying among elite families, continued to be played out in a new field.

Shen Yue and Ren Fang played an essential role in the rise of this new cultural elite. Neither had come from the most elite families, and Shen Yue, moreover, was a native southerner. Both men, however, were regarded as grand literary masters at the turn of century, a status confirmed, even partially established, by their tireless promotion and patronage of younger writers. There was rarely a Liang literary man who had not been appraised by Shen Yue or Ren Fang. Shen Yue alone had commended more than twenty writers and poets, the youngest of whom, Wang Yun (481–549), was forty years his junior. At the beginning of the century, because of their closeness to Emperor Wu and their role in the founding of the dynasty, both Shen Yue and Ren Fang occupied positions of power in the court, and their approval meant not just cultural recognition but political advantage as well. The compiler of the *History of the Liang* (*Liang shu*) said of Ren Fang, "Those he commended were often promoted, and so members of gentry and nobility vied with one another to become acquainted with him. Dozens of guests were constantly in his house." Contemporaries referred to Ren Fang's "core group" as "those who passed the Dragon Gate": Dragon Gate is the legendary rapids on the Yellow River, and it was believed that carps leaping over it would transform into powerful dragons. The historian added that apart from the chosen few, "even scions of noble families could not become part of the group." The exclusiveness of such a close-knit community invoked a cultural aura that had nothing to do with lineage. Granted, none of the select group was really a "nobody," yet neither were any from the most elite clans. The brothers Dao Gai (477–548) and Dao Qia (490–527), members of this group, were descendants of a Liu-Song general whose family background was so humble that he had once made a living by transporting human waste, and Dao Gai was scorned by an aristocrat as "still emitting the stench." In the Liang, however, the Dao brothers became well known because of Ren Fang's appreciation, came to be appreciated by Emperor Wu, and were compared to the famous Lu brothers, Lu Ji and Lu Yun, of the Western Jin.

Another affiliate of Ren Fang's famous group, Liu Xiaochuo, was widely acknowledged as one of the finest Liang court poets. His clan, the Lius of Pengcheng (in modern Jiangsu), boasted over seventy members, male and female, who were good at literary writings. Yet his was merely one of the many "literary families" that flourished in the Liang. Through intermarriages and close associations, these families bound the Liang literary world together in a complex web and strove to define themselves, just as the Liang empire strove to define itself against its northern rival, with cultural, rather than martial, power.

Literary production: catalogues, encyclopedias, anthologies

During the Liang, imperial book collection reached new heights. The imperial library had suffered from a fire at the end of the Qi dynasty, and rebuilding the collection was one of the first things Emperor Wu did upon ascending the throne. Many scholars participated in the task. All Buddhist books were kept in the Park of the Flowering Groves, while non-Buddhist books were housed in the Hall of Literary Virtue and the Quarters of the Imperial Secretariat. The latter amounted to 23,106 scrolls, a quantity that cannot fail to impress when compared to the number of books owned by the Eastern Jin imperial library when it was first founded in the fourth century, which came to 3,014 scrolls (about one-tenth of the Western Jin imperial book collection). The number had also increased since the Yongming era, when no more than 18,010 scrolls were recorded in the imperial book catalogue. As for the Buddhist works, a catalogue compiled by the monk Baochang in 518 recorded 54,000 scrolls.

Private book collecting was also being carried out with a passion. There had never been so many private book collectors gathering books on such a massive scale. As the historian said in the *History of the Sui*, "Emperor Wu of the Liang took great delight in poetry and the Classics, and the entire state was influenced by his penchant. Within the four borders, every household possessed literary writings and histories." At the beginning of the Liang, Shen Yue's book collection boasted 20,000 scrolls, which made him the foremost private book collector in the capital area (later, Crown Prince Xiao Tong's book collection would surpass it). With over ten thousand scrolls Ren Fang came in second. Many of Ren Fang's books were "rare copies." Ren Fang compiled a catalogue of his book collection, which, though lost, was the earliest private book catalogue recorded. Upon Ren Fang's death in 508, Emperor Wu had Shen Yue and He Zong examine this catalogue and take from his collection whatever the imperial library did not have. Emperor Wu's son Xiao Yi (508–554), the prince of Xiangdong, also known as Emperor Yuan (r. 551–554), was an avid book collector all his life, ever since he received his first set of the five Confucian Classics as a gift from his father at the age of five. A chapter entitled "Book Collecting" from his work, *The Master of the Golden Tower* (*Jinlouzi*), gave a detailed account of how he had assembled his book collection. Such accounts would become increasingly common, particularly in late imperial China, but Xiao Yi's is the first we have.

In conjunction with the proliferation of books, Emperor Wu commissioned a series of compilation projects. He commanded Dao Qia to produce an epitome of the Confucian Classics, while another writer, Zhang Shuai (475–527), was put in charge of compiling epitomes of the histories, writings of the Masters, and literary works. Between 505 and 507, three catalogues of the imperial book collection were prepared, by Liu Jun, Zu Xuan (fl. ca 500s), and Yin Jun (484–532). Two catalogues of Buddhist scriptures were put out between 515 and 518. The most extensive catalogue to date was, however, produced by a private individual, Ruan Xiaoxu (479–536), a lifelong recluse who was nevertheless from one of the most prestigious elite clans and a relative of the Liang royal family by marriage. Incorporating an earlier catalogue compiled by Liu Yao (487–536), Ruan Xiaoxu's *Seven Records* (*Qi lu*) was an ambitious undertaking which was intended to include all the books there were in the Liang empire, and recorded 6,288 titles in 44,526 scrolls (some say 30,000 scrolls). Though the catalogue itself is no longer extant, its preface, written in the spring of 524 at Jiankang, is preserved in the seventh-century Buddhist anthology *Expansion of the Propagation of the Light* (*Guang hongming ji*). In the preface Ruan Xiaoxu gave a brief history of book cataloguing from the Western Han to his day, and remarked that *Seven Records* contained many titles missing from the imperial catalogue.

The potential competition and conflict between the public and private claims to cultural authority were even more clearly manifest in the compilation of encyclopedias, another enterprise of literary production closely related to book collection and textual transmission. The "encyclopedia" (*leishu*) was both a way of organizing knowledge and a response to the practical need for the use of references and allusions in one's writings; its categorical structure of "all things," from heavenly bodies down to the tiniest insects, also reflected the understanding of the cosmos, and, as such, represented the affirmation of imperial order. Shortly after Emperor Wu's younger brother asked the scholar Liu Jun to compile *The Garden of Classified Extracts* (*Leiyuan*) in 120 scrolls, Emperor Wu decided to commission an even grander one. The outcome was *The Comprehensive Epitome of the Park of Flowering Groves* (*Hualin bianlüe*) in 620 scrolls. The project, begun in 516, took a group of scholars eight years to complete. Neither survives, but the latter was widely influential at the time, and was carried across the border to the north by book traders.

An intensely Buddhist dynasty, the Liang witnessed the appearance of Buddhist encyclopedias. Early in the sixth century, Emperor Wu commissioned the *Record of Buddha* (*Fo ji*), whose preface, still extant, was written by Shen Yue. In 516, he again commissioned the compilation of *Differentiated Manifestations of Sutras and Laws* (*Jinglü yixiang*), which is the earliest extant Buddhist encyclopedia. Here passages from various sutras are arranged under topical categories, and many themes and images from this work are commonly seen in literary writings. Emperor Wu's third son, Xiao Gang (503–551), also known as Emperor Jianwen (r. 549–551), later organized more than forty courtiers to compile the three-hundred-scroll *Joined Jade Disks from the Treasures of Dharma* (*Fabao lianbi*). Its preface, written in elegant parallel prose by Xiao Yi in 534, survives.

Apart from the compilation of catalogues and encyclopedias, the making of anthologies – literary production in a narrower sense – also flourished in the Liang. Individual literary collections, compiled either by the author or by the author's friend, appeared in large numbers, and many forms and conventions adopted by later editors of literary collections were first established during this period. Following the model of Jiang Yan, Xu Mian (466–535) and Liu Zhilin (477–548) edited their own writings into "Former and Latter Collections." Wang Yun, one of the most famous Liang poets, put together a collection of his literary writings for each office he had held, a practice that set an example for many later writers. Emperor Wu had a separate collection of poetry and *fu* besides a regular collection of literary writings; he also had a collection of "miscellaneous prose." This is one of the earliest known cases in which an individual writer had his writings arranged generically.

The compilation of general anthologies reached a new peak in the Liang. Of the many general anthologies, three survive. These are *Selections of Refined Literature* (*Wenxuan*), a general literary anthology arranged generically and compiled under the auspices of Emperor Wu's eldest son, Xiao Tong; *New Songs of the Jade Terrace* (*Yutai xinyong*), a single-genre anthology of poetry primarily in the five-syllable line compiled by the famous court writer Xu Ling (507–583); and *The Propagation of the Light* (*Hongming ji*), a collection of Buddhist writings from the Eastern Han to the Liang compiled by the monk Sengyou (445–518).

Selections of Refined Literature, the earliest extant literary anthology, exerted a strong influence in the Tang, and is the subject of much modern scholarship, collectively dubbed *Xuan xue* ("the study of the *Selections*"). It was completed in the 520s. According to a Tang source, it made a point of not including any living author. Although this is a debatable point, it is true that *Selections* only includes a very small percentage of Liang writers, and almost completely omits the younger generation. *New Songs of the Jade Terrace*, by contrast, represents contemporary writers very fully. While *Selections* was clearly intended for a general elite audience, Xu Ling explicitly stated in the preface to *New Songs* that it was for a female readership, more specifically for palace ladies. The textual history of *New Songs* is troubled: its most popular edition is a 1633 edition that claims to be the reprint of a Southern Song edition with a preface dated 1215, but this Southern Song edition itself was no more than a patchwork of two printed editions and one manuscript copy. To further complicate the textual problems, the extant versions of the anthology might have mixed in poems from the *Latter Collection of the Jade Terrace* (*Yutai houji*) put together by a Li Kangcheng (fl. ca 778). There is no way of knowing for certain whether the current arrangement of the poems even remotely reflects the original order of the anthology.

These two anthologies are our most important sources of pre-Tang secular literature. In both, Liang literary men worked on the received literary legacy by "fixing" texts as they saw fit and assigning authorship where it was called for; in doing so, they constructed a literary-historical narrative within which they found a place for themselves. It is therefore important to bear in mind that our knowledge and perception of early classical Chinese literature, particularly poetry, are heavily mediated by the sixth-century men of letters. These two earliest extant literary anthologies, despite their special status as such, were produced in the context of many others that have been unfortunately lost, and they differ sharply from each other in terms of compilation purpose, range and standard of selection, and intended readership. In other words, it would be wrong to draw general conclusions about the Liang literary landscape based on a comparison of these two extant anthologies; moreover, their differences should not be understood as a fundamental difference of opinions regarding literature on the part of the compilers. Modern scholars have often taken these two anthologies to represent two "rival literary groups" in this period. Such a view, however, cannot be sustained by any close examination of the literary scene of the Liang.

New Songs was, moreover, compiled for women's reading pleasure, not for didactic purposes like the many "conduct books" for women in contemporary circulation. Although Xu Ling's explicit statement of editorial purpose (i.e. aiming for a female readership) is often not taken seriously by modern scholars, it is substantiated by overwhelming circumstantial evidence. Liang upper-class women, from imperial consorts, princesses, and palace ladies-in-waiting to gentry women, were generally well educated, and there were more known women writers from this period than ever. In 503, Emperor Wu commissioned an encyclopedia of "textual references to women" to be compiled and distributed to palace ladies. Since encyclopedias served the practical purpose of aiding a writer in composition, the compilation of such an encyclopedia indicated that many palace ladies tried their hand at writing. Three of Emperor Wu's daughters, Princesses Lin'an, Anji, and Changcheng, were particularly noted for their literary talents, and a preface to the literary collection of Princess Lin'an, penned by her brother Xiao Gang, is extant. The most famous woman writer of the Liang was Liu Lingxian, the sister of Liu Xiaochuo; some of her poems and a sacrificial address to her husband, written in exquisite parallel prose and often included in later anthologies, have survived.

Literary criticism

The Liang witnessed the first full development of literary criticism in Chinese history. Two important works were produced during this period: Liu Xie's *Literary Mind and the Carving of the Dragon* (*Wenxin diaolong*), written at the turn of the century, and Zhong Rong's *Gradations of Poets*, written between 513 and 518.

Liu Xie came from a northern émigré family of genteel lineage. Some of his ancestors achieved prominent positions during the Liu-Song; by Liu Xie's time, however, the clan's fortunes had declined from any previous glory it had enjoyed. Having lost his father at an early age, Liu Xie never married because of strained financial circumstances. He took up residence in the Dinglin Monastery in the suburbs of Jiankang and became a disciple of the famous monk Sengyou, though at this stage he apparently did not shave his head and take Buddhist vows. During his stay, Liu Xie became widely conversant in the Buddhist scriptures and discourses, assisting Sengyou in the project of classifying the scriptures, cataloguing them, and giving them descriptive summaries. It was presumably during this period that he wrote *Literary Mind and the Carving of the Dragon*, whose completion a scholarly consensus places at around the turn of the century. The title of the work conveys the ambitious nature of his undertaking – the carving of the dragon transforms the traditional derogatory term for literary craft, "carving insects," into a much more sublime model, and yet it paradoxically evokes the pejorative associations and reflects Liu Xie's perennial anxiety about the technical aspect of literature.

The work consists of fifty chapters. The first four chapters are each devoted to the Way, the Sage, the Classics, and the Apocrypha; Chapters 5 to 25 discuss various literary genres, and Liu Xie listed thirty-four genres in total. The second part of the book focuses on a series of basic literary concepts, ranging from rhetorical devices and style to the creative process and readers' reception of literary works. The last chapter functions as an afterword, in which Liu Xie explains the book's title and his intent in composing such a work. In this chapter Liu Xie makes the claim that literature is an extension of the Confucian Classics and that writing literary criticism possesses the same intrinsic value as writing commentaries on the Classics and elucidating the words of the Sage.

Although citing the Confucian Classics as an authoritative model for literature, Liu Xie's immersion in Buddhist texts seems to have given him an edge in analytical discourse. As his primary expository medium, Liu Xie chose to use parallel prose, which sometimes creates no small tension between following the logic of his argument and following the logic of parallelism. In terms of his basic standpoint in relation to the literature of past and present times, Liu Xie theoretically approved of change and transformation, but when dealing with individual writers and period styles, one often senses his anxiety about what he saw as the increasing "ornamentation" in literary writings. Liu Xie's vision of literary history was a continuous process of increasing ornamentation and decadence, which began with the "plain and pure" in distant antiquity and culminated in the "deceptive and new" in the Liu-Song period. According to him, "the nearer we are to our own times, the more insipid literature turns out to be." Liu Xie's views of literature are not, however, always consistent, and considerable modern scholarship on his work is dedicated to explaining the many apparent discrepancies and self-contradictions in the book and finding a coherent system underneath.

Perhaps thanks to Shen Yue's recommendation, Liu Xie embarked on an official career, and served in a series of low posts. He became known to the crown prince, who "received Liu Xie with deep admiration." While Xiao Tong's large library almost certainly contained a copy of Liu Xie's work, whether Xiao Tong had read it and to what extent it influenced him are impossible to know. Liu Xie remained a minor figure in the literary world of the Liang. His name and work were known throughout subsequent dynasties, and received increased attention during the Qing. But never did Liu Xie have the preeminent stature as a critic that he has achieved in modern times: largely under the influence of the European model of the treatise, early twentieth-century Chinese scholars rediscovered *Literary Mind* as a comprehensive and systematic work of "Chinese" literary theory, and the study of this work has become a special branch of learning dubbed "Dragonology." The treatise model is, however, far from representative of the tradition of Chinese literary thought.

It is noteworthy that the two most ambitious works of literary criticism in the period were penned by two minor figures in the sociopolitical world. Like Liu Xie, Zhong Rong was from a northern émigré family, and the most prominent office he held was record keeper, a low-ranking secretarial job on the staff of the prince of Jin'an (Xiao Gang's title before he became the crown prince). *Gradations of Poets*, alternatively known as *Evaluations of Poets* (*Shi ping*), is divided into three sections, ranking 122 poets on three levels (top, middle, and lower) on the basis of their poetry in the five-syllable line. It was evidently influenced by the proliferation of "gradations" or "evaluations" at the time, such as *Gradations of Calligraphers* (*Shu pin*), *Gradations of Go-Players* (*Weiqi pin*), or even Ruan Xiaoxu's *Biographies of Noble Recluses* (*Gaoyin zhuan*), which divide recluses into three ranks, much in the same way as *Gradations of Poets*. These works were in turn inspired by the custom of evaluating people according to their abilities and moral qualities since the late Eastern Han. Another characteristic of *Gradations of Poets* is to point out a poet's literary "ancestry" or "lineage" in terms of his or her style. One again, we see the parallel between the sociopolitical world and the literary culture of early medieval China.

Each section of *Gradations of Poets* has a foreword, which gives a general discourse on poetry. Zhong Rong was more progressive than Liu Xie in terms of generic preference. While Liu Xie still insisted that "poetry in the four-syllable line is the correct form," Zhong Rong remarked that poetry in the five-syllable line "occupies the most important position in literature, being particularly flavorful among various modes of literary expression." Although *fu* was still a venerable form and poems in the four-syllable line continued to be written on formal occasions, poetry in the five-syllable line had become firmly established as the dominant literary genre.

No lengthy work of literary criticism was produced after *Gradations of Poets* throughout the rest of the sixth century, but shorter pieces discussing literature and poetry, in the form of letters, prefaces, or postscripts, were very common. Among these were Xiao Zixian's postscript to "Biographies of Literary Men" in the *History of the Southern Qi* (*Nan Qi shu*), Xiao Tong's preface to *Selections of Refined Literature*, Xiao Gang's letter to his brother Xiao Yi written in the 530s, and sections from Xiao Yi's *Master of the Golden Tower*. It is impossible here to survey these documents at any great length; however, the aggregate of discussion of literary matters does not support the recent scholarly interpretation of three "rival schools" in the Liang, a theory first raised in mainland China in the 1960s and still widely accepted as a received truth.

This view regards the Liang literary world as divided among the "archaic or traditionalist school," with Emperor Wu as its center and Pei Ziye (469–530), historian and writer, as its chief advocate; the "compromise school," headed by Emperor Wu's eldest son Xiao Tong; and the so-called "avant-garde school," led by Xiao Tong's younger brothers, Xiao Gang and Xiao Yi. *Selections* is considered the representative anthology of the "compromise school," while *New Songs of the Jade Terrace* is taken as the anthology par excellence of the "avant-garde school," also known as the "palace-style" group. Xiao Gang is believed to have been the inspiration behind the compilation of *New Songs*, a dubious claim made in a collection of anecdotes almost four centuries later and supported by no textual evidence. The conflict perceived between these two "schools" is based on conventional judgments of moral historiography. Xiao Tong's *Selections of Refined Literature* was seen as canonical and "good," while the so-called "palace-style" poetry championed by Xiao Gang was seen as decadent and immoral.

The claim about opposing schools, however, does not hold well upon closer examination. Granted that tastes and fashions changed with time and individual practices varied from writer to writer, the Liang literary world, though diverse, shared a set of common beliefs and values about the genesis, nature, and function of literature, particularly poetry. Modern scholars too often take a single circumstantial text as the authoritative statement of the author's general position, even though the same author might very well emphasize different aspects of an argument or even adopt different positions under different circumstances to suit the rhetorical purposes of the moment. Since what we have now are only fragments of a once vast textual world, we tend to vest a piece of text with more significance than it might have had in its original context. One example is Xiao Gang's letter to a cousin, thanking the marquis for showing Xiao Gang his new poems; this is clearly a "thank-you" note offering polite compliments on three specific poems by the marquis, instead of a general statement of Xiao Gang's poetic values, which it is often taken to be.

A more serious case is Pei Ziye's treatise "On Carving Insects" (Diaochong lun), commonly regarded as a "conservative" manifesto attacking contemporary literary practice of the "avant-garde school." In its earliest extant source, however, this text did not have a title and was placed squarely in the context of the Liu-Song literary culture, not the Liang. It was the later source, *The Flower of the Garden of Letters* (*Wenyuan yinghua*), compiled between 982 and 987, that gave it a title as well as adding a narrative context to it to make it look like a literary treatise on contemporary (i.e. Liang) literature. In all likelihood, Pei Ziye's "treatise" was taken from his *Essential History of the Song* (*Song lüe*), a work completed in late fifth century, before the founding of the Liang.

Instead of a factional division, the Liang royal family favored the same group of contemporary writers. Liu Xiaochuo and Wang Yun, for instance, were equally admired by Emperor Wu, Xiao Tong, and Xiao Gang. Many of Liu Xiaochuo's poems found their way into *New Songs*, yet he also played a vital role in the compilation of *Selections of Refined Literature*. Likewise, there was a general consensus regarding the past literary canon in the sixth century; this consensus, indicated by a list of "great names," was more or less fixed in the fifth century and set the tone for subsequent reception of early Chinese literature down to our own day. In this context it is particularly important for us to bear in mind the different natures and purposes of the two Liang literary anthologies, for these differences formed the standard of selection.

The Liang literary elite shared an intense critical awareness of the continuity of the literary tradition, as well as the diversity of styles available to be emulated. In the postscript to "Biographies of Literary Men" in the *History of the Southern Qi*, after enumerating three major contemporary styles, Xiao Zixian described his ideal poetry as one

> that is born of natural instincts and yet consults the histories and biographies [for allusions and references]; a poetry that spontaneously responds to inspiration and is not premeditated; a poetry whose language is easy to understand and whose embellishment does not overwhelm its meaning; a poetry that disposes of the ore but keeps the gold; a poetry that is smooth, gentle, graceful, and passionate; a poetry that mixes in lines of ballads and is painless to read out loud; a poetry that is neither too classic nor too popular, but suits the mind just right.

Such statements, couched in terms impossible to refute, reveal familiar elements characterizing the general poetic ideal of the Liang: prosodic excellence and tonal harmony, resistance to obscure language, the presence of both feelings and restraint.

Palace-style poetry

When the term "palace style" (*gongti*) was first coined, it was used to characterize the style (*ti*), not the content, of the poetry written by Xiao Gang and his courtiers after Xiao Gang became the crown prince in 531. "Palace" in this phrase specifically referred to the "Eastern Palace," the official residence of the heir apparent. Frequently simplified and misunderstood as a formally ornamental poetry devoted to the portrayal of life in the boudoir, palace-style poetry was an imaginative and innovative poetry that opened up many new possibilities for later Chinese poets, and its subject matter covered all aspects of elite life.

In the 530s the older court poets such as Liu Xiaochuo and Wang Yun were still active, but a younger generation was rising. Xiao Gang, who was the governor of Yongzhou (in modern Hubei) from 523 to 530, had a group of outstanding scholars and writers in his entourage, including the ten "Scholars of the Lofty Studio," who were charged by the prince with compilation and collation projects. After Xiao Gang became heir apparent, political power was translated into literary influence. Palace style was widely emulated in the capital area and spread to the provinces, disseminated by figures such as Xiao Yi, the prince of Xiangdong, a talented practitioner of this new style. The key members of Xiao Gang's salon were Xu Chi (471–551) and Yu Jianwu (ca 487–551), along with their respective sons, Xu Ling, the compiler of *New Songs of the Jade Terrace*, and Yu Xin (513–581), a major poet of the Southern Dynasties. Xu Chi in particular was credited as the originator of the palace style. The Xus and Yus were so influential in the contemporary literary world that the palace style was alternatively known as "the Xu–Yu style." The central figure of this group was Xiao Gang himself, who was one of the finest, and yet one of the most underestimated, premodern Chinese poets. His extant poems exceed 250, an impressive number from a period when so little survives. In a manuscript culture where textual transmission depends entirely on hand-copying and conscious preservation, the sheer quantity of Xiao Gang's extant work demonstrates a strong interest in his writings.

Palace-style poetry represents a watershed in the development of classical Chinese poetry in ways that go beyond elaborate parallelism and a more strict observation of tonal rules as then understood. It is best defined as a poetry produced against an intensely Buddhist background and profoundly influenced by Buddhist teachings about illusion, illumination, meditative concentration, and visualization. In contrast to earlier poetry, which often depicts the world in generic and unspecific terms and aspires to represent the totality of the landscape, palace-style poetry is concerned with particularity on both temporal and spatial levels, as it attempts to present things as observed in living moments. This poetry is also intensely visual, in the sense not so much of "pictorial images" as of what and how to see; it is characterized by a focused and illuminating look at the minutest details of physical reality. A typical palace-style poem is an act of uncovering and unconcealment, as the poet's gaze brings things into the foreground from the semi-darkness in which they have been hidden; in the meanwhile, because of its engagement with fleeting moments, the palace-style poem perfectly captures what Buddhism teaches about the transience, fragility, and ultimate unreality of the phenomenal world.

We may take for example a couplet from Xiao Gang's poem entitled "Autumn Evening" (Qiu wan). In the foregoing lines, darkness is closing in from all sides, and shadows dominate. The poet then turns his attention to spots of light:

> Tangled clouds, glowing red, are made circular by the limpid water;
> tiny leaves, outlined by a lamp in the air.

Few poets before Xiao Gang had used the word *yuan* ("circular") in the third position of a five-syllable line as a full verb ("make circular"), and with such a strange sense. Because of the grammatical structure in the Chinese original, one might at first think that the first line means something like "tangled ruddy clouds make the limpid water circular." One then realizes that the clouds are reflected in a circular pool and, although "tangled," are confined and given a shape by the pool – a roundness that indicates perfection (in Buddhism *yuan* is used to describe the perfect teachings or enlightenment). Glowing with the sunset red, the clouds grant the pool a momentary splendor. This is the last light of nature. In the next line, the light in the water is transferred to something else, as the poet notices the silhouettes of the leaves outlined by the lamplight. The visual link between the lines is strengthened by the concept *ying*, which refers to "reflections," "shadows," and things seen in "outline," all of which belong to the same category of visual phenomena. In a world gradually sinking into shadows, the poet traces out luminous patterns and forms, and affirms an order created by human effort. The poem represents a moment when, at a time of decreasing visibility, vision is focused on even the smallest change in nature, and, as a result, nature becomes illuminated.

Couplets by earlier masters, such as Cao Zhi's "Trees are blooming in spring splendor, / the clear pool stirs long currents," or Xie Lingyun's "Forests and ravines gather in the dusk colors, / clouds and vapors withdraw the sunset glow," are often more straightforward and linear in their movement; Xiao Gang's couplet, by contrast, intimates a peculiar vision of the world and a peculiar way in which poetry is made to work.

The palace-style poets also perfected the form of poetry in the seven-syllable line. Xiao Gang's quatrain, "Gazing at A Wild Goose Flying Alone at Night" (Yewang danfeiyan), as well as longer pieces such as Wang Bao's (513?–576) "Ballad of Yan" (Yan gexing) and Yu Xin's "Willow Song" (Yangliu ge), are all mature examples of this still rather novel form.

Other literary forms

Fu continued to be a popular form in the Liang. Liang writers were fond of demonstrating their mastery in dealing with traditional subject matter. Shen Yue's lengthy "Fu on Dwelling in the Suburbs" (Jiaoju fu), modeled on Pan Yue's "Fu on Living in Idleness" and Xie Lingyun's "Fu on Dwelling in the Mountains," was composed shortly after he moved into his suburban residence in 507. Even longer were the "Fu on a Southward Journey" (Nanzheng fu) written by Zhang Zuan (499–549), Emperor Wu's son-in-law, in 543, and "Fu on Profound Observation" (Xuanlan fu) written by Xiao Yi, two years later. More interesting to the later reader, however, are shorter fu pieces on less grandiose topics composed during this period. The fu pieces by Xiao Gang, Xiao Yi, and Yu Xin on the topics of lotus-picking and candlelight, for instance, create a free-flowing poetic rhythm by mixing five- and seven-syllable lines in a simple yet elegant language. Such short, lyric fu represented a striking new direction for the genre, so much so that modern scholars frequently speak of a "poeticization" of fu in this period, as the Liang poets also adopted such a mixed meter in some of their poems. The truth is that poetry from the fifth century on has also taken over some of the traits and topics traditionally associated with fu, such as in the aforementioned "poems on things."

Story collections continued to be produced. Ren Fang utilized his large book collection in putting together Accounts of Strange Things (Shuyi ji); Yin Yun (471–529) was commissioned by Emperor Wu in the 510s to gather anecdotes from various histories to produce Small Talks (Xiaoshuo). A similar compilation of anecdotes was Shen Yue's Common Talks (Sushuo), which survives, like the others, in fragments.

Emperor Wu of the Han and the people around him, particularly the courtier Dongfang Shuo, had become the stuff of legend. Stories centering on them had been in circulation from the third century on, such as Tales of Emperor Wu of the Han (Han Wudi gushi), judged to be the earliest of these texts, and the much later Unofficial Biography of Dongfang Shuo. A similar body of materials centering on the lore of the Han emperor famous for his pursuit of immortality was likely produced in the fifth and sixth centuries, despite shadowy claims to much earlier authorship. Compared with earlier accounts of a similar nature, these texts, closely tied to religious Daoism of the Six Dynasties, are much more sophisticated in narrative strategies and ornate in diction and style.

Religious writings also increased in the Liang. Tao Hongjing (456?–536), the famous Taoist recluse who remained on close terms with the Liang royal family, reportedly edited the records left by his disciple, Zhou Ziliang (497–516), about Zhou's encounters with Daoist immortals into a volume entitled *Accounts of Mr. Zhou's Communication with the Mysterious* (*Zhoushi mingtong ji*), and presented it to the throne. Tao himself was responsible for the preservation and editing of the fourth-century Daoist priest Yang Xi's poems.

While biographies of well-known recluses, filial sons, and virtuous officials continued to be produced, hagiographies of religious figures became the new rage in the late fifth century and the early sixth. The Buddhist monk Huijiao's (497–554) *Biographies of Eminent Monks* (*Gaoseng zhuan*) survives more or less in its entirety. Rather than focusing on one special group of monks or on a region, as some earlier works did, it incorporates the biographies of over 250 monks between the first and sixth centuries from the north to the south. Its counterpart is *Biographies of Buddhist Nuns* (*Biqiuni zhuan*), compiled by the monk Baochang around 516. This work records the lives of sixty-five nuns, from the time when monasticism for women was first established in China in 357 to Baochang's own time. Many of the nuns were not only conversant in Buddhist scriptures but also well educated in secular literature; monastery life clearly provided an opportunity for women to follow intellectual pursuits as well as a religious calling.

Huijiao and Baochang's works share the general Liang impulse to organize knowledge and present an orderly account of the cultural past from what seemed to them a privileged vantage point. The monk Sengyou's *A Collection of the Records of the Translated Tripitaka* (*Chu sanzang ji ji*) is an extraordinary work intended as a record of all the translated Buddhist scriptures in the course of five hundred years, from when Buddhism was first introduced into China down to Sengyou's own age. It inadvertently presents us, as no secular source does, with a treasure trove of data about textual transmission in early medieval China. Although the book is exclusively concerned with religious texts, it allows us to catch glimpses of a vast system of manuscripts being produced, reproduced, and circulated across Central Asia and China, a system of words in traffic.

While much extant Liang writing may appear rather impersonal because of its social nature and formalistic elegance, in Xiao Yi's *Master of the Golden Tower* one finds the prince's accounts of his life in touchingly candid, intimate terms and plain, straightforward prose. Xiao Yi had started this work in 522 at the age of fourteen, and it was not completed until one year before his death. In the tradition of the "Masters" who discoursed on various subjects, from the management of the state to the cultivation of self, Xiao Yi wrote on a variety of topics ranging from statecraft and admonitions to his sons to his views on literature. Of particular interest are passages about his parents, particularly his mother, Lady Ruan; his unfortunate marriage; his chronic health problems; his book collecting; his memory of the time when he, as a child, used to pull down the crimson mosquito net during hot and humid summer nights in the south and read until dawn. Sometimes, he confessed, he did not recognize a word or understand a phrase, but this did not prevent him from enjoying the book. It is hard to believe that this was the very person who years later ordered the burning of 140,000 scrolls on the eve of the fall of the Liang and was thus responsible for the largest-scale deliberate destruction of books in Chinese history.

The cultural construction of the "north" and "south"

During the Southern Dynasties the south had finally ceased to be peripheral to the "Central Plains" – the heartland of China in the Yellow River region. The rulers of the Southern Dynasties, Emperor Wu of the Liang in particular, saw themselves as the upholders of the Han–Chinese cultural tradition against a north that had fallen into the hands of the northern "barbarians." The political and military contestation between north and south during this period was translated into antithetical cultural images of the two regions, with the north configured as tough and masculine, while the south was sensuous and effeminate. Such images, which have become standard in the Chinese cultural imagination, were cultural constructs that reduce the great complexities of the real north and south to simplified pictures that served political and cultural purposes. The process of construction reached maturity in the Liang through literary representations, but the antithesis was firmly established only in the early seventh century under the rule of the Sui and Tang, the two northern dynasties that unified China and brought north and south together.

As we will see later, the Sui and early Tang played a key role in setting up the antithesis of the cultural concepts of "north" and "south," but here we will limit ourselves to two groups of texts from the south that were instrumental in shaping the image of the north: a poetic subgenre later dubbed "frontier poetry," and a set of songs commonly regarded as "northern folk songs." These latter songs were performed and preserved by Liang court musicians as part of military music ("Songs for Fife and Drum"), hence representing a north as perceived and constructed by southern aristocrats. We do not know the origin of many of these so-called "northern songs," and some or all of them might have indeed come from the north; what should be stressed, however, is the mediating role of southerners in choosing, performing, and preserving these songs. The proper question to ask is not whether these songs were originally northern or southern, but why they were chosen by the southerners for performance in the southern court. In dealing with these songs we should also separate the issues of music and lyrics; that is, the music of these songs might very well have integrated non-Han music motifs from the north, but the adaptation of the lyrics is a different matter. In most cases, we do not have definitive evidence for the northern origin of the lyrics.

In both "frontier poetry" and the "northern songs," the north is represented with a stylized macho language and dramatized description of the bitter cold; it is an austere and harsh place, characterized by its martial prowess and lack of refinement. In "frontier poetry," the "frontier" is neither the real geographical division line between north and south during this period, nor the southern or southwestern borderland. Instead, it is identified with a specific locale, namely the far north or northwest, the Central Asian frontiers of the Han empire; the frequent use of historical Central Asian place names intensifies the sense of exoticism. It embodies an attempt on the part of the southern elite to imagine a space "out there" – distant and inaccessible in both spatial and temporal terms, functioning as a cultural other to the construction of the southern identity. Reaching its characteristic form first in Bao Zhao, the southern poet who had never left the south, this poetry became a notable phenomenon in the Liang, developed by He Xun, Wu Jun, and particularly Xiao Gang. As the southern court literature exerted a large influence on the northern writers in the sixth century, northern poets eventually adopted the diction and imagery of the north in their own "frontier poetry." Poems on military campaigns and frontier life by famous northern poets are often no more than a pastiche of allusions and images taken from historical and literary sources, modeled on the southern "frontier poetry." Lu Sidao's (535–586) "Ballad of Joining the Army" (Cong jun xing), written in a long tradition of the established *yuefu* title, is exactly such a text. Any authentic experience that the poet might have had is overwhelmed by the rich historical and literary allusions which appear in virtually every line.

The Southland (Jiangnan, literally "south of the Yangzi river") was the complement of the poetic north and found its embodiment in the poetic image of the lotus flower, celebrated in the southern *yuefu* songs performed at court as well as in the court poetry and *fu*. Rich in association in the native

Chinese literary tradition, the lotus, in the regional love songs (*lian*, punning with "passion," also *lian*) as well as in a Buddhist context (representing purity and enlightenment), caught the imagination of southern poets, who made the lotus a symbol of the south. Lotus-picking, an agrarian activity usually performed by women, became a popular topic of poetry and *fu* beginning in the late fifth century. Xiao Gang's "*Fu* on Lotus-Picking" provides a fine example, representing the Southland as a land of sensuality and pleasure against a vast background that is "pure and empty," evocative of the Buddhist vision of the vanity of all sensuous forms. Such a nostalgic, romanticized portrayal of the south produced a lasting impact on later Chinese cultural imagination.

Trauma and diaspora: writing the fall of the south

In 548, Hou Jing, a northern general who had defected to the Liang, rebelled against his benefactor and seized the capital, Jiankang, after a bloody five-month siege. Emperor Wu died in 549; Xiao Gang ruled under Hou Jing's control until he was murdered in 551. Xiao Yi then claimed the Liang throne in Jiangling and defeated Hou Jing in the following year, but the damage was already done. The Hou Jing Rebellion caused massive devastation to the south, wiped out a large part of the southern elite, and effectively destroyed the old social order. In 554 Jiangling fell to the Western Wei army, and Xiao Yi was captured and executed. Three years later, the Liang was overthrown by Chen Baxian (503–559), a southern general from a minor gentry family. The new Chen dynasty lasted only a little more than thirty years and was conquered by the Sui army in 589. Emperor Wen of the Sui ordered the destruction of the entire city of Jiankang: its walls, palaces, and houses were all to be demolished and the land returned to agriculture. The Southern Dynasties had come to an end.

Many Liang writers went north after the fall of the dynasty, either as envoys who were detained or as captives. Some, like Xu Ling and Shen Jiong (502–560), eventually came home; others, like Wang Bao, Yu Xin, and Yan Zhitui (531–591?), never did. Although cultural communication between the north and the south continued throughout the period of disunion, by way of Buddhist clergy, merchants, and state envoys, the displacement of southern writers to the north after the mid-sixth century contributed to the "fusion" of the northern and southern cultures, made a true comparison of north and south possible, and enabled the writers who survived traumatic historical changes to obtain a distance across time and space to reflect on what had happened to their state, their families, and themselves. Much writing after the fall of the

Liang was literally in survivors' accounts, responses to the devastation of the south, which was rightly perceived as the end of an era.

On his way back from the north after his release, Shen Jiong observed his ravaged homeland as he approached Jiankang and wrote in a poem,

> Still apprehensive about the northern cavalry,
> I am ever wary of encountering barbarian troops.
> Only large trees remain in the empty village;
> deserted towns are left with crumbling city walls.
> None of my old friends is around;
> all my new acquaintances have different names.
> A hundred years, thirty thousand days in all,
> this heart-wrenching sorrow in each and every one of them.

His "*Fu* on the Returned Soul" (Guihun fu), of which only parts have survived, portrays in great detail his experiences during and after the Hou Jing Rebellion.

Yan Zhitui, a writer and scholar who had served under Xiao Yi, was taken to the north after the fall of Jiangling. He wrote "*Fu* on Contemplating My Life" (Guan wo sheng fu), giving a full account of his life in a chaotic age. The *fu* is interspersed with Yan Zhitui's own annotations in unrhymed prose, explaining references and furnishing details of the author's personal circumstances as well as larger historical events. Yan Zhitui was clearly writing with an audience in mind – people whom he feared might not be acquainted with what had transpired in the south: northerners perhaps, but also future generations. A devout Buddhist, Yan Zhitui also authored *The Account of Wronged Souls* (*Yuanhun zhi*), a collection of tales intended to illustrate the Buddhist principle of retribution, but also preserving, among other things, poignant details from a vast canvas of brutality and devastation after the fall of the south.

Yan Zhitui's most famous work is *Family Instructions to the Yan Clan* (*Yanshi jiaxun*). It was written over a long period from the 570s until 589 or later. In this work Yan Zhitui laid out a series of rules of conduct for his sons. The man emerging from these lucidly written essays in many ways represented the "average" Southern Dynasties courtier: a learned scholar and a talented writer, Yan Zhitui nevertheless lacked the flair of a Yu Xin or a Xu Ling. Admitting that he had no interest in the abstract discourse of the *Laozi* and *Zhuangzi*, he manifested a down-to-earth philosophy of life. The topics discussed range from children's education to household management, remarriage, scholarship, literary writing, maintenance of good health, mastery of miscellaneous arts such as calligraphy and painting, and various ethical codes. It embodies the vision of the world of a member of the sixth-century Chinese elite; more important, it is characterized by his quest for a way of life both honorable and safe in a dangerous age, and by his painful attempt to establish an enduring value system when everything with which he was familiar had crumbled. Some of his advice might fail to satisfy the more exacting criteria of ethical action of later neo-Confucianism, but Yan Zhitui, writing from early medieval China, was giving less a patriarch's instructions than a survival guide.

Yu Xin, hailed as one of the finest classical Chinese poets, exerted an immense influence on northern literature. After the fall of Jiankang, he joined Xiao Yi's entourage in Jiangling. In the early summer of 554, Yu Xin was sent to Chang'an, the capital of the Western Wei, as an envoy. He was detained and never again returned to the south. A complicated man, Yu Xin suffered from feelings of guilt, shame, remorse, and homesickness, yet his homesickness was of a peculiar quality. To Yu Xin, the south was not merely a physical space, but a land of the past. What Yu Xin had lost and lamented was more than his state, even more than his prince; it was an entire era, a way of life.

Yu Xin's sentiments found expression in his monumental *fu*, "The Lament for the South" (Ai Jiangnan fu), one of the last grand *fu* in Southern Dynasties literature. Like Yan Zhitui's "Contemplating My Life," here Yu Xin situates the account of his personal life within a larger historical context. Yu Xin's highest accomplishments, however, lie in poetry and shorter *fu* pieces, in which he managed to frame and highlight emotional intensity with a masterful formal control and the cultivated grace of the Liang court poet. In Yu Xin's later poems, the intricate parallelism and erudite textual references to earlier literature favored by palace-style poets are dexterously combined with a simpler diction and an apparent ease of expression, which produce a powerful rhetorical force.

The aftermath

In many ways the Chen was no more than an aftermath of the Liang. Its territory was the smallest in all the Southern Dynasties, cramped by the Western Wei (later Northern Zhou) and Eastern Wei (later Northern Qi) to the north, and the Latter Liang, a small state under the rule of the descendants of Emperor Wu of the Liang, to the west. Many of the Chen writers had grown up in the Liang, and Chen literature was a continuation of the Liang court literature in terms of diction and style, only on a diminished scale and lacking the robust energy that characterized their predecessors. Xu Ling, the compiler of *New Songs of the Jade Terrace*, was revered as the grand literary master in the Chen court, but the center of the Chen literary landscape was the much younger Chen Shubao (553–604), the last Chen emperor. Chen Shubao was an avid poetry lover and gathered around him a group of courtiers who were skilled in writing, including Jiang Zong (519–594) and Zhang Zhengjian (ca 527–575). Their poems were elegant formal exercises mostly composed to imperial command at banquets and parties and in the company of palace ladies. Some of the palace ladies with literary talent, such as Yuan Dashe, held the title of "Female Scholar" amd participated in the group composition. Those "particularly alluring" poems would be set to music and sung in the harem.

The poet Yin Keng (fl. 540s–560s) deserves special mention. Coming from an official family, he served in a series of low posts, mainly on the staff of princes, from Liang to Chen. Yin Keng was not a prolific poet, but his extant poems, thirty-four in all, contain memorable lines. The following couplet is taken from a companion piece to Hou Andu's (520–563) "Ascending a Tower and Gazing toward My Homeland" (Denglou wangxiang):

> Cold fields, after the harvest, stand still;
> in the wilderness, sunlight is feeble
> through the smoke of burned stubble.

The autumn scene, imbued with a sense of deprivation and loss after a time of affluence, captures the mood of the south in the aftermath of the Hou Jing Rebellion. Another poem, "Visiting an Empty Temple at Baling" (You Baling kongsi), plays with the double meanings of "empty" (kong; Skt. Śūnyatā), a word with immense resonance against the intensely Buddhist background of the late Southern Dynasties:

> Incense long gone, but the curtain is still perfumed;
> banners are covered with dust, images grow hazy.
> You ask me what I have seen –
> a breeze in the air stirs the heavenly clothes.

The last image – the movement of the robe put on the Buddhist statue – deepens the stillness and desolation of the place. Buddhism was also known as the "Doctrine of Images," since it teaches by way of icons – statues and paintings. In the poet's eyes the deserted temple seems to be imparting a lesson of the illusive and transient nature of worldly glory with the very image of its hollow existence.

IV. The northern court: early fifth through early seventh centuries

An overview

The grand cultural and literary-historical narrative of the Northern and Southern Dynasties, Sui, and early Tang is in many ways one of divergence and convergence of north and south. The Northern Wei dynasty was founded by the Tuoba or Tabgach, a Xianbei people originally from the northeastern part of China and believed to have spoken a Turkic language. The Tuoba rose to power in the course of the fourth century, and changed the name of their kingdom from Dai to Wei in 386. In the early fourth century, while south China was under Liu-Song rule, the Wei carried out a series of military campaigns against neighboring states under the leadership of Tuoba Tao (known posthumously as Emperor Taiwu, r. 424–452), and finally unified north China in the year 439.

Although members of the Han Chinese elite were employed in government service, the Northern Wei court remained largely dominated by Xianbei nobles, until Emperor Xiaowen (467–499) launched a large-scale sinicization program in the 490s. He made Xianbei nobles speak Chinese at court, wear Chinese clothes, and adopt Chinese surnames. The surname of the ruling house itself was changed from Tabgach to Yuan. More importantly, Emperor Xiaowen moved the Wei capital from the old Tuoba power base of Pingcheng (in modern Shanxi) to the former Western Jin capital of Luoyang in 494. Emperor Xiaowen's reform aroused much resentment among the Xianbei and had long-term repercussions for the state as well as for northern literature and culture.

Rebellions of garrison troops, partially caused by intensified ethnic conflicts, broke out in the 520s and eventually led to the empire splitting into two halves, the Western Wei, with its capital in Chang'an, and the Eastern Wei, with its capital in the city of Ye (modern Linzhang, Hebei) in 534. The Eastern Wei, though under the nominal rule of the Tuoba family, was dominated by the powerful Xianbei minister Gao Huan (496–547), whose son deposed the figurehead Tuoba emperor in 550 and established the Qi (commonly called the Northern Qi to distinguish it from the southern dynasty of the same name); the Western Wei court was controlled by Yuwen Tai (507–556), whose heir likewise deposed the Wei ruler and founded the Northern Zhou in 557. Twenty years later, the Northern Zhou conquered the Northern Qi, but the Zhou itself was ended soon afterwards by Yang Jian (Emperor Wen of the Sui, r. 581–604), a tough, astute general who became the first Sui emperor and finally brought China under the rule of a single dynasty.

Yang Jian was not a man of learning or literary sensibilities, and he did not care for the elaborate southern court literary style prevailing in the north in the sixth century. In 584, he issued an edict ordering that all public and private letters and documents be "plain factual records" with no rhetorical embellishments. Later that year a provincial governor was thrown into prison because his memorandum to the throne was "ornate and sumptuous." But Yang Jian's successor Yang Guang (Emperor Yang, r. 605–617), who was married to a Liang princess, was fascinated with the sophisticated culture of the south, made repeated trips to the south during his reign, showed a high regard for southern writers, and eventually was murdered by his rebellious generals in the South.

Yang Guang was an ambitious ruler who engaged in grandiose, expensive civil and military projects and whose vision exceeded his ability. As the Sui crumbled in civil war under his rule, another northern general, Li Yuan, a descendant of the ruling house of one of the Sixteen Kingdoms, rose to prominence and founded the Tang dynasty in 618. Several years later, Li Yuan was forced to abdicate by his son Li Shimin, who had first killed his elder brother, the crown prince, and a younger brother, in a palace coup. Li Shimin, better known as Emperor Taizong, ascended the throne in 626, and began a twenty-three-year rule famous not only for his successful management of the newly unified empire, but also for his successful construction of self-image as a benevolent, respectful, and self-critical Confucian ruler. Many cultural and literary issues were carried over from the Northern and Southern Dynasties into Taizong's court, where we see the last manifestation of the cultural confrontation and integration of the north and south.

Like the Sui, the Tang was founded by a powerful northern elite clan of mixed ethnic origins, but Taizong took care to base dynastic legitimacy on what he perceived to be the orthodox Han Chinese culture. In the fifth century, Emperor Xiaowen of the Northern Wei had executed his crown prince because of the young man's preference for the Xianbei lifestyle and his opposition to the emperor's sinicization reform; similarly, Taizong's eldest son chose to speak Turkic, dress in Turkic clothes and even set up a tent in his residence in imitation of a Turkic khan. Taizong removed him from the position of heir apparent and chose as his successor a younger son, Li Zhi, who embraced the Han Chinese cultural heritage.

Taizong made a conscious investment in various kinds of cultural work contributing to the project of dynasty-building, but the most notable impact that the Sui and early Tang had on literature lay in their active role of judging and transmitting the literary output of the Northern and Southern Dynasties. Judgments passed on southern court poetry in Sui and Tang official discourse were to become the mainstream opinion for a millennium; however, a more profound consequence of the judgments of this period follows from its neglect of the north. It is impossible for us to even begin to understand the northern literature – from its extant quantity to the nature of the literary writings – without taking into consideration the sources that have preserved it.

Despite their rivalry for military dominance and political legitimacy, north and south were never entirely closed off to each other during the period of disunion; various forms of cultural exchange took place by way of traveling monks, merchants, and state envoys (who were often chosen for their articulateness and literary talent); nor was their boundary ever fixed. The northern elite were quite familiar with southern literary writings, and many of them fell under the influence of famous southern writers such as Xie Lingyun, Bao Zhao, Xie Tiao, Shen Yue, and Ren Fang. The southern court, in turn, also marveled at the wit, eloquence, and literary sophistication of the northerners. Emperor Wu of the Liang, upon reading the writings of the northerner Wen Zisheng (495–547) that were copied and taken back to the south by a Liang emissary, praised Wen as a reincarnated Cao Zhi or Lu Ji. An anecdote relates that Chen Qingzhi, a famous Liang general, treated northerners with great respect ever since he came back from his military campaign to Luoyang. When a colleague asked him why he admired the northerners so much, he answered that although "those living to the north of the Yangzi river are always called barbarians," his stay in the north had opened his eyes to the splendid cultural accomplishments of the northerners. We also learn from the dynastic histories that northern writers were no less prolific than the southern writers.

A curious discrepancy, however, appears when we come to the surviving literary works of the northern dynasties: extant northern literature is of a pitifully meager quantity (modern literary histories and anthologies often include Yu Xin, Wang Bao, and Yan Zhitui with the northern poets, although these southerners, who went north in their maturity, were not "northern writers" in a strict sense). The early Tang historian Li Yanshou's preface to "The Biographies of Men of Letters" in *The Southern Histories* (*Nan shi*), however, is merely one-tenth of the length of his preface to "The Biographies of Men of Letters" in *The Northern Histories* (*Bei shi*), which forcefully demonstrates that more significance was assigned to the northern than to the southern literary scene. Another instructive set of figures is the surviving poems of three of the most famous northern writers, commonly referred to as the "Three Talents of the North," Wen Zisheng, Xing Shao (ca 496–561), and Wei Shou (506–572). Wen Zisheng had had a literary collection in about thirty-five scrolls, but his extant poems, including fragments, are eleven in total; from Xing Shao's collection in thirty scrolls, nine poems are left; from Wei Shou's collection of about seventy scrolls, sixteen. All these writers, moreover, were from the sixth century and heavily influenced by the Liang court style. Little Northern Wei poetry survives from the fifth century, and what survives is largely preserved in the *History of the Wei (Wei shu)*, compiled by Wei Shou in the 550s, himself a northerner and a poet.

There seems to have been a strong bias against the northern literature in the early seventh century, the period responsible for preserving most of what we have. The bias is visible not in official discourse but in the act of selection and preservation of literary writings. Although the seventh-century historians always criticized the court poetry of Xiao Gang, Xiao Yi, Xu Ling, and Yu Xin as "the sounds of a fallen state," the encyclopedias of the early Tang showed an overwhelming preference for southern writings as against their northern counterparts. *Classified Extracts of Literature (Yiwen leiju)*, which was presented to the throne in 624 and remains one of the most important sources of pre-Tang literature, contains more than nine hundred selections from Liang poetry, but only four selections from Northern Wei poetry (and of these four selections two were written by Xiao Zong, son of Emperor Wu of the Liang, who went north). Granted, there are only eight individual literary collections by Northern Wei writers recorded in the book catalogue from the *History of the Sui* (comp. 636), but the *History of the Wei*, compiled about eighty years earlier, had mentioned many more writers whose writings "were circulated in the world." In the partially extant *Grove of Texts from the Literature Office*, a large-scale anthology of pre-Tang literature completed in 657, we find two poems from the Northern Wei, but nothing from Northern Qi and Zhou; and of the two poems from the Sui, one is by a southern poet. In contrast, we have thirty-one poems from Liu-Song, Qi, Liang, and Chen, with eighteen of them being Liang poems. The same happens with prose. *Classified Extracts of Literature* includes over six hundred selections from Liang prose, but only forty-three from Northern Wei and Qi; when we come to the Northern Zhou and Sui, the prose selections are almost entirely dominated by those by writers originally from the south, namely Wang Bao, Yu Xin, and Jiang Zong. Of the Northern Wei and Qi prose included in *Classified Extracts of Literature*, 90 percent was by Wen Zisheng, Xing Shao, and Wei Shou, the "Three Talents of the North." In the fragmentary *Grove of Texts* we find one prose piece from the Northern Wei and one from the Sui, but five from the Liang.

An anecdote in an eighth-century work relates that Wei Shou once requested Xu Ling to transmit his literary collection to the south, but Xu Ling later dumped the collection in the water when he crossed the Yangzi river; when an alarmed attendant asked him what he was doing, Xu Ling answered, "I am merely getting rid of an embarrassment for Mr. Wei." Although the veracity of the story is uncertain, it is symbolic of the fate of the rich literary production of the northern dynasties. The north may have conquered the south, but its literary legacy was almost entirely wiped out.

The *History of the Wei* preserves most of the literary writings of the Northern Wei, a dynasty that had lasted a century; this history is also an invaluable source of information about lost writings. For instance, in the early sixth century, a minister Zhang Yi (461–519) presented the throne with seven scrolls of poems he had collected while serving as inspector in the regions of Qi and Lu (modern Shandong) during the reign of Emperor Xiaowen. This poetic collection is no longer extant, and it would have vanished without a trace but for Zhang Yi's letter to the throne accompanying the collection, which is preserved in the *History of the Wei*. The particular nature of the source, however, affects the kind of writings preserved in it; dynastic histories tend to include prose pieces such as edicts, epistles (including petitions to the throne), proclamations, treatises, or even *fu*, rather than poetry. Such a practice is largely responsible for the false impression that the northern literature stressed pragmatic political functions over aesthetic concerns or that *fu* and other prose forms flourished in the North, but not poetry. In fact, of the "Three Talents of the North," Wen Zisheng reportedly did not write *fu* at all, while Xing Shao was considered to be "not good at it." To belittle his fellow writers, Wei Shou claimed that a great writer must base his reputation on *fu*, and, perhaps as a result of such a conviction, Wei Shou included many *fu* in the *History of the Wei* whenever he wanted to showcase someone's literary talent.

It is noteworthy that the compilers of the early Tang encyclopedias were a mixture of southerners and northerners; this shows that their preference for southern writings was a result of the contemporary taste, rather than a bias in favor of one's own native region. If the south won the battle in actual literary influence, it paradoxically suffered ubiquitous public censure. Liang palace-style poetry, to which the early Tang court poetry owed the greatest debt, was most harshly condemned and came to be associated exclusively with boudoir life, projecting an image of the conquered south as effeminate and decadent. The historian of the *History of the Sui* (*Sui shu*) gives the following summary:

> To the south of the Yangzi river, the musical tones are set forth, and a pure sumptuousness is valued; to the north of the Yellow River, the intent of writings is virtuous and hardy, and people prize vital force and substance . . . This is a general comparison between the advantages and disadvantages of the northern and southern writers. Now, if one could take the pure sound from that side and cut down long-winded sentences on this side, so that each will discard its failings and the strengths will be combined, then pattern [*wen*] and substance [*zhi*] will be balanced, and perfection achieved.

Pattern (*wen*) and substance (*zhi*), in complementary antithesis, were concepts with a long history going back to the *Analects*. The combination of pattern and substance to achieve perfection and balance was not a novel idea, but in the historical context of the early Tang such a fusion represented the poetics of a unified empire. To identify the south with patterning and the north with substance was a particular move, indicating that the long period of separation had finally come to an end.

The binary structure of north/south, which began as a geographical and political opposition in the Northern and Southern Dynasties, was soon translated into a cultural division. Both north and south each consciously promoted their own cultural legitimacy and constructed their cultural image in opposition to their rival. After the unification of China, the paradigm of southern cultural dominance versus northern martial dominance, once promoted by the southern court, was displaced into another pair of binary terms, "pattern" versus "substance." While "substance" was considered the fundamental term and the privileged basis for "pattern," the importance of *wen*, a word signifying "pattern" and "form" but also cultural accomplishments and literature, nevertheless remained in the foreground. "Substance" without "pattern" ran the risk of being uncouth, or, even worse, of losing one's identity. The adoption of this particular binary framework placed early Tang historians in a bind, resulting in an ambivalent attitude toward the southern culture ("refined" or "decadent"), even as they identified the north with "substance." Their preference for southern over northern literature further complicated the matter and left future generations with a curious gap between public praise of the northern literature and radical exclusion of the northern writings from encyclopedias and anthologies. As a consequence scholars, critics, and readers have for more than a millennium accepted the paradigm set up by the early Tang court: the "scarcity" of northern literary writings is taken to represent the disinterest of the northern dynasties in literary culture, while southern court literature is regarded with both admiration and contempt. The politically motivated southern image of the north as unsophisticated and crude was thus reinforced and taken for granted.

Northern literature in the fifth and sixth centuries

Throughout Wei, Qi, and Zhou, the Xianbei language, referred to as the "dynastic language" (*guoyu*), was spoken among the Xianbei elite as well as in the army. Works in the Xianbei language were still extant in the Tang, such as *Unclassified Prose in the Dynastic Language* (*Guoyu zawen*), and *Eighteen Biographies in the Dynastic Language* (*Guoyu shibazhuan*). The Wei court musicians had composed "The Dai Songs of Immortal Beings" (Zhenren daige), pre-sumably in the Xianbei language, during the early years of Wei rule; the lyrics were about the founding of the dynasty and the accomplishments of the Wei rulers and ministers. Some of these might have been preserved in a ten-scroll *Immortal Songs in the Dynastic Language* (*Guoyu zhenge*) and an eleven-scroll *Imperial Songs in the Dynastic Language* (*Guoyu yuge*), which were lost after the Tang. One Xianbei song translated into Chinese and entitled "Song of Chile" is preserved in the twelfth-century *Collection of Yuefu Poetry*; it is supposedly the one sung by a Xianbei general, joined in with by none other than Gao Huan, the father of the first Qi emperor, in the year 546.

In the north, poetry and *fu* fulfilled the same social functions as in the south: verses were exchanged between friends, courtiers were called upon to compose poetry at imperial banquets or court gatherings, and eulogies were presented to rulers to celebrate memorable occasions. Because of the scarcity of materials, it is quite impossible to judge the relative proportion of poetry in four- and five-syllable line in the overall literary output of the fifth century; furthermore, poetry in the four-syllable line continued to be written on formal occasions during the same period in the south, so the survival of poems in the four-syllable line alone does not prove the "archaism" of the northern literature as some modern scholars seem to presume; rather it serves to highlight the nature of the sources as favoring the inclusion of poetry composed on formal social occasions.

Gao Yun (390–487), a literary and political luminary of the Northern Wei, had written "*Fu* on the Dai Capital" (Daidu fu, Dai being the for-mer name of the Wei) in the "capital *fu*" tradition; "*Fu* on the Deer Park" (Luyuan fu) was commissioned by Emperor Xianwen (r. 466–471) to celebrate Deer Park, which had been constructed by Emperor Daowu in 399. You Ya (d. 461), another literary courtier, was commanded to write "*Fu* on the Hall of Sumptuous Splendor" (Taihua dian fu). Gao Lü (d. 502), a prolific writer, presented "Eulogy to the Utmost Virtue" (Zhide song) to Emperor Xiaowen upon his succession to the throne in 471; ten years later, after the suppression of a rebellion, Cheng Jun (414–485) presented "Eulogy on Celebrating the Dynasty" (Qingguo song) to the throne. Both eulogies are in the four-syllable line and preserved in the *History of the Wei*. Neither the "*Fu* on the Dai Capital" nor "*Fu* on the Hall of Sumptuous Splendor," mentioned in the *History of the Wei*, is extant, and "*Fu* on the Deer Park" is transmitted only because it was included in a Buddhist source from the early Tang, as a result of the Buddhist associations of the name "Deer Park," where the Buddha had delivered his first sermon.

One of the most notable figures from the first part of the fifth century was Cui Hao (380–450). Cui Hao came from an illustrious northern elite clan; his mother was the granddaughter of the Jin poet Lu Chen. Through his many talents, Cui Hao rose to a powerful position and became a trusted adviser to the emperor, which was unusual for a Han Chinese courtier in the early Wei. In 429 Cui Hao was entrusted with the task of supervising the compilation of the dynastic history. After the project was finished, he accepted the suggestions of two of his assistants to have the history inscribed on stone tablets and set up the tablets in the suburbs of the capital for all to see. Since some of the dynastic events were written in a "comprehensive but not decorous" manner, upset Xianbei noblemen spoke of the matter to Emperor Taiwu, who became furious and had Cui Hao and his entire clan, along with all those who had participated in the project, put to death. Many men of letters associated with Cui Hao, such as Zong Qin and Duan Chenggen, were implicated and executed. Zhang Zhan, another literary companion of Cui Hao, burned all the literary works Cui Hao had sent him and, withdrawing from the public world, managed to die of old age.

In the second half of the fifth century, active literary figures included Li Biao (444–501), Cui Guang (451–523), Han Xianzong (466–499), and Zheng Daozhao (d. 516). Li and Cui, both prolific writers, had exchanged many poems with each other, none of which is still extant. One poem in the five-syllable line presented to Li Biao by Han Xianzong survives from Han's literary collection of ten scrolls. Zheng Daozhao's poems on landscapes, apparently inscribed on stelae, survived fortuitously in a later work on bronze and stone rubbings.

If the execution of Cui Hao and his circle in 450 took a heavy toll of the northern literary community, the second key event in the Northern Wei literary history, namely Emperor Xiaowen's sinicizing reform, marked a literary revival. Emperor Xiaowen himself was a devoted lover of literature and had had a literary collection in nearly forty scrolls during his brief life. It is said that ever since he turned twenty (by Chinese reckoning) in 486, he drafted all the imperial edicts on his own. His sacrificial address to Bi Gan, an ancient loyal minister who was wrongly executed, is a good example of his erudition and stylistic elegance. The more fundamental change in the northern literature brought about by Emperor Xiaowen was the active interest in cultural enterprises assumed by the state.

The sixth century saw the rise of the "Three Talents of the North" and the appearance of many other northern men of letters. The Yang family from Wuzhong (modern Tianjin) is worthy of note. Yang Ni (fl. late fifth century) was a philologist who had had a personal library of several thousand scrolls of books. His clansman, Yang Gu (467–523), was a known writer. Yang Gu's eldest son Yang Xiuzhi (509–582), who served Wei, Qi, Zhou, and Sui, achieved a greater fame among his contemporaries for his poetry and *fu*; he also authored a book on rhymes and *A Record of Past and Present Personages of Youzhou* (*Youzhou gujin renwu zhi*). Amidst the chaos following the collapse of the Northern Wei in 534, Yang Xiuzhi went to the south. It was presumably during this time that he had access to the Liang crown prince Xiao Tong's edition of Tao Yuanming's collection and made a copy of it. He then collated it with two other editions and produced a new edition. Yang Xiuzhi's preface to this new edition, still extant, is one of the earliest writings on Tao Yuanming's collection.

Yang Xiuzhi's younger brother Yang Junzhi composed a set of song lyrics in the six-syllable line in the 540. These lyrics were "lewd and clumsy," but proved immensely popular and sold well in the market under the title "Companion Pieces by Yang the Fifth." It is said that once Yang Junzhi noticed some errors in the copies for sale and tried to correct them; the bookseller, not knowing who he was, scolded him, saying the poems had been authored by "an ancient worthy." Stories like this afford us a precious glimpse into the circulation and transmission of texts in the world of manuscript culture.

One prose work from the Northern Wei that deserves mention is the *Commentary on the Classic of Rivers* (*Shuijing zhu*) by Li Daoyuan (d. 527). The *Classic of Rivers* is a geographical treatise believed to be from the first or second century; in writing the commentary, Li Daoyuan cited copiously from more than three hundred earlier sources, many of which are now lost but for their fragmentary preservation in the *Commentary*. Li Daoyuan is often hailed as a great landscape prose writer; however, due to the loss of the sources, and because citation practice in premodern China does not always make it clear when exactly a citation ends, it is impossible to know how much of the commentary was quoted materials. One of the best-known passages from the *Commentary*, a description of the Wu gorges, often anthologized or cited as representing the supreme achievement of the northern landscape prose, was in fact taken from the fifth-century southern writer Sheng Hongzhi's *Account of Jingzhou* (*Jingzhou ji*). While Li Daoyuan made personal investigations into many of the rivers in the north, he had never traveled to the south, and any description of the southern landscape in his *Commentary* can only be attributed to book knowledge and hearsay. It is remarkable, given the general loss of numerous regional geographic treatises from this period, that the one work that incorporates both north and south, as well as the northern and southern accounts, survives more or less intact; it is also a work that joins the author's real experience and textual landscapes.

After the split of the Northern Wei in 534, the Eastern Wei and its successor dynasty, the (Northern) Qi, got the better share of literary men. Men of letters formed a social and literary circle and participated in group compositions at gatherings. Xing Shao, Yang Gu, Wang Xin (d. 560), Pei Bomao (497–535), and some others once composed dozens of poems together at a party, and the next morning Xing Shao reportedly was able to recite all the poems without missing a single character. After Pei Bomao died from over-drinking, a dozen of his literary friends held a memorial service at his tomb and each composed a poem lamenting his death. They included Wang Xin, Chang Jing (d. 550), Lu Yuanming (fl. 528–537), and Li Qian (b. 508). Wei Shou, being away at the time, also sent a poem. Lu Yuanming and Li Xie (496–544) had once served as emissaries to the south; along with Wei Shou and Wang Xin, they were much admired by the Liang court for their literary sophistication and wit.

Apart from the increasingly sophisticated use of parallelism in poetry and prose, the impact of southern literature on the north during the sixth century can be seen in anecdotes such as one in which Xing Shao criticized Wei Shou for imitating Ren Fang, while Wei Shou countered by accusing Xing Shao of "stealing from Shen Yue." There was an equal interest in Shen Yue's theory of metrics, as seen in Zhen Chen's (d. 524) "Dismembering the Four Tones" (Zhe sisheng), and Chang Jing's "Eulogy on the Four Tones" (Sisheng zan). Shen Yue himself had even written a response to the former treatise. The Northern Qi emperor Gao Wei (556–578) was fond of literature and established the Grove of Literature Office (Wenlin guan) in 573. Some fifty men of letters, both northerners and southerners, served in the office; many of them contributed to the compilation of a literary encyclopedia, *The Imperial Reader of the Hall of Cultivating Literature* (Xiuwendian yulan). The poems left by some of the Grove of Literature Office poets, such as Zu Ting and Liu Ti (525–573), are stylistically indistinguishable from the southern court poetry.

An interesting work from the first half of the sixth century is Yang Xuanzhi's *Record of Luoyang Monasteries* (Luoyang qielan ji). Yang Xuanzhi was a low-level Wei official. Very little is known about his life, but he was certainly not a famous writer of his day. In 547, upon passing by Luoyang, then in ruins, he gave an account of the once splendid Buddhist temples in the city, lamenting the downfall of the former Wei capital.

The Western Wei was sadly short of literary luminaries. In 545, Yuwen Tai commissioned Su Chuo (498–546), his trusted adviser, to compose "The

Great Proclamation" (Dagao), a piece of political prose in archaic style. The *History of the Zhou* states that "all writings [of the Zhou] followed this style from then on." Even if this had been true, the situation did not last long, for only a few years later, Yu Xin, Wang Bao, and other southerners came to the north, constituting a powerful presence on the northern literary scene. Yuwen Tai's eldest son, Emperor Ming (r. 557–560), an accomplished writer himself, showed great regard for Yu Xin and Wang Bao; two of Emperor Ming's younger brothers, Yuwen You (d. 580) and Yuwen Zhao (d. 580), became Yu Xin's patrons and literary disciples, and Yuwen You penned the preface for Yu Xin's literary collection in 579. Yu Xin was also commissioned by Emperor Wu (r. 561–578) to produce new ritual hymns for the Zhou cosmic and ancestral sacrifices; even the setup of the musical instruments followed the Liang model. The unification of China had begun on the cultural level long before the military and political fact.

The conquest of the Qi in 577 by the Zhou and of the Chen by the Sui a decade later brought many men of letters to Chang'an, which became the new cultural center. Since some of the Northern Qi literati had come from the south after the fall of the Liang, it was as much a reunion of the southerners as a convergence of the north and south. The impulse to make cultural comparisons between the north and south and to standardize and unify was seen in discussions about northern and southern pronunciations among a group of eight northern and southern scholars who gathered at Lu Fayan's house in the early 580s; the result of their collaboration was a rhyme dictionary (*Qieyun*) compiled by Lu Fayan, with a preface dated 601.

Besides a high esteem for the southern court style, former northern Qi and Chen writers suddenly found something else in common as courtiers of fallen states. On an autumn day during his stay in Chang'an, the aging Chen courtier Jiang Zong visited the Kunming Pool with two Northern Qi poets, Yuan Xinggong (fl. ca 570s–590s) and Xue Daoheng (540–609); the poems they wrote on the occasion bespeak a profound sense of loss and alienation. A group of former Qi courtiers, including Yan Zhitui, Yang Xiuzhi, and Lu Sidao, all composed poems on the topic "Listening to the Cicada" (Ting mingchan) after their arrival in Chang'an; the one by Lu Sidao, a well-crafted poem in lines of various lengths, expresses his sadness over his displacement in a strange land.

Lu Sidao and Xue Daoheng stood out among the northern writers for their elegant and lucid style in the second half of the sixth century. Xue, five years younger than Lu, outlived him by nearly a quarter of a century and was revered as a grand literary figure in the Sui.

From Emperor Yang to Emperor Taizong

The short reign of the Sui boasted many accomplished writers in its court, both northerners and southerners. Sweeping generalizations were often made in the late sixth century about "cultural and literary differences between the north and south," as seen in Yan Zhitui's *Family Instructions*, or in the preface to the southern poet Xiao Que's literary collection by Xing Shao (the very fact that a northern poet wrote a preface to a southern poet's literary collection signaled a new era). After the Sui unified China, a northern poet, Sun Wanshou, wrote a long poem during his exile to the south, which quickly became famous. Entitled "Being Stationed Far Away in the South, I Send This to Relatives and Friends in the Capital" (Yuanshu Jiangnan ji jingyi qinyou), the poem contains the following couplet: "The south is a land of pestilential vapors, / and always abounds in banished ministers." This couplet, an attempt to reverse the image of the south back to that of the age of Qu Yuan and Jia Yi when the south was peripheral to the center, is ironically based on the southern poet Xie Tiao's well-known line, "The south is a land of charm and beauty." Even as the northern poet belittled the south, he betrayed his indebtedness to the southern literary legacy.

Empeor Yang, a lover of the south, was in many ways the most important cultural figure in the Sui. He was an accomplished poet; his poetry, often stressing the magnificence and propriety of his rule, exemplifies the "imperial poetics" of a ruler presiding over a newly unified empire. One of the characteristics of Emperor Yang's reign was his penchant for extravagant display of dynastic grandeur and power. A variety show of song, dance, gymnastics, magic, and circus known as a "Hundred Plays," banned by his father, was reinstituted by Emperor Yang on an unprecedented scale, once reportedly involving as many as 30,000 performers. Beginning in 606 the show was staged in the capital in the first month of every year; in 607 it was put on for the Turkic khan at a banquet with 3,500 guests. A poem of sixty lines by Xue Daoheng upon watching such a show, written in response to the southern writer Xu Shanxin (558–618), testifies to the opulence of the carnival (Xu's poem is no longer extant).

A much more successful ruler, Emperor Taizong of the Tang nevertheless shared many similarities with Emperor Yang: Taizong, too, loved display, although his was of an image of himself as a virtuous and restrained Confucian monarch. He had grand imperial ambitions, and, as he was intensely aware, he was also the second-generation ruler over a newly unified empire with all its potential instabilities. A statement by Taizong summarizes his attitude:

"Although We have conquered the world with martial prowess, We must rule it with cultural power." Taizong was a competent poet who, like Emperor Yang, was seduced by the southern literature, but Taizong was much more sagacious in his attempts to incorporate southern sophistication into a larger political agenda.

Even before he ascended the throne, Taizong had inaugurated the Office of Literature (*Wenxue guan*), which later became the Office for Extending Literature (*Hongwen guan*). The scholars appointed to the office continued to hold their regular bureaucratic posts, and were frequently summoned into the imperial palace to "discuss literature as well as state affairs" until midnight. Taizong also placed paramount importance on the compilation of dynastic histories, a project that had begun but languished during his father's reign, and was then revived by Taizong in 629 and brought to completion in 636. The *History of the Jin* (*Jin shu*) was compiled between 646 and 648; this time, Taizong took it upon himself to write "the historian's comments" for four of the biographies: those of Sima Yan, the first Western Jin emperor, Sima Yan's father Sima Yi, the poet Lu Ji, and Taizong's beloved calligrapher Wang Xizhi. The choice of these four biographical subjects reflects Taizong's intense personal interest in cultural politics.

In more than one way, the most important literary activities in the early seventh century happened in the court, as Taizong and his courtiers frequently composed poetry together on public occasions. Due to good fortune in the sources, more poems composed on the same occasion have been preserved than ever before, which enables us to see a clear, comprehensive picture of group compositions on such occasions. These poems, elegant and well crafted in their parallel couplets but lacking in individuality, celebrate the splendor of the dynasty as well as confirming the legitimacy of Taizong's reign. The only poet who betrayed a strong personality in such writings was, not surprisingly, Taizong himself, whose extant collection of about a hundred poems remains the largest from this period. Yet the speaker in these poems is more an emperor than a person, as Taizong was so absorbed in playing the part of a monarch that the man disappeared into his role.

Despite public denunciations of the southern dynasties, Taizong and his courtiers had entirely assimilated the southern court style. Taizong maintained a perfect balance between northerners and southerners among his literary courtiers. Just to cite a few well-known names: on the northern side, we have Yang Shidao (d. 647), who often hosted private parties and invited men of letters to participate and compose poetry; Li Baiyao (565–648), the son of the famous public prose writer Li Delin; and Shangguan Yi (607?–664), whose ganddaughter Shangguan Wan'er was going to become the arbiter of literary taste in the next generation. On the southern side, we have Yu Shinan (558–638), the compiler of the encyclopedia *Extracts from Books in the Northern Hall (Beitang shuchao)*; Chu Liang (555–647), who had served Chen and Sui, and his son Chu Suiliang (596–658), a celebrated calligrapher; and Xu Jingzong (592–672), the son of Xu Shanxin.

One exceptional figure in this period was Wang Ji (ca 590–644), who did not belong to the court group and wrote a kind of poetry remarkably free from court rhetoric. Wang Ji came from a distinguished northern elite clan, but had had an uneven official career marked by several resignations from low-level offices. In his own writings, he cultivates a self-image as a wine-loving eccentric, consciously opposed to the aristocratic circles in the capital and modeled upon such Wei and Jin literary figures as Ruan Ji and Tao Yuanming. The simplicity of Wang Ji's poetic diction has also led scholars to remark on the influence of these earlier figures on Wang Ji's poetry, but Wang Ji's greatest debt is to his immediate predecessor Yu Xin, whose poetry and *fu* incorporate simple diction and easy syntax nevertheless couched in well-wrought parallel couplets. In the late eighth century there appeared an abridged edition of Wang Ji's collection, edited according to the contemporary "return to antiquity" ideology; this abridged edition found its way into printed editions in late imperial China, and became the dominant edition. A fuller edition of Wang Ji's collection in the form of three manuscript copies, "discovered" in the 1980s, almost doubles Wang Ji's *oeuvre*, and shows a Wang Ji who is rather different from the image of a rustic poet conveyed in the abridged edition. This Wang Ji is much more polished, has a decidedly "contemporary feel," and shows a profound indebtness to southern literary culture even as it manages to be free from the more formal, more ornate court style. Wang Ji himself might have been fascinated with a backward gaze, but his poetry prefigures a new era in literary history.

4

The cultural Tang (650–1020)

STEPHEN OWEN

Overview

The cultural Tang does not correspond exactly with the political dynasty, founded in 618 and lasting until 907, by which time it had ceased to be a viable polity for a quarter of a century. We begin our cultural Tang with Empress Wu's rise to power in the 650s and carry on into the first decades of the eleventh century, over half a century after the Song dynasty was established. This period is bounded on one side by the reign of Emperor Taizong (r. 627–649), the final phase of northern court culture and the full assimilation of the sophisticated legacy of the south. On the other side our period ends with the rise of the great political and cultural figures of the eleventh century, such as Fan Zhongyan (989–1052) and, most of all, Ouyang Xiu (1007–1072), writers who were to give Song literati culture its characteristic stamp.

Three hundred and seventy years is too long a span to constitute a meaningful literary-historical period, but comparison of literary culture at the beginning and end of this long era can bring out some of the fundamental changes that occurred. In the 650s, literature was centered almost entirely in the imperial court; by the end of the era literature had become the possession of an educated elite, who might serve in government, but whose cultural life was primarily outside the court.

Both before and during the Tang there were writers who used literature in a very personal way; it is not surprising that these were often the writers who continued to be read in later ages. At the same time, however, it is important to remember that literature was primarily a social practice, shared by an increasingly widening community. The Tang inherited a system of classical prose genres and poetic subgenres and extended it. Most of those prose genres and poetic subgenres were tied to specific occasions in life. As the social sphere of literature spread outward from the court, the capacity to compose competent prose and verse was expected, whether carrying out functions in the civil bureaucracy or going to a party with friends. Although much of this literature tied to social occasion was routine, it in no way precluded genius; indeed, many of the greatest pieces of the era were composed in response to a social obligation to write.

In the mid-seventh century, skill in literary composition was one among many routes to win social distinction and imperial recognition. This would be expressed in Chinese by the term *ming*, both "name" and "reputation." In the first part of our era, making a name for oneself was primarily dependent on the state, whether through imperial favor or, increasingly, through the institution of the literary examination (*jinshi*). Over the course of the eighth and ninth centuries, public recognition of literary "reputation" gradually passed to a much larger community of judgment. Although success in the literary examination remained a compelling aspiration for most, the dissociation of literary merit from state validation reached the point where true literary talent often came to be associated with failure in public life. By the ninth century, we find many who defined themselves as "poets" (and even a few who defined themselves as prose writers), approximating the European tradition's idea of poetry as a unique vocation in life. This process by which literary practice became separated from the authority of the state on the general level (as opposed to the recluses of earlier periods) helped define a whole new sphere of cultural life for the elite.

The Tang transformation of literary culture made this era a new beginning in the history of Chinese literature. In the mid-seventh century writers still took their older models from *Selections of Refined Literature*, representing a tradition that stretched from the Western Han to the beginning of the sixth century; more recent models for both poetry and prose were found in the works of Xu Ling and Yu Xin from the second half of the sixth century. While interest in earlier literature never disappeared, by the ninth century the dominant earlier models for poetry and prose came primarily from the Tang itself, beginning in the eighth century. The manuscript library at Dunhuang, discovered in the early part of the twentieth century, undisturbed since it was sealed in about 1035, included copies of *Selections of Refined Literature*, but the numerous manuscripts of poetry preserved there represent almost exclusively Tang poetry. Although pre-Tang poetry began to gather renewed attention in the fourteenth century, Tang poetry remained the dominant model for most of the rest of the history of classical poetry. The early ninth-century writers Han Yu (768–824) and Liu Zongyuan (773–819) became the first models for "ancient-style prose," the form that dominated prose composition for the next millennium. Although few in the Tang would have recognized their future importance, Tang stories were to provide core plots for much Chinese drama and some fiction.

The *Complete Tang Poems* (*Quan Tang shi*) and its supplements have preserved about 51,000 poems from the Tang and the Five Dynasties. To this should be added approximately ten thousand more poems from the first half-century of the Song, still very much in the Tang tradition. The *Complete Tang Prose* (*Quan Tang wen*) contains about 23,000 pieces (including much documentary material); this has been supplemented several times, with recent additions of large amounts of epigraphic material. Our knowledge of Tang stories depends almost entirely on the early Song compendium *Extensive Records of the Taiping Reign* (*Taiping guangji*) in five hundred chapters, completed in 978 and printed in 981. Since the *Extensive Records* carefully cites its sources for every item included, we can partially reconstruct otherwise lost storybooks and anecdote collections from the Tang and earlier. A number of anecdote collections have survived independently. The Buddhist and Daoist canons have also preserved an extensive corpus of material, including tales, biographies, and verse, which was largely excluded from secular sources. Finally there is the material from the great Buddhist library at Dunhuang. In addition to providing rich sources for religion and social history, the Dunhuang manuscripts preserve a precious window on a marginal Han Chinese literary culture in Central Asia.

Our knowledge of Tang literature depends on what survives, on material accident and acts of conservation that reflect the interests of particular ages and particular individuals. The most important period for gathering and editing Tang literature began at the end of this period, in the last part of the tenth century and in the early eleventh. The hazards of manuscript circulation, with individuals often copying only those texts that pleased them, and the massive destruction of manuscripts during the late ninth century and first half of the tenth, left early Song scholars with extensive, but scattered and fragmentary, remains of the Tang literary legacy. Unlike the itinerant humanists of the European Renaissance, who gathered the remains of Latin antiquity from monastic libraries, most of the editors of Tang literature were civil officials, bound to the single locale of their posts; they gathered what they could, searched, borrowed, and collated.

The case of the poetry of Li Shangyin (813–858), now considered the pre-eminent poet of the mid-ninth century, is a good example. Our present version is due to the efforts of Li Shangyin's early Song admirer Yang Yi (974–1020). Yang Yi began with a collection of somewhat over a hundred poems, poems that would now probably be considered unrepresentative. Over the years Yang Yi diligently gathered until he had 282 pieces. Then a friend serving in the southeast provided a manuscript that brought the collection to over four hundred poems (still substantially fewer pieces than our current version). Yang Yi was not only an ardent admirer of Li Shangyin, he was someone with great political power and an extensive network of friends. If even Yang Yi had such difficulty gathering the scattered manuscript remains of a poet, we can imagine the case for less well-placed editors.

Tang prose by and large continued the range of genres from the pre-Tang period, but some genres achieved a new prominence. The "preface on parting" (*songxu*) became an important independent prose form, its peculiar name perhaps due to its original association with a parting poem. The "account of an excursion" (*youji*) came to be one of the most interesting prose forms, mixing landscape description with reflection. In the ninth century we have a renewed interest in the parable and prose on topics not linked to occasion; the latter sometimes approaches the "essay" in Bacon's sense, if not in Montaigne's.

In the second half of the seventh century, we have the earliest "regulated *fu*" (*lüfu*), following strict balancing of tones as in poetry (though a freer balancing of tones in *fu* existed already in the sixth century). The form did not reach its characteristic form until the eighth century; the "topic" or "title" was followed by a phrase that set the rhymes. There was a strict pattern of exposition, with each section developed using the preset rhyme. This was the kind of *fu* that came to be used in the literary examination. Tang writers developed the full range of topics employed in pre-Tang *fu*, but added many more, including moral topics ("Taking Worthy Men as Treasures"), scenes from the Classics and legend ("Shun Sings 'South Wind'"), and historical scenes.

Poetry was the most common literary form, inviting, as prose and *fu* did not, composition in the context of a group. Sometimes the occasion itself would be the common topic; sometimes a topic might be assigned or multiple topics distributed. Often the rhyme would be assigned. At parties the composition of poetry was regularly part of drinking games, with the last to finish required to drink a cup of ale as a "forfeit."

Composition of poetry at banquets held by emperors, princes, and friends had a long tradition. From the late seventh century on we see less-formal poetry parties held with increasing frequency. Sometimes a group of friends would gather and pay a visit, either by surprise or by prearrangement. Such an occasion required verses from the visitors and the host. Visits, either individual or by a group, often required compliments for the host's dwelling (usually the surroundings rather than the house) and the pleasures of the company enjoyed. Universal rituals of politeness became poetry in the Tang, and in some cases they became poetry that is still read with pleasure.

Qiu Wei, a minor poet of the first half of the eighth century, composed a memorable version of a topic that can be traced back to the Southern Dynasties: "visiting the recluse and not finding him in." In the Tang a "recluse" usually meant simply someone who was neither an examination candidate nor an official; such a person would, however, be celebrated as a recluse in the proper sense. Qiu Wei praised the surroundings of the recluse's dwelling and left, saying that he understood the person from the dwelling and the place, and therefore did not need to meet the man in person. Wang Wei (699 or 701–761) took the social situation yet one more level in an equally memorable poem. A friend visited Wang Wei when he was not in, and Wang Wei wrote to acknowledge the visit, imagining Mr. Su looking for the poet:

> . . .
> A fishing boat, stuck to the frozen shore,
> hunters' fires burning upon the cold moor.
> All there was: out beyond the white clouds,
> a bell's infrequent tolling broke through gibbons' night cries.

Mr. Su's gaze, hoping to discover the returning poet, runs out to the margin of his field of vision, from which comes only the enigmatic sound of a temple bell.

Group excursions likewise called for poems. Perhaps the most memorable was in 752, when a group of poets – including Cen Shen (ca 715–770), Gao Shi (ca 702–765), Chu Guangxi (ca 706–763), and Du Fu (712–770) – together climbed to the top of the pagoda of Ci'en Temple in Chang'an (surviving in modern Xi'an as Greater Wild Goose Pagoda). All marveled at the pagoda's height and the range of vision it provided. From this "perspective" some vowed to follow the truth of Buddhism; others did not; Du Fu saw ominous political problems looming. Although we do not know the sequence of composition, when we read such poems together, we see how they respond to each other, giving each poem in the set a resonance that it lacks when read alone.

Parting had been a common occasion for poetry since the third century. While it varied in the Tang according to situation, it was a social ritual. Friends would sometimes accompany the traveler on the first stage of the journey, then hold a banquet and send the traveler on his way, often the next morning. The parting banquet had its roots in actual ritual, and the highly conventional nature of most parting poems is a good example of how poetry could serve as the individual re-creation of ritual. There are many famous and memorable Tang parting poems; some work through the conventions, but some depart from them altogether.

Most Tang prose letters surviving in the received tradition were composed with the clear intention of preserving them for the author's collected writings, though we may presume they were actually sent. From Dunhuang and elsewhere in the dry sands of Central Asia we have everyday letters. Poetry, however, was commonly used in place of both formal and informal letters. Prose letters would often discuss some intellectual or political issue; verse epistles would tell about what the writer was experiencing or ask about the recipient.

Both prose and verse letters were sent to superiors seeking patronage and preferment. Literature was essential to making a name for oneself, and young writers would often prepare small collections of their poetry and/or prose to circulate among highly placed officials. Some scholars believe that from the last part of the eighth century, tales were used for this purpose as well, showing off the author's style while entertaining the prospective patron.

Poems circulated among friends, and sometimes would spread quickly through a general readership in cities like Chang'an. A recipient of a poem or even a casual reader could compose a "companion piece" (he), responding to the earlier poem. Verse letters and poems presented directly to someone often called for an "answer" (da or chou). Where we have both the original and the answer, we see how necessary the former is to understanding the latter; yet some answering poems are among the most famous Tang poems, even without the poem they were answering.

Poems were composed on travels and on sites visited; meeting someone on a journey also invited a poem. If the poet visited some ancient site, he would write a "meditation on the past" (huaigu); if it was a place associated with his personal past, the poem would be "stirred by traces of [my] past" (ganjiu).

Death was, of course, an important occasion. There were a number of prose genres that took different roles, many of them ritual, in response to death. It seems likely that the composition of grave memoirs (muzhi ming) was an important source of income for some writers. Poetry, too, had its laments, ranging from the personal response to the highly formalized "pallbearers' songs" (wan ge), in the Tang reserved for members of the aristocracy and imperial family.

Yuefu permitted the poet to play a number of stylized roles: the young nobleman (a splendid wastrel), the wandering man-at-arms (righteous, heroic, and sometimes sad), the frontier soldier (eager to gain fame, eager to serve the emperor, lonely for home), the lonely woman (whose man is fighting on the frontier, enjoying himself with courtesans, or simply off wandering). Yuefu used old titles or variations on old titles. Although it had clear roots in the pre-Tang period, a new genre developed in the Tang, closely related to *yuefu* and imperfectly distinguished from it. These were "songs" (*gexing*, to be distinguished from "song lyrics," *ci*, a genre that developed in the last part of our era as new words for popular melodies). "Songs" were often in stanzas and predominantly in the seven-syllable line, and, like *yuefu*, they were distinguished by a manner of presentation rather than by the actual practice of singing. As a rule of thumb, *yuefu* use pre-Tang *yuefu* titles and roles, while "songs" made up new titles and often have the poet himself as a speaker.

The "poem on history" (*yongshi shi*) was a pre-Tang topic that was not very widely practiced in the eighth century, though it became very popular again in the ninth century, both in individual poems and in sets of quatrains on chronologically arranged moments in history. "Poems on things" (*yongwu shi*) were always popular. At one extreme we find Empress Wu's literary courtier Li Qiao (645–714) composing 120 "poems on things," giving a very standard rhetorical treatment of each (the set received a mid-eighth-century commentary by Zhang Tingfang). Like Chinese literary encyclopedias (*leishu*), these poems provided examples of how to treat a topic with the proper allusions. At another extreme we have imaginative transformations of the "thing" in highly specific contexts. Li Qiao gives an exemplary, but very wooden, poem on the "horse." When Gao Xianzhi, a famous general of the Tang's Central Asian armies, arrived in Chang'an in 751, Du Fu wrote on the general's horse.

> The Westland's Protector-General's Turkish blue dapple,
> its fine reputation came here to the east in a flash.
> In the battle line this very horse has been long unrivaled,
> of one mind with its master to achieve great deeds.
> Those deeds achieved, special nurture follows it where it goes,
> and now, wind-tossed, it comes from afar, from Drifting Sands.
> A stallion's manner, never accepting the kindness of the trough,
> a fierce spirit, still longing to seize the advantage in battle . . .

"General Gao's Dapple" may be the product of horse-lore, but the horse is at the same time the counterpart of the great general himself.

The elastic notion of the "ancient" was a powerful force in Tang poetry. Chen Zi'ang's (661–702) "Stirred by Experiences" (Ganyu) from the late seventh century began a legacy of poems, some of which were called "Stirred by Experiences," but many of which went by other titles. A group of such poems were gathered at the beginning of Li Bai's (701–762) poetry collection under the title "Ancient Style" (Gufeng). By easily recognized stylistic and thematic gestures, such poems evoked a sense of intense personal engagement with society and the polity, with the poet as social critic, in ways that were associated with older poetry, particularly poetry from the Han and Wei.

The Tang inherited a map of literary-historical styles, genres, and character types, each with its own associations. Over the course of the Tang, this "map" was extended and more sharply defined. The complexity of such a repertoire enabled combinations and transformations that were original in the best sense of the word. Not only were there new distinctions of type and place, new categories were also added. By the ninth century we have a world of particular detail and nuance that seems close to the lived world.

I. The age of Empress Wu (650–712)

On July 10, 649, Emperor Taizong passed away. His heir, later known as Emperor Gaozong, was a sensible, but weak-willed, young man, whose accession to the throne had been supported by his maternal uncle, the powerful statesman Zhangsun Wuji. The preceding century had witnessed a series of short-lived dynasties, which were sustained by the canniness and charisma of individual rulers rather than by enduring institutions. These dynasties had generally collapsed after the second or third generation, under successors who lacked the gifts of the first emperors. When Gaozong took the throne as the third Tang emperor, the familiar pattern seemed to be repeating itself.

History did, indeed, repeat itself. In Emperor Gaozong's case, however, the power that appeared behind the weakened throne was not that of an ambitious minister, but of his empress, styled Wu Zhao, and known to posterity as Empress Wu. Originally a minor concubine in Emperor Taizong's harem, by 655 she had replaced Gaozong's existing empress and exercised ever greater political control. As Emperor Gaozong's health rendered him increasingly incapacitated, she took over complete control of the empire; after his death in 683, she briefly put her two surviving sons on the throne in rapid succession, then ruled on her own. In 690 she proclaimed her own dynasty, the Zhou, thus ending the Tang after the third actual generation. The Tang was, however, saved for another two centuries because, after her death in 705, her sons and successors bore the Tang imperial surname Li. Albeit unwittingly, Empress Wu was in large measure responsible for giving China her most stable and longest-lived dynasty since the Han.

Her eldest surviving son, Emperor Zhongzong, reigned for five years after Empress Wu's death, but power remained in the hands of court women, primarily his wife Empress Wei and his sister, the formidable Taiping Princess.

The throne then passed to his brother, Ruizong, and after that to Ruizong's son, Li Longji, who was determined to rule as well as reign. With the abdication of his father, Li Longji took the throne in 712 to become the most famous of all Tang emperors, known as Emperor Xuanzong.

Empress Wu's half-century of effective rule and the half-decade of dominance by court women that followed was a unique and underappreciated period in Chinese literary history. The empress favored spectacular rule, frequently changing the reign name with attendant amnesties, staging ceremonies, receiving portents of her legitimacy, and above all transporting the court on grand excursions. She populated her days with events, and her constellation of literary courtiers celebrated each event in turn with the polished rhetoric that befitted the aura that was invested in each. If Emperor Taizong had assumed the role of the self-critical and deferential Confucian ruler, the empress presented herself as divinely authorized (the only possible justification for a woman ruler in a contemporary context); and the function of her literary courtiers was praise and reaffirmation of her legitimacy.

The most enduring strain in the Chinese literary tradition valued not praise, but a persuasive representation of the writer's true feelings and an intense, usually critical, engagement with the problems of society and the polity. As a consequence the writers of her reign most appreciated later were often not the great literary courtiers, but those who were unsuccessful or presented themselves as critics of a woman's empire.

Although we still find members of the powerful old families in Empress Wu's court, the empress wanted her own men, and these were acquired primarily through the literary examination (*jinshi*), which took on a greater importance and new form during her rule. An epitaph recovered from a stele gives the earliest evidence of the most striking feature of literature's ties to political life in the Tang: by 679 the composition of poetry and *fu* was used in the literary examination. These components of the examination were added to the older essay question on policy, ritual, or some moral issue. Throughout the rest of the Tang there were sporadic objections to the poetry and *fu* components of the examination, and several times those components were suspended for a year. They were, nevertheless, very popular parts of the examination, seeming to embody the literary examination's openness to "talent," broadly defined, and hence to the examination's meritocratic promise.

Examination poetry and *fu* preserved the court rhetoric of Empress Wu's age for centuries, long after the style had gone out of fashion outside of court. The topics were set by the examiners and shared by all examinees.

The 679 examination, for example, asked for a poem on the theme "Many Are the Pleasures of Court and Wilderness," a line from Zhang Xie's poem "On History," included in *Selections of Refined Literature*; the *fu* topic was "The Ruler and His Officers Share the Same Virtue." Both the poem and the *fu* required a strict structure of exposition in parallel couplets, eventually with prosodic requirements in balancing tones. It was not a system designed to produce great literary works (though successful works were closely studied for practical purposes), but it was a rhetorical discipline that unified a community of writers and readers for more than three centuries.

The poetry requirement in the literary examination has often been seen as an important stimulus for the flowering of poetry in the eighth century. The relation is more indirect and already apparent in the late seventh century: the increasing promise of office through the literary examination brought together young men with a shared rhetorical training. In the social life of the capital – writing at parties, to friends, and to senior literary men who might be patrons – a less formal poetry developed.

Those who passed the examination and entered the court literary establishment were called upon to celebrate court occasions, but they were often enlisted to work on various scholarly projects. The state played an important role in both sponsoring and authorizing cultural work. We first see this on a large scale in the first half of the sixth century in the Liang dynasty, when Emperor Wu and the princes used literary scholarship as part of a general cultural program to define and strengthen the dynasty. By the seventh century the cultural enterprise was becoming, at least in part, bureaucratized. The state took charge not only of gathering and conserving the textual record, but also of sponsoring large synthetic scholarly projects. Although the center of literary culture shifted from the court to the elite over the eighth and ninth centuries, the state never gave up its claim to be the conservator of past and contemporary culture, including work on the Confucian Classics, history, thought, and more purely literary composition.

Although "literary courtiers," broadly defined, might have had offices throughout the extensive court bureaucracy, two institutions were designated specifically for cultural work. One of these was subordinate to the imperial Chancellery and known in this period as the Office for Extending Literature (*Hongwen guan*); no less prestigious was the Office for the Glory of Literature (*Chongwen guan*) in the crown prince's shadow government. Court cultures everywhere have employed writers to celebrate rulers and their deeds; in China, characteristically, this need was institutionalized in an office that provided both rank and a commensurate fixed stipend. Private scholarship, of course, continued; but on completing their works, private scholars often presented their texts to the throne to gain both the imprimatur of the court and personal recognition.

In the 650s, the first decade of Emperor Gaozong's reign, we can see something of the role of the state in cultural work and its variety. One of the great projects of the first half of the seventh century was a committee, headed by Kong Yingda (574–648), charged with synthesizing and passing judgment on scholarship on the Confucian Classics since the end of the Han. This massive work, *The Correct Significance of the Five Classics* (*Wujing zhengyi*), was first presented to Emperor Taizong in 642. A decade later, in 653, Emperor Gaozong issued an edict that made *The Correct Significance* state-sponsored orthodoxy in the interpretation of the Confucian Classics.

Emperor Taizong had commissioned a set of state-sponsored histories of previous dynasties whose existing histories seemed inadequate. Li Yanshou, a private scholar, undertook briefer and more synthetic versions, *The Northern Histories* (*Bei shi*) and *The Southern Histories* (*Nan shi*). These were presented to the throne in 656, and the imprimatur of the court helped to find them a place in the so-called "standard histories" of dynastic China. In the following year, 657, the famous literary courtier Xu Jingzong (592–672) completed his massive thousand-scroll anthology of pre-Tang literature, *The Grove of Texts from the Literature Office* (*Wenguan cilin*). Here we see another facet of Tang cultural politics. We know that in 686 an envoy from Silla, one of the three kingdoms on the Korean peninsula, came to the Tang court seeking rituals and literary texts and was given selections from *The Grove of Texts*; it was probably in a similar diplomatic context that the anthology made its way to Japan. Although the complete anthology was long lost in China, scattered scrolls have survived in Japan.

The private scholar Li Shan (d. 689) presented his commentary on *Selections of Refined Literature* to the throne in 658. This work, citing the earliest known usage of each phrase in the anthology, set the most common model for subsequent scholarly commentary on literature. The works above, all authorized by the court within a five-year span, are still considered important in Chinese culture and literature.

The grandest of all the court projects was the 1,300-scroll *Pearls of the Three Teachings* (*Sanjiao zhuying*), commissioned by the empress in 699 and completed in 701. This was an epitome of Confucian, Daoist, and Buddhist texts compiled by a large committee of the most distinguished literary courtiers. The epitome itself does not survive, but part of an anthology of poems by its compilers has survived in the Dunhuang manuscripts.

The period of Empress Wu's rule saw a steady stream of anthologies, collections of exemplary couplets, epitomes, and "encyclopedias" (*leishu*, quotations from earlier literature arranged under a systematic set of topics). Since these works are lost, it is easy to overlook their significance; however, in a manuscript culture in which so many complete texts were largely confined to the imperial library, such works seem to have been a primary means by which access to the cultural heritage was acquired. In the preface to a collection of couplets, *Splendid Lines by Poets Old and New* (*Gujin shiren xiuju*), the courtier Yuan Jing wrote of the difficulty of finding the books with which to make a comprehensive selection; in this nine-year project, completed in 670, Yuan Jing acknowledges the central importance of a three-hundred-scroll anthology, one of those court projects, in making material widely available.

The Buddhist church was another site with the institutional structure, the wealth, and the leisure to promote scholarship; no less important, large-scale copying in its scriptoria spread throughout the temples of the empire. In addition to the continuous production of translations of Sanskrit materials (in the Tang primarily done by native Chinese scholars) and commentaries, Buddhist scholars compiled their own anthologies and encyclopedias. In 664 the monk Daoxuan completed the *Expansion of the Propagation of the Light* (*Guang Hongming ji*), an important anthology of earlier pro-Buddhist writings. In 668 the monk Daoshi completed the great Buddhist encyclopedia *The Pearl Grove in the Dharma Park* (*Fayuan zhulin*), which contained not only scriptural material but also retribution narratives.

The seventh century was the last century for major translation projects and the height of Chinese journeys to India, undertaken both under state auspices and as private pilgrimages. The monk Xuanzang (600–664) set off for India without permission, and after a prolonged period visiting the Buddhist kingdoms of northern India and study in a Buddhist university, he returned to Chang'an in 645, where he was received with great honor by Taizong. He devoted the rest of his life to translating the large corpus of Buddhist scriptures that he had brought back to China. On his death in 664 his disciple Huili composed a biography in five scrolls, which was expanded by another disciple in 688 to ten scrolls. Such length was unheard-of in secular biography.

In addition to translation and commentary, Xuanzang also composed *An Account of the Western Regions during the Great Tang* (*Da Tang xiyu ji*) in twelve scrolls, giving concise descriptions of the lands he passed through in his travels. This work has been of great importance for historians of medieval Central Asia and India; for example, one of the cornerstone dates in the history of Sanskrit literature, the approximate period in which the prose-poet

Bāṇa lived, is known because he celebrated a king mentioned by Xuanzang. There was also diplomatic contact with the Indian states; in 664 the imperial envoy Wang Xuance returned to China and composed an account of his travels. Xuanzang traveled over the northern route to India; in 671 the monk Yijing set out for India by the southern ocean route and returned in 691 with Hinayana scriptures; two works of his survive, an account of India and Buddhist practices there and a collection of biographies of earlier monks who had gone to India. Yet another travel account of the Indian pilgrimage was composed by Huichao, a monk from the Tang's closest ally in Korea, Silla, who returned to Chang'an in 727; this has survived in an incomplete version among the Dunhuang manuscripts.

The court culture of Emperor Gaozong's early reign was populated with writers who began their careers during the previous reign. The most famous poet of the 650s and early 660s was Shangguan Yi (608?–664), only a few of whose graceful lyrics survive. Parts of a work on poetics are extant, *An Ornate Roofbeam of Tablet and Brush* (*Bizha hualiang*), with discussions and enumerations of poetic types, kinds of parallelism, and faults in versification, the last of these building on Shen Yue's theory of the "eight faults" of versification. In such works it was common to illustrate each term in an enumeration with exemplary couplets or passages, sometimes followed by a short commentary. Yuan Jing's *Marrow and Brain of Poetry* (*Shi suinao*) is a similar work with surviving sections on euphony and parallelism and is probably also from the 660s. Both of these texts were preserved in Japan; such works on technical poetics fell out of fashion in China and were often lost. This is in striking contrast to technical treatises on calligraphy, of which many have been well preserved, including Sun Guoting's 686 *Handbook of Calligraphy* (*Shu pu*) from the age of Empress Wu.

In 664 Shangguan Yi involved himself in a plot to have the ailing Gaozong remove Empress Wu from power. Informed of what was transpiring, she went and confronted the emperor, who characteristically backed down. The empress then had Shanguan Yi and his entire family executed, sparing only his young granddaughter, whom she took into her service. This was Shangguan Wan'er, whose considerable talents would raise her to become the empress's private secretary in 696 and finally a high-ranking consort of Emperor Zhongzong. She was to become one of the finest poets of the first decade of the eighth century and an arbiter of court literary taste.

The sumptuous rhetoric of court literature, a literature of celebration, had to contend with an enduring strain in the Chinese tradition that distrusted it. For a century and a half cultural critics had lamented the fall of literature from personal engagement and moral seriousness into a fascination with ornament and fine phrasing that seemed like mere play. Such critics often identified moments of radical reform, though such moments always proved to be illusory, merely gradual, or restricted to one person or group. Yang Jiong (650–after 693), himself usually a florid court writer, located one of those apparent moments of reform at the beginning of the 660s, which coincided with the height of Shangguan Yi's popularity:

> In the first year of the Longshuo Reign (661), the style changed in the field of literature. Writers were outdoing one another to construct delicate subtlety; they competed to fashion the most intricate scrollwork . . . They sought success through associations by reflection; they claimed beauty for artificial parallelism. Rugged frame and energy were utterly gone; hardness and vigor were unknown.

The artificial style overthrown was almost certainly the "Shangguan style" (*Shangguan ti*). The writer credited with reforming this sorry state of affairs was Wang Bo (650–676), for whose collected works Yang Jiong was writing a preface. Many of Wang Bo's poems are relatively unornamented, and his works in general have a forcefulness that is indeed distinct from the sometimes mechanical exposition we find in court writers of the era. Wang Bo was, however, sometimes a master of the most florid, ornamental style; and in this, "reform" is hard to see.

Yang Jiong and Wang Bo were counted among the "Four Paragons of the Early Tang" (*Chu Tang sijie*), which also included Lu Zhaolin (ca 634–ca 686) and Luo Binwang (ca 619–684?). Yang Jiong may have felt that Wang Bo changed the fashion for frivolous rhetoric, but Du Fu, writing a century later, refers to his contemporaries' judgment of the "Four Paragons": "Yang, Wang, Lu, and Luo were the style of those days; / 'not serious in their writing' – the sneering never stops." This is hardly a fair judgment, but it does reflect the degree to which even the most serious and "progressive" writers of that age seemed merely flowery from the perspective of the greatly changed literary world of the mid-eighth century.

There were individual connections among the four, but only once – in the winter of 671 – could they all have been at the same place at the same time. They were not a "group" in the later sense, but the four names which, from a later perspective, emerged from this age. Three of them had the attraction of failure, suffering, and untimely but interesting deaths. Wang Bo died at a very early age, probably drowned on an ocean journey in search of his father in Vietnam. Lu Zhaolin spent his last decade suffering from a crippling illness, until at last he drowned himself. Recent scholarship has placed Luo Binwang's date of birth two decades earlier than previously assumed, so he did reach old age. He had a checkered career, including terms of service with Tang armies and several episodes in prison (a not uncommon experience in Empress Wu's reign). In 684, when Empress Wu personally assumed the throne, Luo Binwang joined the rebellion of Xu Jingye and composed a stinging denunciation of the empress that has become a classic of Chinese parallel prose. Luo Binwang presumably died when the rebellion was crushed. Although he did suffer one occasion of "administrative exile" (being posted to a remote and undesirable location), Yang Jiong had a reasonably successful career as one of the empress's literary courtiers.

All four writers were capable of writing in the highly mannered, allusive style of the age, and often did so. Three, however, worked extensively outside the context of the court and its courtiers, which allowed them greater freedom. Lu Zhaolin's best-known works are ballads in the seven-syllable line such as "Chang'an: Ancient Theme" (Chang'an guyi) on the splendor of the great city, but closing with the figure of the isolated scholar. Perhaps his two most remarkable works are in the *sao* style deriving from the *Verses of Chu*, the "Five Sorrows" (Wubei) and the "Resolving Sickness" (Shiji wen), in which his personal suffering is expressed with a historically resonant intensity.

We do not know the works for which the "Four Paragons" were admired in their own day (apart from Luo Binwang's denunciation on Empress Wu, which, as the story goes, led the empress to regret that she did not have the old writer on her side). The works anthologized by later ages show the values of later ages. Wang Bo, for example, composed his *"Fu* on Picking Lotus" (Cailian fu) in a tradition stretching back to the first part of the sixth century; he was clearly demonstrating his rhetorical mastery, outdoing his predecessors in copiousness and allusiveness. Later ages, however, remembered him for a few moving, straightforward poems, for his parallel prose "preface" on the old tower of the prince of Teng (Tenwang ge xu), and for the lovely song attached to the preface that ends: "Where is he now, the prince in the tower? – / beyond the balcony the long river just keeps flowing on."

In 675 the ailing Emperor Gaozong withdrew from active participation in the government, effectively ceding rule entirely to the empress. Among those who passed the literary examination that year were some figures who were to be prominent in court life over the next thirty-five years: Zhang Zhuo (658?–730), Song Zhiwen (ca 656–712), and Shen Quanqi (656–ca 716).

Through most of the Chinese tradition, Zhang Zhuo was known for a collection of anecdotes and a collection of "judgments" (panwen), perhaps the most difficult literary form in the language, in which decisions on legal and ritual matters are tersely presented in elliptical, parallel lines. In the nineteenth century, Chinese scholars rediscovered in Japan a short romance in parallel prose, *The Den of Wandering Immortals* (*Youxian ku*). *The Den of Wandering Immortals* is an elaborate variation on a familiar story of how a wandering scholar encounters a woman or women in his travels, stays with them for an erotic encounter, then leaves. The pleasure of *The Den* is less in the predictable plot than in the literary grace of its telling, its rhetorical banter, mixing vernacular elements with graceful euphuistic prose, interspersed with poems that sometimes are laden with sexual double-entendres. It is quite possible that this is a chance survival from a more widespread genre. There is an extensive commentary probably from the ninth century and, according to Ronald Egan, probably not by a native Chinese.

If we compare this lone work with the tradition of romantic tales that began to appear about a century later, it is easy to see in it the echoes of an aristocratic culture in which women had power at least equal to men. In the later tales the women are often social inferiors (or at best equals) who become eloquent through passion or suffering. The two women protagonists of *The Den of Wandering Immortals* are represented as belonging to one of the most distinguished families of the empire, and their graceful banter of sexual negotiation suggests a self-confidence absent in later heroines. To later ages such a story perhaps lost its appeal because of its disinterest in the representation of deep feeling; however, in their capacity to play with their potential lover, these women belong to an age when social and political hierarchy weighed more heavily than gender hierarchy.

The poets of the "class" of 675, Song Zhiwen and Shen Quanqi, are credited with bringing regulated verse in the five-syllable line to its final form and successfully realizing regulated verse in the seven-syllable line. They share the credit in this with Du Fu's grandfather, Du Shenyan, who passed the literary examination in 671. Tang regulated poetry (including eight-line "regulated verse," the regulated quatrain, and longer recent-style poems) had been slowly evolving since the end of the fifth century. It was first shaped by the systematic avoidance of "faults" in the use of tones and by compositional habits; gradually these two distinct forces converged into something like a fixed form in the first decade of the eighth century, a form that continues to be used. "Recent-style" verse is the general term for poetry that observes a strict balance of tones. "Regulated verse" is its paradigmatic form, consisting of four couplets. Each of its two middle couplets should have internal parallelism, with each word matched categorically in the same position in the other line of the couplet. The consequence is usually grammatical parallelism. Accompanying the empress on an excursion in 696, Song Zhiwen writes,

> Valleys darken, a thousand banners emerge,
> the hills resound, ten thousand carriages come.

"Ten thousand carriages" both represent the scene and are metonymy for the ruler. "Valleys" match "hills"; sight ("darken") matches sound ("resound"); the numbers correspond; "banners" match "carriages" and "emerge" matches "come." The art of the couplet is also the sequence of the lines. Going from "valleys" to "hills," attention moves upward; moving from "darken" to "resound," we go from a negative of light to presence of sound; the numbers increase in sequence, suggesting the gradual emergence of the imperial entourage. The "banners" above the carriages appear first, then the "carriages" themselves; and the process is summed up in the sequence of the verbs "emerge" and "come." This is by no means a particularly artful use of the parallel couplet, but it demonstrates clearly how the relation between particular parallel terms can outline a process.

The last and most important requirement of regulated verse was the pattern of tonal balancing in key syllables in the lines. The initial experiments with tonality in metrics in the late fifth century had distinguished all five tones of Middle Chinese. This had changed to a much simpler distinction between "level" and "deflected" tones, which had a roughly even distribution in the language. The basic principle was, first, that tones alternate in key positions in the line; second, that the pattern of the second line of the couplet be the mirror image of the first line; and third, that each couplet be the mirror image of the preceding couplet.

The appearance of the "recent-style" verse genres, requiring tonal balance and parallelism, produced its counterpart in "ancient-style" verse. In later usage ancient-style verse became a purely formal category, encompassing all poetry that did not strictly follow the rules of recent-style poetry, including poems that were otherwise stylistically indistinguishable from recent-style poetry. In the Tang itself the term "ancient" was generally reserved for poetry and prose that, in values and style, looked back to some vaguely defined earlier era of moral seriousness.

For readers from the mid-eighth century on, the preeminent writer of the second half of Empress Wu's reign was Chen Zi'ang, a native of Sichuan and one of the new men brought to the capitals by the literary examination and prospects of advancement. In the context of contemporary court literary values, his poetry is merely competent. In a few works, however, he touched on dissatisfactions and the lingering desire to reform the style of the age. Soon after his death his devoted editor and admirer Lu Cangyong wrote an independent biography that contributed to his reputation as an outspoken Confucian hero. Chen Zi'ang is remembered for his manifesto given in the preface to a poem entitled "Tall Bamboo" (Xiuzhu pian), restating the conventional story of literary decline in the Southern Dynasties and the possibility of present revival in a plainer poetry of personal engagement. What perhaps distinguished Chen Zi'ang's version of these widely shared values was a polemical intensity that seemed to embody the very engagement he advocated. These values were also seen as embodied in a group of thirty-eight poems gathered under the title "Stirred by Experiences" (Ganyu). Some of these were clearly critical responses to contemporary events; others suggested opinions so perilous that they needed to be veiled in obscurity. The style called to mind that of the third-century poet Ruan Ji, whose poems under the title "Singing My Feelings" were understood as figural criticism of the political situation of his own times. For later readers in the Tang, "Stirred by Experiences" came to represent the "ancient" style, avoiding tonal balancing and the high poetic register of court poetry, and thus suggesting moral judgment and personal concern.

Chen Zi'ang did have difficulties with the empress, but there were few in court who did not. While "Stirred by Experiences" and other pieces do suggest principled criticism of the court, Chen Zi'ang was also sometimes favored by the empress and wrote her praise without embarrassment. Most notably he celebrated the founding of her new Zhou dynasty, which was simultaneously the disestablishment of the Tang. In this Chen Zi'ang is characteristic of the Tang, able to play conflicting roles without showing the contradiction between them.

There was, indeed, much to criticize. Corruption and abuse of power by her favorites and relatives were indeed rampant in Empress Wu's later years; with her abdication and death in 705 the situation grew even worse. The empress's ineffectual son, known as Zhongzong, reigned; but power was contested between his Empress Wei, several princesses, and kinsmen of the old and new empresses. This was also the last and one of the most splendid periods of the literature of court culture. Song Zhiwen, Shen Quanqi, and Du Shenyan were at the height of their powers. It is also the best-preserved period of court culture because a collection of works, *The Account of the Literary Office in the Jinglong Reign* (*Jinglong wenguan ji*), edited by Wu Pingyi and painstakingly reassembled by the modern scholar Jia Jinhua, survived to be copied in large part into a massive Song anthology. Here we find a record of the court outings between 708 and 710, with the poems composed on each occasion.

In the spring of 710, as Zhongzong's brief reign was drawing to a close, we have a fitting epilogue to the era. The courtier and historian Liu Zhiji (661–721) completed his large work on historiography, *The Comprehensive Guide to History* (*Shitong*) in twenty scrolls. This is the summa of the medieval Confucian view of history, in which truth appears through the historical unfolding of the moral order. Liu Zhiji addresses issues of narrative and the way in which language encodes historical meaning. In the preface to this work Liu Zhiji tells us that the work was composed as penance for having been compelled to falsify the record when he served in the court history office, thus violating his principles as a historian. This moment, when a true vocation and its bureaucratic institutionalization were so clearly at odds, suggests the future of literature in the empire.

II. The reign of Emperor Xuanzong: the "High Tang" (712–755)

In late summer of 710, after reigning only five years, Emperor Zhongzong was poisoned, apparently by his Empress Wei and the Anle Princess. The age of grand excursions and poetry parties was abruptly over. Zhongzong's brother took the throne as Emperor Ruizong. Behind the new emperor, however, stood his vigorous and ambitious son Li Longji. Two years later, in 712, Li Longji accepted his father's abdication and became the emperor known in history as Xuanzong. Emperor Xuanzong's reign would end over forty years later, compelled to abdicate to his own son as his empire crumbled around him.

The old community of literary courtiers was broken in the spate of executions and exiles between Zhongzong's death and Xuanzong's final triumph over his aunt, the powerful Taiping Princess, in 713. Zhang Yue (667–730) was one survivor. Once a rising star in Empress Wu's court, Zhang Yue had offended an imperial favorite and been exiled to the far south; he returned as an early partisan of Li Longji and prospered in the new reign. Referred to as "the leader in letters of his generation," Zhang Yue continued to serve Xuanzong as both statesman and literary courtier. Although he has some fine pieces from exile and outside of a court context, he and some other survivors of the older generation helped to perpetuate an ossified version of court poetry in the new reign.

Xuanzong, too, held his formal literary assemblies, celebrating festivities, the departure of officials to take up their posts, and imperial travels. Never again, however, would such formal occasions be the center of literature and taste. Later in his reign Xuanzong created the Hanlin Academy, which was located, significantly, in the Inner Court, the imperial residence, rather than the section of the imperial city devoted to the civil service. Appointment to the Hanlin Academy was by imperial pleasure alone, outside the usual bureaucratic procedures. The Hanlin academicians and attendants of Xuanzong's reign waited on the emperor personally and were often cultural and religious figures from outside the bureaucracy; when a poet was appointed, as Li Bai was for a short period, it was not to write the old court poetry. In short, Emperor Xuanzong was responding to reputations made outside the court.

Great changes were taking place in the world of letters, and some of their variety can be seen in the three most famous poets of Xuanzong's reign. Wang Wei (699 or 701–761) represented the culture of the capital. Wang Wei belonged to one of most distinguished families in the empire; in his youth and young manhood he frequented the courts of princes; he had a good career and wrote often for Xuanzong's court festivities with the opulent formality demanded by such occasions. His training and background were perfect for a literary courtier, yet he made his poetic career out of a rejection of public life with an austere simplicity that was related to his Buddhist faith. His collected poems show that he could write in all the styles then popular, but he most often chose plainness. He celebrated the rustic life, the life of solitude, or the pleasure of particular friends. Beneath his simplicity, however, was a peculiar mind that saw the relationships among the things of the world in a unique way:

> The setting sun goes down beside a bird,
> autumn plains, calm beyond people.

When Wang Wei was referred to as "the master craftsman of poetry of our age" in the 740s, it was a craft informed by the discipline of court poetry but transformed into something different and more profound: it belonged to a poet who used the simplest words to measure the position and motion of the sun in relation to a tiny bird.

Sometime around 743 Wang Wei acquired the estate of the long-dead court poet Song Zhiwen in Lantian, south of Chang'an. The poems he wrote at his estate are among his most famous. He and his good friend Pei Di went through the estate, each writing a quatrain on twenty of its sites. These forty poems were combined in the "Wang River Collection" (Wangchuan ji); they celebrate the rustic world of the region around Chang'an, a quietism that is usually associated with Buddhism, and the divinity that seemed to imbue the locale.

If Wang Wei represented a new transformation of the sophisticated literary culture of the capital, larger social changes were also having an impact on the world of letters. Beginning in the 710s, we begin to see the practice of literature in the provinces – not by dissatisfied courtiers sent out as administrators, but by local writers. Such provincial writers became known by the capital elite because they traveled, but they did not necessarily pass the examination or spend their lives in the capitals.

Meng Haoran (689–740) was just such a provincial, a native of Xiangyang on the Han river. The occasions mentioned in the titles of many of his poems remind us that there were indeed literary circles in the provincial cities, though their work has been largely lost to us. In 712, at the very beginning of Xuanzong's reign, another local poet of the city, Zhang Zirong, ventured north to Chang'an and passed the literary examination. The poetry examination and the gradual opening up of the recruitment process, confirmed by local successes, must have had a powerful effect on the provinces. About fifteen years later, Meng Haoran himself went first to Luoyang to make connections and then to Chang'an in 728 to take the examination himself. Like thousands of others, he failed. Meng Haoran has no extant *fu*, which was half of the purely literary section of the examination; and his work does not suggest the rhetorical training to write a successful examination poem or *fu*. Wang Wei met Meng Haoran that year and was present when Meng set off for home; in the parting poem Wang Wei told him with unusual directness that he should go back to the life of a "recluse" and give up trying to pass the examination.

It is not at all clear that in 728 Meng Haoran was appreciated as a poet or stood out from the crowd of failed candidates. Afterwards Meng Haoran traveled, made more contacts, and in 734 Li Bai, already a rising star, visited Xiangyang and praised Meng Haoran effusively as someone who disdained public office (though again making no reference to him as a poet). Meng Haoran did finally briefly hold one post, a low position on the staff of the writer and statesman Zhang Jiuling (678–740).

Meng Haoran apparently first became known as an eccentric personality, a free spirit who cared only for drinking and poetry. Such an image of disdain for public life was, in fact, a route to enter it; and more than a few of Meng Haoran's poems suggest that he hoped for the kind of recognition that would lead to a public career. The earliest surviving praise of his poetry came after his death, in the preface to his works by his editor and admirer Wang Shiyuan. Wang Shiyuan's praise is hyperbolic and largely conventional; the most suggestive section of the preface, rhetorically confirming Meng's indifference to fame, is the claim that Meng threw away his poems after composing them and that

Wang Shiyuan had to go around and gather the poems from people who had kept them. Wang Shiyuan was writing in the 740s, an age that admired eccentricity and flamboyance, and Meng Haoran's reputation rose. By 750, ten years after his death, the poetry collection was copied out in a fine hand and presented to the imperial library. The eccentric provincial poet had become a cultural luminary.

Li Bai was more than just a provincial. Many scholars suspect that his ancestry was, at least in part, not Han Chinese. He grew up in rural Sichuan and was obviously a voracious reader – though at one point he claimed that he had been a young tough. He was learned but untrained; his writing shows none of the formal discipline that came as second nature to Wang Wei. For Li Bai this was a liberty that enabled him to write in ways that were unprecedented. Li Bai had a theatrical flair; he invented himself, and through his poetry advertised himself, as an eccentric, a drinker, and a Daoist initiate. In 725, he left Sichuan and traveled down the Yangzi seeking patrons, enjoying himself, and studying Daoism. His reputation steadily grew, and in 742 he was summoned to court and given a place in the Hanlin Academy. He never took the examination; it is unlikely that he would have been recommended to do so or that he would have been successful. By the 740s, however, poetic talent no longer needed the confirmation of the literary examination to be recognized.

It is hard to separate the grains of truth from the mass of legend about Li Bai's brief period with Xuanzong – the Chief Eunuch Gao Lishi having to wash his feet, court ladies gathered around on a freezing day breathing warmth on writing brushes so that he could write out edicts for the emperor, coming drunk to an imperial summons. The last of these images is close to how he was portrayed by his devoted admirer Du Fu.

> Li Bai makes a hundred poems with one gallon of ale,
> in the marketplace of Chang'an he sleeps in the tavern.
> The Son of Heaven called for him, he wouldn't board the boat,
> declaring: "Your humble servant is an immortal in his ale."

A few years later, he left court, apparently no longer in favor, and continued his wanderings and his poetry. In striking contrast to Meng Haoran, Li Bai carefully conserved his work and twice asked friends to edit his literary collection (which would be complete only on his death).

Although his *yuefu*, "songs" (*gexing*), and impromptu pieces are his best-known works, his poetry collection contains a large number of less-often read occasional pieces to "friends," many of whom were also probably patrons. We might see Li Bai as one of the first "professional" poets in China. Meng Haoran was probably supported by a local estate in Xiangyang; Li Bai, however, had no visible means to support himself, and his continuous travels throughout the greater part of his career were probably due less to wanderlust than to a continuing need to find new patrons, to get room and board and a tangible token of appreciation. His flamboyant poetic persona was part of his profession, as in the famous *yuefu* "Bring On the Ale" (Jiang jin jiu):

> For satisfaction in this life taste pleasure to the limit
> and never let your golden cup be empty in the moonlight.
> Heaven bred in me talents, they must be put to use,
> I toss away a thousand in gold, it comes right back to me.
> So boil a lamb, butcher an ox, make merry for a while,
> in one sitting you must down three hundred cups.

At the end of the *yuefu*, however, it is clear who should pay for the feast:

> So you, my host, why do you say you're short on cash?
> Go out right now, buy ale – and I'll do the pouring.
> Take the dapple horse,
> take the furs worth a fortune,
> just call for the boy to take them to pawn for fine ale,
> and here together we'll melt away the sorrows of eternity!

Judging from his occasional poems, Li Bai had a large number of such "hosts."

We have many sources for contemporary taste in poetry – other poems, prose works like prefaces, and the rich body of anecdotal literature (of varying degrees of credibility). We should avoid thinking of the period in terms of the poetic canon that formed later, a canon in which Wang Wei, Meng Haoran, and Li Bai have unquestioned centrality (we will reserve fuller comment on Du Fu for the period after the rebellion). There were distinct groups, and taste changed over the more than four decades of Xuanzong's rule. We have a nice anecdote about Zhang Yue and Xu Jian, two elderly literary courtiers from the days of Empress Wu who had survived to become prominent court scholars under Xuanzong, holding a discussion in 728 comparing the old court writers who had participated in compiling *Pearls of the Three Teachings* with the younger generation of Xuanzong's reign. As one might expect, in their view the older writers were perfect, while each member of the younger generation was flawed in some way. Yet it is said that, in 724, Zhang Yue, the director of the Secretariat, had a couplet of the recent poet Wang Wan written on the wall of the hall where he conducted business.

A good comparison of variations in contemporary taste can be seen in two surviving poetry anthologies from the period. The first was *The Outstanding*

Talents of the Dynasty (Guoxiu ji), whose earliest form was completed in 744 by Rui Tingzhang. Although our present version of this anthology seems to have been modified after the rebellion, it is likely that its basic form was mostly unchanged. This was largely made up of regulated verse and gave the greatest representation to one Lu Zhuan, a poet who is now almost entirely unread. The anthology begins with the literary courtiers of Empress Wu's reign and continues through Xuanzong's reign.

The anthology with the greatest subsequent prestige was the *The Glorious Spirits of Our Rivers and Chief Mountains (Heyue yingling ji)*, with a preface by the compiler Yin Fan dated to 753. This anthology includes *yuefu*, "songs," and "ancient-style" verse, along with regulated verse. In his preface Yin Fan tells the standard story of the decline of literature in the late Southern Dynasties and its revival in the Tang, with the final perfection in the reign of Xuanzong. The anthology includes 275 poems by twenty-five poets, working between 714 and 753, with a brief evaluative preface heading the selection for each poet. Lu Zhuan is not included. With the exception of Du Fu, most of whose creative life came later and whose reputation was made later still, we find here not only all the best-known poets of the "High Tang," but also some of the poems that have been continuously anthologized up to the present. The poet–statesmen Zhang Yue and Zhang Jiuling were not included, and in his preface Yin Fan explicitly states that he did not include anyone because of their social prominence or political power. If Zhang Yue was not included, Wang Wan, whose couplet Zhang Yue had written on his office wall, was included (indeed, the anthology is the source of the anecdote).

The cultural changes that were taking place can be seen in the preferences of Emperor Xuanzong himself, whose interests took him outside the closed world of the older court culture. Nowhere is this more evident than in Xuanzong's love of popular music. Imperial taste in music was seen as a weighty matter for court ritualists; music was seen as influencing the general customs of the populace. There was, therefore, some consternation when one of Xuanzong's first cultural acts was the establishment of two music academies (*jiaofang*) dedicated to popular music (714). Protests were made in vain when the Emperor imported professional musicians and women singers to staff these institutions. We have extensive information about titles and performers, much of it from Cui Lingqin's *Account of the Music Academies (Jiaofang ji)*, a nostalgic memoir by a former guardsman composed after the rebellion. In addition we have numerous descriptions of performances in poetry and *fu*. There was a notation system, but the scores have been largely lost, except for some pieces from Dunhuang and later transcriptions from Korea and Japan.

The interpretation of these scores remains, however, a matter of scholarly contention.

Although poetry was generally voiced in a kind of chanting, poems were often sung, particularly quatrains and four-line segments taken out of longer poems. There is a famous story of three poets – Gao Shi, Wang Zhihuan (688–742), and Wang Changling (ca 690–ca 756) – in a tavern, each betting that the singing girls would sing one of his quatrains. While the particulars of the anecdote are probably apocryphal, the anecdote depends on the assumption that a contemporary poet's verses would circulate orally and might be sung in relatively popular venues.

As the poetry of the elite reached tavern singers, the news of the day was often transformed into literary song. We expect the poems we find on grand public events, but we also find poems versifying more general news. In 746 a woman from Donghai killed her husband's murderer; although such acts of private vengeance were generally condoned and admired, a local official had to petition the throne for a pardon. This was material for a Li Bai ballad:

> . . .
> Her silver blade gleams like snow,
> her true heart stirs dark Heaven.
> Every ten paces she leaps up twice,
> giving three shouts the weapons met.
> She hangs his head from the city gate
> and goes kicking and trampling his guts.
> In venting the fury of a spouse
> the Highest Good is bright and clear.
> . . .

We do not know if such pieces were actually sung, but they gestured to ballad traditions, both old literary traditions and popular ones.

As Tang armies penetrated ever more deeply into Central Asia and Silk Road traffic brought an influx of foreign goods and foreign culture, Central Asian music and dance became popular both in the court and in Chang'an. The whirling dances of Central Asia particularly excited Chinese spectators; watching one of these dances, the poet Cen Shen heaped scorn on Chinese native dances as "mere dances" and noise, while the Turkoman "whirl" had divinity. Sometime around 718, the commander of the Liangzhou garrison, one Yang Jingshu, presented to the throne a piece of Central Asian music entitled "Balamen" ("Brahma" in sinified Sanskrit); this seems to have been the basis for the ballet suite "Skirts of Rainbow, Feather Coats" (Nichang yuyi), perhaps the most famous piece of music in premodern China, always associated with the reign and fate of Xuanzong. The actual historical origins of the piece were soon transformed into a popular legend that the dreaming Xuanzong was summoned to the moon by Chang E, the goddess of the moon; he heard the music there and on waking transcribed it from memory. The emperor then gave the score to the imperial music ensemble to practice. A famous flautist, Li Mo, listened to the rehearsals outside the palace wall and memorized the music, by which it entered the world outside the palace.

The legend was part of a cycle of interlocking anecdotes about Xuanzong that took shape after the rebellion, but the motif of the heavenly origins of the music came in part from its new title, "Skirts of Rainbow, Feather Coats," which suggests the Daoist realms of gods and immortals. The new title was clearly linked to Xuanzong's passion for Daoism, which grew in intensity in the 740s. Although Xuanzong's devotion to Daoism was clearly something more personal, sponsorship of Daoism by the Tang imperial house was also good policy, in that the imperial Li family claimed descent from the Daoist sage Laozi (Li Dan). Xuanzong gave Daoism precedence over Buddhism at court and established a series of provincial temples to Laozi, which were, in effect, adjuncts of the imperial cult. With reverent awe Du Fu visited the Laozi temple outside Luoyang:

> . . .
> Its sapphire tiles lie beyond the first chill,
> golden pillars rise beside the Elemental Vapor.
> Mountains and rivers brace well-wrought windows,
> sun and moon hang close on its sculpted beams.
> . . .

Du Fu was not known for his interest in Daoism, and in this, one of his earliest poems, the sacredness of the temple is inseparable from his reverence for the dynasty, whose former rulers were painted on the walls by the most famous of Tang painters, Wu Daozi.

Daoism's arcane terminology and rich pantheon had a particular aura for Tang readers (though it was not popular in later ages). Li Bai often used his knowledge of Daoism in his poetry, but he remained, above all, a secular poet. Others, like his friend Wu Yun (d. 778), wrote an essentially religious poetry of mystical vision. Xuanzong welcomed Daoist adepts; Wu Yun arrived at court at about the same time as Li Bai and, like Li Bai, was given a position in the Hanlin Academy. While Li Bai was making a legend of himself by drinking and writing poetry, Wu Yun was writing discourses to instruct the emperor in Daoist mysteries. In 754, he presented Xuanzong with the *Arcane Net* (*Xuangang*) in three volumes. We cannot date Wu Yun's sets of Daoist poems, "Pacing the Void" and "Roaming as an Immortal," or his several remarkable *fu* on mystical experiences, but he was the outstanding writer of Daoist religious literature in Xuanzong's reign.

Any student of Chinese history knows that as a government China never ceased to be deeply engaged in its foreign relations, as any successful polity must be; there were, however, long periods when the majority of writers and intellectuals were not interested in the world outside China. This was not true in the Tang. Throughout Xuanzong's long reign the Tang was contesting control of Central Asia with the equally expansionist Tibetan kingdom and battling with the Khitan and Xi in the northeast. Tang armies reached what is modern Afghanistan, and in 751 an army under the Korean-born general Gao Xianzhi met an Arab army of the Caliphate at the Talas river. The result was serious defeat for the Tang army, but not a strategically significant one in the short run. In the long run it foretokened the end of the Central Asian Buddhist kingdoms.

Poetry about Chinese military experience in Central Asia had taken on its first mature form in the Southern Dynasties. Needless to say, the Han dynasty military ventures described in such poems were entirely products of the poetic imagination, responding to what poets had read in the old histories. Such poetry became highly conventional, and those conventions continued to dominate frontier poetry in the seventh century, even for a poet like Luo Binwang who personally served with Tang armies.

In Emperor Xuanzong's reign there was a new vitality in frontier poetry. It was not that the historical context had changed: Tang armies had been deeply engaged in Central Asia in Empress Wu's reign. Most of the poets who wrote about the frontier had never been there, as in earlier times. The change was in poetry itself and a new freedom of invention, which was at the same time a freedom of the imagination. Poets lamented the loneliness and suffering of Tang troops, celebrated Tang victories, or wrote of the futility of the wars. Wang Changling writes of approaching the Lintao garrison, on the edge of the frontier:

> I let my horse drink, crossed autumn waters,
> the water cold, the wind like a knife.
> Before the sun sank on the level sands,
> I could see Lintao in the growing dark.
> By the Great Wall they battled in olden days,
> and all say how high their mettle was.
> Brown dust aplenty, both now and then
> and white bones tangled in the brush.

Wang Changling seems to speak here as a personal witness, even though the poem is a *yuefu*, inviting a fictional persona. This and other poems are so vivid that Wang Changling's biographers have endeavored to locate some time in his life when he could have visited the frontier. He may have visited the frontier; he may not have. Ultimately in poems like this it is impossible to distinguish personal experience from poetic imagination.

We can more readily assume some basis in personal experience in Du Fu's "Ballad of the Army Wagons" (Bingju xing), which sets the scene around Chang'an, with a long column of conscripts heading north to the Wei River Bridge and off to the frontier. A bystander elicits a monologue from one of the conscripts, who complains of the length of service, deserted farmland, and the anticipation of a futile death on the frontier. A Tang paper fragment with a few lines of this poem has been found in the sands of Central Asia, testifying that the poem traveled where the troops did.

The two poets most strongly associated with frontier poetry in the period are Gao Shi and Cen Shen. Gao Shi visited the northeastern frontier on several occasions; on one of these he was the local official designated to accompany the conscripts to the army headquarters. His most famous poem from 738 is entitled "Song of Yan" (Yan being the old name for the region where the main army of the northeast was headquartered). "Song of Yan" was a companion piece to someone else's poem, now lost, and its scenes are imagined but vivid. In one stanza he describes an attack in a storm:

> Gloomy, the hills and rivers to the frontier's farthest ends,
> Khitan horsemen charge them, mixed with the wind and rain.
> Troops fighting in the front ranks, just half are still alive,
> while beauties in the general's tent continue to dance and sing.

The final line would not endear him to the commander.

Cen Shen twice served in an administrative post with the Central Asian armies in the 750s and had direct experience of life on the frontier. Writing in the flamboyant descriptive style of the day, Cen Shen described volcanoes, tent banquets in a snowstorm, and the great general Feng Changqing leading the army out of Bugur to meet an enemy incursion.

The Tang was a cosmopolitan dynasty, with travelers going to India and merchants from around the Indian Ocean coming to Yangzhou. The last Sassanian prince, fleeing the Arabs, took up lodging in the northeastern quarter of Chang'an, which had its Zoroastrian fire temples, its Manichean temples, and its Nestorian churches, along with its Buddhist and Daoist temples. Tang visual arts took great pleasure in representing non-Chinese. The best relations were with Silla, the Tang's ally on the Korean peninsula, and Japan, which sent a constant stream of envoys and monks as it absorbed both native Chinese and Buddhist culture. When, in 753, Abe no Nakamaro set off on his return to Japan, Wang Wei and others celebrated his departure with poems, for which Wang Wei wrote an elegant preface in parallel prose.

Popular music, imperial patronage of Daoism, and foreign military adventures, exacerbated by the misrule of Xuanzong's chief ministers in the 740s and early 750s, could not but provoke the austere, moralizing strain in the tradition that was vaguely associated with Confucian values. As in poetry, we see here a shift away from the court to the larger community of the elite. In 729, Wu Jing (670–749), one of the grand old scholars left over from Empress Wu's days, presented the *Essentials of Government of the Zhenguan Reign* (*Zhenguan zhengyao*) in ten scrolls to the throne, giving an idealized picture of Emperor Taizong and his famous Confucian minister Wei Zheng. The image of perfection here held up before Xuanzong was one of cooperative rule between the emperor and his advisers, manifest primarily in the adviser correcting the emperor's failings and the emperor heeding the advice. Xuanzong was, however, Empress Wu's grandson, and he inherited something of her autocratic style of rule.

A more aggressive Confucian moralizing took shape outside the court, closely associated with the legacy of Chen Zi'ang's preface to "Tall Bamboo." From the early 740s we have the preface to a lost anthology of prose by one Shang Heng that divides prose into a hierarchical triad: the prose of the "superior man" (*junzi*), the prose of the "man with aims" (*zhishi*), and the prose of a mere "writer" (*cishi*). The discourse of literary decline (and, by implication, cultural decline) and revival was widely shared. If there is a demarcation that sets the majority of the cultural community off from the Confucian moralizers, it may be found in the majority's affirmation that the reign of Xuanzong had accomplished the desired literary and cultural revival. The Confucian moralizers were not satisfied. We see a cultivated discourse of archaism that was the beginning of an intellectual movement that would bear its fullest fruit at the end of the century, associated with the idea of "restoring antiquity" (*fugu*).

Already in the 740s we have the prose writer Xiao Yingshi (717–768) making comments like, "One must esteem the ancients; I have never paid attention to anything since the Wei and Jin." With such a position went a stylized pride and contempt for the social hierarchy. Xiao Yingshi gained notoriety for satirizing the powerful minister Li Linfu in his "*Fu* on Felling a Cherry Tree."

The most striking figure among the moralists was Yuan Jie (719–772), who, like Du Fu, failed the examination of 747. Du Fu continued to make connections, enjoyed the life of the city, and composed *fu* to catch the emperor's attention. Yuan Jie, by contrast, withdrew to compile three dialogue–essays called the "Imperial Plan" (Huangmo) and a set of moral verses in archaic style, provided with a preface and discussions. Such small collections of writings were designed to catch the attention of patrons, whose support could play an important role in success in the examination. Although he may have had particular recipients in mind who would welcome such a collection, Yuan Jie was out of touch with the temper of the times. In 748 he produced a "Discourse on the Beggar" (Gailun), in which a beggar defends the dignity of his profession in comparison with other kinds of less overt "begging" that were the essence of elite society. By 750, Yuan Jie had withdrawn from the world, grandly styling himself "Master Yuan" (Yuanzi). He finally passed the examination in 754 and after the rebellion went on to serve the troubled empire with distinction as a provincial administrator. In 760 he compiled a small anthology of poets representing what he saw as "ancient" values and moral engagement, entitling it *The Collection in a Satchel* (*Qiezhong ji*).

Tang writers were bound together by networks of friendship and association. Sometimes these bonds centered on shared patrons; when Li Bai celebrated Meng Haoran, he had come to Xiangyang to visit Han Chaozong, also a sponsor of Meng Haoran. Such bonds were also intergenerational, with younger writers aligning themselves with older writers. The story of resurgent Confucian values in Xuanzong's reign can be best traced back to Yuan Dexiu (696–754), not known as a writer but as a moral exemplar. Probably in the late 730s Li Hua's (715?–774?) elder brother made himself Yuan Dexiu's disciple and was a friend of Xiao Yingshi. When Yuan Dexiu died, Li Hua and Yuan Jie wrote funerary inscriptions. These men were in turn associated with the poet Gao Shi and the famous calligrapher and writer Yan Zhenqing (708/9–784). The Confucian credentials of Gao Shi and Yan Zhenqing were confirmed by their service to the dynasty in the rebellion, when so many other literary figures surrendered or fled to the relative safety of Jiangnan.

Li Hua was one of the preeminent prose writers of the age, best known in his own day for his monumental "*Fu* on Hanyuan Palace" (Hanyuan dian fu) of 748, celebrating one of the main palace buildings in Chang'an. To later readers he is best known for his "Lament on an Ancient Battlefield" (Diao gu zhanchang wen), a remarkable piece of lyric prose imagining an ancient battle and turning at last to the futility of war. In many of his writings he belongs to the Confucian moralists and was much admired by Han Yunqing, Han

Yu's uncle, and Han Yu's elder brother, Han Hui, who was responsible for Han Yu's education. Han Yu, writing around the turn of the ninth century, was the preeminent stylist of "ancient prose" (*guwen*) of the dynasty. One of Han Yu's closest friends was the older poet Meng Jiao, who composed a very strange and striking set of ten laments for the long-dead Yuan Dexiu. In this sequence we can see something of the lineages of kinship, personal affinity, and admiration that tied generations together and formed closely knit sub-traditions in the wider field of literature.

From his second year on the throne, Xuanzong's long reign was divided into two reign periods: the Kaiyuan reign (713–741), in which Xuanzong was a very active ruler, and the Tianbao reign (742–756), which witnessed a change in imperial style and the temper of the times. In the Tianbao, Emperor Xuanzong increasingly relaxed his direct involvement in government. Li Linfu ("honey on the lips and a sword in the heart") was his minister. Yang Yuhuan was taken from the harem of one of his sons, the prince of Shou, and became Xuanzong's favorite. The emperor's infatuation with Lady Yang, the "Prize Consort" (*Guifei*, the highest harem rank next to empress), became legendary. When Li Linfu died, one of Lady Yang's relatives, Yang Guozhong, replaced him as chief minister. Every winter the emperor took the court to Huaqing Palace on Mount Li, just east of Chang'an, where the hot springs provided comfort against the winter cold. In a famous passage Du Fu passed the mountain, on a journey north to his family:

> . . .
> At the break of dawn I passed Mount Li,
> the royal throne there on its rugged crags.
> Battle flags stuff the cold sky,
> valley slopes smooth from pounding hooves.
> Steam swells up from Jasper Pool
> to the clacking of the royal guard.
> There lord and courtiers linger in pleasures,
> their music rumbling over vast space.
> All granted baths there wear long ribbons,
> no men with short tunics join those feasts.
> The bolts of silk portioned out in the court
> came from the homes of poor women.
> Their menfolk were flogged with whips,
> collecting taxes to send to the palace.
> . . .

The flamboyance of the first part of the Tianbao turned to apprehension with the increasing tension between Yang Guozhong and An Lushan, the commander of all the armies in the northeast. Finally, late in 755, An Lushan rebelled and quickly took the eastern capital, Luoyang. Then, overrunning the loyalist armies hastily assembled to stop him, his forces marched on Chang'an. In 756 the emperor, Lady Yang, Yang Guozhong, and a handful of attendants and guards fled the capital during the night. At Mawei Station west of the city the guards refused to go on unless Yang Guozhong and Lady Yang were put to death. The emperor reluctantly consented. Afterward the emperor made his way west to refuge in Chengdu. The crown prince went north to assemble loyalist forces, forcing Xuanzong to abdicate in his favor.

The story of Xuanzong's passion for Lady Yang, the rebellion, Lady Yang's enforced suicide, and the disconsolate emperor's longing were the stuff of legend. The richness of verifiable historical material was soon amplified by new incidents and new twists to old incidents. The story and its moments were to become a recurrent theme in Tang poetry and later literature, a way to make sense of the rebellion that changed everything.

III. Buddhist writing

In its attention to and preservation of historical detail, Chinese literature invites literary history. History was the medium in which a writer and work were situated and by which value was granted. Chinese biography was not intended to be the story of the inner "person," but a sequence of offices, contacts, and journeys locating the individual in an imperial space that was both social and geographical. The "inner person" was revealed in writing, contextually situated in the biographical frame.

Buddhism claimed a truth that transcended history. Its illustrative medium was the parable, rather than the exemplary historical story. As Buddhism, particularly in its elite forms, accommodated itself to the Chinese tradition, it acquired a historical record with a level of detail absent in the religion's Indian form. A religious truth more important than history and the imperative to promulgate that truth in a culture that looked for a historical ground sometimes led to the manipulation of the historical record, particularly by popular and rising sects like Chan Buddhism. One consequence was texts that we cannot date with certainty, texts that probably took shape over a period of time, but were often backdated.

The Chan Buddhism we know grew out of a remarkable act of usurpation in the succession of the Chan patriarchy. The Fifth Patriarch Hongren had passed on the succession to his chief disciple, Shenxiu, who passed away in 706. In 732, however, a monk named Shenhui began a systematic and public attack on the Shenxiu lineage, claiming that the true Sixth Patriarch was not Shenxiu, but a monk named Huineng, who had secretly received the Dharma and the mantle from Hongren, and then fled into hiding. Since Huineng represented the "Southern School," the lineage of Shenxiu became the "Northern School," which eventually faded away.

Shenhui's "Southern School" was supported by a work commonly known as the Platform Sutra (Tanjing), set as a sermon delivered by the illiterate Huineng, presumably in the late seventh century. At least some parts of the Platform Sutra seem to come from no earlier than the last part of the eighth century, but it is futile to attempt to date a text that probably grew and changed shape with the needs of proselytizing.

Huineng's illiteracy was more than just a biographical detail; it was central to Chan's anti-scholasticism and a feature of Chan writing with profound consequences for the development of a written vernacular Chinese. Chan was a sect that valued immediacy and orality, yet, like other sects, it depended on writing. Its task was to represent orality in a writing system ill designed for it. The most memorable part of the Platform Sutra is Huineng's "autobiography" at the beginning of the sermon. Huineng tells of coming to Hongren to seek the Dharma and of how he labored in the temple mill. In a rather obvious echo of the secular literary examination, Hongren called on each of the monks to compose a *gatha* (a religious verse) to show his level of understanding. Shenxiu, the chief disciple, wrote his *gatha* anonymously on a wall of the temple; the next day Hongren saw it and singled it out for moderate praise. Working in the mill, Huineng heard of the *gatha* from another monk and went by night to see it. Huineng's illiteracy is essential here: he needs the mediation of another, literate monk to read out Shenxiu's *gatha* to him and to write on the wall his own two responding *gathas*, which show his own perfect understanding. Seeing these *gathas*, Hongren summoned Huineng and passed on his Dharma and the mantle of legitimacy. This is a small drama of the role of writing in Chan, both in the dissociation of enlightenment from the study of sacred texts and in writing's ultimate necessity to confirm such dissociation.

It is important to keep in mind that the Platform Sutra is supposed to be a sermon delivered by an illiterate monk. It is anachronistic in this period to divide written Chinese into "literary Chinese" and "vernacular Chinese." We have no knowledge of the actual spoken language, except in written attempts to imitate it, particularly in this and other Chan texts of the ninth and tenth centuries. We see usages that would be excluded from writing in a higher register, some of which are unique to the Tang and some of which have counterparts in the written vernacular of later periods. In the case of the

Platform Sutra, however, it seems clear that it could have been understood aurally by any audience (presuming the familiarity with Buddhist terms that would have come from listening to Buddhist lectures).

"Poetic Chinese" is usually considered "literary Chinese." It is, however, a linguistic form with distinctive features that can be used in registers varying from those that are immediately comprehensible orally to those that require both reading and significant learning. From a relatively "popular" Buddhist tradition we have two bodies of poetry, one in the received tradition and one largely recovered from the Dunhuang manuscripts.

The corpus of somewhat over three hundred poems attributed to one Hanshan (literally "Cold Mountain") and a smaller corpus to his associate Shide ("Picked It Up") are associated with Chan. Hanshan has often been dated to the seventh century because of a preface (certainly spurious) attached to his collection, but another tradition places him in the 770s. Edwin Pulleyblank has argued that the rhymes used cross the historical divide that separates Early Middle Chinese from Late Middle Chinese. While it is not impossible that some of the poems come from the seventh century, some clearly come from the ninth century. Rather than postulating two "Hanshans," we might understand the corpus as a particular genre and idiom for Chan poetry, with contributions added over the centuries. Attempts to construct a biography discussing Hanshan's marriage, his learning, and whether he took the examination are best seen as a symptom of the desire for a single author with a history; we might better see these elements in the collection as a composite of experiences, along with some standard literary conventions that may have had no basis in experience whatsoever. There seems little question that the collection is constructed as if it came from a single author; the first poem begins by addressing "whoever reads my poems." But, as with Huineng, the Chan tradition had a genius for constructing quasi-historical characters.

Hanshan's poetry survived, but it was not much appreciated in the later reception of Tang poetry. It was, however, admired in Japan; and largely from Japan, it was translated and had a presence in American poetry of the second half of the twentieth century. By this somewhat circular route interest in Hanshan's poetry has been sparked again in China and Taiwan.

The Hanshan corpus contains some of the best religious poetry in the Tang. Sometimes denouncing the folly of human passions and the secular life, its most memorable verses speak of "Cold Mountain," treated as both a place and a state of mind. If secular poetry articulates the response of a historical person (however socially constructed that response might be), Buddhist poetry persuades, preaches, and invites:

I go climbing up the Cold Mountain road,
and Cold Mountain's paths do not end.
Boulders lie heaped in the long ravines,
broad torrents, and plants in the misty spray.
Moss, wet and slippery, not due to rain;
the pines make sounds without using wind.
Whoever is able to pass the world's toils
may sit here with me inside the white clouds.

In the Dunhuang manuscripts were found a large collection of poems under the name Wang Fanzhi ("Wang the Brahmacārin," one who maintains abstinence). Wang Fanzhi's name was known in the received tradition and a small selection of the verses was preserved in the received tradition, but the Dunhuang corpus went far beyond the received texts. Like Hanshan, Wang Fanzhi is dated, by a brief notice in the received tradition, to the seventh century. It is far more likely that this is a composite collection, with pieces added and reworked, but going back no earlier than the seventh century. We have one partial manuscript with 110 poems dated by the copyist to 771 (other manuscripts greatly add to that number). The language is simple, with very vernacular elements, and probably represents a register of popular poetry that we do not see elsewhere in the received tradition. One part of the corpus consists of didactic verses, teaching general social values such as filial piety; some scholars believe such verses were used in elementary education. Another part of the corpus gives a dark vision of life in society and human mortality.

IV. After the rebellion (756–791)

No literary figure of note died in the rebellion itself (Wang Changling was killed by a local official for unknown reasons during those years). The famous writers of Xuanzong's reign by and large lived on and continued to produce memorable work in their later years, work not substantially different from what they had written before the rebellion. Yet the rebellion marked a dividing moment in Tang poetry. The younger generation took a decidedly conservative turn. The strong, inventive poetic personalities of Xuanzong's reign were succeeded by a generation whose chief gift was polish and grace. The major exception was no longer a young man when the rebellion broke out, but not considered one of the significant poetic talents of the day. In his case the rebellion saw the beginning of the most creative phase of his life, which lasted fifteen years until his death in 770.

Lives were caught up in the rebellion. The unlucky were captured by An Lushan and forced to take office in his regime in Luoyang. When loyalist forces retook the capitals, these men were sent back to Chang'an for punishment commensurate with their degree of complicity. Wang Wei was among these men, but his career was saved by a poem he had written in captivity expressing his loyalty to the Tang (and saved no less by his politically influential brother). The prose writer Li Hua was less fortunate; a secretary to Geshu Han, the general charged with the defense of the approaches to the capital, Li Hua had fallen into rebel hands when the army was routed, and he was forced to accept a post. He was sent into exile and withdrew from political life. Li Bai was also at the wrong place at the wrong time. In the relative safety of the southeast, he was recruited by the Tang prince of Yong, who staged a brief rebellion against his brother, the new Emperor Suzong. From his poetry one suspects that Li Bai was seduced by a vision of a new "Southern Dynasties," in which he would play the role of the political figure with panache. The little rebellion was crushed, and Li Bai ended up under a prison sentence, though he was eventually pardoned. He was to die a disappointed man.

Many younger writers fled to the safety of Jiangnan, where new literary networks formed that would dominate the coming decades. There were also bolder spirits. As a local official, Yan Zhenqing organized resistance to the rebels and was a true hero of the dynasty. Gao Shi also served Geshu Han, but escaped capture and made his way to Xuanzong, now the "Retired Emperor," in Chengdu. The large Central Asian armies were being recalled to defend the dynasty in the heartland, and Cen Shen came back to serve in the loyalist court of Emperor Suzong.

As always in Du Fu, there is a level of personal detail that is unmatched by other writers. When those details intersected with large political events, Du Fu earned the name later given him, "poet–historian" (*shishi*). Having taken his family to safety and returned to the capital, Du Fu found himself in the city under occupation by An Lushan's troops. Xuanzong's hasty and secret flight from the capital had left behind most of the large imperial family, who were hunted down by An Lushan's soldiers. In "Lament for a Prince" (Ai wangsun), Du Fu chances on such a prince in Chang'an attempting to hide. In "Lament by the Riverside" (Ai Jiangtou), Du Fu is in the Winding River Park of Chang'an and recalls the visits of Xuanzong and Lady Yang, whose "wandering soul is stained with blood and cannot return." News of the major imperial defeats at the battles of Greenslope and Chentao get back to the city: "The moors vast, the sky clear, no sounds of battle – / forty thousand loyalist troops died on the very same day."

Eventually Du Fu escaped from the city and made his way to Suzong's temporary capital, where he was given the court post of Reminder, whose task was to point out errors in documents and imperial decisions. After a while Du Fu's unfortunate political associations and inexperience earned him imperial permission to go and visit his family, which in turn gave us one of Du Fu's longest and most famous poems, "Journey North" (Beizheng), bearing witness to a land in which "Heaven and Earth bear scars." "Journey North" characteristically weaves together immediate experience with larger political issues. Emperor Suzong had been compelled to ask for help from his Uighur allies, a decision that was as politically unpopular as it was necessary in military terms; Du Fu comments with wonderful ambiguity: "of this sort few are valuable." We can read this as praise of their prowess ("even a few are valuable") or as "the fewer the better."

In 757 the capitals were retaken, though the rebellion was far from over, and never again would the Tang have full control over all the rich provinces of the northeast. Du Fu joined the restored court in Chang'an, but his support for a minister out of favor led to his transfer to a low-ranking post away from the capital. During that period, on an extended trip to Luoyang, he wrote his famous "Three Subalterns" (Sanli) and "Three Partings" (Sanbie), giving vivid accounts of the devastation and social dislocation of the rebellion.

Dissatisfied with his post and perhaps hoping for help from a relative, in 759 Du Fu set off for the town of Qinzhou, northwest of Chang'an. His Qinzhou poems represented a major transformation of his style into an austere regulated verse, sometimes on unusual topics such as "Taking down a Trellis" (Chujia), in which dismantling a gourd trellis becomes a figure for discarding something or someone that has served its purpose. By the end of 759 he again set out with his family for Chengdu; employment by the local commander and figures like Gao Shi in service there contributed to make this the happiest phase of his later poetry. He built his famous "thatched cottage" (caotang, an imagined reconstruction of which is still a local site) near the city. Again he had colleagues with whom to write poetry, but, from the rebellion on, Du Fu was essentially an isolated poet, developing his own idiosyncratic style outside the context of social exchange that had largely defined Tang poetry. There is often an understated lightness about his Chengdu poems, balancing perfect formal control with wry monologue. A local flood, excitedly reported by his son, rises swiftly before the contemplative and unhurried witness:

> As I got out of bed, it rose several more feet,
> while I leaned on my staff, it submerged isles midstream.

Du Fu is sometimes the visionary, but throughout his later work we sometimes find a gentle self-mockery that gives his poetry a rare human depth. Driven temporarily from Chengdu by a rebellion of the garrison, he returned to find his little boat sunk in the mud and waterlogged. He laments the loss, saying how he planned to sail down the Yangzi river to warm and idyllic Jiangnan. The conclusion is characteristic:

> . . .
> Perhaps I could dig up the old one,
> and a new one is easy to find.
> What grieves me is often running away to hide,
> that in this plain cottage I can't stay long.

He has learned that he less wants to set sail down the Yangzi river than to be able to stay in one place, sitting in his boat and inventing poems about sailing down the Yangzi.

Eventually in 765 he did set out from Chengdu, stopping in Kuizhou at the head of the Three Gorges. His few years in Kuizhou were his most productive. It was here that he wrote his sequence of eight "Autumn Meditations" (Qiu xing bashou), using the parallel structure of regulated verse and its mirror image in eight regulated poems to contrast the present world and the past of Xuanzong's reign, the "here" of Kuizhou in autumn and the "there" of old Chang'an in spring, the mortal world and the world of Heaven. This is Chinese poetry at its thickest, dense with patterns that recur in changing forms.

Although there are some lighter pieces from Kuizhou, their tone is much darker than that of the Chengdu years. The relative solitude of composition liberated him; he became visionary, using parallelism and the inherent indeterminacy of poetic Chinese to produce couplets unlike anything done before:

> Myself and the age: a pair of tangled tresses,
> Earth and Heaven: a single thatched pavilion.

In 768 he left Kuizhou and set out further down the Yangzi river to Jingzhou, then on into Lake Dongting to visit the territory of the exiled Qu Yuan. Some of the last poems are as powerful and strange as anything in Chinese poetry.

At least since the Northern Song, Du Fu's roughly 1,400 poems have been read in the context of his life. The earliest extant Song editions are conventionally divided between the large genre categories of "ancient-style" and "recent-style" poems, but within each grouping the poems are arranged in chronological order (though with errors in the chronology). This has remained true for most subsequent editions. Early editions of most other poets are arranged by genre or subgenre. Such a biographical reading is encouraged by the poems themselves: Du Fu poetically constructed his life, and the poems eventually transformed a political failure and minor poet into the most famous poet and personality in the Chinese literary tradition.

Du Fu died in 770, the winter of the fifth year of the Dali reign of Emperor Daizong. The then more celebrated poets of that era came to be known as the "Ten Talents of the Dali Reign" (*Dali shi caizi*). Working largely in regulated verse, these and other contemporary poets perfected a fluency and grace that was immensely influential in the later practice of the form; but there was little true innovation. The definitive anthology of the time, conceived as a sequel to Yin Fan's *The Glorious Spirits of Our Rivers and Chief Mountains*, was *The Fine Officers of the Restoration* (*Zhongxing jianqi ji*) compiled by Gao Zhongwu in 779, the year of Daizong's death. Among its 134 regulated poems by twenty-six poets composed between 756 and 779 there is no Du Fu. Indeed, after his death Du Fu seems to have been largely unknown or ignored for about two decades, when his work was championed by Han Yu, Bai Juyi, and Yuan Zhen.

Many of the well-known poets of this period have left considerable poetry collections, though none approaching the size of Du Fu's. They were admired and often anthologized in later ages, but in the majority of cases we are uncertain about the dates of their birth and death (although we usually know the year in which they passed the literary examination). We know random details about their lives pieced together from the titles of their occasional poems, but those fragments of lives are largely irrelevant to reading their poetry. The contrast with Du Fu is both striking and significant. If Du Fu stands out in an old tradition of reading poetry in the context of the person, these masters of regulated verse have been read in a way more like "pure poetry," without readers asking to know more about the poet's life. These poets were the ancestors of one of the most important strains in Chinese poetry in the ninth and tenth centuries. In the late ninth century, when the critic Sikong Tu (837–908) wanted to describe the elusive quality of a scene created in poetry, he quoted Dai Shulun (732–789), one of the poets of the period.

Liu Changqing, who passed the examination in 733, was the oldest of these poets. Liu Changqing was active even before the rebellion, but he lived on through most of the post-rebellion period. In later centuries he was sometimes much admired as a model for regulated verse in the five-syllable line. Qian Qi passed the examination in 750 and became a friend of Wang Wei, who was a profound influence on his poetry. The poems of figures like Lang Shiyuan (*jinshi* examination passed 756), Li Duan (examination 770), Sikong Shu (examination 771), and Han Hong (examination 755) are often hard to distinguish one from another. Han Hong is best remembered as a romantic hero in a Tang tale, seeking his abducted concubine Miss Liu. There is far more variety in the poetry of Lu Lun (ca 737–ca 788) and Li Yi (748–829), with more old-style poems and *yuefu*, with some of their best-known poems concerning frontier themes. Li Yi is particularly interesting in carrying the post-rebellion style through the turbulent inventiveness of the early ninth century.

Most of these poets spent many years of the post-rebellion period in Jiangnan, where they formed literary networks that included a number of poet–monks, writing almost exclusively polished regulated verse and regulated quatrains. The poet–monk whose works have been best preserved was Jiaoran (ca 720–ca 798), who took his vows after failing the literary examination. Jiaoran was very much a member of the scholar elite and spent much of his time exchanging verses with the community of secular poets. No less part of these Jiangnan literary networks were famous prose writers such as Li Hua; Lu Yu (733–?), now known for the *Tea Classic* (*Chajing*); and Dugu Ji (725–777), a strong proponent of "ancient" prose and values.

The literary groups in Jiangnan in this period also included a Daoist nun, Li Ye (also known as Li Jilan), only sixteen of whose poems survive. A number of women poets in the Tang were, at some point in their lives, Daoist nuns, probably less because of their religious convictions than for the advantages of being registered with the government as clerics. For a woman not attached to a household, Daoist registration offered a freedom of movement that would have been otherwise difficult, if not impossible. Li Ye exchanged poems with Jiaoran, Lu Yu, and Liu Changqing. She was unfortunately in Chang'an in 783 when a rebellious army drove Emperor Dezong from his capital and installed Zhu Ci, one of their officers, on the throne. Li Ye evidently wrote a laudatory poem for Zhu Ci; and when Dezong recovered the throne, she was executed.

This period between the rebellion and the gradual stabilization of the weakened central government in Emperor Dezong's middle years was the most difficult time for the Tang government before the last decades of the ninth century. The eastern provinces north of the Yellow River were largely in the hands of autonomous generals; there had been large-scale militarization in other provinces, whose armies answered to imperial control to varying degrees. The economic core of the empire lay in the grain-producing provinces of the southeast, the region around Chang'an, and the water route (the Grand Canal and the Yellow River) that linked them. In the 760s the

Tibetans took advantage of Tang weakness and swallowed up the prefectures northwest of the capital that had long been Chinese. On a number of occasions Tibetan armies threatened the capital and on one occasion they briefly occupied it. The Tang's Uighur allies, moreover, sometimes turned against them; and even as allies, they often behaved more like an occupying power.

Although writers of the day often did serve in Chang'an, many preferred the southeast, still rich and generally peaceful. Not only was it a center for both poetry and prose writing, we also have prefaces for collections of exchange poems, discussions of ancient-style prose, and a remarkable work on technical poetics, *The Statutes of Poetry* (*Shishi*) by Jiaoran, completed in 789. The preface states in the baldest terms the function of a written poetics: "Its purpose is to instill a sense of natural instinct in those who have no natural instincts." *The Statutes of Poetry* is a sophisticated expansion of older paradigms of technical poetics, enumerating categories, virtues, and failings, with brief discussions and comments on passages.

Although *The Statutes of Poetry* survived independently in China (in a long and a short version, along with another work that may have originally been a section of *The Statutes*), parts were also preserved in a large compendium of primarily Tang poetics made by the Japanese monk Kūkai (774–835), who went to China to study in 804 and returned in 806. This work, *The Secret Treasury of the Mirror of Letters* (*Wenjing mifulun*, Japanese *Bunkyō hifuron*), also preserved the works on seventh-century poetics mentioned earlier, along with a considerable corpus of eighth-century material on poetics preserved under the name of the poet Wang Changling. A different and shorter version of the Wang Changling material was preserved in China. I suspect that, as Wang Fanzhi was the name under which a type of moralizing and pedagogic verse was gathered, Wang Changling was the name under which works of popular poetics were gathered (often illustrating points with "a poem by Wang Changling goes . . . "). It is worth observing that Wang Changling has the largest selection of poems and the longest critical preface in Yin Fan's *The Glorious Spirits of Our Rivers and Chief Mountains*.

The Wang Changling materials contain the enumerated taxonomies that were the staple of poetic pedagogy; for example, the "Seventeen Kinetic Forms" (*shiqi shi*) describing poetic exposition as qualities of motion. *The Secret Treasury* includes a long essay "On Meaning in Literature" (*Lun wenyi*), repeating canonical commonplaces along with practical advice, such as keeping a lamp by your bed to jot down lines that may come when waking in the night. "On Meaning in Literature" also encourages a reflective interval between the occasioning experience of a poem and the actual composition;

this practical fact had been ignored in the presumed immediacy of composition, in which the poem's human "truth" was guaranteed by the fact that it came unreflectively out of the occasioning experience. This is our earliest indication of a more craftsman-like approach to poetic composition that would be transformed in the ninth century into a celebration of poetic composition as a laborious and time-consuming process.

For later readers, the most considerable poet of the era was Wei Yingwu (733?–ca 793), from a decayed branch of the illustrious Wei clan. Beginning his career as one of Emperor Xuanzong's imperial guard, he had a long career in and out of service in Luoyang and Jiangnan. Although many later critics singled out his serene landscape poems, he was, in fact, a very diverse poet and was one of the few poets of this period to compose a number of "songs" (*gexing*) in the old style.

Gu Kuang (ca 727–?) may have been influential in shaping the new poetry that took shape around the turn of the ninth century. He passed the literary examination in 757, taking it at Xuanzong's court in exile in Chengdu. In the post-rebellion period he served with several powerful political figures; according to legend he was thrown out of his one court post for mocking certain courtiers. He had a strong interest in Daoism and eventually withdrew to the major Daoist center at Mount Mao. Gu was a Suzhou native, where the nineteen-year-old Bai Juyi met him in 789. Of interest in this context and in the context of the poetry seeking to "restore antiquity" is a set of poems imaginatively re-creating lyrics of high antiquity, provided with prefaces in the style of the Mao prefaces to individual poems of the *Classic of Poetry*, being explicit about their message. A more mature Bai Juyi was to make his reputation with his "new *yuefu*," imaginatively re-creating what Bai saw as the original role of Han *yuefu*, also provided with prefaces explaining their purport. Gu Kuang's ballads and songs, moreover, link the legacy of Li Bai with the imaginative and narrative poetry of the coming decades.

In 791 Gu Kuang wrote a preface for Dai Fu's *Extending Accounts of Anomalies* (*Guang yi ji*), a large collection of short tales of wonders from the post-rebellion period. Like almost all Tang collections of stories, the original has long been lost, but approximately three hundred of Dai Fu's stories have been recovered from *Extensive Records of the Taiping Reign*. Stern moralists had often disapproved of marvelous tales by citing the *Analects*: "The Master did *not* talk about wonders, acts of force, disorder, or the gods." In a fine piece of fanciful philology, Gu Kuang claimed that scholars had misread the ancient form of the character *shi* ("to show") as *bu* ("not") and thus had perverted Confucius' true model, which was indeed "to talk about wonders, acts of force, disorder, and the gods in order to show [people about them]." It was an ingenious, if philologically unsound, defense of fiction. Gu Kuang then listed an impressive sequence of works, at least partially in chronological order, the kind of list that sometimes accompanied work in more respectable genres, establishing a historical pedigree for the text in question.

Tales of wonders had strong religious dimensions, including Daoist tales of immortals, Buddhist tales of retribution, and the hagiographies common to both religious traditions. Although the tradition of such tales was an old one, the quantity of preserved tales increased after the rebellion – perhaps in no small part because post-rebellion works in general survived more fully.

The literary nature of these tales (apart from those with explicitly religious ends) lies outside the Western distinction between "fiction" and "nonfiction." Like our own tales of wonders (sasquatch or the "Bermuda Triangle"), they both invite and strain credulity; some may believe and others may not, but there is a pleasure in the narrative that is linked to an invitation to credulity. The very short tales were circulated in writing and no doubt provided reading pleasure, but we may reasonably suspect that readers of such tales might retell them to their friends and, in doing so, flesh these bare-bones narratives out into something much longer.

We have longer written narratives from earlier in the Tang, such as Zhang Zhuo's *The Den of Wandering Immortals* mentioned earlier in this chapter. Zhang Zhuo's narrative is clearly for reading rather than telling, delighting in its poems, repartee, and rhetoric. Toward the end of the eighth century, we begin to find the longer tales for which Tang fiction is famous. It is, at least, suggestive that one of the earliest of such tales, "Miss Ren's Story" (Renshi zhuan) by Shen Jiji, is framed with a scene of storytelling set in 781. In other words, it is not unreasonable to suppose that these longer tales are written renditions of the pleasures of actual "storytelling," rather than simply the "story," a plot available for telling a story.

"Miss Ren's Story" begins with one of the most standard plots of Tang tales: a man meets a beautiful woman, goes home with her, sleeps with her, is sent on his way the next morning, and somehow comes back to the site of her "mansion" to discover only a lair of foxes. Shen Jiji's version of the conventional were-fox story is carried out with far more flair and humor than most versions, but the story becomes great by continuing. Mr. Zheng, the deceived male, does not react with horror or disgust, but keeps longing for Ren the fox. Zheng finds her again in human guise and tells her that he does not care that she is a fox, after which she is established as his concubine. The plot twists and turns after that, with a triangle developing between Miss Ren, Zheng, and his rich and powerful in-law Wei Yin; it ends with Miss Ren getting eaten by a hunting dog that frightened her back into her original form.

Although this is, on one level, yet another "fox story," nothing earlier in Chinese prose narrative quite prepares us for the detail, the humor, and the complexity of relationships in "Miss Ren's Story." While most stories tended to be set in almost uninhabited nature, in boats, or in settlements of an indeterminate kind, "Miss Ren's Story" is very much a city story, set in Chang'an; we can still trace the movements of the characters on a map of the city. Representing what had never been represented has the historically local effect of surprise that is sometimes called "realism," as in the crowd scene in the market:

> A dozen or so days passed. Zheng was out and going into a clothing store in the Western Market when all at once he saw her, accompanied by her servants as before. Zheng instantly shouted to her. Ren turned to the side and tried to lose herself in a crowd to avoid him. But Zheng kept shouting to her and pushed his way forward. Finally she stood with her back to him, screening her face from his sight with a fan that she held around behind her. "You know, so why do you come near me?"

Shen Jiji's other surviving story, "The Account upon a Pillow" (Zhenzhong ji) is both shorter and more conventional, though very influential in its later transformations. Here a Daoist sets out to enlighten one Mr. Lu by inviting him to rest on his pillow while the innkeeper steams some millet. In the interval of the cooking, Lu falls asleep and dreams a lifetime, rising to glory and enjoying the heights of pleasure until his death, at which moment he wakes up enlightened.

We cannot date Li Chaowei's "Liu Yi's Story" (Liu Yi zhuan), but scholars sometimes place it in the 780s or 790s. This is also an old narrative theme, on the marriage of a mortal and a water goddess, but Li Chaowei's version is executed with plot complications, dramatic scenes, and rich description.

A caution is necessary here: the scene of storytelling in "Miss Ren's Story" is dated to 781, but that does not really tell us when the story was written. In the case of Li Chaowei's story, the internal dating gives us an even less direct link to the composition of the story. The early decades of the ninth century saw an unusually rich set of fully developed prose narratives, which went hand in hand with other cultural changes that can be traced back to the 790s. While it is tempting to see here an anticipation of ninth-century tales, we may, in fact, be reading ninth-century tales.

We know the fact of Tang oral storytelling, both professional and private, but, of course, we cannot know with any certainty how narratives were elaborated in performance. Chinese history was always a favorite topic for imaginative elaboration in oral storytelling, and such elaborations had a written counterpart in "unofficial history" (*yeshi*), often highly sensational. The reign and fall of Xuanzong provided a rich source for the historical imagination, and while this bore full fruit only in the ninth century, the late eighth century gave us Guo Shi's "The Informal Biography of Gao Lishi" (Gao Lishi *waizhuan*), with anecdotes about Xuanzong's famous chief eunuch.

Readers of later ages were far more likely to read Du Fu, Wei Yingwu, or "Miss Ren's Story" and "Liu Yi's Story" than the poetry or prose of those writers most famous in this period between 756 and 792. The case of Du Fu best represents what was happening. During Emperor Xuanzong's reign, the court no longer defined literary excellence for the elite. In Xuanzong's reign, however, the consensus of elite taste had a lasting impact and in many cases was ratified by history. By contrast, the writers we remember from the early ninth century represented something of an insurgent "counterculture"; these writers have now come to represent the canon so much that it is easy to forget that they were a counterculture. The dominant elite culture of the early ninth century is better represented by Linghu Chu's anthology of 817, *Poems for the Emperor's Perusal* (*Yulan shi*), which includes and extends the poets in Gao Zhongwu's *The Fine Officers of the Restoration*. At the same time Han Yu, Bai Juyi, and Yuan Zhen were celebrating Du Fu's poetry, but Du Fu has no place in Linghu Chu's anthology. A major change was happening, in which the writer or intellectual might be seen as inherently alienated from the polity and the elite community as a whole.

V. The mid-Tang generation (792–820)

In 792 a remarkable group of men gathered in Chang'an to take the examination. Their poetry and prose aggressively affirmed their distinction in a style that evoked the earlier Tang discourse of the "ancient." Li Guan (766–794), the nephew of the famous Li Hua, introduced himself in a letter to a high official: "I, Guan, am simply a commoner from the southeast." Anyone who started a letter that way was implicitly claiming to be much more. In another letter he declared, "My mind is different from other people in the world and my sense of mission is also different." Also in this group was Ouyang Zhan (ca 758–ca 801), who would be the first person from Fujian to pass the literary examination. Both men had made friends with a third candidate, Han Yu, who would go on to become one of the most famous writers of the dynasty and something of a Confucian culture hero. They were joined by a poet from the southeast, already in his forties, Meng Jiao (751–814).

Li Guan, Ouyang Zhan, and Han Yu all passed the examination in a class that was to be called the "list of dragons and tigers" for the number of graduates who eventually went on to distinction. Meng Jiao failed; in his disappointment and rage he composed poems with a harsh force that had never before been seen in Chinese poetry. Han Yu wrote to console him, in the "ancient" style:

> Of those who make friends in Chang'an,
> rich and poor each have their fellows.
> When friends and relations stop by,
> each group has its pleasures as well.
> In the humble room, histories and literature;
> in mansions, the music of pipes.
> How can we say which is more glorious? –
> yet we might tell worthy men from fools.

Poetic consolation for an examination failure was common, but usually very different from this. The set of values implicit here was often repeated in writings by other members of the group. These values held immense appeal for many in the educated elite, whose numbers were growing, while the quota of twenty or so passing the annual literary examination remained constant. The "others" are the rich, powerful, and successful. To be different from those "others," as Li Guan claimed to be, was associated with learning, talent, and moral virtue; it was also associated with the "ancient." The "others" will, out of jealousy and incomprehension, reject the talented and virtuous person. As a result such a singular person will end up in humble circumstances, but may enjoy the pleasures of learning. Moreover, singular talented and virtuous men will find each other and form a community. These are the basic components of a counterculture or an avant-garde, in the Chinese case closely tied to exclusion from publicly authorized cultural power as well as political power. In Meng Jiao's case it was his failure in the examination that demonstrated the failure of "others" to recognize the worthy, but it could apply equally well to someone who was not given an office, or received an office less distinguished than he thought he deserved, or was sent into exile. Some members of this group, including Han Yu himself, did eventually hold moderately high offices, but the following couplet by Meng Jiao best represents the group's conviction about the relation between literature and political power: "Bad poems always get you an office, / good poems leave you merely clinging to the mountains."

Although the claims of singularity ("different from others") and isolation were central to this discourse, it was indeed a community, and in its basic form this community reproduced the structure of other social communities, most clearly in the role of patronage. In Tang political and cultural life, older men with high positions would "recognize" the talent of younger men, then promote and recommend them. Han Yu took upon himself the role of cultural patron of this new community of special people, who were invited to show their distinction by writing that which was "different" (yi), which can also be translated as "strange."

If the best are necessarily rejected by the establishment, and fail, then why did so many of the best pass the literary examination in 792? The common answer is the examiners. Lu Zhi (753–805), Emperor Dezong's best political mind, then out of power, was a supervisor. The official immediately in charge was Liang Su (753–793), one of the most famous prose stylists of the day. Although Liang Su, a student of Dugu Ji, was interested in Buddhism, he very much saw himself in the lineage of the advocates of the "ancient" style in prose, stretching back to Li Hua and Xiao Yingshi.

The particular officials in charge of the 792 examination cannot explain the succession of remarkable writers who appeared in the capital and, sooner or later, passed the literary examination between 792 and 800. Even Meng Jiao passed at last, in 796. Neither can the tradition of discourse on the "ancient" explain all the new, diverse interests appearing in literature. These men formed some close friendships and a network of associations in which a new literary and intellectual culture was disseminated.

In Chang'an in 792 there was also the young Liu Yuxi (772–842), who would become an important poet, and Liu Zongyuan, who was to become a prose stylist equal in fame to Han Yu himself. In 793 we find Han Yu and Meng Jiao in the company of Liu Zongyuan and the young Li Ao (774–836), who was to become Han Yu's foremost disciple as a prose stylist and a Confucian thinker of some consequence. That same year the precocious Yuan Zhen (779–831) passed the examination in the Confucian Classics at the age of fourteen. Yuan Zhen formed a famous literary friendship with Bai Juyi (772–846), who would come to Chang'an and pass the examination in 800. Yuan Zhen wrote of reading an anthology of Du Fu's poetry in 794, the first time we hear of Du Fu's works circulating and being admired in the capital.

In 796 the poet Zhang Ji (768–830) came to pay his respects to Meng Jiao, who in turn recommended him to Han Yu. That same year Liu Zongyuan passed one of the special "palace examinations," which promised an even better career trajectory than the regular literary examination. Li Cheng

(766–842), one of the contemporary masters of regulated *fu*, passed with him. In 798 Li Ao passed the literary examination, along with the prose stylist Lü Wen (772–811) and two other masters of regulated *fu*, Wang Qi (760–847) and Zhang Zhongsu (769?-819). Having achieved candidacy with the help of Han Yu, Zhang Ji passed the examination in 799, along with his friend, the poet Wang Jian (b. 766?). New writers would continue to appear, but we can see here the way in which literary networks were established, with the examinations playing a central role as the site where friendships formed and texts were exchanged. Letters and poems of recommendation and mutual praise built reputations.

The fates of these men would be very different in later life. Liu Zongyuan's initial success and rapidly rising reputation brought him into the government of Wang Shuwen in 805, which lasted only a few months and ended in disaster for those who took part in it. As a result, Liu Zongyuan would spend the rest of his life in administrative exile in backwater prefectures of southern China. The same fate befell Liu Yuxi, but he had the good fortune to live long enough to return to better posts. After struggling to pass the literary examination and get a post, Meng Jiao was at last given the lowest position in the bureaucratic hierarchy, that of county sheriff in the provinces; he quit after a short while and returned to the capitals, living out the rest of his life presumably on the largesse of patrons. Lü Wen served as emissary to Tibet and was for a while held captive in Lhasa. Yuan Zhen went on to eventually become a minister and one of the most powerful figures in court. Bai Juyi finally rose to a distinguished court position, only to retire early and live out the rest of his very long life enjoying himself in Luoyang. However different their fates, the associations formed in these early years lasted; whether living their lives in exile or in the court, the dynasty's excellent post system and the constant traffic of officials ensured that their writings circulated and were read.

These men, by and large, shared a common discourse on the "ancient" as a value. Two qualifications, however, are necessary. First, most writers also wrote in distinctly "unancient" styles when the occasion demanded, without any sense of contradiction. In some venues Bai Juyi celebrated the plainness and clarity of a moral message, but he was also famous for his regulated *fu* and for his "judgments" (*panwen*). Manifestos of a writer's literary commitments should be understood as quite sincere, but at the same time contingent on the particular situation and genre.

The second qualification is that the "ancient" was a vague notion and permitted very different interpretations. For Meng Jiao it could be an almost mystical theme of purity: "Ancient bones have no filthy flesh, / ancient clothes are like moss." In Han Yu the "ancient" involved ethical commitment along with a style and register of diction; rather than reproducing the style of any particular ancient text, however, Han Yu's "ancient" style was imaginative and highly idiosyncratic, considered both difficult and strange. Indeed, strangeness and daring were the qualities sought after and admired by those writers most closely associated with Han Yu.

A very different version of the "ancient" was the use of poetry to speak out on moral and political issues. Although we already see this in some poetry of the 790s, from the middle of the first decade of the ninth century we see many examples of what are called "new *yuefu*," a name taken from a series of poems by Bai Juyi. These "new *yuefu*" directly address contemporary social and political problems. They belonged to the discourse of the "ancient" by their filiation to the *Classic of Poetry* and the Han *yuefu*, which took their name from the Music Bureau (*Yuefu*). In the Tang it was believed that both the "Airs" in the *Classic of Poetry* and the Han *yuefu* came from government institutions that collected popular songs so that the ruler could learn of social problems and abuses directly from the mouths of his subjects. Certain poems by Du Fu were seen as already championing this role for poetry in the Tang. Bai Juyi, Yuan Zhen, Zhang Ji, Wang Jian, and many others set out to continue that tradition.

In a poem of 811 to a friend, Bai Juyi articulated the principle behind such poems, which not only opposed the polished style that was associated with the upper strata of officialdom, but also took aim at the experimental "strangeness" associated with members of the Han Yu group:

> I don't seek lofty euphony,
> I don't strive for strange diction,
> I sing only of the problems of the people,
> wanting the Emperor to learn of them.

In 808 Bai Juyi composed his ten "Songs in Qin" (Qinzhong yin) on topics ranging from a virtuous friend who lived in hard straits to the inflated prices paid for flowers in the capital, in face of the poverty of the commoners. The following year saw the fifty "New *Yuefu*," which followed the model of the *Mao Tradition* version of the *Classic of Poetry* by providing each poem with a short prefatory note, making the target of the poem explicit. Here we find topics ranging from the policy of "palace requisitions," with court eunuch agents depriving an impoverished charcoal-seller of his merchandise, to the wealth of salt merchants, to imperial interest in Central Asian dancers. Yuan

Zhen then produced a series of his own, mostly on the same topics treated by Bai Juyi.

Large political happenings had often inspired poetic response, but never before had contemporary social and political issues become a literary fashion shared by a community of writers. Such serious issues were not the only kind of current events circulating in literary culture at the beginning of the ninth century. We can reasonably expect that young men had always discussed their love affairs, but they were not usually the subject of current writing – or if they were, they were usually figured in a story of meeting a goddess. This changed in the ninth century. We see a fine moment of transition in 801, when Yuan Zhen told his friends about his affair with his cousin Cui Yingying, whom he had deserted. His high literary representation of the affair was in a poem of sixty lines entitled "Encounter with an Immortal" (Huizhen shi), in which convention required that the goddess desert her lover and leave him in helpless longing. By 804 both Yuan Zhen and Cui Yingying had married, and he discussed the affair again with the young Li Shen (d. 846), who wrote a long narrative ballad treating the affair in human terms and using Yingying's name. This survives only in fragments. Yuan Zhen himself then wrote the story in prose, "Yingying's Story" (Yingying zhuan), concealing only his own identity under the name Zhang. In the story he included part of his "Encounter with an Immortal." "Yingying's Story" is perhaps the finest of Tang tales, with credibly human characters represented with all their follies and failings. The prose narrative includes an account not only of the love affair itself, but also of the community within which the story circulated; poems and letters exchanged between the lovers were in turn circulated among a group of young men who discuss the affair, pass judgments, and write poems in response.

Jiang Fang's "Huo Xiaoyu's Story" (Huo Xiaoyu zhuan) cannot be dated, though our extant notices place the author in the 820s and early 830s; the story may well be earlier. It tells the story of the poet Li Yi's affair with Huo Xiaoyu, the daughter of a Tang prince and a courtesan–concubine; when Li Yi's mother instructs him to raise money for an arranged marriage, Li Yi cannot face Huo Xiaoyu and stops communicating with her. Huo Xiaoyu spends her modest wealth trying to get word of him. This becomes known among the young men of Chang'an, and when Li Yi is back in the city he is duped into going to her house in the company of a group of young men. Providing themselves with refreshments, the young men watch while Huo Xiaoyu first denounces Li Yi and then dies. She puts a curse on him that he will never find peace with either wife or concubine. We cannot be certain whether Li Yi's subsequent pathological jealousy is the consequence of the curse or of his own guilt.

Love affairs and their ends produced judgmental gossip, poetry, and narrative prose. The long title of a set of poems by Li He (791–817) evokes this discursive culture: "Candidate Xie had a concubine Gaolian, who went off with someone else; Xie tried to make her stay to no avail, but later she was moved thinking about him. At a party we composed poems making fun of her. Here I add four more." The faithless woman lover comes in for the opprobrium of the community no less than the faithless male lover. The positive stories are about keeping faith, or redeeming oneself after betraying a lover. "Missy Li's Story" (Li wa zhuan), by Bai Juyi's brother Bai Xingjian (776–826), is set earlier in the dynasty, and begins memorably: "The Baroness of Qian, Missy Li, was a whore in Chang'an." Here a Chang'an courtesan consumes the wealth of an examination candidate, leading him to ruin and long suffering; later, finding him a beggar, she takes him in, feeds him, and forces him to study, after which he passes the examination and rises to a high position, taking her with him. Yuan Zhen wrote an accompanying ballad that has been lost apart from a few lines.

The grandest of all love stories was that of Emperor Xuanzong and Lady Yang, which Bai Juyi made into his famous "Song of Enduring Sorrow" (Changhen ge) in 806, with Chen Hong writing a prose version as a companion piece. Lady Yang is here transformed into an immortal who returns to the land of the immortals after her enforced suicide. Xuanzong, always longing for her, sends a Daoist wizard to search for her, and she sends back tokens, promising their reunion in future lives. Although the prose narrative is explicitly the companion piece for the poem, the different protocols of poetry and prose produce interesting divergences in the accounts; for example, in the poem Lady Yang is presented as virginal when Xuanzong found her ("raised deep in the women's quarters where no man knew of her"), while the prose version acknowledges that she had been the consort of Xuanzong's son.

Longer prose narratives often concluded with a judgment by the narrator, touching on the lesson to be drawn. At one extreme such narrative becomes parable, such as Liu Zongyuan's "The Story of the Tree-Planter, Camel-back Guo" (Zhongshu Guo Tuotuo zhuan), who is successful because he follows the nature of the plants; this would have been immediately understood as an analogy for governing well. At another extreme the impulse to offer an explanation can be inadequate for the more troubling stories that interested mid-Tang writers. Liu Zongyuan's "Li Chi's Story" (Li Chi zhuan) tells of a madman in love with the goddess of the privy; he evades the attempts of his friends to stop him and at last drowns himself in the latrine. The story, however, remains darker than Liu Zongyuan's attempt to generalize it as being about the foolishly misplaced likes and dislikes that are common to all.

Modern Chinese scholarship makes a clear generic distinction between parables or pieces like "Li Chi's Story," which are included in an author's "literary collection," and narratives like "Yingying's Story" or "Missy Li's Story," which are treated as "classical tales" (chuanqi) and thus part of the history of fiction. Both types share the generic marker zhuan, which is also the generic marker translated as "biography" in historiography. Some scholars are aware of the problem and will appropriate a piece like "Li Chi's Story" into "fiction" (xiaoshuo), but rarely a piece like "The Story of the Tree-Planter, Camel-back Guo." In the Tang the distinction seems to have been thematic rather than generic. Literary collections generally, with some exceptions, excluded zhuan centered on love affairs, violence, or the supernatural – the categories that Confucius refused to speak about, a theme to which compilers of anecdotes and tales often returned in their prefaces. Such stories did, however, circulate widely and were often included in anthologies reserved for such stories, to be collected at last in the Extensive Records of the Taiping Reign.

It is clear that there was much "improper" writing in circulation, writing that did not survive censorship in the various venues of circulation. Often such censorship was carried out by authors themselves; texts of which an author might have been proud at one stage of his life often came to seem an embarrassment in more mature years and higher social station. As we will see, Yuan Zhen excised a substantial corpus of youthful erotic verse from his official literary collection. Sometimes, however, the suppressed text has returned. From Dunhuang we have recovered a fu by Bai Xingjian, the author of "Missy Li's Story," entitled grandly "The Supreme Pleasure of Sexual Intercourse between Yin and Yang in the World" (Tiandi Yin Yang jiaohuan dale fu), giving a very long and detailed, if flowery, description of the sexual act.

The Extensive Records was dedicated to prose accounts of things out of the ordinary, and the mid-Tang had a passion for the extraordinary and surprising. We find this in poetic representations as well as in prose narrative. Sometimes the intent was humorous, as when Han Yu describes a forest fire as a group of demons working for the Heavenly "Bureau of Heat." Meng Jiao described the Three Gorges as a landscape of pure horror, a great stone maw drooling in its hunger to swallow up the voyager. The poet Lu Tong, one of the group around Han Yu, wrote a long allegorical fantasy on an eclipse of the moon.

Li He was obsessed with death, ghosts, and demons, as in "The Tomb of Little Su" (Su Xiaoxiao mu), where a long-dead singing girl of the Southern Dynasties emerges as a ghostly apparition.

Some earlier poets, such as Li Bai, had a gift for representing scenes that could exist only in words and the mind's eye, but many of the poets of the Han Yu circle went much further. Li He, in particular, was drawn to imagining moments in history and legend. Li He writes the poem that "should have been written" by the Liang court poet Yu Jianwu on returning to Jiankang after fleeing the chaos of the Hou Jing Rebellion; he imagines the First Emperor of Qin in a drunken flight through space and time:

> Qin's king rides a tiger, roams to the earth's eight ends,
> rays from his sword light the sky, the heavens turn sapphire.
> Xihe whips the sun, making the sound of glass,
> ashes from kalpas are all flown away, past and present are conquered.

Xihe is the goddess who drives the sun-carriage; a kalpa is a Buddhist eon, after which the world is burned away and a new one starts. Even examination topics for *fu* might be the rhetorical description of some moment in history and legend, like Bai Juyi's "Emperor Gaozu of the Han Cuts the White Snake in Half" (Han Gaozu zhan baishe fu), a successful submission for the palace examination of 803 that was immediately much studied.

Li Shan, the great mid-seventh-century commentator on the *Selections of Refined Literature*, had provided earlier examples or "sources" for all the problematic phrases in the great anthology; later, in the Song, Du Fu would be praised for his poems in which "every word has its source." Against this enduring norm, the mid-Tang often explicitly valued complete originality. Han Yu praised the prose writer Fan Zongshi (d. ca 821) in exactly the opposite way, saying, "he did not follow a single phrase or sentence of those before him." Although Fan Zongshi was prolific, only two of his prose pieces survive, neither of which is entirely comprehensible. We do not know whether this is due to our own limitations or the consequence of copyists making errors as they copied what they did not fully understand.

The mid-Tang is famous as a period of renewal of intellectual life, but this turn of thought went far beyond the famous theoretical treatises, such as Han Yu's "On the Origin of the Way" (Yuan Dao) or Li Ao's three-part "Letter on Restoring One's Nature" (Fuxing shu). Acts of interpretation and new explanations seem to have become a habit of thought. This appears even on the most basic level: Meng Jiao often concluded his poems with "only now I understand that . . . " or rejects conventional wisdom with "who claims that . . . ?" Han Yu, in particular, was given to unconventional interpretations. When Meng Jiao's infant son died, Han Yu wrote a long poem of consolation, framed as a message brought from Heaven, arguing with some sophistry that it was better not to have a son. Meng Jiao himself wrote a tortured sequence on the destruction of apricot buds by a late spring frost, trying to work out the "message" in the analogy with the death of his infant son. In "A Theory of Heaven" (Tian shuo), Liu Zongyuan reported an argument by Han Yu that human beings, in their violence to nature, are like a rotting sore on the Earth, and whoever harms people is doing Heaven a favor; Liu Zongyuan proposed a counterargument, claiming Heaven's utter indifference. Liu Yuxi then picked up the thread and wrote his own "Discourse on Heaven" (Tian lun). The Chan monk Zongmi (780–841) was a good friend of Bai Juyi and many secular intellectuals, and sometime between 828 and 835 he wrote "On the Origin of Man" (Yuan ren lun), a defense of Buddhism in the secular discursive mode, presumably responding to Han Yu's attacks on Buddhism. It was an age of making new arguments, whether those arguments were serious, whimsical, or some undecidable position between the two.

In this period we sometimes find representations of a cruel, even malicious, Heaven, a notion largely absent in the Chinese tradition since the time Sima Qian suggested it in the "Biography of Bo Yi and Shu Qi." In "Teasing Zhang Ji" (Tiao Zhang Ji) Han Yu explains the hardships suffered by Li Bai and Du Fu by proposing a theory that Heaven deliberately made them suffer in order to make them write great poetry, then sent heavenly messengers down to gather up the poems and take them back to Heaven. Their extant works are only the few pieces that slipped out of the bundle and dropped back down into the mortal world. In "Don't Go out the Gate" (Gong wu chu men) the poet Li He describes a Qu Yuan-like figure hunted down by monstrous creatures, then killed by Heaven to "save" him from being devoured.

If the poems, prose works, and stories often read today represent a particularly creative intellectual and literary culture, it is also important to remember that it was in this very period, between 804 and 806, that the Japanese monk Kūkai visited China and assembled a corpus of poetics representing the conservative traditions of the seventh and eighth centuries; he also reported that the poetics of "Wang Changling" was particularly popular with talents in the capital. Kūkai was not traveling in elite circles, and the "talents," if not a bookseller's advertisement, were not the writers we have been discussing. We should also keep in mind that when Linghu Chu compiled his anthology *Poems for Imperial Perusal* in 817, the only contemporary poet included from those mentioned above was Zhang Ji, and he was represented by a single, quite innocuous quatrain. The innovative writers mentioned above by and large composed their most famous poetry in "ancient-style" verse, but the metrically regulated genres remained the norm of social exchange. These same writers did highly original work in old-style *fu*, but the regulated *fu* of the examinations remained the dominant practice. The problem with a successful avant-garde is that it eventually becomes canonical, and the ocean of banality in which it floats is lost or forgotten. This is as it should be, but it is worth contrasting the age of Xuanzong, when many of the most famous poems were composed by minor figures with only a few surviving verses. That was an age in which poetry was a shared social discourse; in the mid-Tang we are in an age of authors who achieved excellence by distinction from the social norm rather than within it.

The group around Han Yu was by far the most daring in purely literary terms, though Bai Juyi's narrative ballads and poems of social protest had a wider and more lasting effect. Throughout much of his career Han Yu collected men of talent, lectured them, and promoted their interests. In his "Discourse on the Teacher" (Shi shuo) of 802 he first used the term *guwen* as "ancient[-style] prose," and the term has become associated with his prose ever since. Han Yu did not mean imitating the style of any particular ancient text; rather it was his way of reconciling the opposing values of study and spontaneity. Perhaps his most famous statement on "ancient-style prose" was in one of the many letters he wrote to young men who had earlier written to him, showing him their writings and asking for instruction. Han Yu's advice was to read the ancients and write, trying to get rid of all commonplaces and ignoring the opinion of others. Eventually one will reach a stage in which the words will flow out spontaneously and perfectly. The ideas and "aims" of the ancients were to be learned, not their diction. Indeed, the "ancient" prose style that Han Yu created was a Tang prose style, a style that gestured to pre-Qin and some Western Han prose rather than imitating it. Tang formal prose tended to be euphuistic and Senecan; Han Yu created a Ciceronian prose.

Han Yu was intemperate. Tang emperors generally undertook their appointed roles for the Daoist and Buddhist communities, as well as for the Confucian community of the state bureaucracy and elite. All the gods, buddhas, and ancestors received their due, and the state prospered. In 819 Emperor Xianzong prepared to receive a sacred relic, a bone of the Buddha. Han Yu submitted a petition to the throne protesting the act and suggesting that this bone of a foreigner, representing a foreign religion, be promptly discarded for the disgusting thing it was. Perhaps the worst part of the letter was the threat to imperial longevity if Xianzong continued to show reverence to Buddhism. The immediate consequence was Han Yu's exile to Chaozhou, in modern Guangdong, a post almost as deadly to northern officials in reality as in the imagination. The issue may not have been the protest per se, but the very power of Han Yu's aggressive rhetoric. We might add that Emperor Xianzong indeed did die in the following year, perhaps poisoned on purpose, perhaps succumbing not to Buddhism but to an elixir compounded by a Daoist. Han Yu lived to return to a court post, but lost his daughter on the journey south.

Han Yu's poetry runs a wide gamut of styles, sometimes playful, sometimes serious, sometimes archaic, and sometimes painfully human, as in the poem on revisiting the site of his daughter's death when coming back from his Chaozhou exile. His "South Mountains" (Nanshan shi) is a long description of the mountains south of Chang'an, celebrating the richness of the imperial heartland and the order of the world. In the Northern Song the relative merits of "South Mountains" and Du Fu's "Journey North" were debated. Du Fu ended up the victor, with poetry conceived in such a way that largely excluded the kind of continuous invention represented by Han Yu. The final judgment was that he "turned prose into poetry," that he somehow transgressed the proper essence of the genre.

Li Guan died in 794, far too young to fulfill his promise. Ouyang Zhan lived on until soon after the turn of the ninth century. Of that group who gathered in Chang'an in 792 to take the examination, Meng Jiao survived to become an important literary figure. Only one prose work survives; the rest is all poetry, almost entirely "ancient-style" verse. Meng Jiao had already had a poetic career by the time he came to Chang'an; although we can see elements in his earlier poetry that foreshadow his future development as a poet, he was, at best a minor poet. The admiration of Han Yu and Li Guan, along with his failures in the examination, seems to have turned him into something greater. Meng Jiao's poetry is never really beautiful; it is great by its fierce energy. One suspects that he was truly mad, a madness that was only marginally under control in the social world but which found adequate expression in his poetry. Unlike Han Yu, Meng Jiao was not a learned poet, but he invented no less than Han Yu. His poetic sequences, several of which have been mentioned earlier, are remarkable. He also wrote a great deal about his devotion to writing poetry, which made him something of a hero later in the ninth century, when a life defined by poetry became an important value.

The Northern Song turned Meng Jiao from a major figure in poetry to a minor one, and he stayed a minor figure until modern times. The Northern Song judgment was that his poetry "made one unhappy," implying that the function of poetry was to make the reader happy, to put life's difficulties in a bearable light. Perhaps the most devastating attack came from none other than Su Shi (1037–1101), a believer in equanimity, who began a pair of poems on the poet with the line "I hate Meng Jiao's poetry."

Zhang Ji was enthusiastically promoted by Han Yu and Meng Jiao in the 790s, but apart from a few poems in the "ancient" style, strongly showing the imprint of Han Yu, his extant work does not show the group's love of the strange. He also had close connections with Bai Juyi, who has a long poem on reading Zhang Ji's *yuefu*, praising their social value and lamenting that there is no longer an office for selecting such poems to present them to the ruler. Zhang Ji's greatest talents lay in a different direction, which made him an influential figure in the turn poetry took during the 820s; he was the master of a certain kind of regulated verse, making that restricted form sound as natural as speech.

Han Yu was surrounded by a group of lesser poets and prose writers, who often tried to outdo one another in wit and strangeness. The most remarkable of these was on the fringes of the group, Li He, who died in his mid-twenties. The influence of Meng Jiao is clear in some of his poems, but he represented a level of imaginative invention unparalleled by any other poet of the Tang. Han Yu was his examiner for the provincial exams, but in the capital he was not allowed to sit for the literary examination on the technical ground that the *jin* of *jinshi* ("presented scholar," the term for those allowed to sit for the examination) was homophonous with another character used in his father's name, thus violating a taboo. In a famous but unsuccessful defense, Han Yu asked, if the father was known as "humane" (*ren*), then would the son not be allowed the name of "human being" (*ren*).

Li He represented the "poet" in a new mode, or a mode dimly adumbrated by Meng Jiao. According to the account of his sister, he would ride out every day, composing couplets, putting them in a brocade bag; in the evening he would return and put the couplets together into poems. Once he composed a poem, he would lose interest in it and discard it. Earlier in the tradition being a poet was an activity that was only part of a full life; it might be the activity for which a person was best known, but it did not completely absorb the person. The image of the poet as someone entirely absorbed in his art did become prominent in the 830s, over a decade after Li He's death; this in turn is related to the peculiar fate of Li He's collected poems. There is little indication that Li He's poetry had much impact during his lifetime. Certainly some poems must have been known, but we do not find others emulating him as they did Meng Jiao. Before he died, Li He entrusted a manuscript of his poetry to one Shen Shushi, who put it in his luggage and forgot about it. Late one night in 831, fourteen years after Li He's death, Shen Shushi was drunk and, rummaging in his luggage, he found Li He's poems. With a guilt no doubt intensified by his inebriation, Shen Shushi sent a servant to wake up a young writer in his brother's service and ask him to write a preface. This was Du Mu (803–852), who was to become one of the most prominent poets and writers of the mid-ninth century. Roused from his sleep, Du Mu was irritated and refused the request, but Shen Shushi's perseverance finally compelled him to compose perhaps the least laudatory preface to any literary collection in the Tang. Provided with the necessary preface, Li He's collected poems entered circulation and soon came into the hands of a young Li Shangyin, who was to become the most famous poet of the mid-century. It was Li Shangyin who was fascinated by the poetry and took the unusual step of looking up Li He's sister to find out about his life. Li Shangyin's "short biography" (*xiao zhuan*) has many of the features of a Tang tale of the fantastic, with Li He's death being a summons from the Emperor of Heaven to come and write poems for him.

By the early 830s the image of the poet completely absorbed in his craft was already widespread and was centered on a poet very different from Li He, but a poet who also began his career with the support of Han Yu and Meng Jiao. In 811 a monk from the northeast, with the religious name Wuben, set off for Luoyang to make the acquaintance of Meng Jiao and Han Yu. They praised his poetic daring extravagantly. No doubt under their influence, Wuben left the Buddhist community and resumed his secular name Jia Dao (779–843). Only a few pieces in Jia Dao's current collection of poems, however, suggest the mannered extravagance of the Han Yu group. He soon turned to an almost exclusive devotion to regulated verse and craft of the parallel couplet. His story, however, belongs to the next generation, when he became the most prominent example of the devoted poet-craftsman.

While Bai Juyi was on good terms with Han Yu, he represented a very different direction in mid-Tang poetry. With over 2,800 poems, Bai Juyi's is the largest collection of Tang poetry extant, in no small measure due to the extraordinary care he devoted to preparing and preserving the collection. As he lived on to a ripe old age, he added to the collection in installments and had copies made to be deposited with family members and in temple libraries (in one case with the instructions that the manuscript was not to be loaned out). Long regulated poems exchanged with Yuan Zhen and later Liu Yuxi show that he could be as difficult and rhetorical as any contemporary, but in general Bai Juyi prided himself on his plainness and ease. He was arguably the most popular poet of the day. His works went to Korea and Japan, where a Tang manuscript version is still preserved. Yuan Zhen once referred to "printed" versions of his and Bai Juyi's poems, but these were perhaps just single sheets, rather than a collection. This remains, however, the earliest reference to literary works being printed. Probably the most popular works were the long narratives "Song of Enduring Sorrow" and the "Ballad of the Pipa" (Pipa yin). In the latter Bai hears someone playing a pipa (a plucked string instrument with a timbre like that of a mandolin) by night on a river; he finds the performer, who was once a courtesan in Chang'an; she plays for him and tells the story of her former popularity, aging, and getting married to a river merchant.

Bai Juyi developed a genial, rambling poetic style, with a distinct charm. He often treated topics of everyday life as Han Yu did. Han Yu writes of losing a tooth, while Bai Juyi writes of eating bamboo shoots. Bai was a master of the tongue-in-cheek: he could do a mock physiognomy of his portrait in court attire and conclude that such a person was suited only to a life outside of court. His humor was the other face of his unique capacity for moral seriousness, with many poems on the hardships of the common people.

Although they were actually together only briefly, Bai Juyi's closest friend was Yuan Zhen, with whom he composed an extensive "exchange collection" (changhe ji), each poem by one supplied with a companion piece by the other. In his youth, Yuan Zhen had compiled a small collection of poems about women and love, which he subsequently excluded from his collection as he was rising to political prominence. These poems, however, survived independently, and at least some were copied into a mid-tenth-century anthology. Yuan Zhen was a fine poet, but his reputation did not hold up as well as Bai Juyi's. His most famous poem is "Lianchang Palace" (Lianchang gong ci), a long ballad in which the poet encounters an old man at a deserted palace near Luoyang; the old man tells of the days of Emperor Xuanzong and the ruin of the palace and the troubles of the empire since the rebellion.

Most Tang poets spent their careers moving from place to place, either seeking patronage or being constantly sent to new posts. Bai Juyi's long residence in Luoyang in the last part of his life, from 828 until his death in 846, was very unusual. Xue Tao (ca 785–832) was born in Chang'an, but early in her life moved to Chengdu following her father's posting. He died when she was in her teens; rather than getting married, she took on courtesan registry and developed a significant reputation as a poet. Soon she was brought into the establishment of successive governors, where she entertained with her poetry and her wit. She knew Yuan Zhen when he was briefly in Chengdu in 809, and they exchanged poems. Since flirtation was only proper in such exchanges with courtesans, it is hard to decide if there is any substance to the speculations that they had an affair. Late in her life she gave up courtesan registry and took registration as a Daoist nun. A particularly fine paper for writing poems was associated with her. About eighty poems survive from a collection that once circulated in five scrolls.

Liu Zongyuan and Liu Yuxi, former members of the brief Wang Shuwen government, would have probably preferred to travel more. Emperor Xianzong held an unyielding grudge against those who had usurped power during the brief months of his invalid father's reign in 805, and these two writers, who had been part of that government, spent ten years in minor posts in remote provinces. They were briefly recalled to Chang'an in 815, but soon sent back to the provinces. Liu Zongyuan died a year before Emperor Xianzong and never resumed a normal career. Liu Yuxi lived on to pass through more provincial posts and finally return to the center, becoming Bai Juyi's principle poetic correspondent after the untimely death of Yuan Zhen.

Liu Zongyuan's fame as a prose stylist would eventually match Han Yu's own. His prose is quieter, with little of Han Yu's rhetorical fire. He is best known for his parables and his landscape prose, especially a set of accounts of excursions known collectively as the "Eight Accounts at Yongzhou" (Yongzhou baji). These works combine narration, description, and reflective interpretation into a satisfying whole. Liu Zongyuan also left a relatively small poetry collection, which came to be greatly appreciated in the Northern Song for the gentleness and ease of his work.

Liu Zongyuan is dubiously credited with an anecdotal miscellany called Records of Longcheng (Longcheng lu). Such brief accounts of marvels, local customs, political gossip, and circulating anecdotes were not considered high literature in the Chinese tradition, nor would it have been so in the European definition of literature. Such works were, however, read and enjoyed over the centuries and deserve a place in a larger account of literary culture. As with the differentiation of literature and history from tales of love and the supernatural, such miscellanies sometimes took a stand on one side or another of the thematic divide. One larger work of this period is the Supplement to the Dynastic History (Guoshi bu) by Li Zhao, who we know was active in the 810s and 820s. Li Zhao conceived of this work in three scrolls as a continuation of Liu Su's (fl. 740s) Fine Tales of the Sui and Tang (Sui Tang jiahua); Liu Su's book gave anecdotes through the first part of Xuanzong's reign, while Li Zhao's work consisted of anecdotes from the later part of Xuanzong's reign into the 820s. Li Zhao's preface picks up a familiar theme in such works, using what Confucius "did not talk about" as a criterion for exclusion:

Whatever tells of retribution, gives account of ghosts and spirits, or shows dreams and prognostications coming true I have entirely excluded. If it is a record of something factual, investigates the principles behind things, shows encouragement or warning, selects customs, or provides aid in genial conversation, I have written it down.

We can see here the mirror image of Gu Kuang's preface, with Li Zhao excluding precisely what Gu Kuang was defending.

The still larger *New Account [of Tales of the World] of the Great Tang* (*Da Tang [shishuo] xinyu*) by Liu Su (not to be confused with the Liu Su who was the author of *Fine Tales of the Sui and Tang*), in one version given with a preface dated to 807, was meant as a continuation of the fifth-century *A New Account of Tales of the World*. Subdivided into thirty topics in thirteen scrolls, it offers a rich array of anecdotes, not entirely excluding the supernatural, from the founding of the dynasty through the 770s.

When Emperor Xianzong died in 820, he left the empire more secure than it had been since the An Lushan Rebellion. His successor, Emperor Muzong, ruled only about five years before succumbing to experiments with Daoist elixirs; Muzong was useless, but far superior to his teenage son and successor Emperor Jingzong (r. 824–827). Jingzong's wild adolescent behavior evidently convinced the court eunuchs that he was a liability, and they discreetly murdered him after only a few years on the throne. The government managed generally quite well without a competent emperor. Already by the early 820s, however, the creative exuberance of Emperor Xianzong's reign was waning. Meng Jiao, Li He, and Liu Zongyuan were dead; Han Yu began writing regulated verse, and Bai Juyi's "new *yuefu*" phase was over. In the mid-820s the teenage Li Shangyin was studying ancient-style prose, but in 829 he found a patron in Linghu Chu, then a military governor. Linghu Chu encouraged Li Shangyin to give up ancient-style prose and instead master the intricacies of parallel prose; Li Shangyin complied and became a master of the form. We might recall that Linghu Chu had compiled the *Poems for Imperial Perusal* in 817, selecting only conservative regulated verse. A remarkable generation had passed, and in the wake of its passage a more conservative tradition reappeared, a literary style largely unchanged since the 760s.

VI. Last flowering (821–860)

After the palace coup of 827 that ended the brief reign of Emperor Jingzong, Jingzong's brother, also an adolescent, was placed on the throne. In a happier age this young man, Emperor Wenzong (r. 827–840), would have been an exemplary ruler; his moment in history required ruthless determination, and his willingness to reflect and heed the advice of others – the very qualities of Emperor Taizong's greatness – became his weakness. He was afraid of the court eunuchs, for good reason. After a plot to kill all the eunuchs failed in 835, he spent his last half-decade of rule as a helpless and disappointed man.

Wenzong had a real passion for poetry, and in his later years he was said to have proposed creating special Hanlin academicians of poetry. The proposal was blocked by the objections of court officials. Whether historically accurate or not, it is worthwhile to compare this moment with the literary establishment of Empress Wu's reign. Setting aside the obvious fact that no court official would have had the temerity to oppose such a proposal from Empress Wu, Empress Wu wanted literary courtiers of broad competence, who would compose poetry on some occasions, but on other occasions would write *fu*, compose prose prefaces, participate in scholarly compilations, and perhaps draft government documents. Wenzong wanted specifically "poets," which was by this point in history seen as a special gift, distinct from learning or the capacity to write prose. The main court official who was said to have opposed Wenzong's proposal complained that "poets" in this special sense were a disreputable and unreliable lot. Wenzong's regular Hanlin academicians and his literary establishment all, of course, wrote elegant poetry on court occasions, but these were not "poets" in the sense Wenzong wanted. Hanlin Academicians were, at least theoretically, appointed at imperial discretion, and the reason to create Hanlin poets could only have been to bring certain people to court outside the usual bureaucratic process. We do not know whom Wenzong wanted to appoint, but we can infer that he wanted to bring in people outside the court bureaucracy, leaping over the usual procedures of review and promotion. In other words, Wenzong hoped to make the court again a cultural center, implicitly recognizing that the center of culture had moved elsewhere.

If Wenzong lived in quiet terror of his inner court, the eunuch establishment, and the capital army they controlled, his outer court was torn apart by two feuding factions in officialdom, one led by Niu Sengru (780–ca 848) and the other by Li Deyu (787–850). Despite attempts to dignify the enmity between the two men by ideological differences, it was ultimately nothing more than a personal feud, magnified by webs of patronage and obligation. When one faction was in power, the leader and highest-ranking members of the other faction would go off to serve as military governors of the most lucrative provinces. Ever since the An Lushan Rebellion, young men often sought employment with the military governors, who could make appointments to their staffs without going through the usual bureaucratic channels. In earlier periods, however, the protégé would accept an honorable post in the central government if one was offered. Toward the middle of the ninth century we see a new phenomenon: young men would resign from some of the most prestigious starting posts in the central government to take service with military governors. We suspect that the primary reason was financial: the military commands in the provinces absorbed a significant part of the local tax revenue, and writers serving under military commissioners rarely complained of poverty. In this we can see the first phase of the move to a decentralized culture of regional courts.

Some of the old men famous in Emperor Xianzong's reign lived on: Bai Juyi, Liu Yuxi, and Li Shen, who in his youth had written the ballad to accompany "Yingying's Story." About half of Bai Juyi's poems date from after his retirement to Luoyang in 828; although the good anthologist can extract from this huge corpus an engaging image of the old poet, the reader who reads the whole corpus sees a poet who constantly repeats himself. Many younger poets of this era ruthlessly pruned their collected poems; Bai Juyi seems to have carefully preserved everything he wrote, adding new works to his collection, whose quantity he proudly enumerated.

In some circles the polished regulated-verse style of the post-rebellion period had continued to prosper as the highest model for poetry throughout the turbulent inventiveness of the years between 792 and 820. In the 820s writers in this style returned to the center of the poetic stage. Yao He (ca 779–ca 849) was a prominent master of regulated verse in the five-syllable line; his 837 poetry anthology, *The Supreme Mystery* (*Jixuan ji*), selected many of the same poets found in Gao Zhongwu's *The Fine Officers of the Restoration* of 779, with some additions. Yao He was, in turn, closely associated with Jia Dao, the foremost master of regulated verse in the five-syllable line. Jia Dao and the anecdotal lore that grew up around him added a new and attractive twist to the conservative tradition of regulated verse: we see the poet utterly absorbed in his craft, spending time and effort on composition. This was directly opposed to the dominant strain of Chinese poetics, which wanted to see a poem as the immediate response to experience or pent-up feeling. One famous story, almost certainly apocryphal, places Jia Dao walking on a street in Chang'an deliberating the choice of a word in a couplet:

> Birds spend the night on trees by the pool,
> a monk [shoves] / [knocks] at a gate in moonlight.

Han Yu, a high official, was coming along the street with his entourage. Ordinary citizens were supposed to make way, but Jia Dao, oblivious to what was going on around him, blocked the way. Angry attendants dragged Jia Dao before Han Yu, who asked for an explanation. Jia Dao explained his dilemma, and Han Yu responded: "'Knocks' is better." Note that "shoves" would imply that the monk is coming home, while "knocks" would imply that he is paying a visit. The phrase *tuiqiao*, "shoves-knocks," still survives as the term for a careful choice of words in poetry. In this period the phrase *kuyin*, earlier used in its literal sense of "chanting [poetry] in suffering," came to mean "painstaking composition," reciting a couplet over and over again to get the phrasing just right.

There are two implications of such an image of the poet as craftsman. First, poetry can be mastered by effort; second, this work on poetry is not merely mechanical, but comes from complete absorption in the art. Equally important, this kind of poetry used a very limited lexicon and few allusions; success was not dependent on learning. Jia Dao attracted a large number of protégés, but neither Jia Dao himself nor many of his protégés ever passed the literary examination.

The ninth- and tenth-century poets who are now most often read do not belong to the legacy of Jia Dao, but for many in that era he was the dominant figure in the world of poetry. One anecdote records that a later admirer had a statue of the poet cast, before which he repeated Jia Dao's name as others repeated the name of Buddha. Many of his admirers, both in his lifetime and later, came from the provinces, from families with little or no history of service to the dynasty (as was the case with Jia Dao himself). There is, moreover, a close connection between the kind of poetry practiced by Jia Dao and the numerous pedagogic works on poetics from the ninth and tenth centuries; one such treatise is even attributed to Jia Dao himself. The promise of such poetry (closely allied to the promise of Chan Buddhism) was that it required intense devotion and concentration, but not traditional learning, thus making it within the reach of a wider spectrum of the educated elite than anything earlier.

We see the cachet of passionate commitment to writing also in ancient-style prose, with the same exclusivity that we find in poetry. Liu Tui (821–after 874) wrote in a letter, "Eating and drinking I never forget prose; in the darkness I never forget prose. In sorrow and in rage, in illness and merriment, in a crowd and traveling on a mission, I never once fail to have prose on my mind." As was the case with poetry, excellence in prose no longer seemed to promise political success; in 848 Liu Tui theatrically buried his writings, lamenting their futility in "Inscription for the Entombment of My Prose at the Doushuai Temple in Zizhou" (Zizhou Doushuai si wenzhong ming). Obviously he preserved the inscription and continued writing.

The five-syllable poetic line and the seven-syllable line had very different associations. The five-syllable line, preferred by Jia Dao and his followers, had a certain austerity; the seven-syllable line, originally a song line, suggested unrestraint rather than discipline. Among the many possible associations of the seven-syllable line was a certain melancholy panache; this became popular in the 830s and is best represented in the poetry of Xu Hun (ca 788–ca 854), who wrote exclusively in regulated genres. Xu Hun is perhaps best known for his "meditations on the past" (huaigu), occasioned by a visit to some ancient site. The following is a couplet from a poem on visiting the ancient ruins of Luoyang:

> Crows squawk in twilight clouds and go back to the ancient ramparts,
> geese lose their way in the cold rain and descend to the empty moats.

Xu Hun was very popular in the Song dynasty and is one of the only two cases where we possess a facsimile of a Tang writer's works in his autograph. The original manuscript survived into the Southern Song, when it was traced and printed to preserve his calligraphy.

The writer best remembered for the melancholy panache popular in the 830s and 840s was one who perhaps would have preferred fame for his serious political writings. Du Mu was the grandson of the famous Du You (735–812), who had served as chief minister in several reigns. Du Mu made his first youthful bid for literary attention with his "Fu on Apang Palace" (Apang gong fu), probably from 826. This describes the extravagance of the First Emperor of Qin's famous palace as predicting Qin's swift ruin. Du Mu used freely rhymed prose to create a form that was different from the various standard fu types: the popular regulated fu (lüfu), the rhetorical "parallel fu" (pianfu), and the "old-style fu" (gufu), popular among the "ancient" writers of the preceding generation and their younger inheritors, such as Li Deyu. The "Fu on Apang Palace" is considered an important forerunner of the "prose fu" (wenfu) popular in the Northern Song. Anecdote has it that enthusiasm for this work ensured him a place in the graduates of the literary examination.

Receiving a prestigious starting post as an editor in the court literary establishment, Du Mu gave it up after only a few months to take a position with a military governor in the southeast. After a few years he was sent on a mission to Yangzhou, whose military governor was Niu Sengru. This began his association with the Niu Sengru faction and, more importantly, with

Yangzhou, the third greatest city in the empire and its foreign port. It was mistakenly believed that Yangzhou was the city about which Bao Zhao had written his "*Fu* on the Weed-Covered City" (*Wucheng fu*) in the fifth century, describing a city's wealth and extravagance, followed by its ruin. Yangzhou was also the city that Emperor Yang of the Sui had made his southern capital, and it had become strongly associated with sensual pleasures, tinged with the melancholy of impending doom. Although we cannot say with confidence that Du Mu frequented the pleasure quarters of the city more than any other official, he created such a compelling image of its pleasures that the poetic image stuck with the person and with the city:

> Green hills half-hidden in haze, rivers stretch far away,
> autumn ends in the Southland, leaves shrivel on plants and trees.
> By the Twenty-Fourth Bridge on a brightly moonlit night
> at what spot do you have a girl white as jade play on the flute?

Du Mu spent much of his career in the scenic and pleasure-loving southeast, and this is the Du Mu that later readers remembered. In much of his poetry and prose, however, he presented a very different face. He thought of himself as having military talents and composed a commentary on the *Sunzi*, the military classic, along with essays on tactics. The title of his essay "Culpable Words" (*Zuiyan*) anticipates that his arguments will get him in trouble, beginning a minor late ninth-century tradition of collections of outspoken prose. Such collections were entitled with the unpleasant consequences anticipated by the author, such as Luo Yin's (833–909 / 10) *Writings to be Slandered* (*Chanshu*), whose stylized satire and moral posturing supposedly kept him from passing the examination. Du Mu's frequent claim that he would not be heeded or would get into trouble for a particular work is clearly in the lineage of the "ancient-style" writers of the preceding generation.

Later in his life, perhaps aware of his reputation as a rake, Du Mu radically pruned his collected works; since many poems on the pleasures of Jiangnan remain, we can only speculate on what was excluded. Du Mu's drastic editing perhaps inspired the various supplements to his poetry that appeared in the Song. Du Mu was famous for his regulated quatrains, which make up a large proportion of these addenda to his collected poems. Since known works of other poets were often included in these addenda, it is impossible to say how many of the other poems in the addenda are indeed by Du Mu.

In 838, caring for his nearly blind brother, Du Mu made his second visit to Yangzhou. This time Niu Sengru's enemy, Li Deyu, was the military governor. That same year the Japanese monk Ennin reached shore at Yangzhou with a large party of diplomats and clerics, after his boat broke up in coastal waters. Ennin's remarkable and extensive diary in Chinese, kept through to his return to Japan in 847, gives us an incomparable picture of life in Tang China in the mid-ninth century. As is the case with the Chinese accounts of journeys to India, it is filled with those details that only a foreigner would think worth noticing and writing down. We read of the bureaucratic red tape that kept Ennin in Yangzhou awaiting authorization from Chang'an; we read of the modest gifts of gold dust that Li Deyu would hand out on various occasions (giving us a rare glimpse of how the patronage system really worked); we learn how much things cost and the daily life in Chang'an's monastic establishments. We also learn, in great detail, of the effects of Emperor Wuzong's 845 decree, disestablishing virtually all the Buddhist temples and monasteries throughout the empire and laicizing the vast majority of Buddhist clerics.

Emperor Wenzong had passed away early in 840; his successor Wuzong fell under the influence of Daoist advisers, who used the opportunity to advance their old rivalry with Buddhism. The Buddhist church, had, more-over, amassed immense wealth, which was an attractive target for a government beset with economic difficulties, not the least of which was a shortage of metal for currency. The 845 decree was the last in a series of repressive measures against the Buddhist church, and it was carried out with bureaucratic efficiency that caused lasting damage. Du Mu was then prefect in Chizhou, a poor prefecture on the northern banks of the Yangzi; he applauded the edict and no doubt supervised the destruction of the temples in his prefecture. With the characteristic Tang ability to hold contradictory values, however, he lamented an aging laicized monk with nowhere to go:

> His snow-white hair is not an inch in length,
> in autumn's cold, his strength gets weaker still.
> Alone he goes down a path of leaves
> still holding his tattered cassock in hand.
> Twilight among a thousand peaks
> and he knows not where to go.

In spring of the following year, Emperor Wuzong died, reputedly from taking a Daoist elixir. His successor, Emperor Xuānzong (to be distinguished from the famous Emperor Xuanzong of the eighth century), soon rescinded the edict, but the damage was done.

The Buddhist sect that emerged from the so-called "Huichang Persecution" having suffered the least harm was Chan. We have an extensive corpus of "recorded comments" (yulu), attributed to Chan masters dating back to the first half of the seventh century. While we have reason to doubt the historical veracity of dialogues of some of the earlier masters, much of this material clearly comes from the Tang and Five Dynasties; when we come to the ninth century, we can have more confidence in the attribution to individual masters. We have both collections of sayings by individual masters, such as Jiangxi Daoyi (Mazu) from the eighth century, Dongshan Liangjie (807–867), and Linji Yixuan (d. 867), the last two revered as founders of Chan subtraditions. We also have compendia such as the *Record of Passing on the Flame from the Jingde Reign* (*Jingde chuandeng lu*), with a preface dated 1006. The religious message is conveyed through some of the liveliest scenes in Tang writing, with witty dialogues and paradoxes often punctuated by blows from the master's cane. If elite Tang literature is characterized by love of eloquence and its ability to evoke a mood, the recorded comments represent a different, sometimes earthy genius and a different kind of love of language, which always seeks to get beyond mere language.

The most interesting figure of this era in Daoist letters was Cao Tang (ca 797–ca 866), though his Daoism is distinctly of the literary sort. His fame rests on two series, a hundred "Shorter Poems on Wandering as an Immortal" (Xiao youxian shi) and seventeen out of an original fifty "Larger Poems on Wandering as an Immortal" (Da youxian shi). In their conception as a century of quatrains and in their representation of moments in the life of the immortals, "Shorter Poems" seem modeled on Wang Jian's "Palace Lyrics" (Gong ci), composed around 820, representing scenes of the Inner Palace so persuasively that it seemed he had some firsthand knowledge he should not have had. Both centuries belong to a tradition of quatrain vignettes, sketching a moment in a memorable way. The century of quatrains was to become a popular form from the late ninth century on, with "palace lyrics" being one favorite topic. Our extant third of the "Larger Poems on Wandering as an Immortal" suggests that the original was a sequentially arranged set of lyrics for moments in a group of famous stories of the gods and immortals.

Li Shangyin (811/813–858), who was to become the most famous literary figure of the mid-ninth century, was not a Daoist poet, but a period spent studying Daoism left a profound impact on his poetry. As in Europe during the Renaissance and afterward, the discourse on gods and goddesses was conventionally employed in other venues, particularly in reference to the court and love. A segment of Li Shangyin's poetry is "clandestine," implying some situation that is ostentatiously concealed. Taking their cue from the overtly clandestine poems, Chinese critics have sought hidden referents, erotic or political, in a wide range of Li Shangyin's poetry. Primarily since the mid-seventeenth century, numerous divergent interpretations have been proposed for a wide range of his poetry, interpretations taking the form of a contextual scenario that explains a poem. It is worth keeping in mind that if such poems circulated in Li Shangyin's own day – and it is by no means certain that they did – most contemporary readers would have understood their referents no better than later readers. Such poems create a restricted community of those who might understand, perhaps a community as small as the poet and one other person. Insofar as the poet knew that such poems would reach a wider community, he knew that their clandestine aura was their attraction. The poetry here does not lie in finding the "key" that unlocks the secret; it lies in the construction of secrecy itself. The verses, particularly those "Left Untitled" (Wuti), remain some of the most effective in the tradition:

> Your coming was empty words, you left without a trace,
> the moon goes down past the upstairs room, the bell before dawn.
> Dreams of parting far away, crying couldn't call you back,
> the letter hastily finished, ink not yet thick.
> Candlelight half encloses kingfishers sewn in gold,
> the aroma of musk faintly crosses embroidered lotuses.
> . . .

The reference to ink in the fourth line refers to grinding ink, here done with such haste that the ink has not become fully black. The intensity plays against the uncertainty of the situation. Did the other person come or not? He seems to be awake waiting, but then he refers to a dream, yet we don't know if it was a real dream or an actual visit that now only seems like a dream. The fabric in the third couplet suggests a bed, and hence the movement of the poet's attention to the bed, but the empty space in the light is matched by the faint odor of musk, which may suggest that the beloved was there.

Poems like this are a significant minority of the full range of Li Shangyin's poetic work. In many ways Li Shangyin was the true inheritor of the poetry of the first decades of the ninth century. His patron Linghu Chu may have persuaded him to give up ancient-style prose, but he celebrated Han Yu's achievements in public prose in the poem "Han Yu's Stele" (Han bei). In his two-hundred-line "Coming to the Western Suburbs" (Xingci xijiao zuo yibaiyun) he wrote of the abuses of the government and the suffering of the common people. He loved Du Fu, even writing a poem in Du Fu's persona, and the Song literary and political figure Wang Anshi (1021–1086) counted him as the Tang poet who most perfectly followed Du Fu. Li Shangyin wrote poems on history, particularly on the Northern and Southern Dynasties, in which moral condemnation is often hard to separate from sympathy. His "poems on things" (*yongwu shi*) have an unmatched thickness and subtlety. In the hermetic poems suggesting love affairs he continued the early ninth-century culture of romance, giving it a unique intensity. Finally, if Du Mu wrote the preface for Li He's poetry grudgingly and showed Li He's influence only unwittingly, Li Shangyin was the poet who understood Li He's remarkable achievement and transformed his legacy.

Apart from Du Mu, Wen Tingyun was the most gifted of Li Shangyin's contemporaries. Scholars disagree on the date of his birth across a quarter century, between 798 and 824; the date of his death is also uncertain, but is usually given between 866 and 870. Wen Tingyun's literary remains come in various pieces, which may suggest the ways in which literary works were circulating in the mid-ninth century. One large section of his current poetry collection consists of occasional poems and conventional *yuefu*, not unlike other poetry collections from the period. The two scrolls at the beginning of the collection represent isometric songs and *yuefu* in the Li He tradition, so different from the *yuefu* in the following scroll that we suspect these two scrolls must have circulated independently and been added to the more conventional poetry collection. Like Li He, Wen Tingyun often chose dramatic moments from history and legend, along with banquet scenes, scenes of women in the bedroom, and scenes of immortals. Following the main body of the poetry collection, primarily made up of Wen Tingyun's occasional poems, there is a group of very mannered social pieces that were added from an anthology of a coterie in Xiangyang between 857 and 859. This anthology, for example, included a group of comically "poetic" pieces on two singing girls getting into a fight. Finally, there are his now most famous works, song lyrics, mostly in irregular lines and set to known melodies, preserved in the tenth-century anthology *Among the Flowers* (*Huajian ji*).

The lyrics in irregular lines preserved in *Among the Flowers* are considered early examples of "song lyric" (*ci*), a genre fully established only in the Northern Song and attaining legitimacy as a genre only toward the end of the Northern Song. For Chinese readers from the Northern Song on, the "song lyric" was a genre quite distinct from poetry (*shi*), including the literary "songs" (*gexing*) discussed earlier. Like *yuefu*, song lyrics are identified by a tune title. While isometric poems were often sung in the Tang, either to isometric melodies or adapted by singers to heterometric melodies, these "song lyrics" were written specifically for the popular corpus of largely heterometric melodies; their form was dictated by the music, with a fixed number of lines, with rhyme lines dictated by the musical phrasing; each line had a fixed number of syllables, with level or deflected tones required in certain syllables in each line.

If Wen Tingyun himself wrote the song lyrics as they are preserved in *Among the Flowers*, then he would have been one of the earliest literary figures to write song lyrics as they were meant to be sung, but we must allow the possibility that these song lyrics had been modified in a singer's repertoire and were then transcribed as heterometric song lyrics according to the practice established by the tenth century, when *Among the Flowers* was compiled.

Most of Wen Tingyun's song lyrics are scenes of feeling; and insofar as they were performed by professional women singers, they were sketches of moments of longing:

> A single bead of dew, immobile and icy cold;
> reflections on waves
> fill the pool.
> Green stalks and red allure
> tangled together:
> the heart breaks;
> wind on the water, chill.

Such short songs were, as best we know, performed at parties by the attendant singing girls when passing ale to a guest and when urging him to drink. Wen Tingyun's stylized scenes of intense feeling may seem an odd counterpoint to the convivial occasion, but this was apparently the norm. As the song lyric became more literary, such lyrics were read, rather than situated in occasion. Wen Tingyun's song lyrics tend to be highly imagistic, but the irregular line and the moderate use of the vernacular enabled more lively monologic use of the form.

Among those with whom Wen Tingyun exchanged poems was Yu Xuanji (844–868). Yu Xuanji was a native of Chang'an who, after a period as the concubine of an official, took Daoist registration, which permitted freely mixing with literary men and women of the demi-monde. She was charged with beating to death her maid, whose body was discovered buried in her courtyard, and she was executed in the autumn of 868. Many of Yu Xuanji's poems have remarkable force. In "Selling Wilted Peonies" (Mai can mudan) she moves from pathos to pride, figuring herself in the flowers she poetically sells. Confident in her poetic talent, hers was the only voice among Tang women poets to protest the exclusion of women from the examination in "Visiting the South Hall of Chongzhen Lodge, I Caught Sight of Where Recent Graduates Had Written Their Names" (You Chongzhen Guan nanlou du xin jidi timing chu):

Peaks of clouds fill my eyes, letting spring daylight through,
clearly ranged, the silvery hooks appeared at the tips of their fingers.
I hate how this gown of gossamer hides the lines of my poems,
and lifting my head in vain I yearn for my own name on the graduates' list.

"Silvery hooks" referred to beautifully written characters.

Duan Chengshi (803–863) was with Wen Tingyun at Xiangyang and com-piled the anthology from which the coterie poems were taken, including a set of pieces teasing Wen Tingyun for his love affairs. Duan Chengshi is best known for the *Youyang Miscellany* (*Youyang zazu*) in thirty scrolls, the largest miscellany extant from the Tang. This includes not only brief stories of the supernatural and anecdotes, but also random bits of unusual knowl-edge and observations. It is particularly valuable for its accounts of popular beliefs.

Collections of anecdotes and tales appeared with increasing frequency through the ninth century. One of the most influential was *Accounts of Mysterious Marvels* (*Xuanguai lu*) by Niu Sengru. Some of the characters in this collection, like Yuan Wuyou ("Basically Non-existent"), draw on the con-scious fictitiousness of the early tradition of parables and *fu* frame stories, thus bringing prose narrative as close to true "fiction" as it would come for many centuries. There is a *Continuation of Accounts of Mysterious Marvels* (*Xu Xuanguai lu*) by Li Fuyan (775–833), but one story in it post-dates the author. Such collections of stories both grew and shrank in transmission. Something of such variation can be seen in our sole Tang manuscript of a story collection, from Dunhuang, related to Gan Bao's *In Search of the Supernatural*. The title is the same as Gan Bao's collection, but here it is attributed to one Gou Daoxing; some of the stories are roughly the same as in Gan Bao's collection, but there are other later stories included. Embedded poems play a prominent role in Li Mei's *Compilation of the Strange* (*Zuanyi ji*), probably from the second quarter of the ninth century. Lu Zhao's *History of Things Outside the Norm* (*Yi shi*) has a preface dated to 847, by which point, judging by his own claims, he must already have been working on the massive *fu* "The Ocean Tides" (Haichao fu).

Perhaps inspired by Bai Juyi's "Song of Enduring Sorrow," poetry and prose on Xuanzong and Lady Yang became increasingly popular in this period; both Du Mu and Li Shangyin wrote memorably on moments in this popular story. Somewhere around the middle of the ninth century, one Zheng Yu wrote an erudite poem in two hundred lines, provided with his own notes, on visiting Xuanzong's pleasure palace at the hot springs on Mount Li. In addition we begin to find the anecdote collections that would elaborate the legend with incidents, such as Zheng Chuhai's *Miscellaneous Records of the Shining Emperor* (*Minghuang zalu*). Li Deyu wrote a book of oral lore, anecdotes supposedly told by Xuanzong's chief eunuch Gao Lishi to Liu Fang, who told it to his son Liu Mian, who then passed the stories on to Li Deyu's father. In the tenth century we have Wang Renyu's *Neglected Stories of the Kaiyuan and Tianbao Reigns* (*Kaiyuan Tianbao yishi*) and Yue Shi's *The Unofficial Story of Yang Taizhen* (*Yang Taizhen waizhuan*), contributing more fanciful material to the legend of Lady Yang.

When Emperor Xuānzong died in 859, again of an overdose of Daoist elixir, the first in a series of rebellions had broken out in the southeast. Government forces put this rebellion down without difficulty, but a cycle was beginning that would leave the dynasty a hollow shell in little more than two decades. Xuānzong had, on the whole, ruled well, but he left the empire in the hands of his twenty-six-year-old son, known as Emperor Yizong (r. 859–874), who, unable to repair the tottering polity, decided to enjoy its fruits to the fullest while he could.

VII. The fall of the Tang and the age of regional states (861–960)

By the 860s the empire was beginning to break down from troubles within and enemies without. The rich lower Yangzi river provinces had been squeezed for their wealth too long, and peasants were fleeing their land or placing it under the protection of families and institutions that were exempt from taxes. Armies were too large, but any attempt to reduce their size led to revolts or an increase in the unemployed, who often turned to brigandage. The foolish and ultimately helpless Yizong increased his devotion to Buddhism and sent out sporadic edicts deploring the empire's problems.

In 865 Lu Zhao presented his monumental *fu* "The Ocean Tides," accompanied by an elaborate letter to the throne boasting that it had cost the author more than twenty years' labor. Its length is a footnote in Tang literature, though it is hardly ever read. In that same year of 865, Gao Pian (ca 822–887) was the empire's best general. He was from an old military family of the capital army and a poet; he had just been sent with an army to the northern area of modern Vietnam to recover the Tang prefectures that had recently been lost to the aggressive kingdom of Nanzhao. He recovered Annan in 865, and in 866 Jiaozhi. In 866 Choe Chiwon (857–928?) came to China on a merchant ship from Korea to study. He would end up in the service of Gao Pian. In 866 the "ancient-style" poet and prose stylist Pi Rixiu (ca 834–883) failed the examination and gathered his writings on the ills of the day, all in the "ancient" style, in a small collection, *The Marsh of Literature* (*Wensou*). Wen Tingyun most likely died that same year, the end of a generation. Yu Xuanji, with whom Wen Tingyun had exchanged poems, was popular in some capital circles. In the provinces a still relatively young poet–monk with a rising reputation, Guanxiu (831/832–912), was staying at the Buddhist complex on Mount Lu.

Two years later Yu Xuanji would be executed for murdering her maid in a fit of jealousy. We can never know if the verdict was just or if the circumstances were as transmitted, but this was what people believed. After serving with Gao Pian, Choe Chiwon would return to Korea in 883 to become the first famous figure in Sino-Korean literature. Gao Pian would serve the dynasty loyally for more than a decade, rushing to take command wherever the empire was threatened. In 880, whether by treason or the misfortunes of war, Gao Pian failed to prevent Huang Chao and his rebel army from crossing the Yangzi river. He then carved out an independent state in Huainan, one of the empire's richest and most troubled provinces. Willingly or not, Pi Rixiu was to enter the service of the rebel Huang Chao in conquered Chang'an and ultimately to be killed by him. Guanxiu would live on to a ripe old age, finding safe haven at last in Chengdu, in the newly established kingdom of Shu. About a decade after his death, in the third decade of the tenth century, his literary works were printed, so far as we know the first poet in history to have his collected works printed.

In the century between Emperor Yizong taking the throne and the official founding of the Song in 960, there was memorable writing but, apart from the formative stages of the song lyric, little that was truly new. By and large writers in this period carried on the various competing literary values from earlier in the ninth century. In poetry the polished regulated verse that was the legacy of Jia Dao continued to be the most widely practiced form, though the ability to sustain the "high style" diminished. Some poets, most notably Du Xunhe (846–904), brought more vernacular usages into regulated verse. There were prose writers in the "ancient" mode, often adopting the stylized polemical voice of Han Yu. Sun Qiao (d. 884), for example, one of the most famous prose writers of the second half of the ninth century, proudly claimed to follow in the footsteps of Han Yu's disciple Huangfu Shi. Su Shi (1037–1101) quipped, "The person who imitated Han Yu but couldn't equal him was Huangfu Shi; the person who imitated Huangfu Shi but couldn't equal *him* was Sun Qiao." Quite apart from the merits of his judgment, Su Shi's comment suggests an age of epigones. There were likewise poets who modeled their work on Du Fu, Meng Jiao, Li He, and Bai Juyi, "but couldn't equal them."

Emperor Yizong died in 873, leaving the throne to his twelve-year-old son, known as Emperor Xizong. Xizong soon made known his preference for people from the aristocracy and old families; as the dynasty faltered, it fell back on its old base of support, leaving more examination hopefuls to turn to the powerful military officials in the provinces. Rebellions were breaking out, devastating the empire's grain basket in the lower Yangzi delta and further shredding its already tattered social fabric. The deathblow was struck by the rebellion of Huang Chao; the *coup de grâce* would not be administered until a quarter-century later. Having crossed the Yangzi with the complicity of or in spite of Gao Pian, Huang Chao and a large rebel army made their way up first to Luoyang and then to Chang'an, which fell early in 881. Xizong fled to Chengdu, emulating his ancestor Emperor Xuanzong in the mid-eighth century. Huang Chao had imperial pretensions, but his regime soon degenerated into savagery, abetted by the urban mob. The story of Huang Chao's occupation of Chang'an was memorably told in Wei Zhuang's (836–910) very long "Ballad of the Wife of Qin" (Qinfu yin). This was immensely popular, but Wei Zhuang specifically excluded it from his poetry collection; long lost, it was recovered among the Dunhuang manuscripts in about a dozen copies, more than any other single Tang poem.

Loyalist forces eventually rallied, along with their Shatuo Turkish allies. Huang Chao withdrew from the partially ruined capital and was eventually hunted down and killed. The "loyalist" forces then plundered what was left of the great city. By the time Emperor Xizong returned in 885 only a few prefectures around the capital were still under direct imperial control, with the far southern provinces still giving lip service to imperial rule. Almost fifty warlords had partitioned the rest of the empire. During the last decades the dynasty was at the mercy of the warlords who surrounded the shrinking area of imperial control. Young men still came to the capital from the provinces, took the literary examination, and advanced with remarkable speed in a bureaucratic structure that no longer administered much of anything. In most cases those last Tang officials wrote as if nothing had happened. Two more emperors reigned over the remains of the dynasty until Zhu Wen, a local warlord, deposed Emperor Aidi in 907 to establish his own Later Liang Dynasty.

If the military governors were an attractive employment option for intellectuals earlier, the Huang Chao Rebellion and its aftermath sent many writers heading to those provinces that offered a degree of wealth and security.

Power was consolidated by more powerful armies conquering and assimilating weaker ones. A few regions became the most attractive havens: Min, modern Fujian; the area around modern Nanjing, which would become the Southern Tang; Jingnan in modern Hubei; and Sichuan, which became the Shu kingdom. As the large fish ate the smaller fish, the warlords resolved into the "Ten Kingdoms" and the "Five Dynasties," the latter being the name usually given to this period between the deposition of the last Tang ruler and the founding of the Song. In 960 a general of the Later Zhou, Zhao Kuangyin, "reluctantly" gave in to the demands of his soldiers and overthrew his local sovereign, establishing his own Song dynasty. Over the course of the next fifteen years he would reunify the country under a dynasty no less glorious than the Tang.

In the ninth and tenth centuries, the centuries when polished regulated verse was so important to poetic reputation, poetic pedagogy is an essential topic. Tang works in this tradition were sometimes despised by later ages and often did not enter the bibliographical record. Fortunately a Southern Song compendium, *Miscellaneous Records from the Window of Chanting Poetry* (*Yinchuang zalu*), survived, preserving parts of about a dozen ninth- and tenth-century works of poetic pedagogy. Attributions of some of these works to Bai Juyi and Jia Dao need not be taken too seriously. These follow the earlier tradition of technical poetics, with lists and illustrative couplets. In a few cases we have lists of allegorical correspondences; for example, dreaming of roaming as an immortal is supposed to criticize impediments in the relation between the ruler and his officials. *Fu*, still important for the examination, had its own treatises, the unique survival being the *Register of Fu* (*Fu pu*), probably from the second quarter of the ninth century, preserved in Japan.

The *Golden Needle Model for Poetry* (*Jinzhen shige*), attributed to Bai Juyi, postulated an "inner" and "outer" meaning for poetry. The outer meaning was the surface of representation, while the inner meaning worked through allegorical correspondences, intending "praise, criticism, admonition, and instruction." This was a popularization of the Confucian poetics of the *Classic of Poetry*. Elite poetics, however, was taking a very different turn. Already early in the ninth century Liu Yuxi had written, "Poetry is indeed the most intensive kind of writing. When its truth is gotten, the words perish, thus it is subtle and hard to do well. A scene-world is produced beyond the images, thus it has an essence that few can match." Here the essence of poetry is an elusive affect, produced through the representation (the "images," also "likenesses") but transcending it.

We see this carried even further in Sikong Tu:

> Dai Shulun once said, "The scene produced by a poet is the like the warmth of the sun on Lantian, with the fine jade there giving off mist; you can gaze on it, but you can't give it clear definition in the eyes." How can we easily explain such image beyond image, such scene beyond scene?

Invoking one of the regulated verse masters of the post-rebellion period, Sikong Tu here theorizes the poetics of the regulated-verse tradition, a poetry of elusive affect that has nothing to do with "praise, criticism, admonition, and instruction." Sikong Tu's "Gnomic Verse on Poetry [and *Fu*]" (Shi fu zan) gestures to such elusive affect in a way that is only marginally comprehensible. The "Twenty-Four Categories of Poetry" (Ershisi shipin), attributed to Sikong Tu, is either the height of Tang poetry criticism or the most successful forgery in the Chinese tradition. The case is not yet decided, but apart from one highly ambiguous reference, the work was unknown until the Ming dynasty, when it became a huge success. Each of its twenty-four verses evokes a particular quality, and at the very least it is consistent with the poetics Sikong Tu advocated.

Discussion of poets and poetry was common in this period, both in poetry itself and in anecdote collections. One of the favorite forms was telling an anecdote giving the occasion of the poem, like the Occitan *razo*. Meng Qi's *Poems with Their Original Occasions* (Benshi shi) of 886 is the best-known example. The historical veracity of these anecdotes is, in most cases, highly suspect. General anecdote collections like Fan Shu's *Friendly Deliberations at Cloud Creek* (Yunxi youyi) also have a large representation of stories of poets and their poems.

From this period comes probably the most famous of all Tang collections of stories, Pei Xing's *Transmitting the Unusual* (Chuanqi), whose title later came simply to mean "tales." The Daoist Du Guangting (850–933) was a voluminous writer, both of religious and secular texts. His stories of the gods and immortals occupy the fine line between religious texts and tales. His best known secular tale is "The Story of the Man with the Curly Beard" (Qiuran ke zhuan), telling how one Li Jing met a man with a curly beard, who directed him to seek service with Li Shimin, predicting that he would rise to become emperor (Emperor Taizong). Du Guangting was invited to court by Emperor Xizong and fled to Chengdu with him. He accompanied Xizong back to what was left of Chang'an, but on Xizong's death Du Guangting returned to Chengdu, where Wang Jian (848–918) was establishing the Shu kingdom, and lived out the rest of his life there, first in the Shu court and later as a recluse.

As the situation in Chang'an and central China worsened after the Huang Chao Rebellion, Chengdu became a magnet for famous men of letters and developed its own sophisticated local culture. In 900, as if to correct the dynasty's failures in judgment before the dynasty itself expired, Wei Zhuang, still serving in the central court, sent a petition to the throne requesting that fourteen poets be posthumously passed in the literary examination by imperial grace. That same year, Wei Zhuang completed his anthology *Further Mystery (Youxuan ji)*. For the first time a Tang anthology included Du Fu and a selection of poets that begins to resemble the later canon of Tang poetry. The mature judgment of retrospect seems to have already been setting in. Like most officials, Wei Zhuang did not wait for the dynasty's final death throes. In 901 Wei Zhuang accepted an invitation to move to Shu, where he built his house on the site of Du Fu's "thatched cottage" and lived out the rest of his days as a grand old man of letters and ornament of the new regional kingdom. When the Tang breathed its last in 907, the seventy-five-year-old poet–monk Guanxiu was in Shu, where Wang Jian built him a residence and gave him the title "Great Master of the Chan Moon." The most prominent writers of each of the "three teachings" – Confucianism, Buddhism, and Daoism – were all in Shu.

Wei Zhuang, Guanxiu, and Du Guangting all came to Shu in their mature years or old age. When we read the official prose of the next generation of Shu officials, they voice the same public pieties we expect of high officials. A very different image of Shu culture, however, has been shaped by two remarkable anthologies, the *Collection of the Talents (Caidiao ji)* by Wei Hu, probably compiled sometime in the Later Shu kingdom (925–965), and *Among the Flowers* with a preface by Ouyang Jiong dated to 940. *Collection of the Talents* is the longest extant pre-Song anthology of Tang poetry, and it shows a strong interest in poems about women and the immortals. To it we owe the preservation of Yuan Zhen's erotic poems, Cao Tang's "Larger Poems on Wandering as an Immortal," and pieces by Li Ye and otherwise unknown women poets.

With *Among the Flowers* of 940 the song lyric enters datable history. It includes fine songs by Wen Tingyun and his rough contemporary Huangfu Song from the mid-ninth century, as well as a generous selection of the lyrics of Wei Zhuang, representing the preceding generation. It also includes some lyrics by He Ning (898–955), who served in the northern regimes. The rest of the anthology's five hundred song lyrics, however, represent the elite aficionados of song in Chengdu in the first half of the tenth century. While there is some variety in the themes, by and large these song lyrics present scenes of a woman in love, to be performed by women singers for the entertainment of their male composers and their friends at banquets.

The Dunhuang manuscripts also have preserved an extensive corpus of song lyrics, mostly anonymous, to popular melodies, written out in irregular lines. These cannot be dated, but it seems likely that most, if not all, belong to the ninth and tenth centuries. Many may be transcriptions, probably from memory, of songs heard and remembered. There is one collection, *Cloud Ditties* (*Yunyao ji*), which must have been copied. There are two reasonable hypotheses. First, it is possible that writing down song lyrics as they were sung to heterometric melodies was already a common practice in the ninth century and perhaps even earlier; but because this was not an elite practice, such works were not transmitted. In this case the survival of such lyrics in the Dunhuang manuscripts is fortuitous. The second hypothesis does not necessarily contradict the first but restricts it to a local practice in the west and northwest. Something of the stigma carried by the composition of song lyrics can be seen in the northern lyricist He Ning, who is said to have burned his song lyrics when made a minister. Fortunately a few of He Ning's song lyrics have survived in *Among the Flowers*. The elite culture of Chengdu then made the practice of writing such heterometric songs legitimate, and it quickly spread to other kingdoms.

Most of the Dunhuang lyrics are, in fact, on Buddhist topics. There are also sets on popular motifs such as the twelve months and the times of day, which we see again in later popular song. The lyrics that have drawn the most interest since their rediscovery in the twentieth century are the love lyrics, some of which show a lively vernacular aesthetic very different from elite representations of women's voices either in classical poetry or in the song lyrics from *Among the Flowers*. When we read the post-rebellion quatrain "Bowing to the New Moon" (Bai xinyue, attributed to both Li Duan and Geng Wei), a woman goes out into the courtyard and "bows to the new moon," praying for the return of her absent beloved; "no one hears her whispered words," presumably muffled by the wind that whips her skirts. In the Dunhuang song lyric to the same title we do indeed hear the woman's words, and they are not what we might presume from the sentimental scene in the classical poem. To give the first stanza:

> My traveling man's off in another land,
> already now it's the new year, and
>   he still has not returned.
> I am galled by his loves, so like water:
> wherever he roams he strays recklessly

and takes no thought of his home.
Beneath the flowers I point far away,
    and to gods of Heaven and Earth I pray –
up to this very day
    he has left me alone to stay in my empty room.

In contrast to elite pathos, the woman's feelings imagined by the voyeur, here we have a monologue in which the anger and resentment that accompany longing are clearly expressed.

Before leaving Shu, we should mention the Lady of the Flower Stamens, Huarui furen, a consort of Meng Chang, the second and last ruler of the Later Shu kingdom. Her century of quatrains, "palace lyrics" (gongci), follows Wang Jian's famous set, and indeed a number of quatrains are shared between the two collections.

In the early part of the Five Dynasties, the kingdom of Min, modern Fujian, attracted a number of writers, including the senior poets Huang Tao (ca 840–?) and Han Wo (844?–923). Han Wo was the son of Li Shangyin's brother-in-law and close friend, and Li Shangyin had praised Han Wo's talents when he was a boy. Han Wo served the dynasty loyally until almost the very end; Du Fu was very much his model as he documented the numerous flights of the much diminished Tang court. At last in 905, just before the final blow, he fled with his family to Min, where he managed to live to a ripe old age. A collection of erotic, voyeuristic poems, The Perfume Case Collection (Xianglian ji), circulated independently of his more "serious" poems.

Jingnan, in modern Hubei, was significant for two figures, the poet–monk Qiji (ca 864–before 938), who left over 750 poems, and Sun Guangxian (d. 968), who took refuge in Jingnan in about 926. Sun Guangxian wrote the preface for Qiji's poems, but is most famous for his anecdote collection Trifling Words from Northern Yunmeng (Beimeng suoyan), of which twenty of an original thirty scrolls survive.

The numerous anecdote collections from the end of the Tang and Five Dynasties in some cases clearly attest to the desire to preserve a record of a destroyed culture. When we read Sun Qi's Record of the Northern Ward (Beili zhi) on the culture and courtesans of the entertainment quarter in its last heyday, it is important to know that it was composed in 884, in the ruins of the city left in the wake of the Huang Chao Rebellion. Wang Dingbao's (870–941?) Select Anecdotes from the Tang (Tang zhiyan) was completed between 916 and 917; in fifteen scrolls it is one of the largest and most important of Tang anecdote books, with a rich body of information, particularly on the culture of the literary examinations.

The Southern Tang (937–975) emerged from the warring local powers to dominate the rich agricultural lands of the lower Yangzi. Its capital was Jinling, which was old Jiankang, the capital of the Southern Dynasties. When the newly founded Song sought manuscripts to confirm its legitimacy by gathering the textual record, out of the general ruin of China two places provided the riches: Chengdu and Jinling.

In the Northern Song a collection of song lyrics was circulating under the name of Feng Yansi (903–960), a Southern Tang official who became minister. While it is reasonable to suppose that the majority of these lyrics were indeed composed by Feng Yangsi, this is more of a "repertoire" of song lyrics than a literary collection, and there are many song lyrics attributed to others elsewhere. The languid melancholy of Feng Yangsi's lyrics was a style that remained popular for elite parties in the first part of the eleventh century.

The grand man of letters in the Southern Tang was Xu Xuan (916–991). He served in all three reigns of the dynasty; and when the dynasty fell, he was taken into the service of the Song emperor and rose to high positions. Since he drafted edicts for the Southern Tang, he has a great deal of public prose in the sumptuous Tang tradition. Most of his poems are in the usual range of styles that had dominated poetry for a century and a half. In attendance at imperial banquets, Xu Xuan later provided the Song emperor an authentic "Tang" experience, confirming the imperial dignity with court poems in a style virtually unchanged since the days of Empress Wu.

VIII. The new dynasty (960–1020)

For its first half-century the Song continued both the literary and intellectual world of the Tang. New forces were at work, however, and when later Song writers looked back to tell the story of their dynasty's literature, they naturally chose those figures that most perfectly anticipated the direction the dynasty's literature would take. This transformation of Song literary culture can be seen in the fate of Zheng Gu (851–910), one of the most popular poets toward the end of the ninth and tenth centuries. Zheng Gu was a fluent regulated-verse poet in the Jia Dao tradition. Tian Xi (940–1001), one of the most distinguished literary figures in the early Northern Song, began a poem to a friend,

> The *Poems* and *Sao* are too remotely ancient, few truly understand,
> poets in the proper sense have a hundred kinds of mind.
> The mature and agreeable ought to stay with Yuan Zhen's and Bai Juyi's style,
> the fresh and novel can imitate the verse of Zheng Gu and Han Wo.

Tian Xi makes explicit a controversy that was usually only implicit: he rejects the "ancient" in favor of "poets in the proper sense" (*bense shiren*), comprising the two most popular schools of poetry in the second half of the ninth and tenth centuries: Bai Juyi and the tradition of finely wrought regulated verse, here represented by Zheng Gu and Han Wo.

About a half-century later, around the middle of the eleventh century, Ouyang Xiu (1007–1072), the most influential literary man of his day, would write in his *Remarks on Poetry (Shihua)*,

> The fame of Zheng Gu's poetry was at its height at the end of the Tang . . . His poetry was very thought-provoking and contained many excellent lines, but the style was not really elevated. Because it was so easy to understand, people used his poetry for teaching children – even when I was a child, we still chanted his poems. Nowadays his works are not in circulation.

In the course of little more than half a century, the exemplary poet of the "fresh and novel" had become easy and banal poetry for schoolchildren. A major change in literary values had occurred.

The writer still most read from the earliest years of the Song, the years of consolidation, belongs to the Southern Tang. This is Li Yu (937–978), the Last Ruler (Houzhu) of the Southern Tang, who reigned from 961 to 975. He has the distinction of being the first writer of song lyric to use the form to write about his own experiences, particularly on leaving the throne and recalling his lost kingdom under house arrest in Bianjing (modern Kaifeng), the new Song capital.

Like the Tang, the Song began its cultural work by gathering the scattered remains of the manuscript legacy. Both Emperor Taizu and Emperor Taizong sponsored large compilations and printing projects. State-sponsored printing had already begun in the Five Dynasties, with two rival editions of the Confucian Classics produced in Chengdu and Luoyang. In the Shu kingdom, Wu Zhaoyi had been the head of the state printing enterprise, and Song Emperor Taizu had him brought to his capital at Bianjing along with his printing blocks. Early in the dynasty not only were standard editions of the Classics printed, but also the immense Buddhist and Daoist canons. The standard histories were also issued, though the project was not completed until after the middle of the eleventh century, when Ouyang Xiu finished a complete rewriting of the histories of the Tang and of the Five Dynasties.

The modest state library at Bianjing was built up from the collections of manuscripts from Shu, the Jingnan kingdom, and the Southern Tang. From this library came the "four big books." Three of these were by an editorial committee headed by Li Fang (925–996), and the committee included Xu Xuan. These old men belonged to the intellectual world of the Tang and produced court-commissioned projects of the kind that had been done for three centuries; what set their work apart from a long history of large court compilations was a new dynasty with state-supported printing. In practical terms such large Tang compilations of a thousand scrolls required the imperial scriptorium to reproduce, and with few or unique copies they easily vanished in rot or flame. Large Buddhist and Daoist works fared better because the religious institutions had scriptoria throughout the provinces.

The first of the "four big books" was the *Extensive Records of the Taiping Reign*, in five hundred chapters, completed in 978. It is from this compendium, which cited its sources, that the vast majority of Tang tales have been recovered. The second to be completed, in 983, was the *Imperial Reader of the Taiping Reign (Taiping yulan)*, a composite of surviving Tang encyclopedias in a thousand chapters. This was followed in 987 by *The Flower of the Garden of Letters (Wenyuan yinghua)* in a thousand chapters, modeled on the *Selections of Refined Literature* and beginning in the Liang dynasty where *Selections* left off. Unlike the *Extensive Records* and the *Imperial Reader*, both of which were soon printed, *The Flower of the Garden of Letters* was not printed until the early thirteenth century. *The Flower of the Garden of Letters* remains the single most important source for Tang and Five Dynasties writing, representing a substantial percentage of the literary works in the imperial library of the 980s. Not only have many writers otherwise lost been preserved there, we also have a snapshot of the kind of manuscripts that survived. This was the flotsam and jetsam of the manuscript tradition that would never have survived except in this situation where compilers were copying everything they could find to make a "big book." The last of the "big books" was a compendium of documents on government institutions, completed in 1013.

If the flurry of state-sponsored cultural work at the beginning of the Song resembles the seventh century, the level of private scholarship in the Northern Song was unprecedented. In prefaces, colophons, letters, and miscellanies we have a rich testimony to the efforts of Northern Song scholars seeking to recover the remains of Tang literature and collating the manuscripts. Tang literature, particularly poetry, seems to have survived primarily in partial collections or anthologies of a writer's work. Song editors would compare as many versions as they could find (probably only a fraction of what survived throughout China), producing composite editions that sometimes noted variants and sometimes did not. Such comparison of editions did, however, raise scholars' awareness of variants and the nature of manuscript culture. Word of a "fine edition" (*shanben*) would bring requests from other scholars to collate their own copies.

The early Northern Song showed remarkable continuity with the last half of the ninth century and the Five Dynasties in the various styles available for a writer to adopt. Although parallel prose flourished, there was a continuous tradition of admirers of the prose of Han Yu and Liu Zongyuan. Particularly from the end of the Tang on, it was common for such a scholar to claim that no one but himself admired Han Yu and Liu Zongyuan. They were, perhaps, a minority, but the prose of Han Yu and Liu Zongyuan enjoyed, from what we can tell, wider circulation than that of any other Tang prose writer. Liu Kai's (947–1000) short autobiography gives a standard version of the neglect of the ancient style:

> When I turned fifteen or sixteen, I was studying basic reading practices. Master Zhao suggested Han Yu's prose, and after we got a family copy at home, I read it. In those days no one in the world spoke of "antiquity." Being young, there was no one who could share my love, yet from dawn till dusk I never let it out of my hands . . . By the time I reached young manhood, I had achieved a profound grasp of the fine points of Han Yu's prose, and I set my brush to paper to imitate the way he wrote . . . When my father and older brothers heard of this, they were afraid that as a consequence I would not win praise in the age and they warned me that the most urgent task was to follow the fashion of the day. But this did not change my mind in the least, and the heart's devotion to antiquity became increasingly firm. I would talk only of Confucius, Mencius, Xunzi, Yang Xiong, Wang Tong, and Han Yu as the footsteps in which I hoped to follow; and everyone thought that I had gone crazy.

In this account of domestic paideia, Liu Kai retells Han Yu's own compelling myth of singular principles disapproved of by others. In the mid-eleventh century, Ouyang Xiu would tell a similar story in a rather different key.

Taking Tang writers as models was the norm of the day, but Liu Kai carried this into self-naming, adopting the name Jianyu ("shoulder to shoulder with [Han] Yu") and a courtesy name, Shaoyuan ("continuing [Liu Zong]yuan"). In the next generation Han Yu found an even more theatrical admirer in Mu Xiu (979–1032). One story says that he had Han Yu's and Liu Zongyuan's works printed and offered them to any reader who could punctuate them correctly. Mu Xiu won the admiration of the rich and powerful that often accompanied such eccentricity, but he managed to offend or refuse all those who tried to help him.

As discussed earlier, over the course of the ninth century the Tang became the effective literary past, with the pre-Tang era providing models only for advocates of the ancient. There were "masters" and "followers," with the "masters" defining the available styles. In the late ninth century Zhang Wei composed his *Table of Masters and Followers among the Poets* (*Shiren zhuke tu*), in which each style was represented by a single master, with several grades of followers, and each poet given representative couplets. The work begins with Bai Juyi under the heading "Vast Cultural Transformation" (*guangda jiaohua*), invoking the Confucian task of poetry to civilize and reform customs. Such a taxonomy of masters and followers in effect put closure on the poetic tradition and turned all later poets into epigones. Indeed, as we move into the later part of the ninth century, we see for the first time a phenomenon that would continue throughout the rest of traditional China, defining a poet (often a self-definition) by which earlier poet he "followed."

The most famous poet of the early Northern Song, Wang Yucheng (954–1001), saw himself in the lineage of Bai Juyi (in a famous anecdote, however, he was pleased to be compared to Du Fu). Although in the eleventh century Ouyang Xiu was to inaugurate the characteristic Northern Song poetic style by an explicit analogy to the Han Yu group, the Bai Juyi tradition of rambling, genial verse, as if following turns of thought, lay in the background. The somewhat younger Lin Bu (967–1028) made the comparison explicit:

> With wild abandon in the Tang, only Bai Juyi the Tutor,
> moving at will in our Song, there is Huangzhou's Wang Yucheng.

The shift here is a subtle one, but suggests growing Song self-confidence. The Tang model remains attached to the Song poet, but instead of a "follower," Wang Yucheng has been made Bai Juyi's Song counterpart. Ouyang Xiu would use the idea of counterparts to define his own group. The model of Bai Juyi appears throughout Wang Yucheng's poetry, from a fascination with everyday experience to poetry of social engagement, giving accounts of the sufferings of common folk from social abuses. In prose he praised Han Yu, not for style, but for a commitment to moral values.

In one aspect, however, Wang Yucheng remained close to the values of the ninth-century masters of regulated verse, which remained the dominant poetic tradition in the last part of the tenth century: this was making poetry a theme within the poem and proclaiming the unique importance of poetry and his singular devotion to it:

When there is ale before my eyes, I must always get drunk,
beyond my person everything is emptiness but poetry.

The first phase of regulated-verse craft in the last part of the eighth century had been represented by Jiangnan poet–monks; Jia Dao had originally
been a monk; many of the regulated verse masters of the second half of the
ninth century had close ties with poet–monks, and two of the most famous,
Guanxiu and Qiji, were themselves Buddhist monks. That tradition continued
in the early Northern Song with the Nine Monks. The Nine Monks are best
remembered for a passage in Ouyang Xiu's *Remarks on Poetry*:

> Buddhist monks famous for poetry in our present dynasty were nine; thus
> the collection of their works was called *The Poems of the Nine Monks*. It is no
> longer to be found. When I was young, I heard people praising them highly.
> One was called Huichong; I've forgotten the names of the other eight.

Beneath the elegiac tone of comments in *Remarks on Poetry*, Ouyang Xiu was
devaluing the tradition of the craftsmen of regulated verse, declaring them
out of fashion and forgotten. Quite a few poems of the Nine Monks do indeed
survive, representing an art that must have seemed timeless. Huichong even
made a collection of a hundred of his own best parallel couplets and those of
others, preserved in a miscellany of 1087.

In the early Northern Song, regulated verse was also the choice of
"recluses," by this period associated with an aesthetic life. Wei Ye (960–
1019) was one such figure, so successful in staying out of the public eye, as one
legend has it, that Emperor Zhenzong had never heard of him until a Khitan
ambassador declared that he hoped to get a complete edition of his poems.
By far the most famous recluse and regulated-verse master was Lin Bu, a
fastidious eccentric who never married and lived out his life at West Lake
in Hangzhou, refusing posts and even refusing to go into the city. He was
famous for his love of his pet crane and his plum tree: the latter, he said, was
his wife, and the former, his child. Such theatrical solitude won him national
fame as a poet–recluse, and he received gifts of support from the emperor. Lin
Bu wrote exclusively in regulated verse and produced a slim volume of finely
crafted works. When Northern Song fashion changed, and the Late Tang
style was forgotten, Lin Bu retained a place in the Song cultural imagination,
perhaps for a personality of which his poems were an expression.

Yang Yi (974–1020), Li Shangyin's devoted editor, was the leading literary
figure at court at the turn of the eleventh century and represented the age in
both poetry and prose. He was a master of the rhetorical court poetic style

and parallel prose. When the fashion changed, he became the primary target for the Song advocates of the "ancient." What drew the brunt of the attack was the "Xikun style," which supposedly represented the poetic style of the turn of the eleventh century, but was, in fact, only the fashion of a relatively small group of court officials. Xikun, a poetic name for the imperial library, was affixed to Yang Yi's anthology of 250 poems written on shared topics by a group of poets, all eminent officials, the *Exchange Collection of Xikun (Xikun chouchang ji)*, compiled around 1004. Some of the topics distributed were titles of poems by Li Shangyin, and the style of the works in the collection is largely derived from Li Shangyin's most allusive and ornamented work. One Song critic interpreted this as a reaction against Bai Juyi. It was, in fact, a more radical act: rather that choosing from among the conventional range of poetic styles inherited from the first part of the ninth century, Yang Yi recovered a largely forgotten Tang poet and used him as a model from the past to do something new.

If there is one moment that signals the beginning of a new era, it is an anecdote about the ancient-style prose writer Mu Xiu and his friend Zhang Jing (971–1019), a follower of Liu Kai. The anecdote is told by Shen Gua (1031–1095) in his *Written Chat from Dream Creek (Mengxi bitan)*:

> Literary men in past years often admired parallelism in writing prose. In the generation of Mu Xiu and Zhang Jing people first wrote plain prose – in those days they called it ancient-style prose. Mu Xiu and Zhang Jing were going to dawn court together and were waiting for daybreak outside Donghua Gate. When discussing the order of prose, they happened to see a galloping horse trample a dog to death. The two men each gave an account of the event to compare which of them was better. Mu said: "The horse went wild, there was a yellow dog encountered its hooves and perished." Zhang Jing said: "There was a dog died beneath a running horse."

For the first time in the Chinese tradition we see the question of how to represent in words something that exists prior to its representation (even though Shen Gua has to offer his own verbal representation of the event to indicate it). Shen Gua calls it "plain prose" (*pingwen*), suggesting that there is some basic prose that matches the event perfectly; adjudication of the reported competition would favor the less rhetorical.

Even the philosopher Zhuangzi's analogy between language as the fish-trap and truth as the fish was essentially rhetorical; language was pure means. When it was not rhetorical, it was manifestation, a symptom of feeling that one could read like the expression on the face. The "plain prose" described in the anecdote is a new idea of language; it is language as "representation," to be judged by some unrhetorical accuracy in matching something that exists prior to language. As with the call for plain, scientific linguistic representation by the Royal Academy after the English Restoration of 1660, the nature of literature was changed by a changed notion of the relation between language and reality.

IX. Dunhuang narratives
By Wilt Idema

We have only a very imperfect understanding of the literary culture at the various regional courts and power centers from the second half of the eighth century on; this includes the tenth-century courts of the Former and Later Shu regime at Chengdu, and that of the Southern Tang at Nanjing. In one exceptional case, however, that of Dunhuang, our sources provide an in-depth view of a local manuscript culture, down to the first halting writing exercises of beginning students.

In his conquests of the late second century BC, Emperor Wu of the Han had built a string of cities along the northern edge of the Qilian Mountains, linking the heartland of China to the trading routes of Central Asia and separating the Mongol grasslands from the highlands of Qinghai and Tibet, two areas that rarely, if ever, accepted Han Chinese rule. Of these cities Dunhuang was the westernmost garrison. Dunhuang, where the various routes of the Silk Road converged, was both a point of departure for Chinese troops setting off on imperial ventures to assert authority over the oasis towns of Xinjiang and a port of entry for persons, trade goods, and ideas from Central Asia and beyond. The Silk Road trade ebbed and flowed with changes in climate and the fortunes of empires; in that process Dunhuang sometimes flourished. Between the withdrawal of the Han and the rise of the Tang, Dunhuang was a center for local military power and Confucian scholarship, but most of all it was a major regional center of Buddhism. From the fourth century on, Buddhist monks and lay patrons cooperated in building cave temples in a cliff a few miles from the town itself. The rich frescoes in these caves provide a unique panorama of the development of Chinese Buddhist art from the fourth century to the fourteenth, when cave-building at Dunhuang came to an end.

Before the mid-eighth century, Dunhuang was very much part of the Tang empire. Following the rebellion of An Lushan, however, the Tang recalled its Central Asian garrisons, and most of the former Tang possessions in Central

Asia were taken over by the expanding Tibetan empire (until it collapsed due to internal strife in the 840s). The Tibetans also moved into the Gansu region, and in 780 Dunhuang became the last of the Han Chinese cities to submit to the Tibetans, but only on the condition that it would be allowed to maintain its Han Chinese customs. As the Tibetan empire crumbled, in 848 local strongmen took the opportunity to expel the Tibetan garrison. These local rulers in Dunhuang happily accepted titles from the Tang emperors or their successors, but the Tang was in no position to aid the local regime, let alone impose direct rule. For all practical purposes, Dunhuang was a small, independent Central Asian principality, proud of its Han Chinese identity, but also maintaining intensive contacts with the other Central-Asian states, especially Khotan. With the latter it shared a fervent Buddhist culture, which was spared the destruction wrought by Wuzong's suppression of Buddhism earlier in 845. By the middle of the eleventh century, Dunhuang would finally lose its independence when it was absorbed into the Tangut Xixia kingdom.

For reasons that are still not fully clear, shortly after the year 1000, one of the leading monasteries in Dunhuang packed its library in a side-chapel of a cave temple. This chapel was then carefully bricked up, and the wall was painted over. The local climate helped to preserve over 50,000 manuscripts and paintings without damage. This hidden library was discovered only in 1900, after which its contents were dispersed. The major collections are now held in London, Paris, Beijing, and St. Petersburg. These manuscripts have completely revolutionized the study of Chinese culture of the fourth to the tenth centuries. Many works of Tang literature that were believed to have been lost reemerged, and our knowledge of well-established genres was considerably expanded. The Dunhuang library, however, also yielded a considerable body of mostly narrative texts in genres that did not emerge in the print culture of the Song dynasty and beyond, and therefore were completely ignored for nine centuries.

The most common characteristic of these narrative texts is that they were meant to be read out (performed) as part of a ritual or festive occasion, and therefore were written in a highly literary register of the contemporary vernacular language. A few of these texts were composed entirely in verse or primarily in prose; the majority, however, alternated passages in verse and prose. The use of the word *bian* ("transformation") or *bianwen* ("transformation text") in the titles of some of these texts has led to their collective designation as "transformation texts." Scholars initially understood *bian* as the "transformation" of these texts from classical Chinese into the vernacular, but most scholars now believe that these texts concern "transformations," manifestations of Buddhas and bodhisattvas, or miracles and exceptional events in general. The "prosimetric" format has also provoked extensive debate, with some scholars arguing for Indian origins and others preferring an indigenous development.

"Sutra-explanation texts" make up the bulk of modern collective editions of transformation texts, even though such texts are never designated as "transformation (texts)" in the original manuscripts. Some such texts provide line-by-line expositions of the text of a well-known sutra, like the Vimalakīrti Sūtra, the Lotus Sutra, and the Amitābha Sūtra: after a passage of the sutra had been chanted by a cantor, the master provided an exegesis consisting of a prose passage followed by a summary in verse, after which the next sutra passage was chanted. The verse sections employ both the unrhymed six-syllable meter often used in translating Buddhist sutras and the rhymed seven-syllable meter used in Chinese poetry from the third century on. Since the sutras themselves were often large works, such sutra-explanation texts must have been huge compilations; of this genre only fragments (occasionally quite large) have been preserved. Other, shorter (and fully preserved) sutra-explanation texts limit themselves to an exegesis of the sutra title or of a few central lines of text. Sutra-explanations probably formed the staple of large "lectures for the laity." We know the name of one ninth-century Chang'an monk who excelled at this type of performance.

Some sutra-explanation texts are quite scholastic; others extensively elaborate sutra narratives. Short Buddhist narratives not tied to any specific sutra, ranging from accounts of the life of the Buddha Śākyamuni to legends about the piety of female devotees, are provided by a rather homogeneous group of texts, the "tales of causes and conditions" (yinyuan), which are similar to sutra-explanation texts in the prosimetric format and verse forms. Less formal in nature than the sutra-explanation texts, and probably often primarily intended for small female audiences, many of these texts are written in a racy vernacular, not without humor and wit. The "Tale of the Ugly Princess," for example, tells the story of princess who in an earlier life scowled when giving a donation to a monk and was reborn with such an ugly face that even the beggar who was persuaded to marry her was so ashamed of her that he didn't dare to show her to his new noble friends. The contrition of the princess then moves the Buddha to restore her beauty. Another text on the victory of Buddha over Māra, the ruler of the world of desire, gives full rein to the Buddhist propensity for allegory.

Such tales of causes and conditions might be preceded by a narrative or didactic introductory piece, which went by the name "texts to settle the seats" (*yazuowen*) and sometimes circulated independently. One of these, on the topic of the twenty-four examples of filial piety, by one of Chang'an's leading monks, had even been printed, and a copy of this edition was found among the Dunhuang texts.

The verse sections in the remaining prosimetric texts are, as a rule, in the seven-syllable line and do not make use of the rhymeless six-syllable meter. Quite a few of these texts are called "transformation (texts)" in the manuscript titles, although the use of the term in a title is not restricted to works in this format. These texts treat both Buddhist and non-Buddhist subjects. The best-known of the Buddhist works are the "Transformation on the Subduing of Demons," and the "Transformation Text on Maha-Maudgalyayana Rescuing his Mother from the Underworld." The first, composed for the court of Emperor Xuanzong in 749, narrates how the chancellor Sudatta, following his conversion to Buddhism upon meeting with Sakyamuni, tricks the local crown prince into selling his magnificent garden so it may be converted to a monastery. When the established religious authorities protest such importation of heresy, the king orders his priests and the monk Sariputra to hold a contest of their magical powers. In six separate confrontations Sariputra defeats each of these "heretical masters." While the setting of the story is clearly an India of elephants and stupendous wealth, Sariputra's opponents are thinly disguised Daoist priests, with clear echoes of the religious debates often staged in the Tang court.

The "Transformation Text on Maha-Maudgalyayana" recounts a quite different story. Maudgalyayana, who has become a monk, wants to know the whereabouts of his deceased parents; he learns that his father has been reborn in heaven, but that his mother is suffering extreme torments in hell. His visit to the Underworld to rescue his mother provides an opportunity to give a detailed description of the topography, the administration, and the tortures of the many hells. The rescue is eventually accomplished with the help of the Buddha. The legend was linked to the institution of the Buddhist Ghost Festival of the fifteenth of the Seventh Month, and our text was intended for performance on that annual event, urging its audience to make ample donation to the Buddhist clergy for the sake of their deceased parents. This same story was also treated in a tale of causes and conditions and in a short sutra-explanation text. In later centuries the legend would be adapted for the stage and become China's most spectacular religious drama, known in many versions.

Many of the prosimetric texts on non-Buddhist subjects are incomplete. Fragments of two texts tell of feats of arms by the local rulers of ninth-century Dunhuang. Other texts retell traditional stories concerning the relation between Han Chinese and the non-Han inhabitants of the Mongol grasslands, a topic that must have been of particular relevance to the Dunhuang population. We have fragments of the story of Li Ling, a general of Emperor Wu of the Han, who was captured by the Xiongnu and, after Emperor Wu killed all his relatives, eventually joined them. We have the second half of a life of Wang Zhaojun, a palace lady of Emperor Yuan of the Han, who was sent off on a political marriage to a Xiongnu chieftain. There is also a fragmentary adaptation of the tale of Meng Jiang nü, whose husband had died working on the construction of the Great Wall; on a quest to retrieve her husband's body, her weeping causes the Great Wall to collapse. The founding of the Han dynasty was another topic that appears in several texts. One of the few texts that have been preserved in their entirety is the "Transformation Text on Wang Ling." A general of the Han founder Liu Bang, Wang Ling's greatest claim to fame was his mother, who was captured by Liu Bang's opponent Xiang Yu and committed suicide to ensure her son's undivided loyalty to Liu Bang.

It is commonly asserted that texts of this type in performance were accompanied by picture scrolls, showing scenes from the narrative. In a number of texts, each prose section is concluded by a formula which might be translated as "and what did it look like?" Victor Mair has strongly argued that only texts featuring this formula should be considered "true transformation texts." Unfortunately, no accompanying picture scrolls have been preserved, with the possible exception of a scroll depicting five of the six confrontations between Sariputra and his adversaries. Long fragments of a prosimetric text on the career of Wu Zixu and the fifth-century BC wars between the ancient states of Chu, Wu, and Yue lack the "and what did it look like" formula, so this would not be a "true transformation text" by such a criterion. This story of betrayal and revenge and the dangers of women (at least to kings) already had a history of retellings stretching back over a thousand years.

Among the narratives entirely in verse in the seven-syllable line, we find one text of almost a thousand lines, treating another episode from the wars between Liu Bang and Xiang Yu. The hero of this little epic is Xiang Yu's general Ji Bu, who curses Liu Bang and mocks the future Han emperor's lowly origins in front of his troops, thus earning Liu Bang's undying enmity. Following his final victory, Liu Bang excludes Ji Bu from his general pardon, and Ji Bu has to disguise himself as a slave to escape the wrath of the new emperor – he eventually obtains high rank. A much shorter text treats the legend of Dong Yong, one of the exemplars of filial piety.

Verse narrative also appears in "vulgar *fu*" (*su fu*), using the form of the *fu*, but narrative rather than descriptive. One such "vulgar *fu*" treats the tragic love story of Han Peng and his wife: having fallen in love with Han Peng's wife, the evil king of the ancient state of Song condemns Han Peng to serve as a convict laborer; when Han Peng dies, his wife commits suicide. By far the most interesting work in this genre, however, is the "*Fu* on the Swallow and the Sparrow." This is a rare case of a fully developed animal fable in Chinese literature, in which the animals not only display human characteristics but also do the talking. In winter, a sparrow occupies the nest of the absent swallow; when the swallow returns, the sparrow refuses to give up the nest. A fight ensues, and the swallow takes his case to court, where the sparrow, as a local, has many friends. The sparrow is nevertheless imprisoned, and the phoenix, as king of the birds, restores order, urging the little birds to live henceforth in harmony. Its only clear predecessor is "The Hawk and the Sparrow" by Cao Zhi, a much more modest composition. There is another Dunhuang text entitled "*Fu* on the Swallow and the Sparrow," but this text is essentially composed in eight-line stanzas of five-syllable verse. Whereas the previous text was strong in social satire, this text seems more interested in parodying legal language. Another text that is occasionally classified as a "vulgar *fu*" is the "Disputation of Tea and Wine," in which the characters of the title vaunt their own qualities in turn, until both are defeated by Water. This text may well be the script for a little play. Another such disputation confronts Confucius with the boy-wonder Xiang Tuo – the "teacher of ten thousand generations" is consistently bested by the schoolboy (and in an appended poem Confucius has his revenge by killing the brat). Yet another satirical piece portrays a lazy and gluttonous bride.

Many of the texts mentioned above were clearly prepared with performance in mind; they come with directions for the performer, written in a different color of ink or in smaller characters. The narratives entirely in prose lack such indications of a link to the technicalities of performance, which may suggest that they were intended primarily for reading. These narratives distinguish themselves from the classical tales of the time both by their more colloquial level of language and by their greater length. These are fully developed examples of the vernacular story, a genre that was to become prominent later in print culture, especially after the thirteenth century.

Three vernacular tales have been preserved more or less in their entirety. The longest of these tales recounts the legendary life of the fourth-century monk Huiyuan (344–416), who progresses from being a slave of the bandits who have captured him to becoming the triumphant master of Buddhist scholastics in a public sutra–lecture in which he humiliates his monastic rival. A second tale contrasts the shameful way in which the elderly Yang Jian, the founder of the Sui dynasty, wins the imperial throne through the palace plots of his daughter with the heroic exploits of the teenage general Han Qinhu, who first subjugates the Chen dynasty in the south through superior battle formations, and then by his superior archery skills frightens the arrogant Turkic khan in the north into submission, only to be at last called away to become king of the Underworld. The third story concerns the Daoist master Ye Jingneng, a historical figure in the court of Empress Wu, here placed in the court of Emperor Xuanzong. He serves as the emperor's guide on his visit to the moon, but soon becomes aware that the emperor was not born to become an immortal, after which he engineers his own exit from the court. Yet another, rather short text recounts the legend of the mythical emperor Shun, yet another exemplar of filial piety. We also have a fragment of a vernacular tale on Emperor Taizong's visit to the Underworld, where he has to defend himself for the murder of his elder brothers – the emperor escapes only through connections and bribery. This same story would later be taken up in the famous sixteenth-century novel *Journey to the West*.

Although the texts above cannot be dated precisely, beyond their date of copying, most would appear to have been composed in the ninth and tenth centuries. A number were written under the Tang or its successor regimes in the Chinese heartland, but at least some of these texts were written (or edited) for performance at the court of the rulers of Dunhuang. The subject matter of some of the non-Buddhist texts would, moreover, appear to have held special relevance for this small, embattled Han Chinese polity in Central Asia. We also may wonder to what extent the frequent and detailed descriptions of slavery reflect local conditions. While we have scattered references to the performance of transformation texts in the territory of the Tang itself, and while it is tempting to see the Dunhuang materials as typical of Chinese literature as a whole in this period, the number and the contents of these texts would appear to be representative of a quite atypical local Han Chinese culture, in which Buddhism played a far greater role than in China proper.

In their formal features, these texts, especially the prosimetric works, show a clear similarity to the prosimetric genres of literature as we know them from the last imperial dynasties. There is little doubt that there was an ongoing tradition of performing this kind of text, and one can make a strong case for the development of "precious scrolls" (*baojuan*) from "tales of cause and conditions." Manuscripts and imprints of this kind of prosimetrical literature reappear from the fifteenth century on, but by this time it had suffered a great loss of status. While the audience for the Dunhuang narratives probably did not exclude the lower classes, it often did include the highest secular and religious authorities, as with Chaucer reading his *Canterbury Tales* to the English court. Many of the transformation texts display considerable schooling and talent, even if they were not written by the greatest scholars of their day, just as Chaucer would not have been considered a scholar by the Latin clerics of medieval England. Once printing became quite common in eleventh-century China, however, the upper-class listening audience may well have largely changed into individual readers – or have been enticed away by the more spectacular attractions of the rapidly developing theater.

5

The Northern Song (1020–1126)

RONALD EGAN

Overview

In certain ways the Song dynasty (960–1279) continued literary traditions already characteristic of the Tang. The literature that survives was produced by the educated elite, and it continued to be written in a book language, usually called literary Chinese, rather than in the vernacular. Writers were male, with only a few prominent exceptions. The forms of *shi* poetry and the many well-established genres of literary prose continued to dominate. It is only toward the dynasty's end that we begin to see the emergence of drama and fiction written in the vernacular, and that only in very limited quantity.

Despite these continuities, distinctly new styles and modes of expression gradually emerged. A new style of poetry evolved and was established by the mid-eleventh century. It came to be so distinct from dominant Tang styles that already by the century's end, and ever after, the two styles were often simplistically viewed as competing options. Critics were expected to express a preference for "Tang poetry" or "Song poetry" and would-be poets to model their work on one or the other. Another development was that the song lyric (*ci*) attracted increased attention and its scope became broader than the narrow compass it had had during the Five Dynasties. Eventually the song lyric became an important poetic alternative to *shi* poetry, with its own vocabulary, subjects, and expressive function. A whole range of prose writings appeared, including miscellanies, accounts of anomalies, a form of poetry criticism called "remarks on poetry," connoisseur manuals on all manner of aesthetic objects, and travel diaries. Some of these were entirely new. Even those that were not were produced in such increased quantity that collectively they took on an identity quite unlike that of their precursors.

The initial impression of continuity with the Tang fades the more we attend to the substance of Song literature. Part of what is new can be linked to profound changes in society, politics, thought, and material culture that occurred during the Song. The spread of book printing was perhaps the most far-reaching of these in its effects. Although much work remains to be done on the subject, it is clear that it was during the Song dynasty that China underwent the transformation from manuscript culture to print culture, even though manuscripts remained important in book history and textual transmission long after the end of the Song. In the early decades of the Northern Song, printing was still rare: it was mostly confined to Buddhist monasteries and large imperial printing projects of encyclopedias, Classics, and histories, intended primarily for officials and the imperial schools. By the mid-thirteenth century, commercial printers were active in all regions of the empire, and thousands of titles, including works that appealed to merchant as well as elite interests, were in wide circulation. Certainly book printing and increased circulation account for the vast multiplication of the quantity of writing that survives from the Song, when compared to any earlier period. It is likely, as we will see later, that the new availability of print increased not only the survival rates of what was written but even the inclination of authors to compose certain kinds of books.

The dynasty witnessed a revival and ambitious expansion of Confucian thought. Over the course of two hundred years, this Learning of the Way (*daoxue*) or Learning of Principle (*lixue*, conventionally termed "neo-Confucianism" in English) developed a metaphysical system grounded in the old Confucian Classics, now subjected to wholesale reinterpretation, that linked individual moral cultivation with cosmic principles. The Learning of the Way attracted leading intellectuals of the day and was large enough to develop its own internal debates and branches. The question of the proper place of literary work and its relation to moral cultivation was a topic of enduring interest and controversy among the spokesmen and those they viewed as rivals and outsiders. Less well known is the Buddhist revival and the increased integration of Buddhist thinking and modes of expression into elite culture. The Chan and Tiantai schools of Song Buddhism, in particular, made a concerted syncretic effort to reconcile their doctrines with those of Confucianism. Many of the leading poets were Buddhist laymen. Their interaction with monks, mastery of key sutras, and reliance upon Buddhist thought and terminology are evident throughout their verse, to the point that Buddhism becomes an indispensable component of the literature of the period.

Early Northern Song emperors, especially Zhenzong (r. 998–1022) and Renzong (r. 1023–1063), pursued a policy of "giving primacy to *wen*" (*youwen*); that is, to learning, letters, and civil as opposed to martial values. By doing so they helped to set in motion the cultural shift toward bookishness, connoisseurship, and refinement that are often taken as characteristic of the dynasty. But this direction came at a price, as leading thinkers and statesmen were anxiously aware. Peace was maintained throughout the realm, and there was time for great achievements in philosophy, classical studies, historiography, literature, and art. But the northern threat, from the Liao and Xi Xia empires, was held in check only through a series of desperate cessions of borderland territory and treaties that forced the Song state to send large tribute payments annually to the northern empires. Concern that the great peace achieved by the reunification of the empire was unsustainable haunts court policy discussions as early as the 1030s and 1040s. By the 1070s these anxieties, along with the increasingly dire economic needs of the state, led to the sweeping reforms implemented by Wang Anshi (1021–1086). Those reforms polarized officialdom. The political history of the next fifty years was dominated by hostilities between reformers and conservatives, as one group then the other was brought to power, and the reforms alternately implemented and rescinded. It is a dreary story of rampant factionalism and political persecution, and the successive emperors proved incapable of bringing about a reconciliation.

By the time of Emperor Huizong, who reigned from 1100 to 1125, just before the invasion by a new northern rival, the Jurchen state of the Jin, the Song was obviously incapable of defending itself, even against a much smaller rival. The Jurchen invasion brought not just defeat but national disgrace of incalculable proportions. Huizong and his son, the reigning Emperor Qinzong, were captured and taken, along with palace ladies and other members of the imperial clan, back north to the Jurchen capital, where they languished until their deaths many years later. The Song capital of Bianliang (Kaifeng) was overrun and the palaces destroyed. Hundreds of thousands of Song subjects fled before the Jurchen armies, which pushed south all the way to the Yangzi river and beyond. After several chaotic years, the northern half of the Song empire was formally ceded to the Jin, the Song capital having been reestablished at Hangzhou. So began the continuation of the dynasty that ruled over a greatly reduced area, known as the Southern Song (1127–1279). The earlier period of the dynasty came retrospectively to be called the Northern Song. It would be some 250 years before Han Chinese regained control of the Yellow River valley and the North China Plain, the historical heartland.

Emperor Huizong, himself a gifted painter and calligrapher, epitomizes the tension between Song cultural refinement and the problem of maintaining a polity that was viable and capable of defending itself. The literature of the

Northern Song, in all of its richness and earnest engagement with social and political issues, or determination to be freed of the same, should be read against this backdrop of the dynasty's march toward catastrophe.

The relatively underdeveloped condition of Song literary history must be mentioned here. Literary histories of the period do exist, both as individual volumes and as chapters in comprehensive accounts of Chinese literary history. Yet compared to earlier periods, and especially to the well-studied Tang, Song literary history is not well mapped or thoroughly understood. The most salient reason for this is the sheer abundance of Song literary work that survives. We get some sense of this from the fact that it was only in recent years that the first attempts were made to compile "complete" collections of Song poetry and prose. For Tang poetry and prose, such collections have been around for three hundred and two hundred years respectively. The *Complete Song Prose* (*Quan Song wen*) just appeared in 2006. The *Complete Song Poems* (*Quan Song shi*) was not published until 1999. It consists of seventy-two volumes and over 200,000 individual pieces (more than four times the size of the *Complete Tang Poems*), by some nine thousand writers. Given the lateness of the compilation of such works, whatever is said today about the literary history of the period is necessarily selective and somewhat tentative. It will require decades of work by future generations of scholars to refine our understanding.

In what follows, we examine the emergence of a new style of poetry roughly half a century after the dynasty was founded, and trace the development of writing styles through the lives and works of five towering figures: Mei Yaochen (1002–1060), Ouyang Xiu (1007–1072), Wang Anshi, Su Shi (1037–1101), and Huang Tingjian (1045–1105). This is followed by separate sections on the influence of Buddhism on Song poetry and the subgenre of poems on paintings. We turn next to the development of the song lyric, which gradually emerged as an alternative form of poetic expression, tracing its growth through successive generations of writers, including Zhang Xian (990–1078), Yan Shu (991–1055), Liu Yong (*jinshi* 1034), Su Shi, and Zhou Bangyan (1056–1121). The chapter concludes with a survey of prose writings that flourished during the period and expanded the scope of prose expression: the miscellany, remarks on poetry, connoisseur literature, and informal letters.

I. Mei Yaochen, Ouyang Xiu, and the emergence of a new poetic style

The formative stage of what came to be distinctively "Song" in Northern Song literature did not occur at the dynasty's founding in 960 or anytime close to it. In other words, the Northern Song is an example of a time when dynastic change and literary development are distinctly out of sync, belying the widespread assumption in representations of Chinese literary history that the two go hand in hand. The new imperial era would indeed eventually develop a distinctive literary style, but this did not begin to happen until the 1020s and 1030s, roughly two generations after the Song began.

Until then, as we have seen in the foregoing chapter, poetry was dominated by rival schools derivative of mid-Tang or Late Tang styles, which had persisted through the Five Dynasties and on into the new era. There was poetry modeled on Bai Juyi (772–846), such as that produced by Wang Yucheng (954–1001), which emphasized simple language, everyday life, and calm acceptance of worldly circumstances. Although there was room in this style for poems that described the hardships of the common people, the dominant tone was personal, genial, and predictable. There was poetry modeled on Jia Dao (779–843), known as the Late Tang style, which featured meticulous regulated verse on quietude, nature, and deprivation. This was a style embraced by monks and recluses, or literati poets affecting such personae, that celebrated the cold beauty and purity of nature and of life eked out in circumstances of denial and material discomfort. The best known exemplars were the Nine Monks of the early decades of the dynasty. As a radical alternative to these styles, there was lastly the Xikun style, named for a collection of 250 poems written by seventeen imperial librarians around 1004. The group, led by the talented and erudite Yang Yi (974–1020), took Li Shangyin (813–858) as their model. What they seized upon in Li's work was not the subject matter of his hauntingly elusive love poetry, but rather the style of language and presentation he cultivated, marked by the heavy use of allusions and periphrastic diction. The prose manifestation of these same tendencies was a highly learned and ornamental form of euphuistic prose, also known as "parallel prose" (written strictly in strings of couplets, consisting of metrically and grammatically parallel lines), at which Yang Yi also excelled.

These early stylistic options would all eventually be found wanting. The discontent with them that gradually set in was closely tied to calls for political and educational reform, which were themselves inseparable from the conviction that the age had lost its moral underpinning and had given itself over to unprincipled behavior, careerism, and a preference among those holding office for artifice over substance. The reformer Fan Zhongyan (989–1052) began calling in the 1020s for a renewed commitment to the moral cultivation of the lettered class through a return to the Way of the ancient sages and their teachings. There were political as well as ethical dimensions to his vision for change. He wanted a more active and ethical central government that would materially improve the lives of the common people in the provinces. But to achieve this would require that the type of men entrusted with ruling over the people, at all levels, themselves be of high moral cultivation and proven skill. Such improvement of the official class could come only after the civil service examinations were changed to focus upon statecraft and the teachings of the sages rather than on euphonious literary composition, and after the bureaucracy was reformed to ensure that men were promoted on the basis of administrative skill rather than seniority and lineage privilege. A key to Fan's program was a new commitment to the founding of local schools, where young men, the future office-holders, would begin at an early age the process of moralization through education. Instruction in local schools would be steeped in ancient Confucian writings and values. Pernicious beliefs (e.g. in Buddhist and Daoist doctrines) would be rooted out and the local gentry culturally transformed.

Writing was an essential part of this vision and of what needed to be "returned to ancient models." It was not just that the type of subject matter and writing styles favored in the civil service examinations needed to be reformed. Members of the lettered class had to reject the habit of cultivating showy ornamentation whenever they sat down to write, whether it was poetry or prose, at the expense of the substance of what was being said. It was only, the reformers claimed, by redirecting the minds of scholars and men of letters back to the values enshrined in the ancient Confucian Classics that the intellectual shallowness of the time could be overcome.

Fan Zhongyan attracted younger men to his cause, and they became fiercely loyal to him. In 1036 Fan criticized the grand councilor, Lü Yijian (978–1043), for packing the court with toadies. Fan was demoted for his outspokenness, and several of Fan's supporters took the opportunity to declare their disapproval of the court's intolerance of criticism. One of these young men, Ouyang Xiu, wrote a particularly sarcastic letter to a censor who had tactfully kept quiet during this suppression of dissent. Ouyang was himself then demoted and sent to the provinces, but the letter brought him notoriety and ensured he would be returned to prominence at the court once Lü Yijian's power waned.

Ouyang Xiu had distinguished himself in the civil service examinations of 1030, placing first in them, and was then posted to Luoyang, the eastern capital, where he served under Qian Weiyan (962–1034). Qian happened to have in his administration several young men of letters who became fast friends, including Yin Zhu (1001–1047), Xie Jiang (994–1039), and Mei Yaochen. Despite Qian Weiyan's own renown as a master of euphuistic prose, which because of its ascendancy was referred to as the "current style" (*shiwen*), the young men under him were drawn to the "ancient-style prose" (*guwen*) that Fan Zhongyan was advocating. Unlike euphuistic prose, ancient-style prose was not written in strings of couplets. Its rhythm and prosody did not need to fit a predetermined pattern. Consequently, it was more flexible and could readily be tailored to whatever meaning or substance a writer wanted to express. Euphuistic prose, by contrast, imposed a certain tyranny of form over meaning. The writer who chose to express himself in it was obliged constantly to adapt the substance of what he wanted to say to the requirement that he present it in units of parallel lines. Ancient-style prose also dispensed with the dense allusions and other literary ornamentation that was customary in euphuistic prose. A writer who chose the ancient style could thus plausibly claim that underlying meaning – rather than surface texture – was primary in his prose, that it drove and steered the course his language took.

Dissatisfaction with the floridity of the euphuistic style led, in the extreme case, to the view that words themselves were the source of the problem that needed to be solved. Writers thus sought to convey meaning with an absolute minimum of words. What was prized was a terse, clipped style of language in which every word was expected to be meaningful and, indeed, essential. There is a story that the aspiring young writers in Luoyang once competed to compose a prose inscription for a new government hall that had just been completed, each writing in the ancient style. The drafts by Xie Jiang and Ouyang Xiu each ran to over five hundred characters, but Yin Zhu's came in at just 380. Over wine in the evening, Yin Zhu counseled Ouyang to work harder to avoid flaccid organization and unnecessary words. Ouyang tried again, and this time his essay was twenty characters shorter than Yin Zhu's. Yin commended Ouyang for being such a quick study, and thereafter Ouyang devoted himself to the ancient style.

This effort to reform prose writing carried over into poetry. Ouyang and his friends put their energy into poetry in the ancient-style form, turning away from the regulated verse of the Jia Dao school and the Xikun anthology. The preference for ancient-style verse was the poetic complement of the preference for ancient-style prose. What is more, the young activists deliberately incorporated prose or prose-like diction and grammar into the poetic line. They also wrote poems on subjects that had not previously been conventional ones in verse. Because of these various innovations, it was said that the new approach was "to write poetry as if it were prose" (*yi wen wei shi*). While such a characterization may overstate the case, it is not hard to understand why it was applied to the new poetic style.

The Luoyang circle was not the only one that sought to reform poetry by turning to the ancient style. There was an older generation of literati who lived "east of the mountains"– that is, in the lower reaches of the Yellow River (modern Hebei and Shandong) – who had also attacked the Xikun style as excessive and frivolous. But these men, including Shi Yannian (994–1041), Shi Jie (1005–1045), and Du Mo (fl. ca 1030), cultivated a poetic style that was deliberately archaizing, rough, and strange. They quickly developed reputations for eccentricity and cantankerousness. Their "solution" to the narrowness of the early Song poetic styles was itself viewed as too inflexible and mannered. It attracted few adherents. Reminiscing about these early days of stylistic exploration, Mei Yaochen, who was admittedly hardly an objective observer, gave this characterization of the two groups of poets: "The moldy pedants east of the mountains languidly looked askance, / While youthful talents of Luoyang hurried to rally together."

It was Ouyang Xiu, Mei Yaochen, and, to a lesser extent, Su Shunqin (1008–1048) who emerged as the leading poets of the generation, which reached maturity during the 1040s (the Qingli period, known for the political reforms introduced then by Fan Zhongyan, but abandoned soon after). Ouyang, as the longest-lived member of the group, developed into the literary giant of the generation and remained productive and influential through 1070. The corpus of poetry these men collectively produced is large and its range of subjects vast, making it difficult to characterize. The most important part of their work is written in the ancient style, although of course they produced poems in the regulated verse forms as well. They wrote lengthy poems on the plight of commoners. They wrote on historical themes, typically reversing or twisting the conventional viewpoint of a famous person or event. They were also fond of writing on "unpoetic" subjects, including both the distinctly strange or bizarre (e.g. a Japanese sword, swarming mosquitoes, birds of ill omen, an antique stone screen) and the disarmingly mundane (e.g. laborers who made roof tiles, eating clams and picking out lice and finding a flea). In the last group of subjects, we see a fondness for taking on a subject ordinarily thought of as too "vulgar" to warrant poetic treatment, and producing a poem on it as a calculated act, as if to demonstrate that nothing need stand outside the scope of what poetry might include.

Nevertheless, one could find poetic precedents for most of the subjects of their poems, even the unconventional ones. If we want to pinpoint what is new about the output of the leading poets of this generation, it is better to focus on their ways of handling the subjects they chose rather than on the subjects themselves. As has often been observed, there is a discursive quality to much poetry of the Song period and we find that quality evident even in this early generation of writers. Whatever the subject, there is a tendency to treat it in a distinctly thoughtful way, reflecting in the course of the poem on its meaning and implications, whether these be social, historical, political, or aesthetic. To a surprising extent, this habit of treating a subject discursively emerges as an alternative to the tradition of using it emotively or lyrically, as a way to express heartfelt emotions. That is not to say that we do not still find a lyrical or emotive element in the poems. But cogitation and reflection occupy a distinctly prominent role, imparting to this poetry the "intellectual" quality that has often been recognized in it.

This way of writing poetry developed gradually out of the larger effort to redirect learning and approaches to writing generally, to moralize the social elite, and to return to ancient standards of purposefulness in life. In the reform climate of the day, there had come to be something very public about the act of writing, including poetry. Naturally, it was not expected that every poem be explicitly moralistic or didactic. Still, men who had achieved a certain station in life and thus a public persona would not want to produce verse that might be seen as going against the new commitment to a revitalized moral order. The ideal held out for prose writing was that it be meaningful rather than euphonious. This commitment to meaningfulness was then extended to poetry. Whatever the topic one chose to write a poem on, one showed allegiance to the values of the reform movement by treating it in a thoughtful and reflective way, rather than just as a vehicle to display a talent for verbal ornament. Moreover, the continuity now emphasized between personal cultivation, writing, and public values discouraged indulgence in highly personal sentimental expression, even in verse. So it was that leading poets of the day did indeed begin to "write poetry as if they were writing prose."

Mei Yaochen's sizable corpus of poetry (nearly three thousand poems in all) is marked by diction that eschews delicacy and refinement. Mei himself described the quality of language that he strove for as *pingdan*, which could be rendered as "plain" or "mild," or even "bland" or "flavorless." How can blandness be taken as a poetic ideal? This only makes sense in the context of the reform-period values. The language is flavorless so that it does not get in the way of the ideas being expressed. In fact, Mei Yaochen's poetic diction is only "bland" in the sense that it is not ornate and elegant. It is not bland in the sense of being truly transparent and featureless. His poetic diction has a rugged quality. This comes partly from admitting prose-like lines and the grammatical particles of prose, as well as language that is ordinary and sometimes even colloquial. His friend Ouyang Xiu offered descriptions of Mei Yaochen's poetry that focus on this rugged quality of its language. Mei's poetry, Ouyang observed, "gives primacy to what is pure and incisive; its stone teeth are washed in water from a cold stream." Another analogy Ouyang famously used was that of the olive (a subject Mei himself treated in his verse). When you first taste Mei's poetry is it like biting into an olive: it is almost too tart or bitter to keep in the mouth. But after you chew it for a while, its true flavor (and appeal) gradually comes through. Now, an olive is hardly "bland" or "flavorless." This is the special sense of *pingdan* as it is applied to Mei's verse.

As for his subjects, Mei Yaochen had a particular interest in writing about the mundane and even the rustic. Several of his most celebrated poems treat the hardships of the peasants, as well as other aspects of rural life he witnessed as he passed through the countryside. Mei can be outspoken in such poems about local officials' aloofness from the sufferings of the commoners under their control, if not their outright cruelty toward their charges. Observing an elderly naked peasant man carrying his infant grandson, Mei asks what benefit it has brought the man to be registered as "an imperial subject" on the local population rolls. Poems that Mei wrote about the death of his wife and young daughter are distinguished from the earlier tradition of such verse on death in the family by their willingness to present the poet's own inconsolable grief and even anger over the unfairness of such untimely loss of life. In this case, the occasions militated against the general impulse to avoid expressing deeply felt emotions. Indeed, that Mei wrote about these deaths in ways that were not constrained by literary convention was taken to show the sincerity of his grief. In a long epistolary poem he addresses to Ouyang and other literary friends, Mei expresses his views on the function of literature and issues of literary style. He also treats contemporary military and political events in many poems, venting his frustration over perceived injustice and factionalism. One long poem he wrote in 1051, "On Concealment" (Shu cuan), is so outspoken in its criticism of Emperor Renzong and his court that it was eventually suppressed from his literary collection.

Ouyang Xiu is more important than Mei Yaochen as a spokesman for literary reform, and more innovative (as we will see) as a writer and critic generally, but as a poet Ouyang does not have such a readily recognizable style or such stature as Mei. This is partly because Ouyang's range as a poet is extremely wide: he alternately wrote in the styles of Li Bai (701–762), Han Yu (768–824), Meng Jiao (751–814), Bai Juyi, and Tao Qian (ca 372–427). But it is also partly because Ouyang's work in other literary forms, especially the prose genres and the song lyric, tends to overshadow his achievement in poetry.

Mei Yaochen essentially wrote only poetry; Ouyang's literary talent was more diverse.

There are two types of poem that stand out in Ouyang's corpus. One consists of poems of quiet contentment he wrote in bucolic settings, in which he observes the countryside around him, reflects on his situation, sips wine, and amuses himself with simple pleasures. Surprisingly, many of these poems were written during his periods of exile to what most officials would have considered unattractive regions (e.g. Yiling, just below the Three Gorges on the Yangzi river, and Chuzhou, in modern Anhui). Ouyang made these exiles into celebrations of his self-sufficiency and the ability to find, or at least poetically assert, sanguinity amid deprivation and political disfavor. These are the poetic manifestations of the same spirit, marked by equanimity and a capacity for not taking himself too seriously, captured in his famous autobiographical prose account of the Pavilion of the Drunken Old Man. The other type of poem consists of long ancient-style compositions that treat their subject, whatever it is, discursively. Ouyang's most important statement on contemporary poetics is contained in a long poem that characterizes at considerable length the divergent poetic styles of Mei Yaochen and Su Shunqin. Another poem, presented to a friend who is about to take up a position as fiscal commissioner in a coastal region, where salt is produced, features a detailed discussion of the history of the government salt monopoly and all the hardship it has brought upon the commoners through the centuries. Regardless of the subject, these poems evince an advanced ability to incorporate reasoning and even argumentation into verse. Here is an excerpt of one of these ancient-style poems, about the poet's first exposure to a southern variety of clam known, for reasons that escape us, as the "cart clam." Although it is lighthearted in tone, one can still see in it something of the penchant for taking a "low" or "unpoetic" subject and treating it reflectively, as well as for writing verse of social comment or awareness, and, in any case, for avoiding the intensely personal. The "sage founder" referred to in line thirteen is the founding Song dynasty emperor, Taizu.

> ("Upon First Eating Cart Clams")
> Piled high, the clams on the plate,
> They've come from the edge of the sea.
> At first the assembled guests did not know what they were,
> Then, tasting them, exclaimed with delight.
> During the Five Dynasties the empire was divided,
> The Nine Provinces were like a melon sliced up.
> The southeast stopped at the Huai river,
> It had no contact with the central plains.

At that time, people in the northern regions
Lived on food and drink unspeakably coarse.
Chicken and pork were their "unusual dishes,"
Rich and poor all ate the same meals.
But once our sage founder appeared
All under heaven was unified as one.
Southern products came equally from Jiao and Guang
Western delicacies were plentiful from Qiong and Ba.
Goods transported over water arrived in strings of boats,
Land shipments were brought in overflowing carts.
Fresh-water streams yielded fish with delicate whiskers,
The ocean sent powerful sea creatures with spines or teeth.
It was not just high-placed dukes and lords,
People in narrow lanes also gorged on seafood.
But these clams appeared in the capital only recently,
Why, I wonder, did they get here so late?

. . .

The writers associated with Ouyang Xiu recognized him as their leader. He was acknowledged as the preeminent talent in prose, the most prestigious genre, and also the most important and effective spokesman for the call to "restore antiquity." Given the self-consciousness of the group as a literary circle and its commitment to writing in the ancient style and with didactic intent, it was only natural that they cast themselves in the role of Han Yu and his circle of writers, who championed similar causes in the mid-Tang. In this formulation, Ouyang Xiu as leader became the contemporary Han Yu, and others in his circle willingly found their analogues among Han Yu's supporters. Mei Yaochen became Meng Jiao, a correspondence endlessly invoked by Mei and Ouyang that was reinforced by the lack of official advancement that plagued both Mei and Meng. Filling out the parallel, Shi Yannian and Su Shunqin became modern counterparts of Lu Tong (795–835) and Zhang Ji (ca 765–ca 830). This elaborate analogy has both a serious and a comic side, serious in that it grounded the Song writers in an important ideological heritage, and comic in that it provided material for role-playing, mutual teasing, and ingenious poetic imitations.

For us today, however, such assertions of affinity with the Tang circle of poets serve, if anything, to highlight the divergences between the two groups. When we actually read the poetry produced by Ouyang and his friends against that written by Han Yu and his circle, we find a difference in tone and outlook as striking as any similarity in the conscious choice of subjects and forms inherited from Han Yu. Perhaps the most apparent divergence is in the poetic response to setbacks in one's official career. As much as he admired Han Yu, Ouyang Xiu explicitly criticized the Tang writer for allowing himself to indulge in expressions of self-pity, anger, and despair when forced into exile. When Ouyang and others in his group were exiled for their support of Fan Zhongyan in 1036, Ouyang wrote this in a letter to Yin Zhu, who had likewise suffered demotion and removal from the capital:

> Through the ages many men of renown have spoken out fearlessly in court on policy matters, risking their lives without hesitation, and hereby appeared to be men of principle. But if subsequently exiled, they invariably wrote lugubrious and bitter poems, unable to bear their hardship, whereupon they impress one as nothing more than ordinary fellows. Even Han Yu could not avoid this failing.

To complain in poetry about one's lack of worldly success, or to lash out at one's political enemies, was to display a lack of inner cultivation, which should put one above such petty concerns. When he was demoted and sent away from the capital a few years later, Mei Yaochen echoed Ouyang's advice in a poem addressed to Ouyang and other friends. I will look forward, he says, to your poetic correspondence, sent to me "on the wings of birds." Just be sure, he cautions them, that you do not imitate the "sorrowful expressions of little children." This commitment to maintaining a tone of equanimity in the face of worldly setbacks followed from the conviction that the sources of literary expression are internal and should remain unaffected by external circumstances. Comely literary expression, Ouyang told a young man who had written to him for advice, is like the luster given off by gold or jade. It does not result from polishing the surface, but from the inherent properties of the substance itself.

II. Ouyang Xiu and literary prose

Before leaving Ouyang and his generation, we need to comment on their achievement in literary prose. As we have said, the call for the reform of writing first sounded by Fan Zhongyan and others was focused on prose. It was expression in prose, not poetry, that was central to the functioning of the court and imperial bureaucracy. Well before the Song dynasty, the official bureaucracy in China had evolved into a distinctively documentary system of governance. Very little of what was done failed to generate documentation. Often a single action, such as an official's reappointment, say, from one prefectural staff position to the same position in another prefecture, necessitated the composition of several documents. There might, for example, be multiple requests for reassignment submitted by the man concerned, court responses to these requests, and eventually an imperial rescript reassigning the man. Finally, when the man arrived at the new location, he was expected to submit a memorial expressing gratitude for the new position. In a recent typeset edition, Ouyang Xiu's complete writings (excluding the historical works he wrote and his study of the *Classic of Poetry*) fill 2,592 pages. Given that literary Chinese is considerably more semantically "dense" than English, and also that the fonts used for typesetting Chinese permit more characters to fit on a single page than do words on a page of typeset English, if this "complete works" were translated into English it would easily fill five thousand pages. The bulk of this writing is prose, and the bulk of the prose are works that Ouyang composed in some official capacity, whether as local official, court official speaking on his own behalf, or court official drafting imperial decrees (which he did as Hanlin academician). Considering the amount of time and energy that members of the bureaucratic class devoted to writing, it is little wonder that the leading thinkers of the day took different approaches to writing very seriously and discussed them at length.

With Ouyang Xiu's prose it is useful to draw a distinction between what he said as advocate of the reform of writing standards and what he produced as a prose stylist when writing in an unofficial capacity. What is usually said about Ouyang is that he advocated replacing the euphuistic style with ancient-style prose. It would be more accurate to say that in his pronouncements on the subject made for public consumption, he advocated turning away from preoccupation with style itself, any style. His essential position, as we have already seen, was that good writing springs from attending to the cultivation of the self and inculcating in oneself a mastery of the Classics and the values they embody, until one thoroughly understands the purposes and ends of writing. If one only concentrates on this and not on writing per se, then when it comes time to write one will produce sensible and meaningful prose effortlessly.

This may strike us as impractical advice to dispense to aspiring writers. We must, however, understand that it was largely in the context of the civil service examinations that Ouyang considered this the right position and the right advice to give. In Ouyang's day the examination system was expanding as a means for recruiting young men into official service; and given that euphuistic prose was the style expected of civil service examination candidates, young men spent years perfecting their ability to write the decorous and allusive prose that they hoped would impress the examiners. As Ouyang described them, young men of his day began by concentrating on the stylistic sheen of their writing, became obsessed with it as their talent for ornamentation increased, and ended up giving no thought to the ideas or substance of what their writing expressed. This was the approach to writing that Ouyang decried. That this was his perception of the problem allows us to understand why he somewhat paradoxically insisted that the reform of writing styles required that people turn their attention away from stylistic issues.

It was not only the euphuistic style that Ouyang disapproved of. There had been another reaction against the vogue of euphuistic prose, distinct from that associated with Ouyang, Yin Zhu, and the young talents of Luoyang. This was the prose equivalent of the poetic style described earlier, cultivated by easterners, that featured archaizing and strange language as an antidote to the polished ornamentation of the Xikun poets. The leader of this prose movement was Shi Jie, who as a lecturer at the Imperial Academy in the 1040s attracted a large number of followers. Shi Jie was a specialist in the *Classic of Changes*, and perhaps found some of the inspiration for his prose in that archaic text. His way of writing, which was prolix as well as archaizing, was known as the "unorthodox style" (*bianti*), and eventually became so popular among his students that it started to be called the Imperial Academy style. It was criticized in the following way by Zhang Fangping (1007–1091) in 1046, when he was director of the civil service examinations: "Shi Jie, the lecturer, tested students according to his own preferences, which thereafter became the fashion of the day. Presently, writing that is weird, hyperbolic, and inflated is considered exalted, and unrestrained license and prolixity are thought of as a proper amplitude." Ouyang Xiu had a certain respect for Shi Jie's conduct as an outspoken official and man of principle. But Ouyang could not abide Shi Jie's cult of eccentricity. Ouyang Xiu's criticisms of it are contained in letters he wrote to Shi Jie on the subject of the bizarre calligraphy style he used. Ouyang accused Shi Jie of deliberately using the brush in an unorthodox way to win for himself a reputation for being unconventional and superior. When Shi Jie replied that his style was rooted in the archaic script used by the ancient Confucian sages, Ouyang admonished him about the importance of abiding by "enduring standards" (*changfa*). There are certain conventions, Ouyang reminded him, that are universal and essential, and it is unacceptable to reject them by claiming that one is following the ancients. Dissatisfied as Ouyang was with the current style of euphuistic prose, he also disapproved of radical alternatives.

The best-known instances of Ouyang's efforts to reform the way people wrote prose include one text and one official act. The text is an afterword he wrote to his copy of Han Yu's literary collection, in which he described somewhat melodramatically his youthful "discovery" of a tattered and neglected copy of Han Yu's works in his neighbor's library, his Luoyang association with Yin Zhu and conversion to the ancient-style prose, and his subsequent devotion to Han Yu's writings and the values they stood for. The afterword ends with Ouyang repeating aspects of the Han Yu legend that other early Northern Song writers had helped to create: Han Yu had risen from obscurity to prominence, to the point where his works and values had become universally revered, because of the unflagging effort that a few devoted men had put into promoting Han Yu's works.

The official act took place in 1057, when Ouyang Xiu was appointed to oversee the civil service examinations in the capital, his appointment itself being, of course, a highly political choice. Under Ouyang's direction, the examiners that year passed only those candidates who formulated their answers in ancient-style prose and failed anybody who used either euphuistic prose or the Imperial Academy style. This was a sudden and unexpected departure from the way the examinations had always been conducted, and it understandably infuriated the candidates who had spent years practicing the other styles. An angry crowd of failed candidates gathered in the street after the exam results were posted; and when Ouyang himself happened by, they are said to have surrounded and cursed him. Someone went so far as to compose a mock funeral ode for Ouyang and sent it to his home. The whole examinations incident made Ouyang even more famous as the champion of ideological and literary reform.

Ouyang's accomplishment in the field of literary prose goes, in fact, far beyond anything he did either to change writing in the examinations or as the spokesman who called for a return to Han Yu and ancient-style prose. In dozens of accounts (ji, including inscriptions for his own studios and other buildings), prefaces, letters, prose farewells (songxu), and even grave inscriptions, he cultivated a highly personal tone, the likes of which had seldom been seen before in prose. In sharp contrast to his polemical statements about the moralistic sources and purposes of writing, his corpus of prose in these nonofficial genres is toned down and consequently able to accommodate an impressive range of subjects, moods, and themes. Writing about friends and things that are dear to him (e.g. his collection of antique zithers, a tiny fish pond he built for relaxation, a neighbor's garden that he used to play in as a boy, the gift of a zither he makes to a friend, a painting that had belonged to his father, the studio he made for himself in Huazhou and dubbed Pleasure Boat Studio), this prose has a lyrical and poetic quality about it. It may not be sentimental, but it is personal and emotive rather than didactic.

In one sense it is not surprising that Ouyang's pronouncements about reforming writing do not prepare us for this output. It would have been difficult for him to find justifications, even to find language, to support the type of prose he was evidently moved to compose. There was no critical tradition to draw upon to validate an informal tone in prose with a largely autobiographical focus that was almost wholly devoid of moralistic intent. We might even say that insofar as it emphasized the personal over the didactic, this body of prose was at odds with the values and purposes Ouyang championed as a reformer bent on reviving ancient-style prose. Even here, however, Ouyang remained true to the ancient-style commitment to make meaning fundamental and to banish ornament. It was just that, having renounced interest in euphonious prose, Ouyang discovered that a breadth of expression could now be accommodated in nonofficial writings that went far beyond the original reformist vision of insistently "instructive" prose infused with Confucian values.

The statements about prose that come closest to describing what Ouyang actually produced in the field of literary prose are pieces of advice he offered to younger men about what to aim for in writing. Ouyang told the young Wang Anshi that although the writing of Han Yu and Meng Jiao was exalted, he should not always imitate their style. "Seek to write naturally," he urged. To a certain Xu Wudang he gave this advice:

> If you find that your writing is verbose, you should put it aside until another day and edit it, deleting the superfluous words until it becomes sharp and clean. However, do not overdo such deletion. If you do, your words will not flow. You must wait until the final version comes to you naturally, as if it had been in your mind all along.
>
> As for the writing style, on the first draft let the words run freely. But later go back and hold them in check, so that the writing is concise, forceful, and correct. Still, now and then allow a free and unrestrained passage to relax the tone. Do not cling to a single style, then your writing will be masterly.

Earlier, in the account of Yin Zhu's tutelage of Ouyang, we saw the idea of improvement through deletion, and the prizing of a terse, compact style. Here that stance is modified. A new goal of having language that flows freely and is, occasionally, unrestrained and relaxed is introduced to mitigate the previous emphasis on clipped forcefulness. What is common to the two accounts is the focus on language rather than on underlying ideas. In a sense this focus is the antitheses of Ouyang's program as an advocate of ancient-style prose. We are reminded of an anecdote concerning the account Ouyang wrote by invitation for Han Qi's (1008–1075) studio. Several days after Ouyang had already sent him the composition, Han Qi was surprised to receive a messenger who explained that Ouyang had decided that there were some places where the wording was not right, and that he was now sending a revised version. Upon scrutinizing the new version, Han Qi was at a loss to see any changes that had been made. Finally he noticed that in the opening lines Ouyang had added two connective particles (er); the meaning was unaltered but now the lines flowed better. Such was Ouyang's attention to words and prose rhythm.

The year before Ouyang Xiu supervised the examinations, Su Xun (1009–1066), father of Su Shi, introduced himself to Ouyang by way of a letter, a portion of which characterizes Ouyang's prose, contrasting it with that of Han Yu. The letter is hardly a disinterested document. Su Xun surely worded it in a way calculated to please the vastly more eminent statesman and author, and probably designed his description of Ouyang's writing around what he imagined Ouyang would like to have said about it. Still, what Su Xun says is interesting and has a certain validity, even for us today. Han Yu's prose, Su explains, is like the mighty Yangzi river, which flows and twists in powerful turns. The vast flow contains, moreover, a myriad terrifying sea monsters – scaly dragons and other water creatures – that the author keeps mostly concealed, so that people can but dimly glimpse them. Consequently, when people gaze upon the glow of the murky depths and hoary surface, they shrink back in fear, not daring to approach too closely. Ouyang Xiu's writing, he says, is by contrast supple yet ample, twisting this way and that (like a meandering stream) a hundred times. Yet the reasoning is transparent, and free from any gap or break. Even when the spirit and diction rise to a climax, when the words come quickly to clinch a point, they remain leisurely and simple, without any trace of the belabored or forced.

The existence of the unorthodox style appears to have been very significant for the course that Ouyang's own writing would take. His rejection of Shi Jie's literary eccentricity led Ouyang to value the "constant" and "conventional" in a way that proved to be telling. He was put on a track to eliminate euphuistic ornament from prose but not, at the same time, return it to the archaistic and difficult style we associate with Han Yu, despite all his declarations of affinity with Han Yu. Comparison of Ouyang's nonofficial prose with that in the same genres by the leading Tang writers reveals how innovative Ouyang was. The earlier writers have a tendency toward the didactic or the allegorical (political or moralistic) that is less in evidence in Ouyang's informal prose. The earlier writers also tended to direct the expression of personal and lyrical themes into poetry, whereas Ouyang experimented with allowing it into prose.

III. Wang Anshi, the political reformer as poet

Wang Anshi was born in 1021, which made him Ouyang Xiu's junior by fourteen years. His father, Wang Yi, never passed the civil service examination and served only in low clerical posts in prefectural administrations. One could not have foreseen the eminence the son would achieve from the father's record. After passing the civil service examination in 1042, Wang Anshi served for the next sixteen years in various prefectural posts in the Jiangnan and Jiangxi regions. There he observed the problems that were endemic to the lives of peasants and to local administrations in the empire. These included heavy taxation, the exploitation of peasants by wealthy local clans, and local governments run by bureaucrats who were either incompetent or corrupt. Distressed by what he saw, Wang Anshi began to write essays and poetry that addressed these problems. His works came to the attention of leading officials back in the capital, and several times he was recommended for recall and advancement to a court position, but on each occasion he declined. It was not until 1059 or 1060 that he returned to the capital, as a member of the Finance Commission. At that time he took the bold step of submitting to the Emperor Renzong a "Ten Thousand Word Memorial" that outlined the administrative failings he discerned and explained how they could be set right. The primary theme was that there was not currently enough "talent" among the tens of thousands men who constituted the imperial bureaucracy. Such talent could be properly cultivated only with sweeping changes in the "instruction" of promising young men in local government schools, the "nurturing" of the ethical and material lives of the people to the point where social customs were unified, the "selection" of men for official appointment based on their administrative competence, and the "employment" of officials according to their record of performance in office.

It would take nearly another decade before Wang Anshi was given the opportunity to put his vision for bureaucratic reform into practice. In 1067 the indecisive Emperor Yingzong died. Wang Anshi had removed himself from the capital a few years before to go into mourning for his mother. In 1068 the new emperor, Shenzong, summoned Wang Anshi back as a Hanlin academician. Shenzong gave Wang Anshi a personal audience and was impressed by the sharp and candid responses Wang gave to questions about problems facing the realm. In the following year, Wang was promoted as vice grand councilor and began implementing a series of far-reaching reforms that came to be known as the New Policies (*xinfa*). They included measures intended to cultivate bureaucratic talent, but now Wang's program of reforms went far beyond what he had set forth in the "Ten Thousand Word Memorial."

The New Policies aimed to enrich the state, transform social customs, improve the efficiency of the bureaucracy, and restructure the institutions of the central government. Collectively, they were the most ambitious attempt at government reform during the entire dynasty and take their place among the most far-reaching attempts to restructure the state in all of Chinese history. There is hardly any aspect of the fabric of the Song state they did not affect, including taxation, trade and the transportation of goods, neighborhood organizations, military service, local government corvée service, local schools, and the civil service examination system. A key component of the reforms was Wang's intent to make the government more interventionist and even entrepreneurial. Wang lay the blame for many of the economic problems that plagued both the central government (perennial shortage of funds) and the commoners (tax obligations they could not meet) on what he called the "engrossers" (*jianbingzhe*); that is, wealthy clans that acted as landlords and monopolizing merchants. Several of the New Policies were designed to empower the circuit and prefectural administrations to subvert the influence of these engrossers by entering into direct competition with them as conveyers of goods, wholesalers, and lenders. The aim was to break the control wealthy clans and guilds had over local economies and to redistribute land and wealth more evenly. Reforms in schooling and the examination were needed to ensure that the bureaucracy was staffed at all levels by men with the practical and institutional know-how to administer this new order of governance. Wang Anshi composed commentaries on several Confucian Classics, justifying his reforms by finding grounds for them in ancient texts and institutions. Wang's commentaries became the standard interpretations of the Classics, required on the examinations.

The New Policies were as controversial as they were ambitious. They were bitterly opposed by the leading statesman Sima Guang (1019–1086), who considered them dangerously disruptive to the social and political order. Sima Guang withdrew from the court in protest soon after Wang was appointed grand councilor in 1071, and retired to Luoyang to work on his historiographical project, *Comprehensive Mirror for Aid in Governance* (*Zizhi tongjian*), believing that the solutions to the empire's problems were to be found in a careful analysis of historical successes and failures rather than in institutional reform. Even with their most powerful opponent removed from the court, the New

Policies continued to face opposition. Wang insisted on the correctness of the direction he had charted, declaring, "Changes in the empire system are not to be feared, the ancestors need not serve as our model, and what people say in criticism need not be heeded." The emperor, however, occasionally wavered in his support of such a thoroughgoing reform agenda, especially when initial results seemed untoward. Wang Anshi was relieved of his position in 1074 and returned to Jiangning (modern Nanjing). Political infighting broke out among his successors, and Wang was recalled to a second appointment as grand councilor in the following year. By then the political situation had become too fractious, and in 1076 he withdrew permanently from the court. He retired to his estate on Zhong Mountain outside of Jiangning, where he remained until his death in 1086.

The New Policies and struggles over them dominated court politics for the remainder of the Northern Song, from the 1070s through the 1120s. There was a brief period when they were completely rescinded, the Yuanyou era of the 1080s, but afterward their advocates regained power and reinstituted many of them, albeit in somewhat altered form. They were still generally supported by Emperor Huizong, whose lengthy reign ended just one year before the Jurchen invasion of 1126 and the loss of the northern half of the empire. Even after that loss, support for many of the principles of the New Policies continued on through the early decades of the Southern Song. It was not until 1155, with the death of Qin Hui, the grand councilor during the restoration era, that the New Policies and Wang Anshi's learning and commentaries were finally abandoned for good. Thereafter they were often viewed as a foolhardy attempt to do away with norms and principles of governance that had evolved through history. The New Policies came to be blamed for the loss of the north, which weighed on the minds of Han Chinese poets and patriots through the Southern Song and the ensuing Mongol Yuan dynasty.

Wang Anshi was also a major poet. To us it may seem unlikely that a man who rose to the very apex of political power in a state as vast and bureaucratically complex as Song dynasty China could possibly have had the time, energy, and talent to be a leading poet. Thus even some modern Chinese critics have assumed that it was only after Wang Anshi stepped down from office and removed himself to Zhong Mountain that with his newfound leisure he turned to writing poetry. But this was demonstrably not the case. Wang Anshi wrote poetry throughout his life, and there is no period that shows a dearth of achievement, even if the nature of that achievement changes through time. Wang Anshi took full advantage of the preference that had already been established by the poets of the preceding generation to compose a style of verse that was distinctly full of ideas, viewpoints, and opinions, even political ones. There is thus an important element of this style of verse that is readily compatible with Wang's political interests and aspirations.

Indeed, the most striking feature of Wang's early poems is their engagement with social issues. These poems date from the 1040s and 1050s, when Wang held positions in the Jiangnan prefectures and must have had ample opportunity to witness rural life as he traveled from post to post. He composed poems on many aspects of peasant life, including the harvesting of salt from the sea (illegal because it violated the government's salt monopoly), a summer drought in Shuzhou that threatened the rice crop, and the laborious work of picking mulberry leaves, raising silkworms, and the weaving that went into silk production. Wang consistently sided with the peasants, expressing sympathy for their plight and outrage at the way they were exploited by those who ruled over them. A certain cleverness in these poems gives the political criticism its edge. One of the terms used to designate the cricket in Chinese literally means "to hurry weaving" (cuzhi), because the drone of the insect is thought to resemble the whirring of the spooler or loom. Among the wealthy class, there had long been the pastime of catching crickets and training them to fight, then pitting one cricket against another, as the respective owners looked on and placed bets on the winner. A concise quatrain entitled "Cricket" describes such a match in its opening couplet: the combatants are placed inside a golden bowl, while the proud owners look on drunkenly. The poem abruptly shifts its focus in the second couplet to the insect as it is perceived by impoverished families, whose women stay up late at night working at the loom, hurrying to produce silk to meet their tax obligation. How many of such families, Wang asks, can even afford to keep enough of the silk they produce to make tassels for their shoes?

Some of the poems present unexpectedly complex reasoning regarding policy issues. A poem entitled "Reducing the Number of Soldiers," in twenty-six lines, addresses a topic that was being hotly debated at the court. In order to protect its northern border, the Northern Song maintained a large army, garrisoned in numerous strategic places spread across the northern prefectures. A large portion of the annual imperial income was needed to sustain this army. The army was a principal cause of the perennial debts run up by the court (which had to be covered by borrowing from the reserves held by the emperor). Hence some officials recommended diminishing the size of the army. Naturally, there were also those who were apprehensive about the consequences such a reduction might have for border security. In his poem, Wang does not support either side of the argument. Instead, he points out that certain changes must be implemented first before any cuts are made in the number of troops. Specifically, the quality of the generals must be improved, and a way must be found to ease the transition from active soldier to farmer before large numbers of young men are sent home to the countryside:

> Someone here says we must reduce the number of soldiers,
> I say to do this straight away should not be our first step.
> Today our generals are not properly chosen,
> It is with the size of our armies that we guard our borders.
> If the first line of assault is defeated in an attack,
> The troops behind them remain strong and intact.
> By sending our larger numbers against the smaller enemy
> We prevail even when caught in a crisis.
> Our generals are of insufficient talent,
> Their strategies are second-guessed by subordinates.
> If troops are reduced, there will be no reinforcements in case of a defeat,
> The barbarians will advance to drink from the Qin river.
> If you say this reasoning is incorrect,
> Then by what criteria would you have us reduce the troops?
> Our soldiers are accustomed to being arrogant and lazy,
> Send them home: do you think they will farm the land?
> Not farming nor producing silk either,
> Their need for food and clothing will be the same as active troops.
> The right time will come to reduce the number of soldiers,
> But it must be done in the proper sequence of steps.
>
> . . .

Whether or not one finds Wang's suggestions compelling, what is striking is that they are presented in a poem. We would normally expect to find this type of policy discussion in a prose memorial or essay.

It is not only the subject matter of these early poems that commands interest. It is already evident at this stage that Wang is a craftsman of rare talent, able to construct lines and couplets that, despite the meticulous care that has gone into their construction, still read smoothly and naturally. A poem he wrote upon spending an autumn evening at a way-station in the countryside contains this couplet:

> My sickly frame is first to sense the early wind and frost,
> My dream of home is unaware of the distance across mountains and rivers.

The parallel lines, with their dense texture of correspondence and contrast between matching phrases, aptly evoke the hardships of sojourning in an unfamiliar landscape.

A long poem on a portrait of Du Fu shows Wang Anshi's poetic orientation and choices in literary history. In the mid-eleventh century, Du Fu was on his way to becoming recognized as the supreme poetic talent, but there was still room for some disagreement. Ouyang Xiu had declared his preference for Li Bai over Du Fu, saying that although Du surpassed Li in the intensity of effort he put into composition, Li was clearly superior in innate genius. Su Shi would later say that the poetic tradition reached its culmination with Du Fu. Still, among earlier poets it was Tao Qian that Su Shi most revered and sought to emulate in poetic style. Su Shi also owed much to Li Bai and to Bai Juyi.

It is against this background of a range of poetic allegiances and rankings in the mid-eleventh century, when Du Fu had not yet become the "sage of poetry" in everyone's eyes, that Wang Anshi's treatment of Du Fu is interesting. Wang clearly identified with Du Fu, expressing the wish at the end of his portrait poem that he might somehow bring the poet back to life and join him as a friend. Wang's poem makes reference to several of Du Fu's most celebrated compositions, giving particular attention to his famous compassion for the commoners. The opening of Wang's poem is the most revealing. Wang asserts that Du Fu's poetry is a match for the "primal life force" (*yuan qi*) of the universe, that its energy can open up the heavens themselves and turn round the earth. This hyperbole gives way to the following thought: considering the great variety of creatures and objects that fill the world, including everything beautiful and ugly and large and small, in ten thousand distinct forms, how is it possible that Du Fu's brush could have captured and represented them all? This appreciation of poetic breadth and scope, without regard for any particular viewpoint or sentiment – that is, a talent for encompassing subjects that precedes even the expression of commiseration – is a conspicuously writerly assessment of the Tang poet. There seems to be implicit in this judgment a sense of poetry standing on its own, not serving any larger ideological or didactic purpose, that augured well for the author's own future development as a poet.

In the middle period of Wang Anshi's life, from the late 1050s through his tenure as leader of the reform government, we find that his output as a poet continues to be filled with poems that may readily be linked to his public life and political views, although the private and nonofficial side of his life also finds expression in verse. From the years before he came to power at the court, there are poems that present idiosyncratic treatments of standard themes, many of them historical ones. It is likely that by writing such compositions Wang Anshi was trying to attract attention. The best-known example is a lengthy poem on Wang Zhaojun, the Han dynasty imperial concubine who was married off to the Xiongnu chieftain when he asked to form a marriage alliance with the Han state. So numerous were his palace ladies, that the Han emperor, Yuandi, had never laid eyes on Wang Zhaojun, and at her farewell ceremony he was shocked to see how beautiful she was. One version of the story lays the blame for the emperor's ignorance on the palace painter, Mao Yanshou. Mao had been directed to paint for the emperor's perusal portraits of all the palace ladies. Before painting Wang Zhaojun, he asked her for money to ensure a flattering portrait. She rebuffed him, and Mao retaliated by representing her as unattractive. After the emperor realized that he had been tricked, he had Mao Yanshou put to death. It was, however, too late to save Wang Zhaojun. She had already been sent from the palace to the distant north, and her tearful journey into Xiongnu lands and her tragic fate once she got there inspired numerous poems, ballads, and legends. In some versions of her story, she commits suicide just as she is about to leave Chinese territory. In others, she marries the Xiongnu chieftain and bears him a son. Later, when the chieftain dies and the son of a previous wife succeeds him, she is forced to follow Xiongnu custom and marry her own stepson. The alleged event exacerbated Chinese outrage over her fate.

Wang Anshi's handling of the Wang Zhaojun theme is distinctly original. First, midway through the poem, he asserts that she was so beautiful her likeness never could have been rendered in a painting and consequently that the emperor's execution of Mao Yanshou was "unjustified." This is already a significant departure from the standard narrative of the story. But the concluding lines are even more striking. Subverting the tradition of Wang Zhaojun as a pitifully unfortunate figure, Wang tells us that when her family received the bitter letters she sent them from the north, they wrote back to her saying this: be as content as you can be where you are and do not think of us. "Don't you remember how Ajiao was confined inside Long Gate Palace? / When one meets with frustration in life there is no north or south." Ajiao was an earlier Han palace lady, known as Empress Chen. When she lost Emperor Wu's favor, she was locked up inside Long Gate Palace, where she spent lonely and miserable years. In other words, someone like Ajiao, whom the emperor neglects, though she is still kept in the palace, is as pitiful as someone forced out to barbarian lands. The political implications are clear: if the emperor does not heed an official's advice, that official might as well be in foreign exile as present at the court.

This poem was written in 1059, when Wang was at the court, right around the time of the "Ten Thousand Word Memorial." The poem attracted considerable attention. Matching poems (poems on the same theme and using Wang's rhyme words) were soon written by the leading statesmen and poets of the day, including Ouyang Xiu, Sima Guang, Liu Chang (1019–1068), and Mei Yaochen. Wang was clearly making a reputation for himself as a man of singular and revisionist viewpoints.

We find a similar flair for novelty in the way Wang Anshi used literary and historical allusions. Wang is quoted in Cai Juhou's *Remarks on Poetry* (early twelfth century) as saying this on the subject:

> Poetry suffers from having too many allusions. The problem is that poets select only those allusions that match the subject of their poem, arranging them by category. This is like collecting together references on a certain subject. Even when it is done well, what good is it? If, however, one can manage to invest an allusion with one's own meaning, borrowing an ancient event to express new intent, so that altered expressions emerge unpredictably, then any number of allusions may be used without detracting from the poem.

We may readily find lines in Wang's poetry in which he puts this idea into practice. Consider a couplet in a quatrain he wrote about a friend's mountain dwelling that looked out over a lovely landscape of hills and rivers:

> A single river guards the fields, encircling them in a band of emerald.
> Two mountains shove open the door, sending their green inside.

The language is drawn from the *History of the Han*. In its western border regions, the Han established a system of "state farms" (*tuntian*), in which soldiers were stationed on unoccupied land and directed to work it as farmers. These military colonies were supposed to become self-supporting, or even to return surplus crops to the state, and were used as a buffer against the threat of enemy incursion into Chinese territory. As they worked the land, the soldiers were said to be "guarding the fields" (*hutian*). A second borrowed phrase comes from the biography of Fan Kuai, one of Emperor Gaozu's (r. 202–195 BC) loyal generals and advisers. During the period of Qing Bu's revolt, when Gaozu lay ill in the palace, orders were given that no one would be allowed to come into the ailing emperor's presence. But the impetuous Fan Kuai could not tolerate the thought that the emperor should be thus isolated when ill and facing a crisis. So he approached the room where Gaozu was confined, and "shoved open the door (*paita*) and went straight in." In Wang Anshi's couplet these two allusions are ingeniously applied to features of the landscape that stretched out before the friend's villa. A few decades later, Huang Tingjian would formulate the poetic ideal of "touching iron and transforming it into gold" (*diantie chengjin*), and other related notions. What Wang Anshi did with his creative use of earlier phrases anticipated Huang Tingjian's ideal.

At the height of his power in the early 1070s, Wang Anshi was a magnet for political invective, directed at him by those who were adamantly against his reforms and what were perceived as his authoritarian methods. Even someone as self-confident as Wang may have had moments of self-doubt. In poems of this period Wang seems to be seeking to reassure himself that he should not allow the torrent of criticism to cause him to swerve from the course he had set. His detractors labeled him a latter-day Shang Yang, the statesman of the early fourth century BC who persuaded the rulers of Qin to adopt Legalist thought and to rule by harsh law and intimidation rather than through moral suasion. Wang Anshi responded with a poem praising Shang Yang for being candid, a man of his word, and for ensuring that every law was efficiently and effectively enforced. Another of Wang's poems from this period, entitled "The Crowd," proudly declares its author to be unaffected by the outcry against his reforms:

> The hubbub of the crowd, why should I contend with it?
> Their praise would not delight me nor their censure distress me.
> . . .
> The weight of something is not determined by them,
> Beauty and ugliness are what I deem them to be.

Wang's resignation from his second brief term as grand councilor in 1076 ushered in the third and last stage of his work as a poet, while he lived out his life in retirement in Jiangning. There is a distinct change in the tone and subjects of his poetry during these final years. His verse becomes more personal, reflective, and frequently Buddhistic in tone and subject. It was during this period that Wang wrote commentaries on Buddhist sutras, frequently exchanged poems with Buddhists who also lived on Zhong Mountain, and wrote poems matching those of the Tang monks Hanshan and Shide. It is interesting to see that artistically this change of focus is not accompanied by a slackening of effort or effectiveness. On the contrary, it is clear that Wang's commitment to producing innovative and technically demanding verse remained as strong as ever. It is just that his attention became newly directed in these final years. The landscape vistas, mountain neighbors, and abbeys and monasteries in the vicinity of his mountain estate now fulfilled his needs for poetic subjects. Rarely any more does he feel compelled to comment on the social and political issues that had so consumed his previous years.

A shift in formal preferences accompanies this change, with some interesting consequences. Previously, Wang had favored ancient-style verse. Now, he became more interested in regulated verse, and especially the quatrain in the seven-syllable line. Thus formally, and in other respects as well, Wang's poetry began to move closer to Tang dynasty verse, and to separate itself from the poetic styles cultivated by the earlier generation of Song poets. Around 1070, Wang joined with his friend Song Minqiu (1019–1079) in compiling an anthology of Tang poetry. Song Minqiu, who as book collector specialized in Tang poetry, is said to have owned manuscripts of 103 individual poetry collections from the period. Their anthology, *A Selection of One Hundred Tang Poets (Tang baijia shixuan)*, was compiled to be printed: it was Wang's and Song Minqiu's way of promoting familiarity with Tang poetry. Wang was, in other words, a student of Tang poetry and, as we have seen, was particularly devoted to Du Fu. Wang's poetry, especially that of the later years, was perceived early on as being stylistically close to Tang models. Some critics disapproved of this affinity, charging that Wang aped the manner of the Tang poets but could not, in fact, match their brilliance. Others insisted that as indebted as he may have been to the great writers of the Tang, Wang still managed to be distinctive. We recall that in the preceding generation leading poets compared themselves to Han Yu and his circle. These divergent poetic assessments of Wang Anshi anticipate the debate over the nature of the Tang/Song poetic divide and the relative merits of the two styles of poetry, a debate that would set the parameters of much of the critical discussion of poetry through the Ming and Qing periods.

There is a studied cleverness in Wang's verse of these final years that exceeds in frequency and quality anything he produced earlier on. A quatrain entitled "Noonday Pillow" ends with these lines:

> Peeking at me, the birds call me from my wavering dream,
> Across the river the mountains provide an undulating sorrow.

"Wavering" applies both to the speaker's unsteady dream and to the warbling sound of the birds' songs. "Undulating" applies both to the uneven sadness, which twists and turns inside him, and topographically to the rolling hills. Another poem concludes this way:

> Touched by the wind, duck-head emerald glistens brightly,
> Turning in the sunlight, goose-bill yellow hangs down delicately.

The emerald in the first line is the color of the spring water, reflecting the greenery around it. The yellow in the second line is the budding willows growing on the river's edge.

Precedents for such couplets may be found in Tang or other earlier verse. But in Wang's late quatrains, these couplets *are* the poem; that is, they are not embedded somewhere in a string of lines but are instead offered up as the conclusion and climax of the poem. The persona of the poet is largely effaced. The poet as a thinking and feeling person fades from view. It is the cleverness of the wording that is on display, rather than the sentiments of the poet. Even when the voice of a distinct persona is heard, it is still the unexpectedness of what he says that is featured, rather than his emotions. A quatrain inscribed on a Chan meditation hall, which opens with the poet and his friend waking from sleep, ends this way:

> I asked the monk what he had dreamed of,
> He said he had forgotten, not that he hadn't dreamed.

Another poem presents the poet gazing out upon the mountain landscape where he dwells:

> Beneath my thatched eaves I sit facing it all day,
> When not a single bird calls, the mountain is even more deserted.

The last line contravenes a much-admired line from a Tang poem: "A birdcall makes the mountain seem even more deserted."

In literary history, the Jiangxi School of poetry is sometimes traced back to Wang Anshi, even though it was not fully developed until a few decades after his death and lasted well into the Southern Song. In such an understanding, that school's preoccupation with ensuring that "every word" has a literary precedent was ultimately derived from Wang Anshi's studied approach to the poetic art, even though he did not articulate it as such or set out to found any such school.

For us today, Wang Anshi's dual roles as political reformer and literary innovator have greater claims upon our interest than any role he played in the founding of the Jiangxi School. Wang remains one of the premier examples in Chinese history of the compatibility of official eminence and literary talent. In his earlier years the two areas of activity overlap to some degree, as his poetic subjects and unorthodox viewpoints complemented his political aims and boldness as a reformer. In his final years, however, the two could no longer be perceived to coincide or to nurture each other, because he ceased to have a political life. It is then we clearly see that Wang's work as a poet was not in any sense contingent upon his identity as a political leader. It was simply a part of this remarkable man, coexisting with the other components of his life and personality.

IV. Su Shi

Oddly enough, the greatest writer of the period had a life that was bound up inextricably with Wang Anshi's New Policies. Su's outspoken criticism of the reforms occasioned the first in a series of setbacks in his official career, and these in turn brought to full fruition his literary talent.

Su Shi was a celebrity in his own day. His life is thoroughly documented in his own voluminous writings and those of his friends and admirers. He himself is the subject of much of the poetry he produced, and this circulated in numerous printed editions from the time he was aged just over thirty. Su Shi happened also to be a skilled calligrapher, and so the manuscripts he produced, whether of poems, notes, or colophons on other people's painting or calligraphy scrolls, were likewise in high demand and could fetch a handsome price (as he was well aware). The spectacular vicissitudes of his career, which included some of the highest appointments in Emperor Zhezong's court, but also arrest and imprisonment, as well as exiles that were increasingly distant and harsh, added to the aura of celebrity that surrounded him. Su reacted creatively to each set of new circumstances he encountered, using the great variety of his experiences to expand as a writer. Aside from being a poet, he was also an intellectual who developed a complex body of thought about issues that impinged on his life, including governance and loyal opposition, learning and self-cultivation, the way a person should view and respond to the world around him, involvement with "things," transcendence of possessiveness, and the relationship between poetry and the visual arts (calligraphy, painting).

Su Shi was brought to prominence at the age of twenty by his performance in the civil service examination of 1057, in which he placed second among the three hundred who passed that year (out of the several thousand who took the exam). This was the examination supervised by Ouyang Xiu, mentioned earlier. Su Shi would attract even more attention four years later, when he and his younger brother, Su Zhe (1039–1112), together passed a special "examination by decree" that was given irregularly and only to persons of extraordinary promise. The fifty essays Su composed for this exam, on themes that he himself selected, amount to a ringing call for reform of a corrupt and unresponsive imperial bureaucracy. He makes specific recommendations for changes in border policy, in taxation and land distribution, and in the evaluation and promotion of officials. We may first think that this call for reforms by Su Shi anticipates the reform agenda Wang Anshi would develop a decade later. The two men did share dissatisfaction with the status quo, but the visions of a new order that the two offered were fundamentally different. Behind his specific recommendations, Su conveyed a deep antipathy for government by strict policy or regulation as opposed to a more flexible and humane approach that allows for discretion, compassionate intervention, and accommodation of people's needs. At the most abstract level, Su insisted on the validity of human emotions as the ultimate source for all ritual and, by implication, all values. What is fundamental to the human condition is not a tendency toward either good or wickedness but the capacity to have affections. Governance should be attuned to the emotions of the populace and not constrain it to act in ways that are contrary to those emotions. "Good" and "bad" are not defined by Su solely by reference to traditional Confucian virtues and vices. What is "good" is that which leads to communal well-being, and what is "bad" is that which benefits only certain individuals.

The years that immediately followed the decree exam were uneventful ones for Su. By the time Su returned to the capital in 1069 to resume his official career, after a period of mourning for his father, Emperor Shenzong had acceded to the throne and was in the process of adopting and implementing Wang Anshi's radical program of reforms. Su was still but a junior figure at the court, but he joined with those who vigorously protested against Wang Anshi's reforms. Despite his relative lack of experience and standing, Su was a vociferous opponent of the New Policies. Su submitted his own "Ten Thousand Word Memorial" in which he analyzed and argued against one after another component of Wang's program, asserting that they were ill-conceived and unworkable, and would do great harm to the people. Wang's primary aim, as Su understood it, was to enrich the central government, rather than to make it a better custodian of the welfare of the people. Wang's means were also wrong. His program would feature just the type of reliance upon strict policy that Su abhorred. The reforms would be inflexibly applied, mandated from the central government, and uniformly imposed upon all districts without regard for local variation. Su's critique gives particular attention to what Wang had done to the Censorate, one of the court's primary organs charged with policy evaluation, rectification, and criticism. During earlier times, Su observes, censors had been attuned to public opinion and when policies met with popular opposition, censors had fearlessly represented the public outcry in their communications with the emperor and court. But now the censors remained quiet, despite widespread public opposition to the reforms. It was, Su said, because Wang Anshi had packed the Censorate with timid underlings, and so its ability to generate policy criticism had been destroyed.

Seeing that Emperor Shenzong continued to support Wang Anshi and was unaffected by objections to the reforms, many of the elder members of the so-called conservative party removed themselves from the court and went elsewhere in full or partial retirement from official service. These included Sima Guang, Ouyang Xiu, Fu Bi (1004–1083), Lü Gongzhu (1018–1081), Fan Chunren (1027–1101), and Wen Yanbo (1006–1097). Su Shi, being younger and still at the start of his career, did not have this option. Instead, he requested to be reassigned to the provinces. Su began in 1071 what would be nearly a decade of service as vice prefect or prefect in Hangzhou, Mizhou (in Shandong), and Xuzhou. Ironically, in these posts Su was obligated to implement and administer the local component of the reforms he so strongly opposed.

Su Shi's opposition to the New Policies led him to develop a philosophical stance that went far beyond questions of governance. Wang's reforms themselves, especially the New Learning (xinxue) associated with his re-interpretation of the Classics, had a philosophical dimension. Su developed his own ideas on learning, moral cultivation, and mastery of the Way as an alternative to Wang's New Learning. Key ideas in Su's thought are that the Way cannot be approached if one sets one's mind directly on that goal, and that it cannot be found by looking "within." Instead, the Way must be discovered through learning in diverse subjects (astronomy, geography, music, the calendar, rituals, and so on) rather than selective concentration on a few Classics and introspection, as the New Learning directed. A related thought was that different individuals will devise for themselves different means to acquire the Way. Thinking and writing styles will vary, as they should. One of the problems with the New Learning, according to Su, was that it mandated only a single way of thinking and writing, so that everyone sounded the same.

During these years in the provinces, Su Shi attributed the hardships of peasant life he saw to the misguided reforms that had been adopted by the court. But Su no longer memorialized in protest, evidently because he sensed the futility of doing so. What he began to do instead was to allow criticisms of the New Policies into his many personal writings, both prose and poetry. Many of these compositions he sent to friends, either because they had requested that he write something for them (e.g. an inscription for a studio) or just for the pleasure of sharing it. His references to the New Policies often took the form of sarcastic references to the "enlightened rulership" that had the country in its grip. These observations surface haphazardly in his various writings. Sometimes they seem to intrude gratuitously upon the subject at hand, as if Su could not suppress a nagging hostility to the reforms.

Famous and talented as Su was, his writings were in high demand. It was Su's misfortune to live just at the time when bookshops were discovering that there was money to be made by using the emergent technology of book printing to produce unauthorized collections of poetry, especially, it seems, Su's poetry. Selections of his writings, including, of course, those that spoke disparagingly of the reforms, circulated widely. Some of them naturally made their way back to the capital, where they came to the attention of the leaders of the reform administration. A decision was evidently made at the court to make an example of Su. An order was issued for his arrest. He was brought back to the capital under armed guard and thrown into the Censorate prison. He was charged with having slandered the emperor and leading ministers. Su eventually pled guilty to most of the charges against him and even elucidated obscure passages in his writings that contained veiled criticisms of the reforms, evidently convinced that such cooperation might lessen his punishment. Those who brought charges against Su wanted him to be executed, but for reasons that are unclear his punishment was reduced. He was sent in exile to the backward town of Huangzhou on the Yangzi river. The exile was for an indefinite period. He was stripped of his salary and had no means to support himself and his family.

In Huangzhou, Su Shi reached maturity as a writer. He used his time there to reflect on his experiences and personality, explore new modes of writing, and develop inner resources that would sustain him in the midst of deprivation. In his second year he ran out of what little savings he had to support himself and his family. Su received permission to clear an abandoned piece of land, then irrigated it and planted vegetables and rice. The plot of land was known as East Slope (Dongpo), and Su, in a calculated effort to show how he could adapt to the life of an ordinary farmer, began to use the name as his name, calling himself "the layman of East Slope" (or just "East Slope"), the appellation by which he is known to history. Poems he wrote at Huangzhou show remarkably little bitterness over his new lot in life. He explored the unfamiliar countryside, boated on the Yangzi, and befriended local gentry. By the time Su was finally allowed to leave Huangzhou in 1084, he wrote of his reluctance to depart from that place of exile, and declared his hope of returning some day.

A year after Su Shi left Huangzhou, Emperor Shenzong died and the government was taken over by Empress Dowager Gao, ruling on behalf of her child son, the future Emperor Zhezong. The empress dowager had long been opposed to the New Policies, and soon took steps to recall the conservatives, who set about dismantling the reforms. The eight years of this

Yuanyou reign period (1086–1093) were to be the only time for the remainder of the Northern Song that the anti-reformers were in clear control of the court.

One might have expected this to be Su Shi's time of glory as an official. Finally, after fifteen years in the provinces and in exile, he was recalled to the capital and given the prestigious position of Hanlin academician. Almost immediately, however, Su became embroiled in a disagreement with Sima Guang and other senior members of the conservative group over the abandonment of one of the reforms, the Hired Service System. Su believed that this single reform, which levied a tax on local families in order to provide funds to hire staff for local government offices, was superior to the former system of requiring local families to staff those positions themselves on a rotating basis. Su staked his political future on drawing a distinction between the vast majority of the reforms, which he said deserved to be rescinded, and this one, which did not. In the euphoria of the sudden ascendancy of the conservatives, however, Su's position was extremely unpopular and made him many new enemies, who viewed him as something of a traitor to the anti-reform cause. In his defense, Su invoked a larger principle. Throughout his political career, he pointed out, he had consistently been wary of any unanimity of opinion or rush to change the course of government policy. He had always stressed the importance of loyal dissent and policy criticism. Those bent on dismantling the New Policies were now making much the same type of mistake as the reformers had made years before: partisan momentum rendered them incapable of evaluating each separate policy on its own merits, and created a climate that was intolerant of any minority viewpoint, which was promptly denounced as disloyalty.

Su's protestations went unheeded. He requested reassignment to the provinces, and spent the next several years shuffling back and forth between the capital and prefectural posts. Each time he returned he found himself attacked. Wording in memorials and examination questions he had written was twisted by his enemies, who "discovered" in it slander of former emperors. Dismayed, Su observed that at least when he had been arrested in 1079 for what he had written, there had been some basis for the charges brought against him. This time his enemies were "saying white is black and west is east." Again he requested provincial assignment. In his various governorships in Hangzhou, Yingzhou, and Yangzhou, he threw himself into efforts to improve local conditions and to save life, including famine relief, bridge building, and water conservancy.

The politics at the court swung again in 1093. Empress Dowager Gao died and Emperor Zhezong, then eighteen, took control. He returned the reformers to power and the conservatives quickly found themselves the target of a reprisal. Su Shi was singled out for harsh treatment. He was exiled to Huizhou in the distant south (near modern Guangzhou). In all, he would spend the next seven years in the pestilential south. In 1097 Su received an even worse banishment. He was now directed to go to Hainan Island, off the southern tip of modern Guangdong Province. At the time, Hainan was largely aboriginal and was known to be full of malaria and other tropical diseases. This new exile was much like a death sentence.

At Hainan, Su Shi used poetry even more determinedly than before to show that his spirit would not be broken. A strange disjunction entered his conduct and writings. The first thing he did upon arriving on Hainan Island was to buy wood for his coffin. In letters to relatives back on the mainland (he was accompanied to Hainan only by one son, Guo), Su complained of his deprivation, poverty, and ill health. "Send any medicine you can," he wrote, "it doesn't matter what medicine it is." He described the ignominy of laboring in the mud to fashion a hut to live in. But when he wrote poetry he sounded sanguine, even content. He turned to his project of writing matching poems to Tao Qian's entire corpus, and managed to sound more satisfied with his situation than Tao had been in considerably more favorable circumstances. Su finished writing commentaries on the *Classic of Changes* and the *Classic of Documents*. When he was finally reprieved in 1100 and allowed to return to the mainland, as a result of a brief attempt at political reconciliation back in the court, he was decrepit and sickly. Nevertheless, on the boat trip back he wrote that his stay on the island had been "the best pleasure outing of my whole life." He made it back to Changzhou, just north of Taihu Lake (Jiangsu), where his family awaited him on farmland he had purchased some years before. He died there in 1101, a few months after his return.

The attempt at reconciliation at court was short-lived. Under Cai Jing (1046–1126) as grand councilor, a new and particularly aggressive campaign was launched against the conservatives, or, as they were now called, the Yuanyou faction. Hundreds of members of the faction were now blacklisted and banned from office. Stelae listing their names and denouncing their treachery were displayed by imperial decree in every county throughout the empire. Once again, Su Shi was singled out for humiliation, this time posthumously. His writings, together with those of several writers associated with him, were officially proscribed. All copies of their works were to be destroyed, together with any woodblocks used to print them. It was even ordered that any inscriptions Su Shi left, whether carved onto stone or written in his own hand on walls or tablets, also be tracked down and smashed. The ban remained in effect until the 1120s. It was lifted just before the Jurchen invasion that ended the Northern Song and the court's infatuation with the reform ideology.

The proscription is significant in literary history as the first time the Song court attempted to eradicate an entire group's literary work. The court clearly appreciated that the availability of their writings in printed form posed a new kind of threat to its ability to regulate thinking and write the history of recent reigns. The ban set an ominous precedent that would not infrequently be followed by imperial courts of later ages. It is impossible for us to know today what effect the proscription had. The sources are contradictory on this issue, some saying that the banned writings continued to circulate, if covertly, and others asserting that until the 1120s no one dared to mention in their own writings the proscribed Yuanyou period authors, as they were called. There was, in any case, a great resurgence of interest in the writings of Su and his followers with the establishment of the Southern Song, when Su began to be looked upon as a literary and cultural icon.

Su Shi's life has been reviewed at some length here because it is through the prism of his eventful life that his writings have always been viewed. Reading Su's poetry or prose, one is usually aware what period of his life the works are from, partly because he so thoroughly roots them in his immediate circumstances, and in the place occupied by that period in his entire life history. Even today there is a strong sense of place and period attached to Su's works. In recent years, scholarly conferences on Su have been convened in the People's Republic in many of the places that were important in his life, including Meishan (his hometown), Xuzhou, Huangzhou, Huizhou, Hainan Island, and Changzhou. Those who study him assemble in these places partly to pay tribute to Su's courage in the face of political persecution.

Su's poetry continued the intellectual tendency of the preceding generation. If anything, Su took this quality to a new level of achievement. Despite the political trouble his writings landed him in, actually Su did not use poetry as a forum for the consideration and elucidation of political issues nearly as often as Wang Anshi had done. The intellectual component of Su's verse was more reflective and philosophical than political. He regularly took particular experiences of daily life and used them as a springboard to reflect upon larger issues that transcended his immediate needs and interests. For example, sailing down the Grand Canal toward Hangzhou, he was held up at Sizhou for three days by an adverse wind. His boatmen prayed to a local god in a nearby Buddhist temple, and soon a favorable wind arrived. Su wrote a long poem reflecting on these events, in which he observed how misguided it was to suppose, as his boatmen did, that the god actually heeded the prayer and changed the wind on their behalf. Would not this inconvenience travelers going in the opposite direction (who also had the option of praying)? If this were the way gods worked, Su observed, they would be conflicted indeed! Su turned the event into a meditation upon the relation between mortals and divine power. In another boating poem, "One Hundred Pace Rapids," Su reflects on different conceptions of time and movement. The initial subject is Su Shi's experience of negotiating a section of river rapids in a small skiff. At first we are treated to a string of fanciful analogies for the swiftness of the current as it carries the boat along:

> It is like the hare dashing, a hawk dropping from the sky on its prey,
> A powerful horse charging down a steep slope.
> A broken string flies off the instrument, an arrow is shot from a bow,
> Lightning flashes past a crack, dewdrops are shaken from lotus leaves.
> The mountains on all sides are a blur, winds buffet my ears,
> Surging droplets of water form a thousand whirlpools.

But then Su reflects that changes brought on by the passage of time, considered historically or even cosmically, have even more rapidity than the fast current:

> Finding joy in such danger yields a moment of exhilaration,
> But I'm just like the river god who thought his domain was supreme.
> Our lives, riding on change, flow forward day and night,
> In an instant the process moves beyond distant kingdoms.
> As we struggle, all befuddled, in our drunken dream,
> We don't believe brambles will engulf the bronze camels.
> But before you know it a whole kalpa has passed,
> Making these rapids seem slow by comparison.

Finally, Su's eye alights on the holes bored in streamside rocks for the oars of punters, who since ancient times had labored to propel their boats upstream against the swift waters. This reminder of all those who passed by this spot, those who exerted themselves so intently and now have vanished completely, leads to a concluding resolution:

> Look at those grey rocks on the bank–
> Beehives of punters' holes drilled in them since ancient times.
> Let my mind never affix itself to any thing or place,
> Then the Creator's transformations will not bother me.

Su's poems are marked by an exuberance of metaphor and figurative language. What ultimately does life resemble? he asks in an early poem. A wild goose alights on melting snow and mud, he answers, leaves some tracks and then abruptly flies away, and once it does no one can say where it has gone. The bird analogy occupies fully half of the eight-line poem. A playful quality often informs Su's metaphors, traceable to the outlandishness of the comparisons offered. Many of them involve personification or otherwise project the animate upon a lifeless thing: what is the departing year like (written on New Year's Eve)? A snake slithering down a hole. Different calligraphic styles ("short, tall, plump, thin") are likened to different historical female beauties, each with her own appeal. West Lake is a beautiful woman whose "makeup" has been effectively applied. Reading Meng Jiao's poetry is like eating tiny fish: you pick carefully through it only to end up feeling what little you have obtained is not worth the effort. My life, he says, is like an ant on a millstone. As it tries to crawl to the right, the revolving stone carries it to the left. Su Shi delights in presenting these fanciful comparisons.

A quality of bemusement with himself runs through Su Shi's poetry. He is forever observing himself as if detached from his own literary persona, and offers a running commentary on his own actions and behavior. Bai Juyi had been fond of this mode of presentation, and Su borrowed it from him and developed it in his own way. When he was leaving Xuzhou and his post as governor there, and evidently being sent off with great fanfare, his eye alighted on a pair of stone statues of officials that flank the road. How many governors have they seen arrive and depart? he asks. If they could, they would burst out laughing at all this needless fuss being made over my departure.

Much has been made of Su's ability to withstand material deprivation and political persecution, and not indulge in self-pity. This has earned him the admiration of readers through the centuries. In fact, Su does occasionally write sorrowful verse, whether on a dismal Cold Food day in Huangzhou or on mid-autumn moon festivals when he is thinking of his distant brother. But he does not dwell on such moods. His ability to view his situation with detachment served as an antidote to poetic dolorousness, despite the trenchant circumstances of his eventful life.

V. Huang Tingjian and the Jiangxi School of poetry

Inevitably, a figure as charismatic as Su Shi attracted his share of supporters and followers. A group of younger writers came to be associated with Su, as members of his literary circle, from the 1070s on. This group included Huang Tingjian, Qin Guan (1049–1100), Chao Buzhi (1053–1110), Zhang Lei (1052–1112), and Chen Shidao (1052–1102).

Huang Tingjian and Chen Shidao have special significance, not so much for their relationship with Su, or for any affinity their work has with his. No poet after Su manages to sound much like him, as often as they tried. Huang Tingjian and Chen Shidao are important for another reason. In the last decades of the eleventh century the foundation was being laid for a new poetic style, one that would become ascendant during Huizong's reign and last well on into the early part of the Southern Song. In time this came to be known as the Jiangxi School of poetry. The origins of this "school" are, as mentioned before, sometimes traced back to Wang Anshi, or even to Ouyang Xiu. In its early articulation, however, the school's origins are most often traced to Huang Tingjian or to Chen Shidao, although Chen, unlike the other three men, was not from Jiangxi. In fact, only a portion of the poets who were later said to "belong" to the school were Jiangxi natives. Not only did the Jiangxi School have little to do with the place it is named for, there is also little evidence that the men credited with starting it had any intention of creating a poetic school. It is only in retrospect that critics and later poets, eager to give a name to the new approach to poetry, and happily discovering that certain of its precursors had a common geographic origin, posited the existence of this school and identified Huang Tingjian and Chen Shidao as its founders. This first occurred some twenty years after the two men's deaths. The heyday of the Jiangxi School was the last decade of the Northern Song and the first few decades of the Southern Song. Its influence can be seen long thereafter, reaching virtually to the end of the Southern Song in the late thirteenth century. Nevertheless, as early as the start of the Southern Song, the Jiangxi School came to be criticized for its narrowness and predictability. One after another of the major Southern Song poets renounced allegiance to it, as it came to be as roundly maligned as it once was championed.

When one first turns to Huang Tingjian's poetry, it appears so unlike that of Su Shi that one may wonder how it was that "Su and Huang" could ever have been linked together or used as a phrase to designate the poetic style of the Yuanyou era. It happened because the two men were friends, had careers that were intertwined, often exchanged poems, shared the same anti-reformist politics, and consequently had parallel periods of exile. For all that they had in common, however, their work as poets is sharply divergent. Yet each clearly admired the other's verse.

What is remarkable about Huang Tingjian's poetry is not the subject matter, viewpoints expressed, or sense of personality conveyed (all of which are indeed striking in Su Shi's poetry). What is remarkable is the dense semantic texture of the line and couplet, which must often be pondered, its syntax "unpacked" or its allusions identified and explicated, before its sense becomes clear. For example:

> The viscount of Tube City does not have the appearance of eating meat,
> Brother Square-Hole has written a letter breaking off relations.
>
> [*Guanchengzi wu shirou xiang,*
> *Kongfang xiong you juejiao shu.*]

"The viscount of Tube City" alludes to a fanciful biography Han Yu had written about the writing brush, in which the brush is personified and has an official career. At the end of its "life," the writing brush is enfeoffed as a viscount of Tube City, an actual place whose name, appropriately enough, doubles as a synonym for "brush." The second half of the first line may make perfectly good sense read literally, but recognition that it, too, involves an allusion adds another dimension to its meaning. Ban Chao (32–102) commanded Chinese armies on the Han empire's western frontier for some thirty years, during which time he distinguished himself with victories over the Xiongnu. As a young man, however, he worked as a scribe, laboriously drafting documents for others in order to support his elderly mother. It was only after he encountered a physiognomist who discerned in his "appearance" (*xiang*) signs that he would eventually rise to great distinction and become "an eater of meat" that Ban Chao gladly threw away his writing brush and went off to join the army. In the opening line, then, Huang Tingjian refers to himself as a latter-day Mr. Brush (not just because he was known as a poet but also because at the time he wrote these lines he held an editorial position in the Imperial Secretariat) who, however, is *not* fated to be relieved of his writing duties or to rise high and achieve great deeds.

"Brother Square Hole" is a droll euphemism for money, because Chinese coins had square holes in their middle and were "as treasured as older brothers." Also, it happens that the word for "hole" (*kong*) doubles as a surname, so that the Chinese for "square hole" (*kong fang*) sounds like a plausible personal name. Letters written to terminate relations were an established type of letter, with ancient precedents. Line two means that Older Brother Money will have nothing to do with our poet. In other words, not only is Huang fated to remain undistinguished and unknown, he is also destined to remain poor. This is how Huang disparages himself in the opening couplet of a poem sent to a friend.

Not all of Huang Tingjian's lines display such challenging complexity of meaning. He does not, after all, manage to put a literary allusion or two into every single line. But even when he does not, the craft evident in the selection and placement of words is still noteworthy, as is the demand placed upon the reader to find his way through the words to the dense meaning that they convey:

> Peach and pear in spring wind, a single cup of wine,
> Rivers and lakes in night rains, ten years by lamplight.

There are no specific allusions here. Moreover, the words are all utterly commonplace. They are stock poetic phrases, really, bordering on cliché. And yet the meaning actually is not obvious and, as it turns out, not simplistic either. It requires a considerable amount of thought to figure it out. The lines are the second couplet in a poem Huang sent to a friend with whom he had grown up. The two men had traveled to the capital to take the examinations ten years before these lines were written. Subsequently, as each began his official career, the two were separated and had not met again. The opening couplet says this: "I live on the northern sea, you on the southern, / Too far apart even to entrust letters to wild geese to carry." Line three ("Peach and pear . . .") recalls the last springtime the two friends were together, when they took the examinations. The line evokes an enjoyable setting, in which the friends sat outside beneath flowering fruit trees and enjoyed a single cup of wine. Why "a single cup"? Probably to show the intimacy of the two friends, or perhaps also their impoverishment, which did not detract from their enjoyment of each other's company. The following line describes, in dismal terms, the life each has had in the ten intervening years, traveling from one dreary provincial appointment to another, plying the rivers and lakes. "Night rains" is particularly effective, because the phrase is usually used in descriptions of reunions between friends or loved ones, who stay up talking late into the night while it is raining outside (as in "night rains, adjoining beds," *yeyu duichuang*). But in Huang's usage there is no comfort or consolation to be found in the "night rains," and the staying up late, suggested by the mention of the lamp, is a sign of unrelieved loneliness. This couplet has been much praised by critics through the ages for its use of such ordinary language to convey such depth of meaning and emotion.

Huang Tingjian gave more attention to regulated verse, particularly in the seven-syllable line, than had any major Song poet before him. Huang thus built on the direction Wang Anshi explored in his final years, carrying the distinctly Song poetic style, which had originally been developed in ancient-style verse, over into the regulated forms. The result is a poetic *oeuvre* that gives as much prominence to regulated verse as we find in the writings of major Tang poets, but now with the characteristic Song dynasty flavor of intellectuality and discursiveness. To be able to write in the more restrictive forms and yet be true to the new preferences of the age was Huang's special accomplishment.

The only significant shift in subject matter we find in Huang's collection is the general diminishment of poems that deal with the plight of the common people, which had been such an important part of the works of earlier poets. From the 1080s on, national politics became so fractious that Huang and others moved away from the poetry of political content or protest. Avoiding such engagement, Huang turned his attention to the ordinary events of private life. Huang found his own personal world – captured in such subjects as brewing tea, social outings, potted plants, and works of art – more than sufficient as the vehicle through which he would develop his literary talent.

Apart from writing poetry, Huang Tingjian also wrote about writing poetry. In numerous letters, colophons, prefaces, and remarks (quoted by others), Huang set forth his views on how to compose and how to evaluate poetry. His statements, many of which were offered as advice to aspiring younger men, tend to have an ad hoc quality, as he keeps changing the terminology, the metaphors, and the particular direction of his injunctions. Nevertheless, there is an unmistakable consistency to the general drift of his comments and what he holds out as poetic ideals. His best-known dictums include these: "Take the commonplace and make it elegant, take the old and make it new" (*yi su wei ya yi gu wei xin*); "Touch iron and transform it into gold" (*diantie chengjin*); "Not a single word lacks a literary provenance" (*wu yizi wu laichu*); "Change the bones and steal away the embryo" (*huangu duotai fa*) – this refers to repeating meanings found in earlier poems but either in new diction (bones) or in a new form and shape (embryo); "Develop an appreciation for ancient models and then express yourself in new and original ways" (*linglüe gufa sheng xinqi*). All of these statements or ideals involve the relationship of poetic diction to the history of earlier usage. Whatever the particular image or advice, clearly Huang is focused on the issue of poetic language vis-à-vis the literary past. He gives equal attention to the need for novelty and the need to have language that is, after all, rooted in the past or steeped in earlier uses, even if it is marvelously transformed.

Elsewhere Huang writes of the importance of attending to the overall "arrangement" and "disposition" of each composition. In this case he is apparently speaking not about particular lines or phrases but about the general organization or structure of a composition. The act of writing, he says, is like staging a play. You must arrange everything properly on the stage and plan the order of everything to be presented before allowing the play to begin. As for the unit of the line, Huang dwells on the idea that each "line must have an 'eye'" (*juzhong you yan*), that is, some element that animates it, making it memorable. He also speaks often of "the structure of the line" (*jufa*), by which he means the semantic and syntactic organization of the individual line. It is high praise from Huang when he tells his friends that the structure of their lines is "incisive" or "fresh and exceptional," or approaches what he finds in Du Fu's verse.

Huang Tingjian is certainly not the first Chinese poet to give critical attention to the workmanship that goes into poetry writing. But there may be something distinctive in the emphasis he places on "study" and familiarization with the poetic tradition as the key to the cultivation of poetic skill. We have seen that his concept of innovation is inseparable from mastery of earlier usage, and indeed that he demanded that every word have a literary provenance. The advice that Huang gives to younger writers is consistent with these notions: "I'm afraid you have not read enough"; "You must read intently one thousand chapters"; "Your reading of the Jian'an poets as well as the works of Tao Qian and Du Fu has not yet entered your spirit."

The underlying assumption here is that reading is the key to developing skill as a poet. This is different from a conviction simply that writing poetry is hard work, or that good poems result only from painstaking effort and self-conscious crafting. Huang may well have subscribed to such beliefs too, but what we find in his letters of advice to young men about the importance of reading is a separate issue. Writings by ancient poets must be pored over to the point where they "enter your spirit" (*rushen*) and you gain complete control and mastery over them, so that your own poetic diction, when you turn to composition, is informed by a venerable history of poetic usage.

Huang's insistence upon such a readerly approach to poetic composition might be seen as a significant departure from conventional ideas about literary composition. Of course one could find antecedents for Huang's injunctions about the need for would-be poets to master earlier writings. In Huang's thinking, however, literary works from past ages seem to be the primary, if not the sole, repository and source of poetic know-how and inspiration. Implicitly, Huang rejected the traditional view that poetry is grounded either externally in "the world" that the poet observes and reacts to, or internally in himself with all his aims and affections. For Huang the grounding remains external, but what it consists of is the highly specialized external domain of the written word.

It is tempting to link Huang Tingjian's distinctive orientation with the spread of book printing in the last decades of the eleventh century, as recently suggested by Wang Yugen. We know that the printing of literary collections of all kinds as well as historical works and Classics increased dramatically from roughly the 1060s on. It was in mid-century that bookstores in the cities began to compete with printing by government agencies for the growing market for books in print. We know this mainly from complaints that leading literati, including Ouyang Xiu and Su Shi, voiced over the explosion of printed books and, surprisingly enough, the deleterious effect they perceived it to have upon learning, memorization, and recitation, and respect generally for the written word. Su Shi says that in his youth he encountered older scholars who told him that when they were young (i.e., around the year 1000) it was difficult to get their hands on a copy of *Records of the Historian* or *History of the Han*. When they did, they would gladly copy out the entire text by hand, so that they would possess a copy. But today, Su goes on, merchants in the marketplace carve woodblocks and print out ten thousand pages a day of books by all manner of authors. The present-day student has an abundance of writings available to him, and can obtain them readily. The unfortunate result, Su says, is that young men leave their books tied shut and do not even look at them.

Su's observations are offered in an obviously conservative frame of mind. He apparently longs for the old days when books were hand-copied and accordingly treasured. Su's comments are, in fact, part of an inscription he wrote for a friend's private library, which is said to have consisted entirely of manuscripts that the friend personally copied out. So Su's expression of disdain for printed books is entirely appropriate, almost predictable, in such a context.

Literati of the period rarely expressed a welcoming attitude towards the new technology of book printing. Still, they could hardly have been untouched by the dramatic changes that the spread of book printing was having on their world. Like it or not, they were caught up in a technological revolution with far-reaching consequences. Within the space of a generation or two, during the last half of the eleventh century, books went from being precious and difficult to reproduce to being abundant and readily disseminated. Elite literati may have decried this transformation and have been offended by the low quality of bookstore imprints, not to mention the widespread piracy printers engaged in, but they could not have been unaware of or unaffected by the enhanced availability of books.

It is likely that Huang Tingjian's singular idea of the grounding of poetry and poetic talent is related at least in part to the new availability of books. Books were easier to obtain than ever before, so Huang counsels aspiring poets to pore over them to sharpen their compositional skill. His advice reflects an understanding of poetry that would have been difficult to arrive at fifty or a hundred years earlier, but seems a sensible reaction to the altered circumstances of his time, when it was no longer unreasonable to assume that anybody who wanted to could obtain copies of the works of the Jian'an poets, Tao Qian, and Du Fu, not to mention the standard histories and the Classics. "Not a single word lacks a literary provenance" only makes sense when one is confident that the written record from the past, in its richness, is widely available.

Huang's program for developing poetic skill seems designed to get those young men whom Su Shi describes to untie their books – devalued because they had become so easy to obtain – and to study them. Rather than simply decry the new circumstances ushered in by the advent of book printing, Huang Tingjian developed an approach to composing poetry that took advantage of the print revolution and posed a new challenge to would-be poets that fit the times and altered the old assumptions about the nature of poetry.

After he first met Huang Tingjian, Chen Shidao went home and burned all his poems, having resolved to study Huang's methods. By the time of his death in 1105, Huang had many younger followers who imitated his dense and erudite style. Late in Emperor Huizong's reign, Lü Benzhong (1084–1145) compiled a diagram of the Jiangxi School that sketched a poetic "genealogy" that began with Huang and listed various branches of descendants. But even as the sense of excitement over the founding of a "school" and its novel approach spread, doubts began to be expressed over the excesses of the Jiangxi style, which included a determination to be novel to the point of strangeness, an overabundance of allusions, and a self-conscious crafting of language that often showed through and compromised the feeling of natural expression. One by one, the major poets of the early Southern Song would announce themselves to be dissatisfied with the Jiangxi School style and develop new directions.

VI. Buddhism and poetry

The subject of the relationship between Buddhism and poetry requires some comment here. There was a revival of Buddhism during the Northern Song, which began in the earliest years of the period as Emperor Taizu relaxed state suppression of the religion and took steps to extend state support to Buddhist institutions (if also to ensure that they remained under state control). Early imperial printing projects included the printing of the entire Buddhist canon.

Buddhism was better integrated into Song society than it had been in the Tang, and there was less open ideological hostility between Confucian and Buddhist thinkers than in earlier periods. The idea that the relative lack of polemical attacks between the two schools reflected a condition of Buddhism in decline has recently been challenged and must now be set aside. The number of monasteries, and of monks and nuns, was, in fact, larger in the Song than in previous periods. Leading Buddhist spokesmen such as Zanning (919–1001), Qisong (1007–1072), and Dahui Zonggao (1089–1163) actively sought to avoid ideological or institutional confrontation with the state. They strove instead to develop syncretic modes of thought that reconciled Buddhist and Confucian values. They also reached out to the lay community and trained disciples among the literati, including some thinkers important in the Song Confucian revival. Finally, within the Buddhist movement, certain schools such as Chan and Tiantai that were less oppositional to state and literati ideals gained new importance. Consequently, Buddhism became more ubiquitous in Song society and culture than it had ever been before. It certainly is ubiquitous in the elite literature of the period.

Several Buddhists were known as talented poets during the period and left their own collections of verse or literary writings. The Northern Song line of Buddhist poets began with the Nine Monks, mentioned earlier, and continued in each succeeding generation, with Zhiyuan (976–1022), Zhongxian (980–1052), Foyin (1038–1098), Daoqian (Canliao, b. 1043), and Zhongshu (Senghui, d. ca 1104), known for his song lyrics, and Huihong (1071–1128). Huihong is of particular interest as the leader of the "Lettered Chan" (wenzi chan) movement, which eschewed the traditional mistrust of words and writing of the Chan school and sought to reconcile Chan practices with scholarly reverence for texts of all kinds. Although the worlds of the literati and Chan monks had always been associated with each other, Lettered Chan brought the two so closely together that they became almost indistinguishable. Huihong cultivated the tone of lay poets in his verse, and one can read pages of his literary collection without ever realizing that he was a monk. This secular tone of his works was pointedly commented on by Wang Anshi's daughter, who upon reading a couplet he wrote about how thin he had become in springtime with his longing to return home – a peculiar thing for a monk to say, but a thoroughly conventional sentiment for a literatus to express – is said to have remarked, "This monk is nothing but a romantic!" As a movement, however, Lettered Chan was short-lived. In the early Southern Song, Dahui effectively brought it to an end with his own new synthesis, which emphasized introspection on key phrases contained in gongan cases (kanhua chan).

There were, however, no Northern Song Buddhist poets who attained the stature of their counterparts in the Tang, such as Jiaoran or Jia Dao, much less the modern acclaim given to Hanshan. The Song Buddhist poets befriended leading literati of the time and exchanged poems with them, yet they were overshadowed by their lay friends. These Buddhist poets had only limited success in cultivating their own poetic style, perhaps because the mutual assimilation of literati and monastic worlds was so thorough. It was not their fate to develop a niche for themselves in literary history, as their counterparts had done in earlier times. Several recent anthologies of Song poetry, in wide circulation today, contain not a single poem by a Northern Song monk.

Turning away from monk–poets themselves, we find a richer subject in the influence Buddhist thought had upon poetry in general and upon literary thought. The imprint of Buddhism on the lives of leading literati is unmistakable in all generations of Northern Song writers. Yang Yi became interested in Buddhism in middle age, and when serving in Ruzhou studied under the Linji School master Yuanlian. Many of Yang Yi's poems refer to the constant social contact between himself and other high officials and their "friends from empty gates." Yang joined these monk friends in translating Buddhist sutras, and was appointed by Emperor Zhenzong to be co-editor of the *Record of Passing on the Flame from the Jingde Reign* (*Jingde chuandeng lu*; comp. 1004–1007), a major compendium of Chan stories and biographies.

Despite the imperial promotion of Buddhism, if the occasion demanded Buddhism could still be castigated as a pernicious foreign doctrine that misled the people. There is thus considerable evidence among the literati of contradictory pronouncements and behavior, depending on the social and ideological circumstances that informed them. Ouyang Xiu provides a case in point. In his public persona as statesman and official, he presented himself as a staunch advocate of Confucian values and opponent of Buddhism. But in his personal life, he befriended Buddhist monks, visited them in their monasteries, and wrote prefaces to their literary collections, professing admiration not just for their poetic talent but also for their character. It was in middle age and later that Ouyang seems to have become increasingly interested in Buddhism. He met with Qisong and expressed admiration for the monk's learning and literary work. The retreat that he built for himself and made famous in his poems when governor of Yangzhou, Pingshan Hall, was adjacent to a monastery. In his last years Ouyang began to call himself "layman" (*jushi*), a term with unmistakable Buddhist overtones. It was in those final years that Ouyang Xiu wrote colophons to the massive collection of rubbings of stone inscriptions that he had accumulated over the years, which he called *Collected*

Records of the Past (Jigu lu). His collection included many Buddhist inscriptions, especially those from temples constructed in the northern kingdoms of the Northern and Southern Dynasties period. Writing about those inscriptions, and thinking evidently about his own image in posterity, Ouyang still felt the need to declare himself an opponent of the religion the writings promoted. At the same time, Ouyang accepted the inscriptions into his collection, and even observed in his colophons that their calligraphic style, which he characterized as powerful and unconventional, had particular appeal. The tension we glimpse here between attraction and disapproval is characteristic of Ouyang's complex reaction to things Buddhist.

With the eminent writers of the next generations, Wang Anshi, Su Shi, and Huang Tingjian, such conflicted treatment of Buddhism largely vanishes, as does any effort to veil personal enthusiasm for Buddhist values. The three men are similar in the prominent role that friendship with monks played in their lives, their thorough familiarity with key sutras, and the widespread borrowing of Buddhist language and ideas in their literary work. Wang Anshi wrote a commentary on the Vimalakīrti Sūtra (Weimojie jing), another on the Śūrangama Sūtra (Lengyan jing), of the Tiantai school, and a third on the Avatamsaka Sūtra (Huayan jing), of the Huayan school. Unfortunately, these commentaries do not survive (neither do the ones he wrote on the Confucian Classics as part of the New Learning), but they are well attested in Song bibliographies and other sources. Su Shi was capable of suggesting, half in jest no doubt, that in an earlier life he had been Huineng (638–713), the sixth Chan patriarch. He also claimed that he always kept a copy of the Śūrangama Sūtra beside his bed. A more plausible and revealing statement is one he made in a letter to the retired Wang Anshi in the course of recommending Qin Guan to him. The younger Qin, Su says, "is widely learned in historical writings and biographies, and has completely mastered Buddhist writings." Here we see the importance Su, and Wang by implication, attached to Buddhist learning, as something that could be referred to as being on an equal footing with knowledge of standard historiography. As we know, Su Shi's literary collection contains hundreds of Buddhistic compositions: essays, accounts of monasteries, poems and informal letters addressed to monks, inscriptions (*ming*), eulogies (*song, zan*), Buddhist verse or *gāthā* (*jie*), offertories (*shuwen*), and prayers (*zhuwen*). So many of these are scattered through Su's works that the notion of collecting them together in one place suggested itself to Ming scholars who were jointly interested in Su and Buddhism. The result, entitled *East Slope's Delight in Chan (Dongpo chanxi ji)*, was compiled at the end of the sixteenth century, and was reprinted in 1621 by the famous writer Ling Mengchu. Modern editions have kept the work in print today. As for Huang Tingjian, the learned commentaries on his verse produced in the Southern Song make it clear that his work on non-Buddhist as well as Buddhist subjects is full of references to the Lakāvatāra Sūtra (Lengqie jing), the Sutra of Original Enlightenment (Yuanjue jing), the Platform Sutra (Tanjing), in addition to the sutras mentioned earlier, as well as to the *Record of Passing on the Flame*, the *Treatise on Prajñā-pāramitā (Da zhidu lun)*, and various monks' "recorded comments" (*yulu*).

There are other ways that Buddhist writings may have influenced the writings of these eminent lay poets, aside from the adoption of Buddhist subjects and terminology and allusions to Buddhist texts. One that has been discerned is the structure or manner of exposition. Thus Qian Qianyi (1582–1664) said that when he read certain of Su Shi's funerary biographies, for example those for Sima Guang and Fu Bi, he marveled at the narrative structure, which is highly anecdotal and also departs from the convention of strictly linear chronology, and could not think of any precedent. Later, reading sections of the Avatamsaka Sūtra, he discovered strikingly similar passages of narrative. Those, he concluded, must have been the inspiration for Su's unconventional method.

Aside from the borrowing of particular techniques or ideas, there was also a general orientation or frame of mind widespread among poets that surely was influenced by Buddhist thought. A succinct description of this orientation is found in a passage of Su Shi's poem addressed to his monk friend Canliao about the relationship between Buddhism and artistic expression in calligraphy and poetry. In the poem Su Shi explicitly took issue with Han Yu's opinion on the matter. Han Yu had expressed doubts that a monk he knew, Gaoxian, could ever realize his goal of becoming an outstanding calligrapher because his religious training had taught him to suppress or transcend his affections. Han Yu said that it is precisely strong feelings, lodged in brushwork, that make for superior calligraphy in the draft-script style, and therefore Gaoxian had little chance of ever producing good work. (It evidently did not occur to Han Yu that the celebrated "wild draft script" by the monk Huaisu could serve as a powerful counterexample to this argument.) Su Shi had a very different idea of the relationship between the affections and artistic expression. Here is the relevant section of Su's poem:

> Tuizhi [Han Yu] said that draft-script calligraphy
> Is capable of reflecting all worldly affairs.
> Worry, sadness, and all other disquietudes
> May be lodged in the darting of the brush.

But he wondered about the Buddhist monk
Who looks upon his body as an empty well.
Meekly, he gives himself to the mild and plain,
Who will elicit boldness and fury from him?
When I consider this I see it is incorrect.
True ingenuity requires no illusion.
If you want your poetic phrases to be marvelous
You need not be averse to emptiness and quietude.
With quietude you comprehend all movement,
With emptiness you take in ten thousand scenes.
You observe the world as you go among men,
You examine yourself reclining on a cloudy peak.
The salty and sour mix with all other tastes,
Between them there is a perfect flavor that endures.
Poetry and Buddhist are not incompatible,
I submit this view for your consideration.

The line about "illusion" refers to the backhanded compliment with which Han Yu ended his discussion of Gaoxian: the monk, Han Yu conceded, might yet become competent as a calligrapher since Buddhists are so knowledgeable about illusion.

Su Shi's immediate motive in writing this poem was to counsel Canliao not to make his poetry so full of affections and literary brilliance. According to Su, his monk friend was writing poetry that was insufficiently monk-like. In the course of making this argument, Su develops an idea about artistic expression that is based upon the Buddhistic ideals of selflessness and transcendence of the affections. We note that in Su's thinking here "emptiness" and "quietude" are not ends in themselves. They serve to enhance the artist's awareness both of himself and of the world around him. It is that enhanced perception that subsequently informs his artistic expression. This account of the poet's mental and emotional state correlates well with Su's own ability to view his circumstances dispassionately, for which he is so admired. It may also readily be linked to the tendency of Northern Song poetry to favor the reflective mode over that of the expression of intense emotions. Su's invocation of the quality of the "mild and plain" (*danbo*, synonymous with *pingdan*) invites us to consider the Buddhist dimension of Song aesthetic preferences, or at least the compatibility of those preferences with monastic ideals.

Chan in particular came to provide for poets and critics a language and conceptual framework for thinking about poetry. We usually think of the late Southern Song critic Yan Yu (twelfth century) in connection with this application of Chan terminology to poetics. But as Stephen Owen has pointed out, the analogy was already in widespread use earlier in the Song. Terms for linguistic devices used in Chan to convey teachings in "irrational" ways entered discussions of poetry. These devices, widespread in *gongan* stories and discussions between masters and disciples preserved in recorded comments, included all manner of puns, jokes, and riddles (*dahun*); avoidance of broaching a subject head-on (*bufan zhengwei*); taking a dead snake and bringing it back to life (*sishe nongde huo*); crafting language that contradicts ordinary usage (*fanchang hedao*); mixing the uncooked with the cooked (*shouchu zisheng*); and not treading the path of reasoning (*bushe lilu*). On a higher level, parallels were drawn between Chan enlightenment and poetic inspiration or insight, between the period of arduous training necessary before religious enlightment and the literary apprenticeship needed prior to poetic achievement, and between Chan schools and lineages and poetic schools and models.

At the heart of this appropriation of Chan terminology and ideas by literary critics lay a sense of similar purposes and dilemmas. Chan sought to bring the adept to enlightenment but acknowledged that words were inadequate to convey the highest teachings, much less to describe the enlightened condition. Chan then developed illogical or nonlogical ways of using language to overcome its own limitations, a critical discourse that named and discussed these methods, and anecdotal literature that illustrated how they worked in practice.

It had long been a fundamental principle of literary criticism that the "meaning" conveyed by a poem lies beyond words. This notion is fine so far as it goes, but it is not going to be very useful to an aspiring poet. In Chan discussions of uses of language to convey meanings in indirect or nonlogical ways, literati found a ready-made body of thought and terminology that could easily be appropriated for their own purposes. The idea, for example, that a good line must have an "eye," some aspect beyond the individual words that conveys nonverbal meaning and makes it "alive," was derived from the Chan concept of the "dharma eye" (*fayan*). The Chan sense is that the true teaching of the school lies outside of the words of any sutra, but that it may yet be couched inside special lines. The requirement that special lines be made potent by having a "gate of mystery" (*xuanmen*) is a similar idea. The notion that such a "dharma eye" is comparable to meaning that cannot be put into words is found in the *Blue Cliff Record* (*Biyan lu*): "There is no impediment to lines that have eyes and meaning that lies outside words." It is no accident that the earliest discussion of "eyes" in poetic lines was written by Huihong, the leader of the Lettered Chan school. Huihong describes how Huang Tingjian used the term to discuss the excellences of poems by Wang Anshi and Su Shi. Many other critics then followed suit, as they argued over and refined the concept as it applied to poetry. Such a concept gave literati a means to identify, analyze, and discuss nonverbal meaning, and ways to convey it, that they had previously lacked. We consequently find that discussions of poetry recorded in the remarks on poetry form are full of Chan terms for particular uses of language, such as those cited earlier. As has recently been demonstrated by Zhou Yukai, even Huang Tingjian's famous dictums about "touching iron," "changing the bones," and "stealing away the embryo" were widely used in Chan writings before they were ever applied to poetry.

VII. Poems on paintings

Northern Song poets were increasingly drawn to painting as a subject to be treated in verse. Su Shi and those associated with him strove to elevate the stature of painting and worked out the basic values and principles of what came to be known as "literati painting" (*wenren hua*), the tradition that would dominate Chinese painting history for the rest of the imperial era. Poems that take painting as their subject, which played an important role in this articulation of a new approach to the art, are known as "poems inscribed on paintings" (*tihua shi*). Many of them, though not all, were actually inscribed on a painting. In Northern Song times, this was normally a painting done by someone other than the poet, a painting the poet saw or was shown in another person's collection. It might be an ancient work or a contemporary one painted by a friend. Tang paintings survived into the Song, of course, but a Tang painting by a well-known artist was rare and extremely valuable. In any case, the poet would keep a copy of the poem he wrote, whether or not he first inscribed it on the painting, and eventually the poem would become part of his literary collection.

Poems on paintings were already an established subgenre during the Tang. Du Fu wrote more than two dozen of them, in which he reflects on the complexities of the relationship between painting and life, as well as between painting and poetry. But painting remained for Du Fu and most Tang poets something quite extrinsic to their lives. Painting was something done by a person from another walk of life, something to be "observed" like a dance or musical performance. By mid-Northern Song, painting had become more intrinsic to literati life. Many poets dabbled at painting (e.g. Su Shi, Huang Tingjian) or counted true painters (e.g. Li Gonglin (1049–1106) or Mi Fu

(1051–1107)) among their closest friends. Song literati found in Wang Wei a Tang precedent for the ideal *they* developed of being jointly accomplished as painter and as poet, and they never tired of invoking his example to justify their newfound fascination with the visual art. Painting became an important poetic subject. An anthology compiled in 1187, *Paintings with Sounds (Shenghua ji)*, contains hundreds of poems on paintings, the majority written during the Northern Song.

The most interesting poems on paintings do far more than merely give verbal descriptions of the painted landscape, flowers, animals, or persons. A common tactic is to treat the painted images as real, and then tell a story about them that goes beyond the compositional elements of the painting. There is an aspect of virtuosity in this, as the poet sees how far he can move outside the painting, which becomes merely the starting point for an ingenious verbal elaboration upon its images. If the painting is a landscape, the poet may inject himself into the scene and talk about what it is like to live there; if it is a flower or animal painting, he may identify human concerns or qualities of the subject that in fact mirror issues that the painter (or poet) faced in his life.

There was at the same time a new development to which the enhanced interaction between the two arts led. Theoretically minded critics began to formulate ideas about aesthetic principles that were shared by poetry and painting, and calligraphy as well. Strides were made toward developing an aesthetic vocabulary that could equally be applied to poetic words, painted images, and the calligrapher's brushwork. An important one of these was "resonance" (*yun*), itself borrowed from music and now applied to all the arts. In his remarks on poetry, entitled *Poetry Eyes from Hidden Stream (Qianxi shiyan)*, Fan Wen (fl. ca 1122) discussed resonance and the common aesthetic grounding of the various arts at considerable length. As a young man Fan Wen took Huang Tingjian as his mentor, and he would eventually marry Qin Guan's daughter.

The impulse to work out a general understanding of aesthetic principles was accompanied by dissatisfaction with approaches to the arts grounded in literal-minded or representational assumptions. The two attitudes were natural allies: if the arts were truly interchangeable, or if artistic effect and "meaning" transcended the particular media used to convey them, then the issue of how "true to life" those particulars were could no longer be used as the primary standard by which art was evaluated. It was the artist's handling of compositional elements in accordance with universal aesthetic principles that was the key, not the compositional elements themselves and their relation to the real world. Buddhism's emphasis on the illusory nature of all appearances may have had some influence in this impulse to find values elsewhere than in representational aptness.

As an advocate of this notion of artistic liberation, Su Shi had said,

> Anyone who evaluates painting in terms of lifelikeness [xingsi]
> Has the understanding of a child.
> To say a poem must be written a particular way
> Shows you don't know poetry.

Huihong elaborated on these ideas in his miscellany entry entitled "What to Avoid in Poetry." Many people nowadays, he observes, produce verse that has no color or vitality. The constraints they write under limit them to unimaginative autobiographical accuracy, and this makes their verse insipid. A man who is well-off is forbidden to mention poverty, a young man is not supposed to speak of growing old, and so on. On the contrary, Huihong says,

> Poetry is for lodging marvelous viewpoints and extraordinary thoughts [miaoguan yixiang]. It must not be constrained by the carpenter's measuring tools. Wang Wei painted a plantain tree in the snow. Viewing this with the dharma eye, one understands that he was lodging his spirit and emotions in the physical object. The common viewpoint criticized him, however, saying he didn't understand hot and cold climates.

Huihong goes on to quote poetic lines by Wang Anshi and Su Shi in which each man takes leave of his immediate circumstances to reflect broadly on his life. He concludes by quoting a poem he himself wrote on this subject, which ends with these lines: "The plantain tree in the snow transcends hot and cold, / A great steed perceived by the [knowing] eye has no black or sorrel." Huihong's reference to the "dharma eye" in this passage (not to mention his own identity as a monk) reminds us of the influence Buddhism had upon developments in aesthetic thought.

VIII. The song lyric

As seen in the preceding chapter, in the mid-Tang there was already a nascent alternative poetic genre available, the ci or song lyric. Originally, there was probably only a weak and vague sense of this genre being independent of a host of other song forms to which words could be set. Through time, however, and certainly by the Five Dynasties period, the song lyric came to be recognized as a separate poetic genre, consisting of its own set of dozens of tunes. The musicality of the genre is a defining characteristic and sets it apart from *shi* poetry. *Shi* might be set to music and sung, but usually it was not. *Ci* in its early stages was always set to music and sung. Moreover, this was not just any kind of song. It was predominantly the song used in urban entertainment quarters, performed by professional female singers and dancers.

The social context and function of the genre shaped its intrinsic nonformal characteristics. It was performed by women primarily for the entertainment of men. As with urban entertainment songs in many cultures, love in its many moods and guises came to be a favorite subject. It was not just that songs about romantic attachments were welcomed by an audience eager to be diverted for a few hours, as they sipped tea or drank ale. The female performers were in many cases at the disposal of the men who listened to them singing. There must have been many establishments in which distinctions between teahouse, wineshop, cabaret, and brothel were blurred. Romantic liaisons often formed between the men who listened and the women who performed. Given that marriages were arranged by parents and that social contact between men and women was heavily proscribed, such a setting was one of the few in which romantic attachments could occur. This social reality gave impetus to the performance of sentimental songs. A song that treats a woman's longing for an absent or aloof man, or that evocatively hints at the pleasures of lovers alone together, or that describes heterosexual love with surprising openness, had special meaning when performed in a place where attachments between female singer and male listener were commonplace.

Romantic love is certainly not the only subject treated in the song lyric. The many others include those on the seasons, on aging and the passage of time, on flowering plants, on festivals, on travels, on farewells, and on objects. Whatever the focus, however, the song lyric has a tendency to focus on sentimental aspects or perceptions of the subject at hand. The language conventionally used in the song lyric is often spoken of as "feminized" or "effeminate," and the mode of presentation accordingly centers on an aesthetic of delicacy and refinement. Consequently, in thinking about the song lyric in comparison to *shi* poetry, it became customary to observe that "whereas poetry is stern and correct, the song lyric is dainty" (*shizhuang cimei*). A similar critical statement is this: "As a form the song lyric is tender and delicate, and the world it evokes is gentle and dainty." Given that the song lyric developed as it did, written for performance by women, it is hardly surprising that it came to have a gendered stylistic association that stands in contrast to that of its older poetic counterpart. After all, the vast majority of *shi* poets were male and wrote, most of the time, in a male voice.

We know that urban entertainment quarters existed in earlier times. The Tang capital of Chang'an had its "northern quarters," famous as a pleasure district where men went to be entertained by singers and dancers. Surely such districts also existed before the Tang. There must have been entertainment songs that circulated in such settings, and talented women to sing them. The question naturally arises, then, why was it only in the Song dynasty that literati became interested in the urban entertainment song to the extent that they turned to it and made it into one of their own forms of literary expression? Why had this not happened before, and why did it happen when it did, in the eleventh century? Perhaps such questions present the contrasts too starkly. Tang poets did sometimes set new lyrics to entertainment songs. The practice became more widespread in certain elite circles during the Five Dynasties period, particularly at the courts of the Former and Later Shu, hence the appearance of the first literati anthology of song lyrics, *Among the Flowers*. Conversely, even in the Song dynasty, when the song lyric became an important form of literati expression, it was still distinctly secondary to *shi* poetry in stature and centrality. Throughout the dynasty, the quantity of *shi* poetry produced makes that of the song lyric appear minuscule: major writers produced thousands of *shi* poems, and only a few hundred song lyrics. Even after it was established as an important literati form, the song lyric continued to struggle against its merchant-class origins and the elite perception that it was tainted with the "smell of the marketplace." The pejorative terms commonly used at the time to designate the form, such as "little song lyrics" (*xiaoci*) and "the residue of poetry" (*shiyu*), attest to the lingering biases against it.

Despite these qualifications, the fact remains that eleventh-century poets adapted the anonymous songs of the entertainment quarters and made them their own, preserving their formal and expressive distinctions from *shi* poetry, to a degree that was unprecedented in literary history. Explanations of their willingness to do this, to "reach down" socially to a less-than-elite musical form and participate in it, often refer to the commercialization of Song society and the resultant expansion of the size and impact of the merchant class in the cities. The educated elite were more likely to be influenced by merchant-class culture in Song times, this line of reasoning suggests, because the merchant class was larger and played a more central role in society than it ever had previously. One must be cautious about accepting this as the sole explanation of the new literary expression, since a burgeoning merchant class and the commercialization of society are phenomena that have been attributed to just about each period of Chinese history. That said, there is a broad scholarly consensus that the Song marks a new stage in the commercialization of

Chinese society. This is an important factor in the widespread view that the Song ushers in the early modern period of Chinese history, or, to put it another way, leaves behind the "middle ages" of the same. Certainly, based on the textual and pictorial record, it is hard to escape the conclusion that there were features of the Song capitals of Kaifeng and Hangzhou that made them in some ways fundamentally different from the Tang capitals of Chang'an and Luoyang. The Song capitals are considerably less "imperial" than their Tang counterparts. For example, the imperial palaces and parks do not have the dominating presence that they had in the Tang capitals, leaving more space for a merchant class and mercantile activities. As Stephen West has argued, Kaifeng during the Northern Song was a new type of urban space in which the various classes were thrown haphazardly together, the imperial and elite intermingled with merchant-class city dwellers.

Whatever the mix of causes that led eleventh-century men of letters to set their own words to tunes circulating in the entertainment quarters, the result was the gradual development of a second poetic genre that functioned as an alternative to the dominant one of *shi* poetry. The coexistence of the two, so different formally and in their expressive uses, gave rise to a new situation in Chinese literary history. Of course, one could say that poetic alternatives had always existed. There was the ancient choice, available to writers from the Han onwards, between *shi* poetry and *fu*. There had likewise long been the dichotomy between *shi* poetry and *yuefu* and other types of song, not to mention the many subgenres of *shi* itself. Nevertheless, the choice that writers came to have in the Song period between *shi* and the song lyric was a new kind of choice. There had never been anything quite like the song lyric before, as it was developed by literati in the eleventh and twelfth centuries. It offered the possibility of intensely personal and lyric expression, yet of a mode that was instantly recognizable as something distinct from that found in *shi* poetry. There was the gendered divergence between the two, mentioned earlier, and consequent divergences of tone, voice, and subject matter. There were likewise differences in social setting, class provenance, and performative expectations. The song lyric was, in its formative stages, written to be musically performed by a professional (not its author) for an audience. The expectations concerning *shi* poetry were very different. The assumptions about the relationship between the poet and the voice featured in each form were similarly distinct. *Shi* poetry was assumed to be written in an autobiographical mode and to have its observations and affections spring from the life experiences of its author. These assumptions were mostly suspended with the song lyric. Men set words to song tunes that would be performed by women. In the early stages, the focus of the songs is mainly on the sentimental lives of women. Often the persona or voice in the song is that of a woman. Male poets had, of course, used female personae for centuries in *shi* poetry. Usually, however, when they did there was the assumption that the feminine voice was a literary device that allowed the men to express their political frustrations indirectly. The song lyricists who adopted the personae of women when they wrote did not do so for such purposes (the determined efforts of some later critics to interpret song lyrics as political allegory notwithstanding).

As we will see later, the song lyric eventually moved away from a narrow focus on women and dependence upon female personae. Yet because of the form's origins and stylistic identity, after this happened the song lyric remained a poetic mode unto itself, distinct from *shi* poetry. What this meant, in effect, was that Chinese poets had available to them a form of poetic expression for which key expectations regarding *shi* poetry, including the assumptions that it was autobiographical and that its highest purpose was the expression of a man's heartfelt "intent" (usually associated in one way or another with the obligation assumed of the educated elite to serve the state), did not obtain. Song lyricists were free to write in the guise of other persons and to explore the act of writing about experiences they could only imagine, but needed to represent in a persuasive manner if the song was to be credible and effective. The unequal line lengths of the song lyric, a sharp contrast to the regularity of *shi* poetry meter, were particularly well suited to the cultivation of the appearance of spontaneous expression. By virtue of this formal trait, derived from the need to tailor words to musical phrases of varying length, the song lent itself to short emotive interjections, to the inclusion of speech and even dialogue, and to dramatic presentation. Writers who favored tunes that belonged to the category of "long song" (*manci*) took full advantage of its special potential for representing speech and action, as well as psychological introspection, and their compositions moved in the direction of dramatic narrative.

It has become a commonplace in literary history to speak of "Tang poetry and the Song period song lyric" (*Tangshi Songci*), as if the song lyric is the counterpart in the later period of all that *shi* poetry was during the Tang. This is misleading in more ways than one. The song lyric was not the primary poetic form in the Song period, as *shi* poetry had been during the Tang. *Shi* poetry remained the dominant and more prestigious verse form throughout the Song. The saying in question ultimately derives from the myth, widely perpetrated in accounts of literary history, that each major dynasty had its own premier literary genre, just as each had its own ruling clan. But this paradigm has no historical validity. It is particularly deceptive when applied to the song lyric of Song times.

In fact, the history of the song lyric through one hundred years of the Northern Song, from roughly the 1020s through the 1120s, is in large part a history of its gradual elevation in stature and expansion in scope. The form slowly evolved from something that was first viewed as quite frivolous, composed on social occasions "after drinking wine or having tea," to something that was accorded a modicum of respect. The major practitioners of the song lyric during the period each had a hand in this gradual elevation of the form, whether they intended to or not, and their efforts were complemented by late eleventh-century literati who initiated a critical discourse on the song lyric that emphasized its expressive uniqueness and effectiveness. But even at the period's end, the song lyric was still looked down upon, if not dismissed outright, by sober-minded moralists who could not tolerate its feminized language, its sentimentality, and its marketplace origins. The story of the song lyric during this period is one of how a relatively small number of interested poets, evidently attracted by what they sensed were new expressive possibilities, persisted in composing in this form, despite its relative disrepute, and gradually found ways to expand its range and develop it into a genuine alternative to *shi* poetry for a new kind of lyrical expression, thereby making it acceptable to many, if not all, members of the educated elite.

Zhang Xian, Yan Shu

The earliest notable song lyricists of the Northern Song were Zhang Xian and Yan Shu. Their compositions are often said to be stylistically similar to those in *Among the Flowers*. They mostly favor the "short song" (*xiaoling*), which technically is any song form up to fifty-eight characters in length, and they write mostly about feminine loneliness, the passage of the seasons, and parting scenes. While it is true that Zhang and Yan were heavily influenced by the Later Shu anthology, there are aspects of their work in the song lyric that distinguish it from that anthology.

It is important to point out that Yan Shu and Zhang Xian were men of great stature in their day. Yan Shu had been considered a prodigy as a child, for his learning and writing ability. He was awarded an honorary civil service examination degree at the age of fourteen by Emperor Zhenzong and embarked at that age upon his official career. He developed a reputation for wisdom and diplomacy in office. He was appointed Hanlin academician at age thirty-three; by the time he was forty-two he had become assistant councilor, and he eventually rose to the position of grand councilor. Zhang Xian did not have a career of comparable eminence, but he did befriend the most reputable scholars and poets of the day, including Ouyang Xiu, Mei Yaochen, Wang Anshi, and Su Shi. Blessed with longevity, Zhang in his eighties enjoyed a reputation as a senior man of letters, and was looked up to by more talented younger writers.

It is significant that these two men permitted themselves to compose song lyrics, to the point that they developed reputations for their talent in the genre and kept adding to their collections of songs into their old age. It may seem unremarkable that they did this, but not if we recall the way the Shu courts of the tenth century were thought of during the Northern Song. Those courts and the rulers that presided over them were thought to epitomize decadence and frivolous indulgence, and the fondness the ruler and his courtiers showed for the song lyric, drinking parties, and dissolute behavior with the palace ladies were taken as primary manifestations of that decadence. In Northern Song historiography, the song lyrics that were so popular at the Shu courts become the infamous "music of Zheng" that symbolized the moral depravity of the ancient state of Zheng and betokened its early demise. That the Shu kingdoms themselves were short-lived reinforced this assessment of their benighted rule and its connection to licentious song.

As we would expect, then, there is evidence that Yan Shu's and Zhang Xian's enthusiasm for the song lyric met with some disapproval, given the two men's stature. Lü Huiqing (1031–1110), a court official during Shenzong's reign, found Yan Shu's activity as a song lyricist incompatible with his role as grand councilor, saying that a grand councilor ought to make it his priority to rid the realm of the "music of Zheng," rather than contribute to it. Similarly, Su Shi, who seems to have genuinely admired Zhang Xian, declares it a pity that the world knows only to value his song lyrics and ignores his more serious and substantial writings.

In fact, the stature of the song lyric in the early and mid-eleventh century benefited from having thoroughly respectable and talented men, such as Zhang Xian and Yan Shu especially, involved with it. That the grand councilor was known to write song lyrics, over the objections of some high officials, meant that the genre could not easily be dismissed as something fit only for decadent and short-lived regional courts. Moreover, these early writers did more than merely continue the tradition of *Among the Flowers*. They also introduced small but significant stylistic changes. Critics characterize Yan Shu as cultivating a dignified and tasteful aura in his songs, one that verges on the intellectual. Part of what they are reacting to when they give such assessments is that Yan Shu distanced himself somewhat from the excesses of sumptuousness and sentimentality in *Among the Flowers*. The settings in Yan Shu's songs are less ornate and the affections less insistently feminized. In several of Yan's most famous pieces, the person being described is not necessarily female. The focus shifts from a uniquely feminine set of circumstances to one that could be experienced by either gender, imparting a sense of universality. An example follows, "To the tune 'Sands of the Washing Stream' ":

> One new set of lyrics to a tune, one cup of wine.
> Last year's weather, the same old pavilions.
> The twilight sun sets in the west, how many times will it return?
> There's no help for it, the blossoms will fall,
> Swallows I seem to recognize have come back.
> On a scented garden path I pace back and forth alone.

Liu Yong's controversial synthesis

A more radical departure from the style of *Among the Flowers* was that developed by Liu Yong. Liu Yong's songs were closer to the popular tradition of the anonymous entertainment song, as we know from reading the Dunhuang anthologies of such works. Those songs are more colloquial and more direct in their treatment of romantic allure and lovemaking. The aura of aristocratic elegance and affluence that permeates *Among the Flowers* may be thought of as an attempt by the courtiers of Shu to lift the song lyric out of the sordidness of the urban taverns and brothels where it thrived in the ninth and tenth centuries. Liu Yong, by contrast, embraced the "vulgarity" of the popular song tradition and turned it to his own purposes.

The popular image of Liu Yong is that of a roué and a darling of the singing girls. People assumed that his songs reflected his own dissipation and history of love affairs in the pleasure quarters. This was understandable, since many of Liu Yong's songs sound like he is boasting about being a rake. "I would gladly exchange," he had written in one composition, "evanescent fame for a shallow wine cup and a soft song." A number of stories about Liu Yong were inspired by this image of him projected in his songs. It was said that the singing girls would come out to welcome him when he arrived in town. If he mentioned any of the girls by name in one of his songs the price that the lucky girl could demand for an evening's entertainment increased several-fold. After he died, singing girls would gather beside his grave on the anniversary of his death each year to sing his romantic songs in memory of him.

There are also anecdotes that feature the incompatibility of Liu Yong's success as a songwriter and his pursuit of an official career. The emperor is said, rather implausibly, to have personally scratched Liu Yong's name from the list of successful civil service examination candidates, so scandalized was he by Liu Yong's reputation. In fact, we know that Liu Yong did pass the civil service examination and had a moderately successful official career.

These stories aside, we do not really know what effect Liu Yong's songwriting had upon his career, but we do know that the perceived vulgarity of his songs gave rise to a torrent of harsh assessments of his song lyrics by elite critics. While the critics all acknowledge that Liu Yong's songs circulated widely, they pronounce the compositions to be crude in language and lewd in content, and thus to appeal only to "those who cannot read." A sense emerges from the critical disapprobation of Liu Yong that he was perceived as something of a traitor to his class. Here was a man who was educated highly enough to pass the loftiest examinations and hold office, yet he persisted in producing risqué songs about love, written in language that admitted many colloquial elements. He seemed to have lost sight of his social standing and he offended elite tastes.

There is no denying that Liu Yong's song lyrics frequently take us into the bedroom and broach aspects of sexual love more explicitly than do the compositions of any other literati songwriter of the period. Focusing only on this feature of his songs, however, does not do Liu Yong justice as a writer. Although Liu Yong incorporated elements of the bolder popular song lyric tradition into his works, what he created was actually a new synthesis, bridging the divide between the popular and literati approach. He relied more heavily upon the long song than had any earlier literati author, and took advantage of its length and stanzaic divide to represent the introspection of his personae. Typically, the speakers in his compositions, male and female alike, reflect on the joys and pains of romantic attachments, the songs effectively conveying the emotional complexities of such attachments in ways that were quite unprecedented. Another noteworthy feature of Liu Yong's songs is his willingness to use a male voice in them (hence the questionable assumption that he was writing autobiographically). Liu Yong's songs represent a range of moods and anxieties of men caught up in romantic love to an extent not seen in earlier works in the form.

Ouyang Xiu

Ouyang Xiu was prolific as a song lyricist and apparently wrote more pieces in the genre than had anyone before him, including Liu Yong. His productivity is interesting in itself, since it suggests that this prestigious and versatile writer was eager to apply his talent to the lesser poetic form.

In histories of the genre, Ouyang is regularly paired together with Yan Shu, his older contemporary, and said to have produced a stylistically similar body of work. It is true that many of Ouyang's pieces resemble Yan Shu's, especially those written in the short-song form on farewell banquets, loneliness, and the passing of the seasons. But Ouyang occasionally allowed himself more leeway. Roughly one-quarter of his songs are more colloquial in language and less restrained in their presentation of the thoughts or actions of men and women in love. Many of these pieces are in the long-song form. In other words, there is a small but significant portion of Ouyang Xiu's output that is not far removed from the style of Liu Yong's songs, though Ouyang never went as far as Liu Yong did in describing bedroom scenes.

From our vantage point, we might say it is not surprising that a literary talent as eclectic and innovative as Ouyang Xiu would have experimented occasionally with a "lower" style of song lyric that was known to be the favorite of professional entertainers in the pleasure quarters. What is interesting is how persons of Ouyang's time reacted to these experiments with the more risqué style. Certain of the earliest editions of Ouyang's collection of song lyrics seem to have been more or less complete, containing all the songs he wrote. But in the Southern Song, when the image of Ouyang Xiu as a leading statesman, classicist, and historiographer became fixed, the prospect that "the great Confucian of his era" could have written song lyrics that some persons found objectionable became unacceptable. Anthologists as well as the editor who compiled Ouyang's *Complete Works* went through the early collections of his song lyrics and excised the more colloquial and explicit pieces, declaring that they were spurious compositions fabricated by his political enemies and circulated under his name to defame him.

Although such aggressive "editing" was certainly misguided, the idea of Ouyang's enemies taking advantage of his fondness for writing song lyrics to undermine his reputation is not as far-fetched as it might at first sound. Twice during his lifetime Ouyang was formally charged with having had sexual relations with younger members of his clan – a niece and a daughter-in-law – and brought to trial. In both cases – of 1045 and 1067 respectively – the charges against Ouyang were eventually dismissed. Ouyang and his supporters said all along that the charges were trumped up by political rivals who sought to ruin his career. We have it from one of Ouyang's friends that right around the time of the first case, certain "lewd" songs falsely attributed to Ouyang were circulating in the capital. Among the pieces attributed to Ouyang, there are a few that deal with an older man's interest in very young girls, and do so in a titillating way. These particular songs would seem to be well suited to the purpose of persuading people that their author was capable of misconduct with young females. It is also conceivable that the very idea of planting (or exploiting) accusations against Ouyang Xiu for committing sexual crimes, whether or not any slanderous pieces were later fabricated to lend credibility to the accusations, might itself have gained impetus from common knowledge that Ouyang was a man who had a weakness for writing songs about love outside of marriage. In that case, one needs to explain why the likes of Yan Shu and Zhang Xian did not encounter similar difficulties. The answer might be that the type of song lyric they composed did not lend itself to such exploitation by political enemies, or that their enemies were not as resourceful as Ouyang's were.

Su Shi and the turn away from the feminine

As a young man, Su Shi kept his distance from the song lyric. Although he was already productive and celebrated as a poet in his twenties, he wrote few song lyrics until midway through the 1070s, when he was approaching forty. We do not know why he showed little interest in the form as a young man. We may suppose, based on a few stray comments he makes, that he was put off by the contrived sentimentality found in so many pieces and the emphasis placed on tender (i.e. "womanly") attachments, nearly to the exclusion of all else. Su once chided his protégé Qin Guan for writing love songs that sounded to Su like those of Liu Yong.

When Su did begin to write a substantial quantity of song lyrics, his approach was new, and it was so precisely with regard to such issues. He wrote autobiographically, explicitly so, adding prefaces to his compositions that record the circumstances under which they were written. The results were compositions that could no longer be readily detached from their author's life. Su wrote, for example, about missing his brother on the Autumn Moon Festival, visiting Swallow Pavilion outside Xuzhou and dreaming of its former mistress, recalling his first wife on the tenth anniversary of her death, and remembering the late Ouyang Xiu upon passing by his former pavilion outside Yangzhou.

From Mizhou, in about 1075, Su wrote to a friend about his recent efforts in the song lyric, and his excitement about doing something new in the form is palpable:

> As for the clumsy *shi* poems that you request from me, how could I presume to attempt them? I know I cannot refuse you, but just have not yet found the leisure to write them. I have, however, recently composed quite a few

little song lyrics, and although they lack the flavor of those by Master Liu the Seventh (Liu Yong), they are a style of their own. Ha-ha! A few days ago I went hunting in the countryside and caught quite a few animals. I wrote a song lyric about it. If you get a brawny fellow from the northeastern prefectures to sing it, clapping his hands and stomping his feet, and mark time with the shrill flute and drum, it makes for quite a manly spectacle! I am copying it out to amuse you.

A song lyric about hunting is about as drastic a departure from the stock subjects of the genre as one can imagine. Su's advice about how it should be performed is similarly unconventional and obviously intended to be so.

In the history of the song lyric, Su Shi is known as the founder and leading exponent of the "heroic abandon" (*haofang*) style of composition. The piece on hunting marks an extreme of the tendency of that style to replace the feminine bias of the song lyric with masculine subjects and tone. Hardly any other of Su Shi's compositions are so brazenly unconventional. Nevertheless, the "manliness" (or "virility, vigorousness": *zhuang*) that Su points to in his hunting composition would emerge as a key quality of the "heroic abandon" style. Moreover, as we shall see, the need to cultivate the same quality in the song lyric generally was to become an important aspect of making it more acceptable as a literary form.

Su Shi's exile to Huangzhou from 1080 to 1084 played an important role in furthering his work in the form. It is not difficult to understand why this was so. Su had been imprisoned for defaming the New Policies in prose pieces and *shi* poetry. Su's song lyrics had not come up in the trial, while dozens of poems and prose pieces he had written over the years did, and were used as evidence against him. Song lyrics would not have been used against him. They were considered too "frivolous" to figure in a criminal case of such serious proportions (but not too "frivolous" possibly to be used outside the courtroom to defame someone).

In the months following his trial and demotion to Huangzhou, family and friends repeatedly urged Su to give up writing. At one point he vowed to do just that. But, of course, he could not keep his promise. Writing was too ingrained in him for him to stop simply because it had gotten him into political trouble. In Huangzhou, however, he began to give more time and effort to the song lyric, the form that in Su's day avoided political reference and consequently would not implicate him in further trouble. Naturally, he continued to compose *shi* poetry as well, but the song lyric became more central to his expression than it had ever been before. He wrote a number of song lyrics about how content and carefree he was in his new setting, as he explored the unfamiliar countryside. It was in Huangzhou that the song lyric became a major expressive form for Su Shi. It would remain so for the rest of his life.

Already during Su's day there was critical disagreement over his achievement in the form. Many were quick to recognize the originality and effectiveness of his new approach. "In one stroke," the early Southern Song critic Hu Yin observed, Su "washed away all the colored silks and perfumed oils of earlier works." But other critics had reservations. He was said to "write song lyrics as if he were writing *shi* poetry." This observation may contain either a positive or negative assessment, depending on who says it and in what context. It may mean, positively, that Su infused the less prestigious genre with the grander aims and effects of *shi* poetry. But it may also imply that in some sense Su's compositions skewed the genre, turning it into something it was not. Thus it was also said that his song lyrics "were not true to the inherent traits of the form" (*fei bense*), an unambiguously negative assessment. Critics who reacted this way felt that Su's effort to write autobiographically and to expand the scope of the song lyric, so that it was no longer centered on tender attachments, deprived the form of precisely what was distinctive about it. A related complaint was that Su Shi's compositions "could not be sung," meaning that he set words to the prosodic pattern of the tune without considering how they actually fit the melodic line (in tonal register, inflection, vowel quality, and so on). This implied that Su was writing texts to be read, or recited aloud, rather than lyrics to be sung. The gradual separation of at least some writers' song lyrics from music is a phenomenon usually associated with the Southern Song, but Su's approach certainly contributed to that later development.

As for Su Shi's impact and immediate legacy in the song lyric, we find a contradiction. Few writers of the time, even among his own circle, followed his lead. Perhaps they sensed that it required a literary presence and personality as strong as Su Shi's to carry off the autobiographical transformation of the genre successfully, and realized that they themselves could not accomplish it. So they continued to write song lyrics in the conventional mode, which came in time to be designated the style of "delicate restraint" (*wanyue*), in counterdistinction to Su's style of "heroic abandon." There was, however, a change to be seen in attitudes toward the genre among the literati who were younger than Su Shi and who looked up to him. The younger men initiated a critical discourse on the genre, conducted in prefaces and colophons on each other's collections of song lyrics, in which they defended it and put forth arguments about its unique expressive power. They edited their own or each other's collections of song lyrics for circulation. These are activities that we do not find among earlier generations of song lyricists. Su Shi had produced more song lyrics than had any earlier writer, some 350 in all. His corpus began to circulate independently while he was still alive. That the greatest writer of the day was so productive in the form and used it for serious purposes must have had a positive impact upon its stature and encouraged others to see it in a new light, even if younger writers did not follow Su's lead stylistically.

The beginnings of song lyric criticism

Su Shi died in 1101, the year after Emperor Huizong ascended the throne. The new critical discourse on the song lyric dates from early in Huizong's reign, or perhaps a few years earlier. Men who had come under Su Shi's influence in politics and letters begin to write self-consciously about the song lyric, its history, and its capabilities. The most important statements are by Zhang Lei, Li Zhiyi (d. ca 1115), He Zhu (1052–1125), Huang Tingjian, and Yan Jidao (d. ca 1106). The woman poet Li Qingzhao (1084–ca 1155) added her own short historical account of the genre, also thought to date from around the same time.

One of the ideas expressed repeatedly in these statements is that the song lyric is a form that is difficult to write well. Both Li Zhiyi and Li Qingzhao stress this aspect of the form, insisting that it is only through concentrated attention and effort that writers can produce superior compositions. These critics find fault with some prominent authors (e.g. Ouyang Xiu) for not taking the genre seriously enough, treating it as a mere amusement. Li Zhiyi goes so far as to say that the song lyric is the most difficult form to write well, meaning that it is more of a challenge than *shi* poetry. This is quite a remarkable claim, considering the way this "residue of poetry" had conventionally been viewed. Li Zhiyi formulates this ideal for would-be song lyricists: "To attend diligently to the flavor, searching and polishing, so that every word has a source and the genius of the piece is revealed in the final lines; when the words come to an end the thought does not, and when the thought comes to an end the feeling does not." He is applying the sort of standards that had been reserved for *shi* poetry to the song lyric.

The difficult subject of romantic relationships also comes up in these critical statements, as we might expect. Something, after all, would be missing from these attempts to legitimize the song lyric if nothing were ever said about its primary subject matter and the problems it entailed. Naturally, the critics cannot speak too openly about the relationships that developed between male listeners and female entertainers, but they do broach the issue. Yan

Jidao observes, plausibly enough, that the "feelings" that people of his day experience must not be different from those felt in ancient times. He adds that in his song lyrics he sought not just to convey his own longings but also "to record what I saw and heard in the drinking parties of the time, and to give expression to what was on the minds of my fellow revelers." In other words, his songs about love were informed by the flirtations and attachments that occurred in the social gatherings he attended. Yan Jidao even names the singing girls who were kept in the household of one of the frequent hosts of these parties, and describes how they would perform newly composed song lyrics for everyone's amusement. Zhang Lei, in a preface he wrote to He Zhu's song lyrics, takes on the criticism that men who engaged in such romantic attachments, and indeed wrote songs about them, were indulging in saccharine sentimentalism and showing themselves to be "unmanly." Zhang reminds us that even Xiang Yu and Liu Bang, the protean warriors of ancient times who rose up against the Qin dynasty and then battled each other to establish a new empire, had each at one point in their lives extemporized a sentimental song and allowed themselves to shed a few tears. Yet no one had ever suggested that such displays of sentiment (Liu Bang for his hometown and Xiang Yu for his concubine) had compromised the two heroes' manhood.

The example of Yan Jidao and Huang Tingjian's remarks concerning him provide illustrations of the enhanced stature of the song lyric at the end of the eleventh century. Yan Jidao was the youngest son of Yan Shu. Unlike his father, Yan Jidao never distinguished himself in office and had a lackluster career. The father was, aside being from an eminent official, also a leading man of letters who left a huge collection of writings, compiled an anthology of Tang literary works, and dabbled in composing song lyrics. In contrast to his father's wide-ranging literary activities, Yan Jidao seems to have devoted himself exclusively to composing song lyrics. No only did Yan Jidao leave no regular literary collection, he also compiled his own collection of song lyrics, and wrote his own preface to it. He is the first Northern Song writer we know of to take such pains over song lyrics he himself composed. In the preface Yan Jidao explains that versions of the song lyrics he composed over the years at drinking parties were transmitted to the world outside by the singing girls and wine stewards who were in attendance. Later, as the pieces circulated freely, mistaken words were introduced into them. Yan Jidao's act of collecting his song lyrics together (for printing, evidently) was thus an attempt to regain control of them and correct their texts. He evidently could not bear the thought of his compositions circulating in editions he had not prepared.

Apparently not content with having only his own preface to the collection, Yan Jidao approached Huang Tingjian and asked him to write a second preface. Huang was considerably more famous as a man of letters than Yan. Yan must have been concerned that he would be criticized for taking his song lyrics too seriously, and so he sought to attach the imprimatur of the celebrated Huang Tingjian to the collection by way of validating it. Huang could have declined Yan's request, but what he did instead was to take the opportunity to write a defense of Yan's decision to make the song lyric central to his creative life. Predictably, the rhetorical pose Huang strikes is apologetic: he says that Yan Jidao is a man of many "foolishnesses," and we understand that writing nothing but song lyrics is one of them. But Huang makes it clear that each of Yan's "foolishnesses," which the world looks upon as naive or impractical, is in fact a sign of Yan's honesty and integrity. Yan Jidao's song lyrics thus become, in Huang Tingjian's representation of them, the key to understanding his indifference to worldly opinion, a highly estimable quality. Huang even goes out of his way, toward the end of his preface, to recall that he himself had once been reprimanded by the Buddhist monk Faxiu (1027–1090) for composing song lyrics and thus "encouraging promiscuity." Huang brings up this criticism to scoff at it. If Faxiu thought that my works were indecent, he says in effect, what would he have thought of Yan Jidao's? Huang then goes on to recount how much in demand Yan Jidao's song lyrics are in the world, observing that a copy of them fetches a high price in the marketplace. In short, the confidence with which Huang is able to write about Yan Jidao's and his own involvement with the genre, cavalierly dismissing criticism by referring to popular acclaim, suggests that literati were considerably more accepting of the genre than they had been fifty years before, at the time of Ouyang Xiu and Liu Yong. There would always be moralists, Buddhists or Confucians, who disapproved of the song lyric and its focus on romantic love. Its status would never be as unproblematic as *shi* poetry. But clearly, by century's end the song lyric and the expressive possibilities it offered had attracted the interest and even the approval of a broad range of the educated elite.

Yan Jidao, and Qin Guan like him, often used a male persona in their songs. They wrote about men infatuated with women who are described unambiguously as professional entertainers. There are, then, two respects in which these pieces differ from the earlier song lyric that also focused on women. First, the women are no longer elegant ladies sequestered in lavish rooms. They are urban entertainers: they sing, dance, and pour drinks as the readers watch them vicariously through the male persona's eyes. Second, the observing eye is no longer omniscient and aloof. The observer is a male who is at the scene of the woman's performance, or with her later on, and who tends to be very much taken with what he sees. Here is an example from Yan Jidao's collection, "To the tune 'Partridge Sky'":

> Colored sleeves eagerly offered a goblet of jade,
> In those years I didn't mind a face flushed with drink.
> She danced the moon down to the willows beside the inn,
> And sang till the breeze from her peach blossom fan was stilled.
>
> After we parted,
> I always remembered meeting her.
> How many times my soul joined her in a dream!
> Tonight I keep shining a silver lamp on her,
> For fear this meeting is just another dream.

We recall the issue of "manliness" as it came up in connection with Su Shi's innovations in the genre and in Zhang Lei's references to the sentimental songs sung by great warriors of the past. In a song such as this, there is a noteworthy willingness to represent the male as being overwhelmed by female charm – that is, to overcome any apprehension over the "manliness" problem as broached by Su Shi. To a remarkable degree, song lyricists like Yan Jidao were comfortable writing about male vulnerability to ordinary feminine beauty, that of common singing girls in drinking houses rather than that of divine women, palace courtesans, or aristocratic ladies.

Zhou Bangyan

Zhou Bangyan, who flourished at the end of the Northern Song, best represents the culmination of the gradual transformation and elevation of the song lyric we have been tracing. Zhou had a long and quite distinguished career, which began when he attracted Emperor Shenzong's attention in the year 1083 with a long "*Fu* on the Bian Capital." He was rewarded for his literary talent with a position as instructor in the Imperial Academy. Thereafter, he was sent out to the provinces, but he returned to the capital to join Emperor Huizong's court. He then served as vice-minister in ritual offices, where he is said to have overseen revisions of court music, and was eventually promoted to be director of the palace library.

Zhou Bangyan was renowned in his day as a writer of song lyrics. Several stories suggest that Emperor Huizong himself was an enthusiast of his songs. The interesting point about Zhou's reputation is that there is no evidence that his fame as a song lyricist was any impediment to his career. On the contrary, for the last twenty years of his life he seems to have been kept on at Huizong's court largely because of his musical expertise and his talent as a composer of entertainment songs. Furthermore, Zhou did not attempt to radically redirect the genre, as Su Shi had tried. He wrote songs for performance (even writing new tunes himself) and he wrote them about romantic love. This makes even more clear the enhanced acceptance of such compositions, which now made inroads in imperial circles.

Zhou Bangyan gave special attention to the long song, as had Liu Yong before him. Zhou also was interested in using the male persona and in exploring the psychology of the male experience of love, and took full advantage of the length of the long song to do so. But Zhou Bangyan was no Liu Yong in the language he used or the sorts of scenes he described. He avoided the bedroom scenes and references to lovemaking that are so prominent in Liu Yong's songs. Zhou's favorite representation of romance was as a recollected experience, and the images he filled his compositions with are remembered glimpses of the girl the speaker fell in love with. Here is a passage in which the speaker, riding his horse through the pleasure quarters, suddenly realizes he is passing by his former lover's house:

> Silent, I halt there, rooted to the spot,
> Then recall someone naive and young,
> Peeking out through the door.
> In early morning, a yellow palace-style mark drawn lightly on her brow,
> Her sleeves billowed in the wind,
> As she laughed and chatted irresistibly.

Zhou Bangyan also avoided the colloquial language that so offended elite tastes in Liu Yong's works. Zhou's diction is decidedly bookish and difficult. He is fond of incorporating lines from Tang poetry into his songs, giving his works an air of erudition and cleverness, as well as using grammatical inversions and periphrasis, so that no one would say of his works that their language is "vulgar." Zhou Bangyan owes much to Liu Yong in subject matter and general approach to the song lyric, but he found a way to follow Liu Yong's lead without duplicating his style. This was the compromise Zhou Bangyan worked out between what intrigued people about Liu Yong's compositions and the manner of presentation that elite listeners and readers were prepared to endorse.

Nature and the inanimate world in Zhou's compositions, which form a backdrop to his speakers' reflections on their romantic experiences, are rendered with a distinct delicacy and refinement. In this respect the setting is a perfect correlative to the tender sentiments that transpire, or, more often, had once transpired, between the persons presented in the songs. It is as if the speaker, once he or she is awakened to the experience of love, focuses on the aesthetic appeal of every object the eye happens to fall upon. The compositions thus evoke an aestheticized vision of the world, in which even scenes of separation or disappointment in love are replete with endearing beauty. Such a representation of the world may strike some as narrow and verging on the precious. But it is a hallmark of Zhou Bangyan's signature compositions and constitutes an important part of his achievement.

> Wind makes the purple candles flicker,
> Dew moistens the red lotuses.
> Lights in the lantern market gleam on each other.
> As cassia moonbeams stream over the roof tiles,
> And slender clouds disperse,
> The dazzling white moon-maiden prepares to descend.
> Faintly colored and elegant their dresses,
> See the girls of Chu!
> Their slender waists so tiny,
> Plying flutes and drums,
> Their shadows crisscross as they hurry past,
> The lane is filled with perfume and musk.

This composition was written on the Lantern Festival, the first full moon of the new year, when the poet found himself in the south (hence the "girls of Chu"). In its second stanza, not given above, the speaker goes on to recall the splendid ways the festival is celebrated back in the capital, and to regret that he is not there. But we notice that the place he finds himself, where he despairs, is hardly one that lacks for beauty.

With Zhou Bangyan the song lyric reached its Northern Song fulfillment as a form for the exploration of love and other tender attachments to beauteous things. There is no longer a sense that such indulgence in sentiment, even when expressed in a man's voice, is unseemly and that the genre needs to be changed to become respectable. Liu Yong's experiment with incorporating much of the racy colloquial tradition of popular drinking-hall songs has been largely abandoned. Su Shi's effort to make the form autobiographical and to move it away from preoccupation with the romantic and feminine has also been dropped. The song lyric would undergo a number of further stylistic transformations in the Southern Song. But few, if any, masters of the later era would match the unabashed way that love in its many guises, including infatuations and bitter heartbreak, were presented by the last generation of writers to live in the north.

IX. "Nonliterary" prose

We have touched on prose writings earlier, in connection, first, with the call to "restore antiquity" by Fan Zhongyan and, second, with the development of a new style of literary prose by Ouyang Xiu. Ouyang's example as a prose stylist – not just in formal essays and bureaucratic documents, but also in the more informal genres – was passed on to younger writers, including Wang Anshi, Su Shi, Su Zhe, Sima Guang, and Huang Tingjian, and through them to their own followers. A wide-ranging tradition of literary prose, used to treat innumerable subjects and often to express highly personal sentiments, became a distinctive feature of Song dynasty literature.

If space permitted, the scope and features of this literary prose might be traced through the remainder of the Northern Song. This is the prose that is preserved in hundreds of individual literary collections, where it typically constitutes fully half of the work. The analysis of this corpus of literary prose is a task that remains for some future occasion. Given the quantity and range of the material, the undertaking will be a formidable one. It would, nevertheless, be a real contribution to our understanding of literary history to identify, in particular, how this massive body of writing departs from its Tang counterpart in its subjects, language, and expressive purposes. No doubt there would be considerable overlap with the earlier prose tradition. But there are surely innovations as well.

Instead of proceeding with such analysis, we turn here to a body of prose writings that tends to be overlooked in literary histories. We do so not simply to give attention to that which often receives none; we do so largely because in its own way this body of prose may be even more revealing about the distinctive traits of Song thinking about writing and the world than conventional literary prose.

Our focus here will be on the prose that is omitted from individual literary collections, that found in miscellanies (*biji*) and anecdotal collections (*xiaoshuo*). Later, we will expand the survey to include other related forms of "nonliterary" prose (by which I mean only that it is not found in literary collections, not that it lacks literary interest), including remarks on poetry (*shihua*), manuals on connoisseurship (of flowering plants, rocks, tea, and so on), and the informal letter (*shujian*). It is arguably in this massive quantity of material, admittedly disparate and resistant to generalization, except that it would usually be considered utilitarian writing (*bi*) rather than literary work (*wen*, *wenzhang*), that we may glimpse in an unvarnished form the manifestation of distinctly new Song values concerning prose expression.

Miscellanies and anecdotal collections

The miscellany had existed since before the Tang dynasty. Typically, it consisted of mostly short entries on all sorts of subjects. The entries may be arranged by topical category (e.g. astrological phenomena, officialdom, examinations, monks, food and drink, medicine, dwellings, utensils, and so on), in the manner of a *leishu* or encyclopedia. But more often the arrangement of the entries is random and there is no connection between one entry and the next. The completely unsystematic arrangement – the dominant mode – gives the miscellany the unpredictability that is part of its appeal. (An alternate designation for the miscellany, *suibi*, which means something like "impromptu notes," refers explicitly to the lack of any overall organizing scheme.) Depending on its author, the miscellany may be distinctly bookish: it may be essentially a collection of reading notes on the Classics and histories. But it may alternatively consist of "stories" the author has heard that are unsubstantiated by any text. These would usually concern famous persons or notable events. The most weighty and instructive narratives about the past would have already been incorporated into the biographies that constitute the bulk of official histories. What is left for the miscellany compiler to record comprises less important matters, ones that may have little didactic or historiographical value, or that may strain credulity or otherwise be of uncertain provenance and credibility. This is the type of material that is generally referred to in contemporary sources as *xiaoshuo*, which literally means something like "trivial tales," or "inconsequential stories." It will be evident from this description that the rendering "fiction" for the term is apt to be misleading. "Anecdote" or "hearsay" might be a better rendering. In any case, such anecdotes make up a sizable proportion of many Song period miscellanies. Indeed, the Chinese terms for the two are often linked together as one (*biji xiaoshuo*) to designate the works that will here be called "miscellanies."

There is a striking increase in the number of miscellanies produced during the Song dynasty as compared with the Tang. Dozens of the works were written during the Tang. In the Song the number is in the hundreds. The first attempt to gather together and reprint all extant Song miscellanies is taking place as this is being written, a publication project of the Institute for the Compilation of Ancient Books at Shanghai Normal University. To date, only the first few series of a projected ten have been published. The first series alone, in ten volumes, contains some fifty miscellanies, written from the start through the middle of the eleventh century, roughly the first hundred years of the dynasty. The number of works produced in later periods of the dynasty is many times larger.

A question naturally arises about the sheer quantity of this material. The sharp increase of the number of miscellanies in the eleventh century and later coincides with the spread of commercial and private book printing during this time. Is the increase, then, simply a consequence of a higher survival rate among all the works that were written owing to the wider circulation of printed copies?

There is no doubt that the availability of printing enhanced the circulation and hence the survival rate of the miscellanies that were written during the Song. That is true of all types of writing done at the time, and the miscellany must be no exception. Yet it is also clear that the number of works initially produced, before the issue of preservation is taken into account, also increased substantially when compared to the Tang. One of the reasons for that increase seems to have been the new availability of print technology. That is, some authors were apparently motivated in part to produce a miscellany precisely because it could be printed (which was not a feasible option during the Tang). That is not to say that they planned to make money from the printing and sale of their work. It is doubtful that such a motive would have been operative before the Southern Song. Profit aside, the prospect of having hundreds of printed copies of a work circulate, rather than having only a precious few manuscript copies extant, would naturally have been an encouragement to many would-be compilers. We know of at least one miscellany, *A New Account of the Southern Sector (Nanbu xinshu)*, which when it was finished in the mid-1050s was finished in order to be printed. We know because the compiler, Qian Mingqi, son of the man who began the work, Qian Yi, tells us so in his preface. It is likely that there were many other miscellanies compiled with similar intentions, although discretion kept their authors from saying so openly, and that this became ever more common as printing itself became more widespread with each passing decade.

There are certain changes in the contents and authorship of miscellanies from the founding of the dynasty through the end of the Northern Song. Up until the third quarter of the eleventh century, miscellanies may be divided into two general types. There are those that focus on narrating strange or uncanny events and those whose attention centers on the court and its persons of renown. The former stand firmly in the tradition of "anomaly accounts" (*zhiguai xiaoshuo*) from the Six Dynasties and Tang periods. The latter take their inspiration from works such as Li Zhao's *Supplement to the [Tang] National History (Guoshi bu)* of the early ninth century. An example of the former is the very first miscellany to have been produced by someone who lived into the early years of the Song, *Trifling Words from Northern Yunmeng (Beimeng suoyan)*, by Sun Guangxian (d. 968). This sizable work, in twenty chapters, tells of marvelous events that occurred during the Tang and Five Dynasties eras, especially those in the capital cities. Its pages are replete with stories about encounters with gods and spirits, miraculous recoveries from illness, and anomalies (e.g. dogs and cats that speak). Even when the event related is not fabulous, it tends to be decidedly bizarre or grotesque, as for example green-blossoming lotuses whose seeds produce red-blossoming plants, a father who was tricked into eating the flesh of his murdered son, and a youngster who, though seriously ill, was still able to write out a detailed exposé of official corruption at the court. Given this emphasis on the strange, it is not surprising that hundreds of entries from *Trifling Words* were selected into the early Song compendium of such stories, *Extensive Records of the Taiping Reign* (*Taiping guangji*).

The early decades of the Northern Song witnessed the appearance of a number of miscellanies that concentrate on courts and high officials of the Tang and Five Dynasties period, including *Compendium of Recent Events* (*Jinshi huiyuan*), *Recent Events in the Southern Tang* (*Nantang jinshi*), and *Former Affairs of the Five Kingdoms* (*Wuguo gushi*). The impulse to compose such works sprang largely from the apprehension that because of the collapse of the Tang, the political fragmentation that ensued, and the warfare that brought the Five Dynasties period to a close, official history would necessarily be seriously flawed and incomplete. Although the authors of these works readily admit that their compilations are made up mostly of "trivial" material, they nevertheless see themselves as filling out the historical record. They therefore adopt some of the pretensions of regular historians, telling us that they hope their works will serve, in a modest way, to instruct and guide their readers. A more contemporary bent is evident in works that focus on one or another Song official, relating private or little-known events in his life or his witty sayings and exchanges with friends. This type of work was usually compiled after the subject's death by his protégés and admirers. One such work, *The Garden of Sayings by Yang Wengong* (*Yang Wengong tanyuan*), centers on the celebrated official Yang Yi. It records his astute and clever observations on a wide range of subjects, arranged by topical category. Another work, *The Sayings of Ding, Duke of Jin* (*Ding Jingong tanlu*), provides a similar record for Ding Wei (966–1037), who served as grand councilor under Emperor Zhenzong. The interest of such material is that it provides intimate glimpses of the lives and conversation of eminent officials, which would otherwise be excluded from the historical record.

At just about the time of Wang Anshi's reforms, however, we begin to see a new type of focus and tone in the Northern Song miscellany. A new kind of author also begins to become involved with the form. Before this time, leading officials and literary figures generally avoided it. The titles cited immediately above are revealing in this regard. Yang Yi and Ding Wei may have been the subject of such works, but they did not compile them. Again, it is important to bear in mind that these were not considered "literary works" and so it would have been beneath a person like Yang Yi to produce one. This held true for collections of marvel tales as well. The contents of such works bordered on the "heterodox" and fell short of the moral and didactic standards expected of respectable writing. These biases may readily be traced back to the Tang period. Leading literary figures then likewise generally avoided producing miscellanies and collections of marvel tales. (One possible exception is a miscellany attributed to Liu Zongyuan, but as early as the Song the attribution of this work to Liu has been roundly challenged.) We recall the criticism Han Yu attracted for composing a single fanciful tale, "The Biography of Master Brush."

In the closing decades of the eleventh century we begin to see major literary and intellectual figures trying their hand at the miscellany. Ouyang Xiu produced one late in life (in 1067); within a few years so did Fan Zhen (1007–1087, one of Ouyang's assistants for the *New Tang History*), as did the scholar and book collector Song Minqiu. Subsequently, Sima Guang wrote a markedly serious miscellany, which concentrates on Northern Song court history, and so did Su Zhe, whose work consists of political anecdotes from his own time. There is a question about the more wide-ranging miscellany attributed to Su Shi: it is not at all certain that he compiled it himself. But it is clear that he wrote the material that constitutes it, even if it was not brought together until after his death. Su Shi's follower Qin Guan produced a miscellany, which does not survive, as did Lü Xizhe (1036–1114, son of the grand councilor Lü Gongzhu). This new willingness of prestigious literati to involve themselves with the miscellany carried over into the early Southern Song. Ye Mengde (1077–1148), Lu You (1125–1210), and Fan Chengda (1126–1193) all produced such works. The most prolific twelfth-century miscellany writer was the eminent scholar Hong Mai (1123–1202).

The new tone and focus is exemplified by Ouyang Xiu's short miscellany, *Records Written for Returning to the Farm (Guitian lu)*. We might think at first that the title means that the work concerns the act of its author retiring to the countryside, at the end of his official career, and what he did when he settled there. Ouyang's preface, however, makes it clear that these "records" concern events in his life *before* his retirement, and written then too, in order to have reading material to amuse himself with after he withdraws from public life.

The contents of Ouyang's miscellany are closer to the second type mentioned above; there is virtually nothing that broaches the strange or uncanny. Yet there is also an interesting shift that separates Ouyang's work from earlier collections of anecdotes about court life and officialdom. Some of the entries do concern such matters, but many others move outside officialdom altogether, often "lowering" their purview to merchant-class life. Or, if they do treat officials, the entries tend to focus on the mundane and personal rather than on the trappings of power.

There is the entry, for example, about Chen Yaozi (fl. 1030), a Hanlin academician who also served as a military official. He excelled at archery. One day, as Chen was shooting arrows in his garden, an oil peddler happened by. The peddler took the pole off his shoulder, resting awhile, and watched Chen. After some time, Chen, who took great pride in his skill with the bow, called to the man and asked if he were not impressed. "It's just that you're practiced at it," the peddler replied. Angered, Chen demanded an apology. The peddler placed a gourd on the ground and put a coin over its mouth. He then filled a cup with oil and, standing up over the gourd, poured the oil in through the hole in the center of the coin. When he finished there was not a drop of oil on the coin. "I too am practiced at what I do," the peddler said, and went on his way.

The range of subjects in Ouyang's miscellany is broad. He is interested in language and quirks of meaning: he writes about humorous popular sayings, the way temple names are corrupted in speech over time, the variety of terms used for steamed buns, the words stamped on coins, and the origins of recent reign period names. He reflects on the distinctive properties of things: Fujian tea, oranges from his native Jiangxi, the special "brush moistening" presents he gave Cai Xiang (1012–1067) for writing out an inscription for him, and substances that unaccountably act upon other ones as a preservative or ripening agent. Most of all, he is intrigued by unconventional human conduct, as in a gentleman who reverses night and day in his activity and repose, a chess player who defeats all challengers but is unspeakably dirty and crude, men who can drink all day without showing any signs of being drunk, and the wit of Mei Yaochen's wife when she outdoes her literary husband in repartee.

Ouyang does not write about events or people of long ago. Most of his entries concern happenings of his own lifetime, or at least of recent decades. There is also a surprisingly personal touch to several entries. He writes at some length, for example, about the weeks he and five close friends spent sequestered in the examination compound in 1057, grading the exam papers, and the riotous time they had composing poems and sending them back and forth. "Our scribes were exhausted by copying them out, and the servant boys ran back and forth delivering them." They mixed jokes and barbs in the poems, so that when the pieces were read aloud the listeners were overcome by laughter. It was, Ouyang concludes, "one of the marvelous events of our time, the likes of which had never been seen before."

The inclusion of so much material that is quotidian, has no didactic intent, is curious in a worldly but not supernatural sense, or is just plain amusing marks an innovation in the history of the miscellany. Ouyang's purview ranges from the court to the peddler in the street. He may occasionally revert to the role of the court insider who reveals secrets about the lives of the powerful, but that is not his only role or voice. He expands the scope of the miscellany by admitting much of everyday urban life, events of his own time, his own experiences, and his reflections upon what intrigues him and what he does not understand.

There is a story that soon after Ouyang finished his miscellany, news of its existence reached the emperor, who demanded to see it, thinking that it might broach politically sensitive matters. Ouyang, apprehensive that it did indeed contain offending material, hurriedly eliminated many entries, only to find that there was precious little left. With equal haste, then, he supplemented the contents with entirely trivial material, which is what we find in it today. I do not believe this story to be true, but consider it revealing in its own way. This appears to be a tale concocted by someone who did not appreciate the novelty of what Ouyang had done, expected a more conventional work of court-oriented hearsay, and was in fact puzzled to think that a man as eminent as Ouyang Xiu could have produced a work whose entries are so inconsequential. Unable to accept it as it is, he invented an explanation of why it was not something else.

Ouyang Xiu's miscellany, short as it may be, is important for the impact it had on other writers. It is no coincidence that within a few years of his compilation of *Records Written for Returning to the Farm*, other prominent men of letters also began to produce miscellanies (Fan Zhen explicitly refers to Ouyang Xiu's precedent in the preface to his own work). Ouyang's work is also significant for the shift in tone toward the ordinary, contemporary, and personal, as well as the broadening of subject matter to include such a broad slice of life. This was to be the direction that the miscellany developed in during the ensuing decades, as the form proliferated. As much impact as Ouyang had, we cannot say that he was alone. A decade earlier, in the preface to his *Compendium of Recent Events*, Li Shangjiao (fl. 1056) presented an argument for the importance of not overlooking any source of information

("Scholarship truly relies upon breadth and synthesis [of sources]") and the utility of writing down hearsay. Li refers unapologetically to his material as *xiaoshuo* and also to its ability to divert and entertain. Later, in the preface he wrote to his miscellany, Qin Guan would put forth even bolder claims for the value of the unorthodox, amoral, and "uninstructive" record of events that the educated elite normally looked down upon. Where could I go or look, Qin asks rhetorically, that I would not find something of value? Such an attitude, held surprisingly enough by a person who moved in the most elite circles of the literati of his day, supported the new interest in the miscellany. This outlook suggests a broadening and even a social "lowering" of what was considered the proper purview of the gentleman's mind.

Remarks on poetry

The "remarks on poetry" (*shihua*) developed out of two earlier forms of writing. One was the miscellany, with its free-ranging scope and haphazard arrangement. The other was the Buddhist recorded comments, which transmitted the sayings of masters and memorable exchanges between them and their disciples. Unlike the miscellany, remarks on poetry was new as a form, a Northern Song invention. It evidently fulfilled a pent-up need, because after it first appeared, in the 1070s, it caught on quickly and multiplied rapidly. By the end of the Northern Song a few dozen had been written. The proliferation continued through the Southern Song, and we can count some 140 of the works by the dynasty's end. By that time, the remarks on poetry had established itself as the primary form of poetry criticism, flexible enough to accommodate all manner of observations about poetry, including theoretical pronouncements, accounts of literary history, discussions of a single line or phrase, and adjudications of individual talent. The remarks on poetry would remain the most voluminous form of poetry criticism through the end of the imperial era.

The form had its origins in casual conversation about poetry, the kind that was natural in a setting where the writing of poetry was so central to the lives of the educated elite. Hence the *"hua"* ("talk, remarks") in the form's name. What makes one version of a line better than another? Who has produced the most memorable lines on a certain theme? What allusion lies behind a given phrase? Such questions as these would almost inevitably come up when men of letters got together socially. It is not unusual in Northern Song miscellanies to find entries that could equally well have appeared in remarks on poetry. Wang Dechen's (1036–1116) miscellany, *History of the Deer-Tail Whisk (Zhushi)*, even has a section specifically entitled "remarks on poetry." The breakthrough was to recognize that records of such talk and other observations about poetry might be culled from the mixture of other topics dealt with in the miscellany, and that they might circulate separately on their own. It was Ouyang Xiu who had this insight and produced the first remarks on poetry a few years after he finished his miscellany. Again, his precedent had an almost immediate and long-lasting impact, as others followed suit.

It is difficult to generalize about a form that is so sprawling and accommodating. Yet surely one reason for its popularity among poets and critics is that it allowed for the discrete insight or observation that, unlike in more formal essays or treatises on literature, did not need to be situated in a system of values or critical stances. It might be, and was in certain works, but it did not have to be. Being rooted in informal "talk" and, what is more, consisting like the miscellany did of mostly short entries, randomly ordered, the remarks on poetry was notably free of the stifling effect of literary dogmas and the impulse in formal pronouncements to articulate a position on the age-old issue of the relation between literary work and other systems of value (political, moral, social, and so on). Practitioners of the literary art found that in remarks on poetry they finally had a vehicle that allowed them to explore and argue over issues of poetic craft and effect that were of immediate and enduring interest to all readers and writers of poetry.

Connoisseur literature

One way of thinking about the remarks on poetry is that it presents a new type of literary connoisseurship, wherein the attributes of poetic excellence could be explored and analyzed. Seen in this light, remarks on poetry may be linked with connoisseurship writings on a range of other aesthetic objects and pursuits that appeared and spread at the same time. Quantitatively, the largest number of these works are manuals on flowering plants, including the tree peony (*mudan*), herbaceous peony (*shaoyao*), plum, chrysanthemum, lotus, crab apple, camellia, and orchid. There were also manuals on the bamboo and, of course, tea. The body of writing about flowering plants also began with a work by Ouyang Xiu, on the peonies of Luoyang (a city that prides itself on that flower to this day). These manuals discuss the history and cultivation of the plant, as well as popular lore concerning it. In the case of plants that exist in numerous varieties (especially the two types of peony and the chrysanthemum) a considerable amount of space is devoted to listing and describing the various types, with each successive manual on the same plant trying to outdo earlier ones by listing more and more varieties. Aside from plants, connoisseurs of the Song period also turned their attention to art or aesthetic objects, including inkstones, ink, jade, stones, and incense, as well calligraphy and painting. Separate treatises exist for each of these, and in some cases there are multiple and competing works on the same object. Colophons (tiba) on literary works, art, and objects, copied over from the work on which they were originally inscribed, also became abundant and often circulated separately.

The connoisseurship of these aesthetic objects was certainly not new, but in no earlier period do we find such a wealth of writing that transmits knowledge and appreciation of them. We today may be surprised to discover that committing this knowledge to writing was a somewhat problematic act. Yet this is abundantly clear from the works themselves, where we often encounter apologies for their very existence. Traditional ideas about the purpose and proper concerns of writing did not make it easy to justify works about aesthetic enjoyment that could not readily be tied to morally uplifting sentiments. Of course, each object was different in this regard and some posed a special challenge. It was not difficult to justify a treatise on the plum, bamboo, or chrysanthemum, since those plants had long been overlaid with layers of human significance, in which their physical attributes came to be inextricably linked to literati ideals. But the peony had no such significance; if anything it was associated with the dangers of feminine allure. How, then, could one possibly justify writing about it at considerable length and showing oneself to be intimately familiar with all its sensuous qualities and their enhancement through artificial horticultural techniques?

The interesting point is that this body of literature on the enjoyment of aesthetic objects was produced and steadily grew, despite the problems posed by its very existence. Ways were found to justify or excuse the impulse to compose it. There is no question that the literati who created this writing were aware that what they were doing was exceptional. Decades after Ouyang Xiu composed his treatise on Luoyang's peonies, his friend the noted calligrapher Cai Xiang, who in the interim had composed, as if in response to Ouyang, a treatise on the lychee of his native Fujian, copied out the entire text of Ouyang's peony work (some 2,500 characters long) and had the calligraphy engraved on stone, which he kept for his own enjoyment. Shortly before he died, he sent Ouyang a rubbing of the long inscription. It was, Ouyang tells us, one of the few works of his own calligraphy that Cai Xiang ever permitted to be engraved on stone. That Cai Xiang could have so lavished attention upon Ouyang's peony treatise and allowed it to take its place alongside a very select list of other compositions by Ouyang that he ever deigned to write out (the others being formal and didactic compositions) suggests a keen appreciation of the treatise's special appeal. In this act we may also glimpse something of the breadth of interest and delight in new types of prose work that Northern Song literary figures allowed themselves.

Informal letters

The last type of writing we come to is the informal letter, the most humble and ephemeral of all. This kind of document, variously termed *shujian*, *chidu*, and *daobi*, is to be distinguished from its more formal and substantial cousin, the letter (*shu*). The letter had been a staple form of literary expression for centuries, and had long had its place in individual literary collections and literary anthologies (including *Wenxuan*). The informal letter probably had an equally long history, but it had not been considered "literary" and hence was generally not preserved anywhere. The change in the stature of, and attention given to, the informal letter does not appear to have occurred until the eleventh century. We are speaking, here, about a kind of communication that is extremely brief (often just two or three lines) and one that could easily be viewed as purely utilitarian: the most laconic of statements about health, travel plans, concerns about money, food, family, and so on. It is not surprising that the informal letter was late to join the ranks of writings deemed worthy of preservation.

The informal letters that do survive from earlier times were prized not for their content but rather for their calligraphy. Many of the masterworks of Jin dynasty calligraphy, which were copied over and engraved repeatedly, were manuscripts of informal letters written by the likes of Wang Xizhi (321–379) and Wang Xianzhi (344–386). The fact that so many of them are fragmentary hardly matters, since they are "viewed" for their brushwork rather than "read" for their meaning.

Calligraphy surely also played some part in the impulse to preserve the Northern Song informal letter. The two eleventh-century writers with the largest surviving corpora of them are two of the most admired calligraphers, Su Shi and Huang Tingjian. The quantity that the two left is most impressive: 1,500 for Su and 1,200 for Huang. In the complete collection of Su's prose, the informal letters constitute nearly one-fifth of the total number of pages.

At some point, however, these trifling messages began to be appreciated for their ability to convey utterly routine information with an elegance of expression. It is a distinctive aesthetic that is operative here, one that finds in seemingly spontaneous and short missives concerning everyday matters a certain unstudied gracefulness. Naturally, the reputation that men like Su and Huang had built for themselves in more substantial genres informs the reader's appreciation of their informal letters, as one marvels that the imprint of the celebrated personalities carries over into such a lowly form of expression. The heyday of such appreciation came centuries later, in the Ming and Qing, when collections of informal letters by Su, Huang, and others circulated widely. Yet it is impossible to read widely in these informal letters without sensing that the Northern Song authors were already aware of the lithe verbal beauty the form could attain and deliberately strove to perfect it. We might consider this a different manifestation of the ideal of "taking the commonplace and making it elegant" that was applied to poetry. Interspersing humdrum news with jokes, jibes, personal asides, and shrewd observations about contemporary life, these informal letters do indeed have their own special tone and appeal.

Each of the forms of nonliterary prose we have described here continued to be produced in abundance in succeeding dynastic periods. One could say as well that each Northern Song form also contributed to the later development of informal writings (xiaopin wen) of the Ming and Qing dynasties. The masters of that form in later times often invoked Northern Song writers as their inspiration.

North and south: the twelfth and thirteenth centuries

MICHAEL A. FULLER AND SHUEN-FU LIN

I. Literature in the age of "China turning inward"
Shuen-fu Lin

The Northern Song's fall to the Jurchens

In 1114 the Jurchens, a semi-agricultural, fishing, and hunting people based in eastern Manchuria, rose up in rebellion against the Khitan Liao empire, the most powerful northern neighbor of the Song, occupying a vast territory that extended from Manchuria to Inner Asia. Led by Aguda (1068–1123), the Jurchens proclaimed their own Jin dynasty in 1115 and began their destruction of the Liao with lightning speed. They took the Liao Northern Capital at the juncture of Shira Muren river and the Liao river of central Manchuria in 1120. In that year the Jin and the Song formed an alliance against the Liao, agreeing that the Jin would return to the Song the Sixteen Prefectures on the northern border occupied by the Liao, and that the Song would transfer to the Jin the annual indemnities and other obligations they owed to the Liao. The two sides also agreed to launch their coordinated attacks in 1122, with the Jin working to drive the Liao from their Central Capital about a hundred miles south of the Northern Capital, and the Song to take the Liao Southern Capital at the site of present-day Beijing. Because of the Song's failure to meet their side of the agreement, the alliance broke down. Early in 1122 the Jin took the Liao Central Capital and then continued on to take the Western Capital in Datong in modern northern Shanxi as well. Impatient with their Song allies, the Jurchens went on to take the Southern Capital at the end of 1122, and after sacking it, turned it over to the Song.

After Aguda died in the late summer of 1123, his younger brother Wuqimai (1075–1135) succeeded him and completed the conquest of the Liao early in 1125. With the Liao vanquished, the Jurchens began an invasion of the Song in early November that same year, retaking the Liao Southern Capital early in 1126. By the time the Jurchens attacked the Song capital, Bianliang (modern

Kaifeng in Henan), in February 1126, Emperor Huizong (r. 1100–1126) had already abdicated in favor of a son, known to history as Emperor Qinzong (r. 1126–1127). After a long siege, Bianliang fell on January 16, 1127, and the two Song emperors, along with their households, some high officials, and treasures looted from the palaces, were taken to eastern Manchuria. But the Song dynasty did not end there. As fate would have it, a son of Huizong and brother of Qinzong by the name of Zhao Gou (1107–1187) escaped capture. This young prince took the throne himself on June 12, 1127, at what was then the Song Southern Capital in present-day Shangqiu, some eighty-five miles southeast of Kaifeng. With his proclamation as emperor, Zhao Gou (posthumously called Emperor Gaozong) brought an end to the first half of the dynasty later known as the Northern Song (960–1126) and became the first emperor of the Southern Song (1127–1279).

China turning inward

The new Song emperor soon became the target of intensive pursuit by the Jurchens. He and his hastily formed new government were forced to leave the North China Plain and flee as far south as Yangzhou just north of the Yangzi river, then finally across the Yangzi to make Hangzhou (called Lin'an or "Approaching Peace" in the Southern Song) their "temporary capital." The Jurchens continued to press southward and in 1129–1130 even crossed the Yangzi, forcing the emperor to flee Hangzhou and take to the high seas to elude capture. The flight to the south exposed the young emperor, who had up to then lived a life of seclusion, comfort, and security, to situations of uncertainty, extreme danger, and possible death. Even though Emperor Gaozong survived the crisis, his experience must have left a deep mark on his psyche.

During the few years while the Jurchens were pursuing Emperor Gaozong and consolidating their hold on the North China Plain, there were large numbers of loyal Song resistance forces in north China and elsewhere, capable of inflicting enormous losses on the invaders. Emperor Gaozong, however, was always more concerned with his own safety than with attacking his enemies. Even during the 1130s, when a number of such capable generals as Yue Fei (1103–1142), Han Shizhong (1089–1151), Wu Jie (1093–1139), and Wu Lin (1102–1167) repeatedly won victories over the Jurchens, Emperor Gaozong opposed the policy of military confrontation, preferring instead the policy of negotiated peace. The situation was finally stabilized when the Southern Song and the Jin concluded a treaty in 1141–1142, establishing a pattern of peace on the model of the Northern Song treaties with the Liao in the north and the Xi Xia in the northwest, but with terms much harsher and more humiliating than during the Northern Song. The 1141–1142 treaty required the Song to pay annual tribute, to regard itself as a vassal state under the Jin, and to fix the border along the Huai river, about two hundred miles south of the Yellow River and more than a hundred miles north of the Yangzi. After this treaty the two states did attempt to attack each other several times, and new treaties were made as a result, but Song rule was from that time confined to the southern two-thirds of its founder's territory. Because of internal dissension, the Jurchens could not launch major campaigns against the Song after the Chinese defeated them at the battle of Fuli in 1163. From the Song–Jin peace treaty of 1165, which had resulted from this battle, until the time when the Mongols began their conquest of the Southern Song in the 1270s, several decades after they had destroyed the Jin in 1234, the Song was able to enjoy relative peace and ever-increasing prosperity in the rich territory of the south.

Emperor Gaozong was obviously the person responsible for implementing the peace policy, but he handled the situation by delegating power to a surrogate, Grand Councilor Qin Hui (1090–1155), in order to be able to more effectively restrain the aggressive pro-war elements within his court, among the scholar–officials, and in the military ranks, while having someone to take the blame should something go wrong. There is no question that Emperor Gaozong's conduct as a ruler resulted from his struggles in surviving the catastrophic fall of the Northern Song. Concern for imperial safety at all costs also turned his court into one of increasing absolutism.

Emperor Gaozong's style in governing set the tone for a dynastic era very different from the preceding period. The diversity and expansive vigor that had characterized Northern Song politics and intellectual life in the eleventh century gradually disappeared, replaced by a mood of circumspection, retrospection, and introspection. The eminent Song historian James T. C. Liu (1919–1994) has described the cultural transformation that took place in the early Southern Song as "China turning inward," helping turn elite culture in subsequent centuries to greater concern with internal consolidation and refinement, rather than interest in expansion outward to incorporate new ideas and advances. Despite its seemingly weak policy of retrenchment and internal consolidation, in spheres other than elite culture the Southern Song was a great age of social and economic expansion within contracted territory. It hastened the growth of southern China, which eventually displaced the north as the center of Chinese civilization. In particular, the lower Yangzi delta region (historically known as Jiangnan or "South of the Yangzi River"), including the capital, Hangzhou, and the historic cities of Nanjing and Suzhou, became the richest and most populous area in the land. In terms of technological development, commercial activity, urban development, and a sophisticated quality of life, Southern Song China was the wealthiest and most advanced country in the world at that time.

The impact of the Northern Song's fall on learning and literature

In the realm of learning, the Southern Song seemed to have been oriented toward refinement, elaboration, and specialization. Even an intellectual genius like Zhu Xi (1130–1200), the neo-Confucian thinker who had mastered virtually all of the branches of traditional humanities, did more in synthesizing and reordering previous interpretations of the Classics than in contributing original ideas of his own. It might not be incorrect to say that much of Southern Song learning suffered, as James T. C. Liu has argued, "from narrowness, adherence to orthodoxy, insufficient originality, and other similar limitations." At the same time, if the intellectual leaders of elite culture in the Southern Song ceased to expand and reach outward as their predecessors had done in the Northern Song, they certainly accomplished much in extending their values throughout society and culture. *Daoxue*, "Learning of the Way," as Zhu Xi's school of neo-Confucian thought came to be known, became dominant in the Southern Song and in subsequent periods of late imperial history. Southern Song literature's response to the cultural turn inward will be discussed in greater detail later in this section and again in the subsequent sections of this chapter. Let me first comment on the immediate impact on literature of the Northern Song's fall.

In an environment of strong nationalistic sentiments, twentieth-century Chinese scholars have been in the habit of drawing attention to the emergence of "patriotism" as a new element of literature in the early Southern Song. The Jurchen invasion and conquest of northern China aroused a deep resentment against the invaders and a desire to restore the north to Chinese rule. In response to this mood of the time, many writers displayed a tendency to express patriotic feelings and heroic exuberance in their works. One would obviously expect the petitions to the throne and political essays composed by aggressive generals and pro-war scholar–officials such as Yue Fei, Zong Ze (1059–1128), Zhang Jun (1097–1164), Yu Yunwen (1110–1174), Li Gang (1083–1140), and Hu Quan (1102–1180) to contain patriotic indignation and bitter criticism of the peace policy. The response, however, goes well beyond those with a public role debating state policy; patriotic thought and criticism of the policy of the ruling elite are widely expressed in the poetry and song lyrics of writers who lived through the national crisis, such as Zeng Ji (1084–1166),

Chen Yuyi (1090–1138), Zhang Yuangan (1091–1170), Ye Mengde (1077–1148), and Li Qingzhao (1083–ca 1155).

The case of Li Qingzhao, one of the greatest women poets of China, can be used to illustrate the effects of the national catastrophe on the lives and literary careers of the elite during the transitional period. Both Li and her husband Zhao Mingcheng (1081–1129) came from eminent scholar–official families in Shandong. For twenty-five years before the Jurchen invasion, they lived a happy life together. Lacking the ambition to pursue a distinguished official career, Zhao shared with his wife an intense interest in scholarship and literature. They had a passion for collecting works of art and antiquities, especially ancient bronzes. The catalogue they prepared together, entitled *Record of Inscriptions on Bronze and Stone* (*Jinshi lu*), containing some two thousand inscriptions, with their comments, was first published between 1119 and 1125. This work anticipated modern standards in the study of excavated objects. During the Jurchen invasion they lost much of their enormous collection of antiquities and books, leaving still cartloads of them to transport as they fled south. In 1128 Zhao fell ill en route to his new assignment as district governor of Huzhou and died in Nanjing the following year. Li became a widow, living alone in the Yangzi delta region during the last twenty or so years of her life. She continued to work on an improved edition of her late husband's catalogue and wrote a long postscript in which she documented their happy marriage and their joy in producing the book.

Li's accomplishments as a scholar and writer were already recognized during the Southern Song, as evidenced in the fact that her collected poetry and prose under the title *Collected Writings of Li Yi'an* (*Li Yi'an ji*, Yi'an being her literary style) and her collected song lyrics under the titles *Song Lyrics of Gargling Jades* (*Shuyu ci*) and *Yi'an's Song Lyrics* (*Yi'an ci*) were published at that time. These publications have unfortunately long been lost, and all of the existing editions of her literary works, which represent perhaps only a small portion of her total output, are taken from later anthologies. Today we have twenty or so poems and prose essays as well as about fifty song lyrics by this extraordinary writer.

Li was one of the finest poets of the song lyric in Song times, as well as having been one of the first critics of the genre. In her "Discourse on the Song Lyric" (Cilun) she argues that the song lyric constitutes "a distinct household in itself" (*ci bieshi yijia*), with its own distinctive language, subject matter, and musical attributes, different from the well-established *shi* poetry, which lacks a musical setting. Because of her insistence on the genre's intrinsic quality, which is traditionally called "delicate restraint" (*wanyue*), she seldom used the song lyric to express her concerns with politics and the affairs of the state, which were considered subjects more appropriate for poetry than for song lyric. We can see in the small number of her surviving poems that she did write about these subjects. For instance, in "To the Rhyme of Zhang Wenqian's 'Reading the Stele Inscription of Yuan Jie's "Ode to the Restoration"'," she criticizes the Tang emperor Xuanzong (r. 712–756) and his treacherous high officials who brought on the An Lushan Rebellion, almost destroying the dynasty. In the rhetorical mode of using the past as an analogy for the present, the poem implicitly compares Emperor Xuanzong of the Tang with Emperor Huizong and Emperor Qinzong of the Song, and expresses concern for the troubled state of the country. Again, in a poem entitled "Quatrain Written on a Summer Day," she says,

> In life he was outstanding among men;
> In death he remained a hero among the ghosts.
> Today we still sorely miss Xiang Yu
> Who refused to cross to East of the River.

"East of the River" (*Jiangdong*) refers to the lower Yangzi region, especially the area south of the river, from which Xiang Yu (232–202 BC) rose up with his uncle Xiang Liang in 208 BC against the Qin Empire (221–206 BC). Despite his continuous victories over the Qin armies, in 202 BC he was cornered against the Wu river by Liu Bang (256–195 BC), the other contender for the Mandate of Heaven. Too ashamed to return to face the elders of East of the River, Xiang Yu committed suicide, allowing Liu Bang to found the Han dynasty. Implied in this poem is Li Qingzhao's scathing criticism of Emperor Gaozong, who fled with his court to south of the Yangzi river.

In Li Qingzhao's surviving song lyrics we cannot find any examples that contain the veiled or direct political criticism that we see in her poetry. Nonetheless, the song lyrics from her post-1126 period are imbued with melancholy, loneliness, a profound sense of loss, and painful memories of the happier days of the past. In one piece, set to the tune "Forever Meeting with Happiness" (Yong yu le), she recalls the happy days in the Northern Song capital, especially on the day of the Lantern Festival (the Fifteenth of the First Month), when women competed with each other for being smartly dressed. She concludes the song lyric with:

> Now I'm withered and sallow,
> Hair wind-blown and temples dew-white,
> What I fear most is to go out at night.
> I prefer to stay inside the curtains,
> And listen to other people's talk and laughter.

There is no doubt that Li wrote this song lyric while living in Hangzhou. She uses the sharp contrast of her moods in the past and the present to bring out her grief over the ruinous changes suffered by the dynasty and her own family. There is a level of satire at the end when she contrasts her own suffering with the happiness of other residents of Hangzhou, who were totally unconcerned with the state of the country. It is said that the "patriotic" critic and poet Liu Chenweng (1232–1297), who lived through the fall of the Southern Song, always cried whenever he read this song lyric.

After the policy of indemnified peace was firmly established, usually supported by the succession of emperors and an ever-stronger peace faction in the government, patriotic sentiments continued to be expressed in poetry and song lyrics throughout the entire Southern Song, albeit usually more subtly and allusively. All of the major poets and song lyricists, including Yang Wanli (1127–1206), Lu You (1125–1210), Fan Chengda (1126–1193), Xin Qiji (1140–1207), Liu Guo (1154–1206), Jiang Kui (ca 1155–1221), Liu Kezhuang (1187–1269), and Wu Wenying (fl. mid-thirteenth century), wrote some works that express their patriotic concerns. Lu You, who left to posterity more than 9,300 poems, was particularly obsessed with the aspiration to defeat the Jurchens in order to cleanse the national shame and recover the lost territory. His desire to serve the country with his pro-war advice was constantly frustrated by the peace policy, leaving him dejected, isolated, pessimistic, or conversely at times unruly and unrestrained in spirit. He did not have a consistently successful official career, occupying mostly minor positions in local governments. He did work, however, for about a year in 1172 as an assistant to a military commissioner stationed in Sichuan and had the opportunity to be among soldiers in the border town of Nanzheng in southern Shaanxi. This must have been the happiest time in Lu's life, as he wrote many poems expressing his heroic sentiments in forceful, passionate, and beautifully crafted language, especially in the form of regulated verse, of which he was a superb master. During the last twenty-odd years of his life, Lu lived in retirement in his hometown of Shanyin (modern Shaoxing in Zhejiang) among farmers. Although he did write a fair amount of poetry celebrating the carefree enjoyment of everyday life, his patriotic fervor never waned. Even in his deathbed poem entitled "An Instruction for My Son" he wrote,

> I know in death all will turn to nothing;
> Still I grieve that I'll never see all of China united.
> On the day the king's armies bring peace to the Central Plain,
> Don't forget to tell your old man at the family sacrifice.

Unlike most early Southern Song poets, such as Chen Yuyi, Wang Zao (1079–1154), Lü Benzhong (1084–1145), and Yang Wanli, who merely expressed their hopes or indignation concerning national affairs, Lu actually declared that he was more than prepared to throw himself into the fray, "to join the army," "to ride on a horse to attack the enemies," and "to cut off the heads of treacherous enemies by hand and clean out the old capital." Indeed, both the life and the literary works of Lu are filled with patriotic and heroic aspirations.

The case of the great song lyricist Xin Qiji offers an interesting parallel and contrast to Lu You. A Han Chinese born in Jurchen-occupied Shandong, Xin studied under Jin literary masters in his youth. In 1160, when he was only twenty years old, he gathered together two thousand men and joined the peasant resistance forces of 25,000 men led by Geng Jing. In 1161, at his own suggestion, Xin was sent by Geng to Nanjing to negotiate a plan for the Song government to provide leadership for the resistance forces. Geng was unfortunately assassinated by a subordinate, and the resistance forces soon dispersed. Xin was on his way back from a visit to Nanjing when he heard this bad news. He immediately led about fifty brave men and broke into the Jin military camp, captured the rebel assassin, and defected to the Southern Song. Despite his superior qualities as a man of action, however, Xin did not have a successful political or military career, and was fated to be known in history, like Lu You, primarily as one of the greatest writers of his age. In addition to his stubborn attachment to the war faction at the court, his candid and forceful "northerner's" manner was not well suited to the increasingly refined cultural environment of the Southern Song elite. For twenty years after he defected from the Jin, Xin served the government only in lowly official positions. Finally, in 1181, in the prime of his life, Xin was impeached and forced to retire. Although he was later reinstated on several occasions, each time he was dismissed after only a short period of service. He lived in retirement, almost a recluse, on a large estate by Lake Dai in Shangrao, Jiangxi, where he wrote a number of fine song lyrics describing its scenic beauty. Like Lu You, he never allowed the beauty of nature and the comfortable life of a retired scholar to dissipate his expansive and heroic spirit and ambition, as in the following lines from a song lyric set to the tune of "Congratulating the Groom" (He xinlang):

> At midnight I sang wildly, as a stirring solemn wind rises –
> I hear the clanking of the row of metal horses hung from the eaves.
> The south and the north
> Are still split at this moment.

By the late Northern Song, poetry and song lyrics were evolving along lines of ever-increasing technical mastery. The poetry of Huang Tingjian (1045–1105) and Chen Shidao (1052–1102) and the song lyrics of Zhou Bangyan (1057–1121) culminated the developments of these two genres of verse in a poetics that put emphasis on technical perfection, imitation of a few select past masters, display of the author's erudition, and creative transformation of previous works. Huang's works were so admired that he was revered as the founder of the Jiangxi School of poetry during the closing years of the Northern Song. Lü Benzhong of the late Northern and early Southern Song compiled a list called "The Genealogy of the Jiangxi Poetry Society," placing Huang as the founder and Chen as one of the significant early poets of the school. The Jiangxi School had a profound influence on poetry, and to a lesser extent on song lyrics from the late Northern Song to the end of the Southern Song. Similarly, Zhou's song lyrics (with their limitation of subject matter to love, their verbal refinement, and their complete compliance with the qualities of the music to which they were set) also became models for later Northern Song writers to emulate. The fall of the Northern Song had a tremendous impact on this technical orientation in poetry and song lyrics.

In order to write about the national crisis more effectively, writers of the time tried to shake off the fetters of the Jiangxi School poetics and the dominance of Zhou's song lyric art. It is reported that Lü regretted having compiled "The Genealogy of the Jiangxi Poetry Society" and indicated that poets should not model themselves solely on Du Fu and Huang Tingjian, but should also learn from more spontaneous natural talents like Li Bai and Su Shi – especially the latter. Lu You, Yang Wanli, and Fan Chengda, the greatest poets of the early Southern Song, all grew up under the influence of the Jiangxi School and then tried to break away from it to develop their individual styles.

The song lyricists of the early Southern Song also turned to follow the style of "heroic abandon" (haofang), a style associated particularly with Su Shi. Even Li Qingzhao, who closely adhered to the style of "delicate restraint" and was thus harshly critical of Su for writing song lyrics like poetry and for apparently ignoring the musical setting, left several song lyrics in her surviving works that exhibit an expansive and unrestrained style. By his political ardor, forthright character, and boundless energy, Xin Qiji broadened the song lyric to a far wider scope than Su had done before him, further liberating the genre from its chief conventional subject matter of romance and love. A supreme master of this musical–literary genre, Xin was able to freely manipulate the form to express his experiences and aspirations. He extended Su Shi's approach of "writing song lyrics as if he were writing *shi* poetry" (*yi shi wei ci*) still further, to the point where it was said that he "wrote song lyrics as if he were writing prose" (*yi wen wei ci*), involving at times a degree of prosaic discursiveness not seen before. Some of Xin's expressions in the song lyrics are so forcefully direct and outspoken that they border on immodesty and boastfulness. Lines such as "I say a man's heart should be like iron till death; / Look – here I try to use my hands / To repair the crack in the dome of heaven," "How many [in the Southern Song court] are truly skilled in statecraft?," "To flatten the barbarians within a myriad square miles," and "To reorganize the cosmos" can readily be found in his collected song lyrics. Moreover, many of his works are densely studded with literary and historical allusions. Xin's influence on late Song writers surpassed that of Su Shi, who had opened up the possibility of an expansive and heroic style for the song lyric. There were more than fifty noted song lyricists in Xin's own time and later who came under his direct influence, which extended well beyond the circle of writers who were sympathetic toward the war policy. The famous poet, songwriter, critic, musician, and recluse Jiang Kui, for example, not only wrote some song lyrics in explicit imitation of Xin's style, but also employed the "hard" (not the gentle or graceful) language, which is more typical of the style of Su Shi and Xin Qiji, to write about love. In their exuberance and lack of inhibition, however, some followers of Xin's style, such as Liu Guo, changed for the worse and produced works that were composed in rather coarse and unrefined language.

From 1210, the year Lu You died, to the end of the dynasty, the Southern Song was to produce no more major poets of the stature of Lu You, Yang Wanli, and Fan Chengda. Instead, a large number of minor figures appeared who, with few exceptions, were not prominent scholar–officials but private citizens or recluses. Some made their living as professional poets, wandering from place to place, supported by wealthy aristocrats and high officials of the day. Representative of these poets were the "Four Lings of Yongjia" (*Yongjia siling*, referring to Xu Ji (1162–1214), Xu Zhao (?–1211), Weng Juan (fl. turn of the thirteenth century), and Zhao Shixiu (fl. turn of the thirteenth century), four poets from Yongjia, each with the same "Ling" character in their respective literary names); there were also the poets of the *Rivers and Lakes Collection* (*Jianghu shiji*), a collection first published in 1225 by Chen Qi, a book merchant in Hangzhou. The Four Lings and the Rivers and Lakes poets rejected the poetic theories of the Jiangxi school and chose Late Tang poetry, especially that of Yao He (ca 779–ca 849) and Jia Dao (779–843), as their model. With few exceptions (such as Liu Guo and Liu Kezhuang), these poets were disinterested in politics, focusing their attention on their personal and everyday experiences. In an affluent society in which the peace policy almost always carried the day, we can see the creations of the Rivers and Lakes poets as demonstrating diverted energies. It is important to mention that the aggressively activist writers like Lu You and Xin Qiji also produced a substantial amount of such works. The general tendency in the poetry of the Four Lings and of the Rivers and Lakes poets is toward narrowness of vision, refinement, aestheticism, and a lack of intellectual content. Nonetheless, the Southern Song also witnessed some important new developments in the history of Chinese poetry. From the closing years of the twelfth century onward, poetic circles were in fact surprisingly lively. Poetry societies (*shishe*), which had made their appearance toward the end of the Northern Song, flourished in urban surroundings, notably in Hangzhou. Literary organizations of this kind, to which all celebrated poets and scholars of the day belonged, not only sponsored social and literary gatherings in which members could rejoice in fellowship and could write poetry and song lyrics together, but also held competitions in which each participant had to write a poem or song lyric on a common subject using particularly chosen rhyming words.

The case of the song lyric was somewhat different. Unlike *shi* poetry, which already had a long history and attained a height in the Tang dynasty as well as in the late eleventh and early twelfth centuries, song lyric emerged only in the ninth century, in response to the newly introduced banquet music (*yanyue*) from Central Asia. This new genre flourished in the subsequent Five Dynasties (907–960) and attained full maturity in the Northern Song. Although many late Song poets attempted to take new directions in writing poetry, they were never able to completely revive that genre's vitality. By contrast, the song lyric still possessed creative potential. Literary historians generally agree that the song lyric reached its height of sophistication during the Southern Song. Completely within the inward turn of Southern Song culture, a few song lyricists after the end of the twelfth century evolved interesting and novel forms.

On the foundation of an already long literary tradition, literature no doubt continued to flourish in interesting and varied ways in the Southern Song. If creativity seemed to be largely contained within accepted categories, there was a significant rise in the level of professionalism in the production of, and reflection on, literature. And this increasing professionalism also brought about some remarkable achievements.

II. Literature and the Way: the impact of *Daoxue*
Michael A. Fuller

The fall of the north was a national catastrophe, but its central cause was not hard to find. Emperor Huizong may have been a feckless ruler in many ways, but decades of unremitting factional strife within the bureaucracy were yet more crucial in weakening the dynasty before the Jurchen conquest of the north. The questions that confronted the elite stratum in the early Southern Song were why factionalism initially arose and why it persisted with such intensity through the final decades of the Northern Song. Many within the elite simply chose to focus blame on their own particular cast of villains within the contending parties and saw no need to search for more fundamental flaws in the Northern Song polity. Others, however, turned their attention with renewed intensity to a range of institutional and moral failings that had already been topics of discussion before the Jurchen invasion.

Daoxue, the "Learning of the Way," attained its initial identity as part of the conservative reaction to Wang Anshi's New Policies reforms in the mid-Northern Song. During the period of Wang's ascendancy, Sima Guang (1019–1086) attracted a group of scholars to Luoyang who discovered a variety of common concerns. Sima Guang reflected in particular on the dynasty's failure to heed the lessons of history about the need to clearly differentiate the institutional roles of the ruler and his officials. Shao Yong (1012–1077), Zhou Dunyi (1017–1073), and Zhang Zai (1020–1077) focused on finding stable cosmological grounds for moral principles through which to govern. The brothers Cheng Hao (1032–1086) and Cheng Yi (1033–1107), in contrast, turned to the problem of individual moral self-cultivation, of how one can regain the clarity of moral insight attained by Confucius and Mencius. When the conservatives returned to power and drove the participants of the New Policies regime into exile during the Yuanyou reign period (1086–1093), Sima Guang briefly served in the high office of vice director of the Department of State Affairs and vice director of the Chancellery and recommended Cheng Yi as an imperial tutor to the young emperor. When the emperor came of age and began to rule on his own, he restored his father's New Policies advocates to power, and they sent the conservatives into exile once more. Later the regime took the further step of proscribing the writings of all those who participated in the Yuanyou counterreform.

Throughout the partisan struggles of the final years of the Northern Song, students of the Luoyang conservative thinkers kept their master's teachings alive. During the process, the group's marginalized, oppositional role reinforced the centrality of the Cheng brothers' questions of individual moral authority and enhanced the importance of individual moral self-cultivation. After the flight south and the founding of the Southern Song, these questions became increasingly significant for the elite as a whole. First, the number of people participating in the examination system continued to rise, while the number of officials needed to staff the greatly diminished empire dropped. Second, Emperor Gaozong relied on the autocratic approach of his prime minister Qin Gui to carry out the peace policies needed to stabilize his rule. Both the policies themselves and the inflexible techniques used to enforce them alienated a significant segment of the elite stratum. Those members of the elite disenfranchised through failure in the examinations and through opposition to Qin Gui's regime looked for ways to justify both their opposition to the official system and their continuing status as members of a scholar–official elite. Members of the *Daoxue* fellowship (to use Hoyt Tillman's felicitous term) provided increasingly compelling models.

Within elite culture there were debates – which occasionally grew quite fierce – about the claims of the most strident *Daoxue* partisans to have exclusive insight into the Confucian Way (which, they asserted, had been lost since Mencius and revived by either Zhou Dunyi or the Cheng brothers). Within the *Daoxue* community itself, as Tillman argues, there also was a considerable range of approaches to the central question of moral self-cultivation as well as disagreements about which Northern Song scholars were most important in restoring the Way lost for two millennia. During the thirteenth century, however, a broadly accepted *Daoxue* orthodoxy gradually coalesced as the particular interpretations espoused by Zhu Xi came to define the Learning of the Way. When some of Zhu's commentaries were incorporated into the examination system, moreover, his views came to deeply influence the moral, social, and political discourse of the elite as a whole.

The Daoxue *critique of embellished language*

Daoxue encompasses particular communities, doctrines, and practices as well as underlying cultural problems to which those doctrines and practices provided answers. This complexity of *Daoxue* as a phenomenon made a correspondingly multifaceted impact on Southern Song literary history. The truism of Chinese studies of Song dynasty literature is that "literature declined with the rise of the Learning of the Way": this is roughly true, but it is incomplete. The writers most closely associated with the Learning of the Way distrusted belles-lettres and in the end forced a major rethinking of the very nature of aesthetic experience. Yet major Southern Song poets also drew strength from their participation in the *Daoxue* oppositional community. Moreover, Zhu Xi's synthesis, as part of a long-term trend in Chinese culture, provided a solution to aesthetic issues that had grown in intensity during the late Northern Song and created a new foundation for the literary hermeneutics that deeply informed late imperial Chinese literary culture.

The most famous and influential early *Daoxue* pronouncement on literature is Zhou Dunyi's gloss on a statement in the *Zuo Tradition* attributed to Confucius that "if wording is without adornment [*wen*], it will not go far":

> Adornment is that by means of which one conveys the Way. If the wheels and shafts are decorated but no one uses [the cart], this is pointless decoration. How much more so when the cart itself is empty! Adornment of phrasing is a craft; the Way and its virtue are the substance. When one has been careful about the substance and a craftsman writes it, then, if admirable, it will be cherished. If cherished, it will be passed on. The worthy will attain and learn from it, and it will become a teaching. Thus [Confucius] said, "if wording is without adornment, it will not go far." However, even if the unworthy have their father or older brother looking over them and their teacher urging them, they do not learn; and when they are compelled, they do not obey. They do not know to exert themselves over the Way and its virtue and take only the adornment of phrasing as ability, while it is [in fact] just a craft.

Zhou's stance here – and that of the Northern Song *Daoxue* advocates in general – is different from earlier calls for serious writing that "returns to the ancient" manner (*fugu*). For Zhou, debates about style are largely irrelevant and miss the central point: all style is simply an adornment of the moral content. The goal of this adornment should be to make the wording pretty enough for people to read, preserve, and transmit; beyond this function, style has no meaning whatsoever. As Zhou suggests, however, style is not just without content; it confuses people and makes them look for meaning in the wrong places. Cheng Yi voices similar complaints:

> Someone asked, "Does composing [*zuowen*] harm the Way or not?" [Cheng] said, "It is harmful. In writing, if one is not single-minded, one is not skillful. If one is single-minded, then one's resolve narrows to this, and how can it be as large as Heaven and Earth? The *Documents* says 'On playing with things, one loses one's resolve.' Writing also is playing with things."

Cheng Yi sees the writings of the sages of antiquity as forced from them: "The words of the sages and worthies were when they had no choice. If there were this text [*yan*], then this principle would be clear; if this text were not written, there would be a lacuna in the principles [*li*] of the realm." He acknowledges the truism that the Confucian canon is highly accomplished writing throughout, but he argues that this fact has been misinterpreted:

> When people see the Six Classics, they believe that the sages also composed. They do not know that when the sages expressed what had accumulated in their breasts, it simply formed patterned text [*wen*] on its own. This is what is referred to in [the saying] "Those with virtue surely will have texts."

The patterned (*wen*) aspect of the Classics is strictly incidental to their nature as repositories of moral principle.

In their marginalizing of the aesthetic aspects of texts, Zhou Dunyi and Cheng Yi set forth a radical strategy to resolve a growing problem in elite culture. Song dynasty governance and the authority of the scholar–officials who developed and carried out imperial policy rested not on aristocratic privilege or mastery of received cultural traditions but on their creative implementation of the schema for rule embodied in the Confucian Classics. For Song governance to be seen as an articulation of sage principles, however, the Confucian canon had to be deemed both interpretable and self-consistent. Major cultural leaders like Ouyang Xiu forged the distinctive mid-Northern Song ethos through their reading of the canon guided by the humanistic principle that "sage governance did not stray far from human feelings": they assumed that the sages were men writing to other men, and that the basic intentions motivating the canon could be recovered by drawing on a shared human nature. What Ouyang Xiu held to be central in judging interpretations was the correct apprehension of constant patterns of human response to external circumstances preserved in the Confucian canon. These responses include both intentions (dispositions to act) and feelings. Much of the interpretation of the canonical texts, therefore, was a working backwards from texts as records of the sages' inherently correct responses to the sages' inner states that motivated the writing. Rhetorical and aesthetic features of the canonical texts therefore were important guides in the apprehension of the logic of response. This tolerant, optimistic hermeneutic approach proved inadequate when confronted with increasingly strident partisan debates about policies and principles derived from the canonical texts. Early *Daoxue* advocates, confronted with the increasing failure of the hermeneutic of human response to provide unambiguous, univocal interpretations, came to distrust its aesthetic mediation of sage meaning. Instead, they proposed the goal of the direct apprehension of the mind of the sage in which the uncertainties of language and representation no longer matter.

The issue at stake in this debate was nothing less than the nature and locus of meaning. Cheng Yi asserted that the sages wrote only in circumstances when, if they failed to write, the *"li of the realm"* would be incomplete. Here *li* can be translated as "principle," the unchanging reason behind the appearance of objects and events. More particularly, the domain of principle tends to be the ethical. Cheng Yi notes, for example, that "In Heaven it is Fate; *in Rightness, it is Principle*; in people it is Nature; being master of the body, it is the mind, but they in all are one." Principle is metaphysical ("above form," *xing er shang*), outside of time and the processes of transformation, and its primary function is to serve as a guide to moral action. For Zhu Xi, one is assured access to Principle in its unity and completeness because it is in the end identical with human Nature (*xing*), which is similarly "above form." The task of moral self-cultivation is to recover the original mind that in turn gives one access to the Nature. In this process, the student must learn how human desires (*ren yu*) occlude Heavenly Principle and must learn accordingly to still the passions.

While a full account of the *Daoxue* fellowship's discussions about Principle, Nature, and the mind is beyond the scope of this chapter, the important point here is that *Daoxue*, looking within the self and outside of form, confronted a broadly acknowledged failure to find stable meanings that could claim universal assent through the conventional hermeneutics of experience. Rejecting easy access to meaning within the phenomenal, *Daoxue* adherents turned away from *li* as patterns in the world and from human feelings as the guide for governance toward the interiority of Nature and the abstraction of Principle. James T. C. Liu's description of "China turning inward" in this period had literary, ethical, and epistemological dimensions that evolved together with the rise of *Daoxue*.

A literature of interiority and the countermovement outward

When the late Northern Song poet Huang Tingjian proposed the idea that Du Fu and Han Yu had sources for all the language of their poetry, this gesture was not so much a rejection of creativity as an argument for changing the site and material for that creativity. Huang greatly admired his friend, mentor and patron Su Shi, but he also was acutely aware of the problems that arose from Su's approach to writing. Su Shi sought to capture the immanent logic of experience through the supple tracing of the moment of encounter with the objects and events of the world. Since all aspects of experience participated in patterns worthy of articulation, all were subjects for composition. Among these were explicitly political topics like the impact of imperial policy on rural life. Su Shi's caustic wit in writing on political issues ultimately landed him in prison and sent him into exile. Huang argued that biting satire was not proper to poetry and that instead poetry ought to draw its material from within, from the "self and its emotions" (*xing qing*). He presented a model of composition based on mediation, reflection, and inwardness. Such poetry would not withdraw from moral commitments since the self reveals itself through intentions to act and dispositions toward objects – both aspects are part of the term *yi* – and such intentions are inherently moral. Huang Tingjian in his letters constantly stressed that moral self-cultivation was the root from which poetry grew. While the ethical character of Su Shi's poetry sprang as an immediate reflection of the moment of interpretive encounter, Huang Tingjian instead pulled back and sought to articulate not the encounter itself but the shadings and subtle dynamics of the self as it responds to the world; with proper self-cultivation, that response would be morally correct, and the poem would stand as a form of moral self-presentation.

Since Du Fu, the greatest Tang poet, was famous both for his political poetry and for his late poetry of complex response to the world, Huang Tingjian's argument that every phrase Du Fu used had a source in the earlier textual tradition recasts Du Fu's poetry into the form of subtle exploration of the processes of engagement that Huang advocated as an answer to Su Shi's poetics of encounter. For Huang, Du Fu engages the world not through his own isolated subjectivity but through the structures and resources of the culture: what he orders in writing a poem are not the particulars of the phenomenal realm but the meanings these particulars have been given through their prior representation in the textual tradition. Huang Tingjian, in shifting the focus of poetry away from objects and onto human attitudes toward objects, avoids Su Shi's methodological and epistemological impasses. That is, for Su Shi, the deep patterns of the world were, in the end, beyond human knowing: although Su affirmed that humans could translate the patterns of encounter into the structures of writing, he argued that the process of translation in the end was inexplicable. The immediate impact of Huang Tingjian's arguments about poetry was to encourage writers of the next generation to believe, contra Su Shi, that there *was* a method (*fa*) for writing poetry and that they could discover that method by attentively reading and reworking the great poems of the past. This manner of writing poetry – discussed in greater detail below – acquired the name of the "Jiangxi style" after an essay written by Lü Benzhong in which he proclaimed the existence of a "Jiangxi School of poetry" that took Huang Tingjian as its model.

Critics soon condemned "Jiangxi" poetry as a shallow exercise in pilfering obscure phrases from past poets to construct poems with neither aesthetic merit nor affective power. Lü Benzhong himself clearly rejected the narrow stiffness of Jiangxi technique and reportedly regretted writing the essay that started it all. However, the Jiangxi poets represented a deeper shift in poetry – one based on the self-conscious drawing together of the internal resources of poetry at one remove from the immediacy of experience – that proved far more durable than its initial manifestation. Debates about the Jiangxi style in the early Southern Song explore the tension within poetic practice between Huang Tingjian's model of writing as a form of reflection on the self in its construction of a world of human meanings and Su Shi's approach of writing as the trace of an encounter that in itself is a revelation of meanings that include but transcend the human. These debates intersected with *Daoxue* discussions about the nature of the self and its interaction with the world and affected aspects of poetry seemingly distant from the philosophical controversies.

During the Southern Song, the interactions between *Daoxue* and literature occurred in three phases: the early years (roughly 1127–1200) when the debates within the *Daoxue* community were shaping basic positions, a transitional period (roughly 1200–1232) when *Daoxue* proponents served as key members of the networks of elite opposition to the central court, and a late period (1232–1280) when the court coopted *Daoxue* and integrated it into mainstream elite culture. The two most important Southern Song poets – Lu You (1125–1210) and Yang Wanli (1127–1206) – belong to the first period. Both broke with the Jiangxi style early in their careers and explicitly argued that the sources of poetry were in the external world of experience. Both also show in quite different ways the impact of evolving *Daoxue* concerns on literary composition. A variety of new voices that appear in poetry and poetics during the transitional period – the Four Lings of Yongjia, the "Rivers and Lakes" poets, and the critic Yan Yu – reveal how writers were beginning to define themselves within the *Daoxue* conceptual framework. By the final period, major writers like Liu Kezhuang and Wen Tianxiang clearly were drawing on *Daoxue* in their most basic understanding of the act of composition.

The early years: the convergence of aesthetic and philosophical issues in Yang Wanli and Lu You

During his own lifetime, Zhu Xi did not define a *Daoxue* consensus. Although the community committed to learning the Confucian Way agreed that individuals could claim inalienable access to unerring moral authority, what the basis was for that authority and how exactly a person could come to be a sage remained matters of dispute. Both Lu You and Yang Wanli were part of this large community defined in part by social connections, in part by opposition to the policies of Qin Gui, and in part by a shared resolve to realize the Way of the sages in their own practice. Yang Wanli, for example, had excellent *Daoxue* credentials. He took the style name "Studio of Sincerity" (Chengzhai) because he was deeply influenced by Zhang Jun, an official and general who played a key role in the early Southern Song defense against the Jin. Zhang Jun also was the father of the important *Daoxue* scholar Zhang Shi. When Yang Wanli attained a high position in the imperial court, he recommended Zhang Shi, Zhu Xi, and other *Daoxue* figures for court office. Finally, Yang Wanli's commentary on the *Classic of Changes* was highly regarded and at times circulated together with Cheng Yi's. The content of Yang's commentary, however, shows that on central issues he more closely resembled Su Shi than Cheng Yi or Zhu Xi. For Yang Wanli, as for Su Shi, people were participants in a world of constant change, and the very nature of that world and of the role of people in it made knowledge of the processes driving change difficult. Like Su Shi, he argued that it is possible to capture the deeper patterns of the world through writing that follows the flow of experience, but that it is difficult to find stable methods besides suppleness of response.

Yang Wanli's arguments about how people know the world are simultaneously philosophical and aesthetic. They define his stance vis-à-vis both *Daoxue* and Jiangxi poetics, and this convergence of poetic practice, poetics, and intellectual systematizing – this drive to account for what one is doing in terms of larger arguments – reveals the growing impact of *Daoxue* during the early Southern Song. Jiangxi poetics focused on literary method and poetic tradition, and even Lü Benzhong's addition of the idea of a "method of liveliness" (*huofa*) merely complicated the ways of using tradition rather than pointing writers to sources within the world of experience. Yang Wanli decisively rejected the Jiangxi style's self-enclosed couplet-crafting on empirical grounds – the approach was not productive and he found something better – but the "something better" directly related the act of writing to his larger understanding of the human place in the world. As he explains in a preface:

> The Triple Dawn (New Year's morning) of the fifth year of the Chunxi reign was a holiday. On this day, having little official business, I wrote poems. Suddenly it was as if I had an awakening: at that moment I bade farewell to the Tang writers as well as to Wang, Chen, and the Jiangxi masters; and I no longer dared to study them. Afterward I felt a delight: I tried telling one of the young ones to hold a brush while I improvised several poems, and lines flowed out without any of the difficulty of former days. Thereafter, each afternoon, after the clerks had dispersed and the audience hall was empty, I would grab a face-masking fan, pace about the rear garden, climb the old city

wall, pluck medlar and chrysanthemum, and beat my way about the flowers and bamboo. All the myriad images came to present me with material for poems. It seems "beyond my command": before I had responded to the first, the next already pressed upon me. In a torrent, I was unaware of the difficulty of writing poetry.

Yang Wanli discovered that the stuff of poetry was the world of experience. Inwardness and control just do not matter much. This theme of poetry as a barely controlled encounter with the world appears frequently in his poetry:

> ("Late Cold, Composing on Narcissus Flowers and the Lake
>   and Mountains," third of three)
> In refining lines, how can one be without a forge and hammer?
> But when the line's complete, it's not necessarily entirely due to them.
> This old man is not seeking out lines of poetry:
> The lines of poetry have come seeking this old man.

He also returns to the theme of the world impressing itself upon the writer in his discussions of poetry:

> On the whole, in the making of poetry inspiration is the best and recitation second, while social verse comes about when one has no choice. To begin with, I have no intent to write this particular poem, but this thing, this event happens to strike me. My intention also happens to be moved by this thing or this event. The encounter comes first, the response follows, and this poem comes out. How is it my creation? It is Heaven's. This is called inspiration.

This sense of humans participating in meanings that encompass us corresponds with his philosophical account:

> What is the *Classic of Changes* (*Yi*)? The *Yi* speaks of transformation. The *Yi* is the writing in which the sage penetrates transformation. To what does transformation refer? In my view, *yin* and *yang* are the transformation of the Great Ultimate. The Five Phases are the transformation of *yin* and *yang*. People and the myriad phenomena are the transformation of the Five Phases, and the myriad affairs are the transformation of people and the myriad phenomena. From the beginning until now the transformations of the myriad affairs have never ceased

Yang Wanli uses the same terms as the early *Daoxue* thinkers to describe what lies beyond the observable realm, but unlike them, he puts people on a par with other objects amidst the swirl of the world of change. Because the *Daoxue* account still was taking shape and other contending views existed alongside those of Zhu Xi, we need not consider Yang Wanli as explicitly rejecting the particular formulations of Zhu Xi's system. Moreover, while Yang rejects the Jiangxi style's movements of meaning inward, he probably was not explicitly confronting the corresponding inwardness of Zhu Xi and Lu Jiuyuan. During this period, the larger *Daoxue* community continued to debate other compelling alternatives more focused on history, statecraft, and principles to be derived from the vicissitudes of experience. Indeed, the very success of Yang Wanli's commentary on the *Classic of Changes* suggests the variety of positions discussed at the time.

Lu You presents a more complicated case. His mentor was Zeng Ji, who in turn was the student of Lü Benzhong, who was the great-uncle of the important *Daoxue* figure Lü Zuqian. Like Yang Wanli, he was a part of the oppositional pro-war community in which *Daoxue* matured, but he did not share Yang's close connection with the major *Daoxue* advocates. Lu You initially wrote in a crafted Jiangxi manner, but when he was forty-eight years of age he received appointment as an assistant to the military governor (*xuanfushi*) of Sichuan close to the border with the Jin state. The next half-decade of garrison life profoundly changed his views on poetry. He came to realize both the limits of the Jiangxi search for method and the importance of seeing the world in all its variety and substance if one is to write powerful poetry. As he explains in a poem reflecting on his growth as a poet during this period,

> The use of the Heavenly loom and the brocade of clouds is within me,
> [But] the marvelous part of the cutting and forming is not in the knife and ruler.

Like Yang Wanli, Lu You came to stress looking beyond poetry for the source of poetic creativity. Yet, as the couplet above suggests, the role that Lu You assigns to the world is more mediated and at a safer distance than Yang's account of objects and scenes constantly impinging upon him. Lu You in his accounts of writing poetry splits the process into the objects and events that serve as the *material* of poetry, on the one hand, and the intentions and emotions that form the *meaning* of poetry, on the other. Lu You, that is, looks to the inner sources for assessing experience that both Huang Tingjian and the *Daoxue* scholars stressed:

> I suppose that people's emotions are such that when one's sadness and vexation are stirred within and one has no words for it, one then begins to express it in poetry. Otherwise, there would be no poetry. Su Wu, Li Ling, Tao Qian, Xie Lingyun, Du Fu, and Li Bai all were agitated by what they could not bring to an end, and thus their poetry has become the standard [*fa*] for a hundred generations. In our own dynasty, Lin Bu and Wei Ye died

as commoners while Mei Yaochen and Shi Yannian were rejected and never used in office; Su Shunqin and Huang Tingjian died in exile while the Jiangxi poets of recent times were proscribed by inclusion on a faction list, and they all attained reputations for talent. I suppose poetic inspiration [*xing*] basically is like this.

Lu You here asserts poetry's unique ability to express intense internal states, but he is quite consistent (though not completely so) in taking the images of the external world as being the means through which a writer can articulate essentially inner states rather than as having independent meaning of their own. In the middle of a poem about visiting a garden, for example, Lu You makes this act of borrowing objects explicit:

> People say to this white-haired old man,
> "Why are you still as foolish as a child?"
> This old man certainly is not foolish:
> I am borrowing the flowers to bring forth my poem.
> The poem carries the fragrance of the flowers,
> And the east wind does not dare blow . . .

Lu You's distinction between the external occasions for poetry and the internal motives that lead one to respond to those events and objects appears in many forms. It also complicates the significance of his rejection of the Jiangxi style's focus on crafting and the poetic tradition. Lu You's turning outward proves to be at the same time a yet more intense turning inward. He famously wrote in a poem to one of his sons, "If you in fact want to learn poetry, / the effort is outside poetry." Scholars over the centuries have disagreed about what this pronouncement means, but the consensus points to a combination of seeking experience in the world and moral self-cultivation. Lu You's insistence that learning does not count unless it is not only understood but practiced strongly echoes the contemporaneous *Daoxue* focus on "getting it for oneself" (*zide*). He writes,

> As to the Way of the Sages, how could what you formerly practiced day and night be other than this: if one says it, one must enact it, and one takes it to heart rather than merely speaking and hearing it. Beyond this, there is no other way.

Lu You in his comments on poetry and in his approach to writing poetry begins the complex redefinition of poetry in response to the moral foundationalism of *Daoxue*. Although he sees that poetry must engage the world to be meaningful, meaning is in moral terms, in terms of human responses and ethical judgments.

Compared with Lu You, Yang Wanli was the more systematic thinker and had closer ties to the *Daoxue* community, but he proves to be the last major writer of the old order, while Lu You is the first voice of the new.

The early years: Zhu Xi and the transparency of texts

Daoxue's inward turn contributed philosophical underpinnings to Lu You's and Yang Wanli's revisions of the Jiangxi style. Neither, however, confronted the challenge to the literary that was implicit in *Daoxue* views of language, mind, nature, and meaning. Lu You and Yang Wanli seem not to have seen any great need to defend the role of literariness – the conscious crafting of texts – although both acknowledged the limits to what craft alone can achieve. In part this may have been a matter of timing, and in part it may be due to their status on the margin of the core *Daoxue* fellowship. In the larger oppositional community to which they belonged, Zhou Dunyi's attack on the aesthetic aspect of writing was as yet just one position in the discussion. As *Daoxue* arguments began to coalesce around the works of a few central thinkers and to have greater impact in elite culture, however, the issue of the role of the literary grew more urgent.

Most histories of Chinese literature present the major figures in *Daoxue* as moralists who were suspicious of the alluring surface of literary texts. More recent studies seeking to rehabilitate Zhu Xi have stressed that he and his circle in fact appreciated the sensuous life and accepted the pretty accoutrements – like poetry – to a well-ordered life. However, both positions are somewhat beside the point. The central *Daoxue* project was attaining the mind of a sage. *Daoxue* advocates argued that this was possible because we all inherently share the same inner being (seen either as mind or as Nature) with the sages. Moreover, this inner being, since it defies limits of historical transformation, must be above form (*xing er shang*) and free from the uncertainties of the empirically given; it must be identical with Heavenly Principle (*tian li*), and thereby allow us to understand the normative significance (*yi*) of all objects and events that come before us, since this understanding is precisely the definition of sagehood. However, for the *Daoxue* project to work either the sage inner core must prove directly accessible through introspection without the need for guidance from the earlier sages, or the texts left by the sages must prove infallible guides to the recovery of the inner core. In reading canonical texts, the *Daoxue* imperative was to move beyond the historically contingent aspects of its composition to the normative significance behind the represented objects and events, since the reader's act of moving from surface representation to significance was a grasping of the working of the sage mind in the initial creation of the text. This hermeneutic for reading the canon left no room for extraneous crafting: all patterning (*wen*) of the text must arise spontaneously out of – and be integral to – the sage translation of understanding into representation. Nor was there any room for unresolved meanings, indeterminate implications left embodied in the images. This hermeneutic for canonical texts became the model for reading in general and in turn created the norms for proper *Daoxue* writing. It was neither puritanism nor philistinism that led to a distrust of craft but the deep *Daoxue* imperative to guarantee transparency of significance.

During the early years of the Southern Song, the question of the proper role for crafting was far less a matter of *Daoxue* debate than was the role of texts at all in learning to be a sage. Many accounts of the development of *Daoxue* frame the debate in terms of Lu Jiuyuan as the advocate of just recovering the "lost mind," one who saw texts as largely irrelevant, versus Zhu Xi as the more cautious teacher who urged students to rectify themselves through the challenge of fully internalizing key texts of the Confucian canon. However, this account is too schematized, for the impulse to do away with texts was shared more broadly within the *Daoxue* fellowship. One writer, for example, attributed to Cheng Yi the following paean to recovering the lost mind:

> The former sages and the later sages are like matching two halves of a tally. It is not through the transmitting of the sages' way but a transmission of the sages' mind. It is not a transmittal of the sages' mind but a transmittal of one's own mind. One's own mind is not different from the mind of the sages. Vast and boundless, all forms of goodness already are present. If one wants to transmit the way of the sages, one should just broaden and fill this mind. [From a translation by Chu Ping-tzu]

Zhu Xi, however, rejected both the attribution and the argument:

> Now one who learns the way of the sages can know the mind of the sage. Knowing the mind of the sage and using it to regulate one's own mind so that one reaches a point where there is no difference from the mind of the sage: this is the so-called transmission of the mind. How can one say that this "does not transmit [the sage's] way but transmits [his] mind, does not transmit [the sage's] mind but transmits one's own!" Since one already speaks of it as one's own mind, what transmission can there be? How much the less when it is not rooted in clarifying through discussion, preserving [what one has gained], and nourishing [the moral nature] but rather directly "broadens and fills" it? What will one use [as a standard of] correctness as one broadens and fills it? [From a translation by Chu Ping-tzu]

For Zhu Xi, reading the canonical texts was essential in escaping the limitations of one's own subjective experience:

> There is another type of person who has never read texts but says, "I already have become enlightened and attained the principle of the Way. The mind of fear and compassion is like this. The mind of shame and revulsion is like this, and the mind of moral judgments is like this." These are no more than a private opinion, as in the recent [debate over the] imperial temple for distant ancestors.

For Zhu Xi, the canonical texts are essential, but he also argued that their status as supremely well-written texts had been misunderstood:

> [Chen] Caiqing [Wenwei] asked, "The first sentence of Li Han's preface to Han Yu's collection is very good." [Zhu Xi] replied, "You, sir, say it is good. I see it as having a fault." Chen said, "'Aesthetically ordered writing, wen, is a tool to hold together the Way.' Now, since the Six Classics are wen, and all that they convey is the principle of the Way, how is there a fault?" [Zhu Xi] answered, "This is not so. This wen all flows out from within the Way. How could there be such a principle as wen being able to hold together the Way? Wen is wen and the Way is the Way: wen is just like the condiments for one's food. To take wen as holding together the Way would be to take the branch as the root and the root as the branch. Is this acceptable?"

Zhu Xi thus was not opposed to literary endeavor altogether. He wanted its role to be understood as merely ancillary. Thus he criticized Su Shi, whose works continued to be enormously popular in the Southern Song, for obfuscating the place of the literary:

> The Way is the roots and trunk of wen. Wen is the branches and leaves of the Way. Being rooted in the Way, what is expressed in wen therefore also is the Way. The compositions of the sages and worthies of the Three Dynasties all came forth from this way of thinking. Wen is thus the Way. Now, [Su] Dongpo says, "What I call wen must be together with the Way." Thus wen is independently wen, and the Way is independently the Way. He waits until he is composing, then goes to look for a Way to insert. This is his greatest fault. It is just that each time [he writes], the wording is so floridly marvelous that he captures the surface meaning, but at this point he lets [the deeper meaning] slip away unawares.

If one were willing to limit the claims for writing, Zhu Xi had no argument with indulging in composition from time to time:

> It is not unacceptable to write a few lines of poetry occasionally, but there is no point in writing a lot, because that would be just getting mired in it. When

one is not dealing with matters, is calm and self-composed, what could be better than to think over some lines of poetry? At such a time the true flavor issues forth: this is different from those normally considered good poets.

The challenge that Zhu Xi presented to the next generation of writers was to confront the choice he offers: writing of high moral seriousness must find its form spontaneously and must subordinate literary features to the articulation of the Way, or writing is just a pastime.

The early thirteenth century: taking positions on "principle"

Who cared about *Daoxue* philosophy in the early thirteenth century? Was it as marginal as it had been a century earlier? The textual record clearly suggests not: by Zhu Xi's death in 1200 debates drawing upon the *Daoxue* issues of Nature and feelings, the sage mind, principle and desire, and so on were pervasive. The major literary writers of the time exchanged poems and letters with the major contemporary *Daoxue* proponents, and when they argued, they argued in *Daoxue* terms. Both groups were part of a large circulating population of literati on the margins of official political institutions. Some had official rank, while some sought entrée into the official stratum; others sought to be effective within literati society itself; some sought employment in the wider world, while others retired to the life of a rural teacher or landholder. They knew one another through personal contact, since this was a peripatetic group, and they also had access to one another's writings through the active publishing industry. Although most histories of Chinese literature refer to a "Rivers and Lakes Poetic School" during the mid-Southern Song, a better approach is to stress the rise of a socially, politically, and intellectually complex literati culture that encompassed all the figures who appear in modern literary and intellectual histories. The participants in this culture had to confront the *Daoxue* arguments that were part of the contemporary discourse; even if they disagreed with those arguments, they could not avoid framing their disagreements in a shared language that increasingly was shaped by the *Daoxue* conceptual matrix.

To take just one example of the intersection of the literary, intellectual, and political, Bao Hui (1182–1268) had a long and successful career at the local level and by the end of his life served in high court positions. His father had studied under both Lu Jiuyuan and Zhu Xi. Bao Hui exchanged poems with the "Rivers and Lakes" poet Dai Fugu (who never served) and wrote a preface for his collection. Dai Fugu knew Zhao Shixiu and others of the "Four Lings of Yongjia," and also debated poetics with Yan Yu and Wang Ye. Wang

Ye exchanged poems with the major *Daoxue* figure and official Zhen Dexiu, whom Dai Fugu praised in his poetry. The prominent literatus Ye Shi, who had debated with Zhu Xi and came from Yongjia, wrote the funerary inscription for Xu Zhao, another of the "Four Lings of Yongjia," and a colophon for an early collection of Liu Kezhuang's poetry. Liu Kezhuang in turn knew Dai Fugu, helped Zhen Dexiu to compile a literary anthology based on *Daoxue* norms, and wrote a preface to Bao Hui's collection; Liu also was a poet included in Chen Qi's important *Rivers and Lakes Collection*, in which Dai Fugu and Zhao Shixiu also appeared. (However, the original form of the collection is not certain, and the various extant editions differ significantly in their lists of poets.) These are just a few connections extracted from a very dense network that ties these people to one another and to the larger oppositional literati community.

The profusion of ties within the oppositional community during the mid-Southern Song deepened the impact of *Daoxue* arguments on literature. Bao Hui, in discussing poetry, wrote,

> People of old did not write poetry lightly. They did not write many poems, but if a poem did come forth, it surely attained the greatest refinement in the realm. If depicting principle [*li*], then the philosophical interest [*liqu*] was fully presented; if depicting events, then the aspects of the event were all luminously manifest; if depicting an object, then the manner of the object was complete. There were aspects that exhausting knowledge and pushing strength to the limit could not attain, as if it were the spontaneous sound of Creative Transformation [*zaohua*].

Here Bao Hui appears to echo Yang Wanli's vision of the larger patterns of the world expressing themselves through the responses of the poet. Bao Hui's preface to Dai Fugu's poetry, however, suggests that his understanding of principle in fact was in the normative, moral terms of *Daoxue*:

> Poetry of old took principle as central, and Stone-Screen [Dai Fugu] obtained his [poetry] within principle. Poetry of old esteemed resolve, and Stone-Screen's comes from resolve. Poetry of old valued the authentic [*zhen*], and Stone-Screen's comes forth from the authentic. These three all show the depth and distance of his sources, which others cannot reach. Principle is complete in the Classics. If the Classics are clear, then principle is clear. I once heard that there was someone who told Stone-Screen that the poetry of the present dynasty could not reach that of the Tang. Stone-Screen said, "Not so: the poetry of the present dynasty comes from the Classics." This is something people have not understood, but Stone-Screen alone understands.

In this preface, "principle" is "moral principle," and its locus is within the sage mind and the sage texts. The beginning section of a farewell poem Dai Fugu wrote to Bao Hui confirms Bao's interpretation: when the two discussed literature, they did so in solidly *Daoxue* terms:

> Although poetry and prose are different paths,
> Principle and rightness return to one.
> The Airs and the *Sao* have gone through many transformations,
> And the assembled masters of the Late Tang appeared.
> Our dynasty takes the old learning as its teacher:
> The Six Classics are put into practice in our age.
> The assembled worthies support one another,
> And composition returned to the Orthodox Transmission.

Dai's critical comment about the Late Tang masters refers to shifts in contemporary practice. The "Four Lings of Yongjia" strongly advocated returning to the mixture of simplicity, calmness, and crafting associated with the Late Tang style of Jia Dao and Yao He. Their style was becoming popular in the broad literati stratum, and although Dai at times also wrote in the Late Tang manner, he remained ambivalent about its growing importance. His critique is in part framed in the traditional arguments of "returning to the old," but also in part in the new arguments of *Daoxue* moral philosophy.

This mix of old literary and new moral tenets reappears in Dai Fugu's debates about poetry addressed to Yan Yu. Both had participated with Wang Ye in a discussion of Late Tang and contemporary poetry. Dai then wrote a series of quatrains to express his position:

> #1
> Composition follows the age in its ups and downs:
> Completely transforming the Airs and *Sao*, it reached the Late Tang.
> All the age in its chanting puts forward Du Fu and Li Bai;
> People of the time do not discern that there are Chen Shidao and Huang
>   Tingjian.
> #5
> Giving shape to Nature and feelings is my task:
> Dwelling on fine scenery is but childish play.
> An embroidered bag of speech may be remarkable,
> But it is not poetry that is useful among people.

The phrase "chanting one's Nature and feelings" had a venerable history in Chinese poetics. Dai Fugu's poetry shows, however, that *Daoxue* had changed the intellectual system within which the phrase was used. When Dai Fugu and

Bao Hui wrote of Nature, they meant the unblemished, self-complete *Daoxue* Nature defined through the debates of the former generation. "Giving shape to Nature and feelings" in this cultural context acquires meanings unimagined by the author of the "Great Preface" to the *Classic of Poetry*. Poetry brings with it a moral duty to know Nature and cultivate feelings consonant with that Nature that Ye Shi notes in a preface to a commentary on the *Classic of Poetry*:

> Since the beginning of writing, poetry has been foremost in instruction, and King Wen and Wu and the Duke of Zhou were most detailed in their using it. In examining their regulation, when people responded to it in accord, they arrived at those who shared the same virtue with Heaven. In the poems of those already instructed, the Nature and feelings were increasingly clear.

To make the matter even more complicated and deeply enmeshed in contemporary debates, Dai Fugu's two phrases "giving shape to" (*taoxie*) and "dwelling on fine scenery" (*liulian guangjing*) come from an earlier *Daoxue* challenge to poetry that Ye Shi cites in his preface to Liu Kezhuang's poetry:

> Formerly Xie Xiandao [Liangzuo, d. 1102, a student of the Cheng brothers] said that "to *give shape to* [*taoye*] earth-bound desires and depict the manner of things is not so good as the poems of Yan [Yannian], Xie [Lingyun], Xu [Ling], and Yu [Xin] that *dwelled on fine scenery*." Ever since this argument became current, poetry has been abandoned because of it.

In this context, Dai Fugu's claim that "to give shape to Nature and feelings is his task" becomes a morally reenvisioned understanding of poetry that answers Xie Liangzuo's challenge.

There is, however, another way to answer Xie Liangzuo's challenge: to declare independence, to assert that poetry fundamentally just is not about the moral, epistemological, and ontological domain claimed by *Daoxue*. This is Yan Yu's strategy. In *Canglang's Remarks on Poetry*, he famously asserted,

> Now in poetry there is a separate material that does not involve books. In poetry there is a separate interest that does not involve principle. But if a writer is not one who has read much and investigated many principles, then he cannot reach the acme of poetry. [Translation by Stephen Owen, modified]

Modern scholarship has debated what Yan Yu meant by "principle" here. Yan Yu was of the same milieu as Dai Fugu, Bao Hui, and Ye Shi, so there is no compelling reason to assume that his usage of the term differed significantly from theirs. In claiming that "interest" (*qu*) in poetry precisely did *not* involve principle, he turns away from the sort of "philosophical interest" (*liqu*) that Bao

Hui praised. Yan Yu rejects the Late Tang style as too shallow and Song dynasty poetry as too prosy and focuses on the High Tang as the doorway to a domain of self-sufficient aesthetic experience that needs no further justification. In cutting poetry free from the demands of *Daoxue* moral responsibility, Yan Yu altogether eliminates the *Classic of Poetry* – which necessarily blends moral and aesthetic categories – from his account. He simply has students start with the *Chu Ci*, then go on to Han, Wei, Six Dynasties, and Tang poetry.

The impact of *Daoxue* in the mid-Southern Song was to redefine the conceptual landscape within which literature was written and read. The shifts in meaning of such basic terms as Nature, feelings, mind, and *li* (which changed from "pattern" into "principle") – shifts driven by the need to provide compelling solutions to deep problems in the culture – forced writers to rethink their task. They were compelled to make choices about how to participate in the new moral order.

The later years of the Southern Song: a poetics of the moral self

During the middle years of the Southern Song, literati began to accommodate themselves to the *Daoxue* conceptual universe at the same time that they adopted its social commitments and moral justifications for elite opposition to the increasingly autocratic and inaccessible political order. Some writers, such as Yan Yu and the "Four Lings of Yongjia," argued for a poetics that essentially ceded all of the social, moral, and philosophical concerns to *Daoxue* and carved out a realm of craft and "poetry." Others, such as Dai Fugu and many of the "Rivers and Lakes" writers, preserved a space for craft against the encroachments of *Daoxue* but, like Lu You, began to see craft as in service to the difficult task of representing the inner core of the self that *Daoxue* labeled the Nature and the mind. This latter defense of poetry comes to dominate the work of the major late Southern Song writers. Liu Kezhuang and Wen Tianxiang provide the clearest examples.

Liu Kezhuang began writing in the first decades of the thirteenth century. His earliest poetry, from which he saved just one hundred poems, largely was in the Late Tang style of the period. His first published volume of poetry, noted above, shows a shift away from calm landscape verse: since he took Lu You as one of his models and was an ambitious poet, the volume included poems in a broad range of styles and touched upon political issues of the day. It earned the praise of both Ye Shi and Zhen Dexiu and three years later was included in the *Rivers and Lakes Collection*. Two years after Chen Qi published the *Rivers and Lakes Collection*, he, Liu Kezhuang, and other writers in the collection were impeached for slander because opposition to the new emperor's ascension had not died down, and the regime sought to make an example. Although one of Liu's poems in particular was offered as evidence, high-ranking officials at court came to his aid and he retained the low rank of a county magistrate while others in the group suffered demotion and exile.

Liu Kezhuang's early poetry shows two contradictory impulses. On the one hand, he insisted on the poet's right to protest:

> To sorrow over the times, from the start, is the poet's job:
> Don't be surprised that there is much turmoil in my chanting.

On the other, he sought the equanimity that philosophical poise should offer:

> Recently, worldly concerns have ceased:
> Don't be surprised that these small poems are limpid.

Although Liu had been cautioned about the dangers of writing verse, he never backed down from his early commitment. Instead, he sought a poetics that could defend the importance of both modes of writing. The central issue was the value of poems that have no explicit moral purpose. First, Liu Kezhuang argued that there is no harm in an appreciation of the beauties of the phenomenal realm:

> The argument that "toying with wind and moonlight defiles one's behavior" has been current for a long while. In recent times, people have esteemed the Learning of Principle and slighted poetry. Occasionally they write poems, but most of it is no more than versified "recorded sayings" or classics lectures. But Kangjie [Shao Yong] and Mingdao [Cheng Hao] never failed to appreciate "wind, moon, flowers, and willows," and this did not detract from their being great Confucians.

"Toying" with the world was wrong, but that did not preclude more proper responses. More centrally, the responses to the world should accommodate the full range of feelings proper to the human:

> When my child first entered school, I initially selected one hundred quatrains in each of pentasyllabic and heptasyllabic lines to orally teach him . . . My child asked, "Formerly, Du Mu criticized Yuan Zhen and Bai Juyi for 'teaching licentiousness.' Now, among the poems you selected are many 'boudoir feelings,' 'spring longings,' and 'inner palace laments': is that proper?" I said, "The Great Preface says, 'It comes forth from the feelings and Nature and stops with ritual and rightness.' Poems then and now reach this point and stop. Now, Heavenly Principle will not accept the vanishing of what comes from the feelings and Nature, and a sage's brush cannot edit out what stops within ritual and rightness. My young son should know this."

In the end, Liu develops a poetics of "Nature and feelings" in which the objects and events of the phenomenal realm are but occasions to bring forth what is constant in human experience:

> I once said that what *takes feelings, Nature, rites, and rightness as its basis and birds, animals, grasses, and trees as its material* is poetry of the *Classic of Poetry.* That which takes books as its basis and affairs as its material is the poetry of literati . . . Since the "Airs of the States," "Encountering Sorrow," *Selections of Refined Literature, New Songs of the Jade Terrace,* Tribal Bureau [songs], down to Tang and Song, there have been many changes. Nonetheless, what has changed is the *form* of poetry. Throughout a thousand years and ten thousand generations, what has not changed are human nature and feelings. How could your Nature and feelings differ from mine?

Liu Kezhuang solved the problem of how to justify poetry – even that of moonlight and spring longing – by transforming poetry into the project of articulating Nature. He brings to *Daoxue*'s morally pure and difficult-to-know Nature the writer's expertise in recognizing implicit patterns. Poetry depicts not the patterns of the world as such but the always morally informed patterns of human response to the world. This poetry of the self provides a role for the aesthetic in the *Daoxue* world of inwardness of meaning.

Wen Tianxiang is the first major poet of a world of values structured by *Daoxue*. He is primarily famous as the great patriot poet–official who recorded his campaign of resistance to the Mongol invasion in *South-Pointing Record*, wrote the stirring "Song of the Righteous Breath of Life" while in captivity, and finally was executed after refusing to submit to the Mongols. Before Wen Tianxiang began his fight against the Mongol invaders, however, he seems to have had little interest in poetry. Historical accounts instead present him as a model young scholar–official with a strong interest in *Daoxue*. He began his formal studies, for example, with the *Daoxue* scholar Ouyang Shoudao (ca 1209–?). His early poetry reflects his philosophical concerns. On parting from his brother, for example, he writes,

> For ten years we have long traveled together.
> The many gentlemen have lectured aptly and of the essentials.
> As Heaven from the Abyss, we should separate Principle and desire.
> Inside and outside, we should unify knowledge and action . . .

Wen built upon Liu Kezhuang's dualistic formulation of the world as the material for poetry and Nature, feelings, and the moral order as the substance. However, he further reduced the role of the experiential realm when he transformed the traditional idea of poetry "chanting of one's Nature and feelings" into the idea of its manifesting their harmony, a key *Daoxue* concern:

> Poetry is that by which one brings forth [*fa*] the harmony of one's Nature and feelings. Before Nature and feelings are brought forth, the poetry is without sound. Once Nature and feelings are brought forth, poetry has sound. The essence that is shut in by the poetry without sound is made manifest by the traces of the poetry with sound.

Wen took the terminology of the "not yet manifest," the "already manifest," and "harmony" from a crucial passage in the *Zhongyong*: "Before delight, anger, sorrow, and joy have come forth is called 'centeredness'; coming forth and in every case attaining just measure is called 'harmony': centeredness is the great root of all under heaven, and harmony is the state when all under heaven attains the Way." In his theorizing, he had no need to refer to the objects and events of the phenomenal realm that provided the material out of which poetry was crafted, since he envisions a poetry "without sound" more basic than poetry with sound that must wait upon images borrowed from experience.

For Wen Tianxiang, poetry is to express the functioning of the Nature as set forth in the *Zhongyong*. The inwardness of Nature has two aspects: that which is shared by all in common, and that allotment which defines each distinct individual. Wen sees precisely this duality in poetry:

> Things that sing out in the subcelestial realm are many . . . None of these are poor singers. Yet this one and that one cannot sound like each other: each has its own Nature. Poetry is the same: Bao Zhao and Xie Lingyun are naturally Bao Zhao and Xie Lingyun. Li Bai and Du Fu are naturally Li Bai and Du Fu. Ouyang Xiu and Su Shi are naturally Ouyang Xiu and Su Shi. Chen Shidao and Huang Tingjian are naturally Chen Shidao and Huang Tingjian. Bao and Xie not being able to be Li and Du is like Ouyang and Su not being able to be like Chen and Huang. Mr. Zhou Xingchu of my hometown is good at writing poetry . . . I sing of myself. Xingchu sings of Xingchu. This is referred to as "singing of oneself." Although this is so, all sounds are born in the human heart, and why we sing certainly is the same.

When the invasion came, Wen Tianxiang encountered an occasion for writing that perfectly corresponded to the theory he developed out of the interplay of contemporary *Daoxue* thought and views on poetry inherited from Lu You and Liu Kezhuang. Every object and event in his poems written during the invasion and his captivity becomes a token of his loyalty and resistance. At the end of his preface to the now lost *Donghai ji*, the collection of his friend and fellow prisoner Deng Guangjian, Wen explains its creation as the embodiment of a selfhood that can be preserved for generations to come:

> At the time, I was held at the Jinling post station with nothing to do. So I gathered the poems of my friend, wrote them out, and appended relevant material to them. Those who look at them later, relying on the poems to see our shared resolve, surely will be moved by this.

Thus the intensity of Wen Tianxiang's final poetry – far more powerful than anything written on the fall of the north – is made possible by the long process of reshaping literature through the confrontation with *Daoxue*:

> "Jinling Post Station"
> Grasses enclose the old palaces as waning sunlight shifts.
> A lone wind-tossed cloud stops briefly: on what can it depend?
> The view here, mountains and rivers, has never changed,
> Yet the people within the city wall already are half gone.
> The reed flowers that fill the land have grown old with me,
> But into whose eaves have the swallows of my former home flown?
> Now I depart on the road out of Jiangnan;
> Transformed into a weeping cuckoo, reeking of blood, I shall return.

The *xing* of Wen Tianxiang's encounter with the world here fuses with the *bi* of moral allegory. This reenvisioning of poetry was the future: the patriotic poets of resistance at the end of the dynasty continued to draw upon this moral appropriation of the landscape. The poetry of late imperial China – despite its formal, rhetorical, and topical variety – grew out of this shift to an inwardness of meaning that is the key aesthetic legacy of *Daoxue* thought.

III. The social world of literature: groups and clubs and the impact of printing
Michael A. Fuller

In Southern Song China, three interconnected factors – all related to the expansion of printing – significantly enhanced and complicated the organization of the social world of literature. First, a thriving publishing industry made possible broad participation in the examination system. Second, the expansion of printing made knowledge of the past cultural legacy and of new cultural positions – whether *Daoxue* arguments or new poetic styles – more readily accessible to more people in a broader geographic distribution at a quicker pace than had been possible in the time of strictly manuscript transmission. The third factor was the changing nature of what it meant to be a *shi* – a member of the literate elite – that was made possible in part by the broad availability of printed texts.

Printing and examination culture

During the Southern Song, as many as 300,000 candidates at a time participated in the prefectural examinations. Passing this test given at the prefectural seats allowed one to proceed to the capital to take the civil service examination that was the gateway to an official career. The fierce competition in the examinations meant that candidates sought every advantage they could. Since quotas from outlying prefectures, for example, were slightly better than those from cultural centers, some students illegally tried to change their family registry to the easier locale. Knowing what sort of essays and information the examiners might expect also presented a significant advantage. Publishers were only too happy to oblige by selling volumes of successful – or what they at least claimed to be successful – examination essays. The central government, having issued edicts banning such works to no avail, decided to join in the fray by publishing its own volumes culled from the most exemplary of the successful essays. There also was a lively market for the dynastic histories, philosophers, Confucian canonical works, and digests and commentaries on all works that might be included in the exams. The Directorate of Education produced the most authoritative versions, but these were expensive and did not provide the sorts of additional analyses that might aid the test-taker. Private publishers stepped in to meet the demand with cheap, highly accessible editions with many types of annotation and even printed versions of major texts small enough to be smuggled into the examination halls. Government schools and private academies also produced some of the exam preparation materials and, more crucially, provided the sort of training in writing and analysis needed for the examinations.

As the odds of passing the examinations grew increasingly slim, society gradually came to conceive of elite status in broader terms and ambitious young men began to seek other means of making their way in the world. Participating in the examination system itself, for example, rather than actually passing the examination, came to be a marker of *shi* elite status. The withdrawal of the central government from many aspects of community organization, moreover, gave this evolving *shi* elite greater scope for activity at the local level. Finally, as the *shi* saw their fates less entwined with the state, they increasingly asserted their moral independence from and resistance to the succession of autocratic ministerial regimes that presided over the Southern Song government. Within this milieu, new possibilities for creating a contemporary reputation on the edge of or outside the structure of government service emerged. Fame as a teacher in a private academy or exemplary behavior as a local community leader was a way to become known. One's poetry also could establish one as a noble recluse or as an upright man worthy of employment. More generally, writing poetry, attending group composition "events," writing tracts contesting old styles and asserting new ones, and circulating these texts in both manuscript and printed form all were ways of participating in the struggle for distinction in this elite society whose values grew increasingly at odds with the facile cleverness and expedient calculation that the exams came to represent.

Public and private printing in Southern Song China

As in the Northern Song, the Directorate of Education in the capital published the basic books needed in the education of future officials. These consisted primarily of the Confucian canon and the official histories (the dynastic histories plus the *Records of the Historian* and the *Comprehensive Mirror for Aid in Government*). As in the Northern Song, the prints were of high quality and greatly esteemed. Scholars note, however, that few new titles were added to the list and suggest that this was in part a response to the increased printing by local institutions.

During the Southern Song, local government offices increasingly printed books both to meet local educational needs and to earn money to supplement their budgets. Sören Edgren points out that imprints survive from a very wide variety of local offices, many of which have no inherent connection with printing duties: books, for example, were published by fiscal commissions, grain transport offices, tea and salt supervisorates, judicial commissions, and perhaps most commonly by the prefectural envoy storehouse. These local venues for official publishing allowed prefects, as they arrived at their post, to honor former authors from the region, to fulfill their obligation to print the writings of their ancestors, and also to print whatever text they deemed either especially worthy or in demand. For example, when Lu You's son Lu Ziyu became prefect of Yanzhou, he arranged for the printing of his great-grandfather's writings, several of his father's writings, the collections of several early Northern Song figures (Pan Lang, Wei Ye, and Shi Jie), and a collection of anecdotal accounts about the reign of Tang Xuanzong. Lu You also had been prefect in Yanzhou; during his tenure, he had published *New Accounts of the World* (*Shishuo xinyu*), the *History of the Southern Dynasties*, the collection of the Tang writer and official Liu Yuxi, and a collection of his own writings. When Hong Shi, brother of Hong Mai, was prefect of Shaoxing, he had his father's works printed. When his younger brother Hong Zun was prefect in Shaoxing, he had the writings of the Tang author Yuan Zhen printed, since Yuan had once been prefect in the region. And when Hong Mai was district governor of nearby Guiji, he published the first forty-six chapters of his *Ten Thousand Quatrains by Tang Writers*.

A significant aspect of this printing activity is its geographic distribution. While in the Northern Song printing flourished in a few major centers, it appears to have remained somewhat localized. In the Southern Song, by contrast, prefectures throughout the empire availed themselves of the technology. The lists of titles printed by local governments show a division of labor according to the standard categories of Chinese bibliography: the Directorate of Education in the capital published canonical texts and histories (the *jing* and *shi* sections) while local entities focused on philosophers and belles-lettres (the *zi* and *ji* sections). This division breaks down as one gets further from the capital, since the classics and histories grew more difficult to obtain, thus creating a local market for facsimile editions.

Those engaged in private publishing divide into roughly four groups: Buddhist and Daoist temples, private academies, individual sponsors, and commercial printers. As Sören Edgren notes, these distinctions are not perfect:

> Since the commercial and non-commercial aspects of publishing were not always clearly separated at the time, for example, there were Buddhist temples that printed and sold books for a profit . . . The designations are confused by the fact that an institutional religious follower might well publish a book as a private individual, and a private person might publish a book institutionally through the auspices of a family school or ancestral hall. Even the government functioned commercially whenever it offered its publications for sale.

The religious works produced by the temples included massive compilations like the Tripitaka, individual texts like the Lotus, Huayan, and Diamond Sutras, and a host of other more popular rather than elite devotional printings. The records of texts printed by the private academies show that they published the sorts of canonical, historical, and philosophical texts appropriate to their educational mission. The records also show how important the academies were in disseminating the writings of the major *Daoxue* figures from both the Northern and Southern Song.

Private individuals who sponsored publishing include filial sons like Lu Ziyu who dutifully printed the works of their fathers, grandfathers, and earlier ancestors. They also include, significantly, writers who published their own works as well as writings that they thought should be preserved. For example, when Ye Mengde was magistrate of Xuchang county in Henan (between 1118 and 1120), he, Su Guo (Su Shi's son), and local literati gathered for a day of group composition and produced a manuscript text, the *Xuchang chouchang ji*. In 1144 Han Yuanji asked Ye Mengde if a copy of the volume still existed. Han eventually obtained a copy, and in 1175 he happened to be prefect in the printing center of Jian'an at the same time that the grandson of Su Guo held a post there. The two discussed the volume and decided it should be published to preserve the record of voices long since extinguished.

The commercial publishers produced a wide variety of texts. Some, like the much-criticized printers of Masha in Fujian, produced cheap aids for studying for the examinations, books whose texts were densely crowded onto poor-quality paper. Others created extremely fine woodcut prints of canonical and historical materials that reflected careful scholarship and rigorous editing. Ming-sun Poon stresses that commercial printers were quick to respond to market pressures. When, for example, the Southern Song emperor Xiaozong added a test of archery to the civil service examination, such books as *The Enlarged Encyclopedia of Archery* appeared shortly thereafter. Similarly, Poon notes that in Hangzhou, for which the data on booksellers is best, there was a trend toward specialization. Booksellers focused on Buddhist texts, or miscellaneous writings, or classics, histories, or poetry. Commercial printers also were quick to meet demands for a particular book: Edgren cites the example of a text published by the Hangzhou prefectural school in 1139 and pirated in Ninghua in Fujian Province three years later. Commercial printers also met market pressures by differentiating their editions from those of their competitors. While many editions of Han Yu's work existed, one claimed to be a *New Edition of [Han] Changli's Literary Collection Annotated by Five Hundred Scholars with Pronunciation Notes*. Similarly extravagant claims were made for editions of works by Du Fu, Su Shi, and Huang Tingjian. The edition of Su Shi's poetry annotated by the famous Southern Song scholar Wang Shipeng is particularly famous because it was a blatant forgery. Some commercial printers, however, took their vocations very seriously. Zhu Xi, for example, owned a print shop, but defended its commercial nature by arguing that other alternatives for earning money were even worse. At the same time, he also lamented that some publishers acted out of purely mercenary incentives. Chen Qi, an important bookseller in Hangzhou, was an active participant in the poetic circles of his day. He not only printed the volume of contemporary poetry *The Rivers and Lakes Collection*, which gave the name to the poetic milieu, but also published many minor Late Tang poets to make them more generally available.

Poetic style and the literary elite

Huang Tingjian famously claimed that no word in Du Fu's poetry lacked a literary provenance and that poets should follow Du Fu's example in creatively appropriating the language offered by China's written legacy. Writers in the late Northern Song took up this challenge as the most *au courant* mode and thus created the distinctive, difficult Jiangxi style. However, the small coterie of writers who initially espoused the style quickly discovered that to write poetry building upon past texts required either extensive learning or a good source of recherché allusions. When the marketplace provided convenient sources – including well-annotated editions of Du Fu's poetry – leading writers came to damn the style as a form of shallow mannerism. Roger Chartier, a major scholar of European print culture, introduces the ideas of dissemination and distinction to describe a similar pattern in French culture:

> Processes of imitation and popularization . . . need to be thought of as competitive efforts in which any instance of dissemination – whether granted or hard-won – was met with a search for new procedures for distinction. This can be seen in the career of the notion of *civilité*, defined both as a normative concept and as the conduct it demanded. As this notion was diffused throughout the society by appropriation or inculcation, it gradually lost the esteem it had enjoyed among the very people whose social personalities it described. They were then led to prize other concepts and other codes of manners. The same process can perhaps be seen in reading practices, which became increasingly differentiated as printed matter came to be less scarce, less often confiscated, and less socially distinguishing. For a long period, ownership of an object – the book – in and of itself signified social distinction; gradually, different ways of reading became the distinguishing factor, and thus a hierarchy among plural uses of the same material was set up. We need, then, to replace simplistic and static representations of social domination or cultural diffusion with a way of accounting for them that recognizes the reproduction of gaps within the mechanisms of imitation, the competition at the heart of similarities, and the development of new distinctions arising from the very process of diffusion.

These entwined processes of dissemination and distinction lead to what sociologist Pierre Bourdieu calls the "field of cultural production" of an advanced society, where people rely on constantly evolving, mutually defining cultural positions to compete in creating, accumulating, and using cultural capital. When too many writers learned to emulate the Jiangxi style of difficult allusions and tonally syncopated prosody, leading writers called for a new standard. Lü Benzhong, who wrote the essay proclaiming the existence of a "Jiangxi School of poetry," explained in one letter,

Poems like Cao Zhi's "Seven Laments" are broad, vast, deep, and distant and are not something which we composers can attain. This is because they never directed their intention toward their language. Although the Jiangxi scholars of recent times take compass in one hand and right-angle in the other and expend all their effort, they mostly do not know [that they should] go beyond this. They have climbed a hundred-foot pole but cannot advance another inch and have failed to understand Huang Tingjian's intent.

Lü also presented a new standard that only cognoscenti could grasp:

> Those who study poetry ought to come to know the "method of liveliness."
> The so-called "method of liveliness" is when one has the compass and square at the ready but one can go beyond the compass and square, transforming in unpredictable ways and yet not violating [the norms of] the compass and square. In this practice, there is a definable method that is without definition, there is an indefinable method that is definable. If one knows this, I can speak with him about the method of liveliness.

Critics of the next generation then developed the idea of the "method of liveliness" in ways that attenuated its connection to the easily mastered formal techniques of the "compass and square" and stressed its naturalness, spontaneity, and connection with larger processes of creativity. Zhang Yuangan (1091–ca 1170), for example, asserted that "composition comes from the crucible of Creative Transformation [zaohua], and the primal qi joins together within the breast. From ancient times this has been called the 'method of liveliness.'"

By the early Southern Song, the "method of liveliness" in turn proved too successful. Zhou Fu (d. ca 1174) complained,

> Take care not to believe what those who speak of poetry explain about the "method of liveliness." Now what the former generation called the "method of liveliness" was that, having read broadly and exerted great effort, they did not know why [their successful writings] were thus, and yet they were thus, so [they argued that] the "method of liveliness" must be reached through awakening and through effort. Yet people now write a type of unskilled and flavorless phrasing and say "My poem is without difficulty and obscurity: this is the method of liveliness." If it were like this, then one could burn up the *Classic of Poetry* and "Encountering Sorrow."

Claims for the virtues of ease and transparency created the opportunity for counterclaims stressing the importance of crafting that differed as well from the focus on diction and difficult prosody of the Jiangxi style. The Four Lings of Yongjia, who called for a return to the couplet-crafting of the Late Tang style, filled this new niche and were abetted by printers like Chen Qi who made many of the Late Tang poets available to the contemporary audience.

The Four Lings' espousal of Late Tang poetry, however, merely provided a new model to emulate and a new position to attack. Xue Shishi (1178–1228) also was from Yongjia and wrote poetry with the Four Lings, but Zhao Ruhui (*jinshi* 1214), writing a preface to Xue's collections, sought to differentiate him by stressing the poetic virtue of "ancient blandness" (*gudan*) that Zhao saw in Xue's poetry and which he linked to Tao Qian, Xie Lingyun, Du Fu, and Wei Yingwu. The counterposition that became far better known during the Ming was that of Yan Yu, who argued that the poets of Tang Xuanzong's reign – the High Tang poets – were the only Tang poets worthy of emulation. In addition to these oppositional stances arising from within literary discourse, there were also the *Daoxue* advocates attacking the significance of writing poetry at all. It is important to note that as the new positions appeared, the older ones did not disappear but shifted with the new competition. People continued through the end of the dynasty to attack the misguided poets writing in the Jiangxi style. People continued to fight over Du Fu and what it meant to truly understand him: as Ming-sun Poon notes, for example, the very late Southern Song writer Chen Gu (fl. 1279) harrumphed, "Those who do not have Directorate books in their bellies cannot possibly understand Du Fu's poems."

Poetic groups: the social organization of style

The standard histories of Southern Song poetry list the names of the competing styles as they emerge – the Jiangxi School, the Four Lings of Yongjia, and the "Rivers and Lakes School" – and assume the existence of three self-conscious, self-identified groups of practitioners. Each "school" appears to have been well defined. Lü Benzhong provided the list of those in the Jiangxi group. The Four Lings were four well-known poets, while those writers included in the *Rivers and Lakes Collection* can be considered the roster of the "Rivers and Lakes" group. On closer inspection, however, none of this holds up very well. Many of those listed by Lü Benzhong were unhappy with their inclusion, and, in general, comments about Jiangxi poets in the *shihua* literature tend to target unnamed later imitators rather than those on Lü Benzhong's list. There is no evidence at all to suggest that these late practitioners formed a self-conscious group. In contrast, the Four Lings were a very self-consciously defined group, but the significance of their forming a group is open to question. Wang Chuo, writing the funerary inscription for Xue Shishi, recorded that although the Four Lings were the first poets in Yongjia to write in the Late Tang manner, a long list of writers succeeded them in the next generation.

Zhang Hongsheng, the modern scholar who has written the most thorough account of the "Rivers and Lakes" group, argues that it probably is best to treat the Four Lings of Yongjia as simply part of a larger trend to appropriate Late Tang poetry as a reaction against the aesthetic values of the Jiangxi style. Zhang also concludes that using the writers included in the *Rivers and Lakes Collection* to define the group does not work very well. First, there are significant discrepancies between different versions of the text, so who was or was not part of the original anthology is at times hard to say. More crucially, the term had long been used to refer to literati on the margins of official society, and this broader meaning grew increasingly relevant in the political turmoil of the late Southern Song Dynasty. When late in life Liu Kezhuang wrote of his "friends of the Rivers and Lakes Community" (*jianghu sheyou*), he probably referred to this larger group rather than to those specifically included in the original anthology.

The basic questions behind the problems of "schools of poetry" in the Southern Song are in what sort of formal and informal social groups people wrote their poetry and how those groups shaped actual practice. Ouyang Guang has written the most thorough study of extant materials on Song Dynasty poetry groups, and his results suggest that the Four Lings, who developed a program and – in the coherence and longevity of their project – had an impact on poetic practice, were the unique exception rather than the rule. Although there is clear evidence of self-consciously formed "poetry communities" (*shishe*), most of these groups centered on some particular occasion of group composition. Even when a sense of a group identity lingered on after the event or found substantial expression through the creation of a volume, the clubs rarely attained any formal organization. A few clubs seem to have met regularly for writing and criticism, but there is no evidence that any of these endured very long. The group compositions appear to have circulated (seemingly in manuscript rather than print form) and to have been greeted with enthusiasm by other writers, who would express their regrets at not having been at the outing that occasioned the poems and who would send their own poems matching the rhymes and topics used by the group. Ouyang Guang sharply contrasts these groups with the sort of large poetry communities that formed in the Yuan and which mounted impressive poetry competitions in which themes would be announced in the fall, invitations sent out to local poetry groups, and the results announced in the spring. There does not seem to have been a continuous evolution of such groups out of Southern Song practice; the Yuan dynasty clubs were instead a response to the rupture of the Mongol conquest.

The Southern Song poetry groups also seem to have been almost exclusively the domain of the literati. Some were formed by students honing their skill in composition as they studied for the official examinations, but most of those for which records survive seem to have centered on literati with some reputation for poetry. Ouyang Guang finds no evidence of merchant or artisan guild poetry groups even in Hangzhou, where a large enough merchant community existed to have created at least the opportunity for such groups. Although urban society nurtured new performance genres in drama and storytelling, literary distinction seems to have remained defined – at least in extant documents – in strictly literati terms that merchants did not contest.

Literary identity in the Southern Song no doubt had a local component. It was nurtured by the practice of publishing the collections of local writers and those of writers who came to be associated with a place. Local identity, however, did not take the institutional form of long-term clubs for the literati of a particular area. Although Liu Kezhuang was from Putian in Fujian and was well informed about events there, his poetry drew from his broader connections both with the *Daoxue* community and with the "Rivers and Lakes" writers from across the empire. Similarly, Wen Tianxiang was clearly conscious of being from Luling County and Jizhou prefecture, but he looked to the broader tradition to define his role as a writer. The various names of ostensible groups – particularly Jiangxi and "Rivers and Lakes" – prove to be convenient labels for approaches that a writer could take to define himself within the literary culture. They referred to important and distinctive aesthetic values, but they did not point to any larger form of coherent social organization.

IV. Elite literature of the Jin dynasty to 1214
Michael A. Fuller

When the Northern Song fell to the Jurchen invaders, those members of the urban elite who could flee south did so. Still, there does not appear to have been a massive shift in the population of China as a whole, nor does the basic social organization of the countryside in the north appear to have changed. Unlike what would happen in the early Yuan dynasty, the new Jin rulers continued to use the examination system to recruit officials from among the Chinese elite, so that a large class of disenfranchised literati did not develop, with the sort of impact on literature so evident in the Yuan. Nevertheless, writers still had to confront the inescapable facts of the collapse of the Song and the presence of the Jurchen rulers. The Chinese elite was largely isolated from the cultural centers of the south and needed to negotiate the new social, military, and political structures of Jurchen rule. Thus while the literate elite retained fundamental cultural commitments inherited from the late Northern Song, they also confronted new circumstances that challenged those commitments and recast them into new cultural forms.

Because relatively few Jin dynasty texts survive, our knowledge of Jin cultural history remains very limited. Only a handful of individual literary collections have survived intact, and these are from late in the dynasty. Diligent scholars in the Qing dynasty managed to reassemble some collections, and modern scholars have further enlarged the corpus of materials; still, the results are meager when compared to the wealth of texts available from the Southern Song. Given this limitation, the sketch of the development of Jin literature offered below is tentative and leaves many important questions unanswered.

Most studies divide Jin dynasty literature into three periods. The initial phase begins in 1115, when Aguda (1068–1123) proclaimed the founding of the dynasty, and ends with the assassination of Wanyan Liang, the Hailing Prince, in 1161. (Because Wanyan Liang came to the throne through violence, proved a brutal ruler, and met a bloody end, he was given the posthumous title of "prince" rather than "emperor.") So little literature, however, remains from the founding of the Jin until the defeat of the Northern Song in 1127, that the discussion here will begin with the fall of the Northern Song. A middle period, corresponding to the peak of Jin rule, spans the reigns of Emperor Shizong (1123–1189, r. 1161–1189), Emperor Zhangzong (1168–1208, r. 1189–1208), and the Weishao Prince (r. 1208–1213). (The Weishao Prince succeeded to the throne as emperor, but he proved inadequate to the task of resisting the Mongols. He was assassinated and replaced, and his posthumous title was reduced to "prince.") In the final phase, the dynasty declined but literature flourished: this phase begins in 1214, when the Jin moved the capital from present-day Beijing to the old Song capital of Kaifeng because of Mongol military encroachments, and ends with the death of the last Jin emperor in 1234. However, most of the major writers who came to maturity during this final period lived into the Yuan and wrote much of their most important work after the fall of the Jin and under the pressure of dynastic catastrophe. It is best, therefore, to consider their writings as part of the story of the development of Yuan dynasty literature, and accordingly they will be discussed in the next chapter rather than in this.

The early Jin: "borrowing talent from another dynasty"

Zhuang Zhongfang, the Qing dynasty compiler of a major anthology of Jin literature, observed that although writing flourished after the defeat of the Northern Song, the initial period was shaped by quite literal appropriation; that is, by capturing Song dynasty writers. These writers fall into two groups: those who acquiesced to serve the Jin and those who resisted. Among those who served were Cai Songnian (1107–1159), Wu Ji (1090–1142), Yuwen Xuzhong (1079–1146, passed the civil service examination in 1109), and Gao Shitan (d. 1146). The best known among those who resisted the Jin while in captivity are Zhu Bian (d. 1144), Hong Hao (1088–1155), Sima Pu (fl. 1135), Teng Maoshi (d. 1128), and Yao Xiaoxi (fl. 1145).

Cai Songnian was captured while his father was serving in north China in 1125 (that is, before the conquest). He rose to the high rank of right prime minister but eventually attracted the suspicion of the famously bloody-minded Hailing Prince and was killed. Cai excelled in energetic old-style forms and in Su Shi's "unbridled" song lyric style. Cai begins what scholars identify as the characteristically bold and emotionally direct "northern" style of the Jin. Wu Ji, the son of a Northern Song chief minister and the son-in-law of the important Northern Song literati painter and calligrapher Mi Fu, was sent as part of a court mission to the Jin at the end of Emperor Huizong's reign. Because of his reputation as an artist, he was detained in the Jin capital, and after the fall of the Northern Song he joined the Jin Hanlin Academy. Later he also served as a district governor. Wu Ji primarily is known as a writer of *ci* song lyrics. Although his lyrics initially were closer to the Northern Song mainstream, his style evolved while in the north. The following lyric, which Wu reportedly wrote on encountering a former Song palace maid serving wine at a banquet, blends Su Shi's seriousness with the standard *ci* theme of the forlorn woman and is a pastiche of literary allusions:

> In the land of ancient heartbreak of the Southern Court,
> They still sing "Flowers in the Rear Courtyard."
> In former times, the Wang and Xie clans:
> The swallows before their halls,
> Have flown into commoners' homes.
> As if awakened from dream in this encounter,
> A heaven-granted appearance purer than snow,
> Palace coiffure of piled raven.
> The adjutant of Jiangzhou,
> Blue shirt damp with tears:
> Alike we are at Heaven's edge.

Yuwen Xuzhong was sent north on a diplomatic mission by Emperor Gao-zong, the first Southern Song emperor. He was detained by the Jin and served in the Hanlin Academy. He was, however, accused of plotting to rescue the two captive Northern Song emperors and executed. Along the way, he perhaps unintentionally implicated Gao Shitan, another former Song official serving the Jin: as part of their evidence against Yuwen, the Jin accusers noted that he had many maps of China. Yuwen pointed out to them that this was not unusual since, for example, Gao had even more maps than he did. They then arrested and executed Gao as well. Both men were important poets and writers of song lyrics. Like Wu Ji and Cai Songnian, they frequently wrote of their longing for home in a plain manner very different from the crafting of the Jiangxi style of the late Northern Song. Gao laments in "Unable to Sleep,"

> Unable to sleep, I put on my coarse short jacket.
> Dragging a staff, I walk out the gate.
> The moon, close to the mid-autumn, is white.
> The wind after midnight grows pure.
> 'Midst turmoil and separation, I was startled by last night's dream.
> Drifting about, I recall my life so far.
> With tearing eyes, I look to the Southern Dipper:
> I cannot forget my feelings for my former land.

The Jin court detained Teng Maoshi while he was serving as an envoy in 1126; they detained Zhu Bian in 1127 and Hong Hao in 1129. All refused to serve. Teng died in the north and left instructions that his tomb inscription read, "Tomb of Teng Maoshi of Dongyang, Song envoy." Zhu and Hong finally managed to return to the south in 1143 after the peace treaty between the Southern Song and the Jin was signed. Their place in Jin dynasty literary history comes less from any innovations or brilliance of style than from their simple persistence in writing of the desire to go home.

One additional aspect of early Jin literature that is difficult to assess is the large collection of song lyrics written by followers of the new Quanzhen Daoist sect and preserved in the Daoist canon. The *Complete Jin and Yuan Lyrics* has 670 lyrics attributed to the sect's founder, Wang Zhe (1113–1170), who took the Daoist name "Master Double-Yang," and 866 lyrics attributed to his disciple Ma Jue (1123–1184), "Master Cinnabar-Yang." Some of these are straight Daoist verse, some are teaching verse, and others are allegorical lyrics on objects designed to illustrate the Way. Finally, there are many, many laments for the hardships the poets encountered. Only by the time of Qiu Chuji (1143–1227), "Master Long Spring," who has 152 lyrics, do the themes and language of the lyrics begin to largely resemble practices in the larger literati community. In all, however, the Quanzhen Daoist lyrics comprise three-quarters of all extant Jin dynasty song lyrics. We cannot know whether this cache of lyrics by chance preserves one sample of widespread but long-lost writing practices among educated Chinese who stayed away from the capital or whether these particular Daoist masters were uniquely active in writing their own style of lyric for their small Quanzhen audience. The survival of these lyrics reminds us of all that did not survive and that, in the end, our knowledge of the broader character of literati culture in the early Jin remains very limited.

The middle period: the reigns of Emperor Shizong and Emperor Zhongzong: the historical and cultural contexts

Before examining the development of literature during the middle years of the Jin dynasty, it is useful to review briefly the cultural dynamics driving change in the south. As bureaucratic infighting between the "war party" and the regime of Qin Gui replaced the factionalism of the late Northern Song, many officials advocating retaking the north stood by their principles and found themselves demoted to sinecures. Lacking a direct means of influence, many turned to writing and scholarship. As competition in the examination system grew increasingly fierce and created a market for printed materials that promised students an advantage in the struggle, many unsuccessful candidates sought to establish their reputations through writing. At the same time, the government began withdrawing from activity at the local level, leaving the landed elites to seek a new basis for moral authority. They provided an audience for the Learning of the Way and its curriculum guiding the self-cultivation that *Daoxue* advocates considered central to the moral life. The Southern Song thus developed a large, ambitious, and concerned audience; vibrant urban centers; a thriving printing industry; and writers of literary texts who responded to the many crosscurrents of philosophical, political, and aesthetic debates of the period by staking out distinctive positions.

The contexts for writing and the forces shaping literary change in the Jin dynasty were very different as institutions matured during Emperor Shizong's and Emperor Zhangzong's reigns. The primary contrasts with the south were in the nature of the cultural debates, the audience participating in those debates, the circulation of texts, and the role of literature in shaping how writers participated in the larger culture.

The basic question confronting the literate Chinese elite in the north was how to understand their role as men of learning and culture in a society ruled by the Jurchen. Given the clan-based *meng'an* and *mouke* organization of Jurchen society, the Chinese literati had to justify a centralized civil government of the officials appointed by a state bureaucracy. At the level of practice, justification was simple: the Jin rulers already were aware of the efficiency and effectiveness of control over a large sedentary population made possible by a centralized bureaucracy. Indeed, the Jurchen clans' resistance to the Hailing Prince's efforts to impose Chinese models of governance probably derived from their awareness that they were losing power to the ruling Wanyan clan through these reforms. Even though the growing bureaucracy served imperial purposes, nonetheless, the question remained: why staff the bureaucracy with broadly trained generalists rather than specialized clerks? Why choose Confucius over Han Feizi?

The literati idea of *wen* (the "patterned") encompassed aspects of experience ranging from civil government and ritual paraphernalia to essays, poems, and song lyrics. Within this broad understanding of *wen*, the question of its role in Jin society took particular form in the discussions at court about revising the examination system as a tool to recruit officials. Although the Jin had used examinations as one avenue of entry into the bureaucracy from the very beginning of the dynasty, the number of *jinshi* degrees awarded was relatively small. According to the research of Xue Ruizhao, during the nine examinations of Emperor Taizong's reign (1123–1134) approximately seventy candidates passed each year, with the exception of 1128 and 1129, when the numbers jumped to 811 and 140 respectively. During Emperor Xizong's reign (1135–1149), the number rose to about 250 men per examination, for a total of about 1,600, but then dropped again to seventy men per examination during the Hailing Prince's and Emperor Shizong's reigns, though there were times during Emperor Shizong's rule when as few as ten men passed (for a total of about 950 *jinshi* degrees awarded, excluding the Jurchen-language *jinshi* and those awarded by the puppet Qi state). Emperor Zhangzong, during the first year of his reign, increased the allotment to between three hundred and four hundred, but after 1203 the number of those who passed dropped again and steadily dwindled until the dynasty ended. It is of interest that in 1193 (early in Emperor Zhangzong's reign), for example, there were 11,499 officials: 4,705 Jurchen, 6,794 Chinese. Like the Tang, the Jin examination system provided only one relatively small route into government service, even at the height of Jin power during the reigns of Emperors Shizong and Zhangzong. Yet also, as in the Tang, the *jinshi* degree had a power to shape literati culture that far outstripped its actual role in recruitment. In part its power derived from its prestige. The Censorate, for example, played an increasingly important role in providing the emperors with policy criticism, and Emperor Shizong preferred to staff it with *jinshi* degree holders. In part, however, the *jinshi* degree also provided an officially promulgated model for the role of learning in governance. Wang Ruoxu (1174–1243), one of most important cultural figures of the mid- and late Jin, analyzed the four parts of the examination:

> The *fu* was to select talent for drafting documents, the *shi* poem was to choose [men who grasped] the purport of the "Airs" and "Lament" [of the *Classic of Poetry* and *Verses of Chu*], the policy essay was to probe the enterprise of managing the state, and the discourse was to investigate the method of historical reflection. [One can see] what kind of talent would be skilled at all four. (Peter Bol's translation, with modifications)

Wang Ruoxu's argument stressed the value of the accumulated knowledge of the civil order embodied in the Chinese historical tradition, and the moral and emotional truths underlying the belletristic tradition, and it returned to the understanding of *wen* espoused by central cultural figures of the mid-Northern Song like Ouyang Xiu and Su Shi. Yet this was not just nostalgia. Wang's explanation of the examination had to offer reasons why mastery of *wen* gave one authority to exercise power, and it turns out that the mid-Northern Song account provided good reasons. The issue confronting Jin literati here differed deeply from that which engaged Southern Song elites, who needed to explain how learning could justify authority *outside* of participation in the imperial bureaucracy. Although Jin writers often are viewed as backward-looking and derivative, the Jin use of mid-Northern Song models was in fact a creative appropriation to address contemporary issues of justifying *wen* in governance rather than mere repetition of old positions.

Another aspect of the power of the examination in shaping Jin dynasty literati culture is more speculative because the sources are so few. Nonetheless, the examination system seems to have contributed to the creation of the social networks and circulation of texts that culminated in the literary community that supported the distinctive styles of Zhao Bingwen, Wang Ruoxu, Li Chunfu, and Yuan Haowen (1190–1257). During the reigns of Emperors Shizong and Zhangzong, participation in the examination slowly increased. Six years after Shizong came to the throne, the Jin court created the Imperial Academy (*Taixue*), and a decade after that ordered the creation of prefectural schools. Four years later, in 1180, qualifying examinations were held in the prefectures, and over the next decade both schools and prefectural examinations spread. That is, participation in examination culture penetrated ever more deeply into local society. Teachers and texts, printed by the government printing office in Pingshui, circulated more widely. More members of the literate elite learned something close to a common curriculum and shared cultural references. Master–pupil relationships reached beyond local allegiances and spanned the long distance between the Yellow River plains and the Central Capital (modern Beijing). It may well have been that the distance between the political center, where men of talent and ambition went to make their way in the world, and the center of population slowed the process of creating a vibrant literary community: Yuan Haowen noted the irony that the shift of the capital from Zhongdu (with a population of 225,592 households in 1207) to Kaifeng (1,746,210 households) in 1214 marked a disaster for the empire but caused literature to flourish. The effect on writing appeared to be sudden, but it perhaps was the culmination of the slow processes of building literati communities that was aided by the examination system during Emperor Shizong's and Emperor Zhangzong's reigns.

Writing during Emperor Shizong's and Emperor Zhongzong's reigns

Much of what we know about Jin literature comes from Yuan Haowen's determined effort to preserve as much of the dynasty's cultural legacy as possible. After the Mongol conquest, Yuan traveled throughout north China to collect poems for his *Central Region Collection* (*Zhongzhou ji*), in which he added brief biographical sketches of the authors as introductions to the poems he selected. Although later work has supplemented the *Zhongzhou ji*, Yuan Haowen's views continue to deeply inform our understanding of the period. In his biography of Cai Gui (*jinshi* 1151, d. 1174), the son of Cai Songnian, Yuan explains the rise of a genuinely Jin dynasty literature:

> The literati officials [*wenshi*] like Academician Yuwen [Xuzhong], Councilor Cai [Songnian], and Wu [Ji] of Shenzhou must be called men of outstanding talent and courage, but they all are scholars from the Song dynasty, and one cannot discuss them as part of our dynasty's literary current. Thus one can assert that Cai Gui was the progenitor of [our] orthodox transmission, Dang [Huaiying] of Zhuxi followed him, and then Minister of Rites Zhao Bingwen followed next.

Yuan points to successive generations of writers that span the period from 1161 to 1214. The first group of writers to begin defining the distinctive styles of the Jin included Cai Gui, Wang Ji (1128–1194), and Liu Ji, all three of whom passed the civil service examination in 1151. Following them were Dang Huaiying (1134–1211, *jinshi* 1170), Liu Ying (d. 1180, *jinshi* 1174), and Zhou Ang

(d. 1211, *jinshi* 1179). Zhao Bingwen (1159–1232, *jinshi* 1185), the most important writer of the middle period, belongs to a slightly later generation that came to maturity during Emperor Shizong's long reign. The final generation of writers before the transfer of the capital to Kaifeng includes two distinctive but opposed voices – Wang Ruoxu (1174–1243, *jinshi* 1197) and Li Chunfu (1177?–1223?, *jinshi* 1197) – as well as perhaps the best writer from the imperial clan, Wanyan Tao (1172–1232), and Li Junmin (1176–1260), an important writer of lyrics.

Cai Gui primarily was important as a prose stylist and poet and is best known for reintroducing intentional crafting after the earnest simplicity and directness of his father's generation. Earlier writers, for example, had condemned the artifice of writing poems matching rhymes, but Cai Gui revived the practice. Still, his style cannot compare to the mannered inwardness of the Jiangxi writers of the Southern Song at the time. Wang Ji and Liu Ji, like Cai, continued to develop the early Jin plain style with added refinement. Li Chunfu described Liu Ji's poetry as "plain but not crude, limpid but not cold, simple but with structure, light but with flavor." This group of writers seems largely to have been consolidating earlier trends and adding flexibility and suppleness to the plain directness preferred by the writers who lived through the founding of the Jin.

Dang Huaiying, Liu Ying, Zhou Ang, and other writers of the Hailing Prince's reign added boldness and energy to the plain style but also began increasingly to look to the range of styles offered by the canonical poetic tradition. Dang Huaiying is perhaps best remembered for discussing the merits of fleeing to the south with Xin Qiji, when both were students of Liu Ji. Xin Qiji carried south with him the "northern" bold style of song lyric based on Su Shi, while Dang remained in the Jin and eventually rose to the office of policy critic as a Hanlin Academy recipient of edicts. Dang was skilled at several different poetic styles and was the best writer of his generation in both parallel and old-style prose forms. He attained the sort of representational use of abstract wit that was associated with Su Shi, as in the quatrain entitled, "When I Awoke from Sleep, Outside the Gate, the Moonscape Was Like a Painting; a Frosty Wind Blew Steadily and Made a Sound: I Wrote This Quatrain":

The old tree had lived through frost; the many holes were empty.
The moon was bright, and the deep night reverberated with autumn wind.
I then came to understand that the pipes of heaven are not human pipes:
The "blowing of the ten thousand" from the beginning in fact is different.

In contrast, Liu Ying added energy to the plain style to explore mundane and frequently harsh experience in poems like "Ballad of the Shattered Cart," "Sand so Vast," and "Ballad of Repairing the Wall." In "Repairing the Wall," for example, he writes, "When they built it, they used only chicken-shit paste; / The wind and rain having broken it, when dried, it then cracked."

Zhao Bingwen passed the civil service examination in 1185, near the end of Emperor Shizong's twenty-eight-year reign. His rise to prominence as a major cultural figure who served as the trusted adviser to four emperors came in part through his own ability. In part, however, the Jin state, the officials who staffed it, and the literati community that provided the men to serve as officials all had achieved a level of sophistication that made them particularly receptive to the civil and cultural values that Zhao Bingwen embodied. Emperor Zhangzong was not as forceful a personality as Emperor Shizong, but he was an able administrator who implemented important reforms. Despite the constant increase in the Mongol threat, a series of natural calamities, and the Southern Song war of 1206, he believed in the importance of the civil bureaucracy. Zhao Bingwen, as an astute student of the past, offered Emperor Zhangzong the valuable perspective of the Chinese historical record. Zhao also presented the Jin civil elite a comprehensive model for learning from – without becoming mired in – the past that applied to literary as well as political and moral issues.

In his "Letter Answering Li [Jing] Tianying," for instance, Zhao insists that one must learn from men as well as from one's own innate mind. He acknowledges that the writings of the great authors of the past reflect their own distinctive personalities and that, by implication, in the end one should write from the core of one's own self. Still, he argues, it is folly not to learn from the past. Zhao's conclusion that Li should "take the mind of ancient people as his mind" and that it was wrong to "receive [models and methods] from Heaven but not receive [them] from men" has implications well beyond the matters of prose, poetry, and calligraphy that are the explicit topics of the letter. Zhao Bingwen's defense of the aesthetic crafting of texts – of moving beyond the plain, unselfconscious style – extends Su Shi's argument about representational adequacy:

> Writing takes intentions as central, and phrasing is simply to convey the intent. Ancient writing did not esteem empty ornament; it relied on the matter at hand to bring forth the phrasing in order to give shape to that which the mind wished to say. On occasion there is that which the mind cannot say, but it can give shape to it in the patterning [wen]: this is the ultimate in writing [wen].

That is, aesthetic structure provides a second level of organization that extends the representational power of language. This argument makes a pragmatic claim ("it can give shape to it in the patterning") that appeals to experience without the need to draw on any metaphysical grounding and marks the distance between Jin and Southern Song culture.

Zhao Bingwen's own writing reflects his commitment both to past models and to a focus on "conveying the intent." His prose, in both parallel and old-style forms, followed the models of the major Northern Song masters, Ouyang Xiu and Su Shi: it was spare yet elegant and on occasion introduced more crafted elements to keep the text interesting. His particular forte was the informal account (za ji). As a poet, he excelled at imitations, with a preference for High Tang landscape poetry, as in "Imitating Wang Wei's 'Sitting Alone in a Secluded Bamboo Brake'":

> Walking alone in a secluded grove,
> I chat of the obscure and contemplate transformation.
> The western sun half-taken by the peaks,
> It gleams back on rocks within the grove.
> On the rocks, there is much old moss.
> The mountain flowers intersperse red and green.
> The flowers fall: people do not know –
> The mountains are empty, and the waters flow out.

However, Zhao Bingwen also used his imitative impulse to create verse very distinctively marked as Jin dynasty poetry. For example, he uses the model of Wang Wei's "Observing the Hunt" to write of actual battle:

> Below the Wall of Luzhou
> The moon is haloed at dawn as we surround the city.
> The wind high at night as we chop wood for the encampment.
> The sound of horns: the cold water stirs.
> The force of the bows: an isolated swan startles.
> Sharp arrows penetrate the Wu armor.
> Long halberds break the hat-strings of Chu.
> Looking back to where we had fought,
> Dull and dismal, the dusk chill grows.

Like Zhao Bingwen, Wang Ruoxu had a distinguished official career. He studied under his uncle Zhou Ang, who was a friend of Zhao, and shared many of his values. Wang Ruoxu, however, is best remembered as a critic who wrote on all aspects of the Chinese textual tradition. He was deeply committed to learning from the past, but he was not intimidated by it. He, for example, proposed corrections to Ouyang Xiu's and Su Shi's phrasing in some of their most famous compositions. Although he was well aware of trends in the Learning of the Way and wrote a postface to a text entitled *Tracing the Origins of the Learning of the Way*, his sense of the centrality of feelings (*qing*) in governance much more closely resembled Ouyang Xiu's, while his discussion of inherent pattern (*li*) in writing echoed Su Shi, with little impact from the Learning of the Way. Similarly, while he was aware of Southern Song discussions of poetry that stressed crafting, he argued for writing that derived from experience and, like Zhao Bingwen, valued technique committed to representation. In his important and influential *Hunan Remarks on Poetry*, for example, he complains,

> The ancient poets, although with different interests and styles, all took their writing from what they attained themselves. As for their phrasing, conveying the intent and the order [*li*] being consistent, all were adequate to become famous: when did they ever use "line method" [*jufa*] to measure out men? Huang Tingjian's opening his mouth to discourse on "line method" is precisely where he could not reach the level of the ancient people. And his disciples pass along his robe and bowl and proclaim themselves *dharma* successors: how could this be the true principle of poetry!

Wang Ruoxu was a better critic than belletristic writer. In his many analytic essays, he used a lucid, simple style to set out his arguments, but his poetry and other verse forms are not very noteworthy. Perhaps his most famous poems are a series of five quatrains he wrote on returning to his home after the fall of the Jin. In the third he notes,

> The mountain apricots and valley peaches have changed to thorn-bush.
> The dancing terraces and song halls collapsed into ash and dust.
> Since spring arrived, here where I can bear to travel, for what reason
> Does a drifting oriole outside the gate in vain call to people?

Critics have accused Zhao Bingwen and Wang Ruoxu of simply copying the styles and arguments of Ouyang Xiu and Su Shi. While both Zhao and Wang openly admired Ouyang and Su and indeed took positions clearly deriving from these Northern Song models, their appropriations are not simple. Much had changed between Su Shi's death in 1101 and Emperor Zhangzong's ascension to the throne in 1189. Zhao and Wang were leaders of an emerging Jin literati stratum who needed to be able to justify their status as literary men who were also close advisers to the emperor. Ouyang Xiu and Su Shi offered a substantive account of *wen* (the "patterned") that linked civil governance to the facts of human experience; to the philosophical, historical, and literary traditions of writings reflecting on that experience; and to the crafting of texts in the present day. Zhao and Wang saw that the Northern Song account answered Jin dynasty questions, and they took it.

Li Chunfu presented an approach to culture and creativity that, compared to Zhao Bingwen and Wang Ruoxu, looked back less and insisted more on seeking answers within. He passed the civil sevice examination in the same year as Wang and served as a junior colleague of Zhao Bingwen, but he had a rather different sensibility. He was committed to integrating Buddhism and Confucianism and placed greater emphasis on the mind as source. Indeed, many of Zhao Bingwen's and Wang Ruoxu's comments warning of the folly of "taking the mind as teacher" were directed at Li, who was an enthusiastic patron of young men of talent and in a position to influence them. In the end, Li seems to have been more significant for his arguments about writing than for his compositions themselves. Li's surviving comments highlight an important difference between Southern Song and Jin literary thought in general. During the Southern Song, the sense of generic norms grew increasingly strong. Poetry and lyrics both had their "basic coloration" (*bense*), and compositions that violated the norms, even if interesting or compelling, were viewed as a dead end rather than a new approach to explore. Li Chunfu, in contrast, viewed form as a means rather than as an end and had a very expansive view of "poetry":

> People's minds are as different as their faces. When the "sound of the mind" comes forth as speech, the inner order [*li*] of the speech is called *wen*. If it is *wen* and has a segmented rhythm, it is called poetry. Thus poetry is a transformation of *wen*: how can there be a definite form? Therefore in the *Classic of Poetry* the poems are without a definite stanza structure, the stanza without a definite line structure, the lines without definite word-length, and the words without definite sound values. Large or small, long or short, difficult or easy, light or heavy are just to accord with one's intent.

Li Chunfu's insistence on form deriving from content points not only to theoretical differences with Southern Song poetics but also to a difference in practice that appears early in Jin poetry. Jin dynasty poets write about topics rarely broached by their contemporaries in the Southern Song, and they frequently do so in a loose old-style verse form that varies in line length and repeats phrases in a manner that captures the directness of speech and is relatively uncommon in southern writing of the time.

With the removal of the capital to Kaifeng, the city became the center of administration, population, and culture. The elite stratum became increasingly coherent at the same time that it was growing ever more anxious over the Mongol threat. The writers who emerged in this milieu found their distinctive voices in the chaos at the end of the dynasty, and survived into the Yuan dynasty to shape and preserve their accounts of the lost Jin.

V. Professionalism and the craft of song
Shuen-fu Lin

Classical poetry

The poets who lived through the transition from the Northern to the Southern Song (such as Lü Benzhong, Zeng Ji, and Chen Yuyi) and who were born around the reestablishment of the dynasty in the south (such as Lu You, Fan Chengda, and Yang Wanli) all without exception came under the influence of Huang Tingjian and the Jiangxi School. National calamity forced poets to question the validity of Huang's theory and practice. Lü Benzhong regretted having composed "The Genealogy of the Jiangxi Poetry Society" and criticized Huang's poetry for being at times too novel or ingenious. In a preface to a friend's collection written in 1133, he further said,

> One must learn the method of liveliness [huofa] when studying to write poetry. What is meant by the method of liveliness is that one should be equipped with knowledge of the rules and yet be able to go beyond them, and be able to change in an unpredictable way without going against them.

Here Lü is recalling Su Shi's statement about a more spontaneous and free approach to writing (specifically, "to set forth new ideas within rules, and to imply subtle principles beyond the vigorous and unconventional") as the method of liveliness to correct the limitation and rigidity of the Jiangxi School. His slogan of the "method of liveliness" was immediately endorsed by his friend Zeng Ji, who said, "Learning to write poetry is like doing Chan meditation: / One must be careful not to meditate on dead lines."

The great figures of the next generation, especially Lu You, Fan Chengda, and Yang Wanli, all practiced one or another form of the "method of liveliness" in their attempts to break away from the dominance of the Jiangxi School poetics. Lu learned to avoid "meditating on dead lines" from his teacher, Zeng Ji, and emphasized that the best "method" to learn how to write poetry was to stay away from books and to get in touch with life and with the world that exists outside of poetry. Although Lu You was not able to shake off completely the habit of using abundant allusions and sources and of mastering the craft of constructing fine couplets, he criticized as ludicrous Huang Tingjian's opinion that every word in Du Fu's poetry had a literary provenance. Fan Chengda tried to combine the qualities of Su Shi and Huang Tingjian, but to restrain them with gracefulness and vigor (*wanqiao*) in order to achieve a distinctive style of his own. Compared with Lu You and Yang Wanli, Fan Chengda preserved many more of the traits of the Jiangxi School. Like Huang Tingjian, Fan Chengda loved to use obscure allusions and expressions taken from Buddhist scriptures. Nevertheless, late in his life Fan wrote sixty quatrains under the general title of "Miscellaneous Sentiments of the Farm in the Four Seasons" which were lively and realistic depictions of rural life. These quatrains were greatly admired by later scholars and some of them have even been considered superior to the rural poetry of Tao Qian.

The poet who was most frequently associated with a method of liveliness was Yang Wanli. He started out as a student of the Jiangxi School and wrote more than a thousand poems which he later burned. He turned to study the quatrains of Wang Anshi, then turned to learn from the quatrains of Late Tang poets, and finally one day he attained some kind of enlightenment and stopped emulating anybody. He went out to his back garden and also visited an old city where he plucked flowers and bamboos, allowing everything to come to him as material for poetry. Yang's contemporaries praised him for having acquired a way to "take a dead snake and bring it back to life" and to "capture alive [the images of things]." The style he developed after obtaining his method of liveliness is known as the "Yang Chengzhai style" (*Yang Chengzhai ti*), Chengzhai being his literary name. This is a style of poetry that is vivacious, natural, and pungent, involving use of some common sayings and ordinary speech. Yang had not, however, completely liberated himself from the Jiangxi School's theory and practice. He closely followed Huang's principle of having "not a single word that lacks literary provenance." In using common sayings and ordinary speech, he would only use those that had appeared in poetry and prose since the Six Dynasties, or at least in official histories, story texts, and recorded comments of Chan masters. He did not employ ordinary diction indiscriminately. Perhaps the most important aspect of Yang's method of liveliness is his ability to reestablish a direct relationship with real things in the world, especially nature, reinvigorating his sense perception into a dynamic immediacy. He was able to produce many poems that vividly describe the beauty of nature. In general, Lu You, Fan Chengda, and Yang Wanli sought to replace the Jiangxi School's emphasis on prior poetic models and craft with a method of liveliness and a return to the real source of literature (that is, the world of experience), and to replace Huang Tingjian's allusive and difficult style with a more gracefully flowing and artfully crafted style of their own.

Apart from these three masters, few Southern Song poets had the talent and force of personality to make as decisive a break from the Jiangxi School. The great song lyricist Jiang Kui, who was also an accomplished *shi* poet, musician, and critic, went through a process of studying poetry similar to that of these three earlier poets. Being a native of Jiangxi, early in his life Jiang Kui came under the influence of Huang Tingjian, until his creativity was so stifled that he could not utter a word. He then realized that learning or imitation is a disease and shelved Huang's poetry. The poetics of the Jiangxi School, however, remained a significant influence in his poetic career. This is witnessed in the fact that his treatises on poetry, including two prefaces to his collected poetry and his important *White Stone Daoist's Discourse on Poetry* (*Baishi daoren shishuo*), extensively discuss such issues as harmony with the ancients, methods of writing poetry, defects of poetry, organization, chiseling of words, and how to use allusions. The influence of the Jiangxi style is also observable in his song lyrics. Faithful followers of the Jiangxi School continued to be found throughout the thirteenth century. Qiu Wanqing (?–1222), Hong Zikui (1176–1235), Fang Yue (1169–1262), Liu Chenweng, and Fang Hui (1227–1302) are good examples.

The Four Lings of Yongjia and the Rivers and Lakes poets were the major opponents of the Jiangxi School. While the Jiangxi School advocated "relying on books as materials for making poetry" (*zishu yiwei shi*), they recommended "abandoning books to write poetry" (*juanshu yiwei shi*). Instead of the Jiangxi School's fondness for using allusions, they prided themselves on not using them at all. While the Jiangxi school chose Du Fu of the High Tang as its model, they elevated Yao He and Jia Dao to be their idols for imitation. Compared to the views of Yang Wanli's generation, their propositions were narrow, extreme, and radical. The Four Lings and the Rivers and Lakes poets actually never departed very far from Jiangxi theory and practice. Imitation, an important argument in the Jiangxi School poetics, remained strong in their theory of poetry. The only difference is that these later poets picked fewer and minor models to imitate. Some poets in these groups continued the practice of "relying on books as materials for making poetry," except that the books they relied upon were restricted to Late Tang poetry. The most intriguing case is found in the poetry of Liu Kezhuang, the leading figure of the Rivers and Lakes School. Many of his regulated verses composed in the light and spry Late Tang style are studded with allusions and clichés. The Jiangxi style still held sway over these poets who rebelled against the Jiangxi School.

Song lyric

As extensively discussed in the previous chapter, by the late Northern Song, the song lyric, now an established form of literary expression for the literati, had, broadly speaking, developed in two distinct directions. While Su Shi was moving in the direction of "heroic abandon," other writers of the late Northern Song were trying to perfect the finer points of the art within the well-established tradition of "delicate restraint." Like Zhou Bangyan, Li Qingzhao, who lived in the era of transition from Northern Song to Southern Song, closely adhered to the normative subject matter of the genre in depicting tender feelings; she criticized Su Shi for attempting to write the song lyric like *shi* poetry and insisted on total compliance with the structure of "banquet music." In her "Discourse on the Song Lyric" (Cilun) she found fault with virtually every noted writer of the genre in the Northern Song up to her own day. The only person mysteriously left out in her critical evaluation was Zhou Bangyan, who synthesized virtually all previous forms in the style of "delicate restraint." Some modern scholars have speculated that this omission does not mean that Li approved of Zhou's works; rather, she had perhaps not yet known Zhou's works when she wrote the essay. In any event, the essay indicates that Li was a conservative defender of the qualities traditionally associated with the genre and that she set very high standards for all aspects of song lyrics, from singability, harmony between the tones of the words and music, and decorum in language to overall structure, narrative unity, and use of allusions.

Although some people through the ages have criticized Li for appearing arrogant, most scholars believe that her song lyrics have fully met the standards she herself set. One special characteristic of her works is the ability to adhere to the musical qualities and to combine literary and colloquial language to express her feelings. The song lyric set to the tune "Note after Note" (Shengsheng man) is the most famous example of her artistry. This is a piece from her Southern Song period that depicts her sense of sorrow, loneliness, and helplessness. The season is set in autumn. The piece begins with a series of seven sets of reduplicated words (*xunxun mimi / lengleng qingqing / qiqi cancan qiqi*: "search, search, seek, seek, / cold, cold, desolate, desolate, / bleak, bleak, wretched, wretched, sad, sad") describing the parallel complex states of the lyric speaker's heart and the outside world in autumn. It concludes with the visual and auditory image of the rain falling upon Chinese parasol trees at dusk, and the lyric speaker declaring, "How can this word 'sorrow' cover it all?" This work entails a powerful use of fifteen apical and forty-two dental sounds as well as a number of words sharing initials or finals. While Zhou Bangyan employed his cultivation and skill to write about staple subjects most of the time, Li used the song lyric form to express her personal joys and sorrows, celebrating the happiness of her marriage with Zhao Mingcheng, and recording the pain, suffering, and loneliness of her life as a widow living in the South after the fall of the Northern Song. Li's song lyrics, written in refreshingly natural language, had considerable influence in the early Southern Song. Even the hero–poet Xin Qiji, who emulated Su Shi's unrestrained style, wrote some song lyrics in imitation of her. But on the whole Zhou Bangyan commanded an influence larger than Li Qingzhao on Southern Song writers of "delicate restraint," as he was seen as the synthesizer of its developments before the fall of the Northern Song.

Although the explicit division between "delicate restraint" and "heroic abandon" was not made until Zhang Yan of the Ming dynasty, it roughly represents the actual development of the song lyric during the Song dynasty, as outlined above. Song lyricists did in fact produce works in both styles, even though individual writers came to be associated with either one style or the other. Thus Jiang Kui, Wu Wenying, Wang Yisun (late thirteenth century), Zhou Mi (1232–1298), and Zhang Yan (1248–1320?) were said to be in the lineage of "delicate restraint," following from Liu Yong, Qin Guan, Zhou Bangyan, and Li Qingzhao. Zhang Yuangan, Zhang Xiaoxiang (1132–1170), Xin Qiji, Liu Guo, and Liu Chenweng continue the style of "heroic abandon" developed by Su Shi. Southern Song song lyricists in either style were on the whole more sophisticated and professional than their Northern Song predecessors. Southern Song writers generally used more allusions in their song lyrics than before, especially when they used them as figures for their own sentiments or as indirect comments on contemporary situations. If the immense burden of the past drove *shi* poets to seek a method of liveliness, song lyricists faced a less daunting task in building something new on old forms and produced work that reached new artistic heights.

Xin Qiji is an epoch-making figure in the history of the song lyric. He is a writer with a superb skill in depicting a wide range of subjects in a variety of styles. His themes range from heroic and patriotic sentiments and comments on politics and philosophy of life to mundane emotions and representations of the simple and quiet pleasures of rural life. His styles vary from the impassioned and grand, the solemn and stirring, and the dejected and vehement to the gentle and sentimental, the refined and bland, and even the humorous and satirical. Building on Su Shi's pioneering efforts to write song lyrics like poems, Xin extended the range of song lyric further to compose lyrics like pieces of prose, breaking down the generic boundaries among prose, poetry, and the song lyric. He wrote some highly discursive song lyrics on philosophical topics, a practice seldom seen before. He frequently employed colloquial phrases, infusing his works with vitality and freshness. At the same time, his works were often filled with phrases and allusions drawn from such diverse sources as the Classics, historical and philosophical writings, and texts of poetry and fiction. He did all this without sacrificing the distinctive features of song lyric prosody. In all of his song lyrics the strong presence of Xin Qiji's personality can always be felt, placing him squarely in the mainstream of the Chinese lyrical tradition, which views poetry as a medium for self-expression. A heavy use of historical and textual allusions in the song lyric is another characteristic of Xin Qiji's work. About three-quarters of his extant corpus of 626 song lyrics, the largest collection of song lyrics in the Song, contain allusions. With 1,500 allusions in total, this is an average of three allusions per lyric. Such allusive thickness never obstructs the flow of his song lyrics or the strong voice of the lyric speaker. In the piece about parting from a cousin set to the tune of "Congratulating the Bridegroom" (He xinlang), for example, Xin enumerates five incidents of separation in Chinese history as the core of the work and mentions his own experience of the present moment in the opening and closing stanzas as a frame. The allusions serve as parallels for Xin's own experience of parting from his cousin and help to elevate his personal grief over separation to a universal level. He wrote another piece on the balloon guitar (pipa) also set to the tune "Congratulating the Bridegroom." This work consists almost entirely of allusions to stories about the instrument, and there is no reference to direct personal experience. Nonetheless, the reader can detect in it an implicit presence of a strong lyric speaker recounting the sad historical experiences associated with the balloon guitar. Xin Qiji's forceful and at times even wild and unruly personality may have made it difficult for him to break away from the mode of direct self-expression. His influence on later Southern Song *ci* writers was far-reaching. Those writers who were supporters of the war policy such as Han Yuanji (1118–1187), Chen Liang (1143–1194), Liu Guo, Liu Chenweng, and many others all came under his direct influence. Most of these song lyricists were able to emulate Xin's style of "heroic abandon," even if they could not rival his range or level of sophistication. Some of them even tended to be rough and slipshod in their writing.

The career of Jiang Kui, who belonged to a generation a little later than that of Xin Qiji, has often been associated with a new stage in the development of the song lyric during the Southern Song. Despite his talent and cultivation as a writer, artist, and scholar, Jiang was never fortunate enough to pass the civil service examination. He remained a commoner all his life, living as a scholar–recluse–artist under the patronage of wealthy and prominent friends. The scores for the melodies of seventeen song lyrics that he himself composed are the only extant musical material from the Song dynasty song lyric. Both Jiang's adherence to the tradition of "delicate restraint" and his way of life as a scholar–recluse–artist became the career pattern for a large number of song lyricists from the closing years of the twelfth through the thirteenth centuries. Somewhat different from many of the recluse–poets of the time, Jiang was not completely unconcerned with the well-being of society and the state. Subtle expressions of his deep concern for the Southern Song can be found in some of his best-known works. In the piece "Yangzhou: the Long Version" (Yangzhou man), for which he also composed the music, for example, Jiang described what he saw on his visit to Yangzhou in 1176, forty-seven years after it had been ravaged by the Jurchens:

> Through ten miles in the spring wind,
> There's nothing but green shepherd's purse and wheat.
> Since Tartar horses left from spying on the Yangzi,
> Abandoned ponds and lofty trees
> Still detest talk of warfare.

Compared to the bold and flowing style of Xin Qiji's song lyrics, the language we see in these lines is quite subdued. But it is still a hard and vigorous language, distinct from the standard diction of earlier lyrics in the tradition of "delicate restraint."

We know that Jiang Kui had direct contacts with Xin Qiji when Xin, as an old man of sixty-three, was serving as military commissioner in Shaoxing in 1203 and then as district governor of Zhenjiang in 1204. There are four extant works Jiang wrote around this time, using Xin's original rhymes. It is possible that Jiang met his senior contemporary prior to 1203, although we do not have any direct record to prove this. Jiang stated in a short autobiographical account that Xin "deeply admired" his song lyrics. In any event, Jiang must have been familiar with the works of this well-known figure, who appeared to have exerted some influence on him, especially in his extensive use of a hard and vigorous language and of allusions in the song lyric. However, Jiang could well have acquired his habit of using the hard rather than the soft language, and an abundance of allusions, from his intensive study of the poetry of Huang Tingjian in his youth. Jiang Kui, more than Xin Qiji, was the very first poet to use allusions in ways more typical of late Southern Song song lyrics.

In keeping with the conventions of the tradition of "delicate restraint," Jiang's song lyrics are mostly concerned with his life as an unemployed wandering scholar–poet and his experiences of love. He was the first song lyricist in the Southern Song to have written a large number of "song lyrics on objects" (*yongwu ci*) – almost half of his extant song lyrics can be said to belong to this category. Many of these *yongwu ci* are on plum blossoms and willows, and one of his most famous works is on crickets. Many of these works are actually about love, and a few remarkable ones among them are about his romantic experience intermixed with lament for his own life and for the declining Song dynasty. It is in these "song lyrics on objects" by Jiang that two important late Song developments in the genre are found. The two developments are: the creation of what may be called a "spatial form" and a transformation in the direct self-expressive mode, which was dominant up to this time in both poetry and the song lyric.

"Spatial form" is found only in the "long song" (*manci*), which poets after Jiang used to depict complex inner states. The term "spatial form" is used here to distinguish from the "temporal rhythm" commonly found in poetry and song lyrics in both short-song and long-song forms prior to Jiang Kui. "Spatial form" compares a literary text to a visual design that spreads many ideas and emotions out on the "plane" of a page. While temporal rhythm relies on a linear order, spatial design depends on the principles of parallelism, juxtaposition, and correspondence. The transformation in the self-expressive mode took place precisely in the song lyrics on objects that became popular and important during the late Song. In writing such a work, the author withdraws from a position in which the direct expression of his own experience constitutes the expressive core into another position in which he becomes a mere observer of that core, even though that core remains his own complex inner state. The new mode of lyrics on objects that emerged in the late Song represents a significant transformation within the Chinese lyrical tradition, which had previously been predominantly expressive. The shift from the traditional self-expressive mode to one that utilizes an object to reveal an author's complex inner state is nowhere seen more clearly than in the pair of song lyrics on plum blossoms entitled "Secret Fragrance" (Anxiang) and "Dappled Shadows" (Shuying), which Jiang wrote at the request of his patron and friend Fan Chengda in the winter of 1191.

"Secret Fragrance" and "Dappled Shadows" are among the most quoted and admired works by Jiang Kui. The titles are taken from a regulated verse on the plum blossom by the poet–recluse Lin Bu (967–1028) of the early Northern Song and directly from the following couplet: "Dappled shadows hang aslant over clear shallow water; / Secret fragrance wafted in the moonlit dusk." Jiang's lyrics "Dappled Shadows" and "Secret Fragrance" are based on these two coordinate images for the plum blossom, referring to its shape and scent respectively. They are written in a difficult and obscure style. Scholars through the ages have offered diverse interpretations, ranging from taking them as reminiscence of a woman Jiang loved, to expression of sorrow for his less-than-ideal life, to a lament for the capture of the last two emperors of the Northern Song and their palace ladies by the Jurchens in 1127. It is not possible to focus on one interpretation to the exclusion of the alternative readings.

"Secret Fragrance" is the more lucid of the two pieces. Its theme does seem to be Jiang's reminiscence of a woman he loved, with whom he used to pick plum blossoms by West Lake in Hangzhou. The blossom, which is explicitly mentioned in the third line, is not used as a metaphor for the woman but as an object that brings back memories of her to the speaker. Throughout the whole piece, the experiencing subject (the lyric speaker) and the experienced object (the blossom) remain distinct, and the former is the agent that ties everything together.

The strong personal tone of "Secret Fragrance" disappears in "Dappled Shadows." The lyric speaker has given way to the plum blossom in becoming the integrative force in this work. There is a multilayered symbolic framework centered on the material object in "Dappled Shadows." Through the juxtaposition of a series of allusions associated with plum blossoms, Jiang Kui expresses his feelings of seclusion and loneliness in a wanderer's life in times of dynastic decline. If "Secret Fragrance" is concerned with reminiscence of a woman from the perspective of the lyric speaker, "Dappled Shadows" is focused on the experience of seclusion and loneliness that find a symbolic embodiment in the plum blossom. The poetic process in works like "Dappled Shadows," in which the material object has replaced the lyric speaker to become the new lyric center, can perhaps be called "the reification of emotions." "Secret Fragrance" and "Dappled Shadows" are complementary pieces written in two different artistic modes. The allusions used in the second piece consist of references to narrative texts, and textual fragments taken from two poems by Du Fu and a song lyric composed by Emperor Huizong on his journey north as a captive of the Jurchens, all of which are related to the plum blossom. What is peculiar about the use of historical and textual allusions in "Dappled Shadows" is the swift shift from one dimension of time and space to another, from the lyrical present to layers of the past. The juxtaposition of different dimensions of time and space on the same page-plane is what makes the form in which "Dappled Shadows" is cast "spatial."

Once the new aesthetics was evolved by Jiang Kui, with its focus on material objects instead of the lyrical self, its spatial form and its allusive style, it began to attract late Song poets. The pattern of Jiang's life and art became the aspiration of the best poets and song lyricists of the period. His poetry was included in the *Rivers and Lakes Collection*, which appeared soon after his death. Whether or not the direct influence of Jiang is discernible, the younger generation of song lyricists – notably Shi Dazu (fl. beginning of the thirteenth century), Wu Wenying, Zhou Mi, Wang Yisun, and Zhang Yan – all displayed similar tendencies in their works. These writers did not simply imitate Jiang Kui, but rather continued to refine the song lyric and to reach new artistic heights.

Wu Wenying was the greatest song lyricist of the thirteenth century. Although still well within the tradition of "delicate restraint," he developed his works in a direction quite different from that of Jiang. In his important critical text the *Origins of the Song Lyric (Ciyuan)*, Zhang Yan made a distinction between Jiang's style and that of Wu Wenying: he said that Jiang's song lyrics are "transparent and spacious" (*qingkong*), while Wu's are "solid and stuffed" (*zhishi*). He further compared Jiang's works to "a wild cloud that flies alone, moving and stopping without a trace," and Wu's to "a seven-jeweled tower that dazzles the eyes, but when taken apart, the bits do not fit." Crucial to Zhang's comparison is his argument that in song lyrics, especially in the long song, "function words" (*xuzi*) should be used in order to achieve a flowing and "singable" quality. In the song lyric, function words include both particles and certain descriptive adverbs. The primary function of these two types of word is structural rather than image-making, as indicated by the fact that most of them are words that begin a line, relating it to the preceding line or to the speaker's attitude. Unlike Jiang Kui, who effectively made use of many function words, Wu Wenying chose to use as few as possible, allowing his song lyrics to be stuffed mostly with image-producing "content words" (*shizi*). Such a song lyric, without the structural function words, will have a dense, rather than transparent and spacious, quality. Zhang's argument is basically a matter of aesthetic preference, because Wu was a composer as well and certainly knew how to write song lyrics that could be sung. Zhou Bangyan was sparing in his use of function words, while Liu Yong, Li Qingzhao, and Xin Qiji used them often. Wu revived Zhou's "densely luxuriant" (*nongli*) style in the Southern Song.

With the exception of a number of pieces that were composed in response to social occasions, most of the nearly 350 extant song lyrics by Wu Wenying are about remembrance of things and persons in his past, or about lamenting the past and present. There are at least several dozen passionate song lyrics devoted to remembering a woman (or women), composed with similar language and images. Wu's best song lyrics are usually cast in spatial form and in an expressive mode different from that of the traditional lyrical outpouring. Wu is famous for intermingling past and present, the personal and the historical, and for using many allusions. We have seen the technique of merging different dimensions of time and space in Jiang Kui's works, and the frequent use of allusion in Xin Qiji and Jiang Kui. Wu Wenying differs from them in his penchant for seeking out allusions in obscure sources, including legends and myths recorded in gazetteers. The inner states Wu depicts are far more private than those presented in Xin's and Jiang's song lyrics. Wu Wenying is thus a very difficult song lyricist. What is startlingly new in Wu's works is that all too often the author seems to be looking at life and the world through a window of dreams and illusion. Indeed, dream holds a special significance in his life and works. He styled himself "Mengchuang" or "A Window of Dreams" and toward the end of his life changed it to "Jueweng" or "The Old Man Who Has Awakened." The word *meng* ("dream") appears more than 170 times in his collected song lyrics. I should point out that a dream itself reveals a "spatial form" or a montage. In a dream the images that randomly make up the dream events usually come from the sense impressions stored in our memory that belong to different temporal and spatial frameworks. The merging of diverse temporal and spatial boundaries and the appearance of randomness in many of Wu's works are the result of his attempt to write them as if they were direct manifestations of dreams. This sort of structural characteristic cannot be found in song lyrics prior to Wu Wenying.

One of the greatest works in the history of the song lyric is Wu Wenying's "Prelude to the Oriole's Song" (Yingti xu). Containing 240 characters, this song, the music of which was also composed by Wu himself, is the longest in the entire repertory of song lyric patterns. It might have been written late in Wu's life when he revisited alone the places he had lived with a woman or women before. Some of the phrases and events depicted here can be found in many of Wu's works about love, presumably written at different times in his life. Perhaps we can say that similar phrases and images in these works function very much like allusions that refer to some of the most memorable romantic events in his life, even though we do not know what these events were exactly. It is conceivable that "Prelude to the Oriole's Song" is an attempt by Wu Wenying late in his life to integrate the images and expressions referring to his most unforgettable romantic experiences into a grander design.

The piece is divided into four large sections, each with a central theme, which is in turn subdivided into four stanzas, each with its own specific focus. In the arrangement of the large themes of lament for spring, joy of meeting, pangs of separation, and mourning for the dead, the work can be said to have a temporal aspect. It begins with the poet's present thoughts and actions, goes on to depict his recollections of meeting with and parting from his beloved, and returns to the present moment at the very end. But the image fragments that depict his present actions and thoughts are also found in song lyrics about previous occasions. Furthermore, the themes and subthemes are not organized into a whole in any chronological order. Rather, they are spread out as if on a plane, and the unity of the work is maintained through parallels, juxtaposition, and correspondence among these themes and subthemes. "Prelude to the Oriole's Song" is a vast spatial design of Wu's remembrance of a woman or women with whom he was in love. Even though it has not been regarded as a true song lyric on an object, it is clearly not cast in the traditional mode of direct self-expression, but in the mode that characterizes Jiang Kui's "Dappled Shadows." In terms of structure, Wu's "Prelude to the Oriole's Song" is a song lyric on the object of remembrance that constituted his inner state as he wrote this masterpiece. The continuation and further development of the new aesthetics of the song lyric discernible in Jiang's and Wu's works in the last decades of the Southern Song will be discussed in the section on "The fall of the Southern Song."

Prose

The Southern Song did not produce ancient-style prose (*guwen*) writers of the stature of the "eight masters of the Tang and Song" (Han Yu, Liu Zongyuan (773–819), Ouyang Xiu, Su Xun (1009–1066), Su Shi, Su Zhe (1039–1112), Zeng Gong (1019–1083), and Wang Anshi). Nor did it develop any significantly novel forms of nonfictional prose. The most important new development was the "travel diary" that became popular during the period. The earliest bona fide diary in Chinese literary history was *A Family Record in Yizhou in the Yiyou Year* (*Yizhou yiyou jiasheng*) by Huang Tingjian, containing entries from the first day of the first month to the twenty-ninth day of the eighth month in 1105. There was no entry in the entire sixth month, and the entries of six days in the fifth month have been lost. The entries vary in length from one character to more than a hundred. On the basis of the form invented by Huang Tingjian, Southern Song writers produced a number of lively and far more detailed travel diaries. Lu You wrote *Record of a Journey to Shu* (*Ru Shu ji*), detailing his trip up the Yangzi river in 1170 when he received an official appointment in Sichuan. Fan Chengda wrote altogether three travel diaries: *Record of Holding the Reins* (*Lanpei lu*) records his mission to the Jurchen capital in 1170, *Record of Riding the Simurgh (Canluan lu)* records his trip to the southwestern city of Guilin in 1173, and *Record of a Boat Trip to Wu (Wuchuan lu)* describes his trip downstream on the Yangzi from Chengdu to Wu in 1177. Zhu Xi wrote *Record of Baizhang Mountain (Baizhang shan ji)*, describing his trip to Baizhang Mountain in Jiangxi where the Chan master Baizhang Huaihai (720–814) had lived. These are some of the best examples of the travel diary from the Southern Song. Employing plain and logical ancient-style prose, these writers recorded the events on their travels, the beautiful scenery, rural and urban sights, and the daily life of people as they saw it. In addition to being specimens of a fully developed new literary form, these travel diaries are valuable materials for the study of Southern Song life.

The keen attention Southern Song writers gave to professionalism and craft can also be seen in the advances they made in literary criticism. During the Southern Song there appeared a few critical works that had departed from the Northern Song conventions of "remarks on poetry." Many critics turned away from anecdotes and textual study to concentrate their efforts on more comprehensive and fundamental issues. Works such as *Remarks on Poetry from the Cold Season Hall (Suihantang shihua)* by Zhang Jie (fl. early Southern Song), the *White Stone Daoist's Discourse on Poetry* by Jiang Kui, and *Canglang's Remarks on Poetry (Canglang shihua)* by Yan Yu (fl. thirteenth century) provide good evidence of the increasing professionalism in Southern Song critical activities. These are no longer random gatherings of casual notes but intensive treatises expressing the critics' rather systematic and reflective views on poetry. They all criticized the Northern Song tendency to discursiveness, the interest in seeking out allusions and display of erudition, and the polishing of diction; in place of this they argued for a return to a more natural and spontaneous way of writing poetry. Yan Yu developed the existing idea of Chan enlightenment as an analogy for poetic creation. He argued that poetry is for the spontaneous expression of a person's inner feelings, and as such it should be free from explicit philosophizing, bookishness, and the trap of language games. As a corrective to the prevailing practice of imitating Late Tang poetry among contemporary poets of the Rivers and Lakes School, Yan urged poets to take their models from the poetry of the Wei (220–264), Jin (265–420), and, above all, the High Tang periods. In this aspect he remained within a poetics based on earlier models, which had been dominant since the late Northern Song.

Written by Zhang Yan, who lived during the transitional period between the Southern Song and the Mongol Yuan periods, the *Origins of the Song Lyric* is an important critical study on the song lyric. This book is divided into two parts, with the first part devoted to the discussion of music and the second part to the various aspects involved in the creation of texts that are set to music. The work represents the summation of Zhang's efforts of a lifetime of writing song lyrics and studying their craft.

The ancient-style prose writer Lü Zuqian's (1137–1181) work entitled the *Key to Ancient-Style Prose* (*Guwen guanjian*) merits mention. This is the first text solely devoted to the appreciation and writing of ancient-style prose in the history of Chinese literary criticism. The work is primarily an anthology of select works with Lü's general prefatory and interlinear comments of evaluation, appreciation, or explanation of the art of the work. There is also an introductory essay called "Essential Methods of Reading Ancient-Style Prose," in which Lü discusses the appropriate ways of reading the prose works of the Tang and Northern Song masters, as well as how to write good prose and what sorts of flaws to avoid. Lü's *Key to Ancient-Style Prose* began the critical tradition of close reading and interpretation of prose that became popular in the Ming dynasty. The Southern Song was indeed an important period in Chinese literary criticism. The level of sophistication and professionalism observable in the critical works mentioned here is unprecedented.

VI. The pleasures of the city
Shuen-fu Lin

Urban development during the Southern Song

The Song dynasty marked a crucial period in the long history of urban development in Chinese culture. It was during the Song that we see a tremendous growth of cities. It has been estimated that by the late Northern Song, China had one city – the capital, Bianliang (Kaifeng) – with a population of a million; thirty cities with a population ranging from 40,000 to 100,000 or more each; sixty cities having each a population of 15,000; and some four hundred county and prefectural capitals with populations ranging from four thousand to five thousand each. One conservative estimate has it that about 5 percent or more (i.e. over six million people) of China's total population at that time lived in urban environments. Urban growth not only continued during the Southern Song but was more impressive than before. The capital, Hangzhou, had a population of 1,500,000. Many other cities, especially those in the Yangzi delta region, were almost as important as the capital as centers for commerce and culture. As Marco Polo noted in *The Travels of Marco Polo*, when he visited

China after the Mongols had conquered the Southern Song in the late thirteenth century, China had numerous cities of size and magnificence unknown elsewhere in the world. There is no doubt that Song China had the largest cities in the world at the time, and more than its fair share of all the world's smaller cities and towns.

More important than their sheer number and size, as well as more stable growth, traditional Chinese cities, in Song times and afterwards, maintained an intimate relation and a high degree of interaction with the rural areas adjacent to them. Despite the presence of the walls and moats, Chinese cities in the past usually contained rural life and agricultural activities within them, and clusters of urban areas extended outside those boundaries as well. Further, the cities and the adjacent countryside were open for people to come and go freely between them, and so there was always a great deal of daily movement and activity in and out of the cities.

Everyone, urban and rural alike, lived in accordance with the agrarian lunar calendar, which set all of the festivals and holidays throughout the year. The major festivals were the New Year; the Clear and Bright (Qingming) on the third of the third month, when people went to the countryside to sweep ancestors' and relatives' graves; the Double Fifth (Duanwu) on the fifth of the fifth month, when people held boat races; the Ghost Festival on the fifteenth of the seventh month, when both the Buddhist and the Daoist temples performed services for the ghosts; the Mid-autumn Festival, when families gathered together to admire the harvest moon on the fifteenth of the eighth month; and the Double Yang (Chongyang) on the ninth of the ninth month, when people ascended high places to experience the invigorating late autumn air. For each of these festivals and others, special foods were prepared and particular activities carried out. On the major holidays people from the countryside would come into the cities to sell the special foods and products from the land that were needed for the feasting and celebrations, and to enjoy performances and displays. This pattern of open interaction between urban areas and their rural surroundings, already established during Song times, became fully developed in the subsequent dynasties.

Depiction of urban life in literature

There is little realistic description of urban life in poetry and song lyrics. Nonetheless, the growth of the importance of the cities can be seen in the works of some song lyricists and poets. Of the more than two hundred song lyrics by Liu Yong, who traveled to many cities in his life, for instance, about a quarter of them contain some depiction of cities and urban life. In a song

lyric set to the tune "Viewing the Ocean Tide" (Wang haichao), Liu began
with these lines:

> A supreme spot in the southeast,
> The metropolis in all of the Wu region,
> Qiantang has flourished from old.
> Misty willows and painted bridges,
> Green curtains and windscreens –
> There are a hundred thousand households of all sizes.
>
> . . .
>
> In the markets, pearls are displayed,
> Houses brimming with silks,
> Vying with each other for extravagance.
>
> . . .

Qiantang is an old name of Hangzhou. In the following piece set to the
tune "Magnolia Flowers: The Long Version" (Mulanhua man), a piece about
Kaifeng on the Clear and Bright Festival, he offered the following lively
depiction:

> The whole city
> Is out looking at the sights.
> Carved saddles and dark purple carriage curtains rush out to the suburbs.
> In the warm breeze, rich strings and crisp pipes
> Of a myriad families vie in playing new tunes.

And in another piece, set to the tune "Auspicious Partridge" (Rui zhegu), he
opened the song lyric with this portrait:

> Wugui's a romantic place –
> The houses are exquisite,
> High and low, built by water's edge and on hilltop;
> With jade terraces and crimson gates,
> This could be Fairy Hill.
> With a myriad wells, a thousand alleys, and a rich populace,
> It surpasses all thirteen provinces.
> Everywhere you see black-browed girls in painted boats,
> And rouged and powdered women in red mansions.

Wugui refers to the city of Suzhou. From Liu's brief but vivid descriptions, we
know that the Song cities in the eleventh century were places of irresistible
attraction, flourishing markets, and ostentation. Urban life became far more
extravagant and ostentatious in the Southern Song, as we can see in this
quatrain by Lin Sheng:

> Hills beyond hills, and mansions beyond mansions,
> Singing and dancing on West Lake – when will they ever end?
> The warm breeze fumes revelers till they are drunk,
> Simply taking Hangzhou as the capital Bianliang.

As one would expect from good poetry, Liu's and Lin's lines present a powerful, albeit brief and general, sense of how magnificent and pleasurable the cities were in Song times. It is in prose works, however, that we would find more specific and detailed descriptions of urban life.

In *Record of a Journey to Shu*, the travel diary written in 1170 about a journey from Hangzhou up the Yangzi river into Shu (i.e. Sichuan), Lu You wrote on the twenty-third day of the eighth month that he saw in Wuchang (part of modern Wuhan on the south bank), the large city of the central Yangzi, countless merchants' boats tied up in the river stretching for miles along the riverbank. He noted that rows of shops were packed together inside the city walls, and a large market area extended far outside the walls on the inland side. Again, on the twenty-fifth day of the eighth month, he recorded seeing a crowd of several tens of thousands watching onshore a naval exercise on the Yangzi in Wuchang that involved more than seven hundred large vessels, each two hundred to three hundred feet long. Lu's diary offered glimpses of sights and spectacles available to urban and rural residents inside and near inland river cities.

We are fortunate to possess five texts that describe the daily life and customs of Kaifeng (Bianliang) and Hangzhou. They are *The Eastern Capital: A Record of the Dreamland* (*Dongjing menghua lu*) by Meng Yuanlao, with a preface dated 1147; *A Record of the Capital City's Splendors* (*Ducheng jisheng*) by The Old Man Of Forbearance Who Irrigates His Garden (Guanpu naideweng), with a preface dated 1235; *The Old Man of West Lake's Record of Innumerable Splendors* (*Xihu laoren fansheng lu*) by The Old Man of West Lake, possibly sometime after 1235; *A Record of the Millet Dream* (*Mengliang lu*) by Wu Zimu, possibly sometime right before the fall of Hangzhou in 1276; and *Old Events at the Martial Forest* (*Wulin jiushi*) by Zhou Mi, possibly written between 1280 and 1290, after the Song dynasty had fallen. Wulin or "Martial Forest" is another name for Hangzhou. Of the five texts, only *The Eastern Capital: A Record of the Dreamland* is about Kaifeng, while the other four are about Hangzhou. Being the first text about a capital city, *The Eastern Capital: A Record of the Dreamland* became a model for the four texts about Hangzhou. In the accounts of Hangzhou, the four thirteenth-century writers often nostalgically compared contemporary customs and patterns of life with those of the old capital, Kaifeng.

These five texts are invaluable because they surpass the reference to urban life in poetry that we have briefly discussed and even the genre of gazetteers of cities or places in providing extensive details about urban life and customs. They constitute, in fact, a new genre of prose, a sort of journal or notebook devoted to recording the splendors and pleasures of the city. Among the five authors, Zhou Mi is the only one with a reputation as a poet, scholar, and writer. *Old Events at the Martial Forest* is thus written with much more rhetorical flourish than are the other four texts. With the exception of *A Record of the Capital City's Splendors*, the texts devote ample space to the affairs of the court and to the festival days that brought the court and citizens together to celebrate the passing of the important occasions throughout the year. We know that Zhou Mi was a court official, and was thus also a participant in the court rituals described in his text; but Meng Yuanlao, The Old Man of West Lake, and Wu Zimu also demonstrated great familiarity with court life and rituals.

Three points about the five texts merit mention. First, they seem to have been written by their authors rather late in their lives. The authors of *A Record of the Capital City's Splendors* and *The Old Man of West Lake's Record of Innumerable Splendors* used pseudonyms that involved the words *weng* and *laoren* respectively, both meaning "Old Man." In his preface to *The Eastern Capital: A Record of the Dreamland*, Meng Yuanlao indicated that he "had entered the evening of his life." Moreover, "Yuanlao," believed by scholars to be not his real given name but a pseudonym, means "Senior Statesman." In his late fifties when he wrote *Old Events at the Martial Forest*, Zhou Mi clearly stated "I am an old man" in the preface to his text. Wu Zimu is the only author who did not provide any clear clue to his age when he wrote his work. Second, the texts all contain some records of what the authors witnessed and heard. Some of the sources are textual: Wu is found to have copied verbatim from *A Record of the Capital City's Splendors* in places, and Zhou also relied on some contemporary texts that are no longer extant today. Nonetheless, there is no doubt that all five authors wrote their respective works based on substantial direct experiences. Moreover, the authors' experiences are of the daily life and customs of the capitals in times of peace and prosperity, so that each of the five texts consists of remembrances of the good old days directly witnessed by the author. Third, the idea of dream underpins these five texts. With the exception of *A Record of the Capital City's Splendors* and *The Old Man of West Lake's Record of Innumerable Splendors*, the word "dream" is explicitly used in the texts. The title of Meng's journal *Dongjing menghua lu* (*The Eastern Capital: A Record of the Dreamland*) literally means "The Eastern Capital: A Record of the Dream of

Huaxu," alluding to a passage in the "Yellow Emperor" (Huangdi) chapter of the early text *Liezi* in which the legendary Yellow Emperor falls asleep during the day and travels to the Kingdom of Huaxu, a utopian country where people lead a natural existence without government, desires, and ordinary human emotions or values. In the preface to his work written two decades after Kaifeng had fallen to the Jurchens, Meng said that he felt like that ancient person (the Yellow Emperor) who had wakened from a dream in which he visited Huaxu, a land of unlimited happiness. By comparing Kaifeng to the utopian Huaxu, Meng wanted to drive home the idea of the illusory nature of the seemingly perfect life of unending happiness in the Northern Song capital. The title of Wu Zimu's journal, *Mengliang lu* (*A Record of the Millet Dream*), contains an allusion to the story "The Account upon a Pillow" (Zhenzhong ji) by the Tang writer Shen Jiji (ca 750–800). "The Account upon a Pillow" tells the story of a poverty-stricken young scholar who encounters a Daoist wizard at an inn. After hearing the young man's complaint about his own miserable life, the wizard gives him a pillow and causes him to fall into a dream in which he experiences a lifetime of wealth, status, and glory. His dream, however, lasts only a short while because, as he wakes up, the pot of golden millet the innkeeper is preparing for him is still not yet cooked. By use of the allusion to Shen Jiji's story, Wu adds to the illusory nature a sense of the swift perishability of earthly delights and splendors. Although Wu Zimu might not have written *A Record of the Millet Dream* in 1274 as the preface to our modern received text seems to indicate, there is reason to believe that he had written it before the Mongols captured Hangzhou in 1276. As the affairs of the nation were already in a precipitous state by the early 1270s, it did not require great foresight to sense the impending doom facing the dynasty. In his preface to *Old Events at the Martial Forest*, written after the dynasty had collapsed, Zhou stated clearly that when he recalled his previous experiences, they were all like dreams. Even though the authors of *A Record of the Capital City's Splendors* and *The Old Man of West Lake's Record of Innumerable Splendors* did not refer to dreams, it might not be far-fetched to say that the fear that the glories and splendors of Hangzhou would soon fade like dreams in people's memories was the motivating force behind the writing of their works. This is obviously the case because they both had read Meng Yuanlao's memoir of Kaifeng.

The idea that life can be as illusory as a dream is a very old one in Chinese literature, going back at least as early as the *Zhuangzi*, one of the canonical texts in the philosophy of early Daoism. Many writers since Zhuangzi's (ca 369–286 BC) time – such as Du Fu, Shen Jiji, Yan Jidao, Su Shi, and Chen

Yuyi, to name but a few – have written works touching on the theme of "life is but a dream." For the writers of these accounts of the capitals from the late Northern Song to the end of the Southern Song, the idea of "life is but a dream" conveys a much broader and more compelling meaning. As the allusions used by Meng Yuanlao and Wu Zimu indicate, "dream" refers to a fond dream, not a nightmare or a dream of disappointment. Thus a life that is devoted to passionate pursuit of glory, pleasure, and extravagance is like a fond dream, something that all people would want to have; however, being like a dream, such a life is always illusory and ephemeral, doomed to evaporate quickly. While the authors of the journals on the Song capitals felt lucky to have been born in times of peace and prosperity, they also cautioned their readers to be aware of the dream-like nature of the life of luxury, beauty, and enjoyment recorded in their works. This perception of a good life as simultaneously consisting of two interpenetrating sides of reality and illusion seems to have been widespread among writers and scholars of the thirteenth century. In many of the song lyrics, Wu Wenying seems to capture this perception vividly. In a piece set to the tune "Eight-Rhymed Ganzhou Song" (Basheng Ganzhou), which begins with the line "An endless void, mist to the four distances" (miao kong yan si yuan) written on the occasion of accompanying some colleagues on an outing to Mount Lingyan in Suzhou, Wu Wenying intermingled time and space, past and present, history and myth, the personal and the historical, as well as reality and illusion. Although the work is about Wu's inner state on an outing with friends, it is structured in such a way that it becomes a direct manifestation of a dream. This direct manifestation of a dream experience is something not found in song lyrics prior to the late Song.

According to these five twelfth- and thirteenth-century accounts of Kaifeng and Hangzhou, the two capitals (and in fact other large cities also) were metropolitan areas of great wealth, commercial activity, and cultivated pastimes. They boasted a multitude of fashionable hotels, taverns, restaurants, tea houses, temples, pleasure quarters, and many other places for recreation that could satisfy the refined tastes and the thirst for entertainment on the part of both wealthy inhabitants and visitors. There were shops that specialized in all kinds of luxury products or exotic goods from all over China and other parts of the world. In addition to their wealth and all the amenities of urban life, Hangzhou and other cities (especially those in the lower Yangzi region such as Suzhou, Yangzhou, and Nanjing) were also places of beautiful scenery for people to enjoy. West Lake in Hangzhou, for instance, was always provided with many gaily decorated boats of all shapes and sizes, some of which carried singing girls, games, and other forms of entertainment. Lining the lakeshore were luxurious mansions with enchanting gardens furnished with pavilions, bridges, artificial ponds, streams, grottos, and hills, as well as rare flowers and trees. Magnificent Buddhist and Daoist temples could be found in and around the city. On the many festivals throughout the year, the city itself and the scenic spots on the outskirts were invaded by urban and rural people alike, who came to celebrate their fortunate life, to seek amusement, and to enjoy popular shows and performances.

Entertainments in the Song city

The diversity of entertainments in the Song city was remarkable. Listed in the five capital journals are: comedy, including parodies of country bumpkins; dancing; singing and musical performances; narrative ballads using suites of melodies in the same musical mode; dressing up as students, spirits, or ghosts; foot and hand tricks; shadow and puppet plays; acrobatics; boxing and wrestling; pole climbing; tightrope walking; telling jokes; storytelling, secular and religious, including riddles and puns; magic; football; stave fighting; training walking beasts; flea circus; and more. These entertainments were located in the "pleasure quarters" called *goulan* (linked railings), or *washe, wazi, washi, wasi,* and *wajie,* meaning, as Wu Zimu has suggested in *A Record of the Millet Dream,* "when patrons and performers arrive, it is like piling up tiles [*wa*], and when they leave, it is like tiles falling apart." Intermingled with entertainments were fortunetellers and sellers of medicinal herbs, of clothes, of all kinds of drinks and foods, and of arts and crafts. Also housed in the pleasure quarters were large and profitable theaters that drew patrons numbered in the thousands on any given day. Out of the great diversity of entertainments in the Song city evolved traditional Chinese drama and storytelling.

Traditional Chinese theater developed as a form of drama that integrated the various elements of entertainments: music, song, text, storytelling, acting, dance, acrobatics, costume, and elaborate makeup. Both *zaju* (variety play, farce, later the "northern play") and *zhugongdiao* (medley, "all keys and modes") appeared in the late Northern Song, although no text in either form is extant. It is mentioned in *A Record of the Millet Dream* that the variety play "Maudgalyayana Rescues His Mother (from Hell)" (*Mulian jiumu*) was performed in Kaifeng from the seventh of the seventh month to the Ghost Festival on the fifteenth of that month. The story of Maudgalyayana can be found in the transformation texts (*bianwen*) of the Tang dynasty discovered in the Dunhuang caves, which are narrative texts composed in prose, in verse, or in a mixture of the two, on Buddhist and secular subjects, intended for oral presentation. The Song variety play, however, was a complex form of performance integrating the various amusement arts, rather than simply a form of story-telling. This play about Maudgalyayana, one of Buddha's ten great disciples, who went down to the lowest level of Hell to save his mother's soul, obviously had a serious didactic function. From what we can gather from some miscellanies by Song writers, however, these variety plays were mostly comic. "All keys and modes" (*zhugongdiao*) did not reach its peak of development until about the year 1200, when North China was under Jurchen rule.

The many cities in the north under Jurchen rule continued to be thriving centers of trade, entertainment, art, and culture. The theater likewise continued to develop in the north under the Jin. The political split of the north controlled by the Jurchens and the south by the reestablished Song court led to a bifurcation of theatrical entertainments: in the north the "all keys and modes" (or *yuanben*, "theater guild texts," as they were also called) eventually developed into the Mongol Yuan dynasty's (1279–1368) *zaju* ("northern play"), and in the south a type of drama developed in Wenzhou (in modern Zhejiang) and known as *xiwen* ("drama texts") became popular throughout much of southern China in the twelfth and thirteenth centuries. These two forms of theatrical entertainments are basically similar in being musical dramas and differ only in length, music, and other conventions of performance used. Today we only know the names of hundreds of Jin dynasty "theater guild texts," but only one full text and the fragments of another of Jin entertainment have been preserved. The full text is "The Romance of the Western Chamber (in all keys and modes)" (*Xixiang ji zhugongdiao*) by Dong Jieyuan (fl. 1190–1208), and the one in fragments is the anonymous "Liu Zhiyuan (in all keys and modes)" (*Liu Zhiyuan zhugongdiao*). The former is an elaborate dramatization of "Yingying's Story" (*Yingying zhuan*), a love story by Yuan Zhen (779–831) of the Tang dynasty, in eight chapters, employing fourteen musical modes and 193 suites of melodies. The latter tells the story of the marriage, separation, and eventual reunion of Liu Zhiyuan, the founder of the Later Han dynasty (one of the Five Dynasties), and Li Sanniang, daughter of a well-to-do farmer. There is actually another partially extant piece entitled "Anecdotes of the Tianbao Era (in all keys and modes)" (*Tianbao yishi zhugongdiao*) with some fifty individual suites, but without any connecting prose passages. "All keys and modes" is a form between storytelling and drama, which alternates prose and verse organized in suites to be sung. The genre is called "all keys and modes" because two successive suites used in the sung parts are almost never in the same key.

The five capital journals mention that professional storytellers (*shuohuaren*) constituted an important group of entertainers in the pleasure quarters of the great Song cities. The storytellers included narrators of history, of stories from Buddhist sutras, of legends, of romances, of court cases, of the stories of heroes and of people who moved from rags to riches. Storytelling already flourished in Kaifeng in the Northern Song, and reached a golden age in the Southern Song period. Catering to the urban dwellers who were not as well educated as the literati, the storytellers used the simple vernacular language of the day in their performance. During the second half of the thirteenth century, a number of texts called "simple stories" (*pinghua*) appeared. They tell familiar legends or historical stories in very simple style and language. It has been suggested that "simple stories" were primarily a form of entertainment reading written specially for, and read chiefly by, an urban audience of limited literacy. We have several surviving texts of "simple stories": The *Anecdotes of the Xuanhe Period* (*Xuanhe yishi*) tells the events around the fall of the Northern Song, *A Simple Story of the History of the Five Dynasties* (*Wudaishi pinghua*) describes the chaotic situation from the fall of the Tang to the founding of the Song, and *The Story, with Poems, of How Tripitaka of the Great Tang Obtained the Buddhist Sutras* (*Datang Sanzang qujing shihua*) is concerned with Tripitaka's pilgrimage to India to acquire sutras. The last is the story of the seventh-century monk Xuanzang, whose journey to India was discussed in the Tang chapter above. These examples of *pinghua* reveal a few artistic traits. First, they begin with a prologue verse and end with a concluding verse. Second, the prologue verse is usually followed by a short frame story to introduce the main story. Third, in the main story, verse is frequently used to serve the purposes of description, prove a point, or convey a moral message. Fourth, since these texts are rather long, they are divided into chapters, each with a title outlining what happens in the chapter. The "simple story" is the forerunner of the long narrative works that appeared later in the Ming and Qing dynasties.

VII. The fall of the Southern Song
Shuen-fu Lin

The Mongol conquest of the Southern Song

With the treaty of 1141–1142, the Southern Song and the Jin settled into a pattern of peaceful coexistence. The Jin attempted to violate that agreement twice, in 1161 and in 1216–1220, as they campaigned to the Yangzi river, both times unsuccessfully. On the Southern Song side, the infamous Grand Councilor Han Tuozhou (1151–1207) led the government to declare war on the Jin in 1206, ordering the armies stationed along the Huai border to move northward into Jin territory. Despite an initial minor victory, the Song armies were soon defeated. The Song–Jin treaty stipulations were adjusted twice: in 1165 the Song gained by somewhat reduced annual tribute payments following the 1161 failed Jin campaign; in 1208, as a result of Han Tuozhou's disastrous venture, the higher tribute level of 1142 was reinstituted. On the whole, these military confrontations were short-lived and did not greatly disturb the pattern of peace between the two states. Around the turn of the thirteenth century, however, a new ethnic confederation was being forged by a minor tribal group in the Mongolian steppe. Eventually this new confederation was to bring about the demise of both the Jin and the Southern Song.

The man responsible for the creation of the Mongol confederation was Temüjin of the nomadic Borjigin clan, a brilliant but ruthless military genius, born probably in 1162 or 1167 on the banks of the Onon river in Mongolia. By the turn of the thirteenth century, Temüjin had already achieved military celebrity among the Mongol tribes. At a great tribal assembly held in the spring of 1206 on the banks of the Onon river, he was finally confirmed in the title of Chinggis Khan, meaning "universal ruler," by the chieftains of all of the tribes. Once the tribes were unified under one leadership, nothing could stand in Chinggis Khan's way. In merely two decades from 1206 until his death in 1227, Chinggis Khan wiped out virtually all the kingdoms and empires in the inner zone of the Eurasian continent and conquered Mongolia and Manchuria, laying the foundations of a far-flung Mongol empire. His territory stretched from the Pacific Ocean to the Caspian Sea in Central Asia. Thanks to the Jurchens, who had driven the Song court out of North China in 1126 and established the Jin dynasty, the Southern Song did not become one of the first victims of this nomadic conquest. Indeed, because of the buffer the Jin had provided, the Southern Song was slow in becoming aware of the powerful threat that had emerged in the steppe. Just as Chinggis Khan was consolidating the Mongol tribes into one invincible war machine, the Southern Song was entering one of the most brilliant eras of its civilization.

The Mongol conquest of China, including the North under Jurchen rule, took three generations of leaders. Chinggis Khan began attacking the Jin after 1210, eventually driving the Jin emperor to abandon control of north China in 1215 and move his court from the Jin Central Capital in present-day Beijing to the Southern Capital in Kaifeng. The conquest of the Jin was not completed until 1234 under Chinggis's son Ögödei, who succeeded him as the Great Khan of the Mongol empire in 1229. Ögödei campaigned in Sichuan on the Song's western borders throughout the 1230s. The invasion of Song China was not begun again until after Möngke, a grandson of Chinggis, became the Great Khan in 1251. In 1253, Möngke ordered his second brother, Khubilai

(1215–1294), to invade western China. In that campaign Khubilai defeated the Dali kingdom in 1254, bringing Yunnan under Mongol control. Then in 1258 Möngke personally led an army to invade central Sichuan, with Khubilai leading a column east of the main army to enter Hubei and the central Yangzi region. There were two other military columns in this campaign, one to parallel the main army on a route further west and the other to attack the Song from Yunnan in the southwest. When Möngke fell ill and died in the summer of 1259, all military action against Song China was suspended, leaving one to wonder if he would have accomplished the conquest had he not died.

Khubilai declared himself the successor to Möngke as the Great Khan in 1260 before a small tribal assembly in the Mongol heartland. Contesting Khubilai's claim, his youngest brother, Arigh Böke, also declared himself the Great Khan before a small tribal assembly in the same year in western Mongolia. A civil war between them ensued before Khubilai's armies finally prevailed in 1264. In 1268, two years after Arigh Böke died in captivity, Khubilai began in earnest his conquest of the Southern Song by first laying siege to its stronghold in northern Hubei at the twin cities of Fancheng and Xiangyang on the Han river, a tributary of the Yangzi. Khubilai adopted military operations that differed vastly from all previous Mongol invasions in China, taking a different route into Song territory, using inland naval forces and more sophisticated techniques in besieging and capturing walled cities, and employing Chinese, Korean, and Jurchen, as well as Central Asian experts in naval and siege warfare. The change in strategy was necessary because Mongol cavalry were unaccustomed to fighting in the settled and densely populated agricultural lands in the south, with their many rivers, canals, and mountains. The Southern Song, although generally regarded by Chinese historians as a militarily weak dynasty, still proved to be a slower and tougher conquest for the Mongols than the empires of Central and Western Asia. It took the Mongols five years to seize Fancheng and Xiangyang alone. It then took them another year and a half, beginning late in 1274, to move down the Han river to the Yangzi, and then eastward downstream to take Hangzhou. It was three years after capturing Hangzhou in 1276 that the Mongols were able to wipe out the last resistance organized by Song loyalists, bringing an end to the dynasty.

Unlike all earlier Mongol leaders who were essentially warrior chieftains, Khubilai began to cultivate the company of Chinese advisers as early as in his mid-twenties. By 1260 he had drawn at least sixty advisers with whom to explore the problem of governing north China. Most of these experts were Chinese, but there were Khitans, Uighurs, Jurchens, and others as well. Khubilai began using the Chinese system of reign period titles a few months after he declared himself the Great Khan. Then in 1264 he moved his capital from Karakorum in central Mongolia to Yan (present-day Beijing), the abandoned Jin Central Capital. In 1271, on the advice of Chinese advisers, he proclaimed that his new dynasty would be called the "Great Yuan" (Da Yuan), meaning the "great beginning." All of these acts indicated that he had been preparing for a long time to become the emperor of China, even though Khubilai never actually learned Chinese (except a little spoken language) and never identified with Chinese cultural values. His use of Chinese advisers was solely for the purpose of conquering China and to adopt those practices of Chinese government that he found expedient.

Khubilai's full-scale invasion encountered stiff resistance by military leaders and civil officials, who were intensely loyal to the state and committed to protecting Song territory and civilization. The common people also demonstrated a stronger will to resist than did the Southern Song government. As was the case during the Jurchen conquest of North China a century and a half earlier, "patriotic" sentiments became quite widespread in the writings of the last three or four decades of the thirteenth century. The Mongol policy of favoring other ethnic groups over the Han Chinese, particularly southerners, also aroused deep resentment against the alien conquerors. Some members of the educated elite who lived during this era of the Mongol invasion and dynastic transition took part in resistance activities. After 1279, however, many of the elite followed the pattern of passive resistance, withdrawing from society into private lives devoted to the pursuit of the arts, literature, and scholarship.

Literati-turned-warriors

The national crisis produced a number of "literati-turned-warriors." Wen Tianxiang (1236–1283) was the most famous among this group of educated men. At the age of twenty, he passed the civil service examination. While conferring the first place in the civil sevice examination (*jinshi*) degree upon Wen, Emperor Lizong (r. 1225–1264) remarked, "This is a propitious omen from heaven and an auspicious sign for our Song dynasty." "A propitious omen from heaven" (*tian [zhi] xiang*) was the emperor's reading of Wen's given name "Tianxiang." Wen Tianxiang, however, never received important appointments until he was thirty-nine years old. Prior to 1275 he served in some local positions and lived much of the time as a recluse in his hometown in Luling (modern Jishui in Jiangxi). By early 1275, on the middle Yangzi in Anhui, Mongol forces under Bayan's (1237–1295) command had defeated the Song forces consisting of several hundred thousand men and a fleet of 2,500 ships led by Grand Councilor Jia Sidao (1213–1275). The Mongols were now rapidly approaching Hangzhou. In desperation the Song court appealed to all local leaders to defend the state. In quick response to this appeal, Wen gave up all of his family property to be used for military expenditure, recruited ten thousand or more soldiers from his prefecture, Ganzhou (in modern Jiangxi), and came to join the forces defending the capital. On the nineteenth day of the first month in 1276, with Bayan's armies moving from Gaoting Hill to the northeast of Hangzhou into Huzhou, Wen was appointed grand councilor of the right (*you chengxiang*) and military commissioner (*shumishi*). The next day he was sent to negotiate with Bayan, who summarily had him arrested and sent off to the Mongol capital at Yan. En route Wen escaped with the help of some Song loyalists. By then Hangzhou had fallen and another child emperor was established in Fuzhou (in modern Fujian). Wen came to pay obeisance to the new emperor and was again appointed grand councilor of the right and military commissioner in charge of all Song forces. He was captured late in 1278 and kept in captivity as the Mongols swiftly finished up destroying the remnant resistance forces; in late 1279 Wen Tianxiang was sent off to the capital at Yan. For three years Wen repeatedly refused enticements to serve the Mongols before unflinchingly going to the execution ground toward the end of 1283.

Wen's career as a poet and writer can be divided into two periods, corresponding with his career as a statesman. His poetry from the pre-1276 period is mediocre, showing a dominant influence of the Rivers and Lakes poets. There are even a large number of occasional poems written for physiognomists, fortune-tellers, and diviners. His transformation from minor scholar–official into a minister–general changed all this. The major events and his intense patriotism during the last seven years of his life are all recorded in his poetry. He writes directly, with little attention to rhetorical refinement. There are four collections of poetry from this late period. The last of them, produced while he was in prison in 1280, contains two hundred quatrains in the five-syllable line, all made up of lines taken from Du Fu's poetry. Writing quatrains about contemporary events by combining lines from Du Fu was an act of emulation of the Tang master's achievement as a "poetic historian" (*shishi*). Wen's most representative work is his "Song of the Righteous Breath of Life" (Zhengqi ge) composed in the summer of 1281. In the prose preface to this poem, he describes seven kinds of oppressive humours (also called *qi* in Chinese) in his dark and dirty prison cell. He then indicates that he could survive this situation with his frail constitution mainly because he had cultivated what Mencius termed "flood-like breath of life" (*haoran zhi qi*), a vital spirit formed from accumulated righteousness. In the poem Wen uses strong language to describe how the righteous breath of life permeates the space between heaven and earth, how it has sustained those great men in history in times of extreme adversity, and how it enables him to regard the damp and low-lying cell as a realm of peace and happiness. Since the late thirteenth century, this poem has been widely admired for its expression of the unyielding courage and integrity of a Song loyalist.

Xie Bingde (1226–1289) passed the civil service examination in 1256, the same year as Wen Tianxiang. In 1275 Mongol troops entered Jiangxi where Xie was serving as prefect of Xinzhou. He rose in arms against the enemy, but soon lost his prefecture. His wife was captured and committed suicide, and his brother also died in the war of resistance. Xie changed his name, and fled to a mountain village in Jianyang (in modern Fujian), where he passed his days selling fortunes and teaching students. After the fall of Song, he resisted pressure to serve in the Yuan government; he was arrested by local officials and sent to Yan, where he starved to death in prison. Some of his poems expressing his unyielding loyalty to Song have enjoyed wide circulation in later ages.

An associate of Wen Tianxiang by the name of Xie Ao (1249–1295) deserves mention as well. In 1276 he joined Wen's resistance force, serving in the capacity of military consultant. In 1290, a few years after Wen was executed, Xie went with a few friends to the West Terrace of Yan Guang's (fl. early first century BC) Fishing Terrace on the Fuchun river in Zhejiang to offer a memorial ceremony for their martyred friend. Xie wrote "An Account of Ascending the West Terrace to Wail" to commemorate this event. For fear that their action would get them into trouble with the Mongol authorities, Xie pretended that they were grieving for a certain Tang dynasty Prime Minister Lu. Xie's eulogy has been hailed by some later scholars as a piece of unusual prose "written in blood and tears." As is typical of the writings of the loyalists, much of Xie's poetry after the fall of the Song became ambiguous and allegorical.

The variety of Song loyalist writers

A musician–poet who did not participate in any resistance activity but nevertheless produced works that are invaluable records of the fall of the Song was Wang Yuanliang (1241?–1317?). He was a zither (qin) player serving in the palace during Emperor Duzong's reign (1264–1274). When the Mongols captured Hangzhou, Wang was taken into custody together with members of the imperial household and sent to Yan. He lived there for twelve years before he was allowed to return to his hometown, Hangzhou, to become a Daoist priest. On the Mid-autumn Festival in 1280, he visited Wen Tianxiang in prison and played the zither for the captive. After Wen's death, he wrote nine poems to mourn the martyr, to commemorate Wen's loyalty, and also to express his own deep grief. Wang's most important works are the ninety-eight quatrains in the seven-syllable line collectively entitled "Songs of Huzhou" (Huzhou ge) which depict the journey from Hangzhou to Yan of Empress Dowager Xie, child emperor Gongdi who succeeded Emperor Duzong, and other members of the imperial household. Cast in plain and straightforward language, these poems are poignant expressions of Wang Yuanliang's firsthand experience of the loss of his country and home. A sense of patriotic indignation permeates the entire collection of "Songs of Huzhou" as well as many of his other poems. Some of his contemporaries called his poetry "a poetic history of the fall of the Song dynasty."

One of the most interesting Song loyalists who practiced the pattern of passive resistance after 1279 was the poet–painter Zheng Sixiao (1239–1318). He was a student in the Imperial Academy at the capital when the Song fell. After that fateful event, he changed his given name to Sixiao, suggesting "Thinking of Zhao" – "Zhao" is the surname of the Song royal family, and "xiao" is a part of the character "Zhao." He also gave himself the courtesy name of "The Old Man Who Recalls" (Yiweng) and the *nom de plume* "Placed in the South" (Suonan). He lived the rest of his life as a recluse in a Buddhist temple in Suzhou and named his room there "The Original Cave World" (*Benxue shijie*), with the characters "Benxue" (meaning "Original Cave") serving as an enigmatic reference to the "Great Song." While sitting or lying down, he would never face north, whence the Mongols had come. All of these actions were meant to be symbolic of his loyalty to the Song and of his refusal to give in to the conquerors. He was particularly skillful at painting orchid blossoms in ink. After the collapse of the Song, he painted orchids with sparse blossoms and leaves, and without soil to cover their roots. When asked the reason why, he responded, "The soil has been stolen by the barbarians. Don't you even know it?" Indeed, Zheng was one rare personality among the loyalists who tended to be forthright in expressing his patriotic sentiments.

Unlike Zheng Sixiao, most loyalist writers adopted a subtle and indirect approach to the expression of pain and grief over the Mongol conquest and the destruction of Song civilization. The responses of some of these writers to one historical event can serve as an excellent example. In the twelfth month of 1278, about two months before the Mongols wiped out the lingering Song resistance, a Tibetan lama by the name of Yanglianzhenjia, or Byan-sprin lCan-skya (d. 1292), who had been employed by the Mongols to preside over the Buddhist church in the Yangzi delta area, directed the excavation of six Song imperial tombs and the graves of eminent officials in Shaoxing (in modern Zhejiang). The purpose of the digging was to rob the mortuary treasures in order to build a Buddhist temple. The remains of the Song emperors and their consorts were said to have been uncovered and then abandoned in the wilds. This outrage aroused the fury of some Chinese scholars in the region. One Tang Jue was said to have led a group of young scholars including Lin Jingxi (1242–1310) and Xie Ao to collect and rebury the royal bones in some safe place, and transplanted evergreen ilex trees (*dongqing*) from the palace grounds to the burial site. A week after the excavation, the lama ordered the imperial remains to be collected, mixed with animal bones, and placed at the bottom of a white pagoda, to be named "Pacifying the South" and erected on the old site of the Song imperial palace in Hangzhou. Unaware of the dubious authenticity of the imperial remains, the residents of Hangzhou reportedly grieved over the building of the pagoda in secret resentment. Tang wrote two poems on "The Ilex Trees" cast in obscure language to lament this national tragedy. To emulate Tang's subtle poetic act, all of the references to "the ilex trees" in the writings of the loyalists can be said to allude to this event. The song lyricists at the time did something even more extraordinary.

Early in 1279 fourteen song lyricists, including Tang Jue, Zhou Mi, Zhang Yan, and Wang Yisun, got together in Shaoxing to mourn the desecration of the imperial tombs. In a manner resembling the activity of a poetry society or a song-lyric club, a series of five meetings was held, each presided over by one song lyricist. Five song lyric patterns, sets of specific rhymes, and five objects – namely the incense called "dragon's saliva," the edible water-plant *chun* (*Brasenia purpurea*), the crab, the white lotus blossom, and the cicada – were chosen for the occasion. The fourteen poets, some of the best literary talents of the time, set out to compose altogether thirty-seven song lyrics. The pieces on "dragon's saliva," the *chun* plant, and the crab have been interpreted as referring to the emperors, and those on the remaining two objects, to their consorts. The reasons for the choice of the objects remain difficult to grasp, as all five objects appear irrelevant, except that the dragon is, of course, traditionally a symbol of the emperor. The thirty-seven song lyrics were later put together in one volume under the title *Supplementary Inscriptions of the Song Lyrics* (*Yuefu buti*). To avoid any possible repression from the ruling Mongols, all thirty-seven pieces were made extremely ambiguous and densely allusive. The lushness of language and the very complexity of structure and allegory in these works, which are all "song lyrics on objects," defy adequate translation into English or any brief explanation. Detailed annotation and explication have been done by recent scholars. In many ways, *Supplementary Inscriptions of the Song Lyrics* represents the culmination of a century of developments in the art of the song lyric during the Southern Song, specifically the new aesthetics of spatial form discernible in the song lyrics on objects. In this volume the pain and grief over the destruction of a dynasty, as exemplified in the desecration of the imperial tombs, were expressed in series after series of symbolic luxurious images concentrated on five material objects. By focusing on concrete material objects, the writers were better able to come to grips with the complex emotions of loss, regret, and outrage that constituted their inner states. The creative process employed here is the same as that of reification of emotions we have seen in the song lyrics on objects by Jiang Kui and Wu Wenying. By making the volume, the fourteen poets of the end of the Song paid tribute and showed their continuing loyalty, in a carefully veiled ceremonial act, to the refined and urbane Song civilization that was destroyed by an event in history.

Remembrance and criticism of Song culture

As one might expect, the theme of remembrance of the splendor of the past became important in much writing at the end of the Song and in the early Yuan, especially in the works by the Song loyalists. For the subjects of the Song, the *real* splendor of the past was epitomized by the two capitals, Kaifeng and Hangzhou. Indeed, with their great wealth and culture, these two cities served as the cultural symbol and the central stage of the Northern Song and the Southern Song respectively. With the natural beauty of West Lake and the surrounding hills, Hangzhou was a particularly inviting place. As discussed in the previous section, the five memoirs of the capitals record in detail the life of extravagance and splendor of these two great cities. They are often talked about together within the same works by late Song authors. In the song lyric set to the tune "Congratulating the Bridegroom" (He xinlang) reportedly composed in 1253, for instance, Wen Jiweng (fl. 1250s–1275) wrote,

> That ladle of West Lake's water,
> Since we crossed the River,
> (Has seen) a hundred years of singing and dancing,
> A hundred years of drunken stupor.
> Looking back to Luoyang, that world of flowers:
> A faraway place covered with mists and straggling millet.
> Nobody is ever again seen shedding tears at the New Pavilion.
> Musical ensembles in red attire rock in painted boats –

In the middle of the lake, I ask, is there anyone beating the oars?
The resentment of a thousand generations,
When can it be washed away?
My life ambition has been to clean up the world.

But unlike Jiang Ziya at Pan Stream and Fu Yue at Fu Cliff,
I have yet to be discovered by a true ruler.
On whom can we entrust the affairs of the nation?
The River is but a narrow belt.
All seem to say that we can rely on the River God.
If we ask Recluse Lin on Lone Hill,
He'd just turn his head, smilingly pointing at the plum blossoms in bud.
Alas! affairs of the world, don't we know them already?

Wen Jiweng took second place in the civil service examination in 1253. According-ing to an anecdote found in the late Song and early Yuan text *Miscellaneous Records of Old Hangzhou* (*Guhang zaji*), of which only a number of entries are preserved in other texts today, Wen wrote the song lyric on an outing on West Lake awarded by the central government to those scholars who took the first seventy or eighty places in the examination. Originally from Sichuan in the western region, Wen reportedly wrote it in reply to a question from one of the scholars: "Do you have any scenery like this in Sichuan?" The "River" refers to the Yangzi, and "Luoyang," itself an old capital city, is a metaphorical substitute for Kaifeng. As an outsider to Hangzhou, Wen Jiweng was sharply critical of the life of extravagance, gaiety, and complacency there. Typical of the song lyric in the late Southern Song, this work is studded with allusions. Line 6 in the first stanza alludes to the poem "Straggling Millet" (Shuli) in the *Classic of Poetry*, traditionally read as a piece lamenting the decay of the ancestral temple and palace of Western Zhou (ca 1122–771 BC), overgrown with millet. By use of this allusion, Wen reminded people of their former glo-rious capital now in ruin. "The New Pavilion" in Line 7 alludes to an anecdote in Liu Yiqing's (403–444) *A New Account of Tales of the World* (*Shishuo xinyu*) in which officials of the Eastern Jin dynasty (317–370) who had fled from the north to the south often met at the New Pavilion (Xinting) in Nanjing on fine days to weep together. "Beating the oars" in Line 9 refers to a story about Zu Ti (266–321), a general of the Jin dynasty, who once led his own army and sailed north on the Yangzi. In the middle of the river, he hit the side of his boat and swore that he would recover all the lost land in the north for his country. These allusions are juxtaposed with the image of merrymaking on West Lake to criticize the Southern Song's total lack of concern for the loss of the northern territory.

At the beginning of the second stanza, Wen Jiweng uses three allusions to express his wish to have his talent and ambition recognized by a ruler. Line 1 alludes to Fan Pang (137–169) of the Han dynasty, who was known to have the ambition to "clean up the world." "Pan Stream" is the place where the legendary Jiang Ziya was fishing with a straight hook before he was employed by King Wen (twelfth century BC), father of King Wu who founded the Zhou dynasty (ca 1122–221 BC), and Fu Cliff is the place where, according to legend, Fu Yue was recruited by King Wuding (r. ca 1324–1291 BC) of the Shang dynasty (ca 1766–1122 BC) to be his minister. These three allusions are used by Wen Jiweng as metaphors for himself. He had ambition to clean up the world, but he needed to encounter a true ruler who would employ him. Unfortunately, of course, this is not likely to happen. Recluse Lin refers to the Northern Song poet–recluse Lin Bu (967–1028), a lover of plum blossoms and cranes, who resided in Lone Hill on an islet in West Lake. Lin Bu stands for the many self-proclaimed lofty-minded literati in late Song society. The song lyric ends with a vehement note of the helplessness regarding the situation the Southern Song was in.

In this song lyric written some twenty years before the fall of the Southern Song, Wen Jiweng expressed his acute sense of the impending doom the nation was facing. Many late thirteenth-century literati, however, only described or reminisced about the good life, without much thought given to the nation's fate. The situation for the loyalists after the dynasty's fall was, of course, drastically different. An obsession with remembrance of the past was common, either at the level of personal life or at a level that intermingled the personal with the national. We find many examples of this kind in the song lyrics of Zhou Mi, Zhang Yan, Wang Yisun, and others.

The most remarkable examples of song lyrics on remembrances of things past are to be found in the works of Liu Chenweng, a writer who followed the vigorous and forthright style of Xin Qiji. Like Wen Tianxiang, Liu was a native of Luling. In his youth he spent seventeen or eighteen years moving between Luling and Hangzhou, to take the civil service examination and subsequently to work as a scholar–official. Thus he had ample opportunity to witness the full glory of the capital. After the fall of the Song, he refused to be recruited into service in the Yuan government. In a few song lyrics (notably the ones set to the tunes of "The Willow Tips Are Green" (Liushao qing), "King of Lanling" (Lanling wang), "Forever Meeting with Happiness" (Yong yu le), and "The Precious Tripod Is Revealed" (Baoding xian)), Liu expressed his lament for the fallen dynasty by focusing on remembrance of the celebration of the

Lantern Festival in Hangzhou. "The Precious Tripod Is Revealed," written possibly shortly before the poet's death, is especially a masterpiece. Consisting of three stanzas, this work opens with a stanza depicting the spectacular event in Kaifeng with images of happy revelers. The second stanza begins with the line "Elders still remember things of the Xuanhe era" (to indicate that the depiction in the previous stanza is based on memory of a distant past) and then goes on to describe the Lantern Festival in Hangzhou, focusing on the reflections in West Lake of lanterns from the luxurious mansions along the shore, creating an illusory image of a paradise. The third stanza begins with an image of children on hobbyhorses listening to old people trying in vain to tell them about the singing and dancing of the good old days in Hangzhou. The song lyric concludes with the statement that even if the children had seen those entertainments, the glory of the past would have vanished into a world of dreams by now. There is not a single word of sorrow for the fallen dynasty, nor is there any explicit comparison between past prosperity and the present decline of the capital cities. Yet the whole song lyric is permeated with profound sadness over the fall of Song civilization. This and a number of other song lyrics by Liu Chenweng belong to the best literature produced by a generation of writers who had to live through an era of traumatic dynastic transition.

Contrary to the common trend of obsession with remembrance of the past, a literary scholar by the name of Liu Yiqing (late thirteenth–early fourteenth century) put together a unique text to chronicle the fall of the Southern Song in a somewhat detached fashion. Today we know nothing about the life of this scholar, except that he was a resident of Hangzhou during the period of dynastic transition. Entitled *Anecdotes of Qiantang* (*Qiantang yishi*, Qiantang being an old name for Hangzhou), Liu Yiqing's text consists of ten chapters (*juan*), made up of excerpts from Song dynasty sources ranging from notebooks and miscellanies to some historical documents. Typical of late Song practice, Liu did not indicate the sources from which he had taken material, but some of his sources have been identified by later scholars. He wrote this prefatory note to the text he had compiled:

> Emperor Gaozong made a grave strategic mistake in selecting Hangzhou, rather than Nanjing, to be the capital. [The result of this choice was that] literati and officials knew nothing but to indulge in singing and dancing in the hills and by West Lake, giving no thought to affairs of the world. In the end, they lost their army and harmed their rulers, giving up their land and selling out their country. How lamentable! In reading this book, one cannot fail to be touched by it.

Stated in this note is the theme of the book: the decline and collapse of the Southern Song was chiefly attributable to the extravagant mode of life avidly pursued by its rulers and officialdom. Although most of the materials were taken from notebooks and miscellanies, Liu Yiqing often made slight alterations to, and added comments on, the borrowed material, and took pains in organizing it into a text that shows structure and progression, rather than being a collection of miscellaneous notes and anecdotes. The first eight chapters constitute a short chronicle of the Southern Song from Emperor Gaozong's selection of Hangzhou as the capital to its fall to the Mongols in 1276. Although some events from 1127 to 1276 are referred to, the book is particularly detailed concerning the reigns of Emperor Lizong (r. 1225–1264), Emperor Duzong (r. 1264–1274), and Emperor Gongzong (r. 1274–1276), who became emperor at the age of five. The first four reigns under emperors Gaozong (r. 1127–1162), Xiaozong (r. 1162–1189), Guangzong (r. 1190–1194), and Ningzong (r. 1195–1224) were briefly covered in the first two chapters. Chapter 2 ends with a brief record of the joining of the Mongol and the Southern Song forces in attacking and eventually vanquishing the Jin in 1234. With the buffer state removed, the Southern Song and the Mongols came into direct territorial contact from that point onward. The main topics covered in Chapters 3 through 8 are the persistent and methodical invasion of the Mongols, the intense power struggle among high officials at court, the dominance of powerful ministers such as Han Tuozhou and Jia Sidao, the ineffectiveness of the Song military, the complacency of officialdom. There are also some stories of brave people who sacrificed their lives in defense of the country. Chapter 8 chronicles the major events during the year before the Mongols entered Hangzhou to accept the surrender of the Southern Song court on the twentieth day of the first month in 1276. There is a brief note about the fleeing of two child kings to the seas escorted by a few loyal officials.

Chapter 9 is a day-by-day record, written by the imperial diarist (*rijiguan*) Yan Guangda, of the "northward journey" from Hangzhou to Dadu (present-day Beijing) of the Southern Song emissaries, consisting of Empress Dowager Yang, her grandson the boy emperor, and other high officials of the court, to pay tribute to the Mongol conqueror Khubilai. This record begins on the nineteenth day of the second month of 1276, when the emissaries were taken by their captors to go north, and ends with the ceremony of tribute that took place on the second day of the fifth month of the same year. Liu Yiqing provided no further description of the futile activities of resistance of Song loyalists that continued until 1279, since in a very real and ceremonial sense, the Southern Song perished on the second of the fifth month of 1276. The stories included in the book from Chapter 1 through Chapter 9 follow a general chronological order.

The last chapter of *Anecdotes of Qiantang*, however, is set apart from the preceding nine chapters. It contains a detailed description of the highest level of the civil service examination that was held in the imperial capital. This level of the examination involved two stages: the first conducted by the Ministry of Rites, and the second, for those who passed the first stage, in the palace with the emperor acting as the chief examiner. To be included in the list of scholars who passed the palace examination and were subsequently awarded the degree of "presented scholars" (*jinshi*) was the most important honor that could have come to a man in Song China. Included in the chapter are some details of the ways the "presented scholars" were treated by the central government. Of particular importance was an outing in two pleasure boats on West Lake for the top seventy or eighty scholars, followed by a stroll in an aristocrat's garden where the scholars would receive gifts and a dinner banquet in an extravagant imperial garden. It is obvious that Liu Yiqing includes this Chapter 10 in his text in order to show how much the Song government bestowed honor and prestige upon the accomplished scholars, but unfortunately how "literati and officials knew nothing but to indulge in singing and dancing in the hills and by West Lake, giving no thought to affairs of the world." In a subtle way this chapter echoes the theme stated in the prefatory note.

Between the prefatory note and Chapter 10, Liu Yiqing often depicts the life of indulgence in singing and dancing pursued by the Southern Song elite. He does this by quoting poems, song lyrics, and anecdotes, or by adding comments on passages he cites. It should be noted that Wen Jiweng's composition of the song lyric set to the tune of "Congratulating the Bridegroom" on an outing on West Lake discussed earlier is featured in Chapter 1. Liu Yiqing also several times writes about Jia Sidao's indulgent and decadent life. He comments on this prevailing mode of life in the contexts of "The Mongol Army Crossed the River," "(General) Liu Zheng Surrendered to the Mongols," "The Siege of Xiangyang," "The Fall of Fancheng and Xiangyang," and so on. Thus the main theme remains a subtle, and yet steady and powerful, undercurrent throughout the whole book.

It goes without saying that to explain the fall of the Southern Song solely in terms of the decadent and extravagant mode of life of its rulers and its officialdom is inadequate. Apart from Chapters 9 and 10, Liu Yiqing also includes in his text materials that are of dubious credibility. What Liu Yiqing presents in *Anecdotes of Qiantang* is not a comprehensive and accurate account of Southern Song history but a kind of cultural criticism, a critique of a form of life that contributed to the fall of a dynasty. Given its mixture of authentic historical documents with anecdotal materials, its selection of materials that complement each other to form a coherent view of the fall of a dynasty, its use of numerous poems for artistic purposes, and its arrangement of materials in a chronological order through the first nine chapters, *Anecdotes of Qiantang* should be considered an unusual and remarkable piece of narrative literature compiled by a scholar who witnessed the traumatic fall of a brilliant civilization.

Literature from the late Jin to the early Ming: ca 1230–ca 1375

STEPHEN H. WEST

Overview

China under the Mongols was a time of paradox: the Yuan had the shortest span of any major dynasty, yet the reach of its territory was the most extensive. It was diverse and multiethnic yet was a time in which many peoples were united in a single linguistic–cultural realm. It is also an era the scholarship of which owes much to an interest spawned outside of China by the Mongols' globalized reach. It witnessed the spread of literature in Chinese as far as Samarkand and Uzbekistan; its producers were Buddhists, Christians, Muslims, Chinese, Uighurs, Koreans, and Kazakhs. Whether one calculates the time span of Yuan literature 134 years backwards from its demise in 1368 to the time the Mongols snuffed out the Jin (1234), 107 years to the establishment of the Great Yuan dynasty by Khubilai Khan (1261), or 92 years to its destruction of the Southern Song (1276), it was short-lived. But such neat political divisions, datable to exact symbolic or real moments in the flow of time, obscure the tenacious knit of culture's web, which loosens only through duration of change, reforming and reshaping culture's pattern in small but important ways. While the Yuan's political policies actually did create a significant break in literary continuity and an immediate and recognizable change in the whole cloth of Chinese literature, the dynasty was so short that many of these changes are visible only retrospectively as they unfold more elaborately in later times.

Three major elements mark literature in the Yuan: the first is the maturation of colloquial literature; this continued a development that had become widespread in the Song, but brought it to the attention of a reading audience through print circulation. The language used in these texts made gestures toward performance, adopting either a simple form of demotic classical Chinese or a colloquial style that artistically imitated ordinary speech. In their legitimate Yuan dynasty editions these texts display, in their registers, lexicon, and themes, a high degree of differentiation from the same features in either the contemporary polite canon or later colloquial literature. The second major development was the creation of a body of writers set free from the strictures of preparing for the civil service examinations and for whom writing was an act separated from the need to fashion oneself as a scholar–bureaucrat (*shiren*). Except for prose, which was distinctly associated with *Daoxue* scholars who wrote for the ethical–political purpose of "ordering the world" (*jingshi*), other forms, notably poetry and *fu*, changed radically, reverting, in the former instance, to a more lyrical form reminiscent of the Tang, and in the latter, abandoning the "regulated *fu*" (*lüfu*) that had marked the Jin and Southern Song. The third major element was of course the emergence of ethnic writers as major producers of classical and popular forms.

Whereas in earlier times one can justifiably point to great personalities (for example, Wang Wei, Li Bai, and Du Fu in the Tang, Ouyang Xiu, Su Shi, Wang Anshi, Lu You, and others in the Song) as a way to structure a literary history of polite literature, in the Yuan we find only groups, the "Four Great Poets of the Yuan" (*Yuan shi si da jia*), the "Poetry Society of Moon Spring" (*Yuequan yin she*), or the "Three Elders of Dragon Mountain" (*Longshan sanlao*), and so on. The short duration of the dynasty accounts for a certain curtailed development of a truly "dynastic" polite literature with any recognized individual genius rising above an affiliated group; writers were cut off as recognizably independent buds just as they began to emerge as differentiated petals from a whorl of sepals. The standard histories of Yuan literature acknowledge this and are almost wholly given over to discussions of forms of popular and hybrid literature: northern plays and the colloquial song, with classical letters relegated to a small addendum. In doing so a break is created between the "classical" canon and a new "colloquial" literature, one in which scant heed is paid either to the role or the range of the writer (who often produced in both areas) or to the necessity of textual specificity.

Popular genres include "plain stories" (*pinghua*), which were predominantly historical narratives, northern plays (*zaju*), southern drama (*nanxi*), and colloquial songs (*sanqu*). One of the major problems facing the reader of Yuan popular literature is that the same rules of preservation and philology that govern the textual transmission and editing of classical texts do not come into play with colloquial forms. Despite the fact that none of the early popular genres (except the poetic form of *sanqu*) has any authorship attributed in the Yuan editions themselves, the standard histories of Yuan literature still treat drama retrospectively through authorship assigned in late Yuan and Ming bibliographies, and still treat *pinghua* as a form of "prompt book" for professional storytellers. We know, however, that Ming editors re-created, as much as they edited, northern plays and colloquial songs. For instance, if one compares the language of the extant thirty plays from the Yuan period with that of the Ming rewritings of the same plays, it is clear that historical change and a shift in register both figure. The same holds true to some degree for early colloquial songs: if one examines the corpus of *sanqu* writers as they exist in Yuan editions, it is far smaller than the body of songs that come to form their collected writings at a later date. While it is true that poetry, as well as song, was always subject to expansion, the principles of review, discussion, and selection that accompanied the addition or deletion of classical poetry to a poet's works was missing in the collection of colloquial songs, which were considered for the most part nonserious literature. They were often collected in books of musical or tonic notation that were meant as prescriptive guides to composition, or they were jotted down from hearsay or memory. This is not to say, of course, that many of the Ming versions of these works were not based on Yuan originals, but rather that they had been so heavily edited in the late Ming that they reflect the language and ideology of the editors, not the original writers. Thus, in treating both northern plays and colloquial songs, this chapter will deal only with texts that can be reliably dated to the Yuan period. To write a history based on the textual artifacts, rather than a retrospectively conceived development of literary form, produces a somewhat different picture.

The first dynasty since the Han not to be governed totally by Confucian ideology, the Yuan is also one in which there appear no literary inquisitions. While there is no necessary relationship between adherence to the ethical–political model of Confucianism and literary inquisitions, one seems to exist. Ye Ziqi (fl. 1330–1400), while awaiting execution in the early Ming (he was later released), pondered the nature of Song inquisitions: "The poetic inquisitions of the Song were entirely the fault of the various Confucian scholars." This seems fairly clear when one considers the plight of Fan Zhongyan, Ouyang Xiu, Su Shi, and others who were enmeshed in the bitter factional rivalry of the Song. In all cases, the charges were made through the instrument of the emperor. Chinese rulers were part and parcel of the ethical–literary–political world of government, and persuadable to action through arguments based on supposed ethical or nonethical acts. But it is clear that Yuan emperors had no interest in the factional infighting of Chinese officials at their courts. The Mongols were deeply concerned about any encroachment on their prerogatives to govern or any actions that breached the lines of the strong class and ethnic hierarchies in which they believed, but they simply were not interested in the passions of their Chinese officials about writing. Being themselves only marginally literate, they did not share the deep connection Chinese drew between writing and governance. A classic example is found in the famous incident involving Sangha, a brilliant but power-hungry Tibetan whom Khubilai employed as state minister in the latter part of his reign. After Sangha was purged and executed, some high officials at court tried to exile another minister on charges that he "wrote a poem eulogizing Sangha in the most profuse language." Khubilai responded, "What crime did this writer commit? If eulogizing Sangha is a crime, then who amongst all of the officials at court did not eulogize him? Even I eulogized him."

This lack of interest in Chinese cultural ideals was also reflected in the disestablishment of the examinations, the backbone of the education system and the accustomed path to social and political power. This is usually understood as a prime symbol of the Mongols' dispossession of the literati class (which is defined both as "literati," *shi*, and as "Confucian scholar," *ru*). *Daoxue* under the Song had absorbed much of Daoism and Buddhism into its sophisticated analysis of a metaphysical order of ethics, but these two religions were never acknowledged as equal systems of thought. One of the famous discourses at the court of Khubilai, while he was still a prince, was an argument about the relative merit of each of the three ways of thought, and a direct question: "was the Jin lost because of Confucianism?" This presents us with a paradox again. *Daoxue* became a prominent part of learning in the later Yuan, and we must separate the treatment of "Confucians" (classed as *ru*) as a whole from the gradual acceptance of Zhu Xi's form of *Daoxue* as a nativist ethical–political learning.

From the standpoint of the *shiren*, or "literati," the end of the examinations was a disaster; but from the perspective of literature, it was a quite positive move. After the Mongols conquered north China in 1232–1233, Ögödei, relying on the advice of his minister Yelü Chucai (1190–1244), instituted an examination in 1238, although only on a local level and for the express purpose of supplying local officials. Khubilai later held examinations in 1252, 1271, and 1276. After the conquest of Southern Song in 1276, however, scholars were advanced through a system of patronage, recommended by local or court officials. The examinations were reinstated in 1314, but only as a symbolic act. They were held only on a small scale and were open to abuses. They offered no more than what Fredrick Mote has called "weak promise to would-be Confucian scholars." The examinations were suspended from 1334 to 1340, and altogether only sixteen central examinations were held in the years from 1314 to 1368, promoting only 1,139 successful candidates for the bureaucracy.

This uncoupled writing, as an act, from its most important instrumental use: success in the examinations. As we will see below this detachment played a large part in the "revival of antiquity" (*fugu*) in the Yuan, freeing writers to pursue poetry for its own sake, rescuing it from the poverty of opprobrium, changing the course of *fu* production, and stimulating the creation of texts of popular literature. The picture is complicated.

It is probably prudent to look at the experiences in north and south China as two different models. With the wholesale destruction of the Jin, the literary world of north China was in a shambles after 1233. As Wang Yun (1227–1304) wrote in his 1301 "Record on the Shrine to a Former Academician of the Hanlin Academy, Hu Zhiyu [1227–1295]":

> In the loss and disorder of the last season of the Jin, literati [*shi*] had lost their bearings. The various nobles of earlier generations were rarely at hand, and young students and late starters, once they had no hope of advancing [through the examinations], did not know where to begin properly; some clung stubbornly to the past or buried themselves in out-of-the-way topics, incapable of adapting; some had learned incorrectly or were of small talent, and even in the beginning were of no use. So, the entire world all said, "Confucian scholars [*ru*] hold fast to a singleness without comprehension, wander away from reason, and lack any critical awareness."

Wang is writing this in retrospect, and at a time contemporaneous to that which he describes, there were already pseudo-examinations being held in the north and in the south, yet the topics were not statecraft, but poetry. In both the north, under the Jin, and the south, under the Song, much of the examination system had devolved into a performance of technical skills in the *lüfu* ("regulated *fu*") rather than a deep engagement with the Classics, commentaries, and poetry. As Yuan Haowen (1190–1257) wrote in the north in a memorial stele for his friend Yang Huan (1186–1255):

> At first during the years 1201–1211, those who entered into service considered selection through the examination system the most valued category, and once this path to glory existed, everyone strove with each other to walk it. Everything outside of the examination curriculum, including all of the miscellaneous genres of pen and ink, were pointed to as "a worthless skill." They considered poetry particularly taboo because of its deep potential for violating the rules of the regulated *fu*. There were no more than six or seven notables among the most cultured who were comprehensive scholars of the Classics or celebrated writers of prose.

Dai Biaoyuan (1244–1311), a noted writer and scholar of the Southern Song, expressed a similar opinion at the beginning of the Yuan:

> Many in the current world say that the men of Tang were capable of applying all of their energies to perfecting poetry. But is it only men of Tang? From those who arose from the midst of warfare – Liu Bang, Xiang Yu, and Cao Cao and his son Cao Zhi – they were all capable of it, not to mention civilian scholars. But when it came to men of the Tang, they established poetry as a way to fill out a portion of the examinations. If a man could not do poetry, then he had no way to circulate his name – so they had to become skilled at it. In the recent past, once the various nobles of Bianliang [north China] and the Jiang Zhe region [south China] were no longer selected on the basis of name, the whole affair of poetry was nearly abrogated; should a man not do poetry, it would not harm him becoming a thorough Confucian scholar.
>
> I still remember when I was a youngster and friends with Chen Huifu; we would grasp our pens and our pouches and go out of the gates of our local area to visit famous grandees. Eight or nine out of ten of them were products of the examinations, and the way they succeeded was either through "elucidation of the Classics" or regulated prose. None of them were advanced because of poetry. If one or two appeared among them who had been advanced because of poetry, they were called "a mongrel lot," and no one would deign to use them. Only a few, including Shu Yuxiang [1236–?] of Langfeng in Tiantai and I passed the *jinshi* degree early and took advantage of our spare time to practice poetry. But we still did not consider it an important affair, and each time we droned out a few passages when we were moved by feelings or thoughts we encountered, we stored them away privately in baskets and did not dare show them to anyone. It can be compared to a Daoist master who refines cinnabar or practices inhaling and expelling ethers – it is a secret knack known only within his own poor gates. Even though it is to be highly valued, often it is not something that is completely loved by the whole of mankind. After a while the corrupted practices of the examination system were thoroughly changed, and poetry began to come into its own, but the generation of Yuxiang was already haggard and old, or had passed away. I was also old and losing my hair.

The link was broken between the examinations and government service, and bureaucratic advancement for the most part was accomplished by a system of local patronage and personal recommendations. The abolition of examinations, which included the abolition of the regulated *fu* form, was also important for Confucianism. The regulated *fu* was so highly structured that it had become a performance of acquired objective skills that were judged by their adherence to a set of rules external to ethics. The formalized process, once broken, created the opportunity to reassert the inward-looking ethical values of the idealistic schools of Confucianism, represented best by the commentaries of the Cheng brothers and Zhu Xi on the Four Books. Of course the social capital and power that the patronage system of the examinations produced in the public sphere – based on the lifelong affiliation between examinees and examiners – were utterly destroyed, but other forms of social connections would soon take the examination's place.

It has long been held that Confucian scholars were despised and ill-treated by the Yuan, but this xenophobic tradition apparently lacks substantial proof within the texts themselves. The bedrock proof is most famously quoted from the *History of a Loyal Heart* (*Xinshi*), attributed to the staunch Southern Song loyalist Zheng Sixiao (1239–1318): "The Tatar rules: 1st: officials, 2nd: clerks, 3rd: Buddhists, 4th: Daoists, 5th: physicians, 6th: craftsmen, 7th: hunters, 8th: common citizens, 9th: Confucians, 10th: beggars." But in fact the only Yuan text that mentions such a list is clearly meant to be read as a humorous sarcastic remark about the plight of the "Confucian" vis-á-vis the abolition of the examinations. Xie Bingde (1226–1289) wrote,

> In 1261, [a court astronomer] said, "There is a long-tailed star lodging in a particular asterism . . . and my reading is that the fate of writing is unclear. In thirty years there will be no good writing in China." Confucian scholars gazed toward the blue tower and cursed him, "What kind of a blind codger is he to make such heterodox and misleading statements!" The astronomer laughed when he heard this, saying, "Was I saying that there were particularly no good writings? The Classics will remain, but the Way will be abandoned; the Confucian scholar will exist, but the Way will be destroyed. The examination curriculum will be of no use in the future!" Everyone criticized him for spreading vile rumors.
>
> Sixteen years later it came to pass, and a notable comic made fun of the Confucians, saying, "The laws of our Great Yuan have ten classes of people: 1st: officials, 2nd: clerks – these are the ones who come first. And that they are so valued is because they have some use to the state . . . 7th: craftsmen, 8th: prostitutes, 9th: Confucians, 10th: beggars – these are the ones who come last because they are reviled. The reason they are reviled is because they are of no use to the state! Alas, they are put so low, stuck between prostitutes and beggars – these are Confucians nowadays!"

China's elite might have suffered, but not to the extent that nativist writers would have one believe. Moreover, if this were truly the case, it would be difficult to explain the deep attachment that this same elite held for the Yuan when the Ming conquered it. In many ways, the sentiments of Yuan loyalists were as deeply entrenched as those of the embittered Southern Song loyalists had been seventy years earlier.

The beginnings of a truly "Yuan" literature are complex. Northern and southern China had already been divided for some 107 years (1125–1232) by the time the Jin dynasty fell, and this separation continued for another forty-four years before the Southern Song met its end. In this forty-four-year interregnum, Jin writers dominated the formation of a distinctly northern style. At the end of the Jin there was a remarkable growth of interest in the Tang, rather than the Song, as a poetic model, to the point where a demonstrable conflict emerged not only between factions, but between teacher and disciple as well. As mentioned in the previous chapter, while there were many writers in the Jin who took Su Shi and Huang Tingjian as their models for composition, a sharp break began to emerge between the proponents. Some, like Yuan Haowen, who would be the pivotal figure in a defining the legacy of the Jin, clung closely to Su Shi but, like his friend Wang Ruoxu (1174–1243), began to dissociate Su from the younger Huang. Part of this was a natural result of the clear difference between the original Song writers. Su's emphasis on an intuitive impulse as his true muse was in many ways diametrically opposed to Huang Tingjian, who emphasized the acquisition of talent through study and imitation. Huang's model of poetics, with its carefully graduated steps of mastery of texts and techniques external to the self, provided a much more attainable goal to students, and it spawned the famous Jiangxi School of the Southern Song, which was nearly universally rejected by later Southern Song, Jin, and Yuan writers as being completely imitative and inimical to an intuitive sensibility. For Yuan Haowen, Wang, and other writers of the Jin, Su Shi represented a tradition of antiquity that was more closely based on a spontaneous refined self, and a closer link to the Tang.

This led eventually to reclaiming Tang poetics and a return to the values expressed in the "Great Preface" to the *Classic of Poetry* about the relationship between a refined ethical and aesthetic nature or sensibility and the unmediated expression of that sensibility as it encountered human and natural events. This is a common theme running through much late Jin writing, particularly in Yuan Haowen's prefaces to his contemporaries' poetic collections and in Liu Qi's (1203–1250) miscellany, *A Record of Returning Home to Retire* (*Guiqian zhi*). It is significant that in Liu's work we already find criticism of the debasement of the literati and the growing meaninglessness of the examination system at the end of the Jin. Beginning in 1213 a trend had begun in the bureaucracy to replace literati who had passed the examinations with trained clerks in entry-level positions. While the examinations were not eliminated, there was a general feeling that they no longer served the function of putting learned men into office. The mainstay of the examinations in the Jin, as in the Southern Song, was the regulated *fu*, which had a series of tonal and rhyme stipulations, the mastery of which was one of the primary bases for selection in the examinations. These same rules also were inimical to the mastery of the tonal prosody of poetry (at least in the view of Southern Song and Jin writers).

I. Northern writing to 1300

Clearly the major influence in the north was Yuan Haowen. He emerged from the turmoil at the collapse of the Jin as a major figure in three ways. First, the poetry he wrote during and after the fall of the Jin is undoubtedly some of the finest in the entire tradition, and certainly the most spectacular of his own *oeuvre*. Called "poetry of loss and chaos" (*sangluan shi*) these poems, particularly the seven-syllable regulated form (*lüshi*), have the same density and weight as Du Fu's best, and traditional critics draw a link between the two writers through the term they believe describes both best, "deeply sincere and mournfully desolate" (*shenzhi beiliang*). In his masterly *History of Yuan Poetry*, however, the modern critic Yang Lian points out that despite the heavy influence of Du Fu, Yuan Haowen's poetry demonstrates its own strengths: "whereas Du Fu turned inward to perfect his own poetry during the war, Yuan Haowen simply directly spat out everything he had experienced in the constant warfare." These poems, of which "Three Verses on Qiyang" (Qiyang sanshou), "Five Verses on Affairs after the Imperial Entourage Left to Tour East in the Countryside in the Twelfth Month of the Renchen Year [January–February 1233]" (Renchen shi'er yue jujia dongshou hou jishi wu shou), "Three Verses on Crossing North on the Third Day of the Fifth Month of the Guisi Year [June 12, 1233]" (Guisi wuyue sanri beidu sanshou), and "Continuing the Songs of Young Maidens" (Xu Xiaoniang ge) are considered the best, are somber, well-crafted pieces that reflect his changing state of mind and self-questioning in the few months of the Mongol invasion that they cover in real time. The originality of his works have been noted by major critics like Zhao Yi (1727–1814) and Weng Fanggang (1733–1818), who applaud Yuan for avoiding the repetitious language and themes found in even the best of Song poets – Su Shi and Lu You.

Second, during the early years of the Mongol conquest, Yuan Haowen, thwarted in his ambition to carry the Veritable Records of each imperial reign of the Jin to safety, began to travel through north China seeking to recover historical materials. He built a study at his home in Shanxi where he sorted out his materials and compiled a major historical work, the *Miscellaneous Compilation of Events of the Renchen Years* (*Renchen zabian*), now lost, which became one of the bases of the *History of the Jin*. As he did this, his interest in genealogies of prominent families also provided him a way to make a living by composing an extraordinarily large number of grave inscriptions for northern families. This was a way both to earn income and to amass critical historical and biographical information for his history. The production of texts did not stop with history. Much of his data was gathered orally, and those tales and stories that were clearly not historical he put into a small miscellany, or notebook of legends and tales of the supernatural, which he entitled *A Continuation of the Records of Yi Jian* (*Xu Yi Jian zhi*), a thematic continuation of the great collection of tales compiled by Hong Mai in the Song, the *Records of Yi Jian*.

Finally, Yuan Haowen had immense influence on the first generation of northern writers in Yuan for two reasons. First, he was a local hero in Shanxi, having both contemporary and subsequent influence on the formation of a distinct lineage of Shanxi writers. Second, in Shanxi, and particularly in Shandong where he lived for many years under house arrest after the fall of the Jin, he became a prominent teacher. Yuan created a self-styled persona as a "man from Bingzhou," Bingzhou being an ancient name for the region of southern Shanxi. In his writing he emphasizes this "Bingzhou spirit," as a martial, robust, and patriotic strain that runs back to the Six Dynasties as a defining regional characteristic. Local affiliation had always been a part of Chinese writers' mentalities, but this attachment to place was certainly strengthened during periods when the universal institutions of a shared cultural community were shattered: when the state was sundered and the institutional structures of the Confucian belief system were disbanded or fell into disrepute. Under such circumstances local affiliation becomes a way to construct an enduring identity in a troubled and fractured world.

One of the first recognizable groups to form in the north after the fall of the Jin was the group called the "Various Old Holdovers from the Yellow and Fen Rivers" (*He Fen zhulao*, hereafter the He Fen writers), whose works are found in two collections, *The Poetic Collection of the Various Old Holdovers from the Yellow and Fen Rivers* (*He Fen zhulao shiji*) and the *Collection of the Two Marvelous Ones* (*Ermiao ji*). The eight writers known collectively as the "Various Old Holdovers from the Yellow and Fen Rivers" were all writers of the same era as or a little bit later than Yuan Haowen. The poems of the He Fen writers were collected and anthologized by Fang Qi (ca 1260–1301) who, like Yuan Haowen and the He Fen writers themselves, was from an area in

Shanxi along the Fen river from Taiyuan south to the Fen's confluence with the Yellow River. This valley bore the brunt of the first Mongol invasions of 1213–1214 and was continuously ground zero for the war between the Jin and the Mongols. All of the He Fen writers dropped out of government service with the Mongol victory and spent their lives in and around the area of Pingyang in southern Shanxi. They had each suffered a similar fate: all had gone through the war together, all were friends of Yuan Haowen and other Shanxi writers of note, and all shared a tenor and style in their poetry. Most were in their thirties when the Jin fell, and all lived another twenty or thirty years under the Yuan, a period of time that was the most productive of their lives. The two major writers found in the text are the two brothers Duan Keji (1196–1254) and the younger Duan Chengji (1199–1279), who were brought to the attention of Zhao Bingwen in the Jin who named them the "Two Marvels" (*Ermiao*). In sum, the poetry of the He Fen writers is model poetry of nostalgia for one's former, now lost, state (*yimin shi*). They adopted Yuan Haowen's model of integrity – refusing to serve the new dynasty and working hard to preserve the cultural traditions of the Jin – and this act promoted a "path of correct learning for the He Fen poets," as Che Xi wrote in the Ming. Their poetry of loss and suffering, also akin to Yuan Haowen's, reanimated the Song tradition of interpreting Du Fu and its combination of deep feeling and lyricism. As Yang Zhongde is quoted in Fang Qi's postface to *The Poetic Collection of the Various Old Holdovers from the Yellow and Fen Rivers*,

> If one does not observe the poetry of Yuan Haowen, one lacks a way to understand the learning of the Old Holdovers; if one does not observe the poetry of the Old Holdovers, one is without a way to understand the greatness of Yuan Haowen. If one does not observe the writings of Yuan Haowen and the Old Holdovers, one does not understand the subtlety of many works of Tang authors.

Many of the luminaries of Yuan literature were also Yuan Haowen's students or younger colleagues. Hao Jing (1223–1275), Wang Yun, and Liu Bingzhong (1216–1274) all fell under his influence as a writer and preserver of Chinese culture in a time of chaos. With these students, however, the story of northern literature becomes quite a bit more complex. Hao Jing, for instance, is also considered one of the earliest northern Confucian scholars to accept and promote the Zhu Xi school of *Daoxue*. Hao was the grandson of Yuan Haowen's own teacher, Hao Tianting (1161–1217), and studied directly with his grandfather's student. Hao Jing, like Wang Yun and Liu Bingzhong, had been part of Khubilai's court before he became emperor. When the Mongols had reached a stalemate in their advance against the Southern Song, Hao Jing advised Khubilai to sue for peace, regroup, and then attack with a better plan. This bit of good advice led Khubilai, when he ascended the throne as emperor of the Yuan, to enlist Hao into his government. Hao was immediately sent to the Southern Song as an envoy to discuss peace. He was detained on entry by Jia Sidao (1213–1275), the prime minister of Southern Song, because Jia was afraid that his own defeats at the hands of the Mongols – about which he had lied – would come to light if Hao Jing were to reach the capital. So the northern envoy remained a captive under house arrest for nearly sixteen years, returning only after Jia Sidao was executed after his armies fell to the Yuan commander Bayan. Hao lived only a few months after his release, dying in the Yuan capital, Dadu.

One of the features of Hao Jing's writing is its deep interiority. In his "On Nurturing the Self" (Yang shuo), he wrote,

> The most great, the most firm, nourished without harm, limitless energy that stuffs all between heaven and earth – this is how Mencius nourished his energy. From this angle, the way one nourishes the self is the cause of a sage being sagely, a worthy being worthy, and greatness being great.

And, for him, this energy was generated solely from within as a product of the mind. In "Inner Roaming" (Nei you), he wrote,

> Therefore, as for those who desire to learn transcendent roaming and seek aid from outside [the self], why do they not simply seek it inside? The body never leaves the mat where it sleeps, yet roams outside of the six closures; it is born at the end of a thousand antiquities yet roams to a time before – can those who are restricted solely to the vestiges of their own travels, or the last little parts of what they have actually witnessed, be capable of this? One holds fast to the heart and drives one's energy; and one's enlightenment is correct, one's essence unified. One roams within but does not grow stagnant, one responds to what is outside but does not go out to pursue it. Often in repose, one can act; often still, one can move; often sincere, one can keep from thinking wildly; often in harmony, one does not tremble in anxiety. Once knowing still water – in which all things are still and cannot be transformed – is like a bright mirror, then the shape of all things cannot escape it; it is like the measuring of a balance scale, the measuring weight lies within me. There is no partiality, no reliance, no filth, no stagnation, no harassment, no stirring up. Each thing one meets, one can roam in . . . Once one has roamed, once one has gotten it, then one can wash one's mind and fast, withdraw and store it in the hidden; seeing when it is possible, one produces it from time to time;

when one can make it active, activate it, when one can make it still, still it; when one can prolong it, prolong it, when one can make it quicken, make it quicken. From harboring it, it becomes virtuous action; from performing it, it becomes livelihood. Therefore it is not merely a product of writing. If it is like this, then my unsurpassed Way and my limitless energy are one with heaven, and will need no aid from mountain or stream.

This may be seen as the starting point of Hao Jing's theory and practice of writing, and it is clear that it is also a product of his long captivity. This belief about the ability to rely on nothing outside the self is also part of his critical assessment of writing. In a letter he sent to a friend, "In Reply to a Friend's Discussion of the Principles of Prose" (Da youren lun wenfa shu), he pointed out that in all of the genres of the past, the tradition had picked only a few writers out of thousands as superb:

> For the methods of the *Sao* and *fu*, we base ourselves on Qu Yuan and Song Yu; for the methods of history, on Sima Qian; for the methods of narrative compilations, Ban Gu and Yang Xiong; for methods of stele inscription, Cai Yong; for old-style prose, then on Han Yu and Liu Zongyuan; for the methods of discourse and analysis, on Ouyang Xiu and Su Shi. In the past thousand years, none of the other thousands of prose pieces are considered models. Why? All of the superb writers establish their methods by personally attaining first principles, therefore they become noted and establish methods for others. If you set your mind only on the method of others to write prose, how can you become a noted writer?

As he went on to say,

> Modern writers of prose do not need to look at the methods of others to write, they must only understand the principles behind it; carefully and finely exhaust all of the principles under heaven, then the creator of things "is in *me*"; on the basis of this principle, make these words, write this prose, complete this method – all is done by *me* alone.

The philosophical influence of *Daoxue* is quite clear in Hao's reliance on interiority. But this also becomes a somewhat negative feature of his writing. His literary production has been uniformly praised, but it is primarily because of his status as a figure in the intellectual and political history of the early Yuan. His poetry, noted because of its "eccentric nature" (*qijue*) and extensive use of rhymes that use words ending in -p, -t, and -k stops, tends toward an overly refined and aesthetic verse that invites readers into a deeply subjective world. Whatever value the poems possess in terms of revealing the mental and emotional states of the writer, they are marred by a somewhat careless construction that critics assail for its inability to hold the reader's interest as well as their feeling of "dryness and astringency" (*kuse*).

Wang Yun (1227–1304), like Hao Jing, was an important transitional figure from Yuan Haowen to a truly Yuan style of writing. Again, like Hao, he also succeeded in attaining high political office in the early Yuan, holding important positions in the Hanlin Academy and the Bureau of History. Wang was also the ghost author of most of the edicts issued by Khubilai Khan during the early years of his regency. Only eight when the Jin fell, he studied under a relatively famous Confucian scholar called Wang Pan (1202–1293) and received some direction from Yuan Haowen. His writing significantly contrasts with that of Hao Jing. He was, first, extremely prolific, leaving more than three thousand poems in his *Collection of the Autumn Runnel* (*Qiujian ji*), which is also one of the largest collections of personal writings left from the Yuan. Second, whereas Hao was deeply subjective, Wang's writings tend to be documentary essays of events and places. This holds true not only for his three collections of miscellanies (*biji*), but also for his poetry. Wang was, perhaps, the first of the Yuan dynasty "literary official" (*wenchen*) poets, and he often wrote from a sense of duty. Many of his poems are about conditions in north China during the early Yuan, often unrelieved descriptions of hardships or detailed analyses of current political events, written in an unpolished, repetitive style, full of prosodic miscues. Yet, because of their exquisite detail they are excellent even though sometimes overly discursive reflections of the social and political condition of his times.

Wang, moreover, constitutes an important figure in the development of a distinguishable Yuan style of poetry that harks back to the Tang – if not in practice, clearly in theory. Wang's essay "Preface to Mr. Guo Yi'an's Collected Works" (Yi'an Guo xiansheng wenji yin) continues the critical lineage of Yuan Haowen and the He Fen writers in terms of their veneration of Tang models. In his critique of the poetry of Guo Hao (1194–1268), Wang remarked,

> Although literary texts trace back to and elaborate the Six Classics, honor and set out the various philosophers, and are precisely that part of writing that is well crafted and logical, still their roots must be nourished by the Way and righteousness and their stems and branches must be collected and stored through questioning and learning. There must be a long tradition of study that venerates and refines the structure of their language. They must be ceaselessly composed again and again until they have been worked to a perfection that is smooth and round. One must take self-achievement and instrumentality as the basis, get rid of superfluous gorgeousness and stale

cliché before one can reach the realm of centered harmony or unsullied uprightness.

Mr. [Guo] Zhouqing, in his youth and because of his status as a matriarchal grandson of Zhang Jian, was able to mix with the various famous scholars of the Shanxi and Shaanxi areas like the noble Ma Ge, the Duan brothers, Meng, and Li (?). So the depth of what he has stored away and the breadth of his learning can be said to have a long source in the practices of that tradition. So his prose and poetry are warm and pure, classical and elegant, exhausting at every turn his own ideas. He is able to express completely what he desires to say, plainly and ordinarily yet with deep implicit meaning, gently and without pressure, in the same way he is as a person, full of a surplus of benevolence, righteousness, and the Way and its virtue.

These lines have a striking resemblance to the sentiments expressed in Yuan Haowen's prefaces to the collections of his contemporaries, particularly his "Preface to the *Xiaoheng ji* of Yang Shuneng" (i.e. Yang Hongdao) and his preface to Yang Peng's *Taoran shiji*, where he praises their likeness to the great Tang poets who "did not know there was language beyond that of feeling and human nature." This is more than coincidence. Like Yuan Haowen, Wang Yun was deeply anxious about the preservation of Chinese (specifically northern) culture under the Yuan. Thus Wang's interest in Yuan Haowen may be more inspired by cultural anxiety than by a desire for literary affiliation.

The last link in the northern contribution to a strictly Yuan literary tradition was provided by Liu Yin (1249–1293), a complicated and interesting person. Quan Zuwang (1705–1755), author of supplementary notes to the *Case Studies of Song and Yuan Scholars* (*Song Yuan xue'an*), grouped Liu Yin and Xu Heng (1209–1281) as the two notable Confucian scholars and writers of the early Yuan, although their political attitudes were completely different. Xu willingly served the Mongols, hoping to encourage them to effect Confucian rule in China. Liu Yin refused and, except for a very brief period, held no office in the Yuan, declining a series of requests.

There are many theories about why Liu Yin declined the summons of Khubilai, and it became a source of many discussions in later dynasties. Although he lived a full generation after its fall, he deeply lamented the fall of the Jin; and, as the Mongol conquest of the Southern Song ground on, he also changed from a relatively judgment-free attitude about the Yuan to a stance deploring the loss of the Song. He could not be called "a remnant holdover" from the prior dynasty, and although his own family had served the Jin the loss of the Southern Song seems to have been a traumatic event for him. For instance, he had been eager to serve in government when younger, but his desire changed over time. By the time he was thirty, three years after the Song fell, he wrote,

> Early on I was wild and edgy, as if I was to have some aim in life. But my inner substance was weak and twisted, and before thirty it had already lost any body. When I examine why there was no completion, it truly came from my greed and ineptness . . . When I think back upon my original mind, it now seems so hazy that it appears to be lost. Now here I establish a hall, which is my only ambition. To have students to whom to lecture on learning, to have a place to advance self-cultivation, and to have books to pursue questions to the end, comparing and evaluating incidents, to still be able to make some small contribution to bequeathed words from the past and to those who study in the present – this will soothe my heart in no small way.

Perhaps the best way to understand his sense of loss is to view it not in terms of the demise of a state, but as uncertainty about the preservation of a truly Chinese culture. This may explain both Liu's initial interest in *Daoxue* as a "Chinese way" (*Hanfa*) that could save culture if effected through a political process, and his slight estrangement from its basic principles when it became clear, after Khubilai's falling out with his Chinese advisers, that the Mongols were not interested in cultural preservation. It is, in fact, a complicated process to determine the exact status of writers and thinkers of the early Yuan. It was common in the tradition to that point to see writing and politics or thought as a package in which ethics and sensibility, learning and practice, politics and cultural production were intimately intertwined. This may account, for instance, for the high evaluation of a cultural martyr like Hao Jing, who was an excellent theorist of literature, but only a reasonably good writer. Contemporary people were unable to separate the person as a culture figure from the person as a writer. Gradually, however, because of the rise of literature as an art that had become separated from its instrumental use in the examination system, some expansion of critical opinion was possible. This was important in regard to Liu Yin because, except for one funerary epitaph by his student, there were no other funerary documents for him, which was unusual for a writer with such a large network of relationships. One reason for this lack was the inability of contemporary writers to "make a decisive call after the coffin was closed," as the Chinese put it, about his place *outside* of writing – both his commitment to *Daoxue* and his pessimism about the Yuan court could find no single integral explanation. Having been trained early on in the Classics, Liu turned in his late twenties to the *Daoxue* agenda associated with the Cheng brothers and Zhu Xi. He was not, however, a zealous adherent, particularly in terms of the relationship between philosophical writing and belletristic literary production. Yu Ji (1272–1348) wrote about Liu, "In my perception of our state at the moment of its first unity, could there have been one more firm and courageous or lofty and enlightened among northern scholars than Liu Yin?" Yu is talking here about both Liu's Confucian interests and his literary accomplishment. Like many early Yuan Confucian scholars, Liu Yin did not adhere to the line between literature and instrumental prose that was the earmark of the Cheng–Zhu School, which insisted that the sole purpose of writing was to "transport the Way." This boundary crossing was clear not only for the writers, but for critics as well. This did, however, allow for an analysis of his worth as a writer alone, as in Li Dongyang's (1447–1516) comments in his poetry talks:

> The two who stand as the selected ones of the Yuan are Liu Yin and Yu Ji, each of whom can be called famous, but no one can make a precise call to place one higher than the other. The world often "turns their collar left" for Liu Yin . . . I alone say that, as for being one of high notable station, being forceful and sternly correct, for attacking a redoubt or blunting a point, then Liu has a day's head start. But for hiding the point of the spear, concealing the blade, for being able to produce the marvelous to wrest away a victory, like pearls rolling around a plate or a horse's flight through thin air – at first you do not see the marvelous subtlety, but the deeper you probe, the more there is to get out of it – then there is something to seizing upon Yu. This is *not*, however, a discussion of their integrity as *Daoxue* scholars, but precisely a discussion of their poetry.

This distinction between poetry and *Daoxue* was a crucial element in later assessment of Liu Yin's verse. But, as in so much of literary criticism, it was often the anxieties of the critics that are mostly in play. Hu Yinglin's (1551–1602) comments praise Liu's old-style verse at the same time that they criticize the pedantry of his regulated forms:

> Liu Yin's old-style selections imitate the harmonious simplicity of Tao Yuanming: there are good sentences but no complete poem. His longer song forms imitate Du Fu's . . . works: it is a seasoned pen that travels the length and breadth; and although it sometimes slips over into the Song-like works, still it does not show any of the posturing of the Confucian student. Of all of the seasoned and strong seven-syllable poems in the Yuan, one may say there are only Liu Yin's and no other. But his regulated form and his quatrains with their student pedantry are extremely boring.

This probably says more about Hu Yinglin's obsession with refined subjective states than about Liu's style, but it does point out that there is a certain amount of discursive writing in Liu's regulated forms. If, however, we reconsider Hu's criticism in light of Liu's own temperament – that is, to see cycles of stability, endangerment, and possible extinction as cultural rather than dynastic – the conclusion is that these passages are about the poet's state, not about the objective world. A very good example is a quatrain called "On the Road at Cold Feast," describing the time of year when newly married women went home for a visit to help with cleaning the graves and offering sacrifices to ancestors on the Clear and Bright Festival:

> Hat-tucked flowers fresh and bright: girls home for their first visit,
> Shoulder-borne hoes here and there: people going to the graves;
> Ancient human hearts are present now in meaning,
> Following peach and plum to renew one more time.

The idea that nature and history come and go, and that each is renewed through biology or ritual, is certainly a philosophical statement. But, when we put this poem side by side with a few lines from another, "On Reading History," we can see that Liu finds in these discursive moments a point at which the subject of the poet merges with a greater historical reality, which itself is composed by and of human feeling:

> The records are prolix and chaotic, have already lost any authenticity,
> The judgmental weight of words resides in the writers alone;
> If one evaluates calculating minds word by word by word,
> Will not an endless number have been wronged?

Thus ambiguous motives in his own actions, inconclusive to his contemporaries, somehow resonate with his poetry in the sense that they are concerned both with history and with human renewal through cultural acts. These discursive passages demonstrate how history for him functions not as a marker of dynastic change, but as a represented body of action that offers possible choices of models for being human. Liu has a large body of poems "cherishing the past" (*huaigu*) that, as Yang Lian says, "allow him to savor again human life, and to probe the puzzle of human fate." Thus the discursive passages, so troubling to later critics, can be seen as a natural part of the poet's mentality, existing in a seamless state between subjectivity and the outer world. But this history of the outer world is not objective, Liu says; it "resides in the writers alone," and its only true significance is in its capacity for repetition. Human action, the description of which, or the immediacy of which, is enough for some poets, gains meaning for Liu only when it is buried within a complex process of cyclical repetition in which the past is also the present. Historical processes (and the discussion of them) are never "out there," but are part of the subject of the poet, in whom alone meaning resides.

Liu's poetic criticism, which is elaborated in his essay "Recounting Learning" (Xuxue), is largely derivative of Yuan Haowen. He shows the same sentiments as expressed in Yuan's "Thirty Poems on Poetry," but he seems to have a special distaste for some Late Tang writers: "Certainly it is no way to write poetry if one copies the atrophied weakness of the Late Tang – imitating the pointed novelty of Wen Tingyun and Li Shangyin or intentionally being like the exaggerated strangeness of Lu Tong." Yet his own verses show a remarkable influence from Li He, whom he consciously modeled himself on, saying at one point, "Call me Mr. Liu Changji," Changji being the style name of Li He. Liu was the first northern Yuan poet to vaunt the works of Li He as a fit poetic model.

Liu Yin was, likewise, highly conventional in his prose. He had a definite tendency to see prose as a utilitarian tool to be used for "ordering the world." He acknowledged that the Song prose masters "could be studied" (kexue), but his own interests ran to a discursive prose oriented toward problems. This is seen in the large number of political or philosophical essays and the small number of incidental pieces in his collection. Even in his incidental pieces, philosophical argument takes priority. For instance, in his "Record of Roaming in Mr. Gao's Garden" (You Gaoshi yuan ji), over two-thirds of the text of over three hundred words is given over to a discussion of the "principles of heaven and earth that produce life after life without cease."

The northern tradition of writing was a continuation of the Jin in many ways. The return to Tang models of poetry, the split between those writers who preferred Li Bai and Du Fu and those who were enamored of the Late Tang writers, all have their roots in the discourse of late Jin. What we may see as innovative, perhaps, is due to the fall of the Jin and then the demise of the Song somewhat later: the rise of distinctive regional schools as centers of identity formation, the broad-scale vision of cyclical change in which cultural anxiety replaced dynastic considerations, and the growth of an interiority that was a unique combination of Daoxue and the centrality of "human feeling and emotion" that was, perhaps wrongly, ascribed to the greatest of Tang writers.

II. Southern writing to 1300

When the Southern Song fell, two trends can be clearly discerned: one was the development of the typical phenomenon of the yimin or yilao, "loyalists" or "remnant holdovers" whose minds were very much trapped in the previous dynasty and the trauma of its fall. These poets remained in the south, creating networks of writers whose major output was lament for the fallen Southern Song. The other phenomenon was that dynastic change opened up areas of China that had been closed to the south since the mid-1100s. Thus it offered the possibility for exploration and travel. A large number of northern writers had moved into the south with the mass migration from the north in the 1120s, but the flow now reversed, spearheaded by Buddhist and Daoist monks who traveled out of piety or curiosity to the great temple complex at Mount Wutai in Shanxi or to Dadu, the new capital. Because the split between north and south had been so rigorously enforced in the preceding 150 years, the reclamation of the north seems to have replaced the inherent tendency in earlier periods to see a distinct tension between elements of what could have been called "Chinese" culture: northern and southern temperament and styles. The free flow of travel under Pax Mongolica afforded a new sense of unity, in which Chinese culture surged back into a geographical area that had been non-Chinese for some time, in a total environment in which intra-heartland differences were replaced by a distinction between Chinese and non-Chinese culture.

Since the *yimin* of Southern Song have been treated in earlier chapters, we will begin our discussion of southern writers with a closer examination of the major cultural phenomena and writers that had a lasting influence on Yuan writing.

One of the implications of the end of the examination system is that writers, particularly practitioners of the poetry (*shi*) genre, entered into a compensatory cultural space that the examinations had formerly occupied. Poetic competitions in the south, particularly, resurrected the formative ideals and structure of the examination system but placed literary composition, as an act independent of political mobility, at the center of the acquisition of social and cultural capital. Instead of testing the shared body of canonical materials that was at the core of the examination curriculum, they created societies that examined writers on their ability to write poetry on a single topic. The practice was not new in China – incidental poetry on one topic by a group of writers was a standard social practice. What was new were the extent of the practice and the creation of mock institutional forms to judge the quality of the work and to award prizes that were shadow accolades of the examination system. The themes of these contests were varied: flowers, colophons on calligraphy and paintings, parting poems, poems celebrating appointments to positions, poetic gatherings, historical sites and events (including Yue Fei's gravesite), and, among a variety of other topics, perhaps most importantly, palace poems and "bamboo songs" from West Lake in Hangzhou. This resulted, for instance, in hundreds of colophons to the works of painters like Gao Kegong (1248–1310) and Zhao Mengfu (1254–1322), and in independently compiled and printed collections of poems on a single theme, with a preface by the convener (see Yang Weizhen, below).

The large gatherings that accompanied these events made specific poetic acts a cultural commodity that was widely negotiable in terms of area and the social spectrum of practitioners, strengthening communication and the cultural bond between writers – much as the examination system had done. Perhaps the most influential and best known of the variety of salons that emerged in south China was The Poetic Society of Moon Spring (Yuequan yinshe), named after Moon Spring in Pujiang, near modern Jinhua. In November 1286, Wu Wei, a retired magistrate who had refused to serve the Yuan, sent out invitations to the poetic societies known to him, asking writers to compose a poem on the topic "Random Inspirations in Field and Garden in Days of Spring" (Chunri tianyuan zaxing) to be submitted to him at his residence in Pujiang on the day of the Lantern Festival, the fifteenth day of the first lunar month, or January 29, 1287. An announcement would be posted on the third day of the third lunar month, or April 16, listing the winners. Some 2,735 poems were collected and judged by a panel of the eminent writers who, having refused to serve the Yuan, made up the society: Wu Wei, Fan Feng (1240–1321), Xie Ao (1249–1295), and Wu Siqi (1238–1301). To assure impartiality, poets used pen names, and the names of the examiners were sealed from view. The responses came from all the major areas of south China: modern Zhejiang, Jiangsu, Fujian, Guizhou, and Jiangxi. Some 280 poems were selected, ranked, and published along with the critical commentary by the judges and the number and amount of awards. This book, *Poems of the Poetic Society of Moon Spring*, is still extant. The top winner was awarded seventy feet of silk, five pens, and five sticks of ink.

There is no doubt that this poetic society, and others as well, were acts of resistance. The selection of a pastoral theme was, as Quan Zuwang noted in the Qing, a clear act of defiance:

The various gentlemen of the Poetic Society of Moon Spring remained resolute at the end of the Song in the style of [Tao Yuanming's] "eastern hedge" and "northern window." They were together at one time, touching the proud trees and looking at the flowing streams, all them the image of the man from the Eastern Jin – they can be called stout men indeed!

This is clear also in the poems themselves. For instance, the first couplet of the highest-ranked poem begins, "Aged me, I have no heart to go to the public world, / In eastern winds in forested valleys I will wander free as a bird."

By instituting these examinations, the poetic society kept the value of writing alive as a cultural act and, at the same time, renewed a literati culture in which social and cultural authority continued to be linked to competition and to the rewards of good writing. In a world falling apart, the ability to continue, even in shadow form, the main institutional feature of Chinese learning provided a sense of continuity and a personal satisfaction. It also introduced one of the main features of Yuan poetry: the collection of poems on a single topic. Rather rare before the late Southern Song, such collections made poetry a highly cohesive social act. It is remarkable that these societies grew completely out of personal interest, over a wide area, in a time when communications were bad. It is also a remarkable characteristic of the Yuan – and the Yuan alone – that there was no interference from the authorities in the development of this purely private and extensive network of communication.

The extensive poetic exchanges on a single topic became standard fare and continued throughout the Yuan in literati circles. As one modern critic wrote, "poetry became the calling card and the identification document of those who participated in nightly revels in gardens." The range of these centers was broad: there were the Uighur Lian Xilian's (1231–1280) gathering in the Myriad Willows Hall (Wanliu tang), located in the southern portion of the Yuan capital (modern Chongwen district, Beijing), Xu Youren's (1286–1341) Country Estate in Guitang (Guitang bieshu) in Henan, Gu Ying's (1310–1369) Wonderful Place amid Jade Mountains (Yushan jia chu) in Kunshan, the famous painter Ni Zan's (1301–1374) Gallery Enclosed in Purity (Qingbi ge) in Wuxi, and Yang Weizhen's (1296–1370) Gallery of Grass Script's Subtlety (Caoxuan ge) in Wuxing. The importance of these locales in terms of production can be seen in the fact that, of all of the poems written between 1341 and 1367, more than one out of every ten was produced in Gu Ying's salon.

At the end of the Yuan these societies continued to exert their influence on Chinese culture and provide a safe cultural space for literati. As Wang Shizhen remarked,

> When the Yuan was lost, the net of the law was loosened and people did not need to serve in office. There were poetry societies in Zhejiang every year, and one or two eminent elders from the earlier dynasty like Yang Weizhen were picked to serve as overseers, and the best of the poems were published

to serve as models. When Rao Jie [d. 1366] was in service to the "False Wu" [at the end of the Yuan] he solicited the poem "Song of the Tipsy Woodcutter" from the various notables. Zhang Jian was first and Gao Qi was second. Zhang Jian was given ten taels of gold and Gao Qi three catties of silver.

The first major Yuan figure from the south was Fang Hui (1227–1307), a native of Anhui. He holds a problematic position in history because he was one of the first officials to surrender to the Mongols. His immediate capitulation is often contrasted with the "great integrity" (dajie) of culture heroes like Wen Tianxiang, Xie Bingde, and Xie Ao, who remained loyal to the Southern Song to the death. Fang served briefly under the Mongols, but then spent the majority of his time moving around in a limited ambit southeast of Hangzhou, where he made a livelihood from his writing. His character was still under consideration in the Qing, when Ji Yun, the famous compiler of the *Complete Treasury of the Four Repositories of Literature* (*Siku quanshu*), called him "the epitome of the completely unethical literatus" (*wenren wuxing . . . zhi ji*). Despite the issue surrounding his character, his poetry and critical works are all accepted as works of depth.

His major work was the *Yingkui lüsui*, an anthology of representative five- and seven-syllable regulated *shi* poems from the Tang and the Song. The title means roughly *The Essentials of the Regulated Verse of the Poets of the Tang and Song*. There are forty-nine thematic chapters to the work, each with a short introduction. Words in a poem that indicate its "eye" (*shiyan*) – its point of critical excellence – he marked with a circle, and he follows each poem with a short critical statement. Compiled in 1282, the work is primarily a critique of late Southern Song poetry, particularly that of the Four Lings and the Rivers and Lakes poets. In compiling this work, Fang Hui wanted to renew the place of the Jiangxi School in the tradition as a corrective to the overly refined and vulgar nature of the two aforementioned schools. He advocated what he called the "one progenitor and three ancestors" (*yizu sanzong*) of Du Fu, Huang Tingjian, Chen Shidao, and Chen Yuyi, which he named the "correct school of poetry" (*zhengshi zhi pai*), and indeed in his critical comments he often refers to these writers as the highest standards of creativity. He also criticized the Xikun style of the early Song. Fang Hui emphasized "correct methods" (*fa*) for both words and lines and stressed that the highest style was "thin and hard" (*shouying*), "seasoned and strong" (*laola*), and had something definite from which it stemmed (*chuchu laili*). He repeated the major points of the Jiangxi School as defining characteristics of good verse: poetry should represent loftiness in its establishment of aims, hard work in its application of the mind, extensive reading, and authenticity in following the masters. He was, however, evenhanded enough to point out the flaws of the Jiangxi School, clearly delineating how it differed from coeval poetic movements, while simultaneously substantiating its role in the development of the Southern Song poetics.

Nearly all of his own 2,715 extant poems were written during the early Yuan and are thus a product of his later life. Like Wang Yun in the north, his collection is marred by a lack of selectivity and by the inclusion of pedestrian pieces. Still, as he said, he had "already pawned his official gowns for cash for wine," and he spent that portion of his life working solely on poetry. His own style gradually changed during his later years, as he remarked himself:

> I was twenty when I started studying poetry, and now I am seventy-six. As for seven-syllable verse, I certainly did practice the style of Xu Hun but I unrealistically looked toward [the standard set by] Huang Tingjian, Chen Yuyi, and old Du; my energies were no match for theirs, so I withdrew to write in the style of Bai Juyi and Zhang Lei . . . As for five-syllable-line verse, I envied Chen Shidao, but after many hard, vain attempts, I also generally withdrew to do an even and easy style [*pingyi*] with some of the techniques of Jia Dao. But no one recognized it.

The other major figure, of course, was Dai Biaoyuan, mentioned above. He was one of a group of writers who had an extensive social network centered on Hangzhou. He is best remembered as a prose essayist, and his selections on the development of poetry during the early Yuan are exquisite rejections of *Daoxue*'s denigration of belles-lettres and an enthusiastic advocacy of the creation of a poetics based on the Tang model. His views can be contested, of course, but his writing offers a rich assessment of the complex relationship between social change, the abrogation of the examination system, and the status of writers. In encouraging a new style, he trod a careful line between advocating Tang poetics and resisting imitation. Unlike Ming critics, he did not limit himself to the High Tang, rather encouraging his students "promiscuously to pluck the fragrant and fat from all plants" offered to them by Tang writers, saying, "brewing up poetry is exactly like brewing up honey. If you stick to one flower" people will be able to taste its origins and be put off by its lack of complexity. He resolutely resisted imitation, criticizing the Jiangxi School: "Is it possible not to suffer from likeness if one takes likeness from likeness?" He strove to make his students "write like the Tang but like no particular writer from the Tang." His own poetry, however, is no match for his critical eye.

He gathered in Hangzhou with a group of local writers that included Ni Yuan (1247–after 1328), Bai Ting (1248–1328), and Yuan Yi (1262–1306), all of whom were linked by extensive social networks in which poetry was the primary medium of communication and exchange. This accounts for an extraordinary number of poems sent back and forth as "matching rhymes" or "response poems." Verses of this kind are usually ignored in modern criticism on Yuan verse as artificial, occasional, or lacking in social realism. However, they represent a substantial portion of Yuan writers' works and are lyric explorations of the quality of friendship and the significance of social encounters.

The two most important writers in the network of which Dai Biaoyuan was part were Zhao Mengfu and Yuan Jue, Dai's student. Zhao was the son of one of the Southern Song royal princes and, although enlisted into the bureaucracy at fourteen through his father's privilege, he lived in seclusion for eleven years after the fall of the dynasty in 1276. He was summoned to court by Khubilai Khan and immediately entered government service. As a southerner transplanted to the north, Zhao is a significant figure in the dissolution of the traditional cultural boundary between north and south. He served five emperors, rising to the highest ranks of office, and was posthumously enfeoffed as a "duke" of the state, high recognition from the court. His rise to prominence is truly spectacular when one considers that Khubilai had seriously considered moving all of the descendants of the Southern Song royal house to the distant north and had determined never to employ any of them. Zhao Mengfu is best known today as one of the four great painters of the Yuan, which has overshadowed his skill as a writer. Yang Zai (1271–1323), Zhao's student for more than twenty years and one of the Four Great Poets of the Yuan, wrote in his teacher's biography, "His name and talent have been smothered by his calligraphy and painting. People know about them, but not about his writing; and if they know about his writing, they do not know about his studies of 'ordering the world' [political writings]." A good portion of Zhao's writing, like that of others in the social and literary network, consisted of prefaces, colophons, and inscriptions for friends and colleagues. In these he was incredibly introspective and scrupulously honest about his own feelings and abilities. For instance, when asked to write a preface to a friend's collected works, he noted the following line in a "matching" poem his friend had written about someone else, "His fine ink work is inferior to that of Zhao Mengfu." In his preface, Zhao went off on an uncharacteristic aside, "I do not know this person but if he is good at calligraphy, then he should have been matched against someone from antiquity. How could my calligraphy be worthy of such respect in this age! I am deeply shamed by this, and I requested that this line be excised."

As we can see in this passage, Zhao appears to have been a writer of some self-awareness and at least a modicum of self-doubt. Part of his personal uncertainty was likely due to the conflict between his long service to the Yuan and his hereditary links to the Song house. When he moved from retirement to high office under the Mongols, he was subject to criticism both from his coevals and from later critics as well. He was in fact quite self-aware of the contradictions in his own life. Many of his poems, like his famous "Blaming Myself for Coming out of Retirement" (Zui chu), contain a deep sense of anxiety that, for all its fullness of expression, is never really explained (quotation marks indicate passages quoted from other poems or lyrics):

> In the mountains "Japanese senega is called 'distant ambition',"
> But, out of the mountains "it turns into an insignificant grass."
> . . .
> My sick wife coddles my weak child,
> As we depart far away on this thousand-mile road;
> Flesh and blood "are separated by a life's parting,"
> Who will sweep ancestral graves?
> Sorrow deepens, there's not a single word to say,
> As eyes look to where dark clouds break off in the south.
> Wailing and crying until a heartbreaking wind blows –
> How can I lay plaint to vaulted heaven?

He clearly distanced himself from the Song and realized that dynastic change was "the intent of Heaven" (tian yi) and a natural process. But he still worried that later generations could not forgive his service to the Yuan. As he wrote in his "Self Admonitions" (Zi jing),

> Teeth coming loose, hair falling out, now sixty-three,
> For every event of my entire life I can feel some shame;
> Precisely what remains, pen and inkstone – the emotions are still there –
> I bequeath to the human world for their laughing banter.

Zhao Mengfu is also the first of the "bureaucrat–poets" of the Yuan. This category of poet and of poetry, named "cabinet style" (taige ti) later in the Ming, is one of the elements that distinguish the Yuan from other dynasties. Strictly speaking, it was not until somewhat later that these poets formed a critical mass large enough to be a recognized community of writers. Zhao and Wang Yun in the north represent early proto-examples, but it was not until the generation just before the "Four Great Poets" that cabinet-style poetry became a recognizable fashion that would hold sway over later writers, who often assembled and sometimes printed collections of sustained social exchanges of poems using matching rhymes or the same rhyme words.

The crucial era between early southern writers like Zhao Mengfu and the "Four Great Poets of the Yuan" is usually overlooked in the history of Yuan belles-lettres, written off as a "transitional era" that "prepares the stage" for the great masters. Even the most astute of critics, Gu Sili (1669–1722), considered it transitional:

> When the Yuan arose, it continued the last eras of the Song and Jin. With his resoundingly splendid and highly talented compositions, Yuan Haowen stirred up the Central Plain, and his disciples Hao Jing and Liu Yin carried it on. Therefore, northern learning was at its height during the years 1260–1294 . . . Zhao Mengfu entered into service with the Yuan as a royal grandson of the Song and, elegant and cultured, he capped his whole age. The likes of Deng Wenyuan and Yuan Jue harmonized with [the style] that he set, and the study of poetry took another turn. At this point Yu Ji, Yang Zai, Fan Peng [1272–1330], and Jie Xisi [1274–1334] burst forth together in their time, but the heights they reached in the years 1321–1330 were in reality begun in the years 1297–1320.

While the lineage may not be as cleanly drawn as Gu Sili has made it here, Deng Wenyuan (1259–1328) and Yuan Jue (1266–1327) were instrumental in laying the foundations of the "cabinet writers." Deng served in many posts in the government, including as examiner when the examinations were briefly reinstated in 1314. He is most noted as a prose writer and author of many inscriptions and biographies, as well as one of the first "rescriptors-on-demand" to author institutional documents for the Yuan court. His collected works had largely disappeared by the 1760s, leaving only a small collection of prose to be included in the imperial collection of Qianlong. Earlier, however, Gu Sili in the *Selections of Yuan Poetry* had gathered 115 poems. While not much of a writer, Deng's support of others brought Yuan dynasty prose to a new height. As Gu Sili noted,

> The years 1297–1320 were a period of extended peace, and Deng, with the likes of Yuan Jue and Gong Kui [1269–1329], revitalized the study of prose. All of the scholars in the land gathered around them as they saw the power of this movement. The most famous scholars . . . came from the gates of Deng Wenyuan.

Deng's own writing, most often in the form of responses to requests or products of incidental social exchange, ring with what a modern critic has called "a monotone with no alteration in style from one piece to the next."

Yuan Jue, a student of Dai Biaoyuan, was noted as a literary figure from his youth. He was director of an academy in south China when he was, like many other southerners, recommended to the court by Cheng Jufu (1249–1318), a major figure in the movement of men of letters from the south to the north. Rising rapidly through the central bureaucracy, where he stayed for nearly twenty years, Yuan Jue was instrumental in gathering together the basic source materials for the histories of the Song, Liao, and Jin. He was also a bibliophile and inheritor of a large library. His early training gave him great breadth in learning, but it was, unfortunately, put primarily to service in poems of exchange with other scholars in the central bureaucracy. The range of his poetry stays well within traditional limits: meditations evoked by scenery, matching poems of social exchange, and meditations on the past to lament the present (*diaogu shangjin*).

Like his mentor, Dai Biaoyuan, Yuan Jue was a proponent of the Tang style. As he remarked in a poem entitled "Seconding the Rhyme: Zhongzhang's Poetic Structure Has Already Entered the Stylistic Tone of the Tang" (Zhongzhang shilü yi ru Tang ren fengdiao ciyun): "The structure of poetry and its theory must have that to which it owes allegiance." His own verse, particularly in the longer regulated forms, shows a similarity to the poetry of Li Shangyin. Of particular importance are three short collections he wrote in 1314, 1319, and 1321, when he traveled from the main capital, Dadu (modern Beijing), to the Upper Capital of the Yuan near present-day Duolun in Inner Mongolia. These poetic sequences begin the fad of writing a lengthy series of poems about the annual travel between Beijing and Duolun, which later become a favorite topic of Yuan poetry. His prose draws heavily on the Song masters, and most of it is in the form of edicts, memorials, and memorial inscriptions for high court ministers. His incidental prose, written in the form of colophons, short essays, and notes, is what one critic has called "heartfelt pieces of high intelligence and new opinions" on the people and affairs of his age.

One particularly interesting poet from this era is Song Wu (1260–1340), a person about whom sources are unclear and scholarly opinion is deeply divided. According to the most reliable opinion, the person known as Song Wu has three different collections attributed to him. One is a short collection of thirty-three quatrains in the seven-syllable line written when he was a member of Khubilai's failed campaign against Japan in 1281, called *Chants from the Back of a Whale* (*Jingbei yin*). The second is a work entitled *Collection of Talking in My Sleep* (*Anyi ji*), which contains 101 poems on historical and mythical personalities, each verse appended by a narrative of that figure's life. The editors of the *Siku quanshu* criticize these poems as "suffering from making poetry from discourse" (*yi lun zuo shi zhi bing*). Many of the poems treat people who existed only in fictional tales, and some bibliographers have placed the work in the category of *xiaoshuo*, fictional narrative. The third collection is of more standard five- and seven-syllable verse in both ancient and modern styles. Song Wu is perhaps most important as the first poet to consciously create a poetic style based on Li He and Wen Tingyun. His seven-syllable old-style poetry is often an overwrought imitation of Li He's style. For instance, in a poem he wrote, "On an Old Inkstone," he has the following lines: "Nüwa trod the clouds, departed to patch the heavens, / And left behind this lump of scorched black smoke." Critics claim that he often overreaches in these poems due to a desire to say something different and new within the received style. This often results in an ineffective astringency that "leaves a dry taste in the mouth." But by no means is all of his collection written in imitation of the Late Tang. Many of his verses, particularly his five-syllable new-style poetry, often probe the values of friendship and loyalty, and the poems attributed to him about the campaign against Japan are striking for their description of the hardships of overland travel through Korea and across the sea.

The period up to 1320 witnessed the northward movement of southern writers, and the creation of a uniquely Yuan style in both prose and poetry, one that blends traditions from north and south. The single feature common to both regional styles was a revival of a Tang epitome as an antidote to the excesses of Song writing. In the case of the north, writers of the Jin saw themselves as the direct inheritors of the Tang style that had passed to them through the Northern Song. For the southern writers, it was more difficult. Many of them were staunch adherents to *Daoxue*, but they all fought against its pedantry and particularly against its pejorative view of expressive literature used to communicate anything but "the [ethical] Way." In the Yuan, *Daoxue* had very little control over the literary scene. Prose continued to be in service to ethics – even though most writers realized it also required a certain elegant stylistic – or to the state, and was either based in ethics or was a tool for "ordering the world." Poetry was another issue. The criticism of Song poetry as overly involved with "principle" instead of "emotion" or of using "prose to make poetry" turned the tide in the Yuan from a corporate sense of ethics that one finds in Song poetry and in Yuan prose to a new poetics of individualism that bespoke the soul of each person. As Yang Weizhen was to say at the end of the dynasty, "because each person has [individual] feeling, each person has [individual] poetry" (*ren ge you qing ze ren ge you shi*).

III. The Four Masters of Yuan Poetry

The large influx of writers from southeast China during the years from 1312 to 1320 included men who moved into the bureaucracy and staffed many of the prestigious academies at court, forming a robust literary circle that was engaged mostly with poems of an incidental nature. Six men rose to high stature: Liu Guan (1270–1342), Huang Jin (1277–1357), Yang Zai, Fan Peng, Jie Xisi, and Yu Ji. Liu Guan and Huang Jin are best known as two members of the "Four Confucian Masters." Both hailed from the same district in Zhejiang and each is noted for his deep learning. Both were exemplars of the traditional scholar–bureaucrat: a literary figure, a Confucian stalwart, and a poet. But in fact their stature as scholars and teachers has certainly been responsible for their overall favorable evaluation as writers. Liu Guan is a good example. Brought from the south because of his deep learning, he was installed in the Imperial Academy in Dadu, where he taught well over a thousand students. His prose writing is deep and rich but, according to modern critics, suffers from a certain meandering convolution. Huang Jin was a good poet who drew heavily on the early period of Chinese *shi* poetry for inspiration, including the Seven Masters of Jian'an and the early Tang writers, particularly Chen Zi'ang, but he is only moderately successful in terms of his own production.

The other four writers have come to be collectively known as the "Four Masters of Yuan Poetry" (*Yuan shi si dajia*), and they were grouped together (although unnamed) from nearly contemporary times. In a preface to Yu Ji's ancestor Yu Yongwen's (1110–1174) collected works, Ouyang Xuan (1283–1357) wrote,

> When everything was united in the beginning of the Yuan, former Confucians from the Jin and Song staffed all of the major cabinet offices; but as for their literary style, the best were stiff and unyielding, the worst, weak and soft, and from time to time all showed the holdover practices [of the former dynasties]. But as days of peace stretched on, those of superlative talent gathered together in the capital; mouth organs and bells [signifying birth and maturation] played off against each other, and poems [sharing the ancient values of] *feng* and *ya* were sung one after the other. So the "music of a well-governed age" daily grew more and more magnificent.

This contextualizes the prevailing critical opinion of the Four Masters by placing them within a context of universal poetic values, and linking their poetic production to the central values of the Confucian (not necessarily *Daoxue*) personality. In doing so, it creates a certain poetic persona for the four – a recognizable blend of worthy minister, proponent of orthodox Confucian values, poet who looked for inspiration in past masters, and advocate of "restoring antiquity."

The four writers all served in the capital at roughly the same time and all served in the Bureau of History, although they all took different avenues to their appointments. Yu Ji, descendant of an important Song ministerial family, went into the bureaucracy almost immediately. The other three had longer waits. Fan Peng was thirty-six before he left home to roam in the capital, where he was purportedly discovered selling hexagram fortunes in the markets by a Yuan minister who took him into his home and then recommended him for service. Yang Zai did not serve until forty, when he was directly appointed to the Bureau of History. When the examinations were reinstated, however, Yang sat for and passed the highest level. Jie Xisi was also put into the Bureau of History and the Hanlin Academy by direct appointment at an advanced age.

They all shared common ideas about writing. First, they all saw the basis of poetry as being "classical elegance and uprightness" (*yazheng*), a description for writing that issues from a refined moral sensibility. As Yu Ji remarked in his "Preface to Hu Shiyuan's Poetic Collection" (Hu Shiyuan shiji xu):

> Poets of the recent generations who are sunk deeply into resentment are often skilled; those who are long on passion are often beautiful; those who are skilled at being moved by regret are incapable of knowing where to turn; those who are extremely dissolute are incapable of being brought back – this is all because they have not attained the uprightness of human nature and sentiments.

This plea for poetry to be indifferent to strong passions, centered in a harmonic balance, and calm and deliberative was echoed by Yang Zai, who opined,

> Making poetry is exactly like making government: the mind must be in an equable state, one's vital energy must be harmonious, one's feelings must be authentic, one's thoughts must be profound. The mainstays must be illumined, the regulations and rules must be balanced, and the teachings of the Classics (warm, pliant, solid, and substantial) must often be circulating within.

They pursued this agenda in two ways. The first was to "venerate the Tang and restore antiquity," and their poetry often reveals muted gestures toward Li Bai, Du Fu, and Li Shangyin, whom they considered standard-bearers of a correct transmission of poetry. The tradition they followed is, in many respects, completely conventional. As Yang Zai remarked, "Poetry should take its material from the Han and the Wei, and should venerate the Tang in terms of the rhythms of its rhymes," and, "In writing prose, whether novel and abstruse, simple and astringent, model yourself on the ancients and do not deign to write the mundane and ordinary language in the custom of the current age." These citations sound very much like those spoken in the Late Tang, the early Song, and the Jin.

The second way, as these quotations suggest, was by strict attention to tonal prosody, parallelism, and a refined vocabulary. The care they took with their work is best illustrated by an example. In his miscellany *Record of a Break from Plowing* (*Chuogeng lu*), written at the end of the fourteenth century, Tao Zongyi (1321–1407) wrote,

> When Mr. Yu Ji and Mr. Yang Zai were together in the capital, Mr. Yang was always saying that Yu Ji could not write poetry. Mr. Yu then took some wine and inquired about the rules for composing poetry. Mr. Yang, once he was sweet with wine, poured all of [the secrets] out and Mr. Yu then thoroughly understood the principle of [how to do] it. He went on to write a poem sending off Yuan Jue as part of the imperial entourage to the Upper Capital. He availed himself of someone else to take the poem he had written and inquire of it from Mr. Yang. Mr. Yang said, "Only Yu Ji is capable of writing this poem." That person asked, "You once said, sir, that Yu Ji was incapable of writing poetry. How can this be?" He responded, "Yu Ji's scholarship is surpassing and once I bestowed on him the rules about how to write poetry – now no one else can reach this level."

> Yu also once showed [these same lines] from the poem to Zhao Mengfu, duke of Wei, "Paths along the cliffs link the mountains, in the morning detain the imperial chariot, / Huts of the Imperial Guard are scattered in the wilds, at night they are given bow cases." The duke said, "Well, it is beautiful, but it would be particularly beautiful if you changed 'mountains' to 'heavens' and 'wilds' to 'stars'." [Paths in the heavens link the mountains, in the morning detain the imperial chariot, / Huts of the Imperial Guard are scattered like stars, at night they are given bow cases.] Mr. Yu was deeply won over by this [reading].

This interest in resurrecting the past as a present model, in copying the style of writers of antiquity, and in the formal elements of verse, has led to what critics, from the Ming to the present, call a "narrowness of topics" and a "lack of creativity." Hu Yinglin remarked in the Ming, "the tenor [*diao*] of Yuan writers is absolutely pure, but the material of their poetry is completely cramped and narrow." The major criticism is that they have far too much incidental poetry that circulates among them as copied rhymes – that is, either using the same rhyme categories of the poem they received or even using the same set of rhyme words. This type of poetry has been particularly scorned in modern criticism, which censures it as a "distant withdrawal from realism" and as lacking social conscience. It is true that many of the poems exchanged at the capital were verses written on demand or request. There are, however, some signal differences from normal court poetry. First, as distinct from virtually every other dynasty, there was no emperor involved in the exchanges or monitoring the exchange. And if these verses lack a measure of social concern or realism, they more than make up for it by a deep exploration of friendship, a concern just as "real" as the feigned persona of a socially conscious poet.

When we examine the corpus of poems exchanged among the four poets, we sense the deep friendship that held between them. Yu Ji's poetry provides a good example. He once called himself "an old seasoned clerk from the Han court" (*Han ting lao li*), which was a reference to his concern for the rules of composition. In his later life, however, he went nearly blind, and this seems to have brought a new depth to his writing. Toward the end of his life, but while he was still in service in the capital, he wrote a poem, "Sending off Graduate Liu Wen, Wenting, to be Registrar of Linjiang" (Song jinshi Liu Wen, Wenting fu Linjiang lushi), for a young and newly enfranchised scholar returning to his hometown to become a registrar. The young man was from a prominent family, noted for their vast library collection, in particular their own publications on the *Spring and Autumn Annals*:

> For a hundred feet Qingjiang's wall is made of stone,
> A thousand peaks of Mount Taihua collect rain's clearing;
> In government offices when will "document envelopes" settle down?
> On fishermen's boats, all day long hook and line are light.
> Your old home is a good place to find scholarship on the *Spring and
>   Autumn Annals*,
> But in the capital they continue to transmit monthly reports.
> I have an old person's concern, and must bother the recorder –
> When you get to your district, please ask after Mr. Fan for me.

An otherwise conventional poem is concluded with an unexpectedly open plea for the young man to look in on Fan Peng, then a sick old man living in Linjiang in retirement. The humanity of these lines is rather typical of Yu Ji as he suffered through the long process of losing his sight, first at the capital and then in retirement. A comment that Li Rihua, the famous art critic, made about Yu's calligraphy could stand as well for his poetry:

I once saw calligraphy that Yu Ji wrote in his later years, after he lost his eyesight; it was messy and disorganized [*hutu liaodao*] but a true presence issued even more from it, and was even more prized. A long period of emulating the rules and of experiencing the meaning and interest of things, all stewed together in his bosom, and, having lost his eyes, he had to execute it on the basis of spirit – so there is a rareness in it that exists beyond intention.

These later poems are among the finest of his collection and breathe a deep sense of humanity:

> ("Finding the Moment")
> A thousand times I comb my white hair, go through a vegetarian fast,
> Only when there is a guest does the brushwood gate begin to open;
> Calligraphy – my eyes so dim I vainly face the bamboo strips,
> Wine – my money pouch is so empty I have long stopped the cups.
> Windborne rain at the northern window where I always sit alone,
> Letters from the southern sea no longer come.
> Ceasing their plowing among the clods, all the youngsters
> Are forced to come and ask about studies, just to comfort this aging face.

Yu Ji's sentiments of friendship, colored by age, are echoed in the poetic exchanges between all four writers, and also in their prefaces written for their (usually deceased) friends. The same sort of unexpected turn to deep feeling in an otherwise "set" piece, a preface written in response to a request, is found in Fan Peng's short essay written for the publication of Yang Zai's collected writings:

> During the Dade reign [1297–1307], I got my hands on my first poem by Yang Zai of Pucheng and when I read it, I was upset that I did not know this man as a person. After he arrived in the capital and our friendship took hold, we would discourse about the Way of elegant poetry, and we always were in perfect happy agreement. At the beginning of the Huangqing reign [1312], both of us were officials in the Bureau of History. We would stay overnight in the bureau whenever there was something to write or compile. When we got off our shift, we would immediately get back together to wander around the offices, sometimes staying out until the moon appeared, and, when it was gone, continuing our conversation by candlelight. We were the only two who remained unchanged in tasking ourselves and in our self-contentment in seasons both cold and hot.

> Later on, I was sent to the coast by the Censorate to Govern the Archives in Nanxian, and Zai passed the *jinshi* examinations in 1315, and was made magistrate of Fuliang. I was transferred to Jiangxi at the same time he was changed to the position of judicial official in Xuancheng. This is why, although

apart for ten years, separated by a thousand miles, our paths going off like this [in different directions], our hearts still remained firm [in the desire to be] together [as friends again] "to count mornings and evenings." But Zai passed away before he could take his post in Xuancheng. Sadly, I weep!

Jie Xisi, the younger bookend to the four, was also a major court figure. He came from a learned family and was widely known as a writer when young. He traveled from his home to the Hunan–Hubei area, where he met Cheng Jufu, who was attracted immediately by his talent and married him to his niece. Jie Xisi went along with Cheng Jufu when the latter went to the capital in 1312. At the age of forty, he was made an emender in the Hanlin Academy and, except for twice in the next ten years when he returned home, he remained in either the Hanlin Academy or the Imperial Academy. In 1329, when Emperor Wenzong established the Guizhang Academy and the position of teacher of the Classics, Jie was the first name on the list. He participated in the project on statecraft in 1330 (the *Grand Compendium of Ordering the World*, *Jingshi dadian*) and was commissioned as one of the overseers of the *Liao History* and *Jin History* projects. He retired at seventy-one. He was an author, like Yu Ji, of many court and ritual documents, and his poetry can sometimes reflect his staid, bureaucratic interests, as this section of a long series of poems, "Remembering Yesterday" (Yizuo) demonstrates (the description is of his responsibility as lecturer on the Classics to the emperor):

In the middle of the Tianli reign the Imperial Library opened,
And teachers of Classics were newly appointed to nurture a host of talents.
Arriving at palace gates to "wait for the clepsydra," I was often the first in line,
Gathering together my books at the lecture mat, I always went home last.
When summoned to the test, I was comforted by Heaven's word.
When topics were divided I did not wait for His servants to urge me on.

He, too, often wrote about friends. As with other poets, Jie's sense of friendship was bound up with nostalgia and a yearning for home, as in the following poem, "Leaving Shuncheng Gate Early in the Morning, I Fondly Remember Taixu" (Xiao chu Shuncheng men you huai Taixu), written a few days after he had sent off one of his companions from the southern gate of the capital:

Walking out of the gate in the southern wall,
I desolately gaze at the road to the South;
In days just past in the wind and rain,
My old friend left right from here.

Nostalgia for his own homeland is inextricably linked to the sadness of parting in a complicated mix of emotions full of ambiguity – sad his friend is gone, happy he will be back in the warm south, and sad that he himself is both shorn of a companion and away from his ancestral home. This mix of nostalgia and friendship, as in Yu Ji's poem above, is nearly always tinged with a feeling of loss. In one of Jie's late poems, "Dreaming of Wuchang" (Meng Wuchang), friendship and loss are deeply intertwined:

> Parrot Island, in front of Yellow Crane Tower,
> In my dream is completely the same as old time roaming.
> Dark green mountains enter athwart into roads to Triple Xiang [Hunan],
> A setting sun evenly unrolls the flow of seven marshes [of Chu].
> Drum and horn, martial and strong, shake the land far off,
> Sail masts, high and low, chaotically tie boats.
> My old friends, though alive, are all scattered apart,
> All alone, south of the pond, I look at white gulls.

As topics that "rescue" their poetry from the criticism of being hackneyed or socially irrelevant, friendship and the related theme of loss ask us to consider what it is that was lost. It seems clear that their point of reference, as suggested in Fan's preface to Yang Zai's poetry, was the intensity of their time together in the capital. As members of the same high court offices, they shared a space that put them at the pinnacle of conventional (by traditional Chinese values) social and cultural power, lights of the brightest age of Chinese culture during the Yuan. But there they were also bound by a deep sense of friendship.

IV. Foreign writers

As mentioned above, the Mongol era was one in which there was a great deal of freedom of movement and a large-scale incorporation of northern and western peoples into the Chinese sphere. From the earliest chapters of Yuan history, names of foreign-born or second- and third-generation foreign writers fill the pages. It may seem strange in the West to consider second- and third-generation-born writers foreign when their native tongue was Chinese, but Chinese historians usually count these writers as "minority" peoples. This is not the place to debate ethnocentricity, but in fact the categorization of the population into hierarchical categories of ethnicity was a native Chinese process that gained force under Mongol rule. People from the west and northwest border areas had long been called *semu*, a term that means either "colored eyes" or "variegated categories." The term had a long history as a native Chinese designation for "foreign-sounding" surnames. A ninth-century writer, Qian Yi, tells us that dispensation was given to foreigners in the examination systems of the late Tang:

> From the Dazhong reign [847–859] onward, whenever the Board of Rites put up the plaque [with the names of the successful candidates for the examinations], they annually selected two or three men who had obscure surnames – these were called *semu*, and people also called them "plaque adornments."

Many of these surnames were mutiple-syllable surnames that indicated the ethnicity of a particular group of peoples: for example Dashi (pronounced "Daiziek" in the older pronunciation, and meaning Tajik, or Persian), Kangli (an early Altaic tribe related to modern Khazaks), or Dašman (Uighur Muslim). In the Yuan, *semu* was used as a racial or ethnic marker for people from non-Chinese tribes from northern Inner Asia and Central Asia. In the Ming one writer listed some thirty-one different *semu* in China, and during the Jin and Yuan these peoples spread into and throughout China as officials, merchants, traders, or gentry inhabitants. Most of them took Chinese names as a social and political convenience, deriving their names from shortening the longer appellations in their native tongues, taking a surname from one word of their ancestor's administrative or military title, or picking a name that denoted their religious beliefs. At the end of the Yuan foreigners were a common feature of life: there were mosques and graveyards, and Nestorian and Manichean churches throughout the length and breadth of what is now China.

The lineage of foreign writers is impressive, and their contributions to the tradition are well documented. In his Qing anthology, *Selections of Yuan Poetry*, Gu Sili wrote,

> From the time the Yuan arose, all of the young from the northwest turned their attention to learning. Once their cultural nourishment was deep enough, their extraordinary talent all appeared together. Guan Yunshi [1286–1324], Ma Zuchang roused up the beginnings with their tradition of beautiful elegance and fresh newness [*qili qingxin*]; and Sadula continued what they had begun. He was fresh without being flippant, beautiful without being over-elegant. He was one who was able to open up a completely new style outside that produced by Yuan Jue, Zhao Mengfu, Yu Ji, and Yang Zai. It was then that Yahu [Yakut, ca 1310–1360], Taibuhua [Tai Buqa, 1304–1352], Nai Xian [1309–?], and Yu Que [1303–1358] each showed off their talent and brilliance, showing off their novelty, competing in their fully mature learning – cannot this be said to bring the splendor of a whole age to its highest point?

One of the earliest and most influential "foreigners" was Yelü Chucai (1190–1244), who shares a birth year with Yuan Haowen. From the royal lineage of the Khitan, Yelü is primarily important as a historical figure, but his writings are the font of some important developments in the Yuan and later. He was appointed to his first post at seventeen years of age after an examination administered personally by Emperor Zhangzong of the Jin, and he moved up quickly through the ranks. When the Mongols took Yanjing in 1215, Yelü was captured. He was sent to an audience with Chinggis Khan, and in 1218, at the age of only twenty-eight, he became Chinggis's trusted adviser, following him on his long campaign through Central Asia to the west. After Chinggis Khan died in 1227, Yelü was a trusted adviser to three successive rulers until his own death. He used his position to put into place land and tax reforms that could feed the Mongol coffers without causing further death or disruption in north China. He was also instrumental in protecting and promoting Jin official literati after the fall of the Jin capital in Kaifeng.

He was a prolific writer of both prose and poetry. He was particularly inspired by his journeys through Central Asia and by his long stay in the region near modern Samarkand, not only by what he personally saw, but also by an opportunity to learn to read the language of his forefathers, Khitan, and to translate Khitan poetry into Chinese. Like most writers, his poems and essays are not uniformly good, but those written in the west are notable for their interested and nonjudgmental engagement with the land and people of Central Asia. When read alongside his lengthy travel diary, *Record of a Journey Westward* (*Xi you lu*), the poems reveal the first of what will become a sustained body of elite literature by foreigners in Chinese exploring the northern and western frontiers as culturally viable and interesting areas, devoid of alienation and fear. As he wrote in the last of a series, "Ten Songs of Hezhong" (i.e. Samarkand):

> Forlorn Hezhong prefecture,
> Those who remained here are sufficient unto themselves:
> Yellow oranges are mixed with honey to fry,
> Plain cakes are sprinkled with powdered sugar.
> Seeking salvation from drought, the river is turned to rain,
> Having no clothes, dirt clods are planted with sheep ["clod-planted-sheep": cotton];
> From the time I came here to the west,
> I no longer remember my own home place.

This love of worlds beyond China proper is a feature that will distinguish the writing of Chinese texts by Yuan writers of foreign origin from their native counterparts. There were foreigners in other dynasties, to be sure, but the rising ethnocentricity that accompanied the Ming ascendancy as well as the problematic relationship between Chinese and "minority" groups from 1644 onward have had a marked effect on the production of writing about foreigners. The lamentable tendency to mark the foreign-born, despite their full participation in the cultural processes of China and Confucianism, as "minority" writers has had a curious effect in modern literary history. Modern critics emphasize the place of these writers within the tradition by making a fetish of how well they write mainstream literature, as though complete mastery of the language and culture were miraculous for someone with a non-Han background. Thus, when these foreign writers are discussed, there is very little interest in what it is in their writing that makes them different. This is particularly true in accounts of writers like Ma Zuchang, Nai Xian, and particularly the great Sadula, where the focus is on their poetic exchanges with native writers like the "Four Masters of Yuan Verse." Once their ethnicity is discussed they are analyzed in the same way as "cabinet" poets, hermit poets, and other features or styles associated with mainstream Han writers.

A particularly good example is Ma Zuchang (1279–1338), a descendant of an Ongüt Nestorian Christian family that had, by his time, been fully sinicized for at least three generations. By his own generation the extended family had evolved from the time of his great-grandfather Ma Yuehenai (Johanan) along two distinct paths. In the list of names that Ma Zuchang wrote in the spirit-way stele (*shendao bei*) for his great-grandfather, one finds a preponderance of Chinese names but also a good proportion of Christian names like Jacob (Yagu), Esau/Jesus (Yishuo), and so forth. Ma Zuchang's direct lineage had clearly shed Christianity for Confucianism, and Ma had a typical literati career track in the Yuan. His father, Ma Run (1255–1313), had served under the Mongols as an official, and he saw to it that his son was educated in the Confucian Classics. Ma Zuchang was a graduate of the first *jinshi* examination held in the Yuan, and he moved through the highest levels of the court bureaucracy. He was broadly recognized as a leading talent of his day and was influential in establishing "cabinet-style" poetry as a major feature of Yuan verse. His seven-syllable quatrains are particularly good, and he was instrumental in beginning the tradition of "bamboo-branch lyrics" (*zhuzhi ci*) that matured under the late writer Yang Weizhen. Despite the popularity of this short form among ethnically Han writers, modern critics like Yang Lian still insist on using it to remark Ma's "minority" talent:

In the poetic circles of the Yuan, [Ma] can be called an expert in the practice of the seven-syllable quatrain. Perhaps this is because the basic form itself is highly refined, and is pregnant with connotative meaning. And it is easy to control, and it seems that all foreigners from the Western Region love this kind of little poem in which it was so easy to express oneself.

If we were to ask precisely what it is that sets Ma and other writers apart, we would have to turn to their poems written "beyond the borders" (*saiwai*), or "at the borders" (*biansai*). There was a deep attachment on their part to the lands of their ancestors, as Ma Zuchang revealed in a poem, "Drinking Wine: Number Five" (Yinjiu diwu):

> Long ago my seventh-generation ancestors,
> Raised horses west of Tao River,
> The sixth moved to the Altai mountains,
> Every day, hearing the sound of war drums.

This acknowledgement of a connection with a foreign past seems possible only in the Yuan, in an environment that did not draw lines of ethnicity around cultural spheres. This is apparent in the writings of Wei Su (1303–1372), Su Tianjue (1294–1352), and other southern-born Chinese who wrote about these foreign-born writers as part of a general cultural enterprise that was incorporative and based on text and ability, not on ethnic background. This general liberalness is also reflected in the poetry of the writers as well. Compare with poems of earlier periods, for instance, these two verses, "Written about Events in He Huang" (Hehuang shu shi), by Ma Zuchang, written about Gansu, an area traditionally associated with invaders:

> Ironclad cavalry in the Altai mountains – their horn bows are long,
> On lazy days out on the plain, they shoot white wolves;
> Lake Qinghai without ripples, spring geese alight,
> Grass grows amid the dunes, "revealing oxen and sheep."

> A seasoned Persian trader transits the flowing sands,
> Listening at night to camel bells, he knows how far the road;
> He plucks out jade, little green stones, by the river,
> Gathers them in to take to the eastern country and trade for mulberry
>   and hemp.

This is, in fact, in praise of Ma's ancestral home in Gansu. It is a moment when a past that has been related to him and the present come together by chance, when the frontier itself is no danger, but is home, when the horn bows of cavalry pose no threat and the moment turns instead to the distant tinkling of camel bells, signifying movement through a world of widespread peace. The stunning last line, in which China becomes a peripheral country located somewhere in the east, centers the poem at the nexus of movement and communication between people, states, and even commodity values. What this suggests is that the subject location of the poet is contingent and able to move (at least mentally) between several distinct places he could call home. For example, if we compare these two verses with another of Ma's short poems, simply called "A Quatrain," we find him firmly placed within a traditional space that could as well be that of any writer from the Tang:

> At a river village, a mountain inn, buildings lie aslant,
> Traveling the length of the long Huai, just coming home;
> Wind and rain, rain and wind for a long sixty days,
> The better half of this year has been spent at heaven's edge.

The examples of Yelü Chucai and Ma Zuchang are meant to demonstrate concretely to some degree what it is that generally makes foreign-born writers different from their native peers and from foreign writers of other times. Poems about areas beyond the passes are certainly the most significant marker. One needs to be careful, however, because some of these themes are picked up later as part of the repertoire of all writers.

The best examples of this are the long sequences of poems written on the annual journey from Beijing to the Upper Capital, near the modern town of Duolun in Inner Mongolia. This annual trip, from the fourth to the ninth lunar month, was a regular feature of court life. This area had been closed off to the Chinese for some three hundred years, starting with the Khitan conquests in the late tenth century. When it opened up to yearly travel, it became a common topos in the writing of most Chinese writer–officials. The poems were usually a lengthy sequence of quatrains in the seven-syllable line, and many of them, in describing life at the Mongol summer court, actually are a type of "poems of the palace" (gongci). For Southern Song writers who lived into the Yuan, this journey provided an apt stage upon which to ponder the rise and fall of dynasties and to view the shifting tides of dynastic fortune played out upon this northern verge. One late writer, Yang Yunfu (1316–1374), composed a series called "One Hundred Rhymes on the Capital on the Luan River" (Luan jing baiyong), or "Random Rhymes on the Capital on the Luan River" (Luan jing zayong), which more accurately can be described as a detailed first-person account of life in the Mongol capital. These were written after the Ming had conquered the Yuan, and are a reminiscence of the scenery, the strange customs, and the splendor of the court by a man who held a post in the food service of the Yuan court.

Not all of the native writing, of course, was shi poetry. Perhaps the most famous short colloquial song ever written, "Autumn Thoughts" (Qiu si), attributed to Ma Zhiyuan from 1332 onward, may in fact have been describing a journey to the Upper Capital. The oldest text in which this poem is found is Sheng Ruzi's *Collected Discussions of the Seasoned Scholar of Shu Studio* (ca 1310) and it is listed as the first in a trilogy of anonymous poems, with the simple notation, "A scholarly friend of mine from the North, has sent me a short lyric of three stanzas [or perhaps three stanzas of short lyrics] on the desert [*shamo xiao ci san que*; this may also be a title, "Three Short Lyrics on The Desert"], and they describe the scenery well." Most people are only aware of the first of this trilogy of short lyrics:

> Withered vine, old trees, sunset rooks,
> Small bridge, flowing water, people's homes,
> Old road, westerly wind, thin nag –
> Evening sunlight falls to the west,
> A brokenhearted man is at heaven's edge.

But, as the two accompanying poems make clear, these lines describe the route to the Upper Capital, which passed by the then-accepted site of the grave of the famous defeated Han General, Li Ling:

> Level sands, fine grass clumped and scattered,
> Crooked creek, flowing water dripping and bubbling,
> On the frontier, clear autumn early cold –
> One sound of new geese,
> Yellow clouds, red leaves, green mountains.
>
> In westerly winds, on the frontier, a barbarian flute,
> In moonlight bright, on horseback, a pipa guitar,
> So much, Wang Zhaojun's hatred –
> By Li Ling's tower,
> Light mist, sere grass, ochre sands.

Here, as in many of the poems about the trip by native Chinese writers, the land has been incorporated into a long historical and mythical narrative about the political relationships between China and the nomadic tribes in the north. Both Wang Zhaojun, who was ransomed to a Xiongnu chieftain, and Li Ling, who was defeated by the Xiongnu, figure prominently as allusive metaphors for the long history of Chinese shame at the hands of northern invaders. There is no real interest in the land between Dadu and the Upper Capital, except as the stage for the latest iteration of Chinese defeat. Compare these poems with three of a series of five that Nai Xian wrote in the later Yuan:

> Autumn's high sky, sandy dunes, thyme plants few and far between,
> Sable-hatted, fox-cloaked, they go out in the evening to circle for the hunt;

Shooting down a white wolf, they string it up on the horse,
And playing the flute at night's halving, return under the moon.

Here, there, everywhere – felt-topped carts of a hundred or more,
Braving snow at the fifth watch, we cross the Luan river;
Tending the yoke, an old crone, used to all the stretches of this trip,
Breaks ice near the bank to water her camels.

By the walls of Wuhuan rain begins to clear,
Purple asters and golden nasturtiums spring up across the land;
I love best the meadowlarks, so full of feeling –
A single pair flies toward me, singing by the side of my horse.

These poems clearly demonstrate a difference between native and foreign-born writers in their assessment of the land beyond China. While it is difficult to assess the level of "authenticity" in any of the poems cited above, what remains visible, from Yelü Chucai to Nai Xian, is an engagement with the physical worlds of the north and northwest as interesting places in themselves, not a transferred metaphorical space. The poems on the frontier by the non-native writers are poems of choice. All of these poets were fully involved with mainstream poetic exchange and were masters of the language and the culture. But they lived in an environment that allowed them the freedom to make choices that post-Yuan orthodoxy and ethnocentrism would severely constrain. It was forbidden, for instance, to write about the Ming court or the Ming imperial family; strong ethnic lines were drawn between Chinese and non-Chinese in terms of cultural purity and authenticity. While Yuan critics were wont to accept non-Han writers as members of a cultural community based on their simple mastery of language and culture, a trend started in the Ming, which culminates in the historical writing of contemporary times, to isolate these writers as non-Han, "minority" poets. Moreover, curiously, the emphasis has been placed not on what is a marker of their foreignness – their ability to engage and accept non-Chinese landscape and peoples – but on their mastery of mainstream traditional topics for versification.

If ethnicity is eschewed as a rationale for categorizing writers, then some writers of foreign descent, such as that most famous of non-Chinese writers, the Mongol Sadula, must be considered part of the general tradition of poetry. For that reason, his contribution will be discussed below.

V. Poetry to 1375

Among the legion of good poets at the end of the Yuan, two names stand out: Sadula (ca 1272–ca 1340) and Yang Weizhen (1296–1370). Both were writing when the "veneration of the Tang" had come to its apogee. In a passage from his preface to the *Selections of Yuan Poetry*, Gu Sili remarked,

> Many Yuan writers took the two Lis as their models. Sadula was good at imitating Li Shangyin, Song Wu excelled at imitating Li He, and Yang Weizhen was a product of the combination. Feng Zizhen [1257–?], Guan Yunshi [1286–1324], and Wang Mian [?–1357] – their language had to startle a person and had absolutely no meaning or principle to it. They did not understand that ox ghosts and snake spirits never made the most superb compositions in [Li He's] "brocade bag" [where he stored his poetry].

Of course, it is difficult to take such a short statement as encompassing all of the poetic trends of the late Yuan, yet it points to one salient fact: the movement to restore Tang sensibilities to poetry had succeeded. In fact, one of the master narratives of Yuan verse is how it adapts the pro-Tang sensibilities of boundary poets like Dai Biaoyuan in the south and Yuan Haowen in the north, and over time comes full blown, "washing away the older customs," as Gu Sili put it:

> The rise of Yuan poetry began with Yuan Haowen. After the period of 1260–1294 it completely washed away the remaining customs of the Song and Jin, and Zhao Mengfu was its leading proponent. From 1314–1329, when literature as a whole began to flourish and great masters tracked together, the best of the lot were Yu Ji, Fan Peng, Yang Zai, and Jie Xisi. From 1341 human talent came out generation after generation, and of the leaders who signified the new, Yang Weizhen was the most virile. And the transformation of Yuan poetry had now reached its peak.

This master narrative holds true in the general sense; but as the cyclical philosophy of China reminds us, things that reach their peak are bound to change, since the moment of highest intensity introduces its own natural reaction and countermotion. The possibilities of this moment are reflected well in the two major poets of the last period.

Sadula was a Muslim, and although perhaps the best poet of the Yuan, is also one of the most difficult to read and understand, in terms of both his life and his works. There are no funerary accounts of Sadula by his contemporaries, a fact that is extremely puzzling. His circle of acquaintances included some of the most renowned poets of the day, including Yang Weizhen, a close friend who took the examinations the same year (1327). The reason for this is unknown – his family may have been too insignificant after his death to matter, he may have had no living descendants, or the documents might have been lost. He never held more than minor posts in his bureaucratic career (he passed the examinations in his late forties or early fifties), and he soon retired to Hangzhou. He became something of a hermit, and no one knows what fate he met. In a preface to *Bamboo Branch Songs of West Lake*, written in 1348, Yang Weizhen mentions that Sadula was already dead, so we know he did not live to see the turmoil of the Yuan's fall.

Sadula was best known for two subgenres of poetry, "palace poems" (*gongci*), quatrains in the seven-syllable line about the minutiae of court life, and sets of quatrains on "traveling to the Upper Capital." Yu Ji expressed the basic attitude of Sadula's peers toward his poetry in positive, but somewhat ambiguous, terms: "He was best at pure emotion, [his poetry] was free-flowing and beautiful as well as fresh and lively [*liuli qingwan*]. All other writers loved it." This is fulsome praise, although in light of Yu Ji's statements about poetry of "pure emotion" as beautiful but in violation of classical models of restraint and indirection, it implies a certain excessive openness in terms of expression. Such openness, however, accounts for the appeal of Sadula's best poems, which were written primarily on current affairs and on "cherishing the past" (*huaigu*), topics which are intimately interrelated.

Sadula is often compared to the progenitor of palace poems, the late Tang poet Wang Jian, but he extended the range of the *gongci* to make comments on current policy and politics. This is something quite rare in the history of poetry and possible only because of the relative freedom of writers to say what they wanted under Mongol rule. One of his most famous works is a critique of the bloody infighting surrounding the succession of rule in the Yuan. The poem and its attendant context are presented in a collection of remarks on poetry by Qu Yu (1347–1433):

> Sadula became famous because of his palace poems; his poetry was fresh and new, elegant and beautiful. He had a style all his own, and for the most part [his poetry] was very similar. It was precisely the one poem, "Recounting Affairs," that spoke of current affairs without taboo. The poem read:

> That year his iron cavalry roamed the deserts,
> And he returned from a myriad *li* to a meeting of two dragons;
> In vain did Lord Zhou and his ministers keep their word,
> For brothers of the house of Han could not countenance each other.
> He only knew that the seal of state had been offered up, sent with three
>   refusals,
> Could he foretell his roaming soul would be separated from the nine layers
>   [of the court]?
> Up in heaven, the Martial Emperor also scatters tears,
> In this world, could flesh and blood have met so wrongly?

What had happened was that the Emperor Taiding had died in the Upper Capital, and Emperor Wenzong came from Jiangling to occupy Dadu, while his elder brother, the prince of Zhou, was far out in the deserts. So Wenzong temporarily took the throne as regent, and sent an emissary to greet his brother. He issued an edict to the four corners of the empire, "I respectfully await my elder brother's arrival, in order to make this heart of yielding the throne a reality." When the Prince of Zhou actually arrived, he was greeted in the Upper Capital, and was given an evening of festive banqueting, but suddenly died. Wenzong then issued another edict, "How could our time together be so short? The chariot of the palace was never driven, and he is posthumously enfeoffed as Emperor Mingzong." Then Wenzong took the throne for real. Sadula's last line speaks to the fact that they were both Emperor Wuzong's sons.

The many poems in Sadula's collection that speak so forthrightly about contemporary political events evince an interest that is also seen in his verses on "cherishing the past." In both types, what emerges is a sometimes judgmental but often indifferent attitude toward the actual events themselves. In both types, the poet attempts to sublimate historical or current events in a kind of emotional state that can ameliorate the ups and downs of historical circumstance (and life) by placing the poetic subject within the scene. For instance, in his "Cherishing the Past at Yue Terrace" (Yuetai huaigu) he muses on the overgrown remains of the first-century capital of Yue in Fujian:

> The old state of the King of Yue, boxed in by mountains,
> The cloudy ethers still encamped in passes of lions and panthers;
> Beasts of bronze secretly accompany autumn's dews as they weep,
> Crows from the sea all turn their backs on evening's rays as they return.
> Personalities from a single age are beyond the wind and dust,
> Heroes of a thousand antiquities are amid the grass and weeds;
> In sun's setting, the partridge cries all the more urgently,
> On the overgrown terrace stands of bamboo are speckled and spotted by rain.

While some *huaigu* poems will make an allusive link between a historical political situation and a current event as indirect criticism (*diaogu shangxin*), this one and others like it make forays into a more universal realm of chaos and uncertainty. The opening lines are standard enough: the overgrown terrace, now surrounded by high mountains, but still bearing the aura of kingship – cloudy vapors and rocks in the passes that crouch like beasts. The bronze statues weep along with autumn for their fallen dynasty, the crows return day after day to roost in the deserted landscape. In the third couplet, however, the straightforward perceptual scene and its allusions are replaced by a subjective complexity. This is accomplished by a contrast of key phrases: "personalities" with "heroes," "wind and dust" with "grass and weeds," and "a single age" with "a thousand antiquities." All of these terms are marvelously ambiguous. "Personalities" (*renwu*) can mean a person of high talent, an important political personality, a person remembered as an important figure in history. "A single age" (*yishi*) likewise can mean "that whole age," "that one era," and even "ephemeral" in the sense of momentary. "Wind and dust" can mean the turmoil of battle, the messy affairs of ordinary life, an official career, and a world of ordinary mediocrity. At one level, of course, the line simply means that the eminent figures of that court and that time are now beyond any political turmoil, beyond battle, beyond the vicissitudes of life, and perhaps even beyond the reach of history. But if we take the reading "momentary" for *yishi*, then we sense a deeper contrast between the ephemeral glory of high position, gone after death, and the endurance of heroes out in the grass and weeds. Again, at the surface level that line may simply mean that the heroes, whom we will revere in history forever, lie buried in the fields. Yet the simple term "grass and weeds" had a long-standing meaning as "among the common people," which yields a meaning, "enduring heroes are those kept alive in the minds of common folk." This interjection of the sensibilities of the poetic subject into the poem now universalizes the contrast as that between momentary worldly success through any of a variety of routes and a memory that is kept alive as part of an oral (or written, one supposes) transmission of one's virtue.

What was a scene cherishing the past now presents us with a universal conundrum, made specific in the life-choices of the poetic persona. Should he continue on the traditional path to social success, or should he not? Should he strive for momentary importance? The poet is stopped from his musings by the call of the partridge, the cry of which sounds like the phrase "you can't go on from here, brother" (*xingbude ye gege*); he is stopped from further exploring the physical place, presented with a tentative answer about his choice, and given warning at the point where subjective preoccupation becomes all-consuming. The poem closes by zooming back to the concrete physical world, now diminished in scope to the ephemeral dots of rain that stain the bamboo's trunk.

He has the ability to meld the past and present together in a moment that both is deeply conscious of history and creates a subjective state that can withstand the vicissitudes of change represented by dynastic fall by placing poetic sentiment within the historical scene. He was deeply fond of *huaigu* poems, and more than half of his lyric verse (*ci*) is dedicated to that topic. An example is his lyric to the tune "Filling the River with Red" (Manjiang hong), entitled "Cherishing the Past at Jinling" (Jinling huaigu), a lamentation of the early dynasties that had their capital near modern Nanjing:

> Splendor of the Six Dynasties has departed with the spring,
> No more waxings and wanings.
> In vain I disconsolately gaze afar,
> But the shape and lay of mountain and river
> Already differ from the distant past.
> A pair of swallows in front of the Halls of Wang and Xie
> Were once recognized at the mouth of Blackcoat Alley.
> Listen to the deep night
> Lonely, striking the orphaned city walls
> The spring bore quickens.
> Ponder events of the past –
> Sorrow is like a weaving,
> Cherish the former state –
> Emptied of old traces.
> Only: desolate mists, sere grass,
> Chaos of crows, setting sun.
> The song "Jade Trees" is broken, the autumn dew cold,
> The "well of rouge" now collapsed, chill-season katydids weep.
> And now it is like this –
> There is only Mount Jiang green
> And Qin Huai azure.

Sadula spent his remaining years as a hermit in and around Hangzhou, drifting out of people's ken and consciousness. His good friend Yang Weizhen, however, lived on into the Ming. Gu Sili considers Yang the "height of the transformation of Yuan verse," and one of the three great pillars of Yuan literature: Yang, Yu Ji, and Sadula.

Yang was also one of three major figures in a salon culture that developed in the south of China during the chaos of the fall of the Yuan. The two major patrons of writers were Gu Ying (1310–1369) and Ni Zan (1301–1374) in Kunshan and Wuxi, respectively; Yang Weizhen was equally influential, if less rich, and had well over a hundred students in the south, where he was considered the literary master of the age. As Wang Shizhen (1526–1590) wrote in his *Chit-chat in the Garden of Arts* (*Yiyuan zhiyan*):

> Gu Ying of my Kunshan and Ni Zan of Wuxi were both as rich as Croesus, and moreover were in possession of talent and integrity, were easy going, unrestrained and freely giving. They were the ultimate of the southeast, but it was Yang Weizhen who truly was the master of this compact. Ni is

particularly acknowledged as unmatched in the affairs of painting. Our exalted emperor [Hongwu] enlisted Weizhen to compile the *History of the Yuan*, and wanted to give him an office. Weizhen wrote the "Ditty of the Old Woman" to demonstrate that he could not be persuaded, so he was released to go back home. At that time Wei Su was an academician in the Hongwen Academy, and he was just then at the height of his prestige. One day his highness heard the sound of sandals, and asked who it was. Taipu hastily responded, "Your aged minister Wei Su." Upset, his highness said, "[Did you think] I thought it was Wen Tianxiang?" He was banished to farm in Linhao, where he died. People take this [different treatment by Hongwu] to evaluate the relative merits of Yang and Wei.

Ni and Gu each distributed their family wealth. Gu went on to paint his own portrait and inscribe it:

> Confucian robes, a Buddhist hat and Daoist sandals,
> In green mountains under heaven my bones can be buried;
> If you speak of where I was a brave dandy in my early years –
> Saddled horses at Wuling, the streets of Luoyang.

People have passed this poem along until this very day. If the richness of Gu and Ni and the grandness of Weizhen are considered like this, they share the same integrity as Tao Yuanming, but reached it by different routes.

Gu Ying, himself a noted poet, constructed a garden to the west of his estate, which he named "A Wonderful Place at Jade Mountain" or "The Grass Hut at Jade Mountain" and used it, from 1348 onward, as a site to host poets and writers in large gatherings for writing contests. From poems that were written for those taking leave from the garden, the early Qing writer Qian Qianyi (1582–1664) listed the name of thirty-seven prominent writers, including Han, Mongols, Uighurs, and Buddhist and Daoist priests. This is only a partial list, of course, and there were probably hundreds. At least eighty names are found in an anthology that Gu Ying published of poems written in the garden. The salon continued from 1348 to 1365, although it met only sporadically in the later years because of the chaos of warfare.

Yang was born in Shaoxing and passed the examinations in 1327. He was appointed as the director of the saltworks near his home, a position he held for nearly ten years without promotion or transfer. Finally, in 1337, he was enlisted as part of the project to compile the histories of the Song, Liao, and Jin dynasties. When they were finished, he submitted a long memorial on the legitimate succession of dynasties, claiming that the mandate had passed through the Southern Song, and that the Liao and the Jin should be considered as secondary states. He was then assigned to a series of low-ranking posts in the Hangzhou area. When Zhang Shicheng (1321–1367) took Suzhou in 1356, he tried to enlist Yang, and although Yang went to see him, he did not stay. The incident caused Yang to run foul of the powerful minister Tas Temur, who sent Yang to Songjiang, outside modern Shanghai. When the Ming took power, Zhu Yuanzhang summoned Yang, who went but wrote the above-mentioned song, which he sent with the note, "how can an eighty-year-old woman, near to death, arrange a second marriage?" Zhu sent a special carriage to bring him to the capital in Nanjing, and then sent him home with honors a few months later.

Yang is most noted for his "old-style *yuefu*," which strove for novelty and were written in imitation of what he considered the "force" or "power" (*shi*) of Li He and Li Shangyin. This seems simple enough, but Yang was an eccentric and complicated writer and critic. His own literary output was stylistically quite diverse. In addition to his *yuefu*, he also wrote a long series of "bamboo branch songs" and compiled an anthology of those pieces written by his contemporaries in a work entitled *An Anthology of Bamboo Branches from West Lake (Xihu zhuzhi ji)*. While his poetry was elusive and sometimes obscure, he was obsessed with making his prose as clear as possible. It was simple and unadorned, and to keep people from possibly misreading it, he even put in interlinear notes at points where possible mistakes could occur.

By the time Yang was writing, the imitation of the Tang had reached a point where, no longer innovative, it had begun to create a repetitive and imitative style that lacked all originality. This was particularly true of poems written in the style of Li He, and it came under the critical eye of Yang Weizhen. He wrote,

> Those who imitate Li He value imitating his force/power; they do not imitate his words. Those who imitate his power find it permissible to tread in his path; those who imitate his words grow daily more distant from him. There are many now who imitate Li He, but they seem only to imitate his words.

This seeming paradox, in which he is set on pursuing "the power" of the ancients while not imitating them outright, is tied to his concept of *qing* (innate passion or sensibility). As he wrote, "Getting poetry from one's teacher is certainly not as fine as getting it from one's own talent. Poetry is a person's passion and nature; because each person has [unique] passion, each person has [unique] poetry. Can something one obtains from one's teacher in any way be one's own poetry?"

This desire for individual expression is balanced against his own practice, which attempts to recover what it was that made ancient writing profound.

In a preface to Yang's poetry, Zhang Yu (1283–1350), his friend and a renowned Daoist poet, wrote,

> From the time of the *Classic of Poetry* onward only "old-style *yuefu*" has come close to not losing the import of *bi* and *xing*. In this current age only Yang Weizhen and Li Xiaoguang can be called "poets" in terms of being skilled at using the old rhyme books of the talents of Wu and at driving [their poetry] with old-style language. Yang Weizhen runs rampant among them, modeling himself on the Han and Wei in prior times, and occasionally partaking of the talents of Du Fu, Li Bai, and Li He. So the wording of his old-style *yuefu* has a resonance of metal and stone not found in this age. It is something people gaze on in admiration but also in awe. Sometimes he also produces dragons, ghosts, snakes, and spirits to dazzle and stir up the eyes and ears of the age – this is also novel.

How do we balance this assessment with Yang's own words, "People of a later age hold the brush and moan and groan, copying vermilion and imitating white to make poetry – can it still be considered poetic?" The answer seems to lie in the balance between the quality of the poet, which he considered innate passion or sensibility, and learning, which he considered necessary but secondary. That is, the power to be a poet was innate; the power to engage with the outside world in the form of direct stimulus or historical meaning was learned. As he wrote, "Although poetry cannot be learned, the place from which it issues cannot be without learning." "Poetry," he wrote, "is based in innate passion and nature" (*shi ben qingxing*). This idea, of course, was not new and can be ultimately traced back to the "Great Preface" to the *Classic of Poetry*. In the Yuan both Zhao Mengfu and Yu Ji were strong proponents of this theory, but their take was quite different from Yang Weizhen's.

For both of these writers, "passion and nature" meant the refined ethical sensibilities of the writer. Yu Ji, in particular, understood it in terms of the traditional Confucian interpretation as "the uprightness of passion and nature" (*qingxing zhi zheng*). Since this refined ethical nature was expressed through poetry in a modulated, harmonic balance full of warmth and ethical feeling, Yu Ji emphasized what we might call "indifferent blandness" (*danbo*) and "quietude" (*anjing*). Much of Yu Ji's writing exemplified these traits. In terms of practice, however, Yang Weizhen was completely enamored of poems of sexual passion and of feasting, the latter being so numerous that people began to identify his poetry by that feature. Hu Yinglin, a great proponent of individuality, for instance, felt let down when he read Yang Weizhen's verse: "I always lament that such great talent is put to such small accomplishments." Yet he also considered Yang the single person who could master all the styles of Liu Yuxi's bamboo branch songs, Li He's "brocade bag" poems, and Han Wo's "perfume case" poetry. So, for Yang, *qingxing* meant one's private passions and nature rather than an ethical state in which everyone would share. Rather than this shared or corporate subjectivity, a universal, even cosmic, sense of ethics, an individual's poetic subjectivity was the sole mark and possession of a personality, and its expression was contingent on immediate circumstance rather than on a timeless and universal state of being.

There is something of the older Southern Song schools of poetry found in Yang's writings. While he opposed the direct imitation, or use, of phrases from the past, he was intent, as Zhang Yu's preface mentioned, on imitating older rhyme patterns, based on old rhyme books from the south. He almost always uses new topics for his "old-style" poems; and when he does use older titles or topics, the poetry is much closer to seven-syllable old-style verse than to *yuefu*. He also likes to use historical incidents; but rather than objectively describing them, he likes to turn them to something new by incorporating his own evaluation of the incident in the poem. Finally, he is obsessively fond of using what is called "rare and marvelous" material and a highly refined and elegant diction in his poetry that sometimes "dazzles" his contemporaries. Thus his truly interesting "old-style *yuefu*" poetry requires an extensive amount of annotation, both of allusions and of his diction, and is not presented here.

His bamboo branch poems, of which he wrote a hundred or more, were enormously popular. These quatrains in the seven-syllable line are witty and seemingly simple. Below are three examples of the most famous:

> In front of Su Xiaoqing's door, flowers fill the tree,
> On top of Su Shi's dike, a girl faces the wine-warmer;
> Southern officials and northern travelers must come to this very spot –
> West Lake of Jiangnan is found nowhere else.
> (Su Xiaoqing was a famous beauty of antiquity; Su Shi a Song writer and
> bureaucrat who created a dike across the lake to store water.)

> I urge you, sir, do not ascend the high southern peak,
> I urge myself not to ascend the high northern peak;
> There are clouds at the southern peak and rain at the north,
> And rain and clouds pushing toward each other sorrows me no end.

> A boat with a cabin at the mouth of the lake, the mouth of the lake, dark,
> A broken bridge in the middle of the lake, the water of the lake, deep;
> The cabin boat without a rudder: this is your intent,
> A broken bridge that has supports: this is my heart.

These little poems are deceptively simple. The second poem, for instance, may be understood as a separation of clouds on one peak, and rain on the other. "Clouds and rain" is an old euphemism for a sexual tryst and the impossibility of them meeting (i.e. of staging a tryst) creates sorrow on the girl's part. Another way to read it is that, since both peaks are clouded over, they are not "sunlit" (*qing*), which is a homophone for "passion." This can be read, then, as the girl chiding her lover for his singular lack of concern while they are separated. In the third poem, the boat without a rudder stays on a true course, never wavering. The broken bridge has supports that keep it standing, though separated, a metaphor for the firmness of the girl's heart. The last line also has a common variant of "has no supports" (*wuzhu*) for "has supports" (*youzhu*). If the variant is used, we can then understand the word "support" (*zhu*) as a homophone for "master" (*zhu*), meaning that the girl is crazy with love and lacks anything to control her mind as her heart is ground down by constant worry.

One poem in particular was very famous. It was supposedly written when Zhang Shicheng had invited Yang Weizhen to be part of his government. At the time, Zhang had just surrendered to the Yuan court and had been awarded dragon-embroidered robes (usually reserved for the emperor) and imperial wine as part of his settlement. Zhang had pressured Yang Weizhen to visit him, and had given him some of the wine to drink. After Yang chanted the following poem, Zhang was happy to see him leave:

> In Jiangnan war fires spring up everywhere,
> From the sea year after year imperial wine is delivered;
> With war fires like this, with wine like this,
> How can this old man ever release his worries?

Yang Weizhen was responsible for a major change in late Yuan poetics: an emphasis on *qing* that presaged the Ming interest in individual passions and sensibility, the opening up of a poetic discourse on "sexual passion" (*seqing*), and a diatribe against imitation and against obsession with poetic rules. It is worth noting in this regard Yang Weizhen's dislike of the regulated form of poetry, with its several tonal and grammatical rules of parallelism. He refused to let people circulate his "new-style verse," and claimed, "poetry reaching to regulated verse was a singular disaster for poets." The only poets he could countenance who wrote in that style were Du Fu and Cui Hao, who, he thought "were unencumbered by tonal rules." His gates produced many poets, including the so-called Four Masters of Wu of the early Ming dynasty: Gao Qi (1336–1374), Zhang Yu (1333–1385), Yang Ji (ca 1334–1383), and Xu Ben (1335–1380).

The last years of the Yuan were filled with political chaos, social turmoil, and warfare. Between the years 1321 and 1332 there were six successions to the throne. Rebellion plagued the south, and from the early 1350s onward there was constant warfare in south China. The generation that bridged these years included several poets who would emerge in the Ming as major literary and political figures. Liu Ji (1311–1375) is often paired with Song Lian (1310–1381) as one of the "great founding ministers of the Ming" (*kaiguo zhi dachen*). But both were already over fifty when the Ming took power, and while their major contributions to the state and their positions as literary lions are most marked in the Ming, they had quite different backgrounds. Song Lian had never held a post under the Yuan, but Liu Ji had already had an extensive career before the end of the dynasty. Song Lian's contributions are primarily from the Ming, but the majority of Liu Ji's important literary works stem from the late Yuan and are engaged with the decline of political power and the hardships of life in an unsettled age.

Liu Ji's literary output during the Yuan included both prose and poetry, the latter of which accounts for the majority of his collected writings. In his public utterances he was a thorough Confucian, but more in the mold of the political rationalist. For him literature, particularly poetry, was to serve the function of ethically ordering the state. He wrote no long treatises, but from his remarks on the poetry of others, his critical (and, one supposes, compositional) standards comprised ethical instruction (*jiaohua fengyu*), ability to stir up a sense of righteousness (*gandong*), and admonishment cloaked in beauty (*meici fengjie*) that was of help to contemporary moral instruction (*you biyu shijiao*). His work anticipates Ming motifs and he was sharply critical of the late Yuan poetry scene, his harsh comments clearly directed at writers like Yang Weizhen and Sadula:

> Now in the world I have not heard of any regulation that prohibits speech, yet the habits of what the eyes see and ears hear have not yet changed, so those who write poetry all consider moaning about the wind and the moon or playing with flowers and birds to be what makes capability. Once they take that position, then they may be high officials or valued men but they do not take the ancients as their model, they determine what is important and what is not among all other men without even considering if they are dealing with jade or just a stone. They blindly quibble, they match this poem and share rhymes with that poem, even form into cliques and schools, and then slander and revile each other. So it turns out that there are none who actually understand the way of poetry.

There is an air of neo-Confucian fundamentalism about Liu Ji's assessments of literature, and an excoriating attitude toward writing in his time. The lineage of writers that he picks is completely the traditional Confucian model, and his reasons for selecting them are quite clear:

> Principle [*li*] is the master in prose, and ether [*qi*] is to give it expression. If principle is not clear, it is empty writing; if ether is not sufficient, there is nothing to convey principle. The burgeoning and decline of writing definitely are concerned with the fortune of the age in which it is written. In the writing of the age of Tang, Yu, and the Three Epochs [of high antiquity], what is sincere inside takes form in language. They did not force it unnaturally to make it crafted; they did not use made-up sounds to endlessly run on, so in their writing principle is clear and ether is crystalline.

For Liu, literature stands in a reciprocal relationship with the world: it is ineluctably shaped by social forces but also has the power to change or transform the world. The question seems to be whether or not one has the willpower to look beyond immediate rewards to attempt to reshape the world in the mold of the ancients.

As one would expect with such a determined personality, there is a concordance between Liu Ji's theory and his own production. His prose and poetry both deal in frank and critical ways with the world of the late Yuan. In *The Master Who Sheds Light on Culture (Youlizi)*, a prose collection he wrote in the 1350s after being cashiered, are 182 chapters that cover all aspects of life from home to the state, from economics, military strategy, and ethics to the supernatural. But all of the anecdotes are marked by a concern for the declining cultural, social, and political conditions of the time and they are unrelentingly critical of its faults. The passages on "The Horse that Can Run Forever" (Qianli ma) and "The Eight Bayards" (Bajun) criticize the inability of the Yuan to advance the worthy, to make use of the capable, and are a direct swipe at the Yuan policy of discriminating against southerners. In "The Eight Bayards" he recounts how, after the eight steeds of King Mu had died, no one knew how to select "real talent" and horses were picked, graded, and stabled according to their status: northern horses the best, mixed-breed horses the second best, and southern horses the lowest rank, used only for delivering documents along the post routes. The impunity with which this condemnation of the Yuan hierarchy (Mongols, other foreigners (*semu*), and Chinese) was made speaks itself to the relative ineffectualness of rule.

His poetry shared this same sense of indignation. As early as the 1350s, when he was involved in the Fang Guozhen insurrection, his direct appeal in a long poem of 128 lines to better the condition of people caught up in warfare and make officials more responsible for stopping local violence cost him his position. In another long series, "Ten Poems Narrating Events after Being Moved by the Times" (*Ganshi shushi shishou*), he laid the blame for popular insurrections at the feet of rapacious and corrupt local officials and a failed central authority.

If Yang Weizhen's version of *yuefu* was imaginative re-creation of the style of Li Bai and Li He, Liu Ji turned back to the anonymous "old *yuefu*" attributed to the Han. While still writing in the context of Yuan creative invention, there is already a hint of the mid-Ming in his view of the literary past as a repertoire of texts and titles, each inviting a single imitation. We often find poems that are constructed of phrases and motifs of old poetry, woven together in a creative way, as in his version of the Han ballad "Dew on the Shallots":

> Do not strum the zither from Shu,
> Cease for a while blowing the ocarina of Qi.
> Those at the feast mat listen in silence together,
> Listen to my poem, "Dew on the Shallots":
> Yesterday a strapping seven-feet tall,
> Today I am a corpse, dead.
> In vain kith and kin fill the hall,
> Where has the ether of my soul flown?
> Gold and jade were what I loved before,
> Now they are put away and stored in baskets;
> Girdle pendants are what I loved before,
> Now they hang, cold and ignored, in the sighing wind.
> Wife and concubine are what I loved before,
> They sprinkle tears by the empty window;
> Guests and visitors are what I loved before,
> Now dispersed, each gone east or west.
> Those who hated me now share their happiness,
> Those who were close now share their grief.
> I have ears, but hear no more,
> I have eyes, but see no more.
> I am like that fire on the candle,
> Once extinguished, no light remains.
> I am like those clouds in the void,
> Once they disperse, no shape is left.
> A human life never reaches one hundred,
> But what if it could?
> Who can take their own two hands
> To reverse those waters flowing to the east?

> Every hero from antiquity to now
> Has returned to mountain's bend
> If you have wine, then be happy
> And listen to my ballad of "Dew on the Shallots."

The indignation and frankness of his poetry and prose of social criticism and the depressive nature of his writing on nature or ruminations on life are both illustrative of his mentality during this era of decline and warfare. They help explain his early decision to move into Zhu Yuanzhang's camp. His later poetry, including the famous "Two Ghosts" (Er gui), a highly allegorical piece about his position within the Ming bureaucracy, are more rightly a product of a new age. The long poem of 1,200 words relates how two spirits, Jielin and Yuyi, who were overseers of the sun and moon, were dispatched to the mortal world by the heavenly emperor, where they were separated for fifty years. When the world falls into turmoil, they meet to attempt to set the order of the world right again, move the two poles in alignment, and enlighten the common folk so that they "trod in the way of benevolence and righteousness and honor their fathers and teachers." Unknowingly, the two ghosts anger the heavenly emperor, who locks them away in a silver cage, and they must wait for the emperor's anger to cease before they can return to heaven. The poem has traditionally been understood as an allegory of the career of Liu Ji and Song Lian, and an expression of Liu Ji's frustration at being held back from reestablishing a Confucian order and at not being allowed to fully accomplish his desire. Although the circumstances had changed, he was still haunted by an inability to find release from his anxiety and frustration.

VI. A note on the *fu*

As noted above, the examinations were sporadic in the Yuan. From 1233 to 1313 there were only periodic provincial examinations to select Confucian intendants (*ru*) to co-administer local areas with Mongol governors known as *Daruhachi*. The first eighty years resulted in three major events: the use of examinations at the local level, the institution of an examination curriculum in local schools and academies (*shuyuan*), and a long debate at court about the proper procedures for selection and how to properly set an examination.

The early provincial tests combined three areas: the "discussion" (*lun*), the "meanings of the Classics" (*jingyi*), and the "regulated fu" (*lüfu*). Of the twenty-four known successful candidates, ten passed on the basis of the regulated *fu*. We know from a remark in Su Tianjue's "Inscription for the Grave Stele of

Master Zhang, Jiexuan, Former *Ru* Professor of the Zhending Route" that these examinations "employed the old form of the Song and Jin," which laid primary emphasis on the regulated *fu*. People recommended for direct appointment in this early period were also

> to be examined on the basis of topics proposed by education intendants of each circuit together with the literary officers of the Surveillance Commission of each province, who will use one example of their work on a Classic and one of regulated *fu* [*cifu*]; they will examine the complete texts for excellence in composition.

Paradoxically, while early writers supported the use of the regulated *fu* in the examinations, practically none of them wrote in that style. Hao Jing, for instance, wrote only *gufu*, "ancient-Style" *fu*; and in his work on literary sources, *Record of Tracing Antiquity* (*Yuangu lu*), he placed *fu* in the category of "poetry" (*shibu*). He moreover compiled a work, now lost, called *The Ancient-style Fu of our Dynasty* (*Huangchao gufu*). His contemporary, Wang Yun, also wrote only ancient-style *fu*, but he defended the use of the regulated *fu* in the examinations:

> In writing one should come out of the examination system. Otherwise, not only will one not match the proper structures and regulations, but one's writing will also be indiscriminate in its reach, unruly, unorganized, and undisciplined – just like trying to enter and exit without a proper doorway. Even if younger generations do not work at the examination curriculum, they should still read through the parallel prose and regulated *fu* of the Tang; this cannot be neglected. There are many subtle points of excellence in their structure and layout.

Through practice, rather than pedagogical need, the ancient-style *fu* gradually gained ascendency until, by 1314, when the examinations were reintroduced, it had supplanted the regulated *fu* as a major component of the examinations. Simultaneously it had entered perforce into the curriculum of the academies. *Fu* production in general blossomed after it gained a foothold in the examinations. It was, moreover, sometimes a direct path to appointment, a text offered to seek support for a position. In the period from 1234 to 1313, there were thirty-five notable *fu* writers and 180 extant *fu*; in the latter half of the dynasty, from 1314 to 1368, there were some two hundred writers and 720 extant *fu*, with some writers producing as many as ninety that were worthy enough to retain in their collected works. All of these were major writers like Yuan Jie, Ma Zuchang, Xu Youren, Yang Weizhen, Song Lian, Liu Ji, and others.

In earlier times, ancient-style *fu* had been primarily part of writers' reper-toires of pure literature and were kept separate from their endeavors in the examination. The combination of using ancient-style *fu* in the examinations and the growth of print culture, however, seems to have dissolved the bound-aries between examination *fu* and their social and literary influence, both in terms of providing at hand a range of model *fu*, and in terms of what was expected to be won from reading them. Immediately after the examinations were first held, a commercial book appeared throughout China called *Exem-plary Texts from the Examinations* (*Huishi chengwen*). This text was followed in 1341 and 1344 by two others: the *Literary Selections from Three Areas of the Exam-inations* (the extant edition is entitled *Newly Printed and Arranged by Category: Selections from the Three Fields of the Examinations – Xinkan leibian Sanchang wenxuan*) and *Selections from Three Fields of the Examinations in the Imperially Sponsored Examinations of the Yuan* (*Yuan dake sanchang wenxuan*). The 1341 anthology was an attempt to gather together all texts, including *fu*, from the three sections of the eight examinations that had been held since 1314, while the second, the 1344 collection, anthologized only those texts from the 1341 test. Both compendia represented writing only from the areas of Jiangxi, Hunan and Guangzhou, Jiangsu, and Zhejiang in south China. Titles of five other *fu* anthologies are known, only three of which are extant. The two that were lost were clearly primers: *The Level and Line for Ancient-Style Fu* (*Gufu zhunsheng*) and *Topics for Ancient-Style Fu* (*Gufu ti*). The other three are pure anthologies that in some cases include the examiners' comments on the works. These are Su Hongdao's *Fu on the Stone Drums from the Jiangxi County Examinations of 1314* (*Yanyou jiayin ke Jiangxi xiangshi shigu fu*) and two anonymous works: *Fu on the Uncarved Jade of Jingshan from the Huguang County Examinations of 1335* (*Yuantong yihai Huguang xiangshi Jingshan pu fu*) and *Ladder to Clouds in the Blue* (*Qingyun ti*).

While these seem to be simple collections of models to emulate, the focus of the collectors was clearly not simply on technique. In the preface to the *Literary Selections from Three Areas of the Examinations* (1341), we find:

> The texts of the successive examinations are dignified and broad of vision; they were gathered examination after examination, and the cases accumulated until they filled baskets. If we were not to fish out their subtleties or cull the very fine ones, it would be to the detriment of scholars of "new knowledge." The days of reclusion in mountain forests grow long, but the aspiration of wind and clouds stretches far indeed. Therefore I love to read and discuss in detail these writings with those who elevate me through their friendship, copying those that are the best into several chapters, entitling it, *Literary*

Selections from Three Examinations. Our intent is to make it easier to peruse them and to clarify the proper form to be copied and by this to bestow them on learners – it was never to recklessly dare to evaluate the literature of this sub-celestial realm.

The preface indicates the dual nature of the compilation: a textbook of model *fu*, but also a social instrument, a space where reading and discussion of the text give the works a life beyond mere stylistic copying. This moment of sharing in the present – a purely literary and social act – also creates a tension between historicized production and enduring values. The anthology makes clear that the purpose of learning is not to master mere form, but to forge a direct link to the masters of the past. For instance, the preface to the subsection on *fu* in the 1341 edition suggests,

> For the middle section of the examinations, our sagely court used old-style *fu*, and those who composed *fu* were able to immediately wash away the corruption of sound and tonality of recent years [i.e. the Song and Jin], and restore and carry on the complete vigor of the ancients [i.e. the Zhou and Han] – so marvelous, so grand. Someone has meticulously copied out texts of the upper and middle category from the eight examinations that have taken place since the *jiayin* year [1314], and each and every selection that can be used as a model has been carved, according to category, on the printing blocks. If readers become familiar with these, it would definitely be easy to trace out the past steps of Jia Yi, Song Yu, Ban Gu, or Yang Xiong, should one wish.

This preface transfers the idea of a universal quality from technique (sound and tonality) to an original moment of creation – an expression of a refined human state – that endures through time as that ethical moment's homologous literary expression. This argument was carried on in the second anthology (1342), which was a conscious imitation of the earlier one:

> In examinations past and present it has been a longtime custom to select officials on the basis of literature. Although the genres may be different, every single person has been selected on the basis of literature. Now, since animating ether [*qi*] is the basis of literature, any burgeoning of a single era will inevitably possess literature for that single era. From this we can see that this court's selection of literati on the basis of Classical elucidations and ethical behavior is not something one can consider superficial. The examinations were disestablished and then begun anew; once begun, they flourished. The generic styles were exquisitely worked and finely detailed, and the writing was precisely on the mark. If they were not those truly capable of being enlightened by the Classics, how would they attain the subtlety of complete penetration of principle, like the enlightened state of Chan, in which one

can see the nature of each and every thing? Was it not by this? It causes them to be able to cumulatively perfect their actions so they can sustain their inner selves, to fill up their *qi* and by this to create literature – is this not to be considered beautiful? The literary selections of the past three courts are already circulating, and now I have selected the blossoms of the later examinations and carved them again on printing blocks, hoping to expand the experience of those who come later and to shed light on the grand refulgence of the literature and *qi* of an entire era. Those who peruse this must find something they can take from this.

Qi, as an animating spirit of an age, is shaped by the world around it, and creates literature from a current context, but it is linked to all times by universal ethical principles that must be internally perfected by every writer in order to be able to respond in writing to the material world around him. What the anthologist hopes the reader will take away is the knowledge that texts produced in the current world have the same value as those from the past, but only because once beyond the materiality of the present (in its physical, social, or political state) there is something that is eternal and identifiable as literature, that links all writing together as refined expression of a perfected human consciousness.

Two unavoidable trends came from joining the ancient-style *fu* to the examinations: a tendency to copy directly and repetitively and the increasing neo-Confucianization of these texts. Both of these trends were products of inferior writers or inferior poems by good writers guilty of political and governmental opportunism. But they do not represent the whole of ethical experience in the Yuan, in many respects a complicated and nonconforming age. We can certainly see the "sour and rotten" taste of the *Daoxue* writers, particularly in the later writers, but since the Yuan was more tolerant than either the Song or the Ming, even *Daoxue* writers were quite eclectic in terms of orthodox sources. Moreover, while Zhu Xi's commentaries eventually gained ascendency, they were used primarily as "a brick to knock on the door," according to a modern critic, and the writers, once in the position won by their opportunism, simply rejected the whole of *Daoxue* "like a used pair of sandals."

The emphasis on *qi* and on lyrical expression rather than on exposition and mastery of formal rules clearly placed the *fu* in the category of poetry rather than prose for most writers. In one of the first histories of the *fu*, Zhu Yao's (ca 1320–1370) *Discrimination of the Forms of Ancient-Style Fu (Gufu bianti)*, we can see his struggle both to give *fu* a place in literature and simultaneously to acknowledge the *fu*'s place in the examinations. There, as a literary exercise, it was, as Wu Cheng said, a way "to completely understand the writing of the ancients and thereby perfect that style." Zhu Yao's text proceeds along familiar lines. Like the early *fu* writers Ban Gu, Zuo Si, and Huangfu Mi, Zhu emphasized that *fu* was "an offshoot of ancient poetry" (*gushi zhi liu*), and that it had derived from *fu* among the "six kinds of significance" (*liuyi*) of early poetic theory, further evolving from the *Lyrics of Chu*, themselves a "changed" form of the "Airs of the States" of the *Classic of Poetry*. This opinion was shared by Yang Weizhen, who also thought that the *sao* form of the *Lyrics of Chu* derived from the "Airs of the States" and, like the *Classic of Poetry*, could be put to music. Zhu Yao argued against those who understood the meaning of the word *fu* only in the sense of "exposition":

> Ancients considered "Airs," "Odes," and "Hymns" as the three "warps," and took "exposition," "comparison," and "affective image" as the three "woofs" [of the fabric of poetry]. Are not the warps the standard of the *Odes*? And are not the woofs the flowering adornment of the *Odes*? When [a writer] makes the warp an unvarying standard and makes the woof flowering adornment, then the full form of the *Poem* begins to be visible, and compositions that chant at length of human nature and feeling possess that which is not narration, clarification of principle, or the extolling of virtue, of which prose is constructed!

> This is precisely where poetry and prose differ. *Fu* originally stemmed from the *shi*, therefore writers of *fu* should take *shi* as the generic form and should not take prose as the form. In later generations people mostly do not understand the mutual reliance of warp and woof or the mutual necessity of having both an unvarying standard and flowering adornment. So there is nothing on which to rely to issue forth prolonged chanting and there is no reason for nature and feeling to be made visible. Ask what they create *fu* from, and they say, "*Fu* means exposition," as though it stems from exposition and nothing more. I am afraid that if their *fu* is particularly only a type of expository prose, then how can one name it *fu*?

The emphasis on poetry created a certain set of critical variables used in the Yuan as standards of assessment for the *fu*. Like poetry, upon which it was based, it relied on human feeling and empathy as the major elements, with "events and categorizations as secondary." Drawing heavily on the "Great Preface" to the *Classic of Poetry*, Zhu argues that these feelings "take shape in words without a person understanding it," and they "match principle without a person knowing how." Because the best *fu* should be an unmediated expression, they should possess an inner beauty that inspires aesthetic appreciation at the same time as they express ethical principle. Zhu negotiates the relationship between aesthetics, words, feeling, and ethics by outlining the two major failures of the *fu*: being too obsessed with the metrical pattern and being too expository:

> Human feeling takes shape in words without a person's understanding it, and words match principle without one knowing how. Feeling takes shape in words, therefore it is beautiful and can be appreciated; the words match with principle, so its ethical pattern can be emulated. Its beauty and the fact that it can be appreciated both issue from human feeling, although it appears to come from words; that its ethical pattern can be emulated seems to issue from principle, but in reality comes from the words. Because it is possessed of both human feeling and words, those who read it will have the subtle purport of "being moved to action." Because it is possessed of both words and principle, those who read it will possess the bequeathed tonalities of "singing it out." If one should perhaps lose it in terms of human feeling, and be inclined toward words and not inclined toward meaning, then it does not possess the subtlety of "moving one to action" – so, what can it have to do with ethical pattern? *This* is precisely the [metrically overworked] parallel style of later *fu* writers. Or perhaps it is lost in terms of wording, and it is inclined toward principle and not toward words, then it does not possess that which is bequeathed from the unmediated "singing it out" and so what does it have to do with beauty? *This* is precisely the expository style of *fu* of later writers.

Finally, the critical standard by which the *fu* was measured was its ability to revive the values of antiquity. The path that *fu* writing and criticism developed along was the same as that of other genres of literature in the Yuan. It sought to revive the "human feeling" of the past that had been lost in the Song and Jin. Unlike poetry or ancient-style prose, however, it went far back to the late Zhou, the Han, and the Three Kingdoms to find its inspiration. It drew first and foremost from its progenitor, the *sao* of the *Lyrics of Chu*, and its ancestors, the great Han dynasty *fu*, particularly those of Ban Gu and Jia Yi, and even from the shorter and more "lustrous" (*yarun*) pieces of Cao Zhi, although his place in the lineage suffered because his works were a "slightly weakened" form (*dan cha weiruo er*).

VII. Colloquial literature in the Yuan

Until the advent of broadcast media, oral performances in a variety of forms were the medium of pleasure and education for the mass of people in China. These could be historical tales, fictional stories, drama, rhymed verses sung to an accompaniment, farces, or drama. Except for the brief snapshots that short descriptive prose passages or poems provide, there is no way to track the origins of these stories, to verify their development, or to assume any constancy in how they were performed. From such little moments frozen in time we can at best discover the kinds of instruments used, the place a performance was held, or the bare fact that they treated such-and-such a topic. The actual experienced time of their performance can never be recovered.

In the surviving textual artifacts we find ourselves in a maze. Drama is a perfect example. Northern drama (*zaju*) was a form that began sometime in the mid-thirteenth century. It was a play of four acts and each act was composed of one long suite of songs all composed to the same mode. The songs were framed within prose dialogue, and while there were usually four to six actors in each play, only the lead male or the lead female role would sing through the entire play. Like other Chinese plays, the dramas used "role types" instead of characters. There were the male lead, the female lead, the second male, the clown, the comic, the second female, and a few others. Role types usually played on a single character in the play, but there are many instances where the lead changed characters throughout the play. Likewise, in different dramas, depending on their function in the play the same character could be played by a different role type. There is a plethora of material *about* performance, but a paucity of actual scripts or libretti. The lengthier textual materials – long lists of short performances, bibliographies and short biographies, treatises on how to sing, on what not to do when writing – provide a context for us to link names to dramas, and they offer tantalizing hints of possible forerunners of what appears in later colloquial fiction and drama; but they are very misleading when used incorrectly. The surviving secondary sources on performance are all from the middle of the fourteenth century.

Sounds and Rhymes of the Central Plain (*Zhongyuan yinyun*) was published around 1324 by Zhou Deqing (1277–1364), who was famous among his peers for his knowledge of music and tonal structures. His work is divided into two major sections. The first is a formulary of contemporary rhymes. A tonal language, Chinese had four tones. The fourth set of tones, called "entering tones," all ended in stops – -p, -t, or -k. This tone category disappeared in northern dialects along with the stops, and was redistributed in the other three. Southern dialects still retained that fourth category, and Zhou prescribed the way that vernacular lyric (*qu*) should be written in a northern fashion. He entitled this part of his book "the basis of correct language" (*zhengyu zhi ben*) and "the source of transformed elegance" (*bianya zhi duan*). These two phrases gesture toward the discussion of language and meaning in the "Great Preface" to the *Classic of Poetry*, and are meant to firmly place his version of the *sanqu* within the realm of polite poetry by drawing a link between the correct use of rhymes and the ethical purport of texts. This part of the work has been an important source for linguists who have discussed the phonological changes of post-fourteenth-century Chinese. The second section of the work, entitled "Setting the Proper Precedents for Correct Words and Writing Lyrics" (Zhengyu zuoci qili), includes an important primer for composition called "Ten Rules for Writing Lyrics" (Zuoci shifa). In this latter section the author cited many lines from contemporary colloquial songs and some dramatic arias to substantiate the points he was making (in both positive and negative terms).

Zhong Sicheng's (ca 1279–ca 1360) *The Register of Ghosts* (*Lugui bu*), with prefaces dated 1355, 1360, and 1366, is a bio-bibliography of dramas and dramatists that Zhong knew about. This is the major source for bibliographical information on his contemporaries. His entries are divided into the following categories:

1. Those famous nobles, already dead, from the previous generations who have *yuefu* [*ci*, colloquial songs, or arias] circulating in the world.
2. Those famous nobles of the present.
3. Those famous nobles, talented writers, already dead, from the previous generations who have compiled dramas circulating in the world.
4. Those famous nobles, talented writers, already gone but known to me, for whom I have compiled a biography and lamented their passing with the tune "Song of Skimming the Waves" [*Lingbo qu*].
5. Those talented writers already dead, personally unknown to me.
6. Those talented writers of the present known to me – I have recorded their names in full, their actual events, and the dramas that have been compiled.
7. Those talented writers of the present of whom I have heard but do not personally know.

This presents a matrix of three doublets of contrasting variables – famous noble / talented writer, dead/alive, known/unknown – that are tantalizing as possible indices to cultural fame or to professional skill, to the dating of people and works, and to the depth of knowledge of the writer. None of the lines is drawn clearly, although "famous noble" (*minggong*) seems mostly to refer to literati writers of song lyrics in the Song tradition (*ci*) and colloquial songs, while "talented writer" seems to indicate a professional dramatist. Like the *Sounds and Rhymes of the Central Plain*, this record has been used as a sourcebook for information, but little work has been done on it as an integral text, particularly in relation to other secondary sources in the later Yuan.

The *Treatise on Singing* (*Changlun*), by an anonymous person with the pseudonym of Yannan Zhi'an, can be dated reliably to 1341–1346. This small work of some thirty-one entries is difficult to understand because of its use of technical terms when discussing the methods of singing. It basically covers several areas. It discusses the appropriateness of songs to gender and status:

> Each of the three religions favors something different: Daoism sings of sentiments, Buddhism sings of human nature, and Confucianism sings of natural principles.

> Things taboo in singing: amateurs do not sing the songs of professionals; wastrels do not sing the songs of those who have achieved success; males do not sing voluptuous songs; females do not sing manly verses. Southerners do not sing *qu* style and northerners do not sing *ge* style.

The text also discusses intonation, breathing, and modulation of rhythm. It distinguishes the professional categories of singers (specialists in "small songs," "altar songs," "songs for pacing the void," "vending songs," and so on) as well as the topics that singers could offer up to audiences. Each of these topics – iron cavalry, lotus picking, winter scenes, river scenes, wine songs, and so on – is linked to a specific "location" in which a song of any topic would be aptly performed: in a group of entertainers, in the boudoir of an unhappy maiden, at the riverbank with a woman trader, with palace entertainers, for example. The text is careful to lay out the ethical, spatial, and socially and ethically hierarchical venues for singing. It is, moreover, the first text to link the modes of Chinese music with defined emotional overtones, something that may have existed but is now unrecoverable from the actual lyrics. Finally, the *Treatise on Singing* is the first text to define a regional distribution of song lyrics:

> Generally, there are set places for singing colloquial songs [*qu*]: in Dongping [Shandong] one sings the "Magnolia Flower" [Mulan hua man]; in Daming [Shandong] one sings "Groping for Fish" [Mo yu'er]; in the [Jin dynasty] Southern Capital [Bianliang] they sing "Fresh Hawfruit" [Sheng zhazi], and in Zhangde [Anyang] they sing "A Wooden Peckmeasure of Sand" [Muhu sha], and in Shaanxi, they sing "Three Reprises of Yang Pass" [Yangguan sandie] and "Black Lacquered Crossbow" [Heiqi nu].

While the *Treatise* makes a clear linkage between place and tune, it remains unclear whether that link is one of origin – that the songs arose in those places and have some regional quality about them – or whether it is making a comment about the appropriateness of singing those tunes in that location. For instance, Shaanxi was the province from which one left China proper to travel to the west and northwest, usually on military campaign by traditional poetic association, and it would make sense that songs of parting through the pass that led west (Yang Pass) and about crossbows would be associated with that area.

The final important secondary source from this period is the *Collection of the Green Bower (Qinglou ji)*, bearing a preface of the year 1360 by its author, Xia Tingzhi. This text was the first of a doublet that Xia planned to write about actors and actresses known to him. In the single volume he finished, he treats some 150 actresses under 116 main titles. The text is a wealth of information despite a certain bias toward women well trained in literature, those who possessed good memories, and those who could write. That is, he concentrates on actresses who were either kept as mistresses (not legitimized as actual concubines) by high officials or those who were in regular literary correspondence with literati. His own predilections are shown in his preface when he argues that later Yuan drama was well beyond the farce skits and comedies of the early period:

> Farce skits are for the most part no more than teasing and ridicule, but northern plays [*zaju*] are not so – there are plays about ministers and officials, about mothers and sons, husbands and wives, brothers, and friends. All of these can make human relations more substantial and can beautify the transformative power of ethics. They cannot be spoken of in the same breath as the literary tales of the Tang, the southern drama of the Song, or the farce skits of the Jin!

One can equally assume – and it is borne out by the anecdotes – that he also chose to select those actresses who had remained faithful to their lovers, who had become good wives, or who were congenial companions who would not make their literati paramours step over the boundaries of the "Five Constant Human Relations" of Confucianism that he outlined in his preface.

Despite these tantalizing secondary sources, we have very few scripts or libretti of northern plays left from the Yuan; and of those that remain, none has authorship attributed to it. Even in the *Sounds and Rhymes of the Central Plain*, where the author cites lines from several dramas – *The Dream of Yellow Millet*, *Yueyang Tower*, *The Duke of Zhou Acts as Regent*, and from the third act of the second play of *The Story of the Western Wing* – he never assigns authorship. This is particularly interesting since he does cite Ma Zhiyuan's name in connection with a particular song-set as the "perfect" colloquial songwriter, yet he fails to mention Ma as author of either *Millet* or *Yueyang*, both of which are attributed to Ma in Zhong Sicheng's bibliography.

There are thirty independent printings of verifiable Yuan northern plays that have been grouped together since the eighteenth century and have become known by the collective title of "thirty *zaju* in Yuan editions" (*Yuankan zaju sanshi zhong*). As a set of texts stored together, they can be traced back to the library of the Ming scholar, bibliophile, and dramatist Li Kaixian (1502–1568). Although the genre of *zaju* is primarily associated with the large cities of northern China, only four of the thirty texts claim to have been printed in Dadu, the capital. Almost double that number of plays (seven) claim to derive from Hangzhou, the former Southern Song capital and, by the Yuan, one of the major printing centers of China. While the majority of plays specify no place of printing, it seems plausible to assume that most of them also stem from Hangzhou. Some texts advertise themselves as *xinkan* ("newly printed") and others carry the legend *xinbian* ("newly composed"). Both phrases can refer either to an original work or to a revised edition. The physical appearance of the woodblock printings reflects a craftsmanship that ranges from good to very poor. The orthography is that common to other Yuan texts, although the quality of the printing can actually change in a significant way even within a single edition; this has a profound effect on representation of both lyrics and stage directions.

Authorship for these plays has been traced by Ming and Qing scholars and bibliophiles through later editions that bear an author's name, through musical formularies, and through bibliographies, particularly Zhong Sicheng's *The Register of Ghosts* and Zhu Quan's (1378–1448) *A Formulary of Correct Sounds of an Era of Peace* (*Taihe zhengyin pu*). Some of the thirty plays in the Yuan editions are not found in these lists of playwrights and their plays; in some other cases the titles as found in the Yuan editions and those in these catalogues are not exactly identical, making any identification tentative. The printed plays are of two kinds. Five of the thirty plays only consist of the four suites of arias of the lead performer and have no (or extremely few) appended "plot prompts" (*guanmu*), which in the context of the Yuan editions texts mean stage directions and cue lines. The other twenty-five plays not only present the arias but also print stage directions, cue lines, and some incidental prose dialogue. Despite the fact that these fuller editions contain no prose dialogue for the secondary characters in the play, some of them still claim to be "full editions" (*diben*) or "complete editions" (*zuben*), a designation that refers to the fact that they reproduce the arias in their entirety. Modern scholars, however, used to editions that have been prepared for reading and which provide full dialogue for all characters, have found these editions strangely "defective" and have wondered why the plays were printed in such a format. The most persuasive explanation is that the plays were not primarily printed for the benefit of performers or readers but for the benefit of listeners. Many members of the audience, then as now, may have had trouble following the lyrics of the arias as sung in performance. In contemporary China it is normal practice when traditional plays are performed to project the text of the arias alongside or over the stage, and these texts may have performed the same function for listeners. This would also explain why so many more texts were printed in Hangzhou than in Dadu: while Hangzhou may have been only a minor center of *zaju* performance, its audience rarely had a full command of the northern dialect in which the plays were composed and performed. In order to provide the audience with a text of the arias, the printers made use of the most complete texts at their disposal, the role text of the male lead or female lead.

It is clear in the Yuan editions texts that we are presented with either "female texts" (*danben*) or "male texts" (*moben*), scripts written for a single dramatic lead. A close look at the stage directions will confirm this. For instance, the following is from the opening passage of "A Beauty Pining in Her Boudoir: The Pavilion for Praying to the Moon" (*Baiyue ting*):

> *After* OFFICIAL AND LADY *have entered and spoken – after being summoned – and after you enter dressed as* FEMALE LEAD *together with* MEIXIANG *– act out greeting* OFFICIAL. *After* OFFICIAL *has spoken – act out parting, emotionally. Act out offering the cup.* Father, you are so old. Please be careful on your trip. *After* OFFICIAL *speaks – act out wiping away your tears.*

This short passage reflects the grammatical structure of the stage directions, in which a moderate imperative follows clauses marked by the particle for completed action, indicating that these directions are written only for the actor or actress who is going to play the female lead. Spoken lines are cue lines for the arias that follow; here, the cue lines "Father, you are so old. Please be careful on your trip" leads into a song of parting between father and daughter:

> Rolling up the earth, a wild wind blows frontier sands,
> Sunlit in the sparse wood, evening crows caw.
> I offer to you this cup of "flowing sunset" filled to overflowing.
> If I could but detain you half a moment –
> For, in a moment's space we will be far apart, each at an edge of heaven.
> (*Reprise*)
> About to depart, your whip urges on the skinny nag.

After the OFFICIAL *has spoken:*

> What you will see are "white bones strewn like hemp across the Central Plain."
> Even though, during this campaign,
> You bear the burden of "heaven collapsing and earth crumbling away,"
> You must think of us, mother and daughter, and come home soon.

No other characters are given speaking lines in the plays, no stage directions are written for them. Any stage directions that mention other players are clearly for the convenience of the lead role: they provide the sequence and types of other actors' performances so that the lead is able to keep track of stage appearances, to enter at the correct moment, and to properly time his or her performance. This practice accurately reflects what we know of the structure of early acting troupes, which, although constituted of a "family" of actors, were supported by a single star performer. Other members of the acting troupe – the secondary characters, the clown, and so on – probably only had set scenes to perform or only smaller parts of dialogue that could be easily memorized. The arias represented different problems for the lead singer – in addition to a complicated mixture of linguistic register and metrical requirements, they had to be sung, not spoken. Other performances onstage were easier to manage: they were set routines or set speeches. Even fuller texts from the Ming palace or late Ming commercial editions that write out all the speeches often note the presentation of many of these routines only by stage directions.

There can be little doubt, then, that these early texts were based on performance and represent a work of a completely different nature than those found in the later collections. One indication of this is that, of the sixteen plays that are known in more than one edition, the Yuan editions texts, with a few exceptions, always have a significantly larger number of arias when compared with their later counterparts. The performance of the lead singer was more substantially and proportionally highlighted.

As fragmentary as these plays are, they represent an earlier tradition of textual production and are artifacts of a time before drama had passed through the hands of court or literati editors. These texts were not subject to ideological rewriting in order to make them conform to the Confucian norms and values of the elite; and, since they appealed to a broad spectrum of Yuan society from high to low, they certainly reflect popular culture of their time. They are more outspoken in their representation of what we might term the "common" world – a world of crime, sex, and violence, and of love in which the latitudes of behavior are quite wide. The language is more directly critical and less squeamish about portraying violence in politics and the corruptibility of humans.

The full form of the Yuan northern play is found only in late Ming editions that have undergone considerable editing and ideological changes under the hands of editors. Since the main body of the northern play will be treated later, the reader is referred to that section for a fuller discussion of its formal features.

The obverse case holds true for the south, where we have texts, but little commentary. We have three early southern plays (*nanxi* or *xiwen*). The major difference between northern *zaju* and southern *xiwen* is that whereas in the former genre all the arias are assigned to a single singer, in the latter all actors have singing roles. The tunes employed in southern plays were popular southern songs and were not organized into suites according to musical mode as in northern *zaju*. In general, southern plays are of much greater length than northern *zaju*, and began as regional drama in the coastal areas of eastern Zhejiang and then spread to the capital, Lin'an (modern Hangzhou), and beyond. In a work entitled *Trivial Talks* (*Weitan*), Zhu Yunming (1460–1525) remarked,

> Southern plays [*nanxi*] appeared after the Xuanhe reign era of the Northern Song [1119–1125], around the time of the "Southern Crossing" (ca 1125–1126), and it is designated as "Wenzhou comedy." I have seen old official documents, and there was an official proscription by Zhao Hongfu that listed several titles, like "Chaste Maiden Zhao and Cai the Second Esquire"[*Zhao Zhenü Cai Erlang*] and others; but in fact there were not many.

Zhao Hongfu, an otherwise obscure person, was a lateral cousin of the Emperor Guangzong, Zhao Chun, who ruled from 1190 to 1195. The simple fact that he issued such a proclamation banning performance of southern plays clearly indicates just how popular the form had become by the end of the twelfth century. Xu Wei (1521–1593), the great Ming scholar and dramatist, also wrote in his work on theater, *A Sequential Record of Southern Lyrics* (*Nanci xulu*),

> Southern plays began in the reign of Emperor Guangzong of the Song, and their first successes were those plays by Yongjia playwrights such as "Chaste Maiden Zhao" and "[The Heartbreaker] Wang Kui." Some people say that the form was already spreading everywhere during the Xuanhe reign period and actually reached its high point during the "Southern Crossing."

If we take these two late passages together (and can trust them), we can construe that the southern play was created around 1120 in Wenzhou (i.e. the coastal area of modern Zhejiang) and that it had reached the capital, Lin'an, by the 1190s. It then became the prevalent form over a wide range of Zhejiang and Fujian. By the end of the Southern Song (1276) it had even spread to Jiangxi, as witnessed by Liu Xun's (1240–1319) remarks in his "Biography of the Lyric Poet Wu Yongzhang": "By the Xianchun reign period [1265–1275], Yongjia comedy had appeared. Vile youths altered it; thereafter lascivious singing became popular and 'correct sounds' ceased." This charge of lewdness was repeated by Liu Yiqing in the semihistorical text *Affairs from Qiantang* (*Qiantang yishi*), where the "southern play on Wang Kui" appears in a list of plays that "teach lasciviousness" (*xiwen huiyin*). Southern plays continued to flourish in China south of the Huai river during the Yuan, despite the almost total silence of our sources. Northern plays had made inroads into the south following the Mongol conquest of the area, but they barely spread beyond major urban centers such as Hangzhou, where they may have primarily appealed to northerners who had fled to Hangzhou during the Jurchen and Mongol invasions. One of the three surviving southern plays (*A Playboy from a Noble House Opts for the Wrong Career, Huanmen zidi cuolishen*) borrowed two long suites from northern plays and may represent a greater tendency on the part of southern plays to experiment with the inclusion of plots, songs, and song-suites from northern plays.

From various sources, we are able to deduce the titles of some 182 known early southern plays (*nanxi*), but almost none of these plays survive, although a few have survived in heavily revised editions from the sixteenth century. Other fifteenth-century printed editions have been unearthed in recent archaeological excavations, but none that can be reliably dated to the Yuan. Three plays have been preserved in a single stray volume of the *Yongle dadian*, a huge imperial compilation completed in 1407 of which only a limited number of volumes have survived the ravages of time, fire, and looting. These three plays are *Top Scholar Zhang Xie* (*Zhang Xie zhuangyuan*), *A Playboy from a Noble House Opts for the Wrong Career*, and *Little Butcher Sun* (*Xiao Suntu*) These three are known collectively as "three southern plays from *The Grand Encyclopedia of the Yongle Era*" (*Yongle dadian xiwen sanzhong*). One among the three, *Top Scholar Zhang Xie*, is conventionally dated to the late Southern Song, although there is no hard evidence of its existence prior to 1407. The others are clearly Yuan. These three plays are the product of corporate authorship, produced by "talents" (*cairen*) of "writing societies" (*shuhui*): *Top Scholar Zhang Xie* was composed by the "Writing Society of the Nine Hills" (Jiushan shuhui), *A Playboy from a Noble House* is noted as "newly compiled by talents of old Hangzhou" (*gu Hang cairen xinbian*), and *Little Butcher Sun* is a product of the Writing Society of old Hangzhou" (Gu Hang shuhui). Together they formed the last chapter of the large section of the *Yongle dadian* devoted to *xiwen*. It is not clear, however, to what extent they are representative of the genre in the fourteenth century, since it appears from the title catalog of the *Yongle dadian* that the average southern play was much longer, each occupying a single chapter.

The second major colloquial form of the Yuan is historical fiction, called "tales told in plain style" (*pinghua*), annalistic historical tales written in a mixture of classical Chinese (the preferred language of performance texts) and colloquial. There are eleven, possibly twelve of these tales left. The first five of these were all printed by the Yu Family Bookstore in Jian'an, Fujian between 1323 and 1325.

Newly Printed, Fully Illustrated, Told in Plain Style: The Documents of King Wu's Attack on Zhou (Xinkan quanxiang pinghua Wuwang fa Zhou shu) – the title is somewhat misleading, since the majority of the work details the perversity and cruelty of the last emperor of the Shang Dynasty, Zhou, in order to create a pretext for King Wen's and King Wu's decision to wrest the empire from him. The work is heavily based on passages from the *Classic of Documents* and *The Records of the Historian.*

Newly Printed, Fully Illustrated in the Zhiyuan Era: The Plainly Told Tale of the Three Kingdoms of 1321–1323 (Zhiyuan xinkan quanxiang Sanguo zhi pinghua) – beginning with the end of the Eastern Han and ending with the death of Zhuge Liang and the rise of the state of Jin, the story relies both on historical works like the *History of the Three Kingdoms* and on Sima Guang's historical annals, the *Comprehensive Mirror for the Aid of Government (Zizhi tongjian)*; it also incorporates many episodes that must have circulated as popular tales about that era. For instance, the *pinghua* is consistent in demonizing Cao Cao, the founder of the Wei, and vaunting Liu Bei, the Shu-Han emperor. This stands in stark contrast to the historical sources, which establish the state of Wei as the legitimate successor state following the Han. Some critics think this may reflect the Southern Song and Yuan mentality of Han Chinese, in that it promotes Liu Bei as the person who could reestablish the might of the Han dynasty, establishes a contention between a legitimate southern dynasty (Shu-Han) and a usurping northern court (Wei), and represents Liu Bei as an idealized emperor, as opposed to a tyrannical and autocratic ruler. The language of the text is very uneven, but it does incorporate a good amount of rhymed text and poetry, as well as a "first session" (*touhui*), which sets the frame for the rest of book – a session in hell where three wrongly executed heroes from the Han are sent back into the world of humans as leaders of the Three Kingdoms. This is a feature not found in other *pinghua*, and is closely related to the so-called "wedge" (*xiezi*) of later fiction.

Another text has been recently discovered, called *A Brief Account of Events of the Tripartite Split (Sanfen shilüe)*. Like the *pinghua*, it is divided into three chapters. The head title of the first two chapters bears the same characters as the *pinghua: Newly Printed, Fully Illustrated in the Zhiyuan Era: The Plainly Told Tale of the Three Kingdoms of 1321–1323*, but each page is separately titled *Newly Printed . . . in the Year 1294*. It is clear from its style that it was a product of the same publisher as the *pinghua*, the Yu Family Bookstore of Jian'an (Jian'an Yushi shutang). The two works show little difference in text, although the printing style of the 1294 edition is less elegant than that of 1323. The cover title may have been added to the first edition of Yu's series of *pinghua*, to create consistency among the titles, although the page blocks themselves were clearly from another edition. When the *pinghua* was reissued in 1323, new blocks were cut and the "1294" disappeared from the text.

Completely Illustrated Yue Yi Has Designs on Qi: The Last Part of the Plainly Told Tale of the Annals of Seven States (Quanxiang Yue Yi tu Qi qiguo chunqiu pinghua houji) – obviously the second part of a series, the tale recounts the conflicts between the states of Yan and Qi in the Warring States era, and particularly between the generals Yue Yi and Sun Bin. The text makes ample use of the markers of orality, particularly the rhetoric of an intrusive narrator, direct questioning of the audience, and the use of others' speeches as well as poems to provide evidence for the narrator's judgments about historical events. For instance:

> Let's now speak of the soldiers of Qi's complete annihilation of the state of Yan – nothing visible but those crows cawing in the setting sun, the grass dark and the slopes overgrown, with no sign of human cooking fires anywhere. What filled the eye were yellow flowers, purple creepers, thorns and prickles covering the ground everywhere. How could the state of Yan have been so desolate? There's a poem as evidence
>
> > The palace court has transformed into a desolate overgrown land,
> > The six grasses and three streets are now encampments in the fallows;
> > Now deserted and silent, the country of Yan, after its defeat by Qi –
> > The setting sun shines fading light, how it cripples our emotions!

This narratorial rhetoric is an artifact of oral storytelling, used by the author of the written text to set the context of the reading experience in the world of common knowledge, unbounded by the need for textual certainty and outside the closure of orthodox learning.

The remaining two texts in the Yu Family series are the *Completely Illustrated: The Plainly Told Tale of How Qin Swallowed up the Other Six States (Quanxiang Qin bing liuguo pinghua)*, also known as *The Tale of the First Emperor of Qin (Qin shihuang zhuan)*, and the *Completely Illustrated Continuation of the Plainly Told Tale of the History of the Former Han (Quanxiang xu Qian Hanshu pinghua)*, also known as *Empress Lü Beheads Han Xin (Lühou zhan Han Xin)*. The former sticks very closely to the story of the Qin First Emperor, relying mainly on the

Records of the Historian, and the latter remains true to the events recounted in the *History of the (Former) Han*.

One text, the original of which is no longer extant, was found in Hangzhou in 1901 in a very small-sized edition. This work, known as the *Tales Plainly Told from the History of the Five Dynasties (Wudaishi pinghua)*, contains stories based on the states of the Five Dynasties era (907–960): the Liang (first half preserved), the Tang, the Jin, the Han (first half preserved), and the Zhou. While first published with a notation that it was a Song text, it is clear from the orthography, the format of the edition, and the frequent use of imperial names that were taboo in the Song, that it stems from the latter part of the Yuan.

The *Events of the Xuanhe Reign (Xuanhe yishi)* is, as Wang Liqi demonstrated, also probably a *pinghua*. The second part of the text is based on a classical story called *A Firsthand Account by Southern Remnants (Nanjin jiwen)*, but the first section draws freely on historical sources, imperial edicts, memorials, miscellanies, and poetry. The tale tells the story of the fall of the Northern Song and the exile of the last two emperors to the hinterlands of Manchuria, where they both pass away in captivity. It is remarkable for its frank portrayal of violence.

One final text is the *Summary of Events of Xue Rengui's Campaign against the Liao (Xue Rengui zheng Liao shilüe)*, which has been recovered from the *Yongle dadian*. The work is divided into three subjects: the rationale for Tang attacking Liao, Xue Rengui's rise and his success in battle, and finally the conquest of the Liao. The core of the book is the central part, which bears much likeness to stories in fiction and drama about the rise of a lowly commoner to high position (*faji biantai*). Unlike the works called *pinghua*, it is not annalistic, but rather has one continuous narrative thread, unbroken by divisions.

Together, these works show several distinct characteristics. First, they are extremely long. When compared to other forms of early prose narrative (*xiaoshuo*), they are nearly three times the length of any other story. Their annalistic form is the major reason for this length – as popularized versions of history they have to cover a certain period of time in a fashion that allows for the development of interior plot lines and the evolution of character over a certain number of episodes. These are clearly texts to be read, not copies of oral prompt books, and the retention of artifacts of oral presentation, as noted above, is meant to stage the context of reception. The texts called *pinghua* are divided into three major chapters, and each chapter is divided into several subsections. These subsections provided a natural chain of events that link episodes together, and can also link characters across major chapter breaks.

This format of breaking a narrative into discrete "sessions" or episodes (*hui*) is most likely the basis of the chapter divisions of later Chinese fiction.

Second, each work has an opening poem (*shangchang shi*) and a closing poem (*xiachang shi*), and in some works every chapter has the same. The openings are usually one or two poems in the seven-syllable line that capture the whole sweep of history covered either by the book or by each individual chapter, provide a type of historical evaluation, or expose the facts that caused the events to be covered. The closing poems summarize the lessons to be learned from the reading and levy judgments about the actions that are a cautionary lesson for the audience. This format, too, is found in other forms of fictional writing and particularly in the longer fiction of the Ming and Qing.

Third, they use an annalistic form of narrative. This is in the great tradition of Chinese history and is the single most important structure of the *pinghua*. They stay very close to authorized historical accounts but also sometimes intersperse more popular accounts, in an attempt to maintain both historical accuracy and interest. Before beginning the main text of the tales, they often provide a short sweeping narrative meant to illustrate the principles of historical evaluation and assessment. This is followed by a generalized description of the times and background of the period they will cover. These generalized discussions not only provide tools for the audience to be able to share the narrator's judgments of the events, but they also provide a background narrative thread that links together the formal structure of successive blocks of time with different events and people in a meaningful and cumulative way.

Fourth, the language of the texts is a comfortable combination of classical and colloquial Chinese. For the most part they utilize the classical language of the historical sources they mine, sometimes simplifying it to create a rhythmic repetition of measures in the prose line, and they often insert poems, memorials, or letters as a way to pique the reader's interest. Sometimes colloquial and vernacular language is used, but as Wilt Idema has pointed out, the colloquial passages never flow as well as the classical. They sometimes seem disruptive and out of place. When compared to later fiction, both short and long, the colloquial nature of the texts suffers greatly. At the same time, it should be remembered that much performing literature in China used a simple, even demotic, form of classical Chinese for the simple reason that it has a basic parallel structure that makes it fit well with chanting to a percussion accompaniment.

It should be clear how much later fiction is indebted generally, and specifically, to these historical tales told in the plain style. Not only did they provide the basic structure of the long tale, but they also inspired later writers of fiction. The *Romance of the Three Kingdoms* (*Sanguo yanyi*) owes a great deal of its shape to the *pinghua* of the same period, as does the *Investiture of the Gods* (*Fengshen yanyi*) to the story of *King Wu's Attack on Zhou*, and the *Water Margin* (*Shuihu zhuan*) to the *Bequeathed Affairs of the Xuanhe Reign*.

VIII. *Sanqu*: a new form of hybrid poetry

A new poetic genre emerged during the late Jin and early Yuan, the colloquial song (*sanqu*), which matured quite rapidly under the early Yuan to become a favorite form of lyric expression. It had close roots both to vulgar songs (*liqu*) and to popular songs (*suyao*) and close ties to music from the north and northeast that had migrated into China just prior to the Jurchen invasion. This was first remarked on by the Southern Song writer Zeng Minxing (1118–1175), who wrote,

> My father once said that he was a visitor in the capital during the last days of the Northern Song, and the vulgar in the streets and alleyways often sang foreign songs, titled, "A Foreign State Comes to Court," "Four States Come to Court," "Six States Come to Court," "Prologue to the Barbarian Shield," or "Tumbleweed Flowers." The language was extremely coarse but all of the men of worth sang them.

This matches what we understand of the performance milieu of the late Northern Song, when music from the north came to the capital through Shanxi, and was adapted into prosimetric literature and long-song suites used as accompaniment for performances of various types. It also points to a trend that would develop in the Yuan: the appropriation of vernacular songs by literati ("men of worth").

This new form of music-song is sometimes called "leftovers of the song lyric" (*ciyu*), but this is a mistake since it did not actually develop directly from the *ci*. Rather, it derived from similar origins and followed the same path of development, beginning as performance and moving up the scale of respectability until it adapted some of the rhetorical and literary devices of earlier forms of poetry and the lyric. The song lyric seems to have become more confining over the Five Dynasties, Song, and Jin as it moved away from its performance origins to become more decorous in terms of its rhetoric and style as it tended toward the "classically elegant." The void that it left in popular forms of music and song was filled to a large degree by the colloquial song. Perhaps the main difference between the two, at the end of their respective processes of maturation, is that the colloquial song – written in an environment when colloquial literature as a body of texts accepted on its own terms was becoming an acceptable literati style – never lost its own colloquial nature. There is also some internal evidence for this: in addition to changes wrought by new music (and musical instruments), the language used in the colloquial songs underwent significant change. Changes in rhyme structure brought on by the change in tones and finals of words, the extensive use of binomial expressions, the frequent inclusion of long three- and four-syllable onomatopoeic phrases, the use of inserted nonmetrical phrases, and the consequent ability to reflect varying levels of social and linguistic register were to remain significant features of the songs, no matter who wrote them. Another reason, of course, is that the *qu* form was also used in the arias of northern plays, sharing many melodies with colloquial song; thus colloquial song could never really be separated from its performance context.

The void that the colloquial song filled in some respects had also been created by the overly discursive nature of Song and some Jin verse. In his early Yuan memoir, Liu Qi had remarked,

> Poetry should be based on setting forth the emotions of happiness and anger, grief and joy; if someone reads it and there is nothing that moves him, it is not poetry. I have observed that the poetry of poets of these later generations has all probed the wealth of the lexicon to the limit, has pulled in all kinds of learning, and it is truly stunning. But if you read it and it is unable to affect you, then how can it be valued? So, I once said to my now deceased friend, Wang Feibo, "In the Tang and before, poetry was in poetry [*shi*], when it came to the Song it was in 'long and short lines' [i.e. the *ci*], and poetry is now in the coarse songs of the vulgar world [*sujian liqu*], in the likes of the so-called 'ditties of font and earth' [*yuantu ling*]." Feibo said, "How do you know that?" I said, "When the ancients sang out their poetry they all put forth that which their hearts desired to say; if someone chanted them, it sometimes caused them to weep. The poetry of modern writers simply adheres like mud to the stated topic, the event to be covered, and to [tonal and rhyme] rules associated with the lines. It is as if they were going to seize fame from new cleverness – even though people will say it is good, there are few poems that can actually move a person. It is completely unlike popular or coarse songs in terms of revealing true emotions which, opposed to [current] *shi* poetry, can rile up a person's blood and vital ether." Feibo agreed with this.

As the *Treatise on Singing* remarked (see above), the colloquial song developed in a distinctly regional way, with different songs associated with different places in north China in its early stages. Later its production became centralized in the capital Dadu, and then spread southward, as writers clustered around the Hangzhou area. This move southward is tied closely to a tendency for the colloquial song to come closer (within the strictures of its language) to the poem and the song lyric in sensibility. For the main part, however, the writers of the colloquial song in the north remained those of the lower social and political ranks. Certainly, the most illustrious names of the time wrote colloquial songs, but only as a sideline. Its real producers were specialists in the form, and many of them were dramatists as well.

Colloquial songs gradually became a form of hybrid literature, particularly after the center of production shifted to Hangzhou, incorporating many of the tried-and-true themes of the poem and the song lyric, and often utilizing entire lines from well-known poems from the classical canon. In this sense, it was a combination of the two worlds into which Chinese often divide their literature: the classically elegant (ya) and the vulgar or common (su). This notion of "vulgar" of course is tied closely to the colloquial language that colloquial songs used, and which in the end differentiates it from other forms of poetry. This combination, found even in songs by the most learned, is a radical departure from the norms of polite verse, and allowed colloquial songs to reach across many social boundaries, giving them broad appeal to a wide literate audience both inside and outside elite circles. One seldom finds, particularly in early colloquial songs, the reticence, indirection, or muted metaphors and analogies of poetry. Instead, the colloquial songs tend to create a different world of poetic sensibility based on direct expression, uncolored by rhetorical flourish. A good example of this is Bai Fen's (ca 1280–1320) "Song of Parrot Island" written to the tune "Black Lacquered Crossbow":

> I live in a house by the side of Parrot Island,
> Just an illiterate fisherman;
> A little leaf of a flatboat amid the blossoms of the waves,
> Sound asleep in the rainy mists of Jiangnan.
> When I awake, verdant mountains fill my eyes,
> Shaking off my green rush raincoat, I go home;
> I figure in the past I wrongly blamed Old Man Heaven –
> He worked hard to find me a place.

Translation can scarcely bring out the effortlessness of the language of this poem, its register so perfectly appropriate to the speaker, its simple description of action, and its completely frank expression of feeling that hides no subtext. Whereas a classical poem might describe the action of the fisherman in the third person and then speak with muted reticence about him as a symbol of the mysterious communion between a cosmic order and a human subject, this colloquial song, through action and a direct sense of materiality, speaks of the same far-reaching and all-encompassing sense of communion from the standpoint of an actor who is in perfect concord with the flow of the natural world. One can also see here the clear affinity of this dramatized scene with plays or oral performances in song.

This verse also shows us the characteristics of colloquial songs' formal structure. This is a single song, one of two major *qu* forms, the other being the long suite. The actual name of this singular poetic form in its own day was *yuefu*, a term that was used first to distinguish the single poem, also called "little song" (*xiaoling*), from the extended suites (*taoshu*), which were also used as the musical element of northern plays. The *xiaoling*, also known as the "leaf" (*ye'er*), is the shortest and earliest of the colloquial songs. It has affinities with the quatrain of poetry and the short-song lyric, although again, the influence of performance kept the language of colloquial songs much more ordinary. In one sense, however, it partakes of the general trend in all of Chinese poetics toward short, evocative lyrics, as in this anonymous song:

> (*Xianlü* mode; to the tune "Parasitic Grass")
> I had a few lines of heart-to-heart words
> That originally I wanted to say to him.
> In front of the god's image I cut off my black silky hair,
> Behind my parents' back, I made a secret tryst at the lakeside mountain,
> Cold, frosty and chill, moisture soaked my light silk stockings.
> We had barely met, when it turned out differently from what I hoped –
> Better you had never come, just to return my perfumed silk handkerchief.

Chinese music was divided both by the pentatonic scale and by modes. Each of the twelve modes has a number of songs associated with it, and each song has a title. Thus this piece, titled "Parrot Island," is sung to the tune titled "Parasitic Grass," which belongs to the *Xianlü* mode. Each tune has a specific metrical pattern, although that structure can be expanded by the use of "padding words" – short introductory or intrusive phrases that were not part of the metrical beat. For instance, "Parasitic Grass" should have a metrical structure of 3–3–7–7–7–7–7; the first two lines should be a parallel couplet; lines three, four, and five should be what are called a "tripod leg" parallelism (*dingzu dui*); the last two lines should be a parallel couplet. The vagaries of translation obscure this feature in the above poem, but another to the same tune, entitled "Drinking," by Bai Pu (1226–1306), one of the finest *xiaoling* poets, provides a transparent example:

> After a lengthy drunk, what obstacle stands in the way?
> Before you're sober, what worries can you have?

Wine dregs pickle the two words "merit" and "fame,"
Unfiltered wine marinates a thousand years of "rise" and "fall,"
Brewer's yeast buries ten thousand spans of "rainbow" and "halo"
  ambitions.
Those <u>not</u> making the grade all laugh at how wrong Qu Yuan was,
<u>But</u> those who know me well fully explain how right Tao Qian
  turned out to be.

The underlined words are the extrametrical "padding words," effectively changing the wording to 6–6–7–7–7–8–8, although the metrical lyrics would still be sung to the original pattern. This use of extrametrical words gives a greater flexibility and a more colloquial feel to the poems; in terms of meaning they are integral. They are used to a lesser degree in the short songs and can be seen as an artifact of drama, where there is a more distinct need to carry over into the sung arias the colloquial language of spoken dialogue. These fillers have their own rules: they can be used at the start of a song, or in the middle, but never at the end.

The short songs can be combined in sequence (*chongtou xiaoling*), or two short songs can be put together in what is termed "carry-over" songs (*daiguo qu*). The former are poems on the same general topic, linked together by content, and grammatically similar if not parallel. Each short song must be able to stand independently, and each must be written to a separate rhyme. There is no limit to the number of times the song can be repeated. For instance, this sequence by Zhang Kejiu (ca 1280–1354), entitled "Joyful Inspiration of the Four Seasons" (Sishi lexing), is written to the four rhymes -uan, -ang, -ing, and -ui. It is in the *Zhonglü* mode, and to the tune of "Flower Vendor Songs" (Maihua sheng):

Spring
Dong, dong, sound the pipes and drums, the east wind is warm,
In the garden at this place, all the sights are beguiling,
"The whole spring long I burn money to buy flowers."
I roam for fun in the eastern suburbs,
Enjoy feasts at West Lake.
Joyously happy – fill the cup and urge me on to drink!

Summer
Crystal clear azure rays add something to lapping waves,
In this garden of green apricots wine is warmed until fragrant,
Melons float, plums sink, snow ice is chilled.
Gauze mosquito nets and rattan woven mats,
Quickly filtered new brew.
Joyously happy – fill the cup and sing soft and low.

Autumn
The saddled horse snuffles and whinnies, autumn clouds are cold,
A whole stretch of western mountains now a brocade screen of pictures,
For two words, "merit" and "fame," I am lonely and adrift.
Completely at ease by his eastern fence,
Tao Qian finally went home.
Joyously happy – the three paths of the hermit in his old state.

Winter
Dark winds in the four wilds, carmine clouds are dense,
Swirling and whirling in the long void, propitious snow flies,
Inside gold-speckled curtains we hold each other tight and laugh.
The felt shade is dropped low,
Fill the cup with those chalcedony waves.
Joyously happy – after we're drunk, we'll get drunk again!

The other way in which single songs may be combined, the "carry-over," is a pair of different tunes in the same mode the lyrics of which are written to the same rhyme. In the following set, by Xue Angfu, the two songs belong to the *Shuangdiao* mode, and the musical tune notation is "To the Tune 'Chu Skies Extend Forever' Carried Over to 'Prologue to Clear River'" (Chutian yao daiguo Qingjiang yin).

Flowers open, people are truly happy,
Flowers fall, spring seems drunk.
Spring is drunk – there will be time to sober up,
People grow old – happiness is hard to count on.
"A whole Yangzi of spring waters flows on,"
"Ten thousand dots of poplar flowers fall."
Who says they are poplar flowers?
"Dot by dot, they are the tears of those who take their leave."
Turn the head, there is a "fresh breeze from ten thousand miles away,"
Far off, indistinct, there is no edge to heaven.
Sorrow comes with the rising tidal bore,
The tide ebbs, sorrow never retreats.
How much worse as "evening winds quicken again!"

The second major colloquial song form was the lyric-suite (*taoshu*), composed of two or more songs using the same rhyme, belonging to the same mode (songs from other modes could be borrowed if the mode was a harmonic), and concluding with a coda (*weisheng*). If the last song of the suite was a "carry-over" then no coda was necessary. The long suite was truly a Yuan innovation. Earlier performing forms – the "all keys and modes," drum songs, and dance music – had begun to use the suite form, but only in a sporadic fashion. The basic change from earlier performance music was this: earlier songs were usually composed of two stanzas and each song was independent; the colloquial song-suite grouped several songs, all of a single stanza, together in a modal sequence and used the same rhyme throughout. These modal sequences became highly standardized, but not completely inflexible, during the Yuan. The longer suites could be used to sustain lengthy narratives and often covered a single episode in an extensive manner, although they also retained a lyrical core. Because of the use of the suite as the major structuring element of northern plays, colloquial songs written in that form show more similarity to the lexicon and rhetorical strategies of drama and other performing literature. This includes a much more extensive use of padding words and much more colloquial usage than one finds in the colloquial short song.

Generally, one finds a far more dense set of rhymes in colloquial songs than in other forms of verse. In many tunes all lines rhyme, and in some six-syllable lines there is a second internal rhyme at the third syllable, or two internal rhymes at the second and fourth positions. The density of rhymes and close-rhymes in the songs ushered in changes to poetic composition, primarily due to the difficulty of sustaining the rhymes over a long sequence. This was solved partially by collapsing previously separate categories of rhyme together into a single acceptable rhyme group that reflected more accurately the flexibility of living language. Polite poetry still used the rhyme patterns that had long diverged from real language. Yuan Haowen noted this in establishing "ten admonitions" to keep in mind himself when writing poetry, "Do not be a female entertainer who rhymes *ren* ["person"] and *hun* ["soul"]" (*buwei pipaniang ren hun yun ci*). These two words, kept distinct in the rhymes of poetry and the song lyric, were available to the performer as a single rhyme category. Another change, of course, was the distribution of the traditional fourth category (ending in -p, -t, -k) into the other three. While not all of the early colloquial songs or northern plays abide by the categories that Zhou Deqing established in the *Sounds and Rhymes of the Central Plain*, very few works from the later period deviate from it. This is important because it demonstrates that Zhou's work did not necessarily reflect any particular form of spoken language (note the regional distribution of *qu* mentioned in the *Treatise on Singing*), but codified a literary and perhaps stage language that became prescriptive during the gradual rise of *qu* from a true performance art to one of literary, written production. As a final difference between classical poetic forms and the *qu* in general, words could rhyme not only more liberally in terms of their finals, but also across all categories of tone. This flexibility goes hand in glove with the deployment of dense rhyme clusters and made it much easier to sustain long suites that had by necessity to use the same rhyme throughout.

There are roughly 4,280 colloquial songs left from the Yuan, of which 3,800 are short songs, by some two hundred writers. The writers themselves come from three major backgrounds. Many, like Yang Guo, Liu Bingzhong, Wang Yun, Yao Sui, Zhang Yanghao (1269–1329), and others, were eminent scholars and high officials. Others, like the famous Guan Hanqing, Ma Zhiyuan (ca 1250–1324), and Zhang Kejiu, were lower-level bureaucrats; and the third group, best exemplified by Qiao Ji (1280–1345), were literati who never served in any capacity. While it is misleading to say that any group, or any person, wrote in one particular form or on one particular topic, there seem to be some overall predilections associated with each. The high ministers often saw the colloquial song as a form of social criticism like the "new *yuefu*" of the mid-Tang, and they wrote on rather traditional topics like landscape, in which they speak of solace, or of the rise and fall of earlier dynasties. It is tempting to see their ruminations as a reaction to the Mongol displacement of the literati, but in fact most of their poems find counterparts in earlier works under native Chinese dynasties. What makes them different is the language. For instance, in a poem written by Zhang Yanghao, in the best tradition of poems lamenting the past, we find a typical directness:

(Mode: *Zhonglü*; title: "Lamenting the Past at Tong Pass"; tune: "Sheep on a Hillside")
Peaks and pinnacles seem to rush together,
Waves and breakers seem to be angry.
The Mountain and the River, one within, the other without – the road through Tong Pass.
I gaze far away at the Western Capital,
My mind hesitant, uneasy –
I am heartbroken by those places yet to pass, once all Qin and Han,
Untold thousands of palaces and foretowers now all turned to dirt.
They arose – the common people suffered,
They fell – the common people suffered.
(*Tong Pass: at the narrows where the road runs from Shaanxi to Henan on the Yellow River, near Mount Hua; the ancient state of Jin was guarded by "mountains within" and by the "River outside."*)

Many in the second group wrote poems bluntly critical of the government. Liu Shizhong (ca 1270–1324), for instance, wrote two long suites "Sent to Governor Gao" (Shang Gao jiansi) that are a very harsh condemnation of the handling of severe drought by the government and of the corrupt practices in the use of paper currency in the Jiangxi area. And Sui Jingchen's famous "Gaozu of the Han Returns Home" (Gaozu huan xiang) is a biting and satirical look at an emperor coming home in his new clothes. Eremitism also seems to be another favorite topic, and their works are speckled with titles like "Hanging up the Official Hat" (Gua guan), "Returning to Retire" (Guiyin), "Peacefully Withdrawing" (Tian tui), "Living in the Mountains" (Shan ju), and even "Sentiments of the Daoist Way" (Dao qing). In some senses, their writing does betray the pressures they must have been under as local bureaucrats directly involved with taxation and law at the local level. A third topic, not unexpected from this group, is a kind of hedonistic landscape poetry, a large portion of which is devoted to West Lake in Hangzhou. Clearly the best representative of this particular trend is Zhang Kejiu. Among his many poems on West Lake, we can see the power of place to shape the poetic moment:

(Mode: *Nanlü*; tune: "One Spring of Flower"; title: "Returning from the Lake")
"A far sky" to let fall "colored sunsets,"
"Distant waters" to contain autumn's mirror.
"Flowers as red as a person's face" –
"Mountains as green as Buddha's head" –
5 Vivid color surrounds us like a screen.
Kingfisher-green cold, the path through piney clouds,
A girl's laugh, a span of eyebrow's kohl.
I take along the soft and delicate thick with perfume,
What need to poeticize "slender reflections of slanting blossoms?"

(To the tune "Liangzhou")
10 I take her jade-white hand and tarry amid brocade blossoms,
I recline on the "folding chair and point to silver pitchers."
Chang E never married, suffered in her loneliness,
Consider Xiaoxiao of those years,
And ask, "Where is she, my love?"
15 Dongpo's talent and style,
Xizi's startling beauty –
"Each always just right" has left a name for all times.
We two walk alone together in this very place,
At Six-One's Spring Pavilion the poem is completed.
20 This night of triple five, in front of the flowers, below the moon,
Ten and four strings, under my fingers, give birth to the wind.
My love
Full of passion
Lifts the red ivory clappers to match the beat of "Yizhou Ditty,"

25 The myriad pipes are quiet,
   The mountains four sides about are still,
   Muffled sobs are the sound of water falling from spring's flow,
   Cranes are resentful, gibbons alarmed.

(Coda)
   Dhyana caves in steep cliffs sound metal chimes,
30 Dragon palaces at the bottom of waves shimmer with crystals.
   Night ethers are fresh.
   The power of wine now sober,
   Precious seal-script smoke disappears,
   The jade clepsydra sounds,
35 We come back laughing, it seems near eleven,
   How much better than shivering at Ba Bridge, treading in snow to find
      plum blossoms?

This poem is also a wonderful demonstration of how later southern colloquial songs appropriate lines from canonical texts and rework them. The opening couplet is a reference to two lines from the early Tang writer Wang Bo's (649–676) "On Prince Teng's Gallery" (Tengwang ge xu), "Falling sunset rays fly together with one lone duck, / Distant heavens are the same color as autumn's water." These lines were part of every schoolboy's lore, and it is difficult to tell here whether they were used as a direct allusion or simply sprang to mind as a cliché of ordinary discourse. The next couplet (lines three and four) begins to frame a set of contrasting realms. The first line is an allusion to another poem cliché by this time, Cui Hu's "Inscribed at an Estate South of the Capital City Wall" (Ti jingcheng nan zhuang), about a meeting between a young student in Chang'an and a girl from whom he begs a drink of water. By this time, the story and the poem already had been part of the performance repertoire for many years, and were a fairly standard way of evoking "red" as a color of lust and love:

    Last year on this day, in this very doorway
    Her face and the peach blossoms shone red upon each other;
    Who knows where her face has gone,
    But peach blossoms still laugh in the spring wind, just like before.

Zhang contrasts this allusion to a line from Lin Bu (967–1028), a noted hermit and ascetic who lived at West Lake in the early Northern Song. The phrase in quotation marks in line four is taken directly from Lin's "West Lake," "Spring-time waters are purer than the blue of a monk's eyes, / Evening mountains are as congealed as the green of Buddha's head." Zhang follows this in line nine with a reference to Lin's "Little Plums in a Mountain Garden," "Scattered shadows athwart, slanting across water clean and shallow, / A subtle fragrance afloat, stirring the moon in the yellow dusk." Thus the opening couplet, with its brilliant sunset and mirror-like distant waters, provides us with the two poles the poem will work against: color for appreciation, and a mirror for reflection. This trope is continued in the second couplet, which turns perceptual metaphors into material similes: the red of the flowers like a woman's face, and the green of the mountains like the Buddha's head. The poet asks us to make a choice between two historically and literarily authorized readings made possible at West Lake: a disappearance into the refulgent sensuality of its landscape or an ascetic withdrawal to reflect on the illusory and transitory nature of existence and its attachments. In the couplet leading up to his pointed satire in the last line, the author presents us with a choice of how we might choose to read the halcyon colors of the mountains that surround us: they can become a cold path of asceticism and reflection (line six) or we may choose to read them as a blazon, the partial embodiment of a beautiful woman (line seven). His choice of the thick perfume and yielding softness of a feminine companion over the subtle fragrance and scant wisps of plum branches leaves no doubt about his desire or his purposeful rejection of the possibility that Lin Bu offered. Yet he had read directly against part of the tradition to make this decision, and although choosing to reject asceticism, by that very rejection he also authorized it as an alternate possibility, thereby retaining an element of choice as a soft but perceptible background note to the rest of the poem.

In "Liangzhou," discussion of scenery is quickly supplanted by a description of the activities that take place between the couple. In line eleven, the poet adopts a phrase from Du Fu's "Ballad of a Young Man" (Shaonian xing) a poem that describes a brash and impetuous young man:

> Who is that on the horse, that white-faced youth
> Who dismounts near the step and sits in the chair for one?
> He communicates no personal or family name, impetuous in the extreme,
> And pointing to the silver pitchers, he asks to taste the wine.

This clever allusion betrays the headstrong nature of the poet in the song and leads into the materiality of the opening couplet of "Liangzhou," where the lovers' touch, physical comfort, and sensory pleasures of wine and flowers lead to a theme of *carpe diem*. The rising of the moon brings to mind the story of Chang E, who stole and consumed the elixir of immortal life before she fled to that orb, there to live eternally alone in a state of unfulfilled desire.

The beauty of the physical moon, full on the fifteenth of the lunar month, thus creates another paradoxical reading – it is a symbol both of a union of full love, and of eternal loneliness when desire for life overwhelms that for love. In a standard, almost cliché, manner, Zhang then turns to other forms of immortality: beauty and writing, to Su Xiaoxiao, a famous courtesan of West Lake, immortalized for her beauty, and then to Su Shi, the literary lion of the Song. These three touchstones all signal a kind of immortality that is set against the passion of the moment. The allusion to Su Shi is to his famous poem, the first to equate West Lake with the most famous seductress of the Yue area, Xi Shi:

> ("Drinking on the Lake: First Clear, Later Rain")
> When rays on the water roll and glisten, clearing is just right,
> When mountain colors are misty and vague, rain is exactly marvelous;
> To make a comparison between West Lake and Xi Shi,
> Lightly made up or heavily powdered, each always just right.

Zhang's allusion to this poem seals the perfect match for the two lovers and their self-recognition as avatars of the most famous beauty and renowned poet of West Lake, but it does so by making the claim in a way that unites landscape and human beauty. What keeps this piece from being a hackneyed collection of clichés is Zhang's awareness that it is place itself that produces both poetry and beauty. He takes the concept out of the abstract (lines twelve to seventeen) and into the material world, where he and his lover reenact the roles played by Su Xiaoxiao and Su Shi: the music of the courtesan (lines twenty-one to twenty-eight) and the poem produced on the spot (line nineteen). Furthermore, he ties it all directly to the site: "we two walk alone together *in this very place*." Now, "this place" can be both the stage where history or personal abnegation tied to West Lake can be played out again, but it also is that particular place at that particular time. That is, it is both the enduring power of the landscape to shape human activity, and also the creation of one moment of subjective experience that belongs to Zhang and his lover alone. The poem resolves this completely in favor of the latter moment. Lines twenty-one to twenty-eight are a pale reflection of Bai Juyi's famous "Ballad of the Pipa" (Pipa xing) that are evoked by the allusion in line twenty-seven to "muffled sobs." Lines twenty-one to twenty-eight, in fact, are a rereading of three key couplets in Bai's poem that describe the sound and affect of the pipa:

> Chattering and chirping, the talk of orioles gliding beneath the flowers,
> Muffled sobs, the flow of the spring riffling below the ice,

Its water turns cold and sluggish, the strings congeal and break,
Congealed and broken, unable to communicate, the sound momentarily
    ceases.
Another hidden sadness and dark vexation is born,
And now the absence of sound bests its presence.

Bai Juyi's original poem finally resolves in a moment of sadness with the narrator weeping silently in the sleeves of his gown, lamenting a life's lost moments. "Returning from the Lake," however, forsakes that reading, which the author has clearly led the reader to anticipate, for one that comes to an end with the laughing couple returning home at eleven o'clock in the evening. The power of music to still nature, so beautifully rendered in the original Bai Juyi piece ("now the absence of sound bests its presence"), is tacitly acknowledged, but what emerges from Zhang's lyrics are the sounds of humans: the bells of the Chan temple. They are a muted reminder of what the other choice, asceticism, offered in the beginning. They remain marginally present, the last sound of the poem itself, to challenge the brashness of the poet's choice, a subtle reminder of how ephemeral the moment of passion and pleasure will be.

Zhang Kejiu is considered the best of what modern critics have come to call the "graceful" (*qingli*) school of *qu* writing. The other two are the "exuberant" or "heroic abandon" (*haofang*) and the "serious" (*duanjin*). These terms, coined by twentieth-century critic Ren Ne, are actually based on a short comment by the late Qing writer Liu Xizai (1813–1881), who classified comments Zhu Quan had made earlier about each *qu* writer into three distinct realms, "The various evaluations in *A Formulary of Correct Sounds of an Era of Peace* in sum only have the three categories of 'deep feeling,' 'expansive exuberance,' and 'graceful beauty'." Ren acknowledged that his category "serious" really had no defining characteristics, and later critics have unanimously separated *qu* only into the two remaining linguistic and aesthetic schools. Generally speaking, the *haofang* style can be classified as forthright, exuberant, and directly emotional. The *qingli* school, on the other hand, is considered elegantly graceful and much closer to the traditional high-culture values of classical elegance. In terms of their linguistic differences, the *haofang* writers tend to use more colloquial language, very few allusions (except popular stories), and what critics call language of "true color" (*bense*), a difficult term, but one that here means something like truthfulness to register, social position, or context. The *qingli* school, as Zhang Kejiu's poem above demonstrates, uses carefully crafted sentences, refined language, and allusions from classical works, and it tends to value indirection, circumlocution, and reticence, which keep the emotions of the text in a state of potentiality – feelings unexpressed directly, but hinted at through muted gesture. These classifications into general schools fail in the end, however, except at the most general or extreme level, for the simple reason that colloquial songs were never directly tied to an ethically refined authorial subject in the same way as traditional poetry. It was often generated from a dramatized objective scene or from a sense of play. Moreover, each writer often wrote in a variety of styles, using a variety of language. Here, too, context dictated choice.

For instance, the Uighur writer Guan Yunshi wrote of Guan Hanqing, best known as a dramatist, that his colloquial songs were beguiling, "like a young beauty approaching the wine cup." While Guan Hanqing's colloquial songs do in fact often deal with romance and love, the phrase certainly does not fit all of his songs, many of which were written in the *haofang* style. Guan Hanqing, along with Ma Zhiyuan, is considered one of the two best poets of the northern *haofang* style, and in both cases the "exuberance" of their work is tied to their production as dramatists. A suite by Guan Hanqing gives some idea of the difference between the northern style and that represented later by *qingli* writers like Zhang Kejiu in the south. The suite is identical in terms of mode and tune to Zhang's and written about the same area, Hangzhou and West Lake:

> (Mode: *Nanlü*; to the tune "One Spring of Flowers"; title: "Hangzhou Prospect")
> A brocade and embroidery precinct of the whole known world,
> The most *fengliu* place within the surrounding seas,
> A state newly attached to the Great Yuan court,
> An old world map of the lost Song house
> 5 Waters efflorescent, mountains rare,
> Every single place worth playful wandering –
> The whole area just too rich and noble!
> Filling the city – brocade hangings and curtains to screen the wind,
> The whole a bubbling place – a confluence of smoke from kitchen fires.
>
> (To the tune "Liangzhou" number seven)
> 10 Over a hundred neighborhoods – streets and avenues checkerboard square,
> More than a myriad households – lofts and galleries jutting here and there,
> And not half a strip of vacant land.
> Porticos in pines along traces of bamboo,
> Plots of simples along flowery tracks,
> 15 Tea gardens and rice-paddy paths,
> Bamboo hollows and prune-plum streams.

Every stretch a line of a poem's title,
Every step a leaf to be painted for a windscreen.
The western salt yard just like a single strip of white agate,
20 The color of Mount Wu, a thousand layers of halcyon jade.
O, gaze afar at the myriad acres of Qiantang River's glazed tiles –
And there are more clear streams and green waters,
Where painted boats come and go in idle play.
Zhe River Pavilion is hard against,
25 Hard against long strange rocks on precipitous cliffs and high peaks:
All worthy of admiration, worthy of inscription.

(Coda)
House after house disappearing and reappearing alongside waters flowing
in channels,
Loft and gallery rising and climbing to protrude beyond the halcyon mist –
Thus the gaze far off at the imposing force of West Lake's evening
mountains.
30 After looking here, and peering over there –
Even had I bice and vermilion in hand, the brush is impossible to set to silk.

The decided ambiguity of the opening couplet sets the tenor of the piece. The phrase "brocade and embroidery" is often used to refer to the beauty and bounty of a national land in classical writing, but in colloquial texts it conjures up the phrase "a strip of brocade," a term used to describe the future of young lovers or their prospects for marriage. Likewise *"fengliu"* carries multiple meanings. It can refer to eminent and heroic figures (*fengliu renwu*), but it also carries the clear meaning in Guan's time of a "player," a suave and debonair playboy. It can also be used to refer to their sexual encounters (*fengliu jiashi*). Thus the suite begins by using Hangzhou as a stage: in the first sense it is a national arena in which heroes have contested for the founding of new states and lost their old empires, but it is also presented as a site that anticipates material and bodily pleasures.

The eye of the perceiver is far above, looking down on Hangzhou as on a landscape prospect or a map, and it moves across that space in very specific fashion, first giving the totality of the sensations of its place. Although the descriptions of the place on the surface are about the landscape, the poet uses a vocabulary that is tinged with hints of love and seduction. This is, he seems to say, not a place to mourn the loss of the Song – the poet acknowledges its loss – but a stage of living action. It is a place worth playing in, one filled with richness and teeming with a leisured and rich populace whose liaisons and activities are screened by curtains of delicate embroidery. This density of human habitation and activity takes it out of historical time and places it immediately before the eyes – one particular place at one particular time, an environment rich with opportunity and interest. In the first half of Liangzhou Number Seven, the landscape is broken down into discrete, orderly segments: checkerboard wards, constrained horizontally but limitless in height, completely occupied. It is overgrown with trees and shrubs, but all are set to human use: porticos, paths, gardens, and agricultural paddies. As the poet enters the landscape, a sudden change occurs. If we have followed to this point, we have come from a singularity (a map of the world) to a diversity of activity, still seen from above, to localized experiences along the paths and banks of Hangzhou's rivers and gardens. Just at the point where the poet has experienced all of the possible bypaths, he acknowledges that "every stretch" and "every single footstep" he has taken has become productive. Image is overtaken by imagination. The song now begins to move back out to a view from afar, but in doing so, it lets the poet's subject claim the place, re-create it, and reimagine it through writing. He seems to be describing the sights: salt yards, mountain greenery, blue waters, cliffs, peaks, and houses, but we may also see the metaphors he uses as linguistic creations from those very sites. Salt yards turn into white agate, the mountains produce the metaphor of the kingfisher, the cliffs of mountains, the strange and tortured shape of rocks. One may ask, in fact, if it is the poet who creates the metaphor or if it is the place that shapes the linguistic expression. At this point it is nearly impossible to separate the poet, the moment of inspiration, and the place as simultaneously productive forces. All are bound together at one place and at one time in a situation that is unique and unrepeatable. When the poet emerges at the end of the poem, his view is resolutely horizontal: instead of peering down from above, he is literally enwrapped in place through his own imagination of it, overwhelmed by the productive force of West Lake.

These two suites of poems, "Returning from the Lake" and "Hangzhou Prospect," superbly demonstrate the differences to be found in the language and style of colloquial songs. After the center of poetic production shifted to the south in the period around 1320, the exuberance and directness of the colloquial song was slowly displaced. The earlier ties to popular songs and to popular performance literature were loosened, and the four great topics of the northern style – landscape, romance, cherishing the past, and a lyrical style that was highly dramatized – gradually gave way and the colloquial song moved closer to the norms of polite poetry. This included writing a form of social criticism, of which Liu Shizhong's "Sent to Governor Gao" is a good example, and also diminished the role of bravado and direct cynicism found in some of the earlier colloquial songs, replacing it with a much more muted style. In the composition of colloquial songs produced later and in the south, there is far more rigor about rules of composition, more concern about using the techniques of traditional verse, including emphasizing parallelism, tonal regularity, using allusions, and even directly incorporating lines from poems and song lyrics.

These changes are reflected clearly in the writings of Zhou Deqing, who was concerned in his "Ten Rules for Writing Lyrics" with excising many of the earthier styles and language of the original tradition. While his book provides us with excellent insight into later rules for composition, it must be seen as part of a project to "clean up" the colloquial song as it moved into more mainstream poetic discourse where it claimed kinship, through its adaptation of traditional poetic strategies and citations, to classical poetry. Another product of this upward move was the anthology, and while we have four extant middle-period Yuan collections of colloquial songs, they were all culled and edited primarily by southerners. Two of the most influential, both by Yang Zhaoying, were the *Newly Compiled Songs: Harmonious as Spring and White as Snow* (*Yuefu xinbian Yangchun baixue*), with a 1310 preface by Guan Yunshi, and *Songs of Peace: New Sounds from Inside the Court and Out* (*Chaoye xinsheng taiping yuefu*), prefaced 1332, a continuation to his earlier work. There are also two anonymous works, the *Collected Jade of Songs of Notable Worthies Arranged by Category* (*Leiju mingxian Yuefu qunyu*), which gathers only *xiaoling*, and the *New Sounds of Songs that Accord with the Rules of the Pear Garden* (*Liyuan anshi Yuefu xinsheng*). These last two works are particularly important since they contain songs not found elsewhere. There is a clear preference in these anthologies for the works of the *qingli* school of writing, which indicates their limited usefulness in providing a comprehensive picture of the development of the colloquial song.

IX. Epilogue

No short history can give any age the credit it deserves; all narratives can be defined by what they omit. This is particularly true for the Yuan and of this essay. The dynasty has been understudied in the West even though it has become a cottage industry of scholarship in China in the past ten years. Among the omissions of this chapter are fine literary miscellanies like Tao Zongyi's *Record of a Break from Plowing* or Liu Qi's *A Record of Returning Home to Retire*; a plethora of *ci* poems by Quanzhen Daoists; travel records, including the western journey diaries of Yelü Chucai and the Taoist Qiu

Chuji and diaries of travels to Chittagong and places in Southeast Asia; also omitted were five late Yuan southern plays, *The Story of the Lute* (*Pipa ji*), *The Thorn Hairpin* (*Jingchai ji*), *The White Rabbit* (*Baitu ji*), *The Pavilion for Praying to the Moon* (*Baiyue ting*), and *She Kills a Dog to Admonish Her Husband* (*Shagou ji*). The Western-language materials on these topics are slim, but the works are a vital part of understanding an age when a nonconformist literate class developed; when classical Chinese literature was, if not undermined, at least shaken by a rising colloquial tradition fed by shared interests across class lines and by the possibilities of a new print culture; and when the foreign played a part in Chinese culture that, to this day, has never been repeated.

Select bibliography

Chapter 1: Early Chinese literature, beginnings through Western Han

Boltz, William G. *The Origin and Early Development of the Chinese Writing System*. New Haven: American Oriental Society, 1994.

Durrant, Stephen W. *The Cloudy Mirror: Tension and Conflict in the Writings of Sima Qian*. Albany: State University of New York Press, 1995.

Graham, A. C. *Disputers of the Tao: Philosophical Argument in Ancient China*. La Salle: Open Court, 1989.

Hawkes, David. "The Quest of the Goddess." *Asia Major* n.s. 13 (1967): 71–94.

————. *The Songs of the South: An Ancient Chinese Anthology of Poems by Qu Yuan and Other Poets*. Harmondsworth: Penguin, 1985.

Hightower, James Robert. *Han Shih Wai Chuan: Han Ying's Illustrations of the Didactic Application of the Classic of Songs*. Cambridge, MA: Harvard University Press, 1952.

————. "The Han-shih wai-chuan and the San chia shih." *HJAS* 11 (1948): 241–310.

Karlgren, Bernhard. *The Book of Odes*. Stockholm: Museum of Far Eastern Antiquities, 1950.

Keightley, David. *The Ancestral Landscape: Time, Space, and Community in Late Shang China, ca. 1200–1045 B.C.* Berkeley: University of California, Center for Chinese Studies, 2000.

Kern, Martin. "Ritual, Text, and the Formation of the Canon: Historical Transitions of Wen in Early China." *TP* 87, nos. 1–3 (2001): 43–91.

————. *The Stele Inscriptions of Ch'in Shih-huang: Text and Ritual in Early Chinese Imperial Representation*. New Haven: American Oriental Society, 2000.

————. "Western Han Aesthetics and the Genesis of the Fu." *HJAS* 63 (2003): 383–437.

Knechtges, David R. *Court Culture and Literature in Early China*. Aldershot: Ashgate, 2002.

————. *The Han Rhapsody: A Study of the Fu of Yang Hsiung (53 B.C.–A.D. 18)*. Cambridge: Cambridge University Press, 1976.

Legge, James. *The Chinese Classics*. 5 vols. Hong Kong: Hong Kong University Press, 1960 (first published 1861–1872).

Lewis, Mark Edward. *Writing and Authority in Early China*. Albany: State University of New York Press, 1999.

Li, Wai-yee. *The Readability of the Past in Early Chinese Historiography*. Cambridge, MA: Harvard Asia Center, 2007.

Loewe, Michael, ed. *Early Chinese Texts: A Bibliographical Guide*. Berkeley: The Society for the Study of Early China and The Institute of East Asian Studies, University of California, 1993.

Nylan, Michael. *The Five "Confucian" Classics*. New Haven: Yale University Press, 2001.

Owen, Stephen. *Readings in Chinese Literary Thought*. Cambridge, MA: Council on East Asian Studies, Harvard University, 1992.

Qiu Xigui. *Chinese Writing*. Trans. Gilbert L. Mattos and Jerry Norman. Berkeley: The Society for the Study of Early China and The Institute of East Asian Studies, University of California, 2000.

Schaberg, David. *A Patterned Past: Form and Thought in Early Chinese Historiography*. Cambridge, MA: Harvard Asia Center, 2001.

Van Zoeren, Steven. *Poetry and Personality: Reading, Exegesis, and Hermeneutics in Traditional China*. Stanford, CA: Stanford University Press, 1991.

Waley, Arthur. *The Book of Songs: The Ancient Chinese Classic of Poetry*. Ed. Joseph R. Allen. New York: Grove Press, 1996.

Wang, C. H. *From Ritual to Allegory: Seven Essays in Early Chinese Poetry*. Hong Kong: The Chinese University Press, 1988.

Watson, Burton. *Records of the Grand Historian*. 3 vols. Hong Kong: The Chinese University of Hong Kong Press, 1993.

Xiao Tong, ed., *Wen xuan or Selections of Refined Literature*. Trans. David R. Knechtges. 3 vols. Princeton, NJ: Princeton University Press, 1982, 1987, and 1996.

Yu, Pauline. *The Reading of Imagery in the Chinese Poetic Tradition*. Princeton, NJ: Princeton University Press, 1987.

Chapter 2: From the Eastern Han through the Western Jin
(AD 25–317)

Asselin, Mark L. "'A Significant Season': Literature in a Time of Endings. Cai Yong and a Few Contemporaries." Ph.D. diss., University of Washington, 1997.

Cutter, Robert Joe. "Cao Zhi and His Poetry." Ph.D. diss., University of Washington, 1983.

————. "Cao Zhi's (192–232) Symposium Poems." *CLEAR* 6, nos. 1 and 2 (1984): 1–32.

————. "The Incident at the Gate: Cao Zhi, the Succession, and Literary Fame." *TP* 71 (1985): 228–262.

Diény, Jean-Pierre. *Les dix-neuf Poèmes anciens*. Paris: Presses Universitaires de France, 1963.

————. *Les Poèmes de Cao Cao (155–220)*. Paris: Collège de France, Institut des hautes études chinoises, 2000.

————. "Les Septs Tristesses (Qi Ai). À Propos des deux versions d'un poème à chanter de Cao Zhi." *TP* 65 (1979): 51–65.

Frankel, Hans H. "Cai Yan and the Poems Attributed to Her." *CLEAR* 5, nos. 1 and 2 (1983): 133–156.

————. "Fifteen Poems by Ts'ao Chih: An Attempt at a New Approach." *JAOS* 84 (1964): 1–14.

————. "The Chinese Ballad 'Southeast Fly the Peacocks.'" *HJAS* 34 (1974): 248–271.

Gong Kechang. *Studies on the Han Fu.* Trans. and ed. David R. Knechtges, with Stuart Aque, Mark Asselin, Carrie Reed, and Su Jui-lung. American Oriental Series Vol. 84. New Haven: American Oriental Society, 1997.

Holzman, Donald. *Chinese Literature in Transition from Antiquity to the Middle Ages.* Variorum Collected Studies Series. Aldershot, Brookfield, Singapore, and Sydney: Ashgate, 1998.

————. *Immortals, Festivals and Poetry in Medieval China.* Variorum Collected Studies Series. Aldershot, Brookfield, Singapore, and Sydney: Ashgate, 1998.

————. *Poetry and Politics: The Life and Works of Juan Chi, A.D. 210–263.* Cambridge and New York: Cambridge University Press, 1976.

————. *La Vie et la pensée de Xi Kang (223–262 Ap J.C.).* Leiden: E. J. Brill, 1957.

Idema, Wilt, and Beata Grant. "Ban Zhao." In *The Red Brush: Writing Women of Imperial China,* 17–42. Cambridge, MA: Harvard Asia Center, 2004.

Kroll, Paul W. "Seven Rhapsodies of Ts'ao Chih." *JAOS* 120, no. 1 (2000): 1–12.

Lai, Chiu-mi. "The Art of Lamentation in the Works of Pan Yue: 'Mourning the Eternally Departed.'" *JAOS* 114, no. 3 (1994): 409–425.

————. "River and Ocean: The Third Century Verse of Pan Yue and Lu Ji." Ph.D. diss., University of Washington, 1990.

Makeham, John. *Balanced Discourses.* Beijing: Foreign Languages Press and New Haven: Yale University Press, 2002.

Miao, Ronald C. *Early Medieval Chinese Poetry: The Life and Works of Wang Ts'an (A.D. 177–217).* Münchener Ostasiatische Studien, Band 30. Wiesbaden: Franz Steiner, 1982.

Owen, Stephen. *The Making of Early Chinese Classical Poetry.* Cambridge, MA: Harvard Asia Center, 2006.

Watson, Burton. *Chinese Rhyme-Prose: Poems in the Fu Form from the Han and Six Dynasties Periods.* New York and London: Columbia University Press, 1971.

Xiao Tong, ed., *Wen xuan or Selections of Refined Literature.* Trans. David R. Knechtges. See Chapter 1.

Chapter 3: From the Eastern Jin through the early Tang
(317–649)

Cai, Zong-qi, ed., *A Chinese Literary Mind: Culture, Creativity, and Rhetoric in* Wenxin Diao-long. Stanford: Stanford University Press, 2001.

Campany, Robert Ford. *Strange Writing: Anomaly Accounts in Early Medieval China.* Albany, NY: State University of New York Press, 1996.

Chang, Kang-i Sun. *Six Dynasties Poetry.* Princeton, NJ: Princeton University Press, 1986.

Dien, Albert. *Six Dynasties Civilization.* New Haven: Yale University Press, 2007.

————. ed. *State and Society in Early Medieval China.* Stanford, CA: Stanford Univesity Press, 1990.

Faxian. *The Travels of Fa-hsien (399–414 A.D.), or, Record of the Buddhist Kingdoms.* Trans. H. A. Giles. Cambridge: Cambridge University Press, 1923.

Frodsham, J. D. *The Murmuring Stream: The Life and Works of Hieh Ling-yün.* Kuala Lumpur: University of Malaya Press, 1967.

Ge Hong. *To Live as Long as Heaven and Earth: An Translation and Study of Ge Hong's "Traditions of Divine Transcendents."* Trans. Robert Ford Campany. Berkeley: University of California Press, 2002.

Hightower, James Robert. *The Poetry of T'ao Ch'ien.* Oxford: Clarendon Press, 1970.

Holcombe, Charles. *In the Shadow of the Han: Literati Thought and Society at the Beginning of the Southern Dynasties.* Honolulu: University of Hawai'i Press, 1994.

Johnson, David. *The Medieval Chinese Oligarchy.* Boulder, CO: Westview Press, 1977.

Kao, Karl S. Y., ed. and trans. *Classical Chinese Tales of the Supernatural and the Fantastic: Selections from the Third to the Tenth Century.* Bloomington: Indiana University Press, 1985.

Kieschnick, John. *The Eminent Monk: Buddhist Ideals in Medieval Chinese Hagiography.* Honolulu: University of Hawai'i Press, 1997.

Knechtges, David R. *Court Culture and Literature in Early China.* Variorum Collected Studies Series. Aldershot: Ashgate, 2002.

Kroll, Paul W., and David R. Knechtges, eds. *Studies in Early Medieval Chinese Literature and Cultural History: In Honor of Richard B. Mather and Donald Holzman.* Provo, UT: T'ang Studies Society, 2003.

Lin Shuen-fu, and Stephen Owen, eds. *The Vitality of the Lyric Voice: Shih Poetry from the Late Han to the T'ang.* Princeton, NJ: Princeton University Press, 1986.

Liu Yiqing. *A New Account of Tales of the World.* Trans. Richard B. Mather. Minneapolis: University of Minnesota Press, 1976.

Mather, Richard B., trans. *The Age of Eternal Brilliance: Three Lyric Poets of the Yung-ming Era (483–493).* Leiden: Brill, 2003.

———. *The Poet Shen Yüeh (441–513): The Reticent Marquis.* Princeton: Princeton University Press, 1988.

Owen, Stephen. *The Making of Early Chinese Classical Poetry.* Cambridge, MA: Harvard University Asia Center, 2006.

———. *The Poetry of the Early T'ang.* New Haven: Yale University Press, 1977.

Pearce, Scott, Audrey Shapiro, and Patricia Ebrey, ed. *Culture and Power in the Reconstitution of the Chinese Realm, 200–600.* Cambridge, MA: Harvard Asia Center, 2001.

Qian Nanxiu. *Spirit and Self in Medieval China: The Shih-Shuo Hsin-Yu and Its Legacy.* Honolulu: University of Hawai'i Press, 2001.

Rouzer, Paul. *Articulated Ladies: Gender and the Male Community in Early Chinese Texts.* Cambridge, MA: Harvard Asia Center, 2001.

Swartz, Wendy. *Reading Tao Yuanming: Shifting Paradigms of Historical Reception (427–1900).* Cambridge, MA: Harvard Asia Center, 2008.

Tian Xiaofei. *Beacon Fire and Shooting Star: The Literary Culture of the Liang (502–557).* Cambridge, MA: Harvard Asia Center, 2007.

———. *Tao Yuanming and Manuscript Culture: The Record of A Dusty Table.* Seattle: University of Washington Press, 2005.

Xiao Tong, ed., *Wen xuan or Selections of Refined Literature.* Trans. David R. Knechtges. 3 vols. Princeton: Princeton University Press, 1982, 1987, 1996.

Xu Ling, ed. *New Songs from A Jade Terrace.* Trans. Anne Birrell. London and New York: Penguin Books, 1986.

Yu Xin. *The Lament for the South: Yü Hsin's "Ai Chiang-nan fu."* Trans. and annotated by William T. Graham Jr. Cambridge: Cambridge University Press, 1980.

Chapter 4: The cultural Tang (650–1020)

Bryant, Daniel, *Lyric Poets of the Southern Tang: Feng Yansi (903–960), and Li Yu (937–978).* Vancouver: University of British Columbia Press, 1982.

Chou E. Shan. *Reconsidering Tu Fu: Literary Greatness and Cultural Context.* Cambridge: Cambridge University Press, 1995.

Demiéville, Paul. *L'Oeuvre de Wang le Zélateur (Wang Fan-tche). Poèmes populaires des T'ang, VIII–IX siècle.* Paris: Collège de France: Institutut des hautes études chinoises, 1982.

Frodsham, J. D. *Goddesses, Ghosts, and Demons: The Collected Poems of Li He (790–816).* London: Anvil Press Poetry, 1983.

Hartman, Charles. *Han Yu and the T'ang Search for Unity.* Princeton: Princeton University Press, 1985.

Hawkes, David. *A Little Primer of Tu Fu.* Oxford: Oxford University Press, 1967.

Kroll, Paul W. *Meng Hao-jan.* Boston: Twayne, 1981.

Larsen, Jeanne. *Brocade River Poems: Selected Works of the Tang Dynasty Courtesan Xue Tao.* Princeton: Princeton University Press, 1987.

Liu, James J. Y. *The Poetry of Li Shangyin.* Chicago: University of Chicago Press, 1969.

Mair, Victor H. *Painting and Performance: Chinese Picture Recitation and Its Indian Genesis.* Honolulu: University of Hawai'i Press, 1988.

————. *T'ang Transformation Texts.* Cambridge, MA: Harvard University Press, 1989.

————. *Tun-huang Popular Narratives.* Cambridge: Cambridge University Press, 1983.

Nienhauser, William, *et al. Liu Tsung-yuan.* New York: Twayne, 1973.

————. *P'i Jih-hsiu.* Boston: Twayne, 1979.

Owen, Stephen. *The End of the Chinese "Middle Ages": Essays in Mid-Tang Literary Culture.* Stanford, CA: Stanford University Press, 1996.

————. *The Great Age of Chinese Poetry: The High Tang.* New Haven: Yale University Press, 1980.

————. *The Late Tang: Chinese Poetry of the Mid-Ninth Century (827–860).* Cambridge, MA: Harvard Asia Center, 2006.

Rouzer, Paul. *Writing Another's Dream: The Poetry of Wen Tingyun.* Stanford, CA: Stanford University Press, 1993.

Sanders, Graham. *Words Well Put: Visions of Poetic Competence in the Chinese Tradition.* Cambridge, MA: Harvard Asia Center, 2006.

Schafer, Edward H. *The Divine Woman: Dragon Ladies and Rain Maidens in T'ang Literature.* San Francisco: North Point Press, 1978.

————. *The Golden Peaches of Samarkand: A Study of T'ang Exotics.* Berkeley: University of California Press, 1963.

————. *Mirages on the Sea of Time: The Taoist Poetry of Ts'ao T'ang.* Berkeley: University of California Press, 1985.

————. *Pacing the Void: T'ang Approaches to the Stars.* Berkeley: University of California Press, 1977.

_____. *The Vermillion Bird: Tang Images of the South*. Berkeley; University of California Press, 1967.

Shields, Anna Marshall. *Crafting a Collection: The Cultural Contexts and Poetic Practice of the Huajian ji* 花間集 *(Collection from among the Flowers)*. Cambridge, MA: Harvard Asia Center, 2006.

Varsano, Paula M., *Tracking the Banished Immortal: The Poetry of Li Bo and Its Critical Reception*. Honolulu: University of Hawai'i Press, 2003.

Waley, Arthur, trans. *Ballads and Stories from Tun-huang*. London: George Allen and Unwin, 1960.

_____. *The Life and Times of Po Chü-i 772–846*. London and New York: Routledge, 2005.

_____. *The Poetry and Career of Li Po 701–762*. London, and Boston: George Allen and Unwin, 1979.

Warner, Ding Xiang. *A Wild Deer amid Soaring Phoenixes: The Opposition Poetics of Wang Ji*. Honolulu: The University of Hawai'i Press, 2003.

Yates, Robin D. S. *Washing Silk: The Life and Selected Poetry of Wei Zhuang (834?–910)*. Cambridge, MA: Harvard Council on East Asian Studies, 1988.

Yu, Pauline. *The Poetry of Wang Wei*. Bloomington: Indiana University Press, 1980.

Chapter 5: The Northern Song (1020–1126)

Bol, Peter. *"This Culture of Ours": Intellectual Transitions in T'ang and Sung China*. Stanford, CA: Stanford University Press, 1992.

Chang, Kang-i Sun. *The Evolution of Chinese Tz'u Poetry: From Late Tang to Northern Sung*. Princeton: Princeton University Press, 1980.

Chaves, Jonathan. *Mei Yao-ch'en and the Development of Early Sung Poetry*. New York: Columbia University Press.

Egan, Ronald. *The Problem of Beauty: Aesthetic Thought and Pursuits in Northern Song Dynasty China*. Cambridge, MA: Harvard Asia Center, 2006.

_____. *Word, Image, and Deed in the Life of Su Shi*. Cambridge, MA: Council on East Asian Studies, Harvard University, 1994.

Fuller, Michael A. *The Road to East Slope: The Development of Su Shi's Poetic Voice*. Stanford, CA: Stanford University Press, 1990.

Grant, Beata. *Mount Lu Revisited: Buddhism in the Life and Writings of Su Shi*. Honolulu: University of Hawai'i Press, 1994.

Gregory, Peter N., and Daniel A. Getz Jr., ed. *Buddhism in the Song*. Honolulu: University of Hawai'i Press, 2002.

Hightower, James R., and Florence Chia-ying Yeh. *Studies in Chinese Poetry*. Cambridge, MA: Harvard Asia Center, 1998.

Palumbo-Liu, David. *The Poetics of Appropriation: The Literary Theory and Practice of Huang Tingjian*. Stanford, CA: Stanford University Press, 1993.

Sargent, Stuart Howard. *The Poetry of He Zhu (1052–1125): Genres, Contexts, and Creativity*. Leiden: Brill, 2007.

Wang, Yugen. "Poetry in Print Culture: Texts, Reading Strategy, and Compositional Poetics in Huang Tingjian (1045–1105) and the Late Northern Song." Ph.D. diss., Harvard University, 2005.

West, Stephen H. "Spectacle, Ritual, and Social Relations: The Son of Heaven, Citizens, and Created Space in Imperial Gardens in the Northern Song." In *Baroque Garden Cultures: Emulation, Sublimation, Subversion*, ed. Michael Conan. Washington, DC: Dumbarton Oaks, 2004, 291–321.

Yang, Xiaoshan. *Metamorphosis of the Private Sphere: Gardens and Objects in Tang–Song Poetry.* Cambridge, MA: Harvard Asia Center, 2003.

Yoshikawa Kōjirō. *An Introduction to Song Poetry.* Trans. Burton Watson. Cambridge, MA: Harvard Yenching Institute, 1967.

Yu, Pauline, ed. *Voices of the Song Lyric in China.* Berkeley: University of California Press, 1994.

Chapter 6: North and south: the twelfth and thirteenth centuries

Bol, Peter K. "Chao Ping-wen (1159–1232): Foundations for Literati Learning." In *China under Jurchen Rule*, ed. Hoyt C. Tillman and Stephen H. West. Albany: State University of New York Press, 1995, 115–44.

————. "Seeking Common Ground: Han Literati under Jurchen Rule." *Harvard Journal of Asiatic Studies* 47, no. 2 (1987): 461–538.

Cavallo, Guglielmo, and Roger Chartier, eds. *A History of Reading in the West.* Trans. Lydia G. Cochrane. Cambridge: Polity Press, 1999.

Chan, Hok-lam. *The Historiography of the Chin Dynasty: Three Studies.* Münchener Ostasiatische Studien 4. Wiesbaden: Franz Steiner Verlag, 1970.

Chang, Kang-i Sun. "Symbolic and Allegorical Meanings in the *Yüeh-fu pu-t'i* Poem Series." *Harvard Journal of Asiatic Studies* 46, no. 2 (1986): 353–385.

Chartier, Roger. *The Order of Books: Readers, Authors, and Libraries in Europe between the Fourteenth and Eighteenth Centuries.* Trans. Lydia G. Cochrane. Cambridge: Polity Press, 1994.

Chia, Lucille. *Printing for Profit: the Commercial Publishers of Jianyang, Fujian (11th–17th Centuries).* Cambridge, MA: Harvard University Press, 2002.

Duke, Michael S. *Lu You.* Boston: Twayne, 1977.

Edgren, Sören. "Southern Song Printing in Hangzhou." *Bulletin of the Museum of Far Eastern Antiquities* 62 (1989): 1–212.

Fong, Grace S. *Wu Wenying and the Art of Southern Song Ci Poetry.* Princeton: Princeton University Press, 1987.

Franke, Herbert, and Denis Twitchett, eds. *Alien Regimes and Border States, 907–1368: The Cambridge History of China, Vol. 6.* Cambridge: Cambridge University Press, 1994.

Fuller, Michael A. "Aesthetics and Meaning in Experience: A Theoretical Perspective on Zhu Xi's Revision of Song Dynasty Views of Poetry." *Harvard Journal of Asiatic Studies* 65, no. 2 (2005): 311–355.

Hightower, James R., and Florence Chia-ying Yeh. *Studies in Chinese Poetry.* Cambridge, MA: Harvard Asian Center, 1998.

Ho, Ping-ti. "An Estimate of the Total Population of Sung-Chin China." *Études Song (Sung Studies)* Series 1. 1 (1970): 33–53.

Idema, Wilt, and Stephen H. West. *Chinese Theater, 1100–1450: A Source Book*. Ed. Herbert Franke and Wolfgang Bauer. Münchener Ostasiatische Studien. Wiesbaden: Franz Steiner, 1982.

Jin Qicong. "Jurchen Literature under the Chin." In *China under Jurchen Rule*, ed. Hoyt C. Tillman and Stephen H. West. Albany: State University of New York Press, 1995 216–237.

Lian, Xinda. *The Wild and Arrogant: Expression of Self in Xin Qiji's Song Lyrics*. New York: Peter Lang, 1999.

Lin, Shuen-fu. "Space-Logic in the Longer Song Lyrics of the Southern Sung: A Reading of Wu Wen-ying's 'Ying-t'i-hsü.'" *Journal of Sung–Yuan Studies* 25 (1995): 169–191.

————. "Through a Window of Dreams: Reality and Illusion in the Song Lyrics of the Song Dynasty." In *Hsiang Lectures on Chinese Poetry, Vol. 1*. Montreal: McGill University Center for East Asian Research, 2001, 19–40.

————. *The Transformation of the Chinese Lyrical Tradition: Chiang K'uei and Southern Sung Tz'u Poetry*. Princeton: Princeton University Press, 1978.

Liu, James T. C. *China Turning Inward: Intellectual–Political Changes in the Early Twelfth Century*. Cambridge, MA: Harvard University Press, 1988.

Lu You. *The Old Man Who Does as He Pleases: Selections from the Poetry and Prose of Lu Yu*. Trans. Burton Watson. New York: Columbia University Press, 1973.

Lynn, Richard John. "Chu Hsi as Literary Theorist and Critic." In *Chu Hsi and Neo-Confucianism*, ed. Wing-tsit Chan. Honolulu: University of Hawai'i Press, 1986, 337–354.

Mote, Frederick W. *Imperial China, 900–1800*. Cambridge, MA: Harvard University Press, 1999.

————. "A Millennium of Chinese Urban History: Form, Time, and Space Concepts in Soochow," *Rice University Studies* 59, no. 4 (1973): 35–66.

Poon, Ming-sun. "Books and Printing in Sung China (960–1279)." Ph.D. diss., University of Chicago, 1979.

Schmidt, Jeremy D. *Yang Wan-li*. Boston: Twayne, 1976.

Tillman, Hoyt C. *Confucian Discourse and Chu Hsi's Ascendancy*. Honolulu: University of Hawai'i Press, 1992.

Tillman, Hoyt C., and Stephen H. West, eds. *China under Jurchen Rule: Essays on Chin Intellectual and Cultural History*. Albany: State University of New York Press, 1995.

Tsien, Tsuen-hsuin. *Written on Bamboo and Silk: The Beginnings of Chinese Books and Inscriptions*. Chicago: University of Chicago Press, 1962.

Wu, K. T. "Chinese Printing under Four Alien Dynasties: (916–1368 A.D.)" *Harvard Journal of Asiatic Studies* 13, nos. 3–4 (1950): 447–523.

Yang Wanli. *Heaven My Blanket, Earth My Pillow: Poems from Sung Dynasty China*. Trans. Jonathan Chaves. New York: Weatherhill, 1975.

Yoshikawa, Kōjirō. *An Introduction to Sung Poetry*. Trans. Burton Watson. Cambridge, MA: Harvard University Press, 1967.

Yu, Pauline, ed. *Voices of the Song Lyric in China*. Berkeley: University of California Press, 1994.

Chapter 7: Literature from the late Jin to the early Ming:
ca 1230–ca 1375

Chen, Yüan. *Western and Central Asians in China under the Mongols: Their Transformation into Chinese.* Trans. Ch'ien Hsing Hai and L. C. Goodrich. Monumenta Serica Monograph Series: Monumenta Serica, 1966.

Crown, Elleanor H. "Jeux d'Esprit in Yuan Dynasty Verse." *Chinese Literature: Essays, Articles, Reviews* 2, no. 2 (1980): 182–198.

Crump, J. I. *Song-Poems from Xanadu.* Michigan Monographs in Chinese Studies. Ann Arbor: Center for Chinese Studies, 1993.

Idema, Wilt. "Some Remarks and Speculations Concerning *P'ing-Hua*." In *Chinese Vernacular Fiction*, ed. W. L. Idema. Leiden: E. J. Brill, 1974, 69–120.

———. "Why You Never Have Read a Yuan Drama: The Transformation of *Zaju* at the Ming Court." In *Studi in Onore Di Lanciello Lanciotti*, ed. S. M. Carletti *et al.* Napoli: Institute Universiatorio Orientale, 1996, 765–791.

Idema, Wilt, and Stephen H. West. *Chinese Theater 1100–1450: A Source Book.* Ed. Herbert Franke and Wolfgang Bauer. Münchener Ostasiatische Studien. Wiesbaden: Franz Steiner, 1982.

Langlois, John D. "Chinese Culturalism and the Yuan Analogy: Seventeenth-Century Perspectives." *Harvard Journal of Asiatic Studies* 40, no. 2 (1980): 355–398.

Llamas, Regina. "Retribution, Revenge, and the Ungrateful Scholar in Early Chinese Southern Drama." *Asia Major* 20, no. 2 (2007): 75–101.

Lynn, Richard J. *Kuan Yün-Shih.* Ed. William R. Schultz. Twayne World Authors. New York: Twayne, 1980.

———. "Tradition and the Individual: Ming and Ch'ing Views of Yüan Poetry." *Journal of Oriental Studies* 15, no. 1 (1977): 1–19.

Radtke, Kurt W. *Poetry of the Yuan Dynasty.* Faculty of Asian Studies Monographs. Canberra: Australian National University, Faculty of Asian Studies, 1984.

Schlepp, Wayne. *San-Ch'ü, Its Technique and Imagery.* Madison: University of Wisconsin Press, 1970.

Sun, Mei. "Exploring the Historical Development of Nanxi, Southern Theatre." *CHINOPERL Papers* 24 (2002): 35–65.

———. "Performances of Nanxi." *Asian Theatre Journal* 13, no. 2 (1996): 141–166.

West, Stephen H. "Text and Ideology: Ming Editors and Northern Drama." In *The Song–Yuan–Ming Transition in Chinese History*, ed. Paul Jakov Smith and Richard von Glahn. Cambridge, MA: Harvard Asia Center, 2003, 329–373.

Yoshikawa, Kōjirō. *Five Hundred Years of Chinese Poetry 1150–1650, the Chin, Yüan, and Ming.* Trans. John Timothy Wixted. Princeton Library of Asian Translations. Princeton, NJ: Princeton University Press, 1989.

Glossary

Aguda 阿骨打
ai 哀
Ai Jiangnan fu 哀江南賦
Ai Jiangtou 哀江頭
Ai shiming 哀時命
Ai wangsun 哀王孫
Ai yongshi wen 哀永逝文
Ajiao 阿嬌
An Lushan 安祿山
Anji gongzhu 安吉公主
anjing 安靜
Anle gongzhu 安樂公主
Anshi fangzhong ge 安世房中歌
Anxiang 暗香
Anyi ji 嶼嶷集
Apang gong fu 阿房宮賦
babing 八病
Bai Fen 白賁
Bai he fu 白鶴賦
Bai Juyi 白居易
Bai ma pian 白馬篇
Bai Pu 白樸
Bai Ting 白珽
Bai Xingjian 白行簡
Bai xinyue 拜新月
Baichilou fu 百尺樓賦
baijiayu 百家語
Baishi daoren shishuo 白石道人詩說
Baitu fu 白兔賦
Baitu ji 白兔記
Baitu song 白兔頌
Baiyue ting 拜月亭
Baizhang Huaihai 百丈懷海
Baizhang shan ji 百丈山記

Baizhi shi 百志詩
Bajiaolang 八角廊
Bajun 八駿
Ban Biao 班彪
Ban Chao 班超
Ban Gu 班固
Ban Jieyu 班倢好
Ban Kuang 班況
Ban Yi 班壹
Ban You 班斿
Ban Zhao 班昭
Bao De 鮑德
Bao Hui 包恢
Bao Ren Shaoqing shu 報任少卿書
Bao Xi 包犧
Bao Zhao 鮑照
baobian 褒貶
Baochang 寶唱
Baoding xian 寶鼎現
baojuan 寶卷
Baolin 寶林
Baopuzi neipian 抱朴子內篇
Baopuzi waipian 抱朴子外篇
Basheng Ganzhou 八聲甘州
Bati liuji 八體六技
Bayan 伯顏
Bei fen shi 悲憤詩
Bei men 北門
Bei shan 北山
Bei shi 北史
Bei shi bu yu fu 悲士不遇賦
bei wen 碑文
Bei zheng fu 北征賦
Beili zhi 北里志

Beimeng suoyan 北夢瑣言
Beishan yiwen 北山移文
Beitang shuchao 北堂書鈔
Beizheng 北征
benji 本紀
bense 本色
bense shiren 本色詩人
Benshi shi 本事詩
Benxue shijie 本穴世界
bi (brush) 筆
bi (comparison, allegory) 比
Bi fu 筆賦
Bi Gan 比干
bian 變
biansai 邊塞
biansai shi 邊塞詩
bianti 變體
bianwen 變文
bianya zhi duan 變雅之端
Bianzong lun 辨宗論
biao 表
biao ji 表記
Bie fu 別賦
Bielu 別錄
Biezi 別字
biji 筆記
Bing fu 餅賦
Bing shuo 餅說
Bingju xing 兵車行
bingshu 兵書
Biqiuni zhuan 比丘尼傳
Biyan lu 碧巖錄
Bizha hualiang 筆札華梁
Bo Yi 伯夷
Bo Yi Shu Qi liezhuan 伯夷叔齊列傳
Bohu tong yi 白虎通義
Boliang ti 柏梁體
boshi 博士
Bowu zhi 博物志
bu (not) 不
Bu ju 卜居
bufan zhengwei 不犯正位
bushe lilu 不涉理路
buwei pipaniang ren hun yun ci 不為琵琶
　娘人魂韻詞
buxu 步虛

Cai Bojie nü fu 蔡伯喈女賦
Cai Gui 蔡珪
Cai Jing 蔡京
Cai Juhou 蔡居厚
Cai Lang 蔡朗
Cai Lun 蔡倫
Cai Songnian 蔡松年
Cai Xing 蔡襄
Cai Yan 蔡琰
Cai Yong 蔡邕
Caidiao ji 才調集
Cailian fu 採蓮賦
cairen 才人
Cang Jie 蒼頡
Cang Jie xunxuan 蒼頡訓纂
Cang Jie zhuan 蒼頡傳
Canglang shihua 滄浪詩話
Canluan lu 驂鸞錄
Cao Biao 曹彪
Cao Cao 曹操
Cao Cheng 曹成
Cao Pi (187–226) 曹丕
Cao Pí (ca 326–386) 曹毗
Cao Rui 曹叡
Cao Shuang 曹爽
Cao Tang 曹唐
Cao Zhang 曹彰
Cao Zhi 曹植
Caoshi jiazhuan 曹氏家傳
caotang 草堂
Caoxuan ge 草玄閣
Cen Shen 岑參
Cha jiu lun 茶酒論
Chajing 茶經
Chan 禪
Chan fu 蟬賦
Chang di fu 長笛賦
Chang E 嫦娥
Chang Jing 常景
Chang Qu 常璩
Chang yan 昌言
Chang'an guyi 長安古意
Chang'an you xiaxie 長安有狹斜
Changcheng gongzhu 長城公主
changfa 常法
changhe ji 唱和集

Changhen ge 長恨歌

Changlun 唱論

Chanshu 讒書

Chanyue dashi 禪月大師

Chao Buzhi 晁補之

Chao Cuo 晁錯

Chaoye duo huanyu 朝野多歡娛

Chaoye xinsheng taiping yuefu 朝野新聲
　太平樂府

chen (prognostication texts) 讖

Chen Baxian 陳霸先

Chen Chen 陳珍

Chen Fan 陳蕃

Chen Fen 陳玢

Chen Fu 陳孚

Chen Hong (fourth century) 陳弘

Chen Hong (ninth century) 陳鴻

Chen Liang 陳亮

Chen Lin 陳琳

Chen Qi 陳起

Chen Qingzhi 陳慶之

Chen She 陳涉

Chen Shi 陳寔

Chen Shidao 陳師道

Chen Shubao 陳叔寶

Chen Wenwei 陳文蔚

Chen Yaozi 陳堯咨

Chen Yuyi 陳與義

Chen Zi'ang 陳子昂

cheng 成

Cheng Hao 程顥

Cheng Jufu/Wenhai 程鉅夫／文海

Cheng Jun 程駿

Cheng Qianfan 程千帆

Cheng Yi 程頤

Cheng-Han 成漢

Chengzhai 誠齋

Chentao 陳陶

chenwei 讖緯

Chi Chao 郗超

chidu 尺牘

Chile ge 敕勒歌

Chinggis Khan 成吉思汗

chongtou xiaoling 重頭小令

Chongwen guan 崇文館

Chongyang 重陽

Chou lin fu 愁霖賦

Chu 楚

Chu ci (Mao Ode) 楚茨

Chu fu fu 出婦賦

Chu Guangxi 儲光羲

Chu Han chunqiu 楚漢春秋

Chu Liang 褚亮

Chu sanzang ji ji 出三藏記集

Chu Shaosun 褚少孫

Chu sheng 楚聲

Chu Suiliang 褚遂良

Chu Tang sijie 初唐四傑

chuanqi 傳奇

chuchu laili 出處來歷

Chuci 楚辭

Chuci buzhu 楚辭補注

Chuci jizhu 楚辭集注

Chuci tongshi 楚辭通釋

Chuci zhangju 楚辭章句

Chujia 除架

chun 蓴

Chunqiu 春秋

Chunqiu fanlu 春秋繁露

Chunri tianyuan zaxing 春日田園雜興

Chuogeng lu 輟耕錄

Chupu fu 樗蒲賦

Chutian yao daiguo Qingjiang yin 楚天遙
　帶過清江引

Chuxue ji 初學記

ci (song lyrics) 詞

ci bieshi yijia 詞別是一家

Ci shi ji xie fu 刺世疾邪賦

ci zhe wei ye 此之謂也

Ci'en si 慈恩寺

cifu 辭賦

Cilun 詞論

Ciren Wang Yongzhang zhuan 詞人王用
　章傳

cishi 詞士

ciyu 詞餘

Ciyuan 詞源

Congjun xing 從軍行

Cui Guang 崔光

Cui Hao (380–450) 崔浩

Cui Hao (704?–745) 崔顥

Cui Hu 崔護

Cui Lingqin 崔令欽
Cui Qi 崔琦
Cui Shi 崔寔
Cui Yin 崔駰
Cui Yingying 崔鶯鶯
Cui Yuan 崔瑗
Cui Zhiyuan 崔致遠
Cui Zhuan 崔篆
cuzhi 促織
da fu 大賦
Da gao 大誥
Da Jia Changyuan 答賈長淵
Da ke nan 答客難
Da Tang [shishuo] xinyu 大唐[世說]新語
Da Tang xiyu ji 大唐西域記
Da youren lun wenfa shu 答友人論文法書
Da youxian shi 大遊仙詩
Da yunhe 大運河
Da zhao 大招
Da zhi 達旨
Da zhidu lun 大智度論
Da zhuan 大傳
Da Zhuang lun 達莊論
da/chou 答/酬
Dadao qu 大道曲
Dadu 大都
Dafeng ge 大風歌
Dahui Zonggao 大慧宗杲
dahun 打諢
Dai Biaoyuan 戴表元
Dai Fu 戴孚
Dai Fugu 戴復古
Dai gu 代古
Dai Shoulei jiu changlu shi 代收淚就長路詩
Dai Shulun 戴叔倫
Daidu fu 代都賦
Daigu shi 代古詩
daiguo qu 帶過曲
dajie 大節
Dali 大理
Dali shi caizi 大歷十才子
Damuqianlian mingjian jiumu bianwen 大目乾連冥間救母變文
dan cha weiruo er 但差委弱耳
danben 旦本

danbo 淡泊
Dang Huaiying 黨懷英
dangdai shijiang 當代詩匠
dao 道
Dao Gai 到溉
Dao Qia 到洽
Dao qing 道情
Dao'an 道安
daobi 刀筆
Daode jing 道德經
Daoheng 道恆
daojia 道家
Daoqian 道潛 (Canliao 參寥)
Daoshi 道釋
daotong 道統
Daowang fu 悼亡賦
Daowang shi 悼亡詩
Daoxuan 道宣
Daoxue 道學
Daoyi (Mazu) 道一 (馬祖)
Daque fu 大雀賦
Daren fu 大人賦
Daren xiansheng zhuan 大人先生傳
Datang Sanzang qujing shihua 大唐三藏取經詩話
daxu 大序
Daxue 大學
daya 大雅
dayi 大義
dazai 大宰
Dazhuan 大傳
Deng fu 燈賦
Deng Guangjian 鄧光薦
Deng jiangzhong guyu 登江中孤嶼
Deng lou fu 登樓賦
Deng shan 登山
Deng tai fu 登臺賦
Deng Wenyuan 鄧文原
Denglou wangxiang 登樓望鄉
Di 狄
dian 典
Dian jie 典誡
Dian lun 典論
diantie chengjin 點鐵成金
diao 調
Diao gu zhanchang wen 弔古戰場文

Diao Jiasheng wen 弔賈生文
Diao Qu Yuan 弔屈原
Diaochong lun 雕蟲論
diaogu shangjin 弔古傷今
diaowen 弔文
diben 底本
Ding Jingong tanlu 丁晉公談錄
Ding qing fu 定情賦
Ding Wei 丁謂
Ding Yi 丁儀
Ding Yih 丁廙
Dinglin si 定林寺
dingzu dui 鼎足對
Dong Jieyuan 董解元
Dong Yong 董永
Dong zheng fu 東征賦
Dong Zhongshu 董仲舒
Dong Zhuo 董卓
Dongdu fu 東都賦
Dongfang Shuo 東方朔
Dongfang Shuo biezhuan 東方朔別傳
Dongguan Han ji 東觀漢紀
Donghai 東海
Donghai ji 東海集
Donghua men 東華門
Donghuang Taiyi 東皇太一
Donghun hou 東昏侯
Dongjing menghua lu 東京夢華錄
dongpo 東坡
Dongpo chanxi ji 東坡禪喜集
dongqing 冬青
Dongyang Wuyi 東陽無疑
Dou ji shi 鬪雞詩
Dou Rong 竇融
Dou Tao 竇滔
Dou Wu 竇武
Dou Xian 竇憲
Du Du 杜篤
Du duan 獨斷
Du Fu 杜甫
Du Guangting 杜光庭
Du Kui 杜夔
Du Lin 杜林
Du Mo 杜默
Du Mu 杜牧
Du Shang 度尚

Du Shanhai jing 讀山海經
Du Shenyan 杜審言
Du shu fu 讀書賦
Du Xunhe 杜荀鶴
Du Yanian 杜延年
Du You 杜佑
Du Yu 杜預
Duan Chenggen 段承根
Duan Chengji 段成己
Duan Chengshi 段成式
Duan Keji 段克己
Duan Pidi 段匹磾
Duan Ye 段業
Duangan Mu 段干木
duanjin 端謹
duànju (broken lines) 斷句
duǎnju (short poem) 短句
Duanren fu 短人賦
Duanwu 端午
Duanxiao naoge 短簫鐃歌
duanzhang quyi 斷章取義
Ducheng jisheng 都城紀勝
Dugu Ji 獨孤及
dui ge 對歌
duiwen 對問
Dulou fu 髑髏賦
Dulou shuo 髑髏說
Dunhuang 敦煌
Dunhuang shilu 敦煌實錄
Duo shi 多士
E bing fu 惡餅賦
Empress Deng 鄧后
Empress Dowager Deng 鄧皇太后
Empress Dowager He 何皇太后
Empress Yan 閻后
Empress Zhen 甄皇后
Er gui 二鬼
Er jing fu 二京賦
Er shi 二世
ermiao 二妙
Ermiao ji 二妙集
Ernian lüling 二年律令
Ershisi shipin 二十四詩品
Erya 爾雅
fa (bring forth) 發
fa (method, standard) 法

Fa yingtao shu fu 伐櫻桃樹賦
Fabao lianbi 法寶聯璧
Fahua jing 法華經
faji biantai 發跡變泰
fajia 法家
Fan Chengda 范成大
Fan Chunren 范純仁
Fan du fu 反都賦
Fan Jiang 凡將
Fan Kuai 樊噲
Fan Li sao 反離騷
Fan Pang 范滂
Fan Peng 范梈
Fan Shu 范攄
Fan Wen 范溫
Fan Ye 范曄
Fan Yun 范雲
Fan Zhen 范鎮
Fan Zhongyan 范仲淹
Fan Zongshi 樊宗師
fanchang hedao 反常合道
Fang Feng 方鳳
Fang Hui 方回
Fang Yue 方岳
fangji 方技
fangshi 方士
Fangyan 方言
Faxian 法顯
Faxiu 法秀
fayan 法眼
Fayan 法言
Fayuan zhulin 法苑珠林
fei bense 非本色
Feng (Airs) 風
feng (criticism) 諷
feng (sacrifice) 封
Feng Changqing 封常清
Feng Fengshi 馮奉世
Feng fu 風賦
Feng jian shi 諷諫詩
Feng Yan 馮衍
Feng Yansi 馮延巳
Feng Yi 封奕
Feng Zizhen 馮子振
fengliu 風流
fengliu jiashi 風流佳事

fengliu renwu 風流人物
Fengshen yanyi 封神演義
fenshu kengru 焚書阬儒
Fo ji 佛記
Foguo ji 佛國記
Foyin 佛印
fu 賦
Fu Bi 富弼
Fu Chang 傅暢
Fu ji 賦集
Fu Jian 符堅
Fu Kuan 傅寬
Fu Lang 符朗
Fu Liang 傅亮
Fu pu 賦譜
Fu Rong 符融
Fu Sheng 伏勝
Fu Xi 伏羲
Fu Xian 傅咸
Fu Xuan 傅玄
Fu Yi 傅毅
Fu Yuan 傅瑗
Fu Yue 傅說
Fufeng ge 扶風歌
fugu 復古
Fuli 符離
Funiao fu 鵬鳥賦
Furen ji 婦人集
Futu fu 浮圖賦
Fuxing shu 復性書
Fuyang 阜陽
Fuzi 苻子
Gailun 丐論
Gan Bao 干寶
gandong 感動
ganjiu 感舊
Ganshi shushi shishou 感時述事十首
Ganyu 感遇
gao 誥
Gao duhu congma xing 高都護驄馬行
Gao Huan 高歡
Gao Kegong 高克恭
Gao Lishi 高力士
Gao Lishi waizhuan 高力士外傳
Gao Lü 高閭
Gao Pian 高駢

Gao Shi 高適
Gao Shitan 高士談
Gao Wei 高緯
Gao Xianzhi 高仙芝
Gao Yao 皋陶
Gao Yao mo 皋陶謨
Gao You 高誘
Gao Yun 高允
Gao Zhongwu 高仲武
Gaoseng zhuan 高僧傳
Gaoshi zhuan 高士傳
Gaotang fu 高唐賦
Gaoxian 高閑
Gaoyin zhuan 高隱傳
Gaozhai xueshi 高齋學士
Gaozu huan xiang 高祖還鄉
ge 歌
Ge fu 歌賦
Ge Gong 葛龔
Ge Hong 葛洪
Ge ju 葛屨
ge yong yan 歌永言
Geng Jing 耿京
Geng Wei 耿湋
Geshu Han 哥舒翰
gexing 歌行
Gong ci 宮詞
Gong Kui 貢奎
Gong wu chu men 公無出門
Gong yan 公宴
gongan 公案
gongci 宮詞
Gongsun Long 公孫龍
Gongsun Shu 公孫述
gongti 宮體
Gongyang zhuan 公羊傳
Gou Daoxing 句道興
goulan 勾欄
gu 古
gu Hang cairen bian 古杭才人編
gu Hang shuhui 古杭書會
Gu Kaizhi 顧愷之
Gu Kuang 顧況
Gu Rong 顧榮
Gu Sili 顧嗣立
Gu Ying/Aying 顧英/阿英

Gu Yong 谷永
Gu Zhending lu Ruxue jiaoshou Jiexuan
    Zhang Xiansheng mujie ming 故真定路
    儒學教授節軒張先生墓碣銘
Gua guan 掛冠
Guabu shan jiewen 瓜步山碣文
Guafu fu 寡婦賦
Guan ju 關雎
Guan wo sheng fu 觀我生賦
Guan Yunshi/Xiaoyun shihaiya 貫雲石/
    小雲石海涯
Guanchengzi wu shirou xiang
    管城子無食肉相
Guang hongming ji 廣弘明集
Guang yi ji 廣異記
Guangcheng song 廣城頌
guangda jiaohua 廣大教化
Guangshiyin yingyan ji 觀世音應驗記
guanmu 關目
Guanpu naideweng 灌圃耐得翁
Guanxiu 貫休
guanxue 官學
Guanzi 管子
gudan 古淡
Gufeng 古風
gufu 古賦
Gufu bianti 古賦辨體
Gufu ti 古賦體
Gufu zhunsheng 古賦準繩
Guhang zaji 古杭雜記
gui 簋
Gui si fu 歸思賦
Gui tian fu 歸田賦
guifei 貴妃
Guihun fu 歸魂賦
Guiji dianlu 會稽典錄
Guiqian zhi 歸潛志
Guisi wuyue sanri beidu sanshou 癸巳五
    月三日北渡三首
Guitang bieshu 圭塘別墅
Guitian lu 歸田錄
Guiyin 歸隱
Gujin shiren xiuju 古今詩人秀句
Gujin yuelu 古今樂錄
Guliang zhuan 穀梁傳
Guo Ban 郭頒

Guo Chengzhi 郭澄之

Guo Hao 郭鎬

Guo Maoqian 郭茂倩

Guo Moruo 郭沫若

Guo Pu 郭璞

Guo Qin lun 過秦論

Guo Shi 郭湜

Guo Tai 郭泰

Guo Xiang 郭象

Guodian 郭店

guofeng 國風

Guoshi bu 國史補

Guoxiu ji 國秀集

Guoyu 國語

Guoyu shibazhuan 國語十八傳

Guoyu yuge 國語御歌

Guoyu zawen 國語雜文

Guoyu zhenge 國語真歌

Guozi 郭子

Gushi shijiu shou 古詩十九首

gushi zhi liu 古詩之流

guti 古體

guwen 古文

Guwen guanjian 古文關鍵

Guyi 古意

Hai fu 海賦

Haichao fu 海潮賦

Hailing Prince 海陵王

Han (pre-imperial state) 韓

Han bei 韓碑

Han Chaozong 韓朝宗

Han Fei 韓非

Han Feizi 韓非子

Han Gaozu zhan baishe fu 漢高祖斬白
　蛇賦

Han Heng 韓恒

Han Hong 韓翃

Han Hui 韓會

Han Jin chunqiu 漢晉春秋

Han jin fu 漢津賦

Han Lanying 韓蘭英

Han Peng 韓朋

Han Qi 韓琦

Han Qinhu 韓擒虎

Han shi 韓詩

Han shi waizhuan 韓詩外傳

Han Shizhong 韓世忠

Han shu 漢書

Han Tuozhou 韓侂胄

Han Wo 韓偓

Han Wudi gushi 漢武帝故事

Han Xianzong 韓顯宗

Han Ying 韓嬰

Han Yu 韓愈

Han Yuanji 韓元吉

Han Yunqing 韓云卿

Handan Chun 邯鄲淳

Hanfa 漢法

Hangzhou jing 杭州景

Hanlin 翰林

Hanlin lun 翰林論

Hanlin yuan 翰林院

Hanshan 寒山

Hanyuan dian fu 含元殿賦

Hao Jing 郝經

Hao Tianting 郝天挺

haofang 豪放

haoran zhi qi 浩然之氣

he 和

He Changyu 何長瑜

He Chengtian 何承天

He Fasheng 何法盛

He Fen zhulao 河汾諸老

He Fen zhulao shiji 河汾諸老詩集

He Jin 何進

He Ning 和凝

He Shangzhi 何尚之

He xinlang 賀新郎

He Xun 何遜

He Yan 何晏

He Zhu 賀鑄

He Zong 賀蹤

hebo 河伯

Hehuan shi 合歡詩

Hehuang shu shi 河湟書事

Heiqi nu 黑漆弩

Helian Bobo 赫連勃勃

Hen fu 恨賦

Heshang Gong 河上公

Heyue yingling ji 河嶽英靈集

Hong fan 洪範

Hong Hao 洪皓

Hong Mai 洪邁

Hong Shi 洪適

Hong Xingzu 洪興祖

Hong Zikui 洪咨夔

Hong Zun 洪遵

Hongdu Gate 鴻都門

Hongming ji 弘明集

Hongren 弘仁

Hongwen guan 弘文館

Hou Andu 侯安都

Hou Han shu 後漢書

Hou Ji 后稷

Hou Jing 侯景

Houji 后集

Houzhu 後主

hu 壺

Hu Fanghui 胡方回

Hu Guang 胡廣

Hu jia shiba pai 胡笳十八拍

Hu Quan 胡銓

Hu Shiyuan shiji xu 胡師遠詩集序

Hu Yin 胡寅

Hu Yinglin 胡應麟

Hu Yizhou 胡義周

Hu Zhiyu 胡祇遹

hua 話

Hua shanshui xu 畫山水序

Hua Yuntai shan ji 畫雲台山記

Huai fu 槐賦

Huai jiu fu 懷舊賦

Huai sha 懷沙

huaigu 懷古

Huainanzi 淮南子

Huaisu 懷素

Huajian ji 花間集

Hualin bianlüe 華林遍略

Huan Tan 桓譚

Huan Wen 桓溫

Huan Xuan 桓玄

Huan Yi 桓彝

Huanfu Song 皇甫松

Huang Chao 黃巢

Huang Jin 黃溍

Huang niao 黃鳥

Huang Tao 黃滔

Huang Tingjian 黃庭堅

Huang Zu 黃祖

Huangchao gufu 皇朝古賦

Huangde song 皇德頌

Huangfu Mi 皇甫謐

Huangfu Shi 皇甫湜

Huangfu Zhen 皇甫真

Huang-Lao 黃老

Huangmo 皇謨

huangu duotai fa 換骨奪胎法

Huanmen zidi cuolishen 宦門子弟錯立身

Huaqing gong 華清宮

Huarui furen 花蕊夫人

Huaxu 華胥

Huayan jing 華嚴經

Huayangguo zhi 華陽國志

huazan 畫贊

hui 回

Hui Dong 惠棟

Hui Shi 惠施

Huichang 會昌

Huichao 慧超

Huichong 惠崇

Huihong 惠洪

Huijiao 慧皎

Huili 慧立

Huineng 慧能

Huishi chengwen 會試程文

Huiwen ji 回文集

huiwen shi 回文詩

Huiyuan 慧遠

Huizhen shi 會真詩

Hu-lao 虎牢

hun 魂

Hunan shihua 湻南詩話

Huo Xiaoyu zhuan 霍小玉傳

huofa 活法

Hushang gui 湖上歸

hutian 護田

hutu liaodao 糊塗潦倒

Huzhou ge 湖州歌

ji (account) 記

Ji Bu 季布

Ji fu 機賦

Ji guzhong wen 祭古冢文

ji wen 祭文

Ji yuan 集苑

Ji Zha 季札

Jia Chong 賈充

Jia Dao 賈島

Jia Jinhua 賈晉華

Jia Kui 賈逵

Jia Mi 賈謐

Jia Nanfeng 賈南風

Jia Sidao 賈似道

Jia Yi 賈誼

jiaguwen 甲骨文

jiajiezi 假借字

jian (remonstration) 諫

jian (see) 見

Jian yi fu 檢逸賦

jian'ai 兼愛

Jian'an 建安

Jian'an qizi 建安七子

jianbingzhe 兼并者

Jiang Fang 蔣防

Jiang fu 江賦

Jiang Han 江漢

Jiang jin jiu 將進酒

Jiang Kui 姜夔

Jiang Yan 江淹

Jiang You 江逌

Jiang Ziya 姜子牙

Jiang Zong 江總

Jianghu sheyou 江湖社友

Jianghu shiji 江湖詩集

jiangjing wen 講經文

Jiangnan 江南

Jiangxi shipai 江西詩派

Jiangxi style 江西格

Jianyu 肩愈

Jiao Zhongqing qi 焦仲卿妻

jiaofang 教坊

Jiaofang ji 教坊記

jiaohua fengyu 教化諷諭

Jiaoju fu 郊居賦

Jiaoran 皎然

jiaose 腳色

Jiaosi ge 郊祀歌

Jiaozhi 交趾

jie 偈

Jie chao 解嘲

Jie Xisi 揭傒斯

jiedu shi 節度使

Jienan Shan 節南山

jiesheng 結繩

Jigu lu 集古錄

Jijie 集解

Jijiu 急就

Jilong shan 雞籠山

Jin ji 晉紀

Jin jiangzuo wenzhang zhi 晉江左文章志

Jin Shi 靳石

Jin shu 晉書

Jin you fu 近遊賦

Jin zhongxing shu 晉中興書

Jin'an wang 晉安王

jing 經

Jing Cuo 景差

Jing Fang 京房

Jing Ke 荊軻

Jingbei yin 鯨背吟

Jingchai ji 荊釵記

Jingde chuandeng lu 景德傳燈錄

Jinggong tang song 靖恭堂頌

Jingling bayou 竟陵八友

Jingling wang 竟陵王

Jinglong wenguan ji 景龍文館記

Jinglü yixiang 經律異相

jingshi 經世

Jingshi dadian 經世大典

jingshu 經術

Jingu 金谷

Jingye fu 淨業賦

jingyi 經義

Jingzhou ji 荊州記

Jinling huaigu 金陵懷古

Jinlouzi 金樓子

jinshi 進士

Jinshi huiyuan 近事會元

Jinshi lu 金石錄

jinti 近體

jinwen (bronze inscriptions) 金文

jinwen (modern script) 今文

Jinzhen shige 金針詩格

Jiong zhuo 泂酌

Jisheng cao 寄生草

Jiu gao 酒誥

Jiu min 九愍

Jiubian 九辯
Jiuge 九歌
Jiuseng 九僧
Jiuseng shi 九僧詩
Jiushan shuhui 九山書會
Jiusi 九思
Jiutan 九嘆
Jiuzhang 九章
Jixuan ji 極玄集
juan 卷
Juan Dian 圈典
juanshu yiwei shi 捐書以為詩
jueju 絕句
Jueweng 覺翁
jufa 句法
Junchen tongde fu 君臣同德賦
junzi 君子
Juqu Maoqian 沮渠茂虔
Juqu Mengxun 沮渠蒙遜
Juqu wan fu 車渠椀賦
Jurchen 女真
jushi 居士
Juyan 居延
juzhong you yan 句中有眼
kaiguo zhi dachen 開國之大臣
Kaiyuan Tianbao yishi 開元天寶遺事
Kan Yin 闞駰
Kang gao 康誥
Kang Hong 康泓
Kang Senghui 康僧會
Kang Youwei 康有為
Kangjie 康節
kanhua chan 看話禪
kexue 可學
Khitan 契丹
Khubilai 忽必烈
kong 空
Kong Anguo 孔安國
Kong Anguo Shangshu 孔安國尚書
Kong Fang 孔方
Kong fangxiong you juejiao sh 孔方兄有
　絕交書
Kong Huan 孔奐
Kong Rong 孔融
Kong Yan 孔衍
Kong Yingda 孔穎達

Kong Zhigui 孔稚圭
Konghai 空海
Kongque dongnan fei 孔雀東南飛
Kongzi jiayu 孔子家語
Kongzi shilun 孔子詩論
Kongzi xianju 孔子閒居
Kongzi zhengyan 孔子正言
kou you mi, fu you jian 口有蜜，腹有劍
Ku han xing 苦寒行
Kuang Heng 匡衡
Kumārajiva 鳩摩羅什
Kunming chi 昆明池
kuse 苦澀
kuyin 苦吟
Lang Shiyuan 郎士元
Lanling wang 蘭陵王
Lanpei lu 攬轡錄
Lantian 藍田
Lanting 蘭亭
Lao Dan 老聃
laola 老辣
Laozi 老子
lei 誄
Leiju mingxian Yuefu qunyu 類聚名賢樂
　府群玉
leishu 類書
Leiyuan 類苑
Lengjia jing 楞伽經
lengleng qingqing 冷冷清清
Lengyan jing 楞嚴經
li (inherent pattern, principle) 理
li (ritual) 禮
Li Ao 李翱
Li Bai 李白
Li Baiyao 李百藥
Li Biao 李彪
Li Cang 李蒼
Li Chang 李長
Li Chaowei 李朝威
Li Cheng 李程
Li Chi zhuan 李赤傳
Li Chong 李充
Li Chunfu 李純甫
Li Daoyuan 酈道元
Li Delin 李德林
Li Deyu 李德裕

Li Dongyang 李東陽

Li Duan 李端

Li Er 李耳

Li Fang 李昉

Li furen 李夫人

Li Fuyan 李復言

Li Gang 李綱

Li Gao 李暠

Li Gonglin 李公麟

Li Guan 李觀

Li Han 李漢

Li He 李賀

Li Hua 李華

Li hun 禮魂

Li Jing 李經

Li Jing 李靖

Li Junmin 李俊民

Li Kaixian 李開先

Li Kangcheng 李康成

Li Linfu 李林甫

Li Ling 李陵

Li Mei 李玫

Li Mo 李謨

Li Qian 李騫

Li Qiao 李嶠

Li Qingzhao 李清照

Li Rihua 李日華

Li Sanniang 李三娘

Li sao 離騷

Li sao zhuan 離騷傳

Li Shan 李善

Li Shangjiao 李上交

Li Shangyin 李商隱

Li Shen 李紳

Li Shimin 李世民

Li Si 李斯

Li wa zhuan 李娃傳

Li Xie 李諧

Li Xun 李尋

Li Yannian 李延年

Li Yanshou 李延壽

Li Ye (Li Jilan) 李冶 (李季蘭)

Li Yi 李益

Li Yi'an ji 李易安集

Li You 李尤

Li Yu 李煜

Li Yuan 李淵

Li Zhao 李肇

Li Zhi 李治

Li Zhiyi 李之儀

lian (lotus) 蓮

lian (love) 憐

Lian Xixian 廉希憲

Lianchang gong ci 連昌宮詞

Liang du fu 兩都賦

Liang Ji 梁冀

Liang Na 梁妠

Liang Shang 梁商

Liang shu (Liang in the north) 涼書

Liang shu (Liang in the south) 梁書

Liang Song 梁竦

Liang Su 梁肅

Liangjie 良价

Liangli zhuan 良吏傳

Liangzhou 涼州

lianju 聯句

Lianyu duyin 連雨獨飲

Lianyungang 連雲港

Lidai fu 歷代賦

Lienü zhuan 列女傳

liezhuan 列傳

Liezi 列子

Liji 禮記

Lin Bu 林逋

Lin Jingxi 林景熙

Lin Sheng 林升

Lin'an gongzhu 臨安公主

Ling xian 靈憲

Lingbo qu 凌波曲

Linggui zhi 靈鬼志

Linghu Chu 令狐楚

linglüe gufa sheng xinqi 領略古法生新奇

lingshi 令史

Lingyan 靈巖

Linji school 臨濟宗

liqu 俚曲

liqu 理趣

Liu An 劉安

Liu Bang 劉邦

Liu Bei 劉備

Liu Bian 劉辯

Liu Biao 劉表

Liu Bing 劉昞

Liu Bingzhong/Kan 劉秉忠/侃

Liu Bozong 劉伯宗

Liu Cang 劉蒼

Liu Chang (1019–1068) 劉敞

Liu Chang (435–498) 劉敞

Liu Changqing 劉長卿

Liu Chenweng 劉辰翁

Liu Cong (Liu Biao's son) 劉琮

Liu Cong (Xiongnu ruler) 劉聰

Liu Dan 劉旦

liu de 六德

Liu De 劉德

Liu Fang 柳芳

Liu fu 柳賦

Liu Guan 柳貫

Liu Guo 劉過

Liu Hong 劉宏

Liu Ji (1311–1375) 劉基

Liu Ji (twelfth century) 劉汲

liu jia 六家

liu jing 六經

Liu Jingshu 劉敬叔

Liu Jun 劉駿

Liu Jun (Liu Xiaobiao) 劉峻 (劉孝標)

Liu Kai 柳開

Liu Kezhuang 劉克莊

Liu Kui 劉逵

Liu Kun 劉琨

Liu Ling 劉伶

Liu Lingxian 劉令嫻

Liu Mian 柳冕

Liu Pi 劉濞

Liu Qi 劉祁

Liu Shizhong 劉時中

Liu Shuo 劉鑠

Liu Su (fl. 742–755) 劉餗

Liu Su (fl. 806–820) 劉肅

Liu Taotu 劉駒駼

Liu Ti 劉逖

Liu Tui 劉蛻

Liu Wu (Han prince of Chu) 劉戊

Liu Wu (Han prince of Liang) 劉武

Liu Xiang 劉向

Liu Xiaochuo 劉孝綽

Liu Xie 劉勰

Liu Xijun 劉細君

Liu Xin 劉歆

Liu Xiu 劉秀

Liu Xizai 劉熙載

Liu Xu 劉昫

Liu Xun 劉塤

Liu Yan 劉偃

Liu Yao 劉杳

liu yi 六藝

Liu Yi zhuan 柳毅傳

Liu Yilong 劉義隆

Liu Yimin 劉遺民

Liu Yin 劉因/駰

Liu Ying 劉迎

Liu Yiqing (fifth century) 劉義慶

Liu Yiqing (thirteenth century) 劉一清

Liu Yong 柳永

Liu You 劉友

Liu Yu 劉裕

Liu Yuan 劉淵

Liu Yun 柳惲

Liu Yuxi 劉禹錫

Liu Zhen 劉楨

Liu Zheng 劉整

Liu Zhiji 劉知幾

Liu Zhilin 劉之遴

Liu Zhiyuan 劉知遠

Liu Zhiyuan zhugongdiao 劉知遠諸宮調

Liu Zongyuan 柳宗元

liubian 流便

liuli qingwan 流麗清婉

liulian guangjing 留連光景

Liushao qing 柳梢青

Liushi 柳氏

Liuyi shihua 六一詩話

Liuyu fu 流寓賦

lixue 理學

Liyuan anshi Yuefu xinsheng 梨園按式樂府新聲

Lizhi fu 荔支賦

Longcheng lu 龍城錄

longhu bang 龍虎榜

Longshan sanlao 龍山三老

Lu 魯

Lü An 呂安

Lu Bao 魯褒

Lü Benzhong 呂本中

Lü Buwei 呂不韋

Lu Cangyong 盧藏用

Lu Chen 盧諶

Lu Chui 陸倕

Lu Fayan 陸法言

Lu Gao 陸杲

Lü Gongzhu 呂公著

Lü Guang 呂光

Lü Huiqing 呂惠卿

Lu Ji 陸機

Lu Jia 陸賈

Lu Jiuyuan 陸九淵

Lu Jue 陸厥

Lu Kang 陸抗

Lu Lingguang dian fu 魯靈光殿賦

Lu Lun 盧綸

Lu shi 魯詩

Lu Sidao 盧思道

Lu song 魯頌

Lu Tong 盧仝

Lü Wen 呂溫

Lü Xizhe 呂希哲

Lü Xun 呂巽

Lu Xun 陸遜

Lü Yijian 呂夷簡

Lu You 陸游

Lu Yu 陸羽

Lu Yuanming 盧元明

Lu Yun 陸雲

Lu Zhan 陸展

Lu Zhao 盧肇

Lu Zhaolin 盧照鄰

Lu Zhi 盧摯

Lu Zhi 陸贄

Lu Zhonglian 魯仲連

Lu Zhuan 盧僎

Lu Ziyu 陸子遹

Lü Zuqian 呂祖謙

Luan jing baiyong 灤京百詠

Luan jing zayong 灤京雜詠

lüfu 律賦

Lugui bu 錄鬼簿

Lühou zhan Han Xin 呂后斬韓信

Lun du fu 論都賦

Lun heng 論衡

Lun wen 論文

Lun wenyi 論文意

Lunyu 論語

Luo Binwang 駱賓王

Luo gao 洛誥

Luo Han 羅含

Luo Yin 羅隱

Luoshen fu 洛神賦

Luoyang qielan ji 洛陽伽藍記

Lushan fu 廬山賦

Lushan ji 廬山記

Lushan shenxian shi 廬山神仙詩

Lusheng 盧生

lüshi 律詩

Lüshi chunqiu 呂氏春秋

Luyuan fu 鹿苑賦

Ma Fang 馬防

Ma Ge 麻革

Ma Qian du lei 馬汧都誄

Ma Rong 馬融

Ma Ruichen 馬瑞辰

Ma Run 馬潤

Ma Xu 馬續

Ma Yu 馬鈺

Ma Yuan 馬援

Ma Yuehenai/Johanan 馬月合乃

Ma Zhiyuan 馬致遠

Ma Zuchang 馬祖常

Mai can mudan 賣殘牡丹

Maihua sheng 賣花聲

Ma'nao le fu 瑪瑙勒賦

manci 慢詞

Mao 毛

Mao Heng 毛亨

Mao shi 毛詩

Mao shi zhengyi 毛詩正義

Mao shi zhuan 毛詩傳

Mao shi zhuan jian 毛詩傳箋

Mao xu 毛序

Mao Yanshou 毛延壽

Mawangdui 馬王堆

Mei Gao 枚皋

Mei Sheng 枚乘

Mei Yaochen 梅堯臣

Mei Ze 梅賾

meici fengjie 美刺諷戒

Meishan 眉山

Men you ju ma ke xing 門有車馬客行

meng 夢

Meng Chang 孟昶

Meng fu 夢賦

Meng Haoran 孟浩然

Meng Jia 孟嘉

Meng Jiang nü 孟姜女

Meng Jiao 孟郊

Meng Ke 孟軻

Meng Qi 孟棨

Meng Wuchang 夢武昌

Meng Yuanlao 孟元老

meng'an 猛安

Mengchuang 夢窗

Mengliang lu 夢粱錄

Mengxi bitan 夢溪筆談

Mengzi 孟子

Menxia sheng 門下省

Mi Fu 米芾

Mi Heng 禰衡

Miao Kai 繆愷

miao kong yan si yuan 渺空煙四遠

Miao Xi 繆襲

Miaode xiansheng zhuan 妙德先生傳

miaoguan yixiang 妙觀逸想

Min zhi fumu 民之父母

ming (charge) 命

ming (inscription) 銘

ming (name) 名

Mingdao (Cheng Hao) 明道 (程顥)

minggong 名公

Minghuang zalu 明皇雜錄

mingjia 名家

Mingxiang ji 冥祥記

Mo yu'er 摸魚兒

moben 末本

Möngke 蒙哥

Mongol 蒙古

mouke 謀克

Mozi 墨子

Mozuizi 磨嘴子

Mu men 墓門

Mu shi 牧誓

Mu tianzi zhuan 穆天子傳

Mu Xiu 穆修

mudan 牡丹

Muhu sha 木斛沙

Mulanhua man 木蘭花慢

Mulian jiumu 目蓮救母

Murong Chao 慕容超

Murong Chui 慕容垂

Murong Huang 慕容皝

Murong Jun 慕容儁

muzhi ming 墓誌銘

Nai Xian / Nasen 迺賢

Nan du fu 南都賦

Nan Qi shu 南齊書

Nan shi 南史

Nanbu xinshu 南部新書

Nanci xulu 南詞敘錄

Nanhua zhenjing 南華真經

Nanjiao fu 南郊賦

Nanjin jiwen 南燼紀聞

Nanlü 南呂

Nanshan shi 南山詩

Nantang jinshi 南唐近事

nanxi 南戲

Nanzhao 南詔

Nanzheng fu 南征賦

Nanzong 南宗

Nei pian 內篇

Nei you 內遊

Neiye 內業

Ni gu 擬古

Ni Ke cong yuanfang lai 擬客從遠方來

Ni Wei taizi Yezhong ji 擬魏太子鄴中集

Ni Xi zhongsan Yong song 擬嵇中散
〈詠松〉

Ni Yuan 倪遠

Ni Zan / Ting 倪瓚 / 斑

Nichang yuyi 霓裳羽衣

Niu Sengru 牛僧孺

nong jia 農家

nongli 穠麗

Ögödei 窩闊台

Ouyang Jiong 歐陽炯

Ouyang Shoudao 歐陽守道

Ouyang Xiu 歐陽修

Ouyang Xuan 歐陽玄

Ouyang Zhan 歐陽詹

paita 排闥

pan 盤
Pan Lang 潘閬
Pan Yue 潘岳
panwen 判文
Pei Bomao 裴伯茂
Pei Di 裴迪
Pei Qi 裴啟
Pei Songzhi 裴松之
Pei Xing 裴鉶
Pei Yin 裴駰
Pei Ziye 裴子野
Pengze 彭澤
Pi Rixiu 皮日休
pianfu 駢賦
Pin jia fu 貧家賦
ping 平
Pingcheng 平城
pingdan 平淡
pinghua 平話/評話
Pingshan tang 平山堂
pingwen 平文
pingyi 平易
pipa 琵琶
Pipa ji 琵琶記
Pipa xing 琵琶行
Pipa yin 琵琶吟
Po Qin 繁欽
qi (breath, vitality) 氣
qi (seven) 七
Qi (state) 齊
Qi ai 七哀
Qi fa 七發
Qi fu 祈父
Qi ji 七集
Qi lu 七錄
Qi shi 齊詩
Qi shu 齊書
Qi Xie ji 齊諧記
Qian Mingyi 錢明逸
Qian Qi 錢起
Qian Qianyi 錢謙益
Qian shen lun 錢神論
Qian Weiyan 錢惟演
Qian Zhongshu 錢鍾書
Qianfu lun 潛夫論
Qiang Zhongzi 將仲子

Qiangrong 羌戎
Qianguo furen 沔國夫人
Qianji 前集
Qianli ma 千里馬
Qiantang yishi 錢塘遺事
Qianxi shiyan 潛溪詩眼
Qiao Ji 喬吉
Qiao qingyi fu 誚青衣賦
Qiao Xiu 譙秀
Qieyun 切韻
Qiezhong ji 篋中集
Qiji 齊己
qijue 奇崛
qili qingxin 綺麗清新
Qilüe 七略
qin (zither) 琴
Qin fu 琴賦
Qin Guan 秦觀
Qin Hui 秦檜
Qin Jia 秦嘉
Qin shi 秦誓
Qin shihuang zhuan 秦始皇傳
Qinfu yin 秦婦吟
qing (clarity) 清
qing (feelings, passion) 情
qing (minister) 卿
qing (sunlit) 晴
Qing Bu 黥布
Qing miao 清廟
Qing shi 情詩
Qing yi fu 青衣賦
Qingban 青坂
Qingbi ge 清閟閣
Qingbo pian 輕薄篇
Qingguo song 慶國頌
qingkong 清空
Qingli 慶歷
qingli 清麗
Qinglou ji 青樓集
Qingming 清明
qingtan 清談
qingxing zhi zheng 情性之正
Qingyun ti 青雲梯
Qinzhong yin 秦中吟
qiqi cancan qiqi 淒淒慘慘戚戚
Qisong 契嵩

675

Qiu Chi 丘遲
Qiu Chuji 丘處機
Qiu Lingju 丘靈鞠
Qiu si 秋思
Qiu wan 秋晚
Qiu Wanqing 裘萬頃
Qiu Wei 邱為
Qiu xing bashou 秋興八首
Qiu xing fu 秋興賦
Qiuhu xing 秋胡行
Qiujian ji 秋澗集
Qiuran ke zhuan 虬髯客傳
Qiyang sanshou 岐陽三首
qu 趣
Qu Ping 屈平
Qu You 瞿佑
Qu Yuan 屈原
Quan jin biao 勸進表
Quan Jin wen 全晉文
Quan nong fu 勸農賦
Quan Song shi 全宋詩
Quan Song wen 全宋文
Quan Tang shi 全唐詩
Quan Tang wen 全唐文
Quan Zuwang 全祖望
Quanxiang Qin bing liuguo pinghua 全相秦並六國平話
Quanxiang xu Qian Hanshu pinghua 全相續前漢書平話
Quanxiang Yue Yi tu Qi qiguo chunqiu pinghua houji 全相樂毅圖齊七國春秋平話
Quanzhen (Daoist sect) 全真
qusheng 去聲
Ranran gusheng zhu 冉冉孤生竹
Rao Jie 饒介
ren (human being) 人
ren (humane) 仁
Ren Fang 任昉
ren ge you xin ze ren ge you shi 人各有心則人各有詩
ren yu 人欲
Renchen shi'er yue jujia dongshou hou jishi wu shou 壬辰十二月車駕東狩後即事五首
Renchen zabian 壬辰雜編

Renshi zhuan 任氏傳
renwu 人物
rijiguan 日記官
ru 儒
Ru Huazi gang shi Mayuan disan gu 入華子岡是麻源第三谷
Ru Pengli hu kou 入彭蠡湖口
Ru Shu ji 入蜀記
Ruan Ji 阮籍
Ruan Xian 阮咸
Ruan Xiaoxu 阮孝緒
Ruan Yu 阮瑀
Rui Tingzhang 芮挺章
Rui zhegu 瑞鷓鴣
rushen 入神
rusheng 入聲
Ruyin 汝陰
Sadula 薩都剌
saiwai 塞外
San jia shi 三家詩
Sanbie 三別
Sandu fu 三都賦
Sanfen shilüe 三分事略
Sanfu yan 三婦艷
sangluan shi 喪亂詩
Sanguo yanyi 三國演義
Sanguo zhi 三國志
Sanjiao zhuying 三教珠英
Sanli 三吏
sanqu 散曲
sao 騷
Sao ti 騷體
semu 色目
Seng You 僧祐
Sengzhao 僧肇
seqing 色情
Shagou ji 殺狗記
shamo xiao ci sanque 沙漠小詞三闋
shan 禪
Shan Daokai 單道開
Shan ju 山居
Shan Tao 山濤
Shan wen 善文
shanben 善本
Shang Gao jiansi 上高監司
Shang Heng 尚衡

Shang shu 商書

Shang song 商頌

Shang Ting 商挺

Shang Yang 商鞅

shangchang shi 上場詩

Shangguan ti 上官體

Shangguan Wan'er 上官婉兒

Shangguan Yi 上官儀

Shangjun shu 商君書

Shanglin fu 上林賦

shangsheng 上聲

Shangshu 尚書

Shangshu zhengyi 尚書正義

Shanhai jing 山海經

Shanju fu 山居賦

Shanpo yang 山坡羊

shanshui 山水

Shao gao 召誥

Shao nan 召南

Shao Yong 邵雍

Shaonian xing 少年行

shaoyao 芍藥

Shaoyuan 紹元

Sheli fo 舍利佛

shelun 設論

Shen Gua 沈括

Shen Jiji 沈既濟

Shen Jiong 沈炯

Shen Pei 申培

Shen Quanqi 沈佺期

Shen Shushi 沈述師

Shen Yue 沈約

Sheng Hongzhi 盛弘之

Sheng min 生民

Sheng Ruzi 盛如梓

Sheng wu ai le lun 聲無哀樂論

sheng zhazi 生查子

Shenghua ji 聲畫集

Shengsheng man 聲聲慢

Shenhui 神會

Shennü fu 神女賦

Shenwu fu 神烏賦

Shenxian zhuan 神仙傳

Shenxiu 神秀

shenzhi beiliang 深摯悲涼

shi (gentry) 士

shi (oath) 誓

shi (poetry, poems) 詩

shi (scribe) 史

shi (show) 示

shi ben qingxing 詩本情性

Shi bu yu fu 士不遇賦

Shi Chong 石崇

Shi Dazu 史達祖

shi fu 詩賦

Shi fu zan 詩賦讚

Shi Hu 石虎

Shi ji 詩集

Shi ji chao 詩集鈔

Shi ji zhuan 詩集傳

Shi Jie 石介

Shi Jingyin 史敬胤

Shi Le 石勒

Shi ping 詩評

Shi shu 碩鼠

Shi shuo 師說

Shi suinao 詩髓腦

Shi Yannian 石延年

Shi yi lun 釋疑論

Shi You 史游

Shi Zhou 史周

shibu 詩部

Shide 拾得

shihua 詩話

Shiji 史記

Shiji wen 釋疾文

shijia 世家

Shijiamouni 釋迦牟尼

Shijing 詩經

Shipin 詩品

shiqi shi 十七勢

Shiqu ge 石渠閣

shiren 士人

Shiren zhuke tu 詩人主客圖

shisan jing 十三經

Shisan zhou zhi 十三州志

shishe 詩社

shishi 詩史

Shishi 詩式

Shishi shan 石室山

Shishuo 世說

Shishuo xinyu 世說新語

677

Shitong 史通

shiwen 時文

shiyan 詩眼

shiyi 十翼

shiyi 拾遺

Shiyi ji 拾遺記

Shiying 詩英

shiyu 詩餘

shiyue 詩曰

shizhuang cimei 詩莊詞媚

shizi 實字

shouchu zisheng 熟處自生

Shouyang shan fu 首陽山賦

shouying 瘦硬

Shu (document, monograph) 書

Shu cuan 書窜

shu er bu zuo 述而不作

Shu huai 述懷

Shu pin 書品

Shu pu 書譜

Shu Qi 叔齊

Shu Xi 束皙

Shu xing fu 述行賦

Shu Yuexiang 舒嶽祥

Shuangdiao 雙調

Shuanggudui 雙古堆

shuhui 書會

shui 說

Shui lin 說林

Shui nan 說難

Shui yuan 說苑

Shuihu zhuan 水滸傳

Shuijing zhu 水經注

shujian 書簡

Shujing 書經

Shuli 黍離

shumishi 樞秘使

Shun 舜

Shun ge Nanfeng fu 舜歌南風賦

Shun shui 順說

shuohuaren 說話人

Shuowen jiezi 說文解字

shuqi 書契

shushu 數書

Shusun Tong 叔孫通

shutang 書堂

shuwen 疏文

Shuyi ji 述異記

Shuying 疏影

Shuyu ci 漱玉詞

shuyuan 書院

Shuzhai laoxue congtan 庶齋老學叢談

Shuzhi fu 述志賦

si (longing) 思

si (lotus filaments) 絲

Si xuan fu 思玄賦

Sibu yaolüe 四部要略

Sikong Shu 司空曙

Sikong Tu 司空圖

Siku quanshu 四庫全書

Sima Guang 司馬光

Sima Jizhu 司馬季主

Sima Pu 司馬樸

Sima Qian 司馬遷

Sima Rangju 司馬穰苴

Sima Rui 司馬叡

Sima Tan 司馬談

Sima Xi 司馬晞

Sima Xiangru 司馬相如

Sima Yan 司馬炎

Sima Yi 司馬懿

Sima Zhen 司馬貞

Sima Zhong 司馬衷

siming 司命

sishe nongde huo 死蛇弄得活

sisheng 四聲

Sisheng zan 四聲贊

Sishi lexing 四時樂興

song 頌

Song Gai 宋該

Song Hong 宋弘

Song jinshi Liu Wen, Wenting fu Linjiang
    lushi 送進士劉聞文廷赴臨江錄事

Song Lian 宋濂

Song lüe 宋略

Song Minqiu 宋敏求

Song shu 宋書

Song Wu 宋無

Song Xian 宋纖

Song Ying shi 送應氏

Song Yu 宋玉

Song Yuan xue'an 宋元學案

song yue 頌曰

Song Zhiwen 宋之問

Songshi xuanzhu 宋詩選註

songxu 送序

Soushen ji 搜神記

Su Chuo 蘇綽

su fu 俗賦

Su Guo 蘇過

Su Hongdao 蘇弘道

Su Hui 蘇蕙

Su Jun 蘇峻

Su Qin 蘇秦

Su Shi 蘇軾

Su Shunqin 蘇舜欽

Su Tianjue 蘇天爵

Su Wu 蘇武

Su Xiaoxiao 蘇小小

Su Xiaoxiao mu 蘇小小墓

Su Xun 蘇洵

Su Zhe 蘇轍

Sui chu fu 遂初賦

Sui Guoting 孫過庭

Sui Hong 眭弘

Sui Jingchen 睢景臣

Sui Meng 眭孟

Sui shu 隋書

Sui Tang jiahua 隋唐嘉話

suibi 隨筆

Suihantang shihua 歲寒堂詩話

sujian liqu 俗間俚曲

Sun Bin 孫臏

Sun Chuo 孫綽

Sun Deng 孫登

Sun En 孫恩

Sun Guangxian 孫光憲

Sun Guoting 孫過庭

Sun Qi 孫棨

Sun Qiao 孫樵

Sun Qiong 孫瓊

Sun Quan 孫權

Sun Sheng 孫盛

Sun Wanshou 孫萬壽

Sun Zheng 孫拯

Sun Zhongkai 孫仲開

Sunzi 孫子

Suonan 所南

Suoyin 索隱

Sushuo 俗說

suwang 素王

suyao 俗謠

taichu 太初

taige ti 臺閣體

Taihe zhengyin pu 太和正音譜

Taihua dian fu 太華殿賦

Taiping gongzhu 太平公主

Taiping guangji 太平廣記

Taiping yulan 太平御覽

Taishan yin 泰山吟

Taishi 太誓

Taiwei Yu Liang bei 太尉庾亮碑

Taixue 太學

Taiyi 太一

Taiyi sheng shui 太一生水

Tan Daoluan 檀道鸞

Tan fu 談賦

Tan qin fu 彈琴賦

Tan shi fu 歎逝賦

Tan Sitong 譚嗣同

Tang baijia shixuan 唐百家詩選

Tang guoshi bu 唐國史補

Tang Huixiu 湯惠休

Tang Jue 唐玨

Tang shu 唐书

Tang zhiyan 唐摭言

Tangshi Songci 唐詩宋詞

Tanjing 壇經

Tao Hongjing 陶弘景

Tao Jingyuan 陶敬遠

Tao Kan 陶侃

Tao Qian 陶潛

Tao yao 桃夭

Tao Yuanming (Tao Qian) 陶淵明 (陶潛)

Tao Zongyi 陶宗儀

Taohuayuan ji 桃花源記

Taoran shiji xu 陶然詩集序

taotie 饕餮

taoxie 陶寫

Temüjin 鐵木真

Teng Maoshi 滕茂實

Tengwang ge xu 滕王閣序

ti 體

Ti jingcheng nan zhuang 題京城南莊

tian [zhi] xiang 天（之）祥
tian li 天理
Tian lun 天論
Tian shi dao 天師道
Tian shuo 天說
Tian tui 恬退
Tian wen 天問
Tian Xi 田錫
Tianbao yishi zhugongdiao 天寶遺事諸
  宮調
Tiandi Yin Yang jiaohuan dale fu 天地陰陽
  交歡大樂賦
tianguan 天官
tianming 天命
Tiantai 天台
tianyi 天意
tianyuan shi 田園詩
tianzi 天子
Tianzi youlie fu 天子遊獵賦
Tiao Zhang Ji 調張籍
tihua shi 題畫詩
Ting gao 庭誥
Ting mingchan 聽鳴蟬
Tiying 緹縈
Tongguan huaigu 潼關懷古
Tongwan cheng ming 統萬城銘
Tsui Hu 崔護
tuiqiao 推敲
tuntian 屯田
Tuoba 拓拔
Tuoba Tao 拓拔焘
Wai pian 外篇
Wai qi zhen 外戚箴
waizhuan 外傳
wajie 瓦解
wan ge 挽歌
wang 望
Wang Anshi 王安石
Wang Bao 王褒
Wang Bi 王弼
Wang Biaozhi 王彪之
Wang Bo (fourth century) 王波
Wang Bo (seventh century) 王勃
Wang Can 王粲
Wang Changling 王昌齡
Wang Chong 王充

Wang Chuo 王綽
Wang Dao 王導
Wang Dechen 王得臣
Wang Dingbao 王定保
Wang Fanzhi 王梵志
Wang Feibo 王飛伯
Wang Fu 王符
Wang Fuzhi 王夫之
Wang Guobao 王國寶
Wang haichao 望海潮
Wang Hong 王弘
Wang Ji (fourth century) 王濟
Wang Ji (seventh century) 王績
Wang Ji (twelfth century) 王寂
Wang Jia 王嘉
Wang Jian (fifth century) 王儉
Wang Jian (Tang) 王建
Wang Lang 王朗
Wang Ling bianwen 王陵變文
Wang Mang 王莽
Wang Méng (309–347) 王濛
Wang Měng (325–375) 王猛
Wang Mian 王冕
Wang ming lun 王命論
Wang Pan 王磐
Wang Qi 王起
Wang Qiu 王球
Wang Renyu 王仁裕
Wang Rong (fifth century) 王融
Wang Rong (third century) 王戎
Wang Ruoxu 王若虛
Wang Sengru 王僧孺
Wang Shipeng 王十朋
Wang Shiyuan 王士源
Wang Shizhen 王世貞
Wang Shuwen 王叔文
Wang Su 王素
Wang Wan 王灣
Wang Wei 王維
Wang Xianzhi 王獻之
Wang Xin 王昕
Wang Xizhi 王羲之
Wang Xuance 王玄策
Wang Xun 王珣
Wang Yan 王琰
Wang Yanshou 王延壽

Wang Ye 王埜

Wang Yi (eleventh century) 王益

Wang Yi (first–second centuries) 王逸

Wang Yi (third–fourth centuries) 王廙

Wang Yin 王隱

Wang Yisun 王沂孫

Wang Yuanliang 汪元量

Wang Yucheng 王禹偁

Wang Yun (sixth century) 王筠

Wang Yun (thirteenth century) 王惲

Wang Zao 汪藻

Wang Zhaojun 王昭君

Wang Zhe 王喆

Wang Zhihuan 王之渙

Wangchuan ji 輞川集

Wangsun fu 王孫賦

wangzi 王子

Wangzi Qiao 王子喬

Wanliu tang 萬柳堂

wanqiao 婉峭

Wanyan Liang 完顏亮

Wanyan Tao 完顏璹

wanyue 婉約

washe 瓦舍

washi 瓦市

wasi 瓦肆

wazi 瓦子

Wei (major state, Intrigues) 魏

Wei (minor state, Intrigues) 衛

Wei Ao 隗囂

Wei Hong 衛宏

Wei Hu 韋縠

Wei Jia Mi zuo zeng Lu Ji 為賈謐作贈陸機

Wei Jin shiyu 魏晉世語

Wei Meng 韋孟

Wei Shou 魏收

Wei shu 魏書

Wei Sou 韋謏

Wei Su 危素

Wei Xuancheng 韋玄成

Wei Ye 魏野

Wei Yin 韋釿

Wei Yingwu 韋應物

Wei Zhao 韋昭

Wei Zheng 魏徵

Wei zhi fu 慰志賦

Wei Zhuang 韋莊

Weimojie jing 維摩詰經

Weiqi pin 圍棋品

Weishao wang 衛紹王

weisheng 尾聲

Weitan 猥談

weiyan 微言

weiyi 威儀

wen 文

Wen fu 文賦

Wen Jiweng 文及翁

Wen Qiao 溫嶠

Wen quan fu 溫泉賦

Wen Tianxiang 文天祥

Wen Tingyun 溫庭筠

Wen wang 文王

Wen wang you sheng 文王有聲

Wen Yanbo 文彥博

Wen Yiduo 聞一多

Wen Zisheng 溫子昇

wenchen 文臣

wenfu (prose fu) 文賦

Weng Fanggang 翁方綱

Weng Juan 翁卷

Wenguan cilin 文館詞林

Wenhui 文惠

wenji 文集

Wenjing mifulun 文鏡秘府論

Wenlin guan 文林館

wenren hua 文人畫

wenren wuxing...zhiji 文人無行…之極

wenshi 文士

Wensou/Pizi wensou 文藪/皮子文藪

Wenxi 聞喜

Wenxin diaolong 文心雕龍

Wenxuan 文選

Wenxue guan 文學館

Wenyuan yinghua 文苑英華

wenzhang 文章

Wenzhang liubie ben 文章流別本

Wenzhang liubie ji 文章流別集

wenzi chan 文字禪

wobei 我輩

Wu (state) 吳

Wu Daozi 吳道子

Wu fu 舞賦

Wu Han 吳漢

Wu Ji 吳激

Wu Jie 吳玠

Wu Jing 吳兢

Wu Jun 吳均

Wu Lin 吳璘

Wu Maiyuan 吳邁遠

Wu Pingyi 武平一

Wu Shidao 吳師道

Wu Siqi 吳思齊

Wu Wei 吳渭

Wu Wenying 吳文英

Wu xia 巫峽

Wu xing zhi 五行志

Wu Xinlei 吳新雷

wu yizi wu laichu 無一字無來處

Wu Yue chunqiu 吳越春秋

Wu Yun 吳筠

Wu Zetian (Wu Zhao) 武則天(武曌)

Wu Zhaoyi 毋昭裔

Wu Zimu 吳自牧

Wu Zixu 伍子胥

Wubei 五悲

Wuben 無本

Wucheng fu 蕪城賦

Wuchuan lu 吳船錄

Wudaishi pinghua 五代史平話

Wudu fu 吳都賦

Wuguo gushi 五國故事

wujing 五經

Wujing zhengyi 五經正義

Wulin jiushi 武林舊事

Wuliu xiansheng zhuan 五柳先生傳

Wuqimai 吳乞買

Wushan gao 巫山高

Wusheng ge 吳聲歌

Wuti 無題

wuwei 無為

wuxing 五行

Wuyi xiang 烏衣巷

Wuzhong 無終

wuzhu (has no master) 無主

wuzhu (has no supports) 無柱

xi (military proclamation) 檄

xi (particle) 兮

Xi ji fu 喜霽賦

Xi Kang 嵇康

Xi Xi 嵇喜

Xi Xia 西夏

Xi you lu 西遊錄

Xi zheng fu 西征賦

Xi Zuochi 習鑿齒

Xia shi fu 狹室賦

Xia Tingzhi 夏庭芝

xiachang shi 下場詩

Xiahou Bi 夏侯弼

Xiahou changshi lei 夏侯常侍誄

Xiahou Sheng 夏侯勝

Xiahou Zhan 夏侯湛

xian 險

Xian zhi fu 顯志賦

Xian zhi shi 見志詩

Xianbei 鮮卑

xiang (appearance) 相

xiang (image) 像

Xiang furen 湘夫人

Xiang jun 湘君

Xiang Liang 項梁

Xiang Tuo 項托

Xiang Xiu 向秀

Xiang Yu 項羽

Xiangdong wang 湘東王

Xiangfeng xing 相逢行

Xianglian ji 香奩集

Xiangmo bianwen 降魔變文

Xiangyang qijiu ji 襄陽耆舊記

Xiangzhong fu 湘中賦

Xianju fu 閑居賦

Xianlü 仙呂

Xianqiu Meng 咸丘蒙

Xianzong song 顯宗頌

Xiao Baojuan 蕭寶卷

Xiao Ben 蕭賁

Xiao Chen 蕭琛

Xiao chu Shuncheng men you huai Taixu
　　曉出順承門有懷太虛

Xiao Daocheng 蕭道成

Xiao Gang 蕭綱

Xiao gu 效古

Xiao gu shi 效古詩

Xiao He 蕭何

Xiao Luan 蕭鸞

Xiao Qi 蕭綺
Xiao Que 蕭愨
Xiao Suntu 小孫屠
Xiao Tong 蕭統
Xiao Wangzhi 蕭望之
Xiao Yan 蕭衍
Xiao Yingshi 蕭穎士
Xiao youxian shi 小遊仙詩
Xiao Ze 蕭賾
xiao zhuan 小傳
Xiao Ziliang 蕭子良
Xiao Zixian 蕭子顯
Xiao Zong 蕭綜
xiaoci 小詞
Xiaojing 孝經
xiaoling 小令
xiaopin wen 小品文
xiaoshuo 小說
xiaoshuojia 小說家
Xiaosi fu 孝思賦
xiaoxu 小序
xiaoxue 小學
Xiaoya 小雅
Xici zhuan 繫辭傳
Xie Ai 謝艾
Xie An 謝安
Xie Ao 謝翱
Xie Bingde 謝枋得
Xie Chaozong 謝朝宗
Xie Daoyun 謝道蘊
Xie Fei 謝朏
Xie Fu 謝敷
Xie Hui 謝晦
Xie Huilian 謝惠連
Xie Hun 謝混
Xie hun fu 協婚賦
Xie Jiang 謝降
Xie Liangzuo 謝良佐
Xie Lingyun 謝靈運
Xie Shang 謝尚
Xie Shen 謝沈
Xie Tiao 謝朓
Xie Xuan 謝玄
Xie Zhuang 謝莊
Xielu xing 薤露行
Xihe 羲和

Xihu laoren fansheng lu 西湖老人繁盛錄
Xihu zhuzhi ji 西湖竹枝集
Xijing zaji 西京雜記
Xikun chouchang ji 西崑酬唱集
Xikun ti 西崑體
xin (new) 新
Xin lun 新論
Xin Qiji 辛棄疾
Xin Yuefu 新樂府
xinbian 新編
xinfa 新法
xing (one's nature) 性
xing (poetic inspiration) 興
xing er shang (above form) 形而上
Xing Jingkou zhi Zhuli 行京口至竹里
xing qing 性情
Xing Shao 邢劭
xingbude ye gege 行不得也哥哥
Xingci xijiao zuo yibaiyun 行次西郊作一
    百韻
Xinglu nan 行路難
xingsi 形似
xinkan 新刊
Xinkan leibian Sanchang wenxuan 新刊類
    編三場文選
Xinkan quanxiang pinghua Wuwang fa
    Zhou shu 新刊全相平話武王伐紂書
Xinshi 心史
Xinshu 新書
Xinxu 新序
xinxue 新學
Xinyu 新語
Xiongnu 匈奴
Xiqu ge 西曲歌
Xiuwendian yulan 修文殿御覽
Xiuzhu pian 修竹篇
Xiuzhu tan ganjiao wen 修竹彈甘蕉文
Xiwangmu 西王母
xiwen 戲文
xiwen huiyin 戲文誨淫
Xixiang ji zhugongdiao 西廂記諸宮調
Xiyou ji 西遊記
Xu Chi 徐摛
Xu chou fu 敘愁賦
Xu Gan 徐幹
Xu Guāng (299?–333) 徐光

Xu Guǎng (352–425) 徐廣
Xu Heng 許衡
Xu Huang 徐璜
Xu Hun 許渾
Xu Ji 徐璣
Xu Jian 徐堅
Xu Jin Yangqiu 續晉陽秋
Xu Jingye 徐敬業
Xu Jingzong 許敬宗
Xu Ling 徐陵
Xu Mian 徐勉
Xu Miao 徐邈
Xu Qi Xie ji 續齊諧記
Xu Shanxin 許善心
Xu Shen 許慎
Xu Shu 徐淑
Xu Soushen ji (Soushen houji) 續搜神記 (搜神後記)
Xu Wei 徐渭
Xu Wudang 徐無黨
Xu Xian 續咸
Xu Xiaoniang ge 續小娘歌
Xu Xuan 徐鉉
Xu Xuanguai lu 續玄怪錄
Xu Xun 許詢
Xu Yi Jian zhi 續夷堅志
Xu Youren 許有壬
Xu Zhao 徐照
xuan 玄
Xuan xue 選學
xuanfushi 宣撫使
Xuangang 玄綱
Xuanguai lu 玄怪錄
Xuanhe yishi 宣和遺事
xuanlan 玄覽
Xuanlan fu 玄覽賦
xuanmen 玄門
Xuanxi song 玄墨頌
xuanxue 玄學
xuanyan 玄言
Xuanyan ji 宣驗記
xuanyan shi 玄言詩
Xuanzang 玄奘
Xuchang chouchang ji 許昌唱和集
xuci 虛詞
Xue Angfu 薛昂夫

Xue Daoheng 薛道衡
Xue fu 雪賦
Xue Rengui zheng Liao shilüe 薛仁貴征遼事略
Xue Ruan Bubing ti 學阮步兵體
Xue Ruizhao 薛瑞兆
Xue Shishi 薛師石
Xue Tao 薛濤
Xun Kuang 荀況
Xun Qing 荀卿
xunxun mimi 尋尋覓覓
Xunzi 荀子
Xuxue 敘學
xuzi 虛字
Ya Hu / Yakut 雅琥 / 古
Yan (state) 燕
Yan Du 延篤
Yan gexing 燕歌行
Yan Guang 嚴光
Yan Guangda 嚴光大
Yan Jidao 晏幾道
Yan Kejun 嚴可均
Yan Ruoqu 閻若璩
Yan Shu 晏殊
Yan Yanzhi 顏延之
Yan Ying 晏嬰
Yan Yu 嚴羽
Yan Zhenqing 顏真卿
Yan Zhitui 顏之推
Yang Bing 楊秉
Yang Chengzhai ti 楊誠齋體
Yang Fang 楊方
Yang Gu 陽固
Yang Guang 楊廣
Yang Guo 楊果
Yang Guozhong 楊國忠
Yang Hongdao 楊弘道
Yang Huan 楊奐
Yang Jian 楊堅
Yang Jingshu 楊敬述
Yang Jingzhou lei 楊荊州誄
Yang Jiong 楊炯
Yang Junzhi 陽俊之
Yang Liang 楊倞
Yang Man 羊曼
Yang Ni 陽尼

Yang Peng 楊鵬

Yang sheng lun 養生論

Yang Shidao 楊師道

Yang Shuneng Xiaoheng ji xu 楊叔能小
  亨集序

Yang shuo 養說

Yang Taizhen waizhuan 楊太真外傳

Yang Wanli 楊萬里

Yang Weizhen 楊維貞 / 楨

Yang Wengong tanyuan 楊文公談苑

Yang Xi 楊羲

Yang Xiong 揚雄

Yang Xiuzhi 陽休之

Yang Xuanzhi 楊衒之

Yang Yi 楊億

Yang Yuhuan 楊玉環

Yang Yunfu 楊允孚

Yang Zai 楊載

Yang Zhao 楊肇

Yang Zhaoying 楊朝英

Yang Zhongde 楊仲德

Yang Zhu 楊朱

Yangdu fu 揚都賦

Yangguan sandie 陽關三疊

Yanglianzhenjia 楊璉真伽

Yangliu ge 楊柳歌

yangping 陽平

Yangwu banlü 陽五伴侶

Yangzhou man 揚州慢

Yannan Zhi'an 燕南芝菴

Yanshi jiaxun 顏氏家訓

Yanyou jiayin ke Jiangxi xiangshi shigu fu
  延祐甲寅科江西鄉試石鼓賦

yanyue 燕樂

Yanzi chunqiu 晏子春秋

Yanzi fu 燕子賦

Yao 堯

Yao dian 堯典

Yao He 姚合

Yao Hong 姚宏

Yao que fu 鷾雀賦

Yao Xiaoxi 姚孝錫

Yao Xing 姚興

Yaochi 瑤池

yaoci 爻辭

yaojiao 窈糾

yaotiao 窈窕

yaoyan miaodao 要言妙道

yarun 雅潤

yayan 雅言

yazuowen 押座文

Ye Jingneng 葉淨能

Ye Mengde 葉夢得

Ye Shi 葉適

Ye ting daoyi 夜聽擣衣

Ye ting ji 夜聽妓

Ye Ziqi 葉子奇

ye'er 葉兒

Yelü Chucai 耶律楚才

yeshi 野史

Yewang danfeiyan 夜望單飛雁

yeyu duichuang 夜雨對牀

yi (arts) 藝

yi (different) 異

yi (intention) 意

yi (normative significance) 義

yi (rightness) 義

Yi gu 依古

yi gu wei xin 以古為新

Yi li 儀禮

Yi shi 逸史

yi shi wei ci 以詩為詞

yi su wei ya 以俗為雅

yi wen wei ci 以文為詞

yi wen wei shi 以文為詩

Yi'an ci 易安詞

yidai cizong 一代詞宗

Yijing (Classic of Changes) 易經

Yijing (seventh century) 義淨

Yiling 夷陵

yimin shi 遺民詩

Yin Chun 殷淳

Yin Fan 殷璠

Yin hushang chuqing houyu 飲湖上初晴
  後雨

Yin Jun 殷鈞

Yin Keng 陰鏗

Yin You 殷祐

Yin Yun 殷芸

Yin Zhongwen 殷仲文

Yin Zhu 尹洙

Yinchuang zalu 吟窗雜錄

Ying Qu 應璩

Ying Yang 應瑒

Yingkui lüsui 瀛奎律髓

Yingti xu 鶯啼序

Yingwu fu 鸚鵡賦

Yingying zhuan 鶯鶯傳

Yinjiu 飲酒

Yinjiu diwu 飲酒第五

yinping 陰平

yinyang 陰陽

yinyang jia 陰陽家

Yinyi zhuan 隱逸傳

yinyuan 因緣

yishi 一時

Yiwen leiju 藝文類聚

Yiwen zhi 藝文志

Yiweng 憶翁

Yixi 義熙

Yixuan 義玄

Yiyuan 異苑

Yizhi hua 一枝花

Yizhou yiyou jiasheng 宜州乙酉家乘

yizu sanzong 一祖三宗

Yizuo 憶昨

Yong chansi daoren 咏禪思道人

Yong shi 詠史

Yong yu le 永遇樂

yonghua shi 詠畫詩

Yonghuai 詠懷

Yonghuai shi 詠懷詩

Yongjia siling 永嘉四靈

Yongming 永明

yongshi shi 詠史詩

yongwu ci 詠物詞

yongwu shi 詠物詩

Yongzhou baji 永州八記

You Baling kongsi 遊巴陵空寺

you biyu shijiao 有裨於世教

you chengxiang 右丞相

You Chongzhen Guan nanlou du xin jidi timing chu 遊崇真觀南樓睹新及第題名處

You Dongtian 遊東田

You Gaoshi yuan ji 遊高氏園記

You Nanting 遊南亭

You Shimen shi xu 遊石門詩序

You Tiantai shan fu 遊天台山賦

You tong fu 幽通賦

You Ya 游雅

youji 遊記

Youlizi 郁离子

Youming lu 幽明錄

youshui 遊說

Youwen 右文

youxian 遊仙

Youxian ku 遊仙窟

Youxuan ji 又玄集

Youyang zazu 酉陽雜俎

Youzhou gujin renwu zhi 幽州古今人物志

Yu (culture hero) 禹

yu (illustration) 諭

Yu Chan 庾闡

Yu fu 漁夫

Yu gong 禹功

Yu Ji 虞集

Yu Jianwu 庾肩吾

Yu Liang 庾亮

Yu lin 語林

Yu Que 余闕

Yu Shinan 虞世南

yu xiao zi 予小子

Yu Xin 庾信

Yu Xuanji 魚玄機

Yu Yu 虞預

Yu Yunwen 虞允文

Yuan Bao 袁豹

Yuan Can 袁粲

Yuan dake sanchang wenxuan 元大科三場文選

Yuan Dao 原道

Yuan Dashe 袁大捨

Yuan Dexiu 元德秀

Yuan Haowen 元好問

Yuan Hong 袁宏

Yuan Jie 元結

Yuan Jing 元兢

Yuan Jue 袁桷

yuan qi 元氣

Yuan ren lun 原人論

Yuan Shansong 袁山松

Yuan Shao 袁紹

Yuan Shu 袁淑

Yuan Wuyou 元無有

Yuan Xionggong 元行恭

Yuan Yi 袁易

Yuan you 遠遊

Yuan Zhen 元稹

Yuangu lu 原古錄

Yuanhun zhi 冤魂志

Yuanjue jing 圓覺經

Yuankan zaju sanshi zhong 元刊雜劇三
　十種

Yuanlian 元璉

Yuanren 圓仁

Yuanshang 元尚

Yuanshi si da jia 元詩四大家

Yuanshi xuan 元詩選

Yuanshu Jiangnan ji jingyi qinyou 遠戍江
　南寄京邑親友

Yuantong yihai Huguang xiangshi
　Jingshan pu fu 元統乙亥湖廣鄉試荊山
　璞賦

yuantu ling 源土令

Yuanyou 元祐

Yuanzi 元子

Yue chu 月出

Yue Fei 岳飛

Yue fu 月賦

Yue jue shu 越絕書

Yue Shi 樂史

yuefu 樂府

Yuefu buti 樂府補題

Yuefu shiji 樂府詩集

Yuefu xinbian Yangchun baixue 樂府新編
　陽春白雪

Yueji 樂記

yueling 月令

Yuequan yinshe 月泉吟社

Yuetai huaigu 越／粵臺懷古

Yulan shi 御覽詩

yulu 語錄

yun 韻

Yunxi youyi 雲溪友議

Yunyao ji 雲謠集

Yushan caotang 玉山草堂

Yushan jiachu 玉山佳處

Yutai houji 玉臺後集

Yutai xinyong 玉臺新詠

Yuwen Tai 宇文泰

Yuwen Xuzhong 宇文虛中

Yuwen You 宇文逌

Yuwen Zhao 宇文招

za ji 雜記

Za shi 雜詩

Za ti 雜體

Za yu 雜語

Za zhongxian shiyi fu 雜忠賢失意賦

Zaiqiong ji 在窮記

zajia 雜家

zaju 雜劇

zan 贊

Zanning 贊寧

zaohua 造化

ze 仄

Zeng Baima wang Biao shi 贈白馬王彪詩

Zeng Gong 曾鞏

Zeng Ji 曾幾

Zeng Minxing 曾敏行

Zeng xiucai ru jun 贈秀才入軍

zengda shi 贈答詩

Zhan Fangsheng 湛方生

Zhang Chao 張超

Zhang Daoling 張道陵

Zhang Fangping 張方平

Zhang Heng 張衡

Zhang Hong 張紘

Zhang Hua 張華

Zhang Huan 張奐

Zhang Ji 張籍

Zhang Jiàn 張建

Zhang Jiǎn 張簡

Zhang Jie 張戒

Zhang Jing 張景

Zhang Jiuling 張九齡

Zhang Jun (1097–1164) 張浚

Zhang Jun (307–346) 張駿

Zhang Jun (late third, early fourth
　centuries) 張浚

Zhang Kejiu 張可久

Zhang Lei 張耒

Zhang Rong 張融

Zhang Shi 張栻

Zhang Shicheng 張士誠

Zhang Shoujie 張守節

Zhang Shuai 張率

Zhang Tan 張譚

Zhang Tingfang 張庭芳

Zhang Wang 張望

Zhang Wei 張為

Zhang Wenqian 張文潛

Zhang Xian 張先

Zhang Xiaoxiang 張孝祥

Zhang Xie 張協

Zhang Xie zhuangyuan 張協狀元

Zhang Yan (1248–1320?) 張炎

Zhang Yan (fifth century) 張演

Zhang Yan (third century) 張晏

Zhang Yanghao 張養浩

Zhang Yi 張彝

Zhang Yu / Zezhi / Sizhen 張雨 / 澤之 / 嗣真

Zhang Yuangan 張元幹

Zhang Yue 張說

Zhang Zai 張載

Zhang Zhan 張湛

Zhang Zhengjian 張正見

Zhang Zhongsu 張仲素

Zhang Zhuo 張篤

Zhang Zirong 張子容

Zhang Zuan 張纘

zhangju 章句

Zhangsun Wuji 長孫無忌

zhanguo 戰國

Zhanguo ce 戰國策

Zhao (state) 趙

Zhao Bingwen 趙秉文

Zhao Gou 趙構

Zhao Hongfu 趙閎夫

Zhao hun 招魂

Zhao Kuangyin 趙匡胤

Zhao Mengfu 趙孟頫

Zhao Mingcheng 趙明誠

Zhao Ruhui 趙汝回

Zhao Shixiu 趙師秀

Zhao Yi 趙翼

Zhao Yi (Later Han) 趙壹

Zhao yinshi 招隱士

Zhao Zheng 趙整

Zhao Zhennü Cai Erlang 趙貞女蔡二郎

Zhaoming taizi 昭明太子

Zhe sisheng 磔四聲

Zhebaima fu 赭白馬賦

zhen (admonition) 箴

zhen (authentic) 真

Zhen Chen 甄琛

Zhen Dexiu 真德秀

Zhen lü fu 鍼縷賦

Zheng (state) 鄭

Zheng Chuhai 鄭處海

Zheng Daozhao 鄭道昭

Zheng Feng 鄭豐

Zheng Gu 鄭谷

Zheng lun 政論

Zheng Qiao 鄭樵

Zheng Sixiao 鄭思肖

Zheng Xuan 鄭玄

Zheng Yu 鄭嵎

Zheng Zhong 鄭眾

zhengming 正名

Zhengqi ge 正氣歌

zhengshi zhi pai 正詩之派

Zhenguan zhengyao 貞觀政要

Zhengyi 正義

zhengyu zhi ben 正語之本

Zhengyu zuoci qili 正語作詞起例

Zhengzi 鄭子

zhenren 真人

Zhenren daige 真人代歌

Zhenzhong ji 枕中記

zhi 質

Zhi Yu 摯虞

Zhide song 至德頌

Zhidun 支遁

zhiguai 志怪

Zhijiang 智匠

zhishi (man with aims) 志士

zhishi (solid and stuffed) 質實

Zhiyuan 智圓

Zhiyuan xinkan quanxiang Sanguo zhi pinghua 至元新刊全相三國志平話

Zhong fu 冢賦

Zhong Hui 鍾會

Zhong lun 中論

Zhong Rong 鍾嶸

Zhong Sicheng 鐘嗣成

Zhongchang Tong 仲長統

Zhongfu zhi liuhuang 中婦織流黃

Zhonglü 中呂

Zhongshan (state) 中山

Zhongshu (Senghui) 仲殊 (僧揮)

Zhongshu Guo Tuotuo zhuan 種樹郭橐駝傳

Zhongshu ling 中書令

Zhongxian 鍾顯

Zhongxing fu 中興賦

Zhongxing jianqi ji 中興間氣集

Zhongyong 中庸

Zhongyuan yinyun 中原音韻

Zhongzhang shilü yi ru Tang ren fengdiao ciyun 仲章詩律已入唐人風調次韻

Zhongzhou ji 中州集

Zhou Ang 周昂

Zhou Bangyan 周邦彥

Zhou Deqing 周德清

Zhou Dunyi 周敦頤

Zhou Fu 周孚

Zhou li 周禮

Zhou Mi 周密

Zhou nan 周南

Zhou Ruming 周汝明

Zhou She 周捨

Zhou shu 周書

Zhou song 周頌

Zhou Xingsi 周興嗣

Zhou Yong 周顒

Zhou Yukai 周裕鍇

Zhou Ziliang 周子良

Zhoushi mingtong ji 周氏冥通記

Zhu Bian 朱弁

Zhu Ci 朱泚

Zhu Daosheng 竺道生

Zhu fu 竹賦

Zhu Mu 朱穆

Zhu Quan 朱權

Zhu Wen 朱溫

Zhu Xi 朱熹

Zhu Xuzeng 朱緒曾

Zhu Yao 祝堯

Zhu Yu zhuan 諸虞傳

Zhu Yunming 祝允明

zhuan 傳

zhuang 壯

Zhuang Ji 莊忌

Zhuang Zhongfang 莊仲方

Zhuang Zhou 莊周

Zhuang Zhu 莊助

Zhuangbai 莊白

Zhuangzi 莊子

Zhufu Yan 主父偃

zhugongdiao 諸宮調

Zhuixing 追興

Zhulin mingshi zhuan 竹林名士傳

zhulin qi xian 竹林七賢

Zhushi 麈史

zhuwen 祝文

zhuzhi ci 竹枝詞

zhuzi 諸子

zǐ 子

zì 字

zi bu yu 子不語

Zi ji wen 自祭文

Zi jun zhi chu yi 自君之出矣

Zi Lu 子路

Zi Si 子思

Zi Xia 子夏

zi yue 子曰

Zidanku 子彈庫

Zidao fu 自悼賦

zide 自得

Zijing 自警

ziran 自然

zishu 子書

zishu yiwei shi 資書以為詩

Zixu 自序

Zixu fu 子虛賦

Ziyi 緇衣

Zizhi tongjian 資治通鑑

Zizhou Doushuai si wenzhong ming 梓州兜率寺文冢銘

Zong Bing 宗炳

Zong Qin 宗欽

Zong Ze 宗澤

zonghengjia 縱橫家

Zongmi 宗密

Zou 鄒

Zu Chongzhi 祖沖之

Zu Taizhi 祖台之

Zu Ti 祖逖
Zu Ting 祖珽
Zu Xuan 祖咺
Zuanyi ji 纂異記
zuben 足本
Zui chu 罪出
Zuiyan 罪言
Zuo Fen 左棻

Zuo Qiuming 左丘明
Zuo Si 左思
Zuo you ming 座右銘
Zuo zhuan 左傳
zuoce 作冊
Zuoci shifa 作詞十法
zuowen 作文

Index